Kostas
December 2013

# The Future of Electricity Demand

What will electricity and heat demand look like in a low-carbon world? Ambitious environmental targets will modify the shape of the electricity sector in the twenty-first century. 'Smart' technologies and demand-side management will be some of the key features of the future of the electricity system. Meanwhile, the social and behavioural dimensions will complement and interact with new technologies and policies. Electricity demand will increasingly be tied up with the demand for heat and transport.

*The Future of Electricity Demand* looks into the features of the future electricity demand in light of the challenges posed by climate change. Written by a team of leading academics and industry experts, the book investigates the economics, technology, social aspects, and policies and regulations which are likely to characterize energy demand in a low-carbon world. It provides a comprehensive and analytical perspective on the future of electricity demand.

TOORAJ JAMASB is the SIRE Chair of Energy Economics at Heriot-Watt University, Edinburgh. He was previously Senior Research Associate in the Faculty of Economics and at the ESRC Electricity Policy Research Group (EPRG) at the University of Cambridge.

MICHAEL G. POLLITT is Reader in Business Economics at the Judge Business School, University of Cambridge and Fellow and Director of Studies in Economics and Management at Sidney Sussex College, Cambridge. He is also an assistant director of the ESRC Electricity Policy Research Group (EPRG).

# The Future of Electricity Demand

*Customers, Citizens and Loads*

Tooraj Jamasb
Michael G. Pollitt

CAMBRIDGE UNIVERSITY PRESS
Cambridge, New York, Melbourne, Madrid, Cape Town,
Singapore, São Paulo, Delhi, Mexico City

Cambridge University Press
The Edinburgh Building, Cambridge CB2 8RU, UK

Published in the United States of America by Cambridge University Press, New York

www.cambridge.org
Information on this title: www.cambridge.org/9781107008502



First published 2011

*A catalogue record for this publication is available from the British Library*

*Library of Congress Cataloguing in Publication Data*
Jamasb, Tooraj.
The future of electricity demand : customers, citizens,
and loads / Tooraj Jamasb, Michael Pollitt.
p. cm. – (Department of applied economics occasional papers ; 69)
Includes bibliographical references and index.
ISBN 978-1-107-00850-2 (hardback)
1. Electric power consumption – Great Britain – Forecasting.
2. Energy policy – Great Britain. 3. Energy conservation – Great Britain.
I. Pollitt, Michael G. II. Title. III. Series.
HD9685.G72J36 2011
333.793′2120941 – dc23 2011017973

ISBN 978-1-107-00850-2 Hardback

# Contents

# Figures

# Tables

# Boxes

# Contributors

ELCIN AKCURA is a PhD Candidate at the Electricity Policy Research Group, Faculty of Economics, University of Cambridge.

GRAHAM AULT is Professor at the Institute for Energy and Environment, Strathclyde University.

MARKO AUNEDI is Research Assistant at the Control and Power Research Group, Department of Electrical and Electronic Engineering, Imperial College London.

RÉGINE BELHOMME is Project Manager, Senior Engineer, EDF SA, Research & Development Division, France.

FRANÇOIS BOUFFARD is Assistant Professor at McGill University, Canada. He was previously Lecturer at the School of Electrical & Electronic Engineering, University of Manchester, UK.

AOIFE BROPHY HANEY is a PhD Candidate at the Electricity Policy Research Group, Judge Business School, University of Cambridge.

RAMÓN CERERO REAL DE ASUA is a Control Systems Senior Engineer at Iberdrola Distribución Eléctrica, SAU, Spain.

YU-FOONG CHONG is Consultant at IPA Energy + Water Economics.

JOE A. CLARKE is Professor at the Energy Systems Research Unit, Department of Mechanical Engineering, University of Strathclyde.

FRÉDÉRIC DESOBRY is Research Associate in Signal Processing at the Department of Engineering, University of Cambridge.

HANNAH DEVINE-WRIGHT is Director at Placewise Ltd. She was previously at the University of Manchester.

PATRICK DEVINE-WRIGHT is Professor in Human Geography, University of Exeter and was previously Reader at the School of Environment and Development, University of Manchester.

ALIOUNE DIOP is Engineer at EDF SA, Research & Development Division, France.

DAMIEN FRAME is Research Assistant in the Institute for Energy and Environment, University of Strathclyde.

ELISABETH GARNSEY is Emeritus Reader in Innovation Studies, Institute for Manufacturing, University of Cambridge.

STEPHANE HESS is Reader in Choice Modelling at the Institute for Transport Studies, University of Leeds.

SIMON HILL is Research Associate in Signal Processing at the Department of Engineering, University of Cambridge.

JUN HONG is Research Fellow at the Energy Systems Research Unit, Department of Mechanical Engineering, University of Strathclyde.

NICK HUGHES is UKERC Research Student, Imperial College London and University of Strathclyde.

TOORAJ JAMASB is the SIRE Chair of Energy Economics at Heriot-Watt University, Edinburgh. He was previously Senior Research Associate in the Faculty of Economics and at the ESRC Electricity Policy Research Group (EPRG) at the University of Cambridge.

CAMERON M. JOHNSTONE is Senior Lecturer, Energy Systems Research Unit, Department of Mechanical Engineering, University of Strathclyde.

SCOTT KELLY is a PhD student at the Centre for Climate Change Mitigation Research (4CMR) and the Electricity Policy Research Group (EPRG) at the University of Cambridge.

JAE MIN KIM is Senior Research Fellow at the Energy Systems Research Unit, Department of Mechanical Engineering, University of Strathclyde.

MATTHEW LEACH is Professor in Energy & Environmental Systems and Director of the Centre for Environmental Strategy, University of Surrey.

PEDRO LINARES is Associate Professor at the Universidad Pontificia Comillas, Spain.

CRISTIANO MARANTES is Low Carbon London Solution Manager, at UK Energy Networks in London, UK.

GREGORY MARSDEN is Senior Lecturer in Transport Policy and Strategy at the Institute for Transport Studies, University of Leeds.

HELENA MEIER is Lecturer in Economics at Department of Economics, Heriot-Watt University, Edinburgh, and was previously visiting Researcher at the EPRG.

LAURA M. PLATCHKOV is Research Assistant at the Faculty of Economics, University of Cambridge.

MICHAEL G. POLLITT is Reader in Business Economics at the Judge Business School, University of Cambridge and Fellow and Director of Studies in Economics and Management at Sidney Sussex College, Cambridge. He is also Assistant Director of the ESRC Electricity Policy Research Group.

DANNY PUDJIANTO is Research Associate at the Control and Power Research Group, Department of Electrical and Electronic Engineering, Imperial College London.

DAVID M. REINER is Senior Lecturer in Technology Policy and Course Director of the MPhil in Technology Policy at the Judge Business School, University of Cambridge.

MARIA SEBASTIAN-VIANA is an Expert Engineer at EDF SA, Direction Optimisation and Trading Division, France.

VERA SILVA is a PhD Candidate at the Control and Power Research Group, Department of Electrical and Electronic Engineering, Imperial College London.

VLADIMIR STANOJEVIC is Research Assistant at the Control and Power Research Group, Department of Electrical and Electronic Engineering, Imperial College London.

JEVGENIJS STEINBUKS is Research Associate at the Faculty of Economics and Director of Economic Studies, Sidney Sussex College, University of Cambridge.

GORAN STRBAC is Professor of Electrical Energy Systems, Control and Power Research Group, Department of Electrical and Electronic Engineering, Imperial College London.

JACOPO TORRITI is Fellow in Environment at the London School of Economics. He was previously Research Associate at the Centre for Environmental Strategy, University of Surrey.

PAUL TUOHY is Lecturer, Energy Systems Research Unit, Department of Mechanical Engineering, University of Strathclyde.

GIOVANNI VALTORTA is Head of Network Operation and Maintenance at ENEL Distribuzione S.p.A., Italy.

CATHERINE WADDAMS PRICE is Director of the ESRC Centre for Competition Policy at the University of East Anglia and Professor in Norwich Business School, University of East Anglia.

JIM WATSON is Director of the Sussex Energy Group, SPRU, University of Sussex.

CHERRY YUEN is Group Leader Utility Solutions, ABB Switzerland Ltd, Switzerland.

# Foreword

Until the oil shocks of the 1970s, electricity demand growth was rapid, but then slowed dramatically in developed economies, with subsequent excess capacity. Falling fuel and electricity prices from 1986 then directed attention away from the demand side. That situation has now changed. Ambitious environmental targets, rising electricity prices, rapid technical progress, combined with cheaper and better information and communication technologies, will have a dramatic impact on the electricity sector of the twenty-first century. 'Smart' technologies and demand-side management will be key features of this new electricity system. Social and behavioural changes are also likely to play an important role. Decarbonizing the economy means increasing the share of electricity, which will power cars and heat pumps, reducing the importance of oil and gas but creating new and more concentrated demand patterns. New intermittent low carbon generation and new heavy demand uses will require more flexible and responsive demand, which will require major changes to the design and operation of the electricity system, further increasing its complexity.

The UK led the world in electricity reforms starting in 1990, providing a valuable case study for other countries to learn how, and to what extent, the management of electricity demand can – or cannot – be successfully combined into a competitive energy market environment. The next wave of required reforms offers new opportunities for learning, and although this book concentrates on the UK, it draws numerous insights from, and for, other countries.

This need to reconsider the design and management of the electricity sector led the Engineering and Physical Sciences Research Council (EPSRC) to extend the SuperGen FutureNet Research Programme from 2006 for a further four years with the FlexNet Programme. This had funded a consortium of seven UK university groups bringing together a range of fruitful interdisciplinary collaborations to address the issues. The Flexnet Research Programme builds on the achievements of FutureNet and lays out the major technical, economic, market design, public acceptance and other steps required to create flexible networks. An important part of the project is to showcase lessons to be taken up by the commercial sector, government and regulators. It has studied technologies and options needed for a more flexible energy system, and characterizes future energy demand in a low-carbon world. This will require radically new ways to produce, use, and value and price electricity, while maintaining productivity, comfort and security.

The demand side will need to become more flexible and to allow dynamic interaction between producers and consumers. This was the focus of the 'Customers, Citizens and Loads' (CCL) work stream, coordinated by the University of Manchester, which is the source of the material in this book. The CCL work stream has examined all aspects of electricity demand – economic, technical, political and social – as well as drawing on the expertise of and results from the rest of the FlexNet Programme.

We published the first book based on this work, *Future Electricity Technologies and Systems*, in 2006. It concluded that a low-carbon electricity system by 2050 was technically feasible. In 2008, a second volume – *Delivering a Low-Carbon Electricity System* – outlined what important steps needed to be undertaken by 2020 to put us on track towards such a system. *The Future of Electricity Demand* focuses on a somewhat neglected part of the electricity system, where interdisciplinary work continues to offer significant insights and where there is much to be gained from the sort of research collaboration that has produced this book. We trust you will find it as exciting as we did.

PROFESSOR DAVID NEWBERY
*Director of Research,*
*ESRC Electricity Policy Research Group*
*Professor of Economics*
*Faculty of Economics*
*University of Cambridge*

PROFESSOR TIM GREEN
*Professor of Electrical Power Engineering*
*Department of Electrical and Electronic Engineering*
*Imperial College London*

# Preface

Ambitious environmental targets will modify the shape of the electricity sector in the twenty-first century. 'Smart' technologies and demand-side management will be some of the key features of the future of the electricity system in a low-carbon world. Meanwhile, the social and behavioural dimensions will complement and interact with new technologies and policies. Moreover, electricity demand will increasingly be tied up with the demand for heat and transport.

*The Future of Electricity Demand* explores the features of the future electricity demand in light of the challenges posed by climate change. Written by a team of leading academics and industry experts, the book investigates the economics, technology, social aspects, and policies and regulations which seem likely to characterize energy demand in a low-carbon world. The book begins by looking at the economics and the modelling of energy demand. Next, it examines the technological solutions for achieving active demand, such as smart meters, smart appliances and electric vehicles. It then turns to the social dimensions of energy, and finally to policy and regulatory instruments. It thus provides a comprehensive and analytical perspective on the future of electricity demand.

TOORAJ JAMASB
MICHAEL G. POLLITT

# Acknowledgements

The editors are very grateful to the large number of individuals without whom this book would not have been possible. In particular, we acknowledge the help and support of the UK Research Councils and the SuperGen community, especially the FlexNet consortium of universities. Together they have facilitated the coming together of a wide range of individuals from different disciplines to share their expertise and views on the future of electricity demand in a low-carbon world.

We particularly wish to thank Janusz Bialek, Mark Bilton, Steve Connors, Nick Eyre, Ahmad Faruqui, Gareth Harrison, Benjamin F. Hobbs, Sue Roaf, Sanem Sergici, Fionnguala Sherry-Brennan and Sonia Yeh, all of whom, as external referees, have ensured the quality of the substance covered in the book. We would also like to thank Roger Fouquet and Peter J.G. Pearson, who kindly provided the data for some of the figures in Chapter 1. A special mention must be made to Aoife Brophy Haney and Laura Platchkov, Research Assistants at the Cambridge Faculty of Economics, who successfully managed the entire process through to completion.

We are also grateful to David Newbery, Research Director of the ESRC Electricity Policy Research Group, who continues to inspire us with criticisms and encouragements, Sean Holly, Research Director of the Faculty, as well as Chris Harrison and Philip Good at Cambridge University Press, for their support and work in preparing the book for publication. And last but not least, we extend our sincere thanks to all the authors, without whose unwavering support this book would not have been completed.

TOORAJ JAMASB
MICHAEL G. POLLITT

# Introduction and overview of the chapters

*Tooraj Jamasb, Laura M. Platchkov and Michael G. Pollitt*

## Opening remarks

This book aims to explore aspects of the future demand for electricity in the light of the challenges posed by climate change. In the UK we have a formal target for the reduction of carbon dioxide equivalent emissions of 80 per cent by 2050 (on 1990 levels). Official publications regularly suggest that reducing overall energy demand is an important part of meeting that target. Indeed, in a recent report of the UK Committee on Climate Change (CCC, 2009, p. 22), it was suggested that residential energy efficiency measures could reduce carbon dioxide emissions by 50 million tonnes per annum (or around 10 per cent of the UK's current total emissions) by 2022. The UK is not alone: many other countries have targets and aspirations for the reduction of energy consumption. Meanwhile, the future of energy demand will increasingly be synonymous with the future of electricity demand if the heat and transport sectors are electrified over the coming decades.

Decarbonization of the energy sector is not just about reducing energy demand. Emissions from direct combustion of heat and direct combustion of liquid fuel in vehicles are roughly equal to emissions from power stations. Reducing emissions from electricity production is technically feasible via a combination of renewables, nuclear power and carbon-capture-and-storage equipment. This implies that switching heating and transportation demand for energy from combustion of fossil fuels to heat from electricity (or combined heat and power) and to electric vehicles is important in reducing emissions.

The scale of the decarbonization challenge will depend in large part on the drivers of energy demand. If underlying demand for energy increases due to population growth and increasing wealth then more low-carbon energy production will be required. Projections of energy demand by 2050 vary widely and consequently give rise to large variations in the required amounts of electricity generation. Working out how to delink future energy demand growth from traditional upward drivers of demand will be important for energy regulators and policy makers.

While aggregate demand for energy is made up of industrial, commercial and residential (or household) demand, we focus significantly in this book on domestic demand for electricity. The reason for this is that this is the portion of energy demand (and energy-related carbon emissions) where there are significant untapped possibilities for improvements in efficiency and where much of the recent research interest and effort has been focused. In particular, the emergence of smart metering of electricity (and gas) combined with smarter domestic appliances capable of responding to price and stability signals coming from the electricity grid implies a level of consciousness and responsiveness in energy demand previously seen only in larger industrial and commercial users.

The book focuses on the UK, while drawing substantially on evidence from elsewhere. The UK is an interesting case study globally for a number of reasons. It is a mature economy with slow-growing energy demand where efforts to improve energy efficiency are likely to be an important and noticeable part of any successful decarbonization. The UK has also led the world in terms of policy development. It was one of the first countries to liberalize its electricity and gas markets, to independently regulate its energy networks and to implement targets for substantial long-term carbon emissions reduction. The UK will be an interesting case study for other countries to learn from (positively or negatively) in terms of how (and indeed if) demand-side measures can be combined with and integrated into a competitive energy market environment.

## Structure of the book

This chapter presents the motivation of this book and an introduction to the wider context of economics of energy demand and efficiency. The rest of the book is organized in the following four parts. Part I examines some specific economic aspects of future electricity demand. In Chapter 1, Platchkov and Pollitt provide an introduction to the economics of energy demand and efficiency, laying down some economic fundamentals of energy demand. In Chapter 2, Ault *et al.* outline four rather different scenarios along which demand and its effects on the system can unfold towards 2050. A smart grid requires participation of active customers. Chapter 3 by Torriti *et al.* explores the customer participation options. Given the potential for major changes in the level and pattern of demand, the importance of modelling and forecasting demand is likely to increase. A review of recent trends in modelling energy and electricity demand is presented in Chapter 4 by Steinbuks.

The future of electricity demand will undoubtedly be influenced by technological change and innovative solutions in different areas. In Part II the book turns to technological solutions for achieving the active future demand. In Chapter 5, Hong *et al.* present intelligent demand-side management and control systems at homes and building level, which aim to maximize comfort and convenience for the consumers. They make clear that much of the future development and promise of smart grid and active demand hinges upon the roll-out of smart meters. This is explored in Chapter 6 by Haney *et al.*, who review different functionalities of smart meters and the international experience with these so far, focusing on cost–benefit analysis of roll-outs. In Chapter 7, Silva *et al.* take a different approach and focus on the role of smart domestic appliances that can shift load and use scenario simulations to estimate their value to the system. There is a growing anticipation that electric cars will link energy demand from road transport to household demand for energy. We therefore conclude this part with Chapter 8 by Marsden and Hess presenting a review of the main technological options for electric cars and assessment of the effect of their large-scale adoption on electricity use as well as the peak demand.

The social and behavioural aspects of energy demand complement and interact with the economic and technical features of the electricity system. With regards to active demand this role is likely to grow in importance and is studied in Part III. Chapter 9 begins this part with Haney *et al.* presenting the result of two public opinion surveys on consumer attitudes and actions revealing differences between the roles of the individual as consumer versus citizen and its relevance for the political economy of energy policy. This is followed by a discussion of the local dimension of energy demand (for both electricity and heat) in Chapter 10 by Kelly and Pollitt. Achieving the ambitious climate policy objectives is likely to lead to significant price increases for all customers, and this is likely to be a serious problem for those millions of households (in the UK) already in energy poverty. In Chapter 11, Devine-Wright and Watson explore the centralization versus decentralization options for the UK electricity sector. We examine energy poverty in Chapter 12, where Waddams Price revisits the concept of fuel poverty and distinguishes between households officially characterized as fuel poor and those who consider themselves as such. Chapter 13, by Meier and Jamasb, emphasizes the case of potentially vulnerable groups of households, such as single-mother headed, pensioners and those on benefits.

As mentioned earlier, achieving flexible networks and active demand will require strong policy commitment and implementation. In Part IV we shed light on some relevant policy aspects and areas that can facilitate development of a flexible electricity demand. Chapter 14 by Haney *et al.* reviews the lessons from international experience from *demand-side strategies* towards the residential sector adopted in leading countries. The configuration of electricity networks will be important in facilitating a more active demand side. The implications for *regulatory policy towards networks* are therefore analyzed in Chapter 15 by Jamasb and Marantes. They present a detailed and disaggregated distribution network investment model, the results of which can feed into investment planning and strategies for active networks and demand. Given the myriad possibilities that can be identified on the demand side for electricity, a coherent *research policy* will be essential for the development and implementation of new technologies As an example of a move in this direction, Bouffard *et al.*, in Chapter 17, describe the results of a large-scale European collaborative research initiative for the development of active demand. *Building regulations* can also play a role in facilitating the active demand future. Chapter 16, by Clarke *et al.*, reviews a selection of the EU and UK legislative approaches to energy performance of buildings. Low hanging fruit still exists on the demand side of policies which are cost effective in saving energy (and carbon). As a rather precise example of this, Chong *et al.*, in Chapter 18, describe how a *change in the daylight saving time* in the UK can contribute to electricity demand and emissions reductions. Finally, in Chapter 19, the editors offer some closing reflections on how to create a smarter, more efficient demand side for electricity.

## Overview of the main chapters

### *Part I: The economics*

*Chapter 1: The economics of energy (and electricity) demand*, by Platchkov and Pollitt, lays out some of the important economics foundations of energy demand in general, and electricity in particular. The authors first look at the macroeconomic context. The examination of the different drivers of energy and electricity consumption over time reveals how both are subject to the same drivers – income and price. Taking the example of demand for electric light over the last centuries in the UK, they point out that relative energy prices matter for long-run economic transitions. Long-run demand trends are mirrored in long-run price trends. However, the authors caution against the risk of taking energy demand (and carbon emissions) falls in isolation, as raising the price of energy – and hence reducing consumption – in one country may have little effect at the world level. The authors then examine some of the features of energy service expenditures over time. The share of income spent on energy services is fairly constant over time (around 8 per cent of GDP in the UK since the 1970s), transport fuel is the most significant component, and taxes on energy consumption are an important revenue to the government (around 7 per cent of total tax revenues in the UK). However, the different sectors are very distinct from one another in terms of consumption profiles, and new sources of electricity demand may substantially change total demand and the way electricity is consumed.

Turning to the microeconomic context of energy demand, the authors review some of the physics of energy demand, highlighting the energy efficiency of electric power. Theoretically, large savings are possible; however, the economics is unlikely to support achievement of all the technical potential. A number of challenges need to be taken into account, including how consumers actually behave (rather than should behave). The authors conclude by highlighting the various unknowns that characterize the future of energy demand, such as the scale and shape of the IT changes required, the kinds of innovations that might appear in the heat and transport sectors, who will be the future actors in the energy market, and the uncertainty as to how consumers may react to new technological opportunities.

*Chapter 2*: *Energy scenarios and implications for future electricity demand*, by Ault *et al.*, explores the possible paths along which the UK future electricity system can develop in the long run-up until 2050, with a particular focus on the demand side. These futures are explored through four scenarios: big distribution and transmission, energy services companies (ESCOs), distribution system operators (DSOs) and microgrids. The scenarios build on the insights from a major research project on the future of the UK electricity networks, sponsored by the energy regulator Ofgem. The differences in the scenarios developed are primarily driven by customer participation, environmental concern and institutional governance. The findings highlight the long-term effect of different demand trajectories which are in the rather wide range of 290 and 450 TWh by 2050 as against around 330 TWh in 2000.

*Chapter 3*: *Demand-side participation: price constraints, technical limits and behavioural risks*, by Torriti *et al.*, disentangles some of the drivers of and constraints to demand-side participation in liberalized energy markets, which can bring about significant reductions in electricity prices. Shifts of demand which reduce system peaks could reduce the need for higher marginal cost of generation, offer lower-cost system balancing, decrease grid reinforcement investment and play a key role in achieving ambitious environmental policy objectives, through facilitating greater connection of intermittent renewable generation. However, there are significant constraints associated with the extent to which consumers can manage electricity loads. Those constraints are categorized into (1) price constraints – including price structures and signalling, (2) technical limits in terms of the availability of metering technologies and their cost effectiveness as well as communication technologies, and (3) the behavioural types of constraint, particularly issues of psychological motivation and social acceptance. Those are then illustrated with demand-side participation experience in European countries. The authors then propose and discuss key aspects and mechanisms of an incentive/payment scheme for end-users, taking into account wider economics and behavioural issues.

*Chapter 4*: *Review of recent developments in economic modelling of energy demand*, by Steinbuks, revisits recent developments in the literature on econometric modelling of demand for energy and electricity. The chapter discusses the diverse and complex factors that are in play in accurately modelling the demand for electricity (within the context of the overall demand for energy), such as energy intensity, own and cross elasticities, and the rebound effect associated with energy efficiency. The chapter covers demand for energy in the residential, industrial and transportation sectors. Energy demand modelling can also potentially play a role in better understanding of the factors that influence active demand. The main themes being traced in the chapter include the scope for fuel input substitution, trends in energy efficiency, the impact of changing industrial structure of the economy as a whole, and the nature of technological change.

## *Part II: Technology*

*Chapter 5*: *Demand-side management and control in buildings*, by Hong *et al.*, examines the application of demand-side management and control, or DSM+c, in buildings. The subject of this chapter differs from the conventional view of DSM in that an advanced control system responds to potentially intermittent supply signals and manages the different loads in a building in subtle ways and without compromising the comfort of the users. The DSM+c concept presented in this chapter is based on utilization of the flexibilities that exist in the constituent components of the loads within a building. The control systems are a vital part of the systems and utilize the latest advances in information and communication technologies, including the use of Internet to activate the demand side. Power demand and supply and environmental variables are monitored using sensors connection to Internet-based communication systems.

*Chapter 6*: *Smart metering: technology, economics and international experience*, by Brophy Haney *et al.*, looks at technologies that can enable small users to become active participants in energy markets. The recent emergence of smart meters acts as a platform for both more sophisticated and transparent pricing structures as well as automated demand response, in combination with smart appliances, for instance. The authors start with a discussion of the policy context for smart metering. Metering is a central part in the relationship between energy consumers and suppliers, and different models have been applied worldwide, subject to different drivers. There is still much confusion on what makes a smart meter 'smart', so the chapter clarifies the object of the debate with a presentation of the range of available technologies and their functionalities. It follows on with an economic assessment of smart metering, which is a delicate question due to the sensitivity of different costs and benefits, among others to the chosen roll-out strategy. The subsequent review of the international experiences uncovers various drivers which have shaped different regulatory approaches and technology choices. In Italy, for instance, the initial push came from industry, whereas in Sweden it was the requirement for more accurate customer bills. The authors conclude that technology choice is important, but difficult, and deployment depends on the existing market structure; however, smart meters could add significant value to electricity systems.

*Chapter 7*: *Smart domestic appliances as enabling technology for demand-side integration: modelling, value and drivers*, by Silva *et al.*, describes the role that smart domestic appliances can play in increasing the flexibility of the demand side and contributing to the balancing and security of the wider demand–supply system as well as the network operation. Such appliances account for a considerable share of total domestic electricity consumption, but this fact can also potentially offer benefits to the system. The chapter presents a framework for assessing the economic value of the flexibility of demand and new ancillary services provided by smart appliances through automatic and intelligent modification of their operations. The methodology employed consists of a simulation model of an annual system operation which schedules generation sources and smart domestic appliances, taking into account system security and operational constrains. The model is used to explore case studies of demand shifting and dynamic demand and quantify their effects under different scenarios.

*Chapter 8*: *The scope for and potential impacts of the adoption of electric vehicles in UK surface transport*, by Marsden and Hess, examines some of the key issues associated with large-scale adoption of the main types of electric vehicle, with a particular focus on their potential impact on the electricity system and especially the networks. The electric cars can shift a considerable demand for transport fossil fuels over to the electricity system, a development which poses both possibilities as well as concerns. Among other significant points presented in the chapter, it argues that the effect of large-scale adoption of electric cars will probably not have a major impact on the total electricity demand. At the same time, the load effect of such a trend on the system can be more significant. This in turn implies that the challenges and implications of electric cars for the electricity networks can be more important than their potential impact on the generation segment of the electricity sector.

*Part III: Social dimensions*

*Chapter 9: From citizen to consumer: energy policy and public attitudes in the UK*, by Akcura *et al.*, presents the results from two public opinion surveys conducted in the UK in 2006 and 2008 to draw insights into factors affecting customer attitudes and behaviours. Public support is particularly important in energy policy, where the public is expected to actively contribute by changing lifestyle. Hence, understanding the determinants of customer attitudes and actions will be increasingly important in considering how feasible demand-targeting electricity policies are, and successful policies will heavily depend on how they can influence existing behaviours. The surveys reveal the dichotomy between consumer and citizen, in other words between attitudes/intentions and behaviour/action. The many dimensions involved in individual decision making, which go beyond the very availability of information to encompass social, demographic and exogenous factors, are also highlighted. Policy preferences and attitudes to energy and the environment are found to be very sensitive to the broader economic climate, for instance. This is evidenced by a dramatic shift in energy policy preferences between 2006 and 2008, with the authors finding that in 2006, respectively 26 per cent and 20 per cent of the respondents considered 'increasing the use of renewable energy' and 'reducing the impacts of climate change' as a top priority, a percentage that reduced to respectively 9 per cent and 6 per cent in 2008. Over the last years, concerns dramatically shifted towards fuel poverty, with 41 per cent of respondents considering 'keeping price low' of utmost importance in 2008.

*Chapter 10: The local dimension of energy*, by Kelly and Pollitt, argues that some of the best opportunities for reducing energy demand and carbon emission would require a stronger involvement and leadership from local governments. The contrast is drawn between community energy versus local energy, where the former is typically developed from grassroots (bottom-up), whereas local energy projects are typically undertaken by institutions such as local government (top-down). There is now a growing emphasis on local energy governance. Local governments can and do have a significant impact on both energy production and consumption and will be key stakeholders in the solutions to future energy systems, as they play a vital role in educating, mobilizing and responding to challenges of sustainable development, and are responsible for large areas of policy. Kelly and Pollitt argue that one of the reasons explaining lower energy intensities of some countries, such as Denmark, Sweden or Japan, is the devolved power to local authorities. The evidence suggests the importance of energy services companies as a vehicle for delivering those strategies. The chapter highlights three key success factors for local governments: the recognition of the co-benefits of local energy, a strong political leadership and the use of partnerships.

*Chapter 11*: *Centralization, decentralization and the scales in between: what role might they play in the UK*, by Watson and Devine-Wright, explores the scope for the UK energy system to develop at a range of different scales – from continued large-scale, centralized power plants to small-scale, decentralized heating systems that are integrated into buildings. There has been extensive debate on the potential advantages of decentralized energy for meeting current and future challenges, but there have been only marginal changes until now. The authors ask whether the strongly centralized approach to energy provision that developed in the post-war period can continue to meet the needs of society over the coming decades. They argue that it may be sufficiently flexible to meet the dual challenges of energy security and climate change, but this is by no means certain. They start with some definitions of decentralized energy, which can involve different technologies, institutions, policies and stakeholders. Then they explore and compare the range of scales and actors that distinguishes decentralized from centralized energy systems. The authors highlight the importance of retrofitting the building stock, which has an important social dimension, and hence will partly depend on public acceptance and levels of trust. The barriers imposed by the regulatory framework are also stressed. They conclude that the choice of future energy options is not straightforward, and the extent to which decentralization leads to a more secure or sustainable system depends on the kind of decentralization that is pursued.

*Chapter 12*: *Equity, fuel poverty and demand (maintaining affordability with sustainability and security of supply)*, by Waddams Price, introduces the current debate on fuel poverty, which leads the author to unwrap one of the key dilemmas of the energy policy agenda: the tension between climate change and energy security targets versus affordability. This implies a contradiction at the very heart of the energy agenda, due to the opposite pressures towards energy prices that each of these challenges implies. Waddams Price argues that higher energy prices are crucial for both energy security and the realization of the environmental agenda; and in the UK liberalized context, whether competitive markets remain the best vehicle to deliver affordability is challenged. The very nature of energy demand poses important dilemmas, where most responsive demand comes from low-income households. In parallel, regulators' duties are expanding and being enhanced by new obligations. There is a discussion of a UK household survey of low-income households conducted in 2000 which reveals some striking differences between the official and a more subjective definition of fuel poverty. Half of the 16 per cent of people feeling unable to afford sufficient heating were spending less than 10 per cent of their income on energy expenditure, the official criteria used to classify people as fuel poor.

*Chapter 13*: *Energy spending and vulnerable households*, by Jamasb and Meier, focuses on fuel poverty in Great Britain, in particular on energy spending among households on very low incomes, including pensioners, female single-parent households and benefit recipients. Three factors play a major role in fuel poverty: income, energy prices and energy efficiency. The authors describe how energy spending has changed over time and they shed light on a broader picture of energy spending. The chapter explores the determinants of energy spending of vulnerable groups of households. Using the British Household Panel survey (BHPS), they analyze the number of vulnerable households over time and the drivers of fuel poverty. They find that vulnerable household groups have on average higher levels of energy spending of their incomes than the average household in the sample. They explain this difference by lower levels of insulation, less energy-efficient appliances and less access to different fuels, and different payments methods. Lower-income households may also spend more time at home. The authors conclude that next to financial support, smart metering and social tariffs can play an important part in eradicating fuel poverty. However, their possible impacts need to be carefully examined, including any possible accompanying measures and issues of equity.

### *Part IV: Policy and regulation*

*Chapter 14*: *Demand-side management strategies and the residential sector: lessons from international experience*, by Brophy Haney *et al.*, explores demand-side management (DSM) strategies, including both demand response and energy-efficiency policies. The aim is to uncover what features might strengthen DSM effectiveness. The authors start with a presentation of key features of residential energy demand, in which they discuss the limits to energy indicators and, consequently, cross-country comparisons. Despite the challenges this poses, the importance of residential energy demand within the broader energy demand and its large untapped potential remain salient. This is evidenced by historical energy intensity trends in the sector. The discussion then follows with a review of the barriers to energy-efficiency measures in the residential sector. Then, a number of potential DSM policy responses for addressing these barriers are identified. This reveals the necessity of 'integrated policy strategies' or a portfolio approach, which refers to bundled strategies that seek to simultaneously impact different parts of the market and enhance the strengths of individual measures while compensating for their weaknesses through the use of complementary policies. The authors then look at international experience, in particular Denmark, Germany, Japan and the US, to contrast and shed some light on the UK experience. The chapter concludes with an emphasis on a holistic underpinning approach towards energy efficiency that has clear objectives and mandates, is able to adapt and integrate to the other policy tools in the package, enables participation from all stakeholders and has clear measurement and verification guidelines.

*Chapter 15: Electricity distribution networks: investment and regulation, and uncertain demand*, by Jamasb and Marantes, discusses the importance of capital investments in the electricity networks and its relation to regulatory frameworks and uncertainty. Electricity distribution networks are highly capital intensive, and investment in them is crucial for long-term reliability and expansion of supply. In the UK, and more broadly in Europe, major investments will be needed in the coming years, due to aging assets and the need for a more flexible network. The authors describe the role and operating environment of electricity distribution networks and the main features of the current UK distribution network regulation. They argue in favour of an integrated incentive regulation and single total expenditure measures, to avoid trade-offs between different costs. Then they discuss the various drivers for capital investment: demand growth, energy efficiency and the integration of distributed generation. This leads them to question the ability to forecast demand growth and network investment needs simply on the basis of past trends and macroeconomic variables. The integration of distributed generation, the diversity of non-domestic activity and regional differences are some of the factors arguing in favour of more disaggregated forecasts that enable the assessment of local investment needs. The authors describe an example of such a planning tool and the results it generates. The model uses a long-term maximum electricity forecast methodology developed by EDF that produces highly disaggregated outputs at the substation level. The authors conclude that given the right regulatory incentives, such a site-specific but integrated approach can enhance the long-term economic and operational efficiency of the network.

*Chapter 16*: *The potential impact of policy and legislation on the energy demands of UK buildings and implications for the electrical network*, by Clarke *et al.*, discusses the effects of buildings legislation on future buildings' features and the resulting energy demand. First, the authors present the 2002 Energy Performance of Buildings Directive (EPBD), a major milestone in the promotion of energy efficiency, as well as its update, due in 2011. Comparing the European legislation with the UK building regulations reveals differences in calculation methods and scope, with appliances and equipment energy use still not being included in UK building regulations despite their increasing importance. The authors suggest that building demand might increase in the future and look at the wider factors that might influence it, such as grid carbon emission factors (or primary energy factors), costs of fuels and revenues from selling electricity to the grid, and the impact on energy demand and supply choices. They conclude that the change foreseen in the servicing of buildings could potentially and substantially increase electricity demand and peak loads; and local generation, such as photovoltaic (PV) and combined heat and power (CHP), will not necessarily provide a good match with the peak loads in the UK. They stress the need for a review of regulatory calculation methods.

*Chapter 17*: *The ADDRESS European Project: a large-scale R&D initiative for the development of active demand* by Bouffard *et al.*, presents a description of the results of a major European Union (EU) research and development project, ADDRESS, on active demand. The chapter gives first-hand insights into design, processes and objectives of a major collaborative research project. The ADDRESS project aims to develop a commercial architecture that enables achievement of active demand based around aggregation of demand-side flexibilities, market outlets for demand-side products and services, and the need for benefits and acceptance of active demand across the whole value chain of the electricity system. This chapter illustrates the sorts of large system design questions which are well addressed by collaborative research projects involving stakeholders in several countries each facing similar issues about how to best exploit the technical potential of more active demand.

*Chapter 18*: *Daylight saving, electricity demand and emissions: the British case*, by Chong *et al.*, explores the impact of the changing clock time regime in Britain. Climate change is a strong driver for the reduction of energy consumption and carbon emissions, and reduction in electricity peak demand – generally occurring at 5.30pm – could reduce carbon emissions, generation costs and electricity price. In parallel, today it is easier for policy makers to alter official clock time than to change the habits of the population. Hence, the authors argue that clock time needs to be analyzed in relation to the daily activity patterns of today's urban population, for whom noon is much earlier than the mid-point of their working day. First, the authors review the literature on daylight saving time (DST) on electricity demand and find that a number of studies report saving in overall electricity consumption of 0.5–1 per cent with a better alignment of clock time with the activity patterns of consumers. They find that extending the period of DST could reduce up to 4.3 per cent of daily peak value over the autumn shoulder period. This would have significant price implications, leading to price reductions of 0.6–0.8 per cent over a day, according to their estimate. A number of ancillary benefits, including a reduction in road accidents and death rates, need to be added to the calculation of benefits. Hence, they conclude that a change in clock time regime is a 'low-hanging fruit' measure, which requires minimal time, investment and effort to yield tangible results.

## Conclusions

The motivation for, and the structure of, the present book are inspired by the fact that the literature and debates on the future of electricity demands often run in parallel along disciplinary and specialization lines. However, the nature of the subject matter is inherently interdisciplinary and this book attempts to bring the developments in these areas somewhat closer. This is done with a view to the prospective tightening of climate change policy measures and objectives. However, it is important to bear in mind that most of the ideas and solutions presented in the book are in large degree independent of the climate change debate and as a result of technological progress and developments in energy (rather than emissions) markets, i.e. they are about energy efficiency per se.

The UK presents an interesting case study because it continues to lead in its development of policy towards energy market liberalization and climate change mitigation. This means that many of the issues and options examined in this will also be relevant for other countries aspiring to have a liberalized electricity sector. Hence, the future smart networks and active demand in the UK electricity system will probably unfold in the context of a market-oriented environment. As a result, many of the chapters presented in this book are also mindful of the role of costs, values, prices and markets in the solutions and discussions they present.

The importance of income as a driver of electricity demand suggests that demand is likely to increase at the household and commercial levels in the longer run (having stalled somewhat due to sharp price rises and recession). In addition, the range of energy services which depend on electricity may increase, as heating and transport demand for electricity rise. In principle, increased electrification of the economy is not a problem for energy efficiency, or for the efficient utilization of the electricity system, and indeed there are good reasons to welcome or even encourage such a development. Electricity is a very clean source of energy at the point of consumption and can be produced by a large number of technologies at many different scales. It is rather the issues related to the generation, and increasingly transport, of electricity that are the source of concerns in energy and climate change policy. It is in this context that insights into technical, economic, behavioural and societal aspects of energy demand are important. This book showcases the ways in which the demand side can play its part in achieving a sustainable, secure and competitive energy sector.

Smart networks and active demand can contribute to addressing environmental concerns as well as increasing the resilience of the system and hence the security of energy supplies (Jamasb and Pollitt, 2008). A central message of this book is that while there are certain underlying tensions between the objectives of a liberalized electricity sector and climate change policies, this does not necessarily and automatically suggest a return to the centralized pre-reform system of the past. Rather, the picture that emerges is one of a world where technology, economics, individual behaviour and societal support will interact in ways that are difficult to predict or to manage. What all the authors in this book would hope for is that energy policy will develop in ways which allow a significant portion of the potential for energy and cost savings discussed in the book to be realized.

## References

Committee on Climate Change (2009). Meeting carbon budgets – the need for a step change. Progress report to Parliament, October, London: Committee on Climate Change.

Jamasb, T. and Pollitt, M. (2008). Security of supply and regulation of energy networks, *Energy Policy*, **36**(12): 4584–9.

*Part I*

# The economics

# 1 The economics of energy (and electricity) demand

*Laura M. Platchkov and Michael G. Pollitt*

## 1.1 Introduction

In the UK, electricity demand grew by 2.4 per cent p.a. between 1970 and 2005, to reach a record high of 357 TWh, but then declined to 330 TWh in 2009 following the sharp recession which began in 2008.[1] However, longer-run trends suggest increasing electricity demand globally in the future, and even in the UK. Figure 1.1 shows the trends in electricity consumption in the UK since 1960 for various sectors: residential, public administration, transport, agricultural and commercial sectors, and industrial. In the residential sector, consumption increased by 59 per cent between 1970 and 2009 (DUKES, 2010). The largest household electricity consumption increase is due to consumer electronics, as will be shown later in this chapter. Commercial and public services have used sharply more electricity since 1970, with a rise of 140 per cent to 2009 (DUKES, 2010). Consumption by industry, by contrast, has been decreasing recently, with a steady fall since 2005, partly due to deindustrialization, the recent recession and increased energy efficiency (DECC, 2010a). In the longer run, however, electric vehicles and the electrification of the heat sector (should natural gas decline as the heating fuel of choice) will provide significant new sources of growth in electricity demand.

Figure 1.2 shows the scale of the potential impact of electrification of transport and heat on household electricity demand. Household transport demand for petroleum is around four times the energy value of the electricity used for lighting and appliances.[2] Electrification of water and

[1] See Table 5.1.2 in 'Digest of United Kingdom energy statistics 2010: long-term trends', available at www.decc.gov.uk/assets/decc/Statistics/publications/dukes/324-dukes-2010-longterm.pdf, last accessed 15 October 2010.

[2] Given substantial transformation losses in electricity supply, around 2.5 times the amount of raw energy is required to supply a given level of electricity to the home, so Figure 1.2 exaggerates the relative size of transport demand to lighting and appliance demand, but the scope for increased demand for electricity is clear.

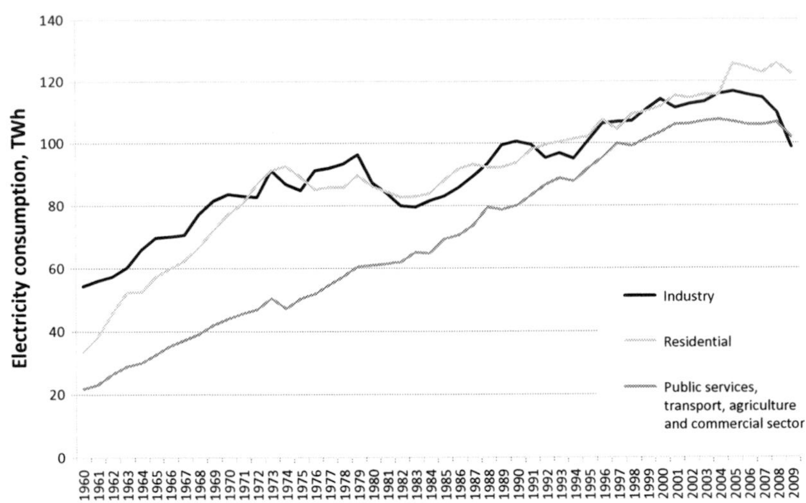


Figure 1.1 UK final electricity consumption by sector, 1960–2009.
*Sources:* 1960–2004: IEA (2010a); 2005–2009: DUKES (2010).

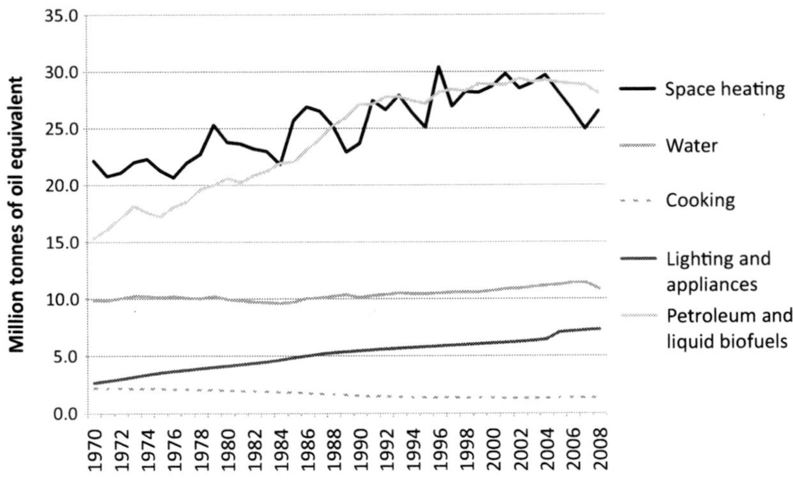


Figure 1.2 UK domestic energy consumption by end use, 1970–2008.
*Source:* DECC (2010b).

space heating, currently largely (though not entirely) supplied via natural gas, would produce a significant rise in demand for electricity.[3]

[3] Around 80 per cent of households are on the gas network; the rest mainly use oil or electricity for heating.

This suggests that income, technologies and demand-side management are keys in understanding the long-term trends of energy and more specifically electricity consumption. Future energy trends are central to policy making. This chapter intends to uncover what lessons can be learned from the empirical evidence. It looks back at the history of energy demand, discusses key technological and price developments as well as the demand-side issues that have led us to where we are now and are likely to continue guiding future energy developments. By doing so, it lays out some economic fundamentals of energy demand, which underpin some of the analysis in later chapters of the book. It is not intended to cover the extensive literature surrounding energy demand (for a recent review of energy demand modelling, see Steinbuks, this volume), but rather to bring together a number of key factors influencing energy demand and to reflect on some likely future developments, in light of current challenges. A number of unknowns are highlighted that testify to the fact that we are now at a crossroads in the history of energy consumption and a number of different paths are possible. The rest of the chapter is organized as follows: in section 1.2 we discuss the long-run macroeconomic context of energy demand; in section 1.3, we discuss the long-run microeconomic context of energy demand; and we offer some initial conclusions in section 1.4.

## 1.2 The long-run macroeconomic context of energy demand

### *1.2.1 The drivers of aggregate energy consumption*

The 2050 decarbonization target context in which many energy and climate policies are framed immediately gives rise to a long-run comparative view of how energy demand is likely to evolve. It is instructive to examine what the evidence of history says about this. Figure 1.3 shows the evolution of energy consumption per head versus GDP per head over the period 1972–2008. The solid line shows a linear relationship through the data. The data show the strong positive relationship between energy consumption and income for most countries. Only Germany and the US show significant reductions over longer periods. In Germany this occurs at a high level of income, while in the US this occurs at a very high level of energy consumption and following the oil price shocks of the mid-1970s and mid-1980s. Figure 1.3 also illustrates (by implication) how rising population contributes to absolute growth in energy consumption.

Figure 1.4 highlights the role of price in explaining the differences in energy consumption between countries. Higher prices are associated with lower levels of energy consumption. Indeed, the oil intensity of GDP (units of oil consumed per unit of GDP) is proportionately reduced for proportionate increase in the average energy price (including taxes). The

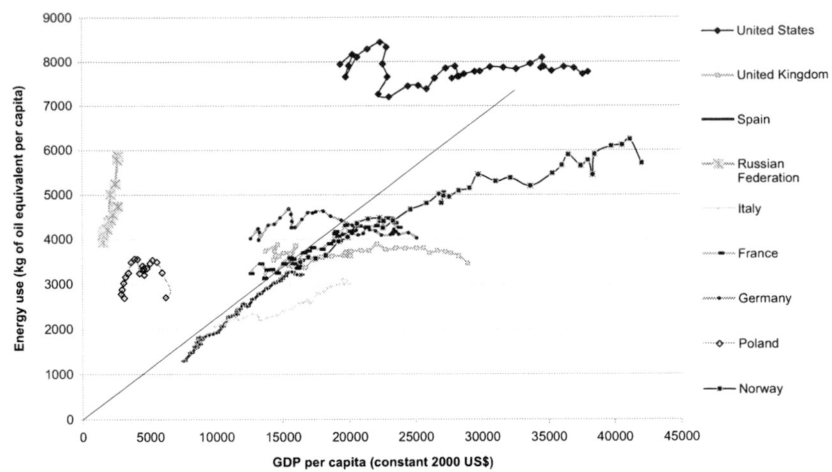


Figure 1.3 Income as a driver of energy consumption – energy use per head versus GDP per head, 1972–2008.
*Source:* World Bank (2010).

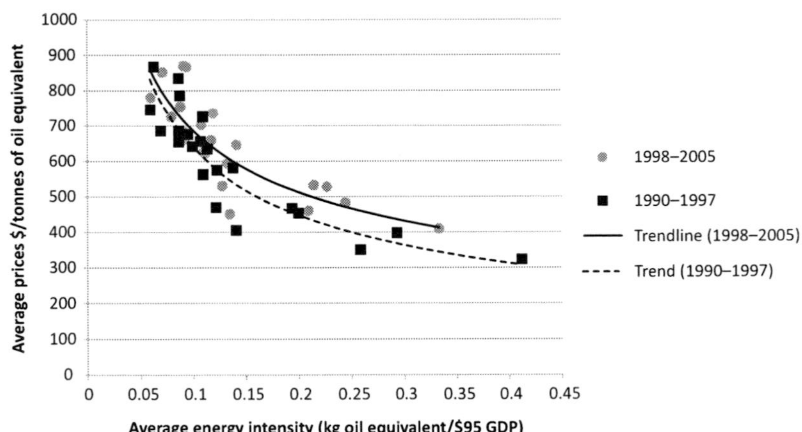


Figure 1.4 Price as a driver of energy consumption – energy intensity versus energy prices. The data points include the following countries: Australia, Austria, Belgium, Czech Republic, Denmark, Finland, France, Germany, Greece, Hungary, Ireland, Italy, Japan, Korea, Luxembourg, Netherlands, Poland, Portugal, Slovak Republic, Spain, Sweden, UK, USA.
*Source:* Data from Steinbuks (2010).

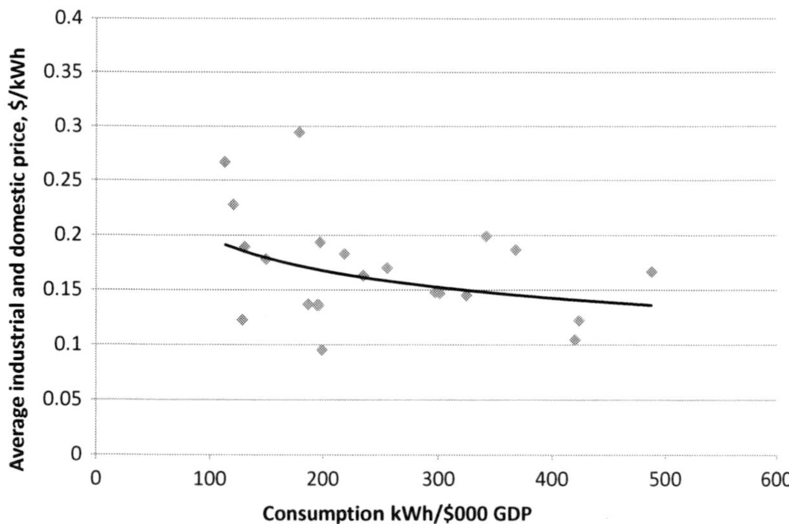


Figure 1.5 Price as a driver of electricity consumption: 2008 data. *Source:* IEA (2010b); Countries: Austria, France, Luxembourg, Slovak Republic, United Kingdom, Belgium, Greece, Netherlands, Spain, United States, Czech Republic, Hungary, Norway, Sweden, Denmark, Ireland, Poland, Switzerland, Finland, Italy, Portugal, Turkey.

fitted line shows the price elasticity of demand for units of energy in an economy which is highly elastic, i.e. 1 per cent increase in average price reduces energy consumption by 2 per cent. Comparison of the 1998–2005 period with the earlier period 1990–7 indicates that the revealed elasticity is increasing between the earlier and later periods. This means that the differences in levels of energy intensity at the same income level significantly reflect price differentials.

Figure 1.5 suggests that the price relationship for electricity demand across countries is similar to that for overall energy demand. Countries that have very high prices (due to taxation) tend to have lower demand for electricity, while countries that have very low prices (due to subsidy) tend to have very high consumption. We can conclude from Figures 1.3–1.5 that price and income are two of the key triggers for both electricity demand and overall energy consumption.

In order for us to gain a perspective on what historians might be saying 100 years from now we can look further back into history. In order to evaluate climate policy, historians in 2110 may look back on the national and international efforts to decarbonize energy systems which began to be discussed seriously in 1988 in the run-up to the 1992 Rio

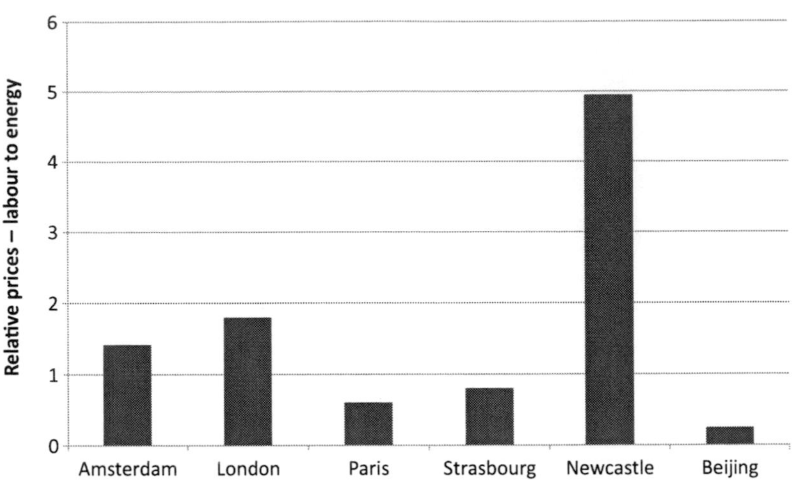


Figure 1.6 The role of relative input prices in long-run economic development: price of labour relative to energy, early 1700s.
*Source*: Allen (2009, Table 6.2, p. 140).

Climate Change Summit and the many modelling exercises which suggested how carbon dioxide levels should evolve to 2100. Figure 1.6 provides some food for that thought experiment. This figure is taken from Allen's (2009) book, in which he suggests that the reason that the industrial revolution took place in northern England and not elsewhere was significantly to do with the relative prices of different inputs to production. In northern England a unit of agricultural labour was expensive relative to a unit of energy (due to abundant cheap coal and relatively productive agricultural workers). This incentivized the use of and innovation in labour-saving, energy-intensive technologies (such as the steam engine). Figure 1.6 shows that in the early 1700s labour was almost five times more expensive relative to energy in Newcastle than it was in Strasbourg (and more than ten times more expensive than in Beijing). The conclusion which we can draw from this is that relative energy prices may have triggered some of the key developments that led to the British industrial revolution, and hence are likely to matter for future long-run economic transitions.

This is a point supported by Fouquet and Pearson (2006), who look at the history of lighting demand in the UK since the 1300s. They focus their discussion of energy demand on the services produced by energy inputs. Energy consumers are not interested in units of energy per se, but rather in the amenities that energy provides (i.e. light, heat, transportation) or *energy services*. Fouquet and Pearson look at how, over a long period,

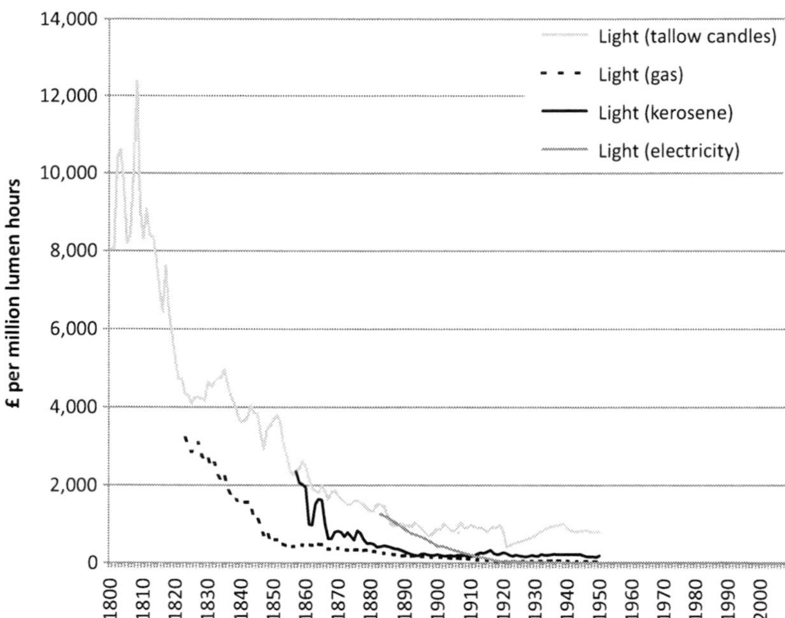


Figure 1.7 How long-run technological change drives prices of energy services: price of light 1800–1950 (2000 prices).
*Source:* Fouquet and Pearson (2006), with kind permission.

technology changes came about as a result of relative costs of different technologies (cheaper technologies emerged) and how falling costs (and associated falling prices) drove consumption of higher levels of energy services consumption. They focus on lighting and the number of lumen hours (i.e. units of light supplied for one hour). Figure 1.7 shows the price evolution of three technologies which emerged over time in the 1800s (initially as niche applications) and then became dominant, as they became cost competitive (on the basis of a mixture of price and convenience grounds). It shows the price evolution of energy services from electric lighting, which is now the dominant technology. The figure makes the general point that the same technology gets cheaper over time but can be overtaken by a new technology.

Figure 1.8 shows the associated impact of the decline in costs and prices on the demand for lighting services. Fouquet and Pearson show that the price of a unit of lighting services in 2000 was 1/3000 of their real level in 1800 and demand per capita had increased 6,500 times. This indicates a very significant price effect (for one element of overall energy demand). This figure shows how long-run demand trends are mirrored in long-run price trends.

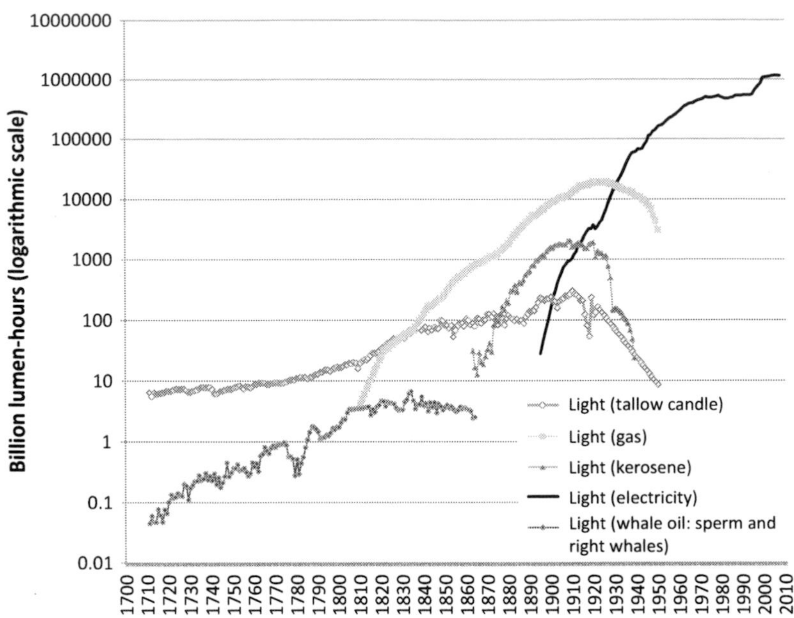


Figure 1.8 How falling prices have driven long-run demand for energy services: demand for light.
*Source:* Fouquet and Pearson (2006), with kind permission.

Given the global nature of the climate problem, it is important to think about global energy demand. Price and income effects on energy demand operate globally. Raising the price of energy in one country will have very little effect at the world level (unless it is a very large country). In particular there might be considerable leakage of energy demand to other countries, such that once the embodied energy (and carbon) in imports is taken into account there is very little reduction in global energy consumption (and carbon emissions). The UK, for instance, has seen significant reductions in the amount of carbon dioxide it has produced domestically since 1990; however it has also seen a significant rise in manufactured imports from developing countries (and relative reduction in domestic manufacturing). Table 1.1 shows this sort of effect at the global level (for an earlier period). Total energy consumption in developed countries has risen less than the GDP effect would have suggested (activity effect) due to a combination of structural effect (i.e. deindustrialization and emergence of developing country manufacturing) and increased energy efficiency (intensity effect). However, in developing countries and China there have been significant increases in energy consumption caused by the rise of their industry and some weakness in the energy efficiency of

Table 1.1 *Global drivers of energy consumption: increase in energy consumption 1973–90*

| | Contribution by | | | |
|---|---|---|---|---|
| Million tonnes of oil equivalent (mtoe) | Activity effect | Structural effect | Intensity effect | Total increase |
| Developing | 322.85 | 99.12 | 136.56 | 558.53 |
| China | 178.65 | 243.90 | −139.80 | 282.75 |
| Developed | 1488.21 | −204.35 | −1069.16 | 214.70 |
| Eastern Europe, former USSR | 503.70 | 29.42 | −210.53 | 322.59 |
| World | 2493.41 | 168.09 | −1282.93 | 1378.58 |

*Source:* Sun (1998, p. 98).

their industry. Table 1.1 cautions against taking a fall in energy demand in one country in isolation from what is happening elsewhere as a sign of progress worldwide.

### *1.2.2 Recent aggregate expenditure on energy services in the UK*

A basic conclusion of the observation of a stable long-run relationship between energy demand and price and income is that the share of income spent on energy services is roughly constant. High prices favour lower energy consumption as consumers experience 'payment resistance', while low prices incentivize increased consumption of energy services. This is illustrated in Figure 1.9. From 1970 to 2008, the average share of total energy expenditure (including electricity, natural gas and liquid fuel) as a share of GDP was around 8 per cent; even with the sharp rise in energy prices in the period to 1982, total energy expenditure increased by only 20 per cent. Prices then fell back substantially as energy efficiency improvements continued to come through in the 1980s and 1990s. A recent resurgence of prices since 2003 (substantially increasing energy prices) has merely taken energy expenditure as a percentage of GDP back towards the average for the entire period.

In 2009 total energy expenditure was £113 billion, of which £17.5 billion was spent on natural gas, £31.1 billion on electricity and £61.2 billion on petroleum (of which £51.5 billion was road transport). Of the total expenditure, a significant share was taxation, with taxes on petroleum being £34.3 billion, with additional VAT being levied on domestic electricity and gas and a climate change levy being raised on industrial and commercial energy use, taking the total tax revenue

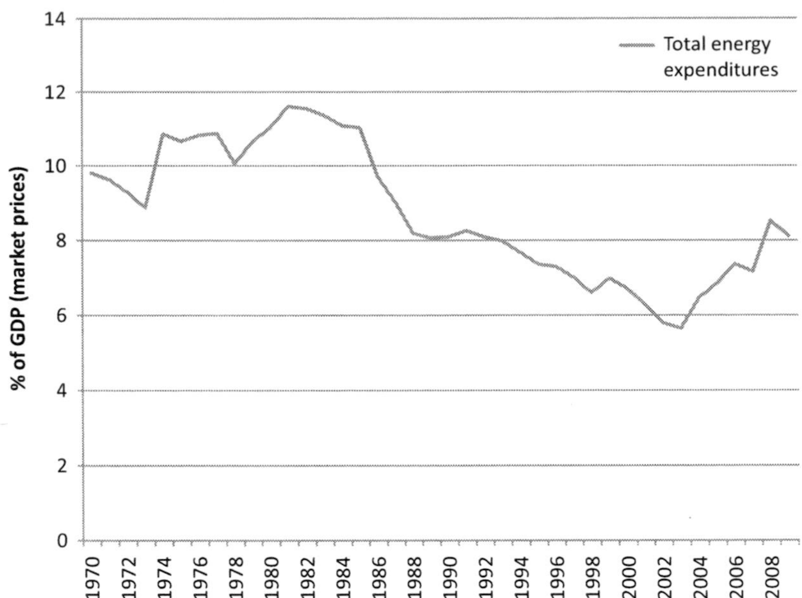


Figure 1.9 UK energy expenditure as a percentage of GDP.
*Source:* Office of National Statistics (GDP at market prices) and DUKES (2010, Table 1.1.6).

to £37.3 billion in 2009 (DUKES, 2010, Table 1.4). These numbers illustrate two important macroeconomic phenomena. First, that transport fuel is the most significant component of energy expenditure and hence a driver of future energy demand (including electricity). Second, that energy is an important source of government tax revenue, with 7 per cent of total tax revenue coming from taxation on the use of energy.[4] This is in addition to taxation of the profits of energy companies and taxes on the production of oil and gas in the North Sea. Any migration of energy demand from heavily taxed liquid fuels to currently lightly taxed electricity will most probably require substantial tax rises on electricity to maintain public finances.

Newbery (2005) points out that energy is not efficiently taxed at the moment in the UK as it does not follow rational approaches of public finance or a sensible carbon tax policy. Indeed, some types of fuels face

[4] Total public sector receipts were £514 billion in 2009–10 (*source*: HM Treasury Public Finances Databank).

very high taxes, whereas others are relatively lightly taxed. Thus liquid fuel for road transport has a high tax rate, whereas aviation fuel and gas for heating have very low tax rates. If taxes truly reflected environmental damage costs (of all types) and international security externalities, then taxes would be significantly increased on the less heavily taxed goods. Taxes should be used to give better price signals on the relative environmental damage of different fuels, to give incentives to reduce energy consumption and to raise tax revenue which can be recycled to reduce the general level of taxation or to support public expenditure (including measures to help the fuel poor).

Substantial components of overall energy expenditure arise from the industrial and commercial sectors of the economy. Indeed, the relative aggregate figures are somewhat misleading as to the position for the household sector. The household sector spends almost twice as much on gas as on electricity (rather than the other way round for the whole economy) and about the same amount on liquid transport fuels as on electricity and gas. This indicates the relative importance of non-transport energy demand for households and the importance of heat demand relative to power demand.

Energy services demand is not synonymous with demand for fuel and power. Energy services (e.g. lighting, heating and transport) are provided by a combination of capital equipment and energy. Expenditure on better household insulation or double glazing of windows is expenditure on energy services because it has a similar ultimate effect to gas-fired central heating in raising the ambient household room temperature in the winter. A car and liquid fuel are both required to provide transport services, and expenditure on one can be substituted for the other at the margin by spending more on a more fuel-efficient vehicle. A low-energy light bulb or a more energy-efficient domestic appliance will cost more money but use less electricity.

Figure 1.10 looks at the expenditure on energy services at the household level and its stability over time. From 1964 to 2008 we see that total consumer expenditure on the main categories of expenditure that are associated with energy services (as a percentage of GDP) fluctuated within fairly narrow bounds. We take energy services expenditure to be reflected in maintenance and repair of buildings and vehicles, capital expenditure on vehicles, fuels and other oils for vehicles and fuels (natural gas, heating oil and coal) and electricity. Not all expenditure on the maintenance and repair of buildings will be energy-services related, but a substantial part will be related to the provision of thermal comfort and can also be substituted for energy expenditure in the future (e.g. solar panels as part of a new roof). Figure 1.10 shows the substantial amount

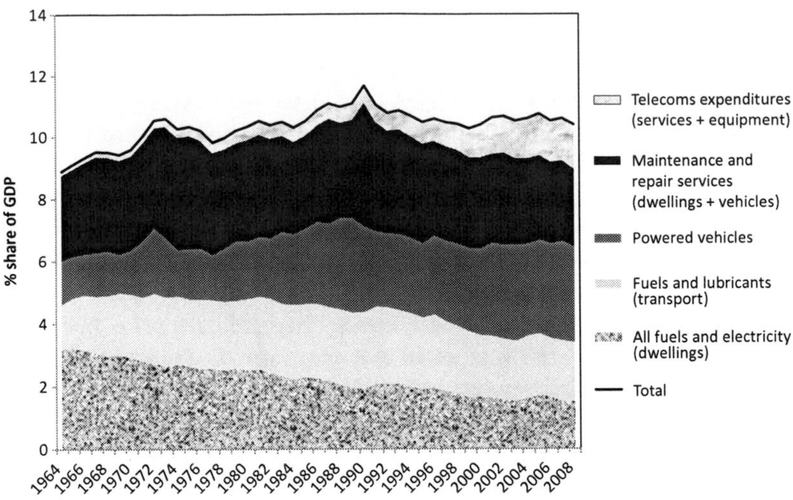


Figure 1.10 UK energy and communications services expenditure as a percentage of GDP.
*Source:* Office of National Statistics.

of expenditure on transport where expenditure on vehicles and on their repair exceeds expenditure on fuel. It also shows a gentle decline in the significance of household energy.

For comparison, Figure 1.10 shows expenditure on various components of communications services. This we take to be initially postal services (which have declined significantly) and latterly telecoms related. Here there is very little direct expenditure on equipment (as much of the equipment is supplied by service providers in return for the payment of usage charges). We return to communications services as a point of comparison with energy services later in this chapter.

An examination of the macroeconomic context of energy demand suggests the size and significance of energy services expenditure. There is substantial scope for diverting the different shares of expenditure between power, heat and transport, and between equipment, maintenance and energy expenditures. While utility companies may be dominant in electricity and gas, major oil companies and major supermarkets are dominant in liquid fuels and a large number of different companies are present in the repair and maintenance of buildings and vehicles. The electrification of heating and transport and the reduction in the size of the markets of liquid fuels will be likely to attract the interest of current liquid fuel incumbents and will create opportunities for substitution of equipment and repair and maintenance expenditures for expenditure on units of energy.

The first report of the Committee on Climate Change (CCC) (2008) in the UK illustrated the importance of electricity demand growth and the emergence of new technologies for reducing electricity consumption. In particular the Committee suggested that without attempts to reduce emissions, electricity demand might rise by 2.5 per cent p.a. (CCC, 2008, p. 55), partly as a result of climate change increasing the demand for air conditioning. However, with the application of new technologies such as LED lighting and efficient air conditioning, electricity demand could be 35 per cent below its baseline figure by 2050 (CCC, 2008, p. 55). However, some research in California points to some ambiguous effects. Indeed, it has been shown that newer buildings (subject to stricter energy buildings standards) might enable higher temperature response, as they are more likely to be equipped with air conditioners and are often larger, so that the cumulative effect on absolute electricity consumption is ambiguous, and the aggregate temperature response can be predicted to increase with new (and more energy efficient) construction (Chong, 2010).[5] Higher temperature response means more incremental electricity use. Even within industrial processes the Committee saw scope for the reduction of electricity demand (by 18 per cent below baseline in 2050 – CCC, 2008, p. 56). It is worth pointing out that these estimates are highly uncertain and that actual demand will significantly depend on outturn prices and incomes.

## 1.3 The long-run microeconomic context of energy demand

We now turn to how the demand for energy (and hence electricity) operates at the level of microeconomics. It is worth beginning by discussing the relationship between the underlying physics of energy demand and the economics of energy consumption, and relating this back to individual behaviour and microeconomics.

### *1.3.1 The physics of energy consumption and its relation to the economics of energy consumption*

MacKay (2008) discusses energy efficiency at the level of the device and the household. He points out that there is a significant variation in existing energy efficiencies of transport and of heating and of household

[5] Chong defines temperature response as the percentage increase (relative to usage on a 65° F day) in electricity use due to a 1° F increase in temperature.

power devices. For each of these energy services, electric power is the most energy efficient. Thus, for household heating a heat pump can convert 1 kWh of electricity into up to 4 kWh equivalent of heat. This implies that a gas-fired power station running at 53 per cent electrical efficiency might be able to deliver electrical heat using half the gas of a gas-fired boiler with '90 per cent efficiency' (pp. 152–3). An electric car uses around 15 kWh per 100 km, around five times less than the average fossil fuel car. This implies that even powered by the existing electricity system an electric car produces a quarter of the emissions per km of the average conventional vehicle (pp. 129–30). Electric household devices are notoriously inefficiently used – in the UK, for instance, 8 per cent of all electricity is used by devices on standby (DTI, 2006, p. 43) and this could be reduced by a factor of more than 10 for many devices. MacKay (pp. 157–8) gives the example of reducing his own household electricity consumption by 50 per cent by reducing standby and installing energy-efficient light bulbs.

Allwood (2010) looks in more detail into the theoretical potential of energy efficiency by examining the underlying material efficiency of production processes. He gives the example of the car where the energy required to power the vehicle is a function of the sum of the aerodynamic drag (of the car through the air), the mechanical drag (of the wheels on the road) and the inertia (which must be overcome to get it moving). He suggests how the force required to move the car at a constant speed can be reduced substantially. This can be done by getting the mass of the car down (by 75 per cent), reducing the friction coefficient (by 93 per cent), reducing the drag coefficient (by 75 per cent) and shortening the frontal area of the car (by 25 per cent). He calculates that the energy required can thus be reduced by 91 per cent. This sort of calculation indicates the scale of the efficiency improvements that are theoretically possible in providing the same level of energy service. These fundamental redesigns of the way energy services are provided substantially exceed the efficiency improvements that are possible in industry from simply producing existing energy-intensive goods more efficiently. Examination of the energy-efficiency savings in the production of steel, cement, plastic, paper and aluminium shows that use of best-practice technology and recycling reduces energy consumption only by less than 50 per cent in most scenarios.

The conclusion we can draw from the above is that large physical potential savings in energy use are possible (often involving increases in the scope of use of electricity). However, the economics of such savings do not currently stack up. For instance, heat pumps are very expensive and involve high capital costs, relative to existing gas-fired boilers. They also involve significant running costs and many would currently be more expensive to run than a gas boiler.[6] There is also the issue of whether the quality of the service provided is comparable. Heat pumps are more intrusive and can take up more space in a household room. Electric vehicles have limited mileage ranges and slower refuelling times. A car which weighs 75 per cent less, is narrower and has very low drag (sitting the passenger lower down) will not necessarily be considered as being as safe, comfortable or stylish as existing vehicles.

Indeed, it is clear from history that there is always a wide range of observed efficiencies in the economy, with the average efficiency of the provision of an energy service being significantly less than the efficiency of the most efficient. New fossil fuel cars and gas boilers are 50–100 per cent more efficient than those of the average fleet. As we saw in Figure 1.7, technologies tend to persist long after the appearance of apparently superior and more efficient ones (which will indeed eventually become dominant). This is partly because initially new technologies are relatively expensive (even for new installations) and partly because of lock-in to existing technologies whereby individuals and companies continue to use existing technologies because they have already invested in them and incurred their up-front capital costs or are uncertain over future energy savings (Hassett and Metcalf, 1993). Thus the average life of energy service equipment, as well as its cost, becomes an important determinant of how the average efficiency relates to the highest available efficiency.

### *1.3.2 The apparent non-rationality of individual energy consumption*

Another important consideration in economics is apparently non-rational behaviour. The idea that energy-efficiency measures which reduce cost will necessarily be implemented is based on neo-classical consumer theory, which says that more is always preferred to less and that individual economic decision makers will always take actions which are in their economic interests. There are a number of important challenges to this, only some of which are genuinely about irrationality.

First, even neo-classical theory suggests the paramount importance of considerations of who benefits as distinct from who bears the cost of an action. Thus, apparently non-rational behaviour may simply reflect

[6] If the average price of 20,000 kWh of gas is 2.61p/kWh and the marginal price of electricity is 9.62p/kWh (a typical tariff on 17 September 2010), a heat pump would need to have a coefficient of performance of greater than 3.31 to reduce *running* costs below that of a 90 per cent efficient gas boiler.

the fact that it is not the same individual (or group of individuals) who benefits from switching off the light bulb or installing energy-saving equipment as the individuals who have to incur the inconvenience (however minor) of taking energy-saving actions. In the commercial sector and in the rented sector this is often exemplified by the tenant–landlord split whereby it is the landlord who has to decide on and organize investment in energy-saving equipment, but it is the tenant who benefits through lower bills (as discussed in Grubb and Wilde, 2008). Within the household there may be competing incentives and perceptions – one of our colleagues was told to remove his energy-saving bulbs by his wife who did not like the quality of the light they produced!

Second, the well-known marginal cost of abatement curve (e.g. CCC, 2008, p. 226) suggests that there are large unexploited energy-efficiency savings in the commercial and household sectors. However, this merely values the benefit of action against its capital cost, not against the time and inconvenience costs which would be incurred to deliver what are often individually small savings which require significant up-front investments of individual or organizational time. Thus even for a commercial business, prioritizing energy-cost savings may come at the expense of sales-enhancing strategies which could have been worked on by the same individuals. Some energy savings may even come at the direct expense of sales, e.g. if keeping shop doors closed (to reduce heating bills) or not visiting clients in person (to reduce transport costs) actually results in less business.

Third, behavioural economics, which looks at how individuals actually behave when making economic decisions, has suggested a number of phenomena which may be increasingly important to take account of in considering the future of energy demand. These include liquidity constraints, expectations, loss aversion, commitment devices and perceptions. Brutscher (2010) investigates these in the context of explaining top-up behaviour by electricity customers using pre-payment meters in Northern Ireland. He starts by observing that individuals top up by significantly less than is rational given interest rates and the costs of topping up (using a Baumol–Tobin model). He finds that given fixed costs of topping up (the opportunity cost of time taken to go online, telephone or buy credit in-store) versus the lost interest on credit balance, individuals should top up 2.3 times a year at £230 per time. What actually happens is that individuals top up around fifty times a year, by £13 each time. Liquidity constraints would suggest that the reason people might do this is because they do not ever have £230. Expectations theory might suggest individuals worry about future changes in prices in ways that might reduce the optimality of their top-ups. Loss aversion might suggest that people worry about the potential for losing larger credit balances (should the meter malfunction or they have to move house). Commitment device theory might suggest that individuals use low top-up amounts in order to force themselves to be more conscious of energy use, because they are forced to check their meter more regularly. Perceptions may matter because intuitively people may prefer spending a series of small amounts rather than a one-off expenditure of the equivalent amount. Therefore we might prefer pay-as-you-go expenditures over lump-sum contracts, even if the lump-sum contract is cheaper (Finkelstein, 2009). Brutscher (2010) finds evidence for perceptions theory as an explanation of actual top-up behaviour in Northern Ireland. One implication of this is that smart meters which facilitate small top-ups may make many consumers less concerned about their energy consumption by making them think they are spending less on energy than they actually are. Behavioural economics may prove to be significant both in explaining observed energy behaviour (with and without smart meters) and in understanding how best to encourage individuals to make more rational energy decisions. This relates to Thaler and Sunstein's idea of nudge theory (2009), where the way information is presented (rather than the underlying financial characteristics) may be very important for the final aggregate outcome and that small changes in the way information is presented might have a significant impact on behaviour.

Fourth, there are serious issues of poverty and vulnerability in the provision of energy services. An estimated 4.9 million households in the UK are currently in fuel poverty (i.e. spending 10 per cent or more of their income on household energy) (see Waddams Price, this volume). This is around 20 per cent of all households; in some regions the figure is more than 40 per cent. Of those households perhaps half are vulnerable households, i.e. households with sick, disabled, children or elderly people who are more vulnerable to cold-related illness (Bolton, 2010) and hence for whom an adequate provision of energy may have serious impacts on health and/or for whom rational decisions about energy consumption may not be possible. Fuel poverty may merely be a component of poverty, but it clearly has implications for the future of energy demand. The fuel poor may be exempted from general pressures to raise energy prices to bring about the long-run transition required by decarbonization targets, or they may be targeted for capital expenditure interventions which reduce their regular expenditure. The poor may exhibit very different income and price elasticities from the national average. Concerns about the nature of the social contract with the poor in transition and developing countries explain large subsidies to reduce energy prices (which are often very poorly targeted). Climate change policy may increasingly come up against such pressures to subsidize final prices for large numbers of customers (hence raising the cost for others).

Finally, it is worth saying that inefficiency and variability in decision making are characteristic of energy markets (and indeed all markets). Wilson and Waddams (2007) analyzed the behaviour of household consumers in choosing electricity and gas suppliers. They found that a significant number of consumers switched to a higher tariff when they intended to switch to a cheaper one, whereas less than half of those switching to get the cheapest price chose the cheapest tariff available at the time of switching. They concluded that this demonstrated a combination of computational mistakes (the 'bounded rationality' of consumers, following Simon, 1947), the fact that factors other than price alone (such as the quality of service) were also important and that companies might make it difficult for consumers to calculate exactly how much they were going to pay under any tariff using so-called 'foggy tactics' (Miravete, 2007), hidden clauses and tiny fonts (thereby being an example of a 'confusopoly'[7]). This was in addition to the fact that 50 per cent of customers had never switched supplier, even though they could have saved money by moving away from the incumbent. It is simply a fact that customers of any given product exhibit high degrees of inertia, value quality of service, are prone to miscalculations or are faced with confusing (and sometimes misleading) information from service providers. Thus apparently optimal solutions spread only slowly through the economy.

One of the ways in which individual energy users might become better informed is via social networks. This could happen for householders through being in touch with other better informed individuals (e.g. friends, family, neighbours, members of social network groups). Or it could happen for companies through interactions with motivated outside stakeholders (such as green non-government organizations (NGOs)). Zhang and Nuttall (2008) use agent-based modelling to show how a supplier-led smart meter roll-out might develop as a result of social and economic influences on individual households. Brophy Haney *et al.* (2009) show how high-street retail companies are more likely to have adopted tougher energy and climate objectives if they have connections with more outside stakeholders of a particular type (most notably academic institutions). Participation in energy-saving clubs can be associated with substantially enhanced demand reduction as participants share ideas (though the likelihood of voluntary participation might be low).[8] Social

[7] This term was introduced by Scott Adams in *The Dilbert Future* (1997).
[8] See Ofgem (2010, p. 9) for some evidence from the UK.

Table 1.2 *Lifetime costs of certain energy-related services*

| | Capital cost £ | Lifetime energy cost £ | Total cost £ | Energy cost % |
|---|---|---|---|---|
| Light bulb 100W | 0.35 | 18.98 | 19.33 | 98.2% |
| Light bulb low energy 100W | 1 | 15.53 | 16.53 | 94.0% |
| Gas boiler | 1000 | 7629.05 | 8629.05 | 88.4% |
| TV | 700 | 540.01 | 1240.01 | 43.5% |
| Fridge | 300 | 159.56 | 459.56 | 34.7% |
| Car (annual) | 2500 | 1000.00 | 3500.00 | 28.6% |
| Computer | 1000 | 48.84 | 1048.84 | 4.7% |
| Mobile phone (annual) | 360 | 1.42 | 361.42 | 0.4% |

Key assumptions: electricity 13p/kWh; gas 3.5p/kWh; 5% discount rate.

capital and its relation to the encouragement of energy efficiency (and more efficient consumption in general)[9] would seem to be an important idea reflected in these results.

### 1.3.3 *How to encourage energy efficiency*

Now we turn to the underlying microeconomics of energy services and discuss how easy it is likely to be to encourage the uptake of energy-efficient products. Energy services are goods which are quantity, place, time and quality specific. They are a derived, or intermediate, demand, in that the final price of the good which requires energy is what consumers in general perceive, rather than just the price of the energy. As the energy cost is less than 100 per cent of the cost of the service this dilutes the impact of changes in energy prices on the final price to which customers respond. This is further complicated in that, although the marginal cost of consuming the product may be substantially made up of the energy cost, individuals may consider only the average total cost (possibly due to pre-commitment to use the product once purchased and also due to bounded rationality).

#### *1.3.3.1 Raising prices*

Table 1.2 shows a rough calculation for the costs of the energy part of certain energy services in relation to the total cost of the service. It

[9] See Pepper *et al.* (2009), who discuss the link between green consumption and sustainable consumption in general. Pollitt (2010) argues for the importance of a more holistic engagement with individuals' religious beliefs in eliciting behavioural change related to the achievement of climate-change policy targets.

is immediately clear why low-energy light bulbs are high up the list of products that individuals are willing to buy in order to save energy. Even for a low-energy light bulb costing £1, 94 per cent of the lifetime cost is the electricity consumed. Having an energy-efficient gas boiler should be high up the list of actions to take if a £1,000 up-front cost is not a problem. Cold-storage services provided by fridges are roughly one-third energy costs. However, for a computer or a mobile phone the energy cost is a small fraction of the total annual cost.

Table 1.2 suggests that doubling the price of electricity or of natural gas is likely to have a significant impact on the uptake of low-energy light bulbs or energy-efficient boilers and energy use per unit of lighting service or heating comfort. However, it is likely to have a negligible impact on incentivizing the purchase of energy-efficient mobile phones. For these energy-related services, agreed energy-efficiency standards might be very important in encouraging the manufacture and sale of more energy-efficient devices. Table 1.2 has a further implication: as energy efficiency improves it is likely to become harder to influence energy demand via price effects. This is because the share of energy in the cost of the service is likely to drop over time (unless the price rises to compensate), thus reducing the incentive to achieve further efficiencies. Income elasticities for certain energy-related services will be very important drivers of energy demand. Income elasticity for additional fridges (at households which already have one) is likely to be low; however only around one-third of UK households currently have dishwashers, while demand for personal electronic equipment is likely to be highly income elastic. Interestingly, it is also the case that energy consumption is rising fastest for the categories of energy service where the share of energy in total costs is lowest, such as personal electronic devices (see Figure 1.11). Power for personal electronic devices (including computing) increased from 19 per cent of total domestic electricity consumption in 1990 to 32 per cent in 2009; by contrast, lighting demand fell from 24 per cent to 19 per cent over the same period.

### *1.3.3.2 Electrification of personal transport*

New sources of electricity demand may emerge which substantially change the total demand for electricity and the way electricity is consumed by the household. The Tesla Roadster[10] stores 53 kWh of electricity and has a maximum power rating of 185 KW (Mackay, 2008, p. 129). Typical daily household demand in the UK is about 10 kWh, with a maximum power of 10 KW. An electric car has a typical charge

[10] The Tesla Roadster is an electic sport car prototype manufactured by Tesla Motors – see www.teslamotors.com, last accessed 27 February 2011.

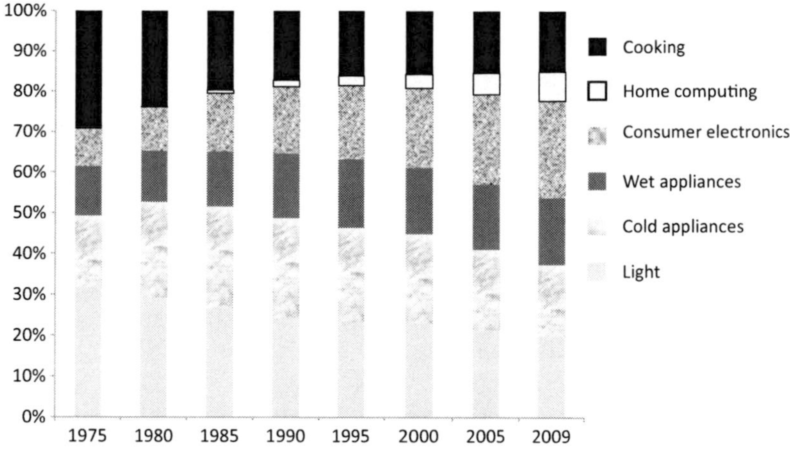


Figure 1.11 Shares of different devices in household electricity demand in the UK, 1970–2009.
*Source:* DECC (2010).

and discharge efficiency of 85 per cent of the electrical energy used to charge the car. The impact of charging an electric car at home would be to substantially shift electricity demand towards the residential sector and to increase aggregate electricity demand. It would also increase the maximum power drawn by the household, though this would substantially depend on the rate of charge required (53 kWh could be delivered overnight in seven hours at 8.91 KW power). Given that the average household consumption at the evening peak in winter is only 1 KW,[11] a significant penetration of electric vehicles charging at home would be a substantial system load. It would also imply substantial infrastructure investments and have significant implications for the grid.

However, electric vehicles offer other possibilities. They offer substantial battery storage capacity to the electricity grid, both when stationary at home and when at places of work. They may thus be very useful in providing short-term back-up at system demand peaks or for dumping electricity to the batteries when supply is at a peak (due to the running of large quantities of intermittent renewables). This sort of link-up between intermittent wind generation and electric vehicle demand is being trialled on the Danish island of Bornholm.[12] Electric vehicles also offer the ability to shift the location of consumption around the grid, with cars

[11] This is based on there being around 25 million homes in the UK and peak household demand of around 25,000 MW (as discussed below).

[12] See www.edison-net.dk.

charging at places of work and discharging at home or vice versa. Indeed, commercial loads could be supported by discharging vehicles during the daytime which then return home to charge up at night.

*1.3.3.3 The size of the elasticities*

The evidence on elasticity of demand with respect to price and income is large but difficult to interpret (see Steinbuks, this volume). There is also a substantial difference between the short-run and long-run responses to a price or income change. Espey and Espey (2004) looked at a number of studies of household electricity demand and found that the median short-run price elasticity for electricity was −0.28, rising to −0.81 in the long run. They found the median short-run income elasticity was 0.15, rising to 0.92 in the long run. This highlights the importance of raising real prices as incomes rise if demand is not to increase over time. For transport Espey (1998) looked at a larger number of studies and found lower median elasticities in the long run. The median short-run price elasticity of demand was −0.23, rising to −0.43 in the long run. Espey also found the median short-run income elasticity of demand was 0.39, rising to 0.81 in the long run. Given that energy costs are currently a relatively small part of the running costs of a petrol-powered car (see Table 1.2) and would decline substantially for electric vehicles, electricity demand for transport would not be particularly sensitive to its own price. Indeed, over time we would be expecting to see price elasticities of demand for energy declining as energy became less significant as a share of the total cost of energy-related service.

*1.3.3.4 Shifting electricity consumption across time and place*

Electricity consumed at different times of the day and year has different underlying resource costs. Figure 1.12 charts the daily variation in prices on the UK power system for three days in 2009. Prices vary considerably. On an off-peak day the price in the power market does not rise above £50 per MWh or 5p/kWh, significantly less than the price paid by residential consumers for each additional unit of power. However, on a median day the price varies between £30 per MWh and £100 per MWh for half-hour periods across a twenty-four-hour period. On the peak day on the system prices reached £800 per MWh or 80p/kWh. For median days there is a strong incentive for large, energy-intensive users to use electricity at night rather than during the day. Smart demand response from commercial and residential users could exploit this underlying price differential, either by reducing consumption or by shifting it to a cheaper time. Residential consumers could therefore reduce marginal generation costs.

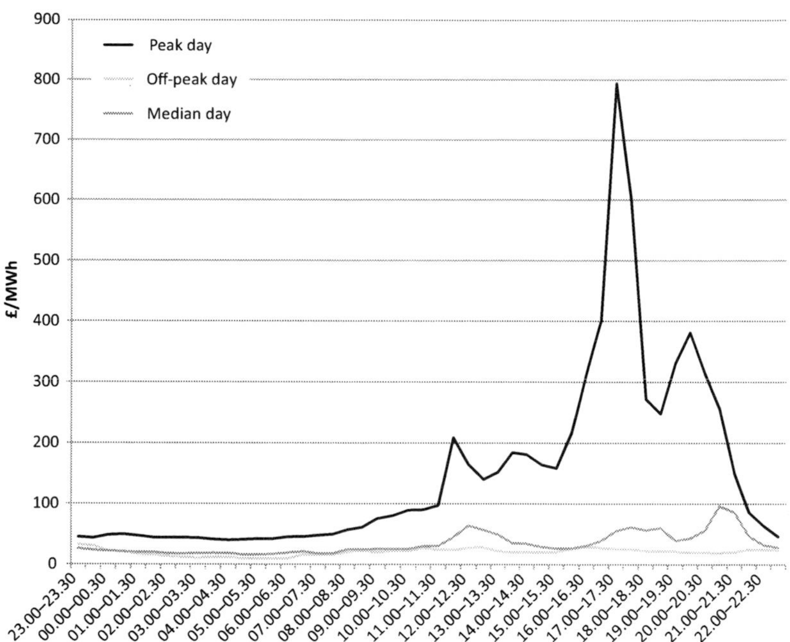


Figure 1.12 UK daily power prices, 2009.
*Source:* APX (2010).

The potential for demand shifting, even by a couple of hours, could be substantial. At the system peak time a disproportionate part of the load is made up of residential demand (45 per cent, against an average of 36 per cent final energy consumption).[13] Figure 1.13 shows the components of household demand at the typical daily winter peak (of 52016 GW in this case). Five per cent of total domestic demand is simply devices on standby, while another 6 per cent is wet appliances such as dishwashers and washing machines, many of which could be run later at night. Another 9 per cent is represented by cold appliances, which could be pre-cooled before the system peak to maintain their target temperature over the peak period before switching back on. Next the 16.5 per cent of demand due to water heaters – these could also be turned on earlier to have hot water available ahead of the system peak. Pre-loading of devices with energy does imply added energy cost due to energy losses, but with better thermal insulation this cost could be kept low.

[13] Thirty-six per cent is calculated as the domestic share of final electricity consumption in 2007, reported in DUKES (2010, Table 5.1, p. 132). The figure of 45 per cent is from Lampaditou and Leach (2005).

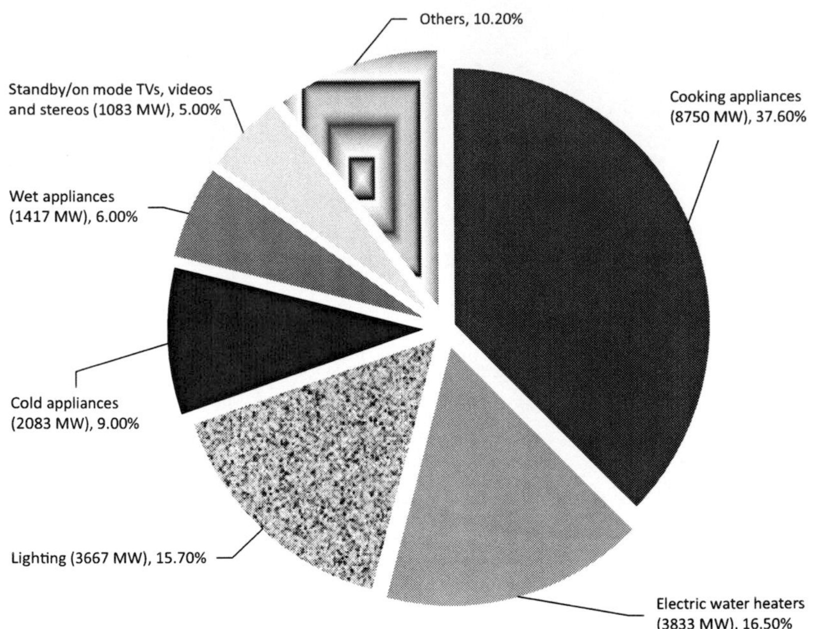


Figure 1.13 The components of household electricity demand at system peak.
*Source:* Lampaditou and Leach (2005).

Residential consumers could also respond to local voltage or national frequency changes (i.e. providing back-up demand response equivalent to back-up generation response). The National Grid spends several hundred million pounds per year on spinning reserve to maintain frequency in the national transmission system.[14] In theory, households could provide a form of virtual spinning reserve. This would be possible if fridges, freezers, washing machines and dishwashers could be interrupted for short periods a small number of times per year in return for a payment related to the current payment for spinning reserve.[15]

A number of economic issues arise with exploiting this potential for demand response. These include the size of the likely benefit relative to

[14] Spinning reserves refer to generators that can instantaneously increase the power they generate, in case of a decrease in frequency, i.e. when load is greater than generation. Electricity system operators are required to maintain a certain amount of spinning reserves in case of sudden surges in power demand.

[15] See Samarakoon *et al.* (2010).

the costs. *Time of use* pricing is relatively straightforward to implement and already exists for a significant number of customers (on Economy 7 tariffs, or the PowerShift tariff in Northern Ireland). This sort of tariff does not require two-way communications with the meter, just a clock in the meter so that charging occurs in line with the charge periods. *Real-time pricing*, where prices change according to spot prices in the market, requires two-way communication with the household meter. This implies additional telecoms costs as well as creating uncertainty about the actual price that the consumer will face. Assuming demand response arising from real-time pricing is to be largely automated via sequential switching off of particular appliances, this requires additional communications infrastructure within the home, and possibly smart controls on the appliances connected to the meter. Contracts could specify the nature of the demand response to real-time prices (e.g. pay a fixed price and get a reduction for limiting consumption to a specified maximum level when the price rises above a certain level on the spot market). *Critical peak pricing* is a limited form of real-time pricing whereby strong incentives to reduce consumption are given at certain times of the year, usually involving a known price paid for a measured response at the critical peak. This requires a two-way communication system, but can be quite basic (e.g. a red light on the meter), aimed at soliciting a manual response by the householder to the signal received.

Brophy Haney *et al.* (this volume) discuss the evidence from trials on the size of the effect from time of use, real-time and critical peak pricing. They conclude that peak savings of up to 15 per cent are possible, with demand reductions of up to 10 per cent, though it is not entirely clear how much of the savings are due to improved information on energy use alone. For the UK, the evidence from Northern Ireland is that the introduction of better prepayment meters (which gave clearer information on energy use) reduced demand by up to 5 per cent (Boyd, 2008).

A further overall consideration is the fact that if there is significant responsiveness of demand, this begins to reduce the marginal benefit of further response, flattening the price curve and reducing the cost of spinning reserve. This reduces the value of additional responsiveness and the incentives to respond if responsive demand receives only its marginal value to the system. In short, responders create positive externalities for other users which would somehow need to be recycled back to the responders. There may also be issues to do with the fact that rich consumers might have more opportunities to benefit from offering demand response (e.g. because they could afford the state-of-the-art household appliances capable of responding and because they use more non-essential appliances) and hence this would exacerbate fuel poverty concerns.

Lampaditou and Leach (2005) conduct a simulation, in line with Figure 1.13 above. They suggest that time of use pricing with water/wet appliances might lead to a 47 per cent decrease in the household morning peak (due to a shift of water heating) and a 6 per cent decrease in the household evening peak (due to a shift of wet appliances). They calculate that this could generate consumer benefits of up to £52 per year per consumer (using average spot prices of random winter day from UK APX 2005). However, if there was direct load control (by the grid) of major appliances at 5–6pm (due to shifting use and better cycling), there could be much greater responsiveness in the evening peak. They suggest that switching off washing machines, tumble driers, dishwashers and cold appliances would cause a 15 per cent household peak reduction (or 3500 MW), rising to a 23 per cent reduction if there was better cycling of water heaters (5500 MW). Clearly these figures represent the upper end of what is technically possible rather than reasonable estimates of the likely uptake of contracts for such response. Silva *et al.* (this volume) present more recent simulations of the benefits of responsiveness from domestic appliances.

Actual household demand responsiveness will be driven by consumer willingness to participate in the contracts that might be offered by suppliers for demand response. A large number of consumers are likely to show no response (in line with more than 50 per cent of consumers who have not switched electricity supplier).[16] Other consumers will respond depending on the size of the benefits available to them (their ability to respond) and their view of the level of control they would like exercised by external parties. Remote control of appliances will raise issues of data security, confidence in the technology and the availability of easy overrides. Uptake will also probably be a function of the extent to which consumers can understand the contracts being offered. It seems likely that simple contracts will be favoured and that widespread use of real-time pricing is unlikely in the current environment. It is also the case that people prefer the insurance that fixed tariffs offer (most consumers currently pay a fixed amount monthly)[17] and hence may well be prepared to pay a premium to avoid exposure to variable tariffs.

A major discussion which has gone on at the transmission level, and to some extent at the distribution level, of electricity networks is the role of nodal (location-varying) prices (Pollitt and Bialek, 2008). These prices allow the reflection of marginal congestion costs around the electricity system. Additional demands located at congested nodes impose both

[16] See Ipsos Mori (2010). [17] See Ipsos Mori (2010).

short-run energy losses and long-run expansion costs on the network as a whole, while additional generation at these loads reduces short-run losses and longer-run expansion costs. Of course, it is already possible to differentiate prices by location alone. However, truly efficient nodal prices vary by time of day and hence nodes heavily congested at the national system peak are not likely to be congested off-peak. At the moment most loads and all households pay the same for electricity from a given supplier within the same distribution network area. Thus it would be possible that there is some quantifiable benefit from varying retail prices more by location than at present. Estimates from Heng (2010) suggest that locational import and export energy prices might vary significantly within the same distribution network. Location-varying charges within distribution networks may be particularly useful in avoiding the need for local network upgrades. All the same, issues arise with location-varying charging as with time-related charging. The idea that individuals living in close proximity might pay different prices according to the condition of the electricity distribution network may raise fairness issues, which may be difficult to explain.

Locational as well as time-varying prices are particularly relevant to transport demand for electricity. We already have place-varying prices for liquid fuel (i.e. every petrol station can set its price independently). It may be useful to have location-varying prices reflecting the efficient cost of supplying electricity to particular parts of the network. In fact, it is possible that transport demand at high levels of penetration could significantly improve the efficiency of operational and capital expenditure on the distribution networks.

## 1.4 Conclusions on the economics of electricity demand

There is much that we can imagine about the potential future of energy demand and its degree of responsiveness. However, there are things that we know we don't know about the energy future.

First, the scale of the IT challenge is unclear until we know what we would like the power system to do and the degree of public acceptability for the massive amounts of data transfer that could be involved.

Second, we don't know what outturn response elasticities could be. The previous estimates vary widely. The London Congestion Charge for vehicles actually revealed an elasticity of demand with respect to price of −0.42 against a value −0.15 predicted (Evans, 2008), leading to significantly more price response and significantly lower charge revenue than predicted.

Third, we don't know what innovations might come along in heat and in transport which might impact back on electricity demand. The recent revolution in telecoms (e.g. the growth of SMS messaging) suggests that we should expect the unexpected.

Fourth, we don't know which diversifying entrants will come into the market (e.g. device retailers, supermarkets, oil and gas majors). Evidence suggests that it is likely that well-positioned incumbents in related sectors will enter if profitable entry opportunities present themselves (Klepper and Simons, 2000).

Fifth, we don't know how consumers will react to the new technological and contractual opportunities. Official trials of smart meters appear to have been disappointing in the UK (Ofgem, 2010), but this may be because of the way the trials have been set up. It may be the case that actual or apparently non-rational behaviour is likely.

Sixth, we are likely to see the exhaustion of the benefit of new demand technologies at relatively low levels of penetration. It may not be worth signing more people up to a new tariff or equipping them with new technology given the increasing marginal cost of persuading additional householders to participate and the declining marginal benefits of them doing so.

In closing, there would seem to be four important messages from our discussion in sections 2 and 3.

*First, higher prices are key to demand moderation.* Prices must rise (nationally and globally) as technology improves to avoid a significant rebound in demand arising from more efficient appliances and higher income. The good news is that economies can and do adjust to high energy prices and consumers may not notice the difference in the long run.

*Second, price signals should be helped by standards.* As income rises and energy service equipment becomes more energy efficient, prices will become a weaker signal, especially for new sources of demand. Energy-efficiency standards will remain important policies driving long-run demand.

*Third, shifting electricity demand is worthwhile* and may be easier and more valuable than actual reduction. This is especially true if there is a rise in electric vehicles and in renewable penetration, which will make the exact time and place of consumption important as well as the quantity. This is an area where new business models are required – and are already emerging – to fully exploit the potential benefits by inducing behavioural change.

*Finally, the full potential for demand reduction and response is unlikely to be fully realized.* The demand side of electricity consumption is decided by the interaction of millions of decisions made by human beings with bounded rationality and mixed incentives. Some of the aspects of such diversity of patterns of consumption have beneficial impacts, such as through load flattening, for instance. However, it always has been and always will be the case that we will look at the current pattern of consumption and be able to identify significant theoretical scope for savings. The hope is that we can achieve as much demand reduction and response as is possible within the constraints.

## References

Adams, S. (1997). *The Dilbert Future: Thriving on Stupidity in the 21st Century*, New York: HarperCollins.

Allen, R.C. (2009). *The British Industrial Revolution in Global Perspective*, Cambridge: Cambridge University Press.

Allwood, J. (2010). Energy and material efficiency, presentation to EPRG Spring Research Seminar, 14 May.

APX, APX Power UK, Available at www.apxendex.com/index.php?id=61, last accessed 19 October 2010.

Bolton, P. (2010). *Fuel Poverty Statistics*, Standard Note SN/SG/5115, London: House of Commons Library.

Boyd, J. (2008). Keypad meters: The Northern Ireland Experience, presentation to Managing residential electricity demand: Learning from experience in the UK and Ontario, St Hugh's College, Oxford, 21–23 May.

Brophy Haney, A., Jones, I.W. and Pollitt, M.G. (2009). UK retailers and climate change: the role of partnership in climate strategies, EPRG Working Paper 0928, Faculty of Economics, University of Cambridge.

Brophy Haney, A., Jamasb, T. and Pollitt, M.G. (2011). Smart metering: technology, economics and international experience, in Jamasb, T. and Pollitt, M. (eds.), *The Future of Electricity Demand: Customers, Citizens and Loads*, Cambridge: Cambridge University Press.

Brutscher, P.B. (2010). Pay-and-pay-as-you-go: an exploratory study into prepayment metering, Presentation to EPRG Seminar, Cambridge, 3 May.

Chong, H. (2010). Building vintage and electricity use: old homes use less electricity in hot weather, EI @ Haas Working Paper WP-211, Berkeley, CA: University of California.

Committee on Climate Change (2008). *Building a Low-carbon Economy – the UK's Contribution to Tackling Climate Change*, London: the Stationery Office.

DECC (2010a). UK Energy in Brief 2010, *Department of Energy and Climate Change*, London: DECC.

DECC (2010b). Energy Consumption in the UK, *Department of Energy and Climate Change*, London: DECC.

DTI (2006). *Energy Review: The Energy Challenge*, London: Department for Trade and Industry.

DUKES (2010). *Digest of United Kingdom Energy Statistics 2010 [DUKES]*, London: TSO.

Espey, J.A. and Espey, M. (2004). Turning on the lights: a meta-analysis of residential electricity demand elasticities, *Journal of Agricultural and Applied Economics*, **36**(1): 65–81.

Espey, M. (1998). Gasoline demand revisited: an international meta-analysis of elasticities, *Energy Economics*, **20**(3): 273–95.

Evans, R. (2008). Demand Elasticities for Car Trips to Central London as revealed by the Central London Congestion Charge, Transport for London, Policy Analysis Division, London.

Finkelstein, A. (2009). EZ-tax: tax salience and tax rates, *Quarterly Journal of Economics*, **124**(3): 969–1010.

Fouquet, R. and Pearson, P.J.G. (2006). Seven centuries of energy services: the price and use of light in the United Kingdom (1300–2000), *Energy Journal*, **27**(1): 139–77.

Grubb, M. and Wilde, J. (2008). Enhancing the efficient use of electricity in the business and public sectors, in Grubb, M., Jamasb, T. and Pollitt, M. (eds.), *Delivering a Low-Carbon Electricity System: Technologies, Economics and Policy*, Cambridge: Cambridge University Press, pp. 229–56.

Hassett, K.A. and Metcalf, G.E. (1993). Energy conservation investment: do consumers discount the future correctly? *Energy Policy*, **21**(6): 710–16.

Heng, H.Y. (2010). Long-Term Distribution Network Pricing and Planning to Facilitate Efficient Power Distribution, Department of Electrical Engineering, PhD Dissertation, University of Bath.

HM Treasury (2010). Public Finances Databank, available at www.hm-treasury.gov.uk/psf_databank.htm, last accessed 19 October 2010.

IEA (2010a). *Electricity Information (2010)*, International Energy Agency: Paris.

IEA (2010b). *Energy Prices and Taxes (2010)*. International Energy Agency: Paris.

Ipsos Mori (2010). Customer Engagement with the Energy Market – Tracking Survey, *Report prepared for Ofgem*, London: Ipsos Mori.

Klepper, S. and Simons, K.L. (2000). Dominance by birthright: entry of prior radio producers and competitive ramifications in the U.S. television receiver industry, *Strategic Management Journal*, **21**(10–11): 997–1016.

Lampaditou, E. and Leach, M. (2005). Evaluating Participation of Residential Customers in Demand Response Programs in the UK. ECEEE 2005 Summer Study, France.

MacKay, D. (2008). *Sustainable Energy – Without the Hot Air*, Cambridge: UIT.

Miravete, E. (2007). The Doubtful Profitability of Foggy Pricing, CEPR Discussion Paper no. 6295, London, Centre for Economic Policy Research, available at www.cepr.org/pubs/dps/DP6295.asp, last accessed 23 February 2011.

Newbery, D.M. (2005). Why tax energy?, *The Energy Journal*, **26**(3): 1–39.

Ofgem (2010). Energy Demand Research Project Review of Progress for the period March 2009 – September 2009, Ref.37/10, London: Ofgem.

Pepper, M., Jackson, T. and Uzzell, D. (2009). An examination of the values that drive socially conscious and frugal consumer behaviours, *International Journal of Consumer Studies*, **33**(2): 126–36.

Pollitt, M. (2010). Green Values in Communities: How and why to engage individuals with decarbonisation targets, Centre for Business Research Working Paper, No. 398.

Pollitt, M. and Bialek, J. (2008). Electricity network investment and regulation for a low-carbon future, in Grubb, M., Jamasb, T. and Pollitt, M. (eds.), *Delivering a Low-Carbon Electricity System: Technologies, Economics and Policy*, Cambridge: Cambridge University Press, pp. 183–206.

Samarakoon, K., Ekanayake, J. and Jenkins, N. (2010). A Demonstration of a Load Control Scheme to Provide Primary Frequency Response through Smart Meters, Poster presented at Flexnet Annual Assembly, May 2010.

Simon, H.A. (1947). *Administrative Behavior*, New York: Macmillan.

Steinbuks, J. (2010). Interfuel Substitution and Energy Use in the UK Manufacturing Sector, EPRG Working Paper 1015, Faculty of Economics, University of Cambridge.

Steinbuks, J. (2011). Review of recent developments in economic modelling of energy demand, in Jamasb, T. and Pollitt, M. (eds.), *The Future of Electricity Demand: Customers, Citizens and Loads*, Cambridge: Cambridge University Press.

Sun, J.W. (1998). Changes in energy consumption and energy intensity: a complete decomposition model, *Energy Economics*, **20**: 85–100.

Thaler, R.H. and Sunstein, C.R. (2009). *Nudge: Improving Decisions About Health, Wealth and Happiness*, New Haven, CT and London: Yale University Press.

Waddams Price, C. (2011). Equity, fuel poverty and demand (maintaining affordability with sustainability and security of supply), in Jamasb, T. and Pollitt, M. (eds.), *The Future of Electricity Demand: Customers, Citizens and Loads*, Cambridge: Cambridge University Press.

Waddams, C. and Wilson, C.M. (2007). Do Consumers Switch to the Best Supplier? CCP Working Paper 07–06.

Wilson, C.M. and Waddams Price, C. (2010). Do consumers switch to the best supplier? *Oxford Economic Papers*, **62**(4): 647–68.

World Bank (2010). World Bank Online Data Catalog, available at http://data.worldbank.org/data-catalog, last accessed 19 October 2010.

Zhang, T. and Nuttall, W. (2008). Evaluating Government's Policies on Promoting Smart Metering in Retail Electricity Markets via Agent Based Simulation, EPRG Working Paper 0822, Faculty of Economics, University of Cambridge.

# 2 Energy scenarios and implications for future electricity demand

*Graham Ault, Damien Frame and Nick Hughes*

## 2.1 Introduction

This chapter sets out four energy scenarios for Great Britain in 2050 that are intended, as a set, to provide insight, assist strategic planning and promote discussion on future electricity networks and the electricity system as a whole. These scenarios were originally prepared by members and associates of the SuperGen FlexNet consortium for Ofgem in the context of their Long-Term Electricity Network Scenarios (LENS) project and benefited from several rounds of stakeholder consultation, workshops and peer review (Ofgem, 2007b, c, d).

The published LENS scenarios included comprehensive narrative sections that, in two parts, described the high-level energy context for networks and then a more specific description of the role of networks and the associated network technologies. In this chapter the scenarios have been distilled from their original form to reduce the detailed focus on networks and draw out implications for electricity demand. However, no new material has been added – there has simply been a reduction in the quantity of detailed narrative. In addition, LENS included a fifth scenario (multi-purpose networks) that explored the effect of see-sawing trends. This scenario brought out interesting implications for investment in network infrastructure and technology; however, within the context of this book's objectives, and in the interests of space, it has not been included here. The four scenarios presented provide an ample set for exploring future electricity demand. Readers interested in the original set of scenarios are referred to the LENS final report (Ofgem, 2008a).

Although the conclusions of the LENS scenarios focused mainly on the implications for networks, a large proportion of the work was concerned with identifying the factors that will influence those future networks. When analyzing influences on future networks, a major consideration was naturally the profile of demand for electricity (influenced by consumers) and the types of generation that would meet that demand. The

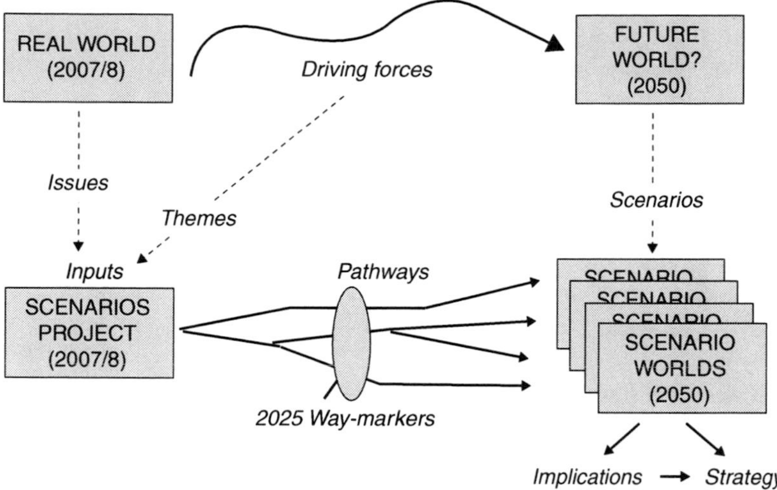


Figure 2.1 LENS scenario terminology.

discussion at the end of this chapter draws out several important issues and questions relating to the nature of electricity consumption, the trajectories for electricity demand growth and the interactions of customers with the power system and the organizations that provide electricity supplies now and in the futures envisaged by the scenarios.

## 2.2 Overview

### 2.2.1 *Scenario development*

In recent years scenarios have been used extensively in the energy industry to provide insights into possible outcomes for the sector in the face of a changing agenda mainly influenced by climate change (with a focus on $CO_2$ emissions) and energy security. Since the use of scenarios was pioneered by the likes of Shell (2003) and Wack (1985a, b) as a tool to address the unavoidable uncertainty associated with planning for the future, scenarios have been acknowledged as playing an important role. Historically they have been particularly successful in challenging preconceived assumptions about the nature of future developments. The use of scenarios provides users with the opportunity to plan robustly against a wider range of possible outcomes.

Figure 2.1 shows the scenario philosophy and terminology used in LENS. Starting with the present real-world situation it can be said that certain driving forces will take us to the future world of 2050. By analyzing the form these driving forces may take, key issues and themes can be derived. Following an iterative process to explore the interaction and development of these issues and themes then allows pathways to be formed and potential world scenarios to be fashioned.

The role of scenarios in planning is therefore not to provide a blueprint or forecast of what 'will' occur. Rather, their role is to present many of the possible developments in the future without prescribing any likelihood to any of the outcomes. Their value is in their combined view of the future and no one scenario should be viewed as the likely or preferred outcome. Each of the scenarios should present a plausible future in its own right and a valuable reference point for the development of strategy to meet the futures presented in all the scenarios.

From this initial definition of the role of scenarios, a methodology (Ofgem, 2007a) to develop the LENS scenarios was established following a thorough literature review in the area of energy and environmental future forecasting and analysis. In some cases, scenarios have been used to demonstrate pathways to a desired future. A future with low $CO_2$ emissions is assumed to be a 'must' and scenarios are developed to demonstrate how that plausibly can be achieved (RCEP, 2000; Tyndall, 2005). Although the reduction of $CO_2$ emissions could well be seen as something that 'must' occur, the LENS project did not specify any elements of the future electricity industry (and networks) that must be achieved. Rather, the purpose was to start with today's situation and explore the range of plausible futures that the electricity industry will need to operate within.

More detailed information on the scenario development process can be found in the original LENS publication. However, it can be summarized by saying that underlying the methodology is a process of detailed and regular consultation with a wide range of industry stakeholders to ensure that a significant number of opinions on the key driving forces were considered. Once established, these driving forces were represented by a set of key themes. The interactions between these themes were used to identify initial scenarios for the high-level energy context, which were then refined and used to identify potential network scenarios through a mapping process. An iterative process considering generation and demand and the input of the high-level context on the resulting network scenarios then produced a final set of scenarios that has a consistent background energy context and emerging network.

### 2.2.2 *MARKAL modelling*

The MARKAL (market allocation) model is a least-cost optimization model which has been used to inform energy policy making in a number of countries and is supported by the International Energy Agency (IEA).[1] The version of MARKAL employed in the LENS project was MARKAL Elastic Demand (MED). This provided the option of exploring the potential for energy demand reduction to be used as a means of achieving the optimal system balance within the constraints imposed.

The LENS scenarios are focused on the UK electricity networks, but are also located within a wider energy system and social context. The scenarios contain intuitively plausible assumptions about various portfolios of energy technologies and their contribution to reducing carbon emissions within the contexts of the scenarios described. The MARKAL model can add a further dimension to the scenarios by exploring in some quantitative detail the trade-offs between various technology options within the system. MARKAL allows the consideration of whole-system interactions and drivers, the competing demands of the various energy-using sectors, which raise further implications for the electricity networks. By considering the simultaneous operation of these numerous interactions in a detailed and quantitative way, the model provides insights into the plausibility of the scenarios and helps to highlight particular challenges or trade-offs which may not have been easily identified through a purely qualitative process.

The model could have been forced (constrained) into reproducing the scenarios exactly, in terms of which energy technologies become used at which times during the overall period. However, the insights produced from this approach would have been limited; the model would have been an illustrative tool rather than an interrogative one. Therefore, rather than focusing on defining the final technology mixes to match the scenarios exactly, the approach has been, wherever possible, to represent key drivers within the model, which the scenario descriptions see as being significant in bringing about the kinds of technology mixes they describe.

In order to generate model runs which explore the kinds of societies and energy systems described by the LENS scenarios, variation of a relatively focused subset of the MARKAL base case data was undertaken. The key 'levers' that were pulled to explore the different dynamics of the LENS scenarios were as follows:

[1] Through the Energy Technology Systems Analysis Programme (ETSAP), an implementing agreement of the IEA.

- *Carbon price.* The MARKAL model can assign varying costs to carbon and apply this to different degrees across the energy-using sectors. While specific environmental policies were not explicitly represented in the model runs, the LENS theme of 'environmental concern', which encompasses both the political will and public tolerance of strong environmental legislation, was represented using the carbon price aspect of MARKAL.
- *Elastic demand.* In conjunction with the carbon price, allowing the system to respond to higher energy prices through reducing demand was a distinguishing feature of certain scenarios and thus of model runs too.
- *Technology development.* Improved performance and reduced cost of particular technologies in some runs represent the effect of sustained society-wide environmental concern over the investment decisions of private actors, as well as in some cases government-led technology-push activities.
- *System constraints.* In scenarios where distribution-level networks were increasingly developed, the model was constrained in its ability to use large-scale transmission, with the assumption that key decisions would have limited the development of major large-scale transmission infrastructure.

Further information on the MARKAL model and its use in LENS can be found in the appendices to the final report (Ofgem, 2008b).

## 2.3 Scenarios

The three main themes that emerged from stakeholder consultation and workshops are detailed below. These were deemed to be key driving forces for future electricity networks, the exploration of which would allow useful and plausible scenarios to develop.

- *Environmental concern (moderate or acute):* the level to which the environmental situation affects the decision making of individuals, communities, private companies, public institutions and the government (on a UK and global basis).
- *Consumer participation (passive or active):* the level to which all types of consumers (commercial, industrial, domestic and public) are willing to participate in the energy market as a whole, and specifically the electricity market and electricity networks, motivated by economic or environmental factors.
- *Institutional governance (market led or government led):* the extent to which institutions will intervene through a variety of mechanisms

Table 2.1 *LENS scenarios and themes*

| | Environmental concern | Consumer participation | Institutional governance |
|---|---|---|---|
| Big transmission and distribution ('switch me on') | moderate | passive | market led |
| Energy services companies ('fix it for me') | acute | passive | market led |
| Distribution system operators (government-led green agenda) | acute | active | government led |
| Microgrids (dynamic green markets) | acute | active | market led |

in order to address specific societal concerns or further overarching policy goals relating to energy use and the environmental and economic implications.

The scenarios that resulted from the development process are listed in the left column of Table 2.1 and the influence of each theme is shown in the subsequent columns (the fifth scenario generated in the LENS process has been omitted, as explained in section 2.1 above).

It is clear that there are other combinations of the main themes (e.g. contexts for scenarios based on moderate environmental concern, with active customers). The scenarios chosen represent the best coverage of the 'scenario space' representing diverse future networks without unduly increasing the number of scenarios to the point where they lose their ease of comprehension and utility. Checks were made to ensure that other combinations of the three LENS themes and other themes did not result in very different network scenarios and in this way the project team consolidated their efforts around these five scenarios.

The modified LENS scenarios, along with accompanying pictograms that allow the electrical network issues to be visualized, are now presented. The symbols used in the pictograms are explained in Figure 2.2. Each pictogram illustrates key qualitative aspects of the scenario narrative:

- It indicates the main forms of **generation and technology** featuring in the scenario, and where they would be **located geographically and within the system**.
- The picture of Great Britain represents the **transmission system**, while the 'call-out bubble' represents the **distribution system**.

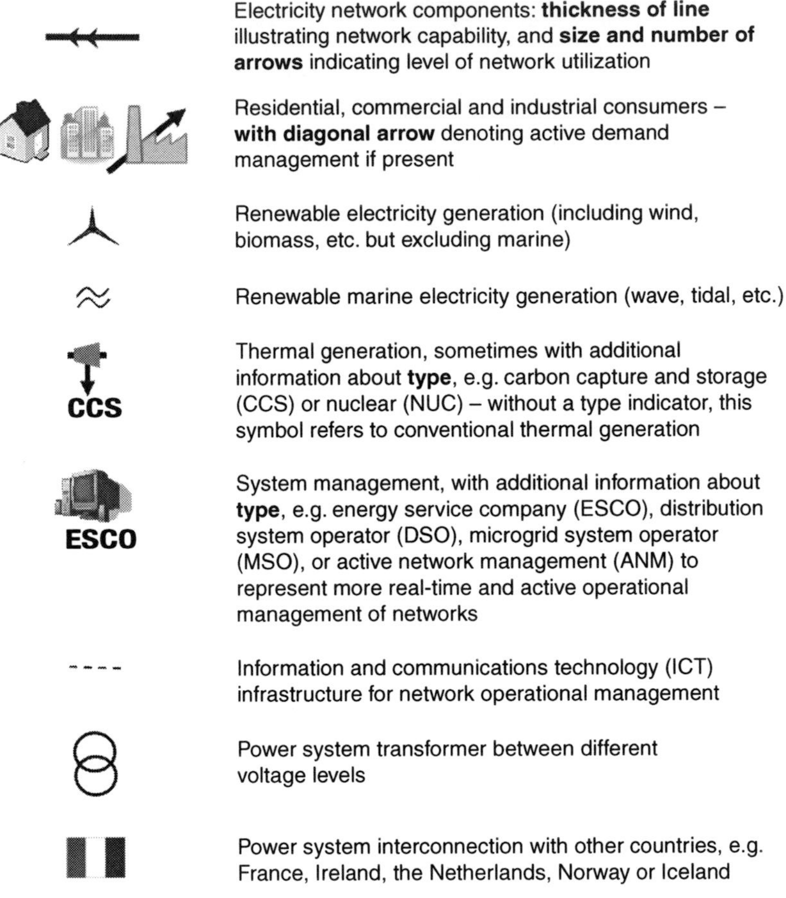

Electricity network components: thickness of line illustrating network capability, and size and number of arrows indicating level of network utilization
Residential, commercial and industrial consumers – with diagonal arrow denoting active demand management if present
Renewable electricity generation (including wind, biomass, etc. but excluding marine)
Renewable marine electricity generation (wave, tidal, etc.)
CCS
Thermal generation, sometimes with additional information about type, e.g. carbon capture and storage (CCS) or nuclear (NUC) – without a type indicator, this symbol refers to conventional thermal generation
ESCO
System management, with additional information about type, e.g. energy service company (ESCO), distribution system operator (DSO), microgrid system operator (MSO), or active network management (ANM) to represent more real-time and active operational management of networks
Information and communications technology (ICT) infrastructure for network operational management
Power system transformer between different voltage levels
Power system interconnection with other countries, e.g. France, Ireland, the Netherlands, Norway or Iceland


Figure 2.2 Key to pictogram symbols.

- The **line thickness** in the picture of Great Britain and the 'call-out bubble' represents the required **network capability** at the transmission and distribution level, respectively.
- The **size and number of arrows** in the picture of Great Britain and the 'call-out bubble' represent the **level of utilization** of the network capacity.
- The 'call-out bubble' shows details of the network architecture in the **distribution system** with locations of active components, such as generation, demand response and control. It distinguishes between **high voltage** (HV), **medium voltage** (MV) and **low voltage** (LV) levels within the distribution system.

## 2.4 Big transmission and distribution ('switch me on')

**Box 2.1 'Big T&D' scenario summary**

- Consumers demand abundant supplies of electricity that require minimum participation on their part.
- Free markets persist as the main mechanism to service the energy requirements of the nation. Society is broadly consumerist and capitalistic.
- The importance of environmental issues to society in general does not grow significantly higher, but there is continued debate and policy development geared towards reducing carbon emissions.
- Fossil fuels are used widely for electricity generation, domestic and commercial energy supplies and transport with ongoing and increasing risks of scarcity in primary fuel supplies and reserves.
- An early drive for low-carbon energy sources sees the development of significant offshore and onshore renewable generation.
- Centralized larger-scale power generation (fossil, nuclear and renewable) retains the highest proportion of electricity production capacity.
- Transmission and distribution (T&D) infrastructure development and management continues largely as expected from today's patterns while expanding to meet growing energy demand and developing renewable generation deployment.
- Network capability-enhancing technologies are deployed to meet the growing demands for network services arising from demand growth. T&D infrastructure is developed with a focus on enhancing capability for integrating renewables at all levels (larger transmission-connected renewable generation and smaller distribution-connected renewable generation).
- The geographical reach of the transmission network is expanded to connect offshore and rural onshore renewables sites and to provide interconnection with European mainland power systems.
- Moderate behaviour change by customers leads to little active demand management. Hence demand growth is unhindered and relatively unmanaged in an operational sense.
- Network companies continue to take the responsibility for providing security and quality of supply.

The moderate level of environmental concern reflects climate change not developing significantly past the effects we observe today. This is either due to inaccuracy of current predictions or because other innovative solutions are found outside the energy sector. An alternative possibility that would have the same effect is that tolerance to climate change increases among developed nations with means to adapt, and although effects of climate change increase, societal concern about it does not. Either way, the current level of urgency will grow in the early years and some international agreements will be achieved in the short term; however, these will be less stringently adhered to as environmental concern plateaus over time. There will be initial emissions capping agreed internationally and this will be broadly adhered to. Nonetheless, there will be a lack of urgency to take further action.

OECD countries will be highly active in securing long-term fossil fuel supply contracts and sources. Fossil fuel will continue to be widely used but it is likely that to meet existing targets for emission reduction carbon capture and storage (CCS) capability will also be developed. Developed countries also continue to increase renewable and nuclear capability as a long-term solution to depleting fossil fuel and in response to rising fossil fuel prices. The momentum to develop offshore and onshore wind capability backed up by strong incentives provides the necessary impetus for a sizeable development of large-scale projects. Nuclear fusion and hydrogen are seen as potential energy sources but remain in developmental stages as the urgency to invest in these technologies does not materialize.

The majority of consumers will maintain a passive attitude to energy use. They desire an uncomplicated energy supply but are also moderately opposed to developments with environmental impact. In particular, network infrastructure developments with high environmental impact receive significant attention as their effect is more immediate and provokes emotional local responses.

Government involvement is primarily directed towards achieving economic and social policies. An element of this will be environmental policy; however, this will not be the strong force it is in other scenarios. Government involvement will not be in any way prescriptive and the market will be left to make its own choices within the soft boundaries set by the government. Carbon trading schemes will continue in a similar form as today but will not develop into sophisticated markets, with a stable carbon price, without the strong environmental focus.

Moderate economic growth and an only moderate focus on environmental issues will hinder continued investment in low-carbon energy technology after an initial surge in response to current government incentives designed to achieve low emission policy targets. Investment will continue in the area of optimizing fossil fuel resources, improving efficiency and reducing cost. The deployments of other generation technology that come about in the early years, i.e. nuclear and offshore renewables, will see investment to drive competitiveness and maximize returns.

Most types of consumers will be reluctant to significantly change their behaviour and will not be motivated by either economic or environmental factors to alter their level of participation in the electricity market. This type of attitude will apply in leisure activities and consumerism where people will persist with current behaviour trends and insist any environmental problems are solved elsewhere. Initial environmental concern will result in consumer demand for agencies that serve and represent them to minimize environmental impact. As the electricity-generation industry moves towards lower emissions, consumers will be satisfied that environmental issues are being addressed and will become less concerned about the source of their energy. Most consumers will demand a reliable, high-quality supply of energy at reasonable cost. Despite the activity of minority groups, it is unlikely there will be significant efficiency improvements and there will be a continuation of today's high energy-use behaviour as powerful drivers and strong government leadership to change consumer behaviour are not present. People will continue to desire older, spacious, less efficient housing and private car use will remain the main choice for transport. Transport will stay predominately fossil fuel based, although efficiency will be improved and hybrid electric vehicles will slowly penetrate the market, providing much improved emissions levels. Rail will gradually become totally electric. Public transport will be improved and there will be some movement to increased use in urban areas. Buses will also begin to electrify by 2050.

Places of employment do not adhere to any strict guidelines on energy efficiency and there will be continued high demands for electricity and space and water heating. Increasing prices of fossil fuels (oil and gas) will have some impact and motivate some energy-saving behaviour; however, reasonably priced electricity will still be available from coal, nuclear and renewable generation for which there is high demand. Natural gas will continue to be used widely for space and water heating in the short to medium term. Approaching 2050, there may be increased migration from gas to electricity as security of supply concern starts to account for depleting fossil fuels and starts to encourage use of electricity generated by a diverse generation portfolio.

Metering and charging will be a passive process for consumers. Supply companies will take responsibility and consumers will pay little attention as long as costs remain within expected boundaries. Consumers will be unlikely to be looking for additional services from their supply company to reduce environmental impact. There may be a gradual development towards more detailed metering providing accurate usage information and using developments in home telecoms to automate readings and billing. This will mainly be a result of natural technological development and a desire from supply companies to optimize efficiency rather than as a result of consumer demand; however, there will be groups of consumers who embrace this as an opportunity to help regulate energy consumption.

The majority of consumers will be reluctant to interact with their supply and the network. They will have a 'switch me on' attitude and be keen for the most economical option without the need for much action on their part. Larger consumers will agree to basic demand management schemes on economic grounds. It is possible that a centralized, largely automated demand-management scheme could be implemented if it required little input from consumers and helped mitigate the impact of any rising costs of power. Overall electricity demand grows in line with long-term trends (since it is relatively unmanaged) and there is a resulting requirement for transmission and distribution systems of greater capability.

By 2050, a transmission network 'backbone' extends to the north of Scotland and branches to the western and northern isles as well as from offshore grids and rural areas up and down the country. The main role for distribution networks continues to be as a conduit for bulk power from the transmission system to consumers and this role grows as load demand increases.

Demand is primarily influenced by individual behaviour changes and there is little technological implication for the development of electricity networks. However, there are some advantages from a general restraint in consumption at peak times and this prevents even greater requirement for network capacity. The network companies expend effort on assessing the likely benefits of the effect of behaviour change on demand levels.

In this scenario, consumers will still contract with supply companies (though there will be more competition as price becomes a bigger issue). Electricity is still viewed as a commodity where consumers pay per unit of energy as opposed to paying for an energy service. There will be a similar structure as today with distribution network operators (DNOs), transmission network operators (TNOs) and a system operator (SO) which charge for connection and system use. The SO is responsible for overall system security, quality and reliability (including system balancing) and will be regulated on its performance in this area to ensure consumers' needs are being met. DNOs will also be regulated to ensure they meet security, quality and reliability standards.

The regulator will still be responsible for the 'natural' monopolies of transmission and distribution networks. The current industry structure

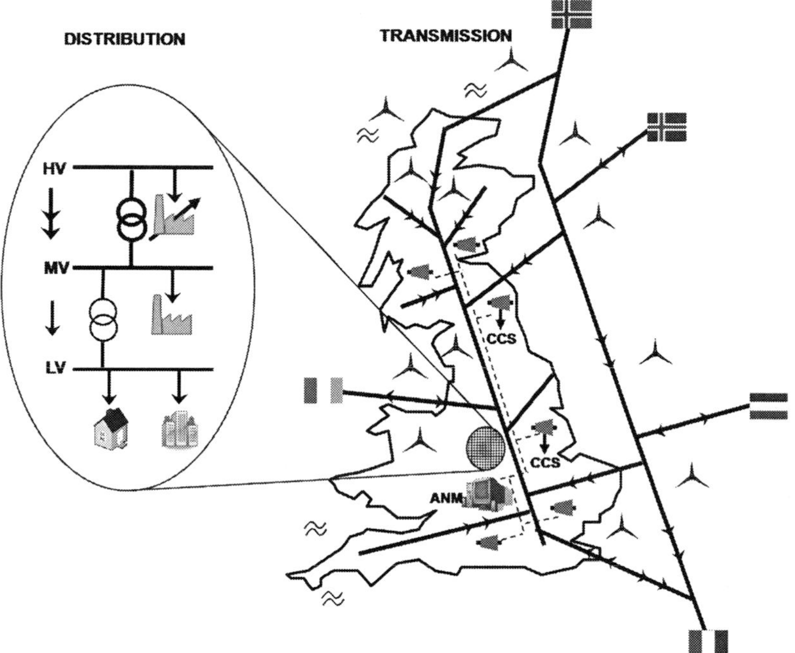


Figure 2.3 Big T&D pictogram.

remains in place, with an independent system operator (ISO) responsible for operating the networks of private, independent, regulated network owners.

The key qualitative aspects of the scenario are represented in Figure 2.3.

### *2.4.1 Modelling results*

This scenario has fewest additional changes compared with the MARKAL reference base case. However, the 'moderate environmental concern' of the scenario justifies a relatively low carbon price and adjustments are made to facilitate investment in large-scale infrastructure.

Other input assumptions applied to this run were energy service demand increases as in the reference case (no elastic demand), capacity and activity constraints on imported electricity double compared with the reference case, and an upper constraint remains in place on plug-in hybrid vehicles, as do all hurdle rates on new technologies.

The results produced by these inputs are described here and summarized in Table 2.2.

Table 2.2 *Big T&D modelling results summary*

| | 2000 | | 2025 | | 2050 | |
|---|---|---|---|---|---|---|
| Total final energy demand (PJ)[a] | 6,189 | | 6,287 | | 6,468 | |
| Transport | 1,855 | 30% | 1,911 | 30% | 2,142 | 33% |
| Residential | 1,961 | 32% | 2,057 | 33% | 1,920 | 30% |
| Other (Industry, Services & Agriculture) | 2,374 | 38% | 2,319 | 37% | 2,407 | 37% |
| Total electricity demand (PJ)[b] | 1,176 | | 1,335 | | 1,522 | |
| Transport | 20 | 2% | 33 | 2% | 85 | 6% |
| Residential | 403 | 34% | 563 | 42% | 587 | 39% |
| Other[c] | 754 | 64% | 740 | 55% | 851 | 56% |
| Total electricity generation capacity (GW) | 84 | | 87 | | 102 | |
| *Large-scale generation:* | | | | | | |
| Fossil (inc. CCS) | 59 | 71% | 44 | 51% | 68 | 67% |
| Nuclear | 12 | 14% | 3 | 4% | 0 | 0% |
| Renewables | 4 | 5% | 31 | 35% | 20 | 19% |
| Interconnectors | 2 | 2% | 5 | 6% | 11 | 11% |
| CHP | 4 | 4% | 3 | 3% | 2 | 2% |
| Storage | 3 | 3% | 1 | 2% | 1 | 1% |
| *Small-scale generation:* | | | | | | |
| Micro CHP | 0 | 0% | 0 | 0% | 0 | 0% |
| Microgen | 0 | 0% | 0 | 0% | 0 | 0% |
| Total electricty generation output (PJ) | 1,288 | | 1,456 | | 1,652 | |
| *Large-scale generation:* | | | | | | |
| Fossil (inc. CCS) | 854 | 66% | 953 | 65% | 1,173 | 71% |
| Nuclear | 282 | 22% | 85 | 6% | 0 | 0% |
| Renewables | 46 | 4% | 245 | 17% | 271 | 16% |
| Interconnectors | 52 | 4% | 137 | 9% | 182 | 11% |
| CHP | 45 | 3% | 31 | 2% | 27 | 2% |
| Storage | 10 | 1% | 6 | 0% | 0 | 0% |
| *Small-scale generation:* | | | | | | |
| Micro CHP | 0 | 0% | 1 | 0% | 0 | 0% |
| Microgen | 0 | 0% | 0 | 0% | 0 | 0% |
| $CO_2$ reductions from 2000 (Mt) | | | | | | |
| Energy system reduction | | 0% | | 14% | | 30% |
| Electricity sector reduction | | 0% | | 16% | | 67% |

[a] 1 PJ = 0.278 TWh.
[b] Sectoral electricity demand figures do not include that proportion of electricity demand that is met by small-scale electricity generation.
[c] Industry, Services, Agriculture, Hydrogen and Upstreams.

There is a steadily growing demand for electricity which is significantly stronger than the overall increase in energy service demand across the system as a whole. The strongest growth for electricity demand is found in the residential sector. As well as growing service demands, this suggests that electricity is becoming increasingly cost effective through the period compared with the direct use of gas, which, though it is used for residential and services space and water heating, becomes increasingly more expensive as continued use moves it up the resource supply curve.

## 2.5 Energy services companies ('fix it for me')

**Box 2.2 ESCOs scenario summary**

- Consumers remain relatively passive towards their energy supply and while the majority of people are concerned about the environment, they strongly believe that it is the duty of government and the market to address the issues.
- Although the belief persists that markets are best placed to service consumer demands at the same time as meeting social and environmental needs, strong intervention to address environmental issues is not ruled out.
- The potential for markets to meet the energy services demands of consumers is realized through the emergence of energy service companies (ESCOs).
- Centralized electricity generation continues to dominate but alongside a relatively strong development of onsite and local/community-scale demand-side participation and smaller-scale generation (e.g. combined heat and power) through the energy service companies.
- The main role for electricity networks is to support a vibrant energy services market. The transmission and distribution infrastructure is required to support a super-supplier or ESCO-centred world.
- ESCOs do all the work at the customer side and the transmission and distribution networks contract with ESCOs to supply network services, allowing the network companies to operate the networks more actively.
- There are wide-ranging developments and vibrant markets in energy services, including microgeneration, onsite heat and power, demand-side management, telecommunications and electric vehicles.
- The services supplied by the networks include transmission system connection to strategic, large-scale renewables and also access to

municipal-scale combined heat and power (CHP) and renewables tailored to local demands.
- System management is aided by the degrees of flexibility provided by 'empowered' customers with high-capability information and communications technologies (ICT).

Environmental concern grows as global average temperature increases and changed weather patterns become apparent and indisputably linked to greenhouse gas (GHG) emissions. Global initiatives will slowly reach full agreement and impose strong mandates for emissions reduction. The current level of urgency will increase steadily and international agreements on emissions capping will be achieved in the medium term. In the UK this results in environmental issues becoming a strong influence on consumer preferences and government policy. For consumers, their decision making will be equally influenced by their relatively passive attitude to energy issues. They desire an uncomplicated energy supply that requires little involvement on their part and will also be opposed to developments with negative environmental impacts.

Government responds to increasingly tough targets for $CO_2$ emissions set in response to strong EU and global mandates. Moving energy generation and use in a new direction via new markets are part 'pull' by private actors in those markets and part 'push' by government through setting market frameworks with targets, penalties and incentives. Light regulation and market incentives are used to address the environmental issues, promote competition and protect consumers' interests. The government identifies areas of importance, such as electricity generation, transport and energy efficiency, and provides general incentives to help overcome the natural barriers in those areas and to promote growth according to environmental targets. Energy efficiency measures will be targeted towards improving the efficiency of products and other electrical loads rather than patterns of use.

A stable carbon price will be established and carbon markets will be developed as firm carbon targets are set and monitored. Many types of innovative markets will emerge in service areas of the electricity sector (for example, carbon accounts) in response to consumer passivity and environmental concern. By being passive, consumers will be prepared to accept some increased cost for additional services that 'assuage their guilt', with minimum effort on their part.

The market opportunity for managed energy efficiency services will stimulate private investment, as will any policy requirement for centralized clean renewables alongside suitable market incentives. Investment in the electricity industry and networks specifically will become a less centrally planned process, with increased competitive tendering and negotiated contracts between buyers and sellers of energy and network services.

Consumers will be reluctant to reduce home energy use via lifestyle changes and will instead look for product manufacturers to increase efficiency and electricity suppliers to provide cleaner power. This type of attitude will apply in work, leisure and purchasing patterns, with individuals persisting with current behaviour and insisting the problems are solved elsewhere. People will continue to desire older, spacious, inherently less efficient housing despite government targets for energy efficiency in housing. Property sector efficiency codes will be on a voluntary basis. The potential conflict here will be met by ESCOs that include home energy efficiency in their portfolio.

By 2050, fully electric vehicles are widely used and commonly provided as part of an energy services contract. Biofuels may also play a part in fleet vehicles. Rail will quickly become fully electric, public transport will be improved and there is some movement towards increased use of public transport in urban areas where good services will be provided and where consumers respond as much to the convenience as to the environmental credentials of public transport. Significant proportions of bus fleets will be electric by 2050.

The UK generation portfolio will maintain a strong centralized element as CCS for existing fossil fuel thermal generation is developed in conjunction with increased use of nuclear power deployed on a large scale to serve the market demand for centralized low-carbon electricity.

This scenario will also see some large developments of renewables – offshore and large-scale wind – as this would be considered the best way of meeting environmental targets with passive consumers in the short to medium term. There is not likely to be widespread development of self-generation since consumers' appetite for such products will be relatively low. However, by 2050 ESCOs will have started to deploy solar and wind microgeneration as cost and performance improvements combine with a high carbon price to make these technologies economically viable. Space and water heating could gradually become an ESCO-provided service and could migrate from gas to network-provided electricity as low-carbon electricity production increases.

These consumers would demand a reliable, high-quality supply of energy at reasonable cost. However, they would express their environmental concern by accepting changes in the industry aimed at reducing emissions and they would regulate their electricity use or participate in demand-side management (DSM) if third-party services could make this happen in an undemanding manner and at a reasonable cost. They would be unlikely to adopt self-generation technology but would be willing to participate in local production of electricity through their ESCO. In the absence of willingly active consumers, demand management is a significant challenge which is addressed by automated DSM schemes provided by the network and managed services from ESCOs to control the growth and high-peak nature of demand. The prominence of ESCOs in this scenario could result in quite significant levels of managed DSM, but with very little action required from consumers.

Metering and charging will be a passive process for consumers. Their energy supply company will be given responsibility and the consumer will pay little attention as long as costs remain within expected boundaries. However, the supply companies will deploy advanced smart metering and charging solutions as part of their overall service provision.

ESCOs will either take the place of a supply company but with added-value services, including efficiency measures and DSM schemes, or they will incorporate a local CHP generation source and manage the supply and demand within an autonomous area. With the combined influence of passive but environmentally concerned consumers and a non-prescriptive but focused government agenda to significantly alter electricity use and generation, the market for ESCOs develops to be the significant characterizing feature of this scenario. The ESCOs themselves provide heat, light and power (as well as other services such as electric vehicles) to contracted customers and naturally have commercial incentives to do this on a cost-minimizing basis. This results in ESCO-owned generation plant onsite, smart meters to manage customer demand, communications links to ESCO customer service and server centres to manage consumption, generation and commercial information. Advanced smart meter solutions are a key enabler of the ESCO service provision.

The dynamics of the electricity supply system with so many interrelated energy services being managed dynamically by competing ESCO firms presents major challenges for the power system operators, including balancing supplies in real time and securing essential supporting network services. However, the general level of exchanges and unexpected energy transfers across the power systems reduce since ESCOs manage customer demand and generation much more dynamically. One major challenge for the system operators is to manage the impacts of major energy market events. It will be expected that ESCOs will respond in similar ways to the same market event and take similar actions with customers' generation, storage and demand, resulting in infrequent but large swings in behaviour affecting energy flows in the electricity networks.

The local generation deployed by ESCOs to serve local demands provides a resource for the distribution network operators, with flexibility

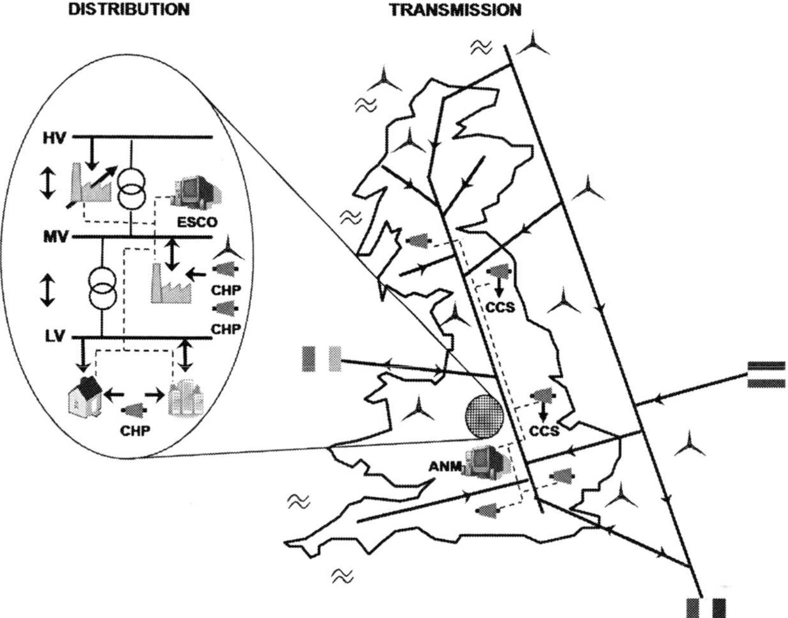


Figure 2.4 ESCO pictogram.

and clear contractual arrangements to use this generation plant to maintain network performance. Network constraints and performance are managed through this interface with ESCOs, and a symbiotic arrangement is achieved where ESCOs rely on the distribution system to balance their obligations by power exchange across the distribution network and the DNOs tap into this embedded, highly managed resource to assist in network operations.

The charging of electric vehicles and the use of the home as a work place present a different challenge to energy service providers, but meeting these new demands falls to the ESCO, which balance all the needs of the consumer and work with local and national resources to meet the demands. The widespread use of electric vehicles is likely to become an important element of onsite energy storage solutions. The hardware deployed at the consumer level will have developed substantially, with onsite monitoring, metering, production, storage and control equipment to meet consumer needs.

The key qualitative aspects of the scenario are represented in Figure 2.4.

Table 2.3 *ESCO modelling results summary*

| | 2000 | | 2025 | | 2050 | |
|---|---|---|---|---|---|---|
| Total final energy demand (PJ)[a] | 6,189 | | 5,961 | | 5,807 | |
| Transport | 1,855 | 30% | 1,635 | 27% | 1,542 | 27% |
| Residential | 1,961 | 32% | 2,054 | 34% | 1,921 | 33% |
| Other (Industry, Services & Agriculture) | 2,374 | 38% | 2,272 | 38% | 2,345 | 40% |
| Total electricity demand (PJ)[b] | 1,176 | | 1,399 | | 1,623 | |
| Transport | 20 | 2% | 100 | 7% | 330 | 20% |
| Residential | 403 | 34% | 563 | 40% | 473 | 29% |
| Other[c] | 754 | 64% | 736 | 53% | 819 | 50% |
| Total electricity generation capacity (GW) | 84 | | 88 | | 121 | |
| *Large-scale generation:* | | | | | | |
| Fossil (inc. CCS) | 59 | 71% | 40 | 45% | 55 | 45% |
| Nuclear | 12 | 14% | 15 | 17% | 13 | 11% |
| Renewables | 4 | 5% | 25 | 28% | 24 | 20% |
| Interconnectors | 2 | 2% | 4 | 5% | 10 | 9% |
| CHP | 4 | 4% | 3 | 3% | 1 | 0% |
| Storage | 3 | 3% | 1 | 2% | 1 | 1% |
| *Small-scale generation:* | | | | | | |
| Micro CHP | 0 | 0% | 0 | 0% | 0 | 0% |
| Microgen | 0 | 0% | 0 | 0% | 17 | 14% |
| Total electricity generation output (PJ) | 1,288 | | 1,526 | | 1,874 | |
| *Large-scale generation:* | | | | | | |
| Fossil (inc. CCS) | 854 | 66% | 759 | 50% | 1,016 | 54% |
| Nuclear | 282 | 22% | 397 | 26% | 334 | 18% |
| Renewables | 46 | 4% | 256 | 17% | 300 | 16% |
| Interconnectors | 52 | 4% | 77 | 5% | 103 | 5% |
| CHP | 45 | 3% | 31 | 2% | 8 | 0% |
| Storage | 10 | 1% | 6 | 0% | 0 | 0% |
| *Small-scale generation:* | | | | | | |
| Micro CHP | 0 | 0% | 1 | 0% | 0 | 0% |
| Microgen | 0 | 0% | 0 | 0% | 113 | 6% |
| $CO_2$ reductions from 2000 (Mt) | | | | | | |
| Energy system reduction | | 0% | | 34% | | 47% |
| Electricity sector reduction | | 0% | | 60% | | 88% |

[a] 1 PJ = 0.278 TWh.
[b] Sectoral electricity demand figures do not include proportion of electricity demand that is met by small-scale electricity generation.
[c] Industry, Services, Agriculture, Hydrogen and Upstreams.

### 2.5.1 *Modelling results*

To represent an increased level of environmental concern, the carbon price input to the model was increased. In this run, carbon price applies only to the electricity and industrial sectors. The model opts for increased energy efficiency and reduces primary energy demand compared with the 'switch me on' scenario. However, the electricity sector as a whole exhibits a growth over the entire period which is greater than that in the Big T&D scenario. As shown in Table 2.3, this increase is almost entirely the result of a massive increase in electricity demand from the transport sector, rising from 20 PJ in 2000 to 330 PJ in 2050.

The model invests strongly in wind power, including in 9.4 GW of offshore wind by 2040, which generates 110 PJ p.a. By 2045, a total of 247 PJ of electricity is generated from wind, with 27 per cent of the total coming from small-scale wind due to the accelerated cost and performance assumptions as part of the ESCO storyline. The success in the model results of microgeneration technologies as well as electrified transport – driven largely by reduced 'hurdle rates' – highlights the potentially important role identified in the scenario storyline of ESCOs in reducing the financial risk and barriers to market access, as well as driving down costs through economies of scale. The model selects significant levels of microgeneration, assuming some form of aggregation and supply–demand management, such as those described in the scenario as being performed by the ESCOs. The technical and institutional feasibility of such an arrangement is an important area to explore.

The main difference between the model and the scenario description is the almost complete absence of CHP technologies in the model results. Natural gas CHP is not considered a sufficiently low carbon option, and biomass resources are used up in other technologies, including transport and thermal power generation.

## 2.6 Distribution system operators (government-led green agenda)

**Box 2.3 DSOs scenario summary**

- The belief develops that stronger government intervention is required in the energy sector to meet consumer demands for energy services and to make a full contribution to the global action to reduce fossil fuel emissions. This move from more market delivery-oriented policies is due to perceived market failures in areas such as delivery of climate change policies and targets, energy security matters and energy prices.

- The decision is made to push for a more electric and more hydrogen economy as part of a cohesive EU initiative.
- Consumers are active in their electricity supplies because of attitudes to the environment and a desire to secure the best possible supply of electricity based on price, service and reliability.
- There is a strong development of larger-scale clean power generation, renewable power generation and a relatively high penetration of hydrogen fuel cells in vehicles.
- Consumers become more active in managing their energy demand and generating electricity in response to their environmental concerns and strong government measures.
- Significant numbers of electricity production facilities are connected to distribution networks, thus reducing the load on the transmission network.
- In addition to its traditional role of connecting centralized thermal generation, the transmission system now acts to provide connections between distribution system operators (DSOs) and to strategic renewables deployments.
- DSOs take much more responsibility for system management, including generation and demand management, supply security, supply quality and system reliability.
- Demand-side management provides greater options for DSOs in system operations but also leads to a generally reduced demand to service.
- DSOs balance generation and demand in local areas with the aid of system-management technologies such as energy storage and demand-side management. Dynamic loads and generation sources make local and regional balancing a key activity for DSOs.

Global climate change develops to a serious degree leading up to 2050. Temperature increases and changed weather patterns become apparent and indisputably linked to GHG emissions. There will be international political consensus and action against $CO_2$ emissions. As a result, tackling climate change will be at the forefront of UK energy policy. There will be a strong perception that electricity generation sources should be environmentally friendly and energy efficiency is an essential matter of national strategic importance.

Public and international pressure combined with lack of progress from liberal market mechanisms will prompt the government to take interventionist action. There will still be a desire to employ liberal market approaches when possible; however, there will be specific cases of strong intervention where market mechanisms are not delivering or are judged to be unable to deliver in the necessary timescales. Regulation will play its part in controlling the market and enforcing some of the interventionist policies. The government will identify areas of importance such as the hydrogen economy and energy efficiency and provide strong leadership, funding and legislation to enable and drive through particular solutions.

The electricity market would be a tightly controlled mechanism for achieving the generation, supply and transmission of power in line with the environmental and economic requirements of society. A centrally planned market will set incentives and rewards to encourage strong investment in renewable generation and decarbonized large-scale thermal generation. Mechanisms such as emission capping and carbon taxation will be applied. The governing institutions will tend to 'pick winners' and use subsidies and taxes to aid the development of particular technological solutions.

A hydrogen economy develops due to strong government-led and EU-wide initiatives on R&D and infrastructure development. The primary use of hydrogen as an energy carrier is in the decarbonization of the transport sector, alongside the much more widespread use of electricity as a clean energy vector for transport. Publicly funded demonstrations and feasibility studies are swiftly followed by strong policy support. The use of electricity from clean sources for transport brings a substantial rise in the electricity demand which is offset only by the same environmental drive bringing strong action on energy conservation and by the use of hydrogen for vehicular transport.

The economic environment will be healthy enough to provide government with the confidence to prompt private investment and fund public investment. Society in general will have become much more environmentally conscious; energy efficiency will have become much more of a priority in all areas of life led by government targets and mandates as well as individual consumer action. Leisure activities and consumer preferences will be influenced by environmental attitudes. Attitudes towards transport and housing will reflect the desire for 'green' lifestyle choices. Consumers will desire energy-efficient housing and be prepared to modify their lifestyles accordingly, i.e. by placing more value on smaller, modern, energy-efficient housing. Older housing will be modified for energy efficiency to attract buyers and to fit with possibilities for taxing houses at sale based on energy efficiency or similar environmental impact measures. This change will happen quickly on the back of strong building regulations imposed by the government on new build due to a strong environmental focus on building policy. The energy 'rating' of a home will be a key part of the house-buying process and government makes this a legal requirement. Demand will be significantly affected by the hydrogen economy and the government promotion of energy efficiency and demand-management schemes.

Use of public transport will be more common as the government invests substantial amounts of public money in improving services. Private car use will still be common, with the electric vehicle or hydrogen fuel cell-powered car prevalent. Cars become more of a short journey transport method. Rail transport will become fully electrically powered as the technology is established and is heavily invested in during the early attempts to reduce emissions. Hydrogen-powered buses will also become more and more widely used in urban areas.

Government action will mean public institutions take the lead in drastically improving office energy efficiency. Self-generation via CHP and possibly wind and solar renewable sources that provide a localized energy resource will also be encouraged. This policy will result in public bodies locating themselves in large, sustainable office parks or promoting home working where employee home energy efficiency is of a high standard. With the government more prone to an interventionist approach, planning decision making will be primarily at a national level, with significant overriding power. The desire for localized planning and rapid deployments may result in clashes with public opinion and local pressure groups on renewable developments and geographic reach of the transmission network.

The export capability of the larger institutions deploying self-generation could become quite substantial and the dual generator/load nature becomes a significant challenge for the network operators. The level of motivation to export will depend on the balance of market-based incentives for consumers to actively trade energy against targets and mandates. Prices for exported electricity are likely to be set centrally.

The majority of domestic consumers will respond positively to government initiatives that push the efficiency agenda and mandate smart meters to encourage/empower consumers to regulate demand. This strong lead from government will parallel EU-wide policy and overcome initial ambiguity on where responsibility for smart meter deployment lay. By 2050 everyone is likely to have a smart meter networked via advanced ICT technology that will have become the standard communications network service provided to most homes. DSM for the domestic consumer will be in response to mandated roll-out of smart meters and energy efficiency targets. A dynamic/automated approach to DSM within commercial agreement with the electricity supplier/local network operator will be welcomed, especially where it is recognized as a means of facilitating intermittent renewable generation. This approach could be supported by government-imposed standards for domestic appliances that align with smart meter use.

For consumers with fuel cell CHP capability, a new factor may emerge in DSM. It could potentially incorporate onsite $H_2$ production where, in times of low demand, excess renewable generation on the grid could be used to produce $H_2$ for later use. This could become an important feature of matching supply to demand.

Variable renewable generation becomes a major part of the electricity generation portfolio as government subsidies and emission taxing make this an attractive economic option for generation companies. As a result, society's energy needs in this scenario will be met by a generation mix that maximizes the potential of localized, renewably generated electricity, CHP (possibly hydrogen) and, latterly, offshore wind and tidal generation. Significant quantities of base load generation in the form of nuclear and fossil fuel with CCS are also still required to supplement the renewable resources.

All of the above means the distribution operations function is much more active, with local balancing, constraint management and market facilitation being taken on by distribution operators. This leads to the emergence of the DSO in contrast to the less active DNO and this is encouraged by government as a convenient vehicle to manage the meeting of energy policy objectives of efficiency, emission reductions and municipal and community-led energy solutions. Demand-side management leads to greater options for the DSO but also a downward pressure on demand to service offset on the upside by greater demand from electric vehicles. Dynamic loads and generation sources make local and regional balancing a key activity for the DSO. The emergence of the DSO is a necessity of the vastly more active situation to be managed within distribution networks.

The DSO develops the network to manage diverse generation and demand-side facilities and this includes energy storage devices, responsive reactive control equipment and a substantial network management system capable of delivering high levels of service from the diverse generation portfolio to managed demand customers. The DSO relies heavily on the functionality provided by networked smart meter technology. In many ways the DSO becomes the centre of the electrical supply system and its role has most bearing on the sources of energy delivered to customers and the other services that customers receive, such as balancing, security, reliability and power quality.

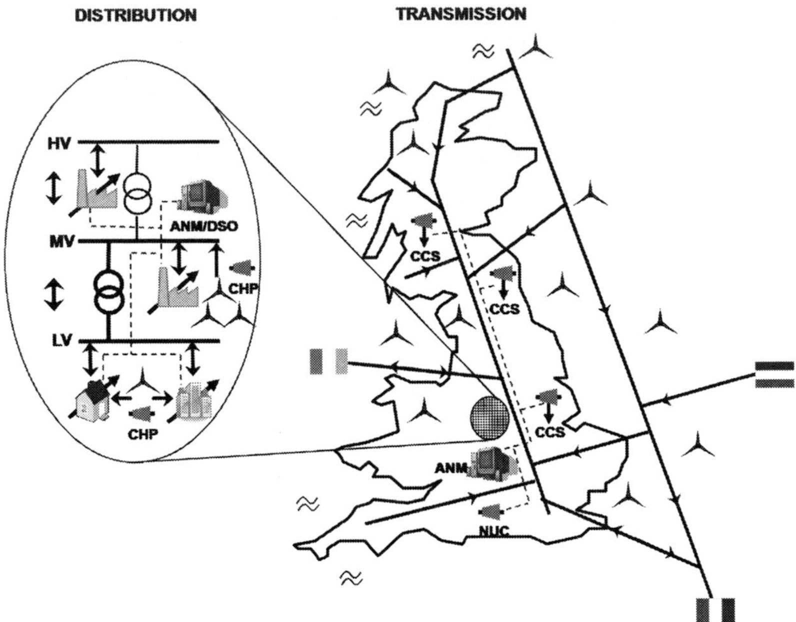


Figure 2.5 DSO pictogram.

The transmission system continues to be operated by a system operator and the degree of cooperation between DSO and SO is very high as the transmission system acts as the conduit from large-scale generation to the DSO. The SO also acts to manage exchanges of power and services (e.g. reserves) between DSOs.

The key qualitative aspects of the scenario are represented in Figure 2.5.

### 2.6.1 *Modelling results*

This run applies a further increase to the carbon price (across all sectors) and allows for the operation of elasticities in energy service demands. This represents a society which, due to rising environmental concerns taking root in a more fundamental way, is prepared to take measures to reduce its demand across all sectors, if encouraged to do so by carbon policies.

The effect of the elastic demand component is the most noticeable element of the primary energy demand mix in this run compared with the 'switch me on' and 'fix it for me' scenarios. As shown in Table 2.4,

Table 2.4 *DSO scenario modelling results summary*

| | 2000 | | 2025 | | 2050 | |
|---|---|---|---|---|---|---|
| Total final energy demand (PJ)[a] | 6,188 | | 5,775 | | 4,910 | |
| Transport | 1,855 | 30% | 1,853 | 32% | 1,292 | 26% |
| Residential | 1,961 | 32% | 1,807 | 31% | 1,625 | 33% |
| Other (Industry, Services & Agriculture) | 2,373 | 38% | 2,115 | 37% | 1,993 | 41% |
| Total electricity demand (PJ)[b] | 1,176 | | 1,102 | | 1,243 | |
| Transport | 20 | 2% | 33 | 3% | 126 | 10% |
| Residential | 403 | 34% | 418 | 38% | 378 | 30% |
| Other[c] | 754 | 64% | 652 | 59% | 739 | 59% |
| Total electricity generation capacity (GW) | 84 | | 83 | | 105 | |
| *Large-scale generation:* | | | | | | |
| Fossil (inc. CCS) | 59 | 71% | 24 | 29% | 27 | 26% |
| Nuclear | 12 | 14% | 19 | 22% | 19 | 18% |
| Renewables | 4 | 5% | 21 | 25% | 22 | 21% |
| Interconnectors | 2 | 2% | 4 | 5% | 10 | 10% |
| CHP | 4 | 4% | 2 | 3% | 0 | 0% |
| Storage | 3 | 3% | 1 | 2% | 1 | 1% |
| *Small-scale generation:* | | | | | | |
| Micro CHP | 0 | 0% | 0 | 0% | 0 | 0% |
| Microgen | 0 | 0% | 12 | 14% | 24 | 23% |
| Total electricity generation output (PJ) | 1,288 | | 1,287 | | 1,501 | |
| *Large-scale generation:* | | | | | | |
| Fossil (inc. CCS) | 854 | 66% | 417 | 32% | 457 | 30% |
| Nuclear | 282 | 22% | 488 | 38% | 502 | 33% |
| Renewables | 46 | 4% | 191 | 15% | 279 | 19% |
| Interconnectors | 52 | 4% | 77 | 6% | 103 | 7% |
| CHP | 45 | 3% | 24 | 2% | 7 | 0% |
| Storage | 10 | 1% | 6 | 0% | 0 | 0% |
| *Small-scale generation:* | | | | | | |
| Micro CHP | 0 | 0% | 1 | 0% | 0 | 0% |
| Microgen | 0 | 0% | 85 | 7% | 153 | 10% |
| $CO_2$ reductions from 2000 (Mt) | | | | | | |
| Energy system reduction | | 0% | | 37% | | 61% |
| Electricity sector reduction | | 0% | | 74% | | 95% |

[a] 1 PJ = 0.278 TWh.

[b] Sectoral electricity demand figures do not include that proportion of electricity demand that is met by small-scale electricity generation.

[c] Industry, Services, Agriculture, Hydrogen and Upstreams.

total primary energy shows a clear and steady downward trend, most evidently between 2005 and 2035.

The scenario storyline outlines an increased importance placed on distribution-level generation, although centralized base load generation still plays a strong role, not least because of the value of the investments already made in these infrastructures. To represent this within the model, an exogenous constraint on the use of the transmission network was applied. The model responds by fully utilizing the onshore wind resource; however, offshore wind is underdeveloped as the model chooses to utilize the available transmission capacity with significant levels of large-scale, centralized low-carbon generation.

With the advanced technology inputs to the model intended to represent this scenario, hydrogen fuel cell cars and buses become cost effective in this run from 2030. As the carbon price is extended to the transport sector, the hydrogen on which these vehicles run has to pay for any emissions associated with its production.

## 2.7 Microgrids (dynamic green markets)

**Box 2.4 Microgrids scenario summary**

- The belief persists that markets are best placed to service consumer demands at the same time as meeting external needs such as tackling environmental issues. Active consumers operate within widespread liberal markets.
- Global action to reduce fossil fuel emissions creates strong incentives for low carbon energy via a firm carbon price and efficient carbon markets.
- Active and concerned consumers radically change their approach to energy and become much more participatory in their energy provision. They are driven by the twin desires to be served at competitive prices and service levels while addressing their desire to have a benign impact on the environment.
- Markets respond to the new demands of consumers and, with supportive frameworks and incentives from government, broadly liberal, free markets rise to the challenges of economic energy supplies with low environmental impacts.
- Renewable generation is prominent and there are relatively high volumes of microgeneration, creating the potential for a radically reformed electricity market with diverse types of generation.
- The self-sufficiency concept has developed very strongly in power and energy supplies, with electricity consumers taking significantly

more responsibility for managing their own energy supplies and demands.

- Individually and collectively, customers actively manage their own energy consumption against their own or locally available supplies, aiming to minimize exports to and imports from the local grid.
- Microgrid[2] system operators (MSOs) emerge to provide the system-management capability to enable customers to achieve this with the aid of ICT and other network technologies such as energy storage.
- Customers take a lead role in their own energy provision and the security, quality and reliability of the supply with the support of the MSO.

Environmental concern grows strongly as climate change develops to a serious degree and is indisputably linked to GHG emissions. OECD countries will take a lead in targeting emissions and moving away from fossil fuel. International agreements leading to firmly established carbon markets will help incentivize low-carbon energy in developing countries.

All of these factors mean climate change will be at the forefront of decision making for individuals, communities, private companies, public institutions and the government in the UK. There will be a strong perception that electricity generation sources should be environmentally friendly and that energy efficiency is essential and a matter of national strategic importance. This will be delivered through markets with appropriate frameworks and bounds. There will be a strong focus on the benefits of decentralized energy and energy efficiency, not only to meet environmental objectives but to reduce reliance on centralized fossil fuel in a world of decreasing supply and increasing prices.

Emissions trading will develop and the resulting market price of carbon will reflect the perceived high cost and consequence of not hitting emissions targets. The carbon market will penetrate to all levels of society and will incentivize consumers and industry to adopt low-carbon technology and solutions.

Planning approaches will be modified to address the demands of developing new generation, network upgrades, self-generation capabilities, new building standards, improved efficiency of older buildings and transport systems, among others. Planning permission for microgeneration projects will become a standardized, fast-track process, removing barriers to uptake. Planning policy will be developed to address the often conflicting objectives of speeding up decisions, reflecting local views and

[2] Microgrid: small-scale, mainly autonomous but still grid-connected power system with demand, energy storage and generation resources and advanced controls to operate the system against objectives.

concerns, addressing environmental impacts, promoting competition and supplier/user negotiations and allowing quicker investment decisions.

Investment in the electricity industry and networks specifically will become a less centrally planned process, with increased competitive tendering and negotiated contracts between buyers and sellers of network services.

Society in general will become increasingly environmentally conscious; energy efficiency will become more and more of a priority in all areas of life. Leisure activities and consumer preferences will be influenced by environmental attitudes. Consumers will desire energy-efficient housing and business will likewise seek opportunities to continue migrating towards more efficient buildings and processes. Greater value will be placed on smaller, modern, energy efficient housing and older housing will be modified substantially for energy efficiency to attract buyers. Government strongly encourages this trend, with reform of building regulations setting zero carbon objectives in the new build and public sectors. This is only one of many policy measures introduced to promote energy saving and remove barriers to microgeneration. Demand will be significantly affected by the high levels of efficiency in consumer energy use and their willingness to participate in DSM schemes.

Transport migrates towards low-carbon options in this scenario. Longer journeys and commuting are avoided where possible and use of public transport becomes more popular. Private car use will still be widespread, mainly for shorter leisure journeys. Hybrid electric vehicles will be the initial preferred choice, moving to fully electrified vehicles by 2050. Hydrogen fuel cell cars are also likely to feature as competition develops between low-carbon options. This is driven by a consumer desire for clean transport and market provision but is also supported by government-led frameworks for the introduction of low-carbon vehicles, such as R&D support, low-carbon transport incentives and mandated obligations. Home charging of electric vehicles will become common, creating a new source of electricity demand with the potential for undersizing of microgeneration installed on a self-sufficiency objective in comparison with the growing demand for electric vehicle charging.

Electrified rail transport will become widely used and will be a booming market, especially for longer journeys and commuting. Buses will also become more and more widely used in urban areas. Alternative fuels will develop for buses, potentially biofuel and hydrogen. The market will lead these developments by responding to consumer demand and government prompting.

Flexible working will become more common as people actively try to avoid unnecessary commuting and a growing preference for living in smaller, more rural communities develops. Advances in ICT and the capabilities of telecommunications networks enable the rise of a digital networked economy, and the emergence of virtual office working practices makes highly distributed workforces a common business model.

Within the domestic sector there could be widespread deployment of micro CHP and renewable microgeneration. As a result of government strategy, public bodies (schools, hospitals, council offices) may have developed CHP, storage and renewable energy sources that reduce these organizations' reliance on their grid connection and centralized energy resource. Industrial consumers could be similar but may have larger generation sources serving multiple factories – power parks. In certain settings these institutions will be central players in community energy solutions, possibly trading within a local microgrid. Centralized generation will be sized to supplement the distributed and microgeneration deployed in local areas and to meet growing demand from new sectors such as transport. Nuclear and fossil fuel with CCS are likely to be prominent as stable high carbon prices incentivize investment in these technologies.

Mechanisms similar to the renewables obligation (RO) are used to promote microgeneration, as are feed-in tariffs at the domestic level. The potential to export low-carbon energy and be rewarded fairly by the market provides additional motivation to develop self-generation technology. These measures have a similar impact as RO certificates (ROCs) have had on onshore wind in recent years and result in the widespread adoption of microgeneration.

Public bodies and industrial consumers will initially participate in DSM in the form of existing commercial agreements with the transmission system operator to limit demand at certain peak times. By 2050 the contracts that cover this will have developed to see such peak management as a more routine rather than an exceptional occurrence, and be available for stepped or emergency load shedding.

The commercial and public sector energy service demands continue to grow, but with the national move for economic and environmentally led activity by consumers of all types this overall demand for energy services will be met by more efficient processes and behaviours, leading to an overall status quo or a decline in energy consumption.

The advent of home-charged electric vehicles will create a demand source as well as a storage capability. The preference for rural living and increased affluence and associated growth in numbers of dwellings and electronic consumables would seem to indicate a significant growth in demand; however, the stringent energy efficiency measures of this scenario (within building regulations and electrical products, etc.) control and reduce the net growth in demand. The majority of space and water heating at present uses gas. It is likely this will migrate to CHP, utilizing existing heat networks where present (high-rise building, power parks, old people's homes, university campuses, etc.) or micro CHP in the domestic setting. Other technology such as heat pumps and solar heating will also be deployed. The overall result is that many energy consumers reduce their reliance on grid-supplied electricity, using distributed and microenergy sources to meet a significant amount of a demand already reduced by energy efficiency measures.

Electricity metering will be a dynamic, real-time process (on half-hourly settlement or even lower resolution), providing advanced levels of information, allowing informed decision making and facilitating various innovative markets such as managed demand, energy consumption capping and scheduling energy use to periods of low prices or high renewables availability. Consumers could make real-time decisions to export excess energy depending on the price available from the local/national network. Domestic consumers will use the advanced levels of information and advanced control technologies to make better decisions on when to use electricity and how best to participate in dynamic local markets. This will result in behavioural DSM and peak smoothing. Automated systems for appropriate domestic appliances may be in place where the system operator has an agreed contract to monitor requirements and balance demand in specific local areas.

One approach being deployed widely is the microgrid where self-sufficiency among individual and groups of customers has developed to such an extent that demand management, energy storage, power quality as well as energy production are coordinated in well-defined customer groups. The role for the distribution network operator might be in operating the microgrids themselves or connecting microgrids to the wider distribution system as virtual or actual private networks. Microgrids will sometimes provide the capability for isolated operation when circumstances dictate – for example, to reduce network access charges or in response to faults or other events in the bulk power system. However, there is often an incentive for microgrids to operate in synchronism with the remainder of the power system for the purposes of selling excess energy or benefiting from the resulting enhanced security and reliability. Although the attitudes within society and the thrust of government policy promote the self-sufficiency and local generation trend, this is not a universal solution and the grid connection is still an essential part of microgrid operation.

Consumers (and their energy management systems with external inputs) will make real-time decisions on whether to export power, locally store power, manage demand, import and various combinations of those actions. There could be a microgrid system operator that may be a

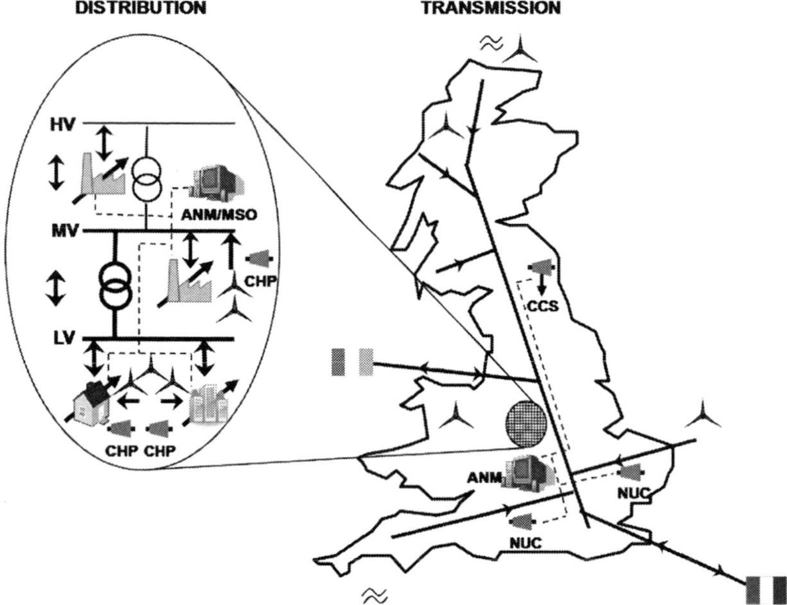


Figure 2.6 Microgrids pictogram.

separate entity or indeed the DSO acting as the MSO in each customer area. The MSO will facilitate these dynamic markets via highly automated intelligent systems. Consumers and generators will be charged by the MSO for connection and system use. Hardware to provide onsite monitoring, metering, production, storage and control equipment will be deployed. Standardization of systems and standards across all MSOs will automate control of the stability of the overall system.

Economies of scale in large-scale renewable energy production and strategic drivers for the exploitation of offshore renewable energy sources will result in the continued investment in large-scale power generation. Centralized thermal generation (especially nuclear) will also continue to play a role in supplementing the increased levels of localized generation. Some large-scale facilities retain the capability to export either hydrogen or electricity to exploit the dynamic markets in both commodity markets. The resulting architecture is a generally reduced transmission requirement but continued geographical coverage. One other important aspect of the higher degree of self-sufficiency within a microgrid and across local groups of microgrids is that supply security can be provided without such heavy reliance on the bulk distribution and transmission systems.

The key qualitative aspects of the scenario are represented in Figure 2.6.

### *2.7.1 Modelling results*

Once again, in order to represent the qualitative storyline in MARKAL, an exogenous constraint on the use of the transmission network has been applied.

As with the DSO (government-led green agenda) run, this run has the model's elastic demand function enabled. A very high carbon price represents a world of very high concern for carbon emissions, where 'climate change will be at the forefront of decision making for individuals, private companies, public institutions and the government in the UK'. This price incentivizes lower-carbon technology choices and also stimulates even greater demand responses, which within the context of the scenario are interpreted as being correlated to a very strong societal willingness to undergo social and lifestyle change.

Total final energy demand therefore ends up at the lowest level of all the runs, 4,558 PJ in 2050 (see Table 2.5). Perhaps the most notable aspect of this severely curtailed energy mix is that demand for natural gas remains almost unchanged from previous runs. This is because natural gas is still being used with very little change for space and water heating in buildings. Although this use is incurring a carbon penalty, the comparatively low carbon intensity of natural gas compared with other fossil fuels means that the penalty is not sufficient to incentivize a major switch to more costly alternatives for providing residential and service heat, particularly when access to electricity for these purposes is limited due to the constraint on transmission.

This run also deploys greater quantities of small-scale generation, and at an earlier time than in DSO (government-led green agenda). The small-scale wind resource is once again fully deployed by 2020 and small-scale solar photovoltonics are already generating significant amounts of electricity by 2015, rising quickly to generate 142 PJ by 2025.

The transport sector again undergoes major transformation, with implications for the electricity sector. In this run hydrogen and electric technologies share the majority of the transport fleets.

## 2.8 Discussion with respect to future electricity demand

The scenarios have explored several aspects of the future of electrical demand informed by the overall trajectory of energy demand (and production). The context for this exploration of the future of electricity demand is in the scenario themes which focused on environmental concern, consumer participation and institutional governance. The scenarios themselves were developed for wider questions than energy or electricity demand alone, but it is clear that electricity demand is a major component

Table 2.5 *Microgrid scenario modelling results summary*

| | 2000 | | 2025 | | 2050 | |
|---|---|---|---|---|---|---|
| Total final energy demand (PJ)[a] | 6,188 | | 5,641 | | 4,558 | |
| Transport | 1,855 | 30% | 1,842 | 33% | 1,255 | 28% |
| Residential | 1,961 | 32% | 1,780 | 32% | 1,431 | 31% |
| Other (Industry, Services & Agriculture) | 2,373 | 38% | 2,020 | 36% | 1,872 | 41% |
| Total electricity demand (PJ)[b] | 1,176 | | 864 | | 1,044 | |
| Transport | 20 | 2% | 33 | 4% | 263 | 25% |
| Residential | 403 | 34% | 271 | 31% | 195 | 19% |
| Other[c] | 754 | 64% | 560 | 65% | 585 | 56% |
| Total electricity generation capacity (GW) | 84 | | 83 | | 113 | |
| *Large-scale generation:* | | | | | | |
| Fossile (inc. CCS) | 59 | 71% | 25 | 30% | 9 | 8% |
| Nuclear | 12 | 14% | 10 | 12% | 27 | 24% |
| Renewables | 4 | 5% | 11 | 13% | 16 | 14% |
| Interconnectors | 2 | 2% | 4 | 5% | 12 | 11% |
| CHP | 4 | 4% | 2 | 2% | 0 | 0% |
| Storage | 3 | 3% | 1 | 2% | 1 | 1% |
| *Small-scale generation:* | | | | | | |
| Micro CHP | 0 | 0% | 8 | 10% | 24 | 22% |
| Microgen | 0 | 0% | 22 | 26% | 23 | 20 |
| Total electricty generation output (PJ) | 1,288 | | 1,203 | | 1,462 | |
| *Large-scale generation:* | | | | | | |
| Fossil (inc. CCS) | 854 | 66% | 423 | 35% | 100 | 7% |
| Nuclear | 282 | 22% | 267 | 22% | 713 | 49% |
| Renewables | 46 | 4% | 151 | 13% | 209 | 14% |
| Interconnectors | 52 | 4% | 77 | 6% | 103 | 7% |
| CHP | 45 | 3% | 19 | 2% | 7 | 0% |
| Storage | 10 | 1% | 6 | 0% | 0 | 0% |
| *Small-scale generation:* | | | | | | |
| Micro CHP | 0 | 0% | 83 | 7% | 142 | 10% |
| Microgen | 0 | 0% | 177 | 15% | 189 | 13% |
| $CO_2$ reductions from 2000 (Mt) | | | | | | |
| Energy system reduction | | 0% | | 36% | | 71% |
| Electricity sector reduction | | 0% | | 74% | | 99% |

[a] 1 PJ = 0.278 TWh.

[b] Sectoral electricity demand figures do not include that proportion of electricity demand that is met by small-scale electricity generation.

[c] Industry, Services, Agriculture, Hydrogen and Upstreams.

Table 2.6 *Total electricity demand across scenarios for years 2000, 2025 and 2050 (in TWh)*

| | 2000 | 2025 | 2050 |
|---|---|---|---|
| Big T&D ('switch me on') | 327 | 371 | 423 |
| ESCOs ('fix it for me') | 327 | 389 | 451 |
| DSOs (government-led green agenda) | 327 | 306 | 346 |
| Microgrids (dynamic green markets) | 327 | 240 | 290 |

of the scenarios. It is interesting to note that the level of consumer participation and overall demand is relatively independent of the institutional governance or environmental drivers. That is to say, high or low levels of demand and high or low levels of consumer participation appear to be able to sit comfortably in plausible futures with different institutional governance arrangements (government intervention, market structures, etc.) and environmental drivers.

The overall electricity demand trajectory in time across the scenarios is quite diverse and there are interesting underlying reasons for this. Table 2.6 compares the electricity demand for each scenario converted from PJ to TWh.

The range of trajectories and outcomes in 2050 for demand across the scenarios is relatively broad. In the Big T&D scenario demand experiences significant and relatively steady growth, while in the ESCOs scenario there is a slightly higher growth path. In the DSOs scenario there is modest rise in demand, with a drop in the early years to 2025 due to far more active consumers and coordinated demand-side management implementation. In the microgrids scenario there is a deeper drop in demand level followed by growth, but not to the level of the year 2000 as a result of even more active consumers and technologies and incentives to support their action to manage their own energy affairs.

The demand growth trajectories are highly dependent on the assumptions in the different scenarios about such factors as technology learning rates and economic characteristics of demand-side and efficiency technologies and also the level of consumer demand elasticity. These issues are described in narrative (qualitative) form within the scenarios and then modelling with MARKAL (MED) adds quantitative detail to this.

The MARKAL (MED) results quantifying significant demand reduction or at least arrest of growth across the scenarios warrant more discussion as this is a significant result (albeit that the modelling runs were set up to explore existing scenarios narratives rather than the other way round). In the MARKAL runs with the elastic demand function enabled

(MED), a trend of demand reductions occurs in the middle of the period as carbon prices rise. In this case overall demand reductions offer a comparatively cost-effective way of avoiding the growing penalty of the carbon price. It is worth considering what would be implied by such overall all-sector energy demand reductions: reduced service and residential electricity demands, which could mean restrictions on energy-guzzling appliances and reduced output of agriculture and industry, which could be interpreted as meaning lower economic growth in the economy as a whole.

As described by the narratives of the two scenarios with the most notable low-growth trajectory for electricity demand, such demand trajectories imply societies in which there is a strong consensus for all actors to accept the reduced use of energy which would be stimulated by a high carbon price and, arguably perhaps, some loss of the benefits of the services which would have been associated with these. In the narratives for these scenarios, this acceptance is driven by a deep-rooted and pervasive environmental concern – it hardly needs to be stated that this would imply some quite significant social changes.

These modelling results should not be interpreted to imply that major demand reductions are the only means of achieving deep carbon emissions reductions but rather that they suggest that if high carbon prices could be created by policy means, at a time when low-carbon technological alternatives were not sufficiently well developed in terms of cost and performance, then an economically rational response could be to reduce energy service demand and forgo the consumption associated with that. This is precisely the effect that can be observed in the middle periods of the DSOs and microgrids modelling runs. However, as low-carbon technologies do become more available, and as their costs start to come down, a rising carbon price need not be associated with energy service demand reductions. In the DSOs and microgrids runs, the accelerated technology development, which begins to pay dividends in the later years, means that despite the mid-period slump in energy service demands, the last 10–15 years sees rising demands in key energy services such as transport and residential electricity.

The assumptions which make these technologies available at reduced costs in later years imply a solid R&D programme in the UK, as well as international consensus on technology development. The runs emphasize that if it was considered desirable to avoid major demand reductions at the same time as achieving considerable emissions reductions, then ensuring that the necessary investment is flowing into various low-carbon technology options (not only in the power sector), and at as early a stage as possible, would be crucial.

## 2.9 Implications and conclusion

The implications of the outcomes for future electricity demand identified in the scenarios and relevant to the objectives of this book are as follows:

- The development of primary power-carrying infrastructure differs across the scenarios, with high demand for network capacity in the Big T&D scenario and lower demand for network capacity in other scenarios. This is driven by overall demand level but also the location of the demand, with more electricity generation closer to loads in the ESCOs scenario.
- One relatively common element across the scenarios is the development of more extensive communications and control infrastructure. Such 'light current' infrastructure extends to varying extents all the way down from transmission systems (dealing with greater numbers of generation sites, interconnectors and demand response), through distribution systems, where distributed energy resources and demand-side management become more prevalent, to customer premises, where ICT-enabled work and home sites become 'linked' into the management infrastructure for the power system. It is evident that among other things ICT is a key enabler for active consumers.
- The level and nature of consumer participation vary across the scenarios from passive to highly active. The nature of consumer activity ranges from the self-motivated or self-initiated action on the part of electricity customers to third party-provided solutions by new market players such as those described in the ESCOs scenario. With consumer activity being one of the main scenario themes, tracking the progress of customer interaction with their electricity suppliers and the electricity networks could provide useful insights into the development trajectory for the electricity system in future years.
- Organizational implications appear to be very important and these differ widely across the scenarios, with new players (e.g. ESCOs, microgrid operators) and new roles emerging over time (e.g. for DSOs managing much more active and complex distribution systems). This changing industry structure and the new cooperative and competitive commercial relationships will be important for consumers to navigate and exploit.
- Changing and diverse organizational arrangements across the scenarios and through time bring with them the ongoing requirement for clarity of responsibilities for security, quality, efficiency and economy of electricity supplies. More complex institutional arrangements combined with complex technical requirements in power systems could provide an unwanted lack of clarity regarding allocation of responsibilities and

it is likely that government and regulators have a key role to play in managing this situation. Once again consumers will know the effects of these changes in the security and quality of supply and service.

- Regulatory arrangements to supervise more complex markets, provide incentives for worthwhile services and reward performance are not trivial. Taking just one example, the reward mechanism for DSOs (or otherwise distribution network companies operating more active distribution networks) would need to recognize the additional resources, challenges, risks and potential for innovation in the distribution companies and reward appropriate risk taking and deployment of resources and innovative approaches. The basis for such a framework of obligations, rewards and penalties might be based on other incentive schemes in operation today, but there might also be reasons why this would not be appropriate. With energy supply customers paying the price for any incentives and feeling the effects of the efficiency of the markets, the outturn of this issue will impact consumers directly in their wallets.
- Interconnectors to neighbouring countries take on various roles in different scenarios, such as bulk import, two-way bulk exchanges based on market operation, and large-scale and small-scale pan-European balancing (due to intermittent renewables and/or microgeneration). The benefits and costs to customers of enhanced interconnection may be significant, but again consumers will ultimately pay for ambitious expansion of the power system.
- Active management of distribution networks (HV, MV and LV) and consumer demand becomes more prevalent in most scenarios. Currently, active management of power distribution networks close to consumers is predominantly a research and development activity, with a few exceptions in deployment. The regulatory and commercial frameworks for active networks and the technical challenges they bring require advances beyond the business models prevalent today.
- Network capacity requirements are relatively similar across some scenarios, with higher network capacity requirements in transmission networks evident in the Big T&D scenario, for example, and with higher network capacity requirements in distribution networks evident in the DSOs and microgrids scenarios. In contrast to this picture of future network capacity are the widely varying levels of network utilization across and within the scenarios. For example, intermittent renewable generation resources will produce a lower utilization of network capacity than high load factor thermal generation but a higher requirement for operational management for system balancing. In distribution networks, the influences of demand-side management, distributed electricity generation resources and energy storage (each in different

measures in different scenarios) will likely make the utilization of network capacity variable across the country and through time. The frameworks for planning network capacity additions, for managing the utilization of the capacity and for charging for the use of the network capacity may need to evolve far from the situation at the time of writing (2010).
- Across the scenarios (to varying degrees) there is projected a future with more (in number and level of activity) active distribution networks. The technological, commercial and organizational arrangements for management of more active networks by the distribution companies is an area where it is likely that more effort will be placed in future. The regulatory arrangements (e.g. incentives and capital expenditure allowances) are also likely to have to adapt to futures with more active distribution networks.
- Energy system modelling shows that consideration of the potential evolution of the networks needs to take a broad view of the drivers, opportunities and technological developments across all energy-using sectors. In particular, transport has been shown to have a significant effect on networks across all scenarios, in terms of increasing electricity demand (for electric vehicles or for hydrogen production) as well as offering an opportunity for load spreading and system balancing with 'plug-in' vehicles. The viability of CHP may also depend on the availability of bioenergy resource, which has numerous other competing uses and interactions with other sectors. It seems clear that planning for the evolution of future networks will benefit from a 'whole-system' view and the trajectory and nature of electricity demand is a major factor in this.

This chapter has set out a number of issues for future electricity demand derived from scenarios for future energy systems with a particular emphasis on power networks. Technological, economic and social issues regarding consumer participation in the electricity system have been prevalent in the scenarios and will continue to be the focus of increased attention as society grapples with the triple challenges of climate change, energy security and the energy economy.

## References

Ofgem (2007a). *Scenarios Development Methodology, Long-Term Electricity Network Scenarios (LENS) Project.* November, Ref 273/07, Available at www.ofgem.gov.uk/Networks/Trans/Archive/ElecTrans/LENS/Documents1/LENS-Scenarios%20Methodology%20-%20v070926.pdf, last accessed 9 February 2011.

Ofgem (2007b). *Long-Term Electricity Network Scenarios (LENS) Report on Scenario Inputs and Second Consultation*. December, Ref 287/07, Available at www.ofgem.gov.uk/Networks/Trans/Archive/ElecTrans/LENS/Documents1/LENSInputs.pdf, last accessed 9 February 2011.

Ofgem (2007c). *Long-Term Electricity Network Scenarios – Initial Thoughts and Workshop Invitation*. June, Ref 146/07, Available at www.ofgem.gov.uk/Pages/MoreInformation.aspx)?docid=61&refer=Networks/Trans/Archive/ElecTrans/LENS, last accessed 9 February 2011.

Ofgem (2007d). *Long-Term Electricity Networks Scenarios Workshop Presentation*. August, Available at www.ofgem.gov.uk/Pages/MoreInformation.aspx ?docid =47&refer=Networks/Trans/Archive/ElecTrans/LENS, last accessed 9 February 2011.

Ofgem (2008a). *Long-Term Electricity Network Scenarios (LENS) – Final Report*. November, Ref 157/08, Available at www.ofgem.gov.uk/Networks/Trans/Archive/ElecTrans/LENS/Documents1/20081107Final%20Report.pdf, last accessed 9 February 2011.

Ofgem (2008b). *Long-Term Electricity Network Scenarios (LENS) Final Report* (Appendices). November, Ref 157/08. Available at www.ofgem.gov.uk/Networks/Trans/Archive/ElecTrans/LENS/Documents1/157018bLENS-Appendices.pdf, last accessed 9 February 2011.

Royal Commission on Environmental Pollution (RCEP) (2000). *Energy – The Changing Climate*. London: HMSO. June. Available at www.rcep.org.uk/reports/22-energy/22-energyreport.pdf, last accessed 23 August 2010.

Shell International (2003). *Scenarios: An Explorer's Guide*, Global Business Environment, 2003. Available at www.shell.com/static/aboutshellen/downloads/our_strategy/shell_global_scenarios/scenario_explorersguide.pdf, last accessed 23 August 2010.

Tyndall Centre for Climate Change Research (2005). *Decarbonising the UK – Energy for a Climate Conscious Future*. Tyndall Centre Technical Report 33. Available at www.tyndall.ac.uk/sites/default/files/tyndall_decarbonising_the_uk.pdf, last accessed 23 August 2010.

Wack, P. (1985a). The gentle art of reperceiving scenarios: uncharted waters ahead (part 1), *Harvard Business Review*, **63**(5): 72–89.

Wack, P. (1985b). The gentle art of reperceiving scenarios: uncharted waters ahead (part 1) and shooting the rapids (part 2), *Harvard Business Review*, **63**(6): 139–50, 1985.

# 3 Demand-side participation: price constraints, technical limits and behavioural risks

*Jacopo Torriti, Matthew Leach and Patrick Devine-Wright*

## 3.1 Introduction

Demand response in domestic contexts may be differentiated into two modes of provision. First, 'automatic' load control involves the direct intervention by utilities to manipulate the performance of domestic appliances using heat or power, without the immediate involvement of domestic end-users. This is sometimes referred to as 'dynamic demand'. For example, in the UK a trial was initiated in December 2009 by a consortium including a fridge manufacturer (Indesit), an energy utility (Npower) and a technology company (RLtec). Three hundred end-users were supplied with 'dynamic demand fridges and fridge freezers', free of charge and the trial involved the monitoring of each device as well as the switching off of appliances for short durations in response to grid conditions.

A second form of demand response can be described as more 'intentional' load control. This involves the direct intervention by domestic end-users themselves, rather than utilities, that would retain total control over the working of domestic appliances and would choose to modify behavioural patterns of energy consumption in response to some form of signal from a utility. This signal is most likely to be a price signal but is not necessarily so – it could involve communicating the availability of energy generated from different kinds of resource (e.g. fossil fuel or renewable) (Devine-Wright, 2003). The signal is most likely to be communicated via a smart metering device, but could alternatively involve a 'traffic light' device that signals the availability of energy via colour-coded signals, or a communication to other forms of ICT via text messages or emails (e.g. mobile phones).

These two forms of demand response are clearly not mutually exclusive – it is possible that a specific household or consumer could accept both forms of response simultaneously, accepting a passive manipulation of certain devices such as fridges or freezers (typically for very short durations) while simultaneously actively monitoring signals from a utility to behaviourally respond over a longer duration (e.g. switching on the washing machine during the night rather than day time). The level of immediate engagement involved in each of these modes of demand response clearly differs, from virtually none in automatic demand response to considerable in intentional demand response.

In principle, demand-side participation can bring about significant reductions in electricity prices, as shifts of demand during peaks could reduce marginal costs (Faruqui, 2005). A participative and responsive demand side would also play an indispensable role in achieving ambitious environmental policy objectives. In practice, the functioning of demand-side participation is underpinned by two necessary conditions and one sufficient one. The first necessary condition regards technical assets. Demand-side participation can be guaranteed only by a high level of exchange of information between the utility and the consumer. The second necessary condition regards behavioural risks. Demand-side participation can work only once behavioural risks stop preventing an adequate level of either 'automatic' or 'intentional' load control. The sufficient condition is with regards to price. Consumers' response to the price fluctuations signalled by the utility can be maximized through a dynamic pricing system. Price-based demand participation implies that time-varying retail prices and dynamic tariffs are a necessary condition for exposing consumers to the price volatility that typically takes place at peak time.

The limitations associated with European experiences of demand-side participation can shed light on the price, technical and behavioural constraints. Despite the progress being made or planned by some countries, notably Italy and the UK, the penetration of smart metering technologies remains generally low, along with the uptake of demand-side participation programmes. What could be done to overcome some of the behavioural and economic constraints to demand-side participation? Psychological motivations and social acceptance shape consumer behaviour and need to be taken into account when proposing new financial tools to encourage demand-side participation.

This chapter commences by introducing the constraints to demand-side participation (section 3.2). It examines how such constraints affect demand-side participation in electricity markets by presenting an overview of European experiences (section 3.3). It provides a description of the social and behavioural aspects of flexibility in demand-side participation, with a focus on issues of psychological motivation and social acceptance (section 3.4). It considers financial schemes to encourage demand-side participation through an incentive/payment scheme (section 3.5). It concludes by making observations on ways to overcome existing constraints on demand-side participation (section 3.6).

## 3.2 The constraints to demand-side participation

A set of constraints which reduces the extent to which the end-user can or chooses to manage electricity loads can be observed in current electricity markets. These constraints relate mainly to technical limits, price and behavioural issues.

### *3.2.1 Technical limits*

Technical limits include availability of smart metering technologies, communication technologies and metering cost effectiveness.

Over the last ten years or so, the availability of smart metering technologies has been limited in the UK, as in other European countries (Frontier Economics, 2007). Current developments within Europe point to a wide roll-out of such technologies. The Energy Service Directive in 2006 in part created the political conditions for investment in smart metering technologies by endorsing that end-users should be the recipients of energy metering whenever technically and financially feasible. The types of technologies vary substantially, including electronic interval meter specification in Italy; 'smart enabled' meters combined with smart boxes in the Netherlands; retrofit devices, which are either clamped, fastened or glued on to meters in Finland; and two-way communication automated meter management in Sweden (Torriti *et al.*, 2010). Moreover, smart metering technologies trials are taking place in most European countries (Brophy Haney *et al.*, 2009 and Brophy Haney *et al.*, this volume).

The way various technologies, such as electronic meters, communicate is vital to effective demand-side participation. Advanced meters with open communication standards might be connected with in-home control and information devices that would automatically communicate with meters and facilitate automated demand participation. Open communication standards also have the potential to reduce costs by encouraging competition among technology providers. Presently the lack of advanced metering infrastructures poses significant limits to allowing demand participation. In other words, the vast majority of current metering systems would require substantial upgrades to support the provision of interval data and extensive investment in billing systems to support large-scale participation in dynamic pricing tariffs. However, around Europe there are plans to deploy advanced metering infrastructures in various European countries, such as Austria, Germany and the Czech Republic.

The costs of electronic meters have long been a practical constraint to demand participation. While production costs of some of the most inexpensive technological solutions have been decreasing over recent years, rendering them affordable, three problems persist with regards to the costs of enabling the most expensive and advanced smart metering technologies.

First, the roll-out costs associated with start-up and implementation remain significantly high. An ERGEG (2007) survey shows that in eleven European countries the penetration level is below 7 per cent, rendering marginal costs of roll-out very high compared with places such as Sweden, Italy, Finland and France, where the penetration level is 20 per cent or above. In a low market-penetration country like the UK, for instance, the cost of a nationwide roll-out of smart meters at a total of £14 billion differs substantially (in the area of £7–£8 billion). In fact, the political consensus on the benefits of smart meters has risen so much over the past year that the roll-out plan will involve the fitting of 26 million electricity and 22 million gas meters by 2020.

Second, regarding the benefits side, most of the debate around the economic potential of demand-side participation in the UK has focused on paybacks to end-users. On this point, the existing studies fall short of estimating the potentially wider impacts of innovation (Bilton *et al.*, 2008). Most studies rely upon the evidence provided by pilot roll-out cases showing that – when fully informed – end-users tend to respond to higher energy prices. However, the long-term economic benefits and carbon-emission reductions have not been fully explored. Section 3.5 of this chapter makes an attempt to investigate possible ways to institute long-term demand participation by considering financial methods to encourage demand-side participation over time.

Third, the most advanced technologies are arguably not yet cost effective. For instance, advanced energy-management systems in commercial buildings and process-control systems in industrial facilities that can reduce load when needed are above reach for most commercial and industrial users, mainly because end-users' awareness of these tools is low. In turn, the price of these technologies is high due to the low level of market penetration, since the marketing infrastructure is in very early stages. In other words, the value chain from the device producer to the retailer is disadvantaged by low levels of cumulative installations and limited experience. The ambiguity around the cost effectiveness of advanced metering systems is illustrated by the difference between some of the early UK cost–benefit analyses commissioned by the Department for

Business, Enterprise and Regulatory Reform – which highlighted that the most advanced smart metering options would have negative net present values – and the final impact assessment (carried out by the Department of Energy and Climate Change). It was noted that this initial negative assessment was partly due to assumptions that limit the value of demand-side management (DECC, 2009). Hence, the final impact assessment on smart meters presents a preferred roll-out option with a positive net present value.

### *3.2.2 Price*

Two types of price constraints restrict demand-side participation. The first type of constraint arises from price structures. Typically, traditional flat rates impede premium prices for those end-users who are willing to follow the market and diversify their electricity usage on a price basis. Where end-users are charged a flat rate per kWh of energy consumed, bills are calculated multiplying the flat rate by the number of kWh used. Flat-rate pricing methods prevent end-users from accessing price fluctuations in wholesale market prices, which normally increase significantly during peak hours. On the contrary, time-varying retail prices and dynamic tariffs expose end-users to the price volatility that occurs during peak hours. A sizeable literature has assessed the impact that dynamic pricing can have on electricity usage, when end-users are charged higher rates when energy is consumed during peak times (Faruqui and George, 2002).

A distinction needs to be made between static time-varying retail prices, generally called time-of-use prices, which are preset for pre-determined hours and days, and dynamic prices, which can change at short notice, often a day or less. In a fully liberalized energy market dynamic retail pricing means that prices for end-users can be adjusted frequently and on short notice to reflect changes in wholesale prices and the supply/demand balance (Borenstein *et al.*, 2002). Dynamic pricing consists of either real-time pricing, which changes every hour or half hour, or critical peak pricing, which allows the retailer to impose a high retail price for a limited number of hours.

The second type of price constraint regards price signalling. The lack of actual signalling prevents customers from operating in a responsive manner in the retail market. The provision of price signals in monetary terms or even simply peak signals (through a red light) has been non-existent under traditional metering systems. The mandatory standards for smart meters are the best venue for deliberating on whether smart meters should require a signalling function.

At the research level recent attempts to overcome the pricing barriers and model behaviour under dynamic pricing have comprised, for instance, occupancy models (Richardson *et al.*, 2008), appliance frequency models (Strbac, 2008; Alvarez *et al.*, 2004) and integrated flexibility demand profile models (Moreno *et al.*, 2004). At a commercial level, ongoing trials are seeking to identify peak usage or high-cost periods via tariffs (Ofgem, 2010a), whereas some suppliers are planning to trial critical-peak pricing where end-users are informed about peak tariffs a short time before peak events (Ofgem, 2010b).

### *3.2.3 Behavioural risks*

The deployment of the appropriate technologies and tariffs is a necessary condition for demand-side participation. However, it is not a sufficient condition as end-users' adaption could be undermined by specific typologies of risks. Risk aversion, unawareness of price-based tariffs and risk of technological obsolescence are some of the most important behavioural risks associated with demand-side participation.

Risk aversion can potentially affect end-users' preferences when it comes to choosing between flat rates and dynamic pricing. When selecting the type of rate (tariff), end-users may focus on the downside risk that their bills can rise if they opt for that rate rather than on the upside potential that they might save money either by changing their load shape or due to their existing profile of consumption across high-cost and low-cost periods. Research by Schultz and Lineweber (2006) shows that end-users who experience time-varying rates report high levels of satisfaction, at least in certain contexts. Regardless of end-user satisfaction rationales, utilities often demonstrate concern about risk aversion by inducing default pricing for (unaware) existing customers, which leads to much higher customer enrolment rather than voluntary opt-in enrolment.

The risk that end-users are either not fully aware of or not capable of understanding the change involved in price-based mechanisms can seriously undermine the successful outcome of demand participation programmes. The historical lack of end-user exposure to dynamic pricing represents a substantial obstacle to their participation. Inertia can be transformed into action as long as at the community level the right prompts are in place (CSE, 2007). The risk of inertial behaviour can be justified by a long-standing predominance of flat rates imposed by the incumbent utility and ultimately contributes to low participation rates in voluntary programmes.

The risk associated with technological obsolescence affects end-users, industry and government. Perceptions of the useful life of price-sensitive control technologies drive concerns for risk of technological obsolescence. End-users, who in countries such as the UK bear the costs for smart metering deployment through higher bills, might think that smart meters could shortly be replaced with newer technologies and not invest time in understanding the functions of smart metering technologies. The risk of technological obsolescence is also extended to the enabling technologies, many of which are still in the development stage. Most of these concerns enhance doubts around the capacity to recover the costs of investments before they need to be substituted. On this issue, the role of government as a risk-taker is key. On the one hand, a strong presence of the state in the mass implementation of advanced metering technologies will favour the price reduction. On the other hand, such presence in the metering market may pose barriers to increased private investment.

## 3.3 Overview of European experiences on demand-side participation

Evidence for the price-related, technical and behavioural constraints outlined in section 3.2 is substantiated by looking at the European experience on demand-side participation. Although there have been several cases of demand-side participation programmes over the past twenty years, their deployment has not been consistent across Europe (Torriti *et al.*, 2010). The participation of the end-user in European electricity markets has been traditionally low besides the engagement of major energy users in system balancing because end-users lack means and a limited number of incentives are in place to respond to price signals (IEA, 2003; Vasconcelos, 2008). A number of factors undermine effective demand-side participation in Europe: the lack of real-time price information reaching the end-user, regulated retail prices, outdated metering technologies, and an approach traditionally averse to demand-side participation.

The lack of real-time price information prevents end-users from accessing price fluctuations in wholesale market prices, which normally increase significantly during peak hours. While some studies estimate different levels of peak reductions in different European countries thanks to demand-side management and demand response, a study by UCTE (2008), the European association of Transmission System Operators, provides forecasts for demand-side participation in European countries. Table 3.1 shows in one column the percentage of smart metering deployment planned for 2010 and in the other column the level of demand-side

Table 3.1 *EU 15 smart metering deployment and demand-side participation projections*

| EU 15 member states | Percentage of smart meters deployment (2010 projection from Enerdata 2008) | Percentage of demand-side participation (2010 projection, from UCTE 2008) |
|---|---|---|
| Sweden | 100% | NA |
| Italy | 90% | 3.00 |
| Finland | 20% | NA |
| Denmark | 10% | NA |
| Spain | 5% | 2.30 |
| Ireland | 5% | NA |
| UK | 1% | NA |
| Germany | 1% | 0.30 |
| France | 1% | 3.00 |
| Austria | 1% | NA |
| Netherlands | 1% | 1.00 |
| Belgium (and Luxemburg) | 1% | 0.02 (Luxemburg) 0.20 (Belgium) |
| Greece | 1% | 0.60 |
| Portugal | 1% | NA |

participation forecasted for some of the EU 15 countries on the basis of TSO estimates of market penetration of price-sensitive technologies, in terms of percentage of peak shifting of electricity use as a consequence of demand-side participation programmes. In the majority of European countries where the penetration level of smart meters is still very low – including the UK – the access to real-time price information is rare and costly. With regards to the economic potential of demand-side participation, this varies significantly depending on assumptions about the day analyzed and the level of demand that is shifted. For instance, a 20 per cent uptake of time-of-use tariffs in the UK has been associated with a 5 per cent potential in load shifts (DECC, 2009). According to Ofgem (2010b), higher shifts of 10 per cent could result in cost savings of up to £1.7 million per day, depending on the day analyzed and the level of demand that is shifted.

Even where the shift has occurred from flat rates to diversified tariffs, under regulated retail prices, time-of-use systems tend to be preferred to real-time pricing. An example of the regulators' preference for time-of-use comes from the country where smart meters have the highest market penetration in Europe. The Italian energy regulator has recently introduced time-of-use for calculating the price of energy with the aim of shifting consumption to periods of lower and cheaper loads (AEEG, 2008). The new pricing system will apply to all end-users in possession of electronic meters, i.e. almost 90 per cent of Italian end-users from 2010. In cases like the Italian one, the predominance of regulated retail tariffs may hinder dynamic premium prices.

The metering technologies in place in most European countries still rely heavily on electromechanical meters, i.e. Ferraris meters. Electromechanical metering technologies require utilities' intervention in order to read electricity consumption. Readings and estimates are subject to errors and less frequent reading than under smart metering technologies, as pointed out in some preliminary trials in the UK (Ofgem, 2010a). Such outdated metering technology prevents the main functions of demand-side participation, including hourly metering reading, information feedback to end-users via in-house displays, automated direct load control and two-way communications. While it is commonly agreed that a wider use of electronic meters than the one currently experienced in Europe would create the bases for most of these functions, the absence of a convincing business case has prevented the deployment of electronic meters. It is also suggested here that the lack of a liberalized metering market in most European countries, apart from the UK, Germany and the Netherlands, can help explain why this replacement has not taken place in Europe to date.

European policy makers' traditionally averse approach to demand-side participation can be justified for three main reasons. First, although the costs of the technologies discussed in this chapter have decreased in recent years, they remain significantly high. Some European countries are unwilling to invest during the current recession and are expecting increases in volumes and reduced marginal costs. Second, many European policy makers and regulators have been focusing on liberalizing tariffs and removing flat rates (Jamasb and Pollitt, 2005). Third, while it is clear what demand-side participation can achieve in terms of demand shifting from peak periods, limited knowledge has been developed about its medium- and long-term energy-saving capacities.

In addition, in EU member states, demand-side participation programmes thus far have focused mainly on industry, as most European utilities include direct load control programmes as part of their DSM strategies, with fixed compensations attributed to small numbers of large industrial end-users. Interruptible programmes for large industries are very frequent, although the mechanisms for compensating industries vary significantly. These supply-led programmes can hardly be interpreted as demand-side participation. In the future, however, large numbers of end-users, including commercial end-users and households, could actively participate through compensations consisting of prices and deliberate shifts in electricity demand in correspondence with peak loads.

## 3.4 Description of the social aspects of flexibility in demand response, particularly issues of psychological motivation and social acceptance

Turning to the motivational bases for engaging in demand response, an important point to note is that the default position for most householders is likely to be a rather disengaged state of energy consciousness, where day-to-day domestic activities are undertaken in a predominantly habitual manner, with little, if any, conscious awareness of energy consumption or engagement with the electricity meter – where energy use is quite 'invisible' (Lutzenhiser, 1993). Although this may not be the case for a minority of householders (encompassing a diverse array of social groups, including energy-literate 'deep greens', those who have inherited frugal habits from childhood or the fuel poor), the implication of habitual behaviour for the majority of particularly fuel-rich householders is that such behaviour will be less amenable to purely information-led approaches to behavioural change. Because of this, successful interventions to promote demand response could take advantage of a physical or material change to the household context (Verplanken and Wood, 2006). Energy-demand examples might include homeowners at the point of replacing a boiler or a radiator system in their existing home, or individuals in the process of moving into a new home before new habits have yet had time to become established.

Provided such contextual changes are taken advantage of, there remain issues of diverse motivational bases to take into account when attempting to promote demand flexibility. Environmental psychologists have empirically identified three motivational bases for pro-environmental behaviour: egoistic, altruistic and biocentric concerns (e.g. Schultz *et al.*, 2005). Interventions to promote flexible demand that concentrate solely upon self-interested motivations (e.g. by availing of financial incentives at the personal level) will be more appropriate for egoistic end-users in comparison with altruistic or biocentric end-users, who in contrast may be more responsive to interventions stressing wider social or environmental benefits. Therefore, it is important for communication campaigns to target the specific audience that they are seeking to influence, with their respective social and environmental values.

It is also important to recognize the social embedding of individual or household energy behaviours. What this means is that regardless of which of the three motivational bases above are pursued, social norms will exist that shape how individuals will respond and by seeking to transform normative behaviour at the collective level (e.g. through community- or area-based approaches), more enduring forms of behavioural change may result. This is a key principle of the social-marketing approach to behavioural change that has recently been adopted by the UK Department for the Environment, Food and Rural Affairs when designing policy strategies seeking to encourage more pro-environmental behaviour. In terms of social aspects of change acceptance, it is also quite possible that an intervention may lead to a form of psychological 'reactance', whereby householders holding diverse values come together with the common goal of rejecting a campaign for change which they interpret as threatening their sense of control over how they behave in their own homes. This might be particularly likely if such an intervention was led by a state organization and sought to pressurize individuals to respond to a collective 'need' (e.g. a response to climate change) that was disputed, considered unjust or inequitable. There remains a possibility, for example, that a roll-out of smart-metering devices could suffer a strong social backlash if interpreted as a surveillance device that undermines established social norms of privacy in the home.

## 3.5 Incentivizing demand-side participation through incentive/payment schemes for the end-user

Section 3 discussed the importance of the lack of asymmetries of information for a high level of demand-side participation. The smart meter roll-outs being implemented by several European governments and utilities will help reduce asymmetries of information by covering the whole consumer population and ensuring immediate access to information regarding consumption. Is perfect information about electricity consumption sufficient to prompt demand-side participation? The energy economics literature (Caves *et al.*, 1984; Faruqui and George, 2005) suggests that the inelasticity of the demand curve for electricity implies that more needs to be done to encourage the consumer to respond to changing electricity prices. The right financial incentives need to be in place.

According to the extensive theoretical literature on demand-side management, one major reason why demand-side participation may not be effective is because of the absence of electricity providers' incentives to encourage demand-side participation (Wirl, 1995). The idea is that providers may see demand-side participation programmes as suboptimal due to the losses associated with reductions in demand which exceed gains associated with marginal decreases in generation costs and imports.

The orthodox rationale is that losses from capital costs, installations and planning demand-side participation should be covered under financial incentive mechanisms such as those for cost recovery, lost revenue, etc. However, in cases such as the UK or Italy, where extensive smart metering roll-outs are taking place, utilities have already faced capital costs (about £340 per household in the UK) and will recoup them from the end-user through higher bills or up-front fees. For this reason, another approach is presented here whereby end-users – and not utilities – are at the centre of a payment-incentive scheme.

The approach suggested here is designed to ensure that the planning costs of demand-side participation programmes are recovered by providers through payments from those end-users who do not react to price signals. In addition, those end-users who proactively engage in shifting their loads and significantly react to price stimuli will be rewarded by paying less for their electricity consumption. This will be in addition to the savings brought about by shifting loads. Because real-time rewards to end-users tend to fail due to the negligible amounts associated with gains (and losses) for a single consumer (Dulleck and Kaufmann, 2004), in the approach presented in this section, the regulator determines cumulative benchmarks which are matched against responses to price signals.

The benchmarks should be set in a way that proportionally penalizes non-active end-users. The financial scheme should guarantee that end-users who have any sort of impediment to responsiveness will not pay excessively for their performance. Moreover, those end-users affected by fuel poverty should not be penalized by the scheme. The following section outlines one possible payment/reward scheme, through which some of the key drivers for and obstacles to expansion of demand-side participation can be explored.

### 3.5.1 *Main features of the incentive/payment scheme for end-users*

While financial incentives are one way of incentivizing demand-side participation, these can be combined with payments for lack of participation of those end-users registered with dynamic pricing tariffs. The rationale behind the incentive/payment scheme for consumer participation is that those end-users who proactively engage in shifting their loads and significantly react to price signals will be rewarded by paying less for their electricity consumption. Those end-users who do not improve their active participation in response to price signals will have to pay penalties. Since the high cost of energy at peak times already economically penalizes end-users, such penalties are tenable, with end-users also signing up to maximum capped-consumption patterns. The aim of the model underpinning the incentive/payment scheme for end-users is to determine the optimal level of incentives and payments given utilities' costs for providing demand-side participation programmes, benchmarks measured through yearly end-user performance and caps set by the regulator.

The economic agents involved in the incentive-payment scheme are end-users, utilities and government. Time runs in a discrete sequence of periods indexed by the number of years. The model works under the assumption that the market where the incentive-payment scheme is introduced is perfectly competitive, so end-users take prices as given. If end-users do not reach the objectives set at the beginning of the year, they pay penalties, i.e. they will have to pay higher bills over the next year. If end-users go beyond objectives, they receive incentives, i.e. they will get lower bills.

Benchmarks are established according to end-users' performance in the previous period. The minimum number of active responses to price signals that each consumer should undertake in one year can be calculated as a percentage of the number of price signals. The maximum number of active responses that one consumer can undertake in one year is based on the number of price signals sent by the utility. Each year end-users are rewarded or penalized according to their actually measured performance.

Unitary reward/penalty parameters are set *ex ante* at the beginning of the period. Reward and penalty parameters are capped by the regulator in order to avoid excessive volatility of retail prices. Every year, the price cap reflects the changes in payments and incentives. The incentive system is funded through penalties paid by those end-users whose responsiveness targets are not met, and for the net difference between incentives and penalties. Hence, determining the planning costs for utilities is vital in order to assess the level of payments (and incentives) which are efficient for utilities.

### *3.5.2 Planning costs*

The costs faced by the utility can be represented as costs associated with demand-side participation plus costs of generation (not associated with demand-side participation). In terms of planning costs, each utility is disposed to pay according to a percentage of demand-side participation programmes, which is also based on the number of programmes implemented by the utility.

While the regulator faces an effectiveness problem (i.e. maximizing incentives and payments, while protecting poor and vulnerable consumers), providers face an efficiency problem (i.e. finding the right level of incentives to demand-side participation programmes). These two different problems can be reconciled in two steps. First, a responsiveness factor could be introduced in the cost of generation faced by utilities. Second, the two different levels of incentives – one for regulators and another for utilities – should be made equal in order to calculate the optimal cost of generation.

### 3.5.3 *Rate effects and value changes*

The incentive/payment scheme outlined so far in this section is not designed to take into account the effect of costs on rates and loads. The costs estimated by the scheme are fed into a financial mechanism that then calculates rates according to a cap-price system. If the resulting rates differ from those assumed in forecasting the loads in the incentive/payment scheme, those loads could be adjusted. Rate determination can be made internal to a model by adding a restriction, e.g. a revenue requirement equation (Braeutigam and Panzar, 1993). This restriction specifies that the revenue received by the utility should cover its cost plus the consumer incentives that will have to be offered for pursuing load shifts. For simplicity, the complications of multiple end-user classes and non-linear rate schedules will be ignored. Calculations related to rate-induced changes in loads are essential both for accurate estimates of the costs of serving those loads and to understand how these would affect the total value received by end-users.

### 3.5.4 *Compensatory weights for disadvantaged electricity end-users*

The incentive/payment scheme implies that end-users are tasked with the objective of improving the way they respond to price signals year by year. The pressure on active participation would be high on all types of end-users. However, the regulator might want to protect those end-users who for various reasons have limited ability to respond when it comes to shifting loads. Weights should be included in the scheme to compensate the negative distributional impacts associated with the introduction of the incentive/payment scheme, particularly on disadvantaged electricity end-users.

First of all, separate levels of incentives and payments might be applied for the fuel poor. One of the criticalities of incentive/payment schemes is that they might increase disparities by penalizing those who strive to pay energy bills. Other elements of impediment to responsiveness (e.g. physical and mobility disabilities, severe illness, number of dependent children) could be factored into mitigation of the incentive-payment scheme.

The financial scheme presented in this section assumes a completely new type of consumer. Active participants will have their performance measured and will either save or pay depending on the improvements to their responses to price signals. The conclusions discuss how such a radical change in end-users' approach to electricity consumption is feasible, taking into account the constraints described in section 3.2.

## 3.6 Conclusions

This chapter disentangles and explores some of the drivers for and constraints to demand-side participation. These are divided into price constraints, technical limits and behavioural risks. Technical limits are defined here in terms of availability of metering technologies, metering cost effectiveness and communication technologies. Price constraints are distinguished between price structures – with flat rates typically preventing consumers from seeing price fluctuations during peak hours – and price signalling – whose absence inhibits efficient electricity consumption and savings from over-consumption during peak periods. Behavioural risks, in the form of risk aversion, risk of technological obsolescence and unawareness of price-based tariffs, are looked at as key elements for effective demand-side participation.

The way in which technical, pricing and behavioural issues limit demand-side participation in electricity markets is exemplified through an overview of European experiences of, and limits to, demand-side participation. Despite more than forty years of attention to demand-side management, the low penetration of new metering technologies, the limited consumer access to dynamic energy tariffs and a traditional aversion to active consumer participation have severely limited the expansion of demand-side participation programmes.

Notwithstanding the technological element, in order to understand what could be done to overcome some of the behavioural and economic constraints to demand-side participation, the chapter considered in some depth, on the one hand, consumers' psychological motivation and social acceptance and, on the other hand, financial methods to encourage demand-side participation through an incentive/payment scheme for consumers. It is clear from this brief discussion that any attempt to devise a specific incentive/payment scheme will open up a series of difficult social and economic issues about responsibility, responsiveness, efficiency and protection of the vulnerable. These issues have been evident for many years in debates about the wider energy market as well as debates about energy-efficiency programmes. Concern about fuel poverty in the UK has, for example, had a strong influence on national energy taxation policy and on energy efficiency programme design, arguably restraining progress (see Waddams Price, this volume). New participatory or tariff schemes need to be designed such that they facilitate the fuel poor and other vulnerable groups to reap the potential benefit of reduced energy bills, for example by ensuring they have access to the necessary infrastructure, such as smart meters. The incentive/payment scheme outlined here has also demonstrated the mechanism by which vulnerable groups could be protected in the short term, if they are ill-equipped to participate.

Greater demand-side participation from consumers in all sectors of the economy needs to be fostered – to aid the efficiency of the power system, to facilitate implementation of intermittent renewable energy, and as part of wider moves towards behaviour change for higher energy efficiency and reduced energy use. The challenges for developing demand-side participation in the residential sector in particular are myriad, and multi-disciplinary. Much of the work done to date has focused to a large extent on technical and financial design of schemes, and their testing among limited groups of homogenous customers. These aspects need to be considered alongside the wider economic and behavioural issues discussed in this chapter if robust schemes are to be developed suitable for utility- or national-scale roll-out.

## References

AEEG (2008). Disposizioni in materia di applicazione delle condizioni economiche del servizio di maggior tutela (corrispettivi PED), di obblighi di registrazione e di messa a disposizione dei dati di prelievo e conseguente adeguamento di TIV e TILP, Decision ARG/elt 56/08. Milan: AEEG.

Alvarez, C., Gabaldon, A. and Molina, A. (2004). Assessment and simulation of the responsive demand potential in end-user facilities: application to a university customer, *IEEE Transactions on Power Systems*, **19**(2): 1223–31.

Bilton, M., Leach, M., Anderson, D., Tiravanti, G., Green, T. and Prodanovic, M. (2008). *Response to Ofgem's Consultation on Domestic Metering Innovation*, London: Imperial College London.

Borenstein, S., Jaske, M. and Rosenfeld, A. (2002). *Dynamic Pricing, Advanced Metering and Demand Response in Electricity Markets*, University of California Energy Institute, Center for the Study of Energy Markets, available at http://repositories.cdlib.org/cgi/viewcontent.cgi?article=1005&context=ucei/csem, last accessed 9 August 2010.

Braeutigam, R. and Panzar, J. (1993). Effects of the change from rate-of-return regulation to price-cap regulation, *American Economic Review*, **83**: 191–8.

Brophy Haney, A., Jamasb, T. and Pollitt, M.G. (2011). Smart metering: technology, economics and international experience, in Jamasb, T. and Pollitt, M. (eds.), *The Future of Electricity Demand: Customers, Citizens and Loads*, Cambridge: Cambridge University Press.

Caves, D., Christensen, L. and Herriges, J. (1984). Consistency of residential customer response in Time of Use pricing experiments, *Journal of Econometrics*, **26**: 179–203.

CSE (2007). Mobilising individual behavioural change through community initiatives: Lessons for tackling climate change, University of Bristol: Centre for Sustainable Energy.

DECC (2009). Impact assessment of a GB-wide smart meter roll out for the domestic sector, 2009, Available at www.decc.gov.uk/assets/decc/consultations/smart%20metering%20for%20electricity%20and%20gas/1_20090508152831_e_@@_smartmeteriadomestic.pdf, last accessed 9 August 2010.

Devine-Wright, P. (2003). Social and Psychological Aspects of using Load Management on the Grid with Intermittent Power Generation, Report produced for the DTI/Econnect Ltd. Institute of Energy and Sustainable Development, Leicester: De Montfort University.

Dulleck, U. and Kaufmann, S. (2004). Do customer information programs reduce household electricity demand? – the Irish program, *Energy Policy*, **32**: 1025–32.

ERGEG (2007). Smart metering with a focus on electricity regulation, Brussels: European Regulators' Group for Electricity and Gas, Ref E07-RMF-04-03.

European Transmission System Operator (2007). Demand response as a resource for the adequacy and operational reliability of the power systems. Brussels: ETSO, Explanatory Note.

Faruqui, A. and George, S. (2002). The value of dynamic pricing in mass markets, *The Electricity Journal*, **15**(6): 45–55.

Faruqui, A. and George, S. (2005). Quantifying customer response to dynamic pricing, *The Electricity Journal*, **18**(4): 53–63.

FERC (2007). Assessment of Demand Response and Advanced Metering. Washington, DC: FERC, September.

Frontier Economics (2007). Smart Metering: A Report Prepared for Centrica. London: Frontier Economics.

International Energy Agency (2003). The Power to Choose – Demand Response in Liberalized Electricity Markets. Paris: IEA.

Jamasb, J. and Pollitt, M. (2005). Electricity market reform in the European Union: review of progress toward liberalization and integration, *The Energy Journal*, **26**: 11–42.

Littlechild, S. (2003). Reflections on incentive regulation, *Review of Network Economics*, **2**(4): 289–315.

Lutzenhiser, L. (1993). Social and behavioral aspects of energy use, *Annual Review of Energy and the Environment*, **18**: 247–89.

Moreno, F., Garcia, M., Marin, G., Lazaro, G. and Bel, A. (2004). An integrated tool for assessing the demand profile flexibility, *IEEE Transactions on Power Systems*, **19**(1): 668–75.

Ofgem (2010a). Energy Demand Research Project: Review of progress for the period March 2009 – September 2009, London: Ofgem, Ref 37/10.

Ofgem (2010b). Demand Response: a Discussion Paper, London: Ofgem, Ref 82/10.

Richardson, I., Thomson, M. and Infield, D. (2008). A high-resolution domestic building occupancy model for energy demand simulations, *Energy and Buildings*, **40**(8): 1560–6.

Schultz, D. and Lineweber, D. (2006). Real Mass Market Customers React to Real Time-Differentiated Rates: What Choices Do They Make and Why?, 16th National Energy Services Conference. San Diego, CA.

Schultz, P.W., Gouveia, V., Cameron, L., Tankha, G., Schmuck, P. and Franek, M. (2005). Values and their relationship to environmental concern and conservation behavior, *Journal of Cross-Cultural Psychology*, **36**: 457–75.

Sibley, D. (1989). Asymmetric information, incentives and price-cap regulation, *RAND Journal of Economics*, **20**(3): 392–404.

Strbac, G. (2008). Demand side management: benefits and challenges, *Energy Policy*, **36**: 4419–26.

Torriti, J., Hassan, M. and Leach, M. (2010). Demand response experience in Europe: policies, programmes and implementation, *Energy*, **35**: 1575–83.

Vasconcelos, J. (2008). Survey of Regulatory and Technical Development Concerning Smart Metering in the European Union Electricity Market, Florence School of Regulation, RSCAS Policy Paper 2008/01, Florence: European University Institute.

Verplanken, B. and Wood, W. (2006). Interventions to break and create consumer habits, *Journal of Public Policy and Marketing*, **25**(1): 90–103.

Vogelsang, I. (2002). Incentive regulation and competition in public utility markets: a 20-year perspective, *Journal of Regulatory Economics*, **22**(1): 5–27.

Wirl, F. (1995). Impact of regulation on demand side conservation programs, *Journal of Regulatory Economics*, 7(1): 43–62.

# 4 Review of recent developments in economic modelling of energy demand

*Jevgenijs Steinbuks*

## 4.1 Introduction

In recent years, climate scientists, economists, engineers and policy makers have paid more and more attention to the possibilities that changes in energy use might introduce for environmental and climate policies. Economists often cite price-induced increases in energy efficiency as critical in addressing environmental problems, such as an increase in $CO_2$ emissions and global warming. For example, the United Nations Framework Convention on Climate Change (2007, p. 39) mitigation scenario foresees that by 2030 energy-efficiency improvements will provide the same services with 15 per cent less energy, and shift the energy supply to more climate-friendly technologies. The International Energy Agency's *World Energy Outlook* (2008, p. 49) projects that improved energy efficiency will lower fossil fuel consumption by a cumulative amount of 22 billion tonnes of oil equivalent between 2010 and 2030, yielding cumulative savings of more than $7 trillion.

Critics of proactive energy and climate policies, meanwhile, argue that reduction in energy demand from such policies will result in economic recession and affect international competitiveness of industrialized countries (Cosbey and Tarasofsky, 2007). In this context, sorting between different effects of changes in energy prices, based on sound econometric methodology, becomes especially important.

This chapter reviews major developments in economic modelling of energy demand.[1] It analyzes four channels which affect energy demand: (i) input substitution, (ii) energy efficiency, (iii) the change in the industrial structure and (iv) technological change. The main findings from a large number of economic studies are summarized, while the major

[1] There is a variety of other approaches to modelling energy use (e.g. thermodynamic, engineering–economic, integrated assessment, case studies, scenario exercises and hybrids of all these). Though these approaches are undoubtedly important for understanding energy use, they are beyond the scope of this chapter.

emphasis of this chapter is on the econometric modelling of energy demand.

This chapter is organized as follows. Section 4.2 surveys the most important developments in the inter-factor/inter-fuel substitution approach to energy demand modelling and summarizes estimated energy demand elasticities. Section 4.3 describes the relationship between energy demand and energy efficiency, based on the evidence from recent micro- and macroeconometric studies. It also discusses the significance of the 'rebound effect' in understanding energy demand. Section 4.4 discusses the effect of change in the mix of industries in the economy on energy demand and presents recent evidence from studies, which decompose changes in the aggregate energy demand into shifts in the structure of sectoral composition and adjustments in the efficiency of energy use. Section 4.5 analyzes the effects of technological change, both exogenous (e.g. resulting from autonomous scientific advance) and energy-price induced. It presents the recent findings from the research in energy and R&D economics and discusses the relationship between technological change and the asymmetric price responses in energy demand models. Conclusions are discussed in section 4.6.

## 4.2 Input substitution

The aim of the input substitution studies is to quantify how the change in *relative* energy prices affects the choice of energy in the optimal input mix to production. The input substitution studies can be divided into two streams. The first stream (inter-factor substitution) looks at the choice of *aggregate* energy input relative to the changes in prices of aggregate inputs to production. This stream is applicable to modelling industrial (e.g. manufacturing and services sectors), residential and transportation energy demand. In the industrial and commercial transportation energy demand, the econometric analysis stems from the behaviour of rational profit-maximizing (cost-minimizing) firms choosing optimal amounts of inputs to production, such as labour, capital, energy and materials. In residential energy demand, the household production model of utility-maximizing (cost-minimizing) households is analyzed.

The second stream (inter-fuel substitution) analyzes the choice of a *particular* source of energy relative to the changes in prices of energy fuels, such as electricity, coal, oil and gas. The central aim of input substitution analysis is to obtain the own-price and cross-price elasticities of energy demand, which are consistent with the economic theory. The economic literature on input substitution started from the pioneering works of Berndt and Wood (1975), Griffin and Gregory (1976) and

Pindyck (1979), and flourished in the 1980s. Because input substitution is defined as a well-known econometric problem, academic interest in it has fallen since then, but occasional studies analyzing this problem appear regularly in the economic literature. Barker *et al.* (1995), Thompson and Taylor (1995), Adeyemi and Hunt (2007) and Kilian (2008) provide excellent surveys on research in this area.

### *4.2.1 Industrial energy demand*

The economic analysis of industrial energy demand starts from the theory of a rational firm that chooses an optimal (profit-maximizing or cost-minimizing) mix of inputs to production function. Under regular assumptions on the firm's production function (see, for example, Chapter 5 in Mas-Colell *et al.*, 1995), one can derive reduced-form (or structural) equations for optimal input demand.[2] The major econometric difficulty for estimating industrial energy demand was the absence of a flexible functional form for the firm's cost function that would allow for cross-interactions between relative prices of different inputs to the production function. This difficulty was overcome with the introduction of the transcendental logarithmic (translog) cost function econometric approach by Christensen *et al.* (1971, 1973). Berndt and Wood (1975) applied the translog approach to model the US industrial energy demand in a four-factor (capital, labour, energy and materials, or KLEM) framework. The major findings were that the energy demand is inelastic, with estimated own-price elasticity close to 0.45. Energy was found to be a substitute for labour and materials inputs, and the complement to capital input to the production function.

Griffin and Gregory (1976) extended Berndt and Wood's (1975) work to a cross-country perspective and found that energy demand is more elastic, with estimated own-price elasticity close to 0.8. Griffin and Gregory (1976) also found that energy is a substitute for both labour and capital inputs. They interpret estimates based on cross-country data as the long-run elasticities, and the estimates based on the time-series data as the short-run elasticities. Consistent with the economic theory, in the long run energy is more elastic than in the short run.

[2] A number of studies (see, for example, Cebon, 1992, DiCanio, 1993, Gabel and Sinclair-Desgagné, 1998, 2001) argue that market failures resulting from organizational inefficiencies, asymmetric information and bounded rationality could prevent firms from being fully efficient, at least in the short run. Atkinson and Halvorsen (1984) demonstrate that this assumption can be relaxed, while being fully consistent with the neo-classical theory of production. The examples of energy demand studies for non-cost-minimizing firms are Atkinson and Halvorsen (1984) and Kumbhakar and Lovell (2003).

A large number of studies followed to replicate the results of Berndt and Wood (1975) and Griffin and Gregory (1976), and most of them found the short-term own-price elasticities of energy demand to be in the range of 0.2–0.5 and the long-term own-price elasticities of energy demand to be in the range of 0.5–0.9 (see Barker *et al.*, 1995 for a survey).[3]

An important limitation in early analyses of Berndt and Wood (1975) and Griffin and Gregory (1976) was the restrictive assumption that the capital stock is allowed to adjust instantaneously to energy price changes. Further analysis in input substitution literature therefore focused on relaxing this assumption and finding more plausible trajectories for the adjustment of the capital stock. Berndt *et al.* (1981) and Pindyck and Rotemberg (1983) estimated a dynamic model, in which energy and capital are highly complementary and the capital stock is subject to adjustment costs (or the capital is 'quasi-fixed'). Because of the adjustment costs, the capital stock moves slowly over time in response to changes in energy prices. Since energy and capital are highly complementary in production, energy moves slowly as well. In the long run, the capital stock adjusts to permanent differences in energy prices and so does energy use.

Atkeson and Kehoe (1999) developed a 'putty-clay' model in which a large variety of types of capital goods is combined with energy in different fixed proportions. Because the capital stock is fixed in the short run, the model delivers low own-price elasticity of energy demand. In the long run, in response to permanent differences in energy prices, agents invest in different capital goods with different fixed energy intensities. As a result, in the long run, energy use becomes responsive to differences in energy prices. Both models rely on the assumption that capital and energy inputs are complements in the short run.

More recent studies (e.g. Thompson and Taylor, 1995), however, demonstrated that capital and energy inputs are likely to be substitutes even in the short run. Steinbuks *et al.* (2009) developed and estimated the vintage capital model, which explicitly incorporates capital stock in the econometric analysis of energy demand, while allowing for capital and energy inputs to be short-run substitutes.

While the structural estimation methods described above provide sound theoretical foundations and robust interpretation of estimated elasticities, a number of studies (e.g. Fisher and Kaysen, 1962, Waverman,

[3] It is important to recognize that the estimated elasticities are highly sensitive to choice of dataset and chosen econometric methodology, therefore reported averages have high standard errors. The same observation holds for the analysis of inter-fuel substitution below.

1992) warned of errors in the measurement of capital stock, which affect consistent estimation and tractability of estimated elasticities from structural econometric analysis. With the development of advanced econometric techniques in time-series analysis, a number of studies attempted to treat capital stock as an unobserved variable. For example, Hunt and Lynk (1992) estimated an error-correction model for the UK manufacturing sector using annual data from 1952 to 1988. Hunt *et al.* (2003) and Dimitropoulos *et al.* (2005) used the structural time-series model to capture non-linear adjustments in unobserved capital stock and technological change with UK quarterly and annual data respectively. These studies found the own-price elasticities of industrial energy demand between −0.2 and −0.3, which is lower than the results from the structural econometric models. Reconciling the results from different methodologies is a difficult problem, which still needs to be addressed.

### *4.2.2 Residential energy demand*

Similarly to the previous section, the economic analysis of residential energy demand starts with the consumer's utility-maximization problem. The solution to this problem yields reduced-form energy demand schedules, which can be further econometrically estimated. The economic literature acknowledges several constraints to estimating residential energy demand. First, residential energy (electricity and gas) price schedules are non-linear, as consumers face multi-part tariffs.[4] As Reiss and White (2005, p. 855) note, 'the demand behaviour of a utility-maximizing consumer thus depends not on the average price, nor any single marginal price, but on the entire price schedule'. The existence of a price schedule with decreasing block tariffs means, in effect, that the consumer faces a downward-sloping supply schedule defined with respect to average price (Taylor, 1975, p. 79). Because the supply curve facing the consumer is no longer perfectly elastic, energy prices and quantities are econometrically endogenous, and the estimates of residential energy demand obtained by the least squares estimation are biased and inconsistent.

Halvorsen (1975) attempted to address this issue by estimating residential energy demand by two-stage least squares, using households' income and utilities' costs of labour and fuel as instrumental variables. Reiss and White (2005) pointed out that the instrumental variable approach used by Halvorsen (1975) and subsequent studies is

[4] A similar (and perhaps even more serious) problem persists in the econometric analysis of industrial energy demand. All previous studies known to the author assumed that energy supply facing industrial firms is perfectly elastic. This problem has yet to be resolved.

inappropriate because the consumption data are aggregated over time and different types of energy-using appliances, and the consumers' actual marginal prices are typically not observed. In the presence of non-linear aggregation, the endogenous marginal price sequences cannot be projected onto any instrument and the instrumental variables estimation is unfeasible. Reiss and White (2005) proposed a generalized method-of-moments estimator, which overcomes these difficulties. Using the data for a large number of Californians they found the average own-price elasticity of residential electricity demand to be −0.4. The estimated own-price elasticity of residential electricity demand was close to unity for the households with electric space heating. Reiss and White (2005) also found that the distribution of estimated own-price elasticities of residential electricity demand is negatively skewed, implying that most households will alter their electricity consumption very little in response to a price change (Reiss and White, 2005, p. 870).

Second, residential energy demand is determined by consumers' use of two fuels – electricity and natural gas. The econometric analysis of households' choice between electric and natural gas-powered appliances is complicated by a significant heterogeneity among the residential customers in terms of their socioeconomic characteristics and preferences. In the presence of such unobserved heterogeneity, households' choice between different types of appliances is econometrically endogenous (Dubin and McFadden, 1984).

A number of studies (Hausman, 1979, Dubin and McFadden, 1984, Dubin, 1985) attempted to model joint determination of appliance demand and use. However, because of data limitations, most of the studies deal with households' fuel demand *conditional* on their durable ownership. For example, Baker *et al.* (1989) estimated a translog model of households' energy fuel demand based on the data for more than 80,000 UK households between 1972 and 1983. They found that the own-price elasticities of residential electricity and natural gas demand were close to − 0.75 and − 0.3 respectively and that they varied across households with different socioeconomic characteristics. They also found that electricity and gas are the gross substitutes for electric appliances, but are gross complements for gas-powered appliances. Thus, an increase in natural gas prices will result in a greater use of electric appliances, whereas an increase in electricity prices will result in less use of gas-powered appliances. Jamasb and Meier (2010) used the data for about 5,000 UK households between 1991 and 2007 and estimated income and price elasticities of energy spending for different socioeconomic groups. They found significant differences in estimated elasticities among different income groups. In particular, the expenditures of low-income households were found to be *more* responsive to electricity price changes but *less* responsive to gas price changes than those of high-income households.

Third, in a similar way to industrial energy demand, households respond to energy price changes by adjusting their appliance stocks. Fisher and Kaysen (1962) estimated a two-stage model, in which the short-run residential electricity demand depended on electricity prices, households' income and capacity utilization of the appliance stock. In the long run, the capital stock adjusts, depending on socioeconomic characteristics, macroeconomic factors and the technological change. However, poor measurement of the appliance stock significantly affected tractability of Fisher and Kaysen's (1962) results. Because measurement of changes in appliance stocks at the household level over time remains an important limitation, a number of studies used implicit econometric techniques to overcome this problem. Silk and Joutz (1997) estimated an error-correction model for residential energy demand using US annual data from 1949 to 1993. Their estimated short-run and long-run own-price elasticities of residential electricity demand were about −0.25 and 0.5 respectively. These estimates were much lower than other studies have found.

### *4.2.3 Transportation energy demand*

The demand for energy in the transportation sector has become increasingly important to policy makers in the context of its increasing effect on climate change.[5] The economic literature on energy demand in the transportation sector is mainly focused on the demand for gasoline in non-commercial cars.[6] As with the literature on residential energy demand, the economic models of demand for gasoline are based on households' utility-maximization process given income and gasoline prices, as well as the number and types of vehicles owned, and the amount of driving for commuting, errands, vacations and personal pleasure (Schmalensee and Stoker, 1999). Early works on energy demand in the transportation sector (Houthakker *et al.*, 1974, Dahl, 1979, Wheaton, 1982), followed by a large number of further studies (see Dahl and Sterner, 1991, Espey, 1998 and Graham and Glaister, 2002 for excellent surveys) estimated a simple linear model of gasoline consumption as a function of gasoline

[5] For example, the UK domestic transport's carbon dioxide emissions increased by 9 per cent from 1990 to 2006 and now account for about 24 per cent of all emissions in the UK's national inventory (Committee on Climate Change, 2008).

[6] For a survey of energy demand in other transportation sectors (particularly in public transportation), see Goodwyn (1992).

prices, disposable income, quantity and characteristics of vehicle stocks and their lagged terms. As gasoline prices and quantities are econometrically endogenous variables, prices of other petroleum fuels (e.g. kerosene or residual fuel oil) were used as instrumental variables. These studies found price elasticities of gasoline demand varied between −0.2 and −0.3 in the short run and between −0.6 and −0.8 in the long run. The income elasticities of gasoline demand were found to be between 0.35 and 0.55 in the short run and between 1.1 and 1.3 in the long run.

While earlier studies gave fairly accurate representation of gasoline demand at the aggregate level, they failed to account for intra-household drivers of gasoline demand, including demographic, spatial and behavioural characteristics. More recent studies have attempted to address these limitations. Schmalensee and Stoker (1999) estimated a reduced-form semi-parametric model of gasoline demand based on a sample of 2,684 US households in 1991. Their most interesting finding was that the elasticity of gasoline demand with respect to the number of licensed drivers had been estimated to be around 0.6 and allowing for this effect cut the estimated income elasticity in half. This finding suggested that rapid expansion in gasoline demand was due mainly to an increased number of cars per household. Schmalensee and Stocker (1999) also found that urban households drove less than suburban households, who drove less than rural households. Gasoline demand was nearly perfectly inelastic for low-income households, possibly because there was a subsistence gasoline consumption level in the US. Yatchew and No's (2001) study of a cross-section of 6,230 Canadian households confirmed Schmalensee and Stoker's (1999) results and also found that price was essentially orthogonal to households' demographic variables. West and Williams (2005) estimated a consumer demand system, modelling jointly labour participation decisions and demand for gasoline using data for 9,706 households in California. They found that miles driven and leisure were relative complements. Based on that finding West and Williams (2005, p. 294) argued that 'the gas tax encourages labour supply by raising the cost per mile driven, producing an additional efficiency gain'. On the contrary, Corporate Average Fuel Economy (CAFE) standards reduce the cost per mile, discouraging labour supply and yielding additional efficiency loss.

Bento *et al.* (2009) estimated a comprehensive model of gasoline taxation for more than 20,000 US households that accounted for both supply- and demand-side responses to policy changes. The model linked the markets for new, used and scrapped vehicles and accounted for the imperfectly competitive nature of the automobile industry. Their estimated elasticity of gasoline demand was about −0.2. Price-induced reductions in gasoline demand came from a decline in average miles travelled. They also found that the size of the vehicle fleet was not responsive to gasoline prices (estimated elasticity about 0.02).

Notwithstanding significant improvements in gasoline demand modelling, the recent studies were based on cross-section or pooled panel data. Overcoming data limitations and estimating a gasoline demand model for a substantially long panel dataset remains an important area for further research.

### 4.2.4 *Inter-fuel substitution*

The previous two sections generally considered energy as a single homogenous input to a firm's production or household expenditure. It is important, however, to recognize that energy comprises different types of fuels facing different price schedules. The distinction becomes especially important in the context of the climate change regulations that affect the price of fossil fuels relative to other fuels. Because the fuel choice in the household production model is relatively unsophisticated and limited to two fuels (electricity and natural gas), most studies on the inter-fuel substitution focused on electricity generation and industrial energy demand. The early econometric analysis of inter-fuel substitution was similar to the econometric analysis of aggregate industrial energy demand. Atkinson and Halvorsen (1976) and Pindyck (1979) applied the translog function econometric approach to model fuel choice in the US electric power generation and international industrial energy demand respectively. Because the choice of energy fuel inputs affects the choice of aggregate energy input in industrial energy demand modelling, estimated energy demand elasticities are biased. To resolve that problem, Pindyck (1979) proposed a two-stage econometric approach. In the first stage, the choice of energy fuels is estimated, holding other factors of production constant. The estimated parameters from the first-stage regression are then used to form the instrumental variable for the aggregate price of energy, which is used in the second stage to obtain aggregate energy demand elasticities.

A large number of studies (see Barker *et al.*, 1995 and Ko and Dahl, 2001 for surveys) attempted to replicate the results of Atkinson and Halvorsen (1976) and Pindyck (1979). For the fuel use in thermal generation of electricity, the average own-price elasticity estimates were between 0.2 and 0.5 for coal, 0.7–1.4 for natural gas and 0.7–3.5 for oil. For industrial energy demand, most of these studies found the own-price elasticities to be about 0.2–0.3 for electricity, 0.8 for oil and about 1 for coal and gas.

An important question raised in the literature on the inter-fuel substitution was whether the translog approach provides the best approximation for modelling the fuel choice. Considine and Mount (1984) developed a linear logit model, which provides an alternative flexible functional form for estimating input demand equations. They argued this functional form is better suited to satisfy restrictions of the economic theory and is consistent with more realistic adjustment of the capital stock to input price changes. Serletis and Shahmoradi (2008) proposed modelling inter-fuel substitution semi-non-parametrically using two globally functional forms – the Fourier and the Asymptotically Ideal models. Jones (1995) and Urga and Walters (2003) compared the predictions of dynamic specifications of translog and linear logit models. Both studies concluded that linear logit specification yields more robust results and should therefore be preferred in the empirical analysis of inter-fuel substitution. It is still unclear how the signs and the magnitude of estimated elasticities from semi-non-parametric models correspond to those from translog and linear logit models.

Another important problem in the empirical analysis of inter-fuel substitution in industrial energy demand is the aggregation problem. Because most empirical studies rely on aggregate macroeconomic data across industries and types of energy use, the estimated elasticities are likely to be biased. Waverman (1992) pointed out that fuels used by the industrial sectors for non-energy purposes, such as coking coal, petrochemical feedstocks or lubricants, have few available substitutes and should therefore be excluded from the data. Jones (1995, p. 459) found that 'excluding fuels used for non-energy purposes yields larger estimates of the price elasticities for coal and oil and indicates generally greater potential for interfuel substitution than when using aggregate data'.

Bjørner and Jensen (2002) estimated empirical models of inter-fuel substitution between electricity, district heating and two other inputs, using a micro-panel dataset for Danish industrial companies. Their estimated cross-price elasticities of substitution for electricity were lower than in the studies based on the macroeconomic data. Bjørner and Jensen (2002) interpreted this difference as an effect of 'derived demand' (or aggregation bias). Steinbuks (2010) applied interfuel substitution models for the twelve most energy-intensive UK industrial sectors, first, using aggregate data, and then, separately for each type of energy use (heating, cooling, machine drive, and ventilation and air conditioning). Similar to the results of Bjørner and Jensen (2002), the estimated own-price and cross-price elasticities for electricity were lower for each type of energy use compared with the results based on the aggregate data.

## 4.3 Energy efficiency

The input substitution studies discussed above concentrate on the shorter-term (or operational) response to energy prices. In the medium term, firms respond to an increase in real energy prices by changing their investment decisions and improving the energy efficiency of their capital stock (achieving smaller energy-input requirements per unit of capital). For example, firms in the commercial sector may insulate their office buildings, and firms in the transport sector may adopt more fuel-efficient vehicles to achieve better mileage per gallon.

Firms' and households' investment response to energy prices is an important channel affecting energy demand in the medium and long run, and several recent empirical studies have attempted to quantify their response at the macroeconomic level. The evidence from these studies is controversial. Sue Wing (2008) estimated a structural econometric model for thirty-five US manufacturing industries and found intra-industry efficiency improvements were small relative to other effects, although they played a more important role in the post-1980 period. Metcalf (2008) adapted an index number-based empirical approach and found that 'roughly three-quarters of the improvements in U.S. energy intensity since 1970 results from efficiency improvements' (p. 1).

Steinbuks and Neuhoff (2010) estimated an econometric model, which separately accounts for operational and investment responses to energy prices, for five manufacturing industries in nineteen OECD countries. They found a large variation in real energy price-induced investment response across sectors, with estimated own-price investment elasticities of energy efficiency of capital stock varying between 0.03 and 0.9. Broadstock and Hunt (2009) estimated a structural time-series model for oil demand in the UK transportation sector for 1967–2007, separately accounting for behavioural, efficiency, price and income effects. They found that energy prices and energy-efficiency improvements had relatively small effects on gasoline demand dynamics, whereas the contribution from income and non-economic factors was relatively large. Li *et al.* (2009) estimated a partial adjustment model for vehicle efficiency of gasoline use for twenty US metropolitan statistical areas between 1999 and 2005. They found that own-price elasticity of vehicle efficiency to gasoline prices is small, varying from 0.02 in the short run to 0.2 in the long run. On the contrary, Busse *et al.* (2009) estimated a reduced-form model using transaction data from a 20 per cent sample of US new car dealers from 1999 to 2008 and found that vehicle fuel efficiency is very responsive to gasoline prices. Specifically, they found that a $1 increase in the gasoline price changes the market shares of the most and least fuel-efficient quartiles of new cars by +20 per cent and −24 per cent, respectively.

At the microeconomic level, there is still limited empirical evidence on the capital stock response to real energy prices. Newell *et al.* (1999) estimated a product-characteristics model of energy-saving consumer durables for three appliances (room air conditioners, central air conditioners and gas water heaters). They found that the energy price had little effect on the rate of overall innovation (introduction of cheaper and more energy-efficient commercial appliances), but it did affect the direction of innovation for some products. Nonetheless, a sizeable portion of capital stock efficiency improvements were independent of energy prices. While Newell *et al.*'s (1999) work is very important from a methodological perspective, its limited scope allows us to make only general conclusions about the effect of energy prices on energy efficiency. Further rigorous work based on large microeconomic data is required to shed more light on this issue.

When studying the effect of energy prices on the efficiency of capital stock in the context of energy demand modelling, it is important to consider the phenomenon known as the 'rebound effect'. This term was first applied narrowly to characterize the direct increase in demand for an energy service whose supply had increased as a result of improvements in technical efficiency in the use of energy (Khazzoom, 1980). Since then, the term 'rebound effect' has been used more broadly to capture wider economic effects.

Greening *et al.* (2000) consider four categories of market responses to changes in energy efficiency: (1) direct rebound effect, (2) secondary use effects, (3) market clearing price and quantity adjustments (especially in fuel markets), or economy-wide effects, and (4) transformational effects. The *direct rebound effect* refers to the original definition of the rebound effect described above. The *secondary use effects* take place because increased efficiency of an energy service raises households' real income and therefore affects consumption of other goods and services, including energy services.[7] If the size of direct or secondary use effects is large enough to affect the interrelationship of prices and outputs of goods and resources in different commodity markets, the entire structure of the economy can change, leading to *economy-wide effects*. Finally, changes in technology also have the potential to change consumers' preferences, alter social institutions and rearrange the organization of production. These potential consequences are known as *transformational effects*.

[7] Greening *et al.* (2001, p. 391) point out that because energy is a relatively minor share of an individual consumer's total expenditures, the secondary effects are probably insignificant.

In a comprehensive survey of the rebound effect, Sorrell (2007, p. viii) concluded that 'the available evidence for all types of rebound effect is far from comprehensive. The evidence is better for direct effects than for indirect effects, but even this focuses on a small number of consumer energy services, such as home heating and personal transportation, within developed countries'. The econometric estimates for the transportation sector show that the rebound effect varies between 2 per cent and 15 per cent in the short run and between 10 per cent and 30 per cent in the long run (see Small and Van Dender, 2007 for a survey). The size of the rebound effect in the residential sector varies between 10 per cent and 58 per cent in the short run and 1.4 per cent and 60 per cent in the long run, with a suggestion that rebound effects are larger for low-income groups (Sorrell, 2007, p. 34). The large measurement error for the estimates of the rebound effect in the residential sector is because of limited data on households' energy use for specific appliances. Davis (2008) attempted to overcome this difficulty by using the data from a quasi-randomized experiment for household clothes washing. He found that during a field trial, households increased 'cloth washing' on average by 5.6 per cent after receiving a high-efficiency washer, implying an elasticity of demand for cloth washing with respect to input (energy and water) prices of −0.06. Based on these estimates, Davis (2008, p. 531) concluded that 'for cloth washers, it appears that only a small portion of gains in energy and water efficiency are offset by increased utilization'. The empirical evidence for the size of the rebound effect in the manufacturing sector remains limited. Bentzen (2004) estimated the dynamic translog model for the US manufacturing sector and found a rebound effect of 24 per cent. Steinbuks and Neuhoff's (2010) vintage capital model simulations for the UK petrochemical sector found a long-run rebound effect of about 35 per cent. Estimating the rebound effect in the manufacturing sector based on rigorous analysis of appliance-level data remains an important area for future research.

## 4.4 Change in industrial structure

Another channel through which the demand for energy is affected in the medium run is through macroeconomic structural effects. Price-induced change in the industry structure of the economy takes place because an increase in the real price of energy services raises the price of intermediate and final goods throughout the economy, leading to a series of price and quantity adjustments, with energy-efficient goods and sectors likely to gain at the expense of energy-intensive ones (Sorrell and Dimitropoulos, 2008, p. 637). Of course, transformation of the industrial structure also takes place for reasons other than changes in relative energy prices, e.g. because of exogenous product and process innovation.

The economic literature is still inconclusive on the importance of price-induced relative to non-price-induced changes in the industrial structure. For example, Metcalf (2008) found no significant relationship between energy prices and the index of industrial structure for the US economy. On the contrary, Sue Wing (2008, p. 21) concluded that 'inter-industry structural change was the principal driver of the observed decline in aggregate energy intensity' and that 'price-induced substitution of variable inputs generated transitory energy savings'. The analysis of the relationship between two variables is further impeded because energy prices are potentially endogenous to the industrial structure – an increase (or reduction) in energy-intensive industries is likely to affect energy suppliers' pricing decisions for industrial customers.

A large number of studies (see Ang and Zhang, 2000 and Liu and Ang, 2007 for excellent surveys) attempted to separate changes in the aggregate energy intensity[8] into impact arising from product-mix (or structure) change and that arising from energy-efficiency change. The majority of the studies utilized the index number techniques to perform decomposition; a smaller number of studies used the input–output analysis. They covered a fairly wide range of countries and time periods over the past three decades. Most of these studies concluded that changes in the aggregate energy intensity for industry have been influenced more by energy-efficiency changes than by structure change. Energy-efficiency improvements were found to contribute strongly to the decline in the aggregate energy intensity for the industrialized countries between 1975 and 2005. On the contrary, the effect of the industrial structure change has been uncertain, leading to either increases or decreases in the aggregate energy intensity. These studies also found that the contributions of energy-efficiency improvements and the industrial structure changes to aggregate energy intensity were different for the industrial countries and the developing countries. The results of the Liu and Ang (2007) analysis suggest that there is greater potential for reducing growth in industrial energy demand through more efficient use of energy in the developing countries.

## 4.5 Technological change

In the long run, a significant channel affecting energy demand is technological change, both exogenous (e.g. resulting from autonomous

[8] Energy intensity here refers to the ratio of energy consumption in industry to the overall level of industrial activity.

scientific advance) and energy-price induced. In earlier studies, technological change was taken as an exogenous parameter, and in most econometric studies of energy demand it was approximated by a time trend. A number of recent studies have attempted to better quantify the effect of technological change. Popp (2002) estimated a structural model, using US patent data as an instrument for scientific knowledge, and found that both energy prices and the quantity of existing knowledge had significant positive effects on innovation in the energy sector.

Frondel and Schmidt (2006) compared energy-price elasticities of capital before and after the oil crisis of the early 1970s. The results of their counterfactual analysis indicated a substantial technological change, but its magnitude was unknown because of the change in economic circumstances. Linn (2008) used plant-level data from the Census of Manufactures to compare the energy intensity of entrants and incumbents from 1967 to 1997. He found that a 10 per cent increase in the price of energy reduced the relative energy intensity of entrants by just 1 per cent. Linn (2008) interpreted this finding as evidence that energy prices and technology adoption have a small effect on energy intensity.

An important issue related to the role of technological change in explaining energy demand is the phenomenon known as the 'asymmetric price response'. One of the early studies on this phenomenon was Mork (1989). Mork investigated the relationship between GDP and real energy prices based on the US data and found that while GDP and real energy prices are negatively correlated when real energy prices are *rising*, the correlation ceases to exist when real energy prices are *falling*. Further research by Walker and Wirl (1993, for the transportation sector), Haas and Schipper (1998, for the residential sector) and Gately and Huntington (2002, for aggregate energy demand) demonstrated that both energy and oil demand respond asymmetrically to energy price changes, with the most elastic response being to new price maxima. Put simply, energy demand was found to be more responsive to an *increase* than to a *decline* in energy prices. Griffin and Schulman (2005) provided econometric evidence that asymmetric price responses in econometric energy demand models actually reflect the effect of energy-saving technical change. Adeyemi and Hunt (2007) estimated a panel data model of OECD industrial energy demand for fifteen countries between 1962 and 2003 and found that the energy-saving technological change was a complement to rather than a substitute for the asymmetric price response. Their preferred econometric specification for OECD industrial energy demand, however, incorporated asymmetric price responses but not exogenous energy-saving technical change.

## 4.6 Conclusions

This chapter has explored major developments in energy demand modelling, focusing on four channels which affect energy demand: input substitution, energy efficiency, the change in the industrial structure and technological change.

While *input substitution* is a well-defined econometric problem, and a large number of studies have focused on estimating own-price energy demand elasticities, there are several issues the researcher should recognize. First, input substitution is a complex problem, which involves trade-offs between different inputs to production functions, which interact in a non-linear way. Measurement of such variables, especially the capital stock, is difficult, and estimates are subject to large measurement error. The econometric techniques allowing for unobserved capital stock yield significantly lower own-price elasticities of energy demand. Second, the adjustment to energy price shocks takes a different time for different inputs to the production function, and the econometric estimates are sensitive to the assumptions on how inputs to production (especially the capital stock) respond to energy prices. Third, energy prices are non-linear for residential (and possibly for industrial) consumers, which makes the energy prices and quantities econometrically endogenous. While econometric methods exist to overcome this problem, the estimation is non-trivial and this issue is frequently disregarded. Finally, most econometric estimates based on the aggregate data are highly imprecise and frequently (e.g. in the cases of inter-fuel substitution and residential demand with non-linear pricing) erroneous.

The policy makers and macroeconomists view price-induced changes in *energy efficiency* as an important source of reduction in the use of fossil fuels, but the econometric evidence on this issue is still limited. Recent studies have shown that the energy-efficiency response to energy prices varies across different industries and households. Rigorous econometric analysis at the microeconomic level is required to quantify the energy-efficiency response to energy prices. Perhaps encouraging news for policy makers is that existing empirical evidence for the transport sector shows that energy-efficiency improvements are irreversible and the rebound effect is relatively small. Still, more analysis at the microeconomic level is required to evaluate the size of the rebound effect in the manufacturing and residential sectors.

The results from a large number of studies that decompose changes in aggregate energy intensity into improvements in *energy efficiency* versus *change in the industrial structure* indicate that it is the former that matters more than the latter in industrialized countries. However, these studies also find that there is significant scope for energy-efficiency improvements in the developing countries. The empirical literature on the determinants of energy efficiency in the developing countries based on sound econometric analysis is virtually non-existent. Very few studies exist on how much of the change in the industrial structure in the developed countries is exported to the developing countries.

Finally, the econometric evidence on *innovation* and *technological change* and the demand for energy is still mixed. While some studies find that energy prices do have an effect on the introduction of new technologies, other studies suggest that energy-saving technological change is largely exogenous. The relative importance of technological change to the other factors discussed above is still unclear. There is also still a debate on whether asymmetric demand response to energy prices reflects the unobserved effects of technological change.

## References

Adeyemi, O.I. and Hunt, L.C. (2007). Modelling OECD industrial energy demand: asymmetric price responses and energy-saving technical change, *Energy Economics*, **29**: 693–709.

Ang, B.W. and Zhang, F.Q. (2000). A survey of index decomposition analysis in energy and environmental studies, *Energy*, **25**: 1149–76.

Atkeson, A. and Kehoe, P.J. (1999). Models of energy use: putty-putty versus putty-clay, *The American Economic Review*, **89**: 1028–43.

Atkinson, S.E. and Halvorsen, R. (1976). Interfuel substitution in steam electric power generation, *The Journal of Political Economy*, **84**: 959–78.

Atkinson, S.E. and Halvorsen, R. (1984). Parametric efficiency tests, economies of scale, and input demand in U.S. electric power generation, *International Economic Review*, **25**(3): 647–62.

Baker, P., Blundell, R. and Micklewright, J. (1989). Modelling household energy expenditures using micro-data. *The Economic Journal*, **99**: 720–38.

Barker, T., Ekins, P. and Johnstone, N. (1995). *Global Warming and Energy Demand*, London and New York: Routledge, Taylor & Francis Group.

Bento, A.M., Goulder, L.H., Jacobsen, M.R. and von Haefen, R.H. (2009). Distributional and efficiency impacts of increased US gasoline taxes, *The American Economic Review*, **99**(3): 667–99.

Bentzen, J. (2004). Estimating the rebound effect in US manufacturing energy consumption, *Energy Economics*, **26**: 123–34.

Berndt, E.R. and Wood, D.O. (1975). Technology, prices, and the derived demand for energy, *The Review of Economics and Statistics*, **57**: 259–68.

Berndt, E.R., Morrison, C.J. and Watkins, G.C. (1981). Dynamic models of energy demand: an assessment and comparison, in Berndt, E.R. and Field, B. (eds.), *Measuring and Modelling Natural Resource Substitution*, Cambridge MA: MIT Press, pp. 259–89.

Bjørner, T.B. and Jensen, H.H. (2002). Interfuel substitution within industrial companies: an analysis based on panel data at company level, *The Energy Journal*, **23**: 27–50.

Broadstock, D.C and Hunt, L.C (2009). Quantifying the Impact of Exogenous Non-Economic Factors on UK Transport Oil Demand. Surrey Energy Economics Centre Working Paper 123, Department of Economics, University of Surrey.

Busse, M.R., Knittel, C.R. and Zettelmeyer, F. (2009). Pain at the Pump: The Differential Effect of Gasoline Prices on New and Used Automobile Markets. Energy Institute at Haas Working Paper 201, Haas Business School, University of California, Berkeley.

Cebon, P.B. (1992). Twixt cup and lip – organisational behaviour, technical prediction and conservation practice, *Energy Policy*, **20**: 802–14.

Christensen, L.R., Jorgenson, D.W. and Lau, L.J. (1971). Conjugate duality and the transcendental logarithmic production function, *Econometrica*, **39**: 255–6.

Christensen, L.R., Jorgenson, D.W. and Lau, L.J. (1973). Transcendental logarithmic production frontiers, *The Review of Economics and Statistics*, **55**: 28–45.

Committee on Climate Change (2008). *Building a Low-carbon Economy – the UK's Contribution to Tackling Climate Change*. London: TSO.

Considine T.J. and Mount, T.D. (1984). The use of linear logit models for dynamic input demand systems, *The Review of Economics and Statistics*, **66**: 434–43.

Cosbey, A. and Tarasofsky, R. (2007). *Climate Change, Competitiveness and Trade*, London: Chatham House.

Dahl, C.A. (1979). Consumer adjustment to a gasoline tax, *The Review of Economics and Statistics*, **61**(3): 427–32.

Dahl, C.A. and Sterner, T. (1991). Analyzing gasoline demand elasticities: a survey, *Energy Economics*, **3**(13): 203–10.

Davis, L.W. (2008). Durable goods and residential demand for energy and water: evidence from a field trial, *RAND Journal of Economics*, **39**(2): 530–46.

DeCanio, S.J. (1993). Barriers within firms to energy efficient investments, *Energy Policy*, **21**: 906–14.

Dimitropoulos, J., Hunt, L.C. and Judge, G. (2005). Estimating underlying energy demand trends using UK annual data, *Applied Economics Letters*, **12**(4): 239–44.

Dubin, J. (1985). *Durable Choice and the Demand for Electricity*, Amsterdam and New York: North Holland.

Dubin, J. and McFadden, D. (1984). An econometric analysis of residential appliance holdings and consumption, *Econometrica*, **52**: 345–62.

Espey, M. (1998). Gasoline demand revisited: an international meta-analysis of elasticities, *Energy Economics*, **20**: 273–95.

Fisher, F.M. and Kaysen, C. (1962). *A Study in Econometrics: The Demand for Electricity in the United States*, Amsterdam: North Holland Publishing Co.

Frondel, M. and Schmidt, C. (2006). The empirical assessment of technology differences: comparing the comparable, *The Review of Economics and Statistics*, **88**: 186–92.

Gabel, L. and Sinclair-Desgagné, B. (1998). The firm, its routines, and the environment, in Tietenberg, T.H. and Folmer, H. (eds.), *The International Yearbook of Environmental and Resource Economics 1998/99: A Survey of Current Issues*, Cheltenham: Edward Elgar.

Gabel, L. and Sinclair-Desgagné, B. (2001). The firm, its procedures, and win–win environmental regulations, in Folmer, H. *et al.* (eds.), *Frontiers of Environmental Economics*, Cheltenham: Edward Elgar.

Gately, D. and Huntington, H.G. (2002). The asymmetric effects of changes in price and income on energy and oil demand, *The Energy Journal*, **23**: 19–55.

Goodwin, P.B. (1992). A review of new demand elasticities with special reference to short and long run effects of price changes, *Journal of Transport Economics and Policy*, **26**(2): 155–69.

Graham, D. and Glaister, S. (2002). The demand for automobile fuel: a survey of elasticities, *Journal of Transport Economics and Policy*, **36**: 1–26.

Greening, L.A., Greene, D.L. and Difiglio, C. (2000). Energy efficiency and consumption – the rebound effect – a survey, *Energy Policy*, **28**: 389–401.

Griffin, J.M. and Gregory, P.R. (1976). An intercountry translog model of energy substitution responses, *The American Economic Review*, **66**: 845–57.

Griffin, J.M. and Schulman, C.T. (2005). Price asymmetry: a proxy for energy saving technical change? *The Energy Journal*, **26**: 1–21.

Haas, R. and Schipper, L. (1998). Residential energy demand in OECD countries and the role of irreversible efficiency improvements, *Energy Economics*, **20**: 421–42.

Halvorsen, R. (1975). Residential demand for electric energy, *The Review of Economics and Statistics*, **57**(1): 12–18.

Hausman, J.A. (1979). Individual discount rates and the purchase of and utilization of energy-using durables, *The Bell Journal of Economics*, **10**: 33–54.

Houthakker, H.S., Verleger, P.K. and Sheehan, D.P. (1974). Dynamic demand analysis for gasoline and residential electricity, *American Journal of Agricultural Economics*, **56**(2): 412–18.

Hunt, L.C., Judge, G. and Ninomiya, Y. (2003). Underlying trends and seasonality in UK energy demands: a sectorial analysis, *Energy Economics*, **25**(1): 93–118.

Hunt, L.C. and Lynk, E.L. (1992). Industrial energy demand in the UK: a cointegration approach, in Hawdon, D. (ed.), *Energy Demand: Evidence and Expectations*, London: Academic Press, pp. 143–62.

International Energy Agency (2008). *World Energy Outlook*, Paris: OECD/ IEA.

Jamasb, T. and Meier, H. (2010). Household Energy Expenditures and Income Groups: Evidence from Great Britain. EPRG Working Paper 1003, Faculty of Economics, University of Cambridge.

Jones, C.T. (1995). A dynamic analysis of interfuel substitution in U.S. industrial energy demand, *Journal of Business & Economic Statistics*, **13**: 459–65.

Khazzoom, J.D. (1980). Economic implications of mandated efficiency in standards for household appliances, *The Energy Journal*, **1**: 21–40.

Kilian, L. (2008). The economic effects of energy price shocks, *Journal of Economic Literature*, **46**(4): 871–909.

Ko, J. and Dahl, C.A. (2001). Interfuel substitution in US electricity generation, *Applied Economics*, **33**: 1833–43.

Kumbhakar, S.C. and Lovell, C.A.K. (2003). *Stochastic Frontier Analysis*, Cambridge: Cambridge University Press.

Li, S., Timmins, C. and von Haefen, R.H. (2009). How do gasoline prices affect fleet fuel economy? *American Economic Journal: Economic Policy*, **1**(2): 113–37.

Linn, J. (2008). Energy prices and the adoption of energy-saving technology, *The Economic Journal*, **118**: 1986–2012.

Liu, N. and Ang, B.W. (2007), Factors shaping aggregate energy intensity trend for industry: energy intensity versus product mix, *Energy Economics*, **29**: 609–35.

Mas-Colell, A., Whinston, M. D. and Green, J. R. (1995). *Microeconomic Theory*, New York: Oxford University Press.

Metcalf, G.E. (2008). An empirical analysis of energy intensity and its determinants at state level, *The Energy Journal*, **29**: 1–26.

Mork, K.A. (1989). Oil and the macroeconomy when prices go up and down: an extension of Hamilton's results, *Journal of Political Economy*, **97**(3): 740–4.

Newell, R.G., Jaffe, A.B. and Stavins, R.N. (1999). The induced innovation hypothesis and energy-saving technological change, *The Quarterly Journal of Economics*, **114**: 941–75.

Pindyck, R.S. (1979). Interfuel substitution and the industrial demand for energy: an international comparison, *The Review of Economics and Statistics*, **61**: 169–79.

Pindyck, R.S. and Rotemberg, J.J. (1983). Dynamic factor demands and the effects of energy price shocks, *The American Economic Review*, **73**: 1066–79.

Popp, D. (2002). Induced innovation and energy prices, *The American Economic Review*, **92**: 160–80.

Reiss, P.C. and White, M.W. (2005). Household electricity demand, revisited, *The Review of Economic Studies*, **72**(3): 853–83.

Schmalensee, R. and Stoker, T.M. (1999). Household gasoline demand in the United States, *Econometrica*, **67**(3): 645–62.

Serletis A. and Shahmoradi, A. (2008). Semi-nonparametric estimates of interfuel substitution in U.S. energy demand, *Energy Economics*, **30**: 2123–33.

Silk, J.I. and Joutz, F.L. (1997). Short and long-run elasticities in US residential electricity demand: a co-integration approach, *Energy Economics*, **19**: 493–513.

Small, K.A. and Van Dender, K. (2007). Fuel efficiency and motor vehicle travel: the declining rebound effect, *The Energy Journal*, **28**: 25–51.

Sorrell, S. (2007). The Rebound Effect: an Assessment of the Evidence for Economy-wide Energy Savings from Improved Energy Efficiency, Working Paper, UK Energy Research Centre.

Sorrell, S. and Dimitropoulos, J. (2008). The rebound effect: microeconomic definitions, limitations and extensions, *Ecological Economics*, **65**: 636–49.

Steinbuks, J. (2010). Interfuel Substitution and Energy Use in UK Manufacturing Sector, Cambridge Working Paper in Economics 1032, Faculty of Economics, University of Cambridge.

Steinbuks, J., Meshreky, A. and Neuhoff, K. (2009). The Effect of Energy Prices on Operation and Investment in OECD Countries: Evidence from the Vintage Capital Model, Cambridge Working Paper in Economics 0933, Faculty of Economics, University of Cambridge.

Steinbuks, J. and Neuhoff, K. (2010). Operational and Investment Response to Energy Prices in OECD Manufacturing. Cambridge Working Paper in Economics 1015, Faculty of Economics, University of Cambridge.

Sue Wing, I. (2008). Explaining the declining energy intensity of the US economy, *Resource and Energy Economics*, **30**: 21–49.

Taylor, L.D. (1975). The demand for electricity: a survey, *The Bell Journal of Economics*, **6**(1): 74–110.

Thompson, P. and Taylor, T.G. (1995). The capital-energy substitutability debate: a new look, *The Review of Economics and Statistics*, **77**: 565–9.

United Nations Framework Convention on Climate Change (2007). *Investment and Financial Flows to Address Climate Change*. Bonn: UNFCCC.

Urga, G. and Walters, C. (2003). Dynamic translog and linear logit models: a factor demand analysis of interfuel substitution in US industrial energy demand, *Energy Economics*, **25**: 1–21.

Walker, I.O. and Wirl, F. (1993). Irreversible price-induced efficiency improvements, *The Energy Journal*, **14**: 183–205.

Waverman, L. (1992). Econometric modelling of energy demand: when are substitutes good substitutes? in Hawdon, D. (ed.), *Energy Demand: Evidence and Expectations*, London: Academic Press.

West, S.E. and Williams II, R.C. (2005). The Cost of Reducing Gasoline Consumption. *The American Economic Review, Papers and Proceedings of the One Hundred Seventeenth Annual Meeting of the American Economic Association*, **95**(2): 294–9.

Wheaton, W.C. (1982). The long-run structure of transportation and gasoline demand, *The Bell Journal of Economics*, **13**(2): 439–54.

Yatchew, A. and No, J.A. (2001). Household gasoline demand in Canada, *Econometrica*, **69**(6): 1697–709.

*Part II*

# Technology

# 5 Demand-side management and control in buildings

*Jun Hong, Cameron M. Johnstone, Jae Min Kim and Paul Tuohy*

## 5.1 Introduction

In order to decarbonize the energy-supply system, policies have been introduced to stimulate an increase in the amount of energy we use from clean and renewable energy systems. With the progressive increase in the quantities of clean and renewable energy-supply systems being commissioned, there comes a point where due to the intermittency and unpredictability of renewables it is difficult to maintain a demand–supply balance. In such circumstances, the traditional control theories of energy supply being demand following cannot be enacted. In order to maintain the integrity of the demand–supply match, the onus of control needs to shift from the supply side to the demand side. Ideally, we would like to have flexibility and infinite control over each load so that control can be enacted which enables the energy demand to become supply following. The control being enacted on each load type would be such that the functionality or comfort levels each individual load is satisfying would not be compromised. Thus, this level of discrete control would result in the building occupant/user being unaware of control measures being enacted. In practice, however, this may not be feasible. Therefore the purpose of this chapter is to explore how we may achieve increased levels of control over individual loads, the impact this will have on introducing flexibility into the demand side, and how this could be implemented at a practical level.

## 5.2 Drivers for DSM and control within buildings

A number of drivers exist to influence and accelerate the penetration of demand-side management (DSM) within the built environment, specifically within the domestic sector. These drivers include evolving energy policy, improved energy efficiency through the use of more efficient appliances, the increased uptake and technological advancements in the microgeneration system, and the development and application of information and communication technologies to control and optimize the energy supply–demand match, while being sympathetic to the building environmental conditions being attained.

### *5.2.1 Energy policy*

Progressive updates in legislation and building regulations, such as the European Union Directive on the Energy Performance of Buildings (EPBD), the 2003 Department of Trade and Industry (DTI) UK Energy White Paper, and the 2007 Scottish Building Standards Agency (SBSA) Scottish Building Regulations, etc., have been brought forward to improve the energy performance of buildings. These improvements to the governing regulations have resulted in the building consenting process being satisfactorily achieved through the demonstration of a reduction in building energy demands and/or the inclusion of small-scale renewable-based microgeneration systems. In order to fully deliver these policies, only two possible approaches can be adopted: either improving the efficiency of energy utilization within the demand side, or through adopting 'green' energy-supply technologies locally on the supply side. Due to the typically stochastic variations in energy delivered from these supply technologies, such as intermittency of renewables and a demand-profile sensitive for low-carbon technologies, optimized control over building plant and loads is essential if we are to reduce and reshape the demand profile. In the longer term, building controls enabling local buildings with optimized energy performance to trade energy supply and demands between them will further facilitate the demand–supply match. In doing so, better performance of these new energy systems should be achievable, improving the demand–supply match and contributing to a reduction in energy demands.

The EPBD (EU, 2002) instructed that by the end of 2005 all EU member states should have brought into force national laws, regulations and administrative provisions for setting minimum requirements for the energy performance certification of buildings. Such certification applies to all new-build and existing buildings subject to major renovation.

Simultaneously, the UK Energy White Paper (DTI, 2003b) begins to address this issue in the context of the important challenge of climate change we are facing and the linkage with the ever-increasing levels of anthropogenic greenhouse gas emissions ($CO_2$). These have been adopted to inform UK energy policy development, specifically focusing on a number of factors, including widespread promotion and uptake of low-carbon technologies (e.g. CHP or micro-CHP systems), the adoption of new renewable and low-carbon energy technologies, and substantive improvements in the energy efficiency of appliances being used and the improvement in the energy performance of the building fabric. These measures are not only aimed at reducing greenhouse gas emissions to target levels, to mitigate the potential damages associated with 'global warming', but also provide a measure of energy security (Hawkes and Leach, 2005, 2007).

The SBSA, an executive agency of the Scottish government, is responsible for the development and implementation of new standards and regulations for buildings in Scotland. In recent documentation, it requires that at least 10 per cent of the annual heating demands for new buildings comes from onsite renewable energy technologies, such as solar, wind or biomass energy (SBSA, 2007).

### *5.2.2 Unused energy*

Research has shown that a significant amount of energy is wasted in delivering energy services that are not actually used or required by users/occupiers. These include the heating/cooling of unoccupied spaces and rooms, localized overheating or overcooling to make up for temperature variations over larger floor areas, power consumed as a result of appliances in standby or inoperative mode, and consumers' use of needlessly energy-intensive appliances. If effective measures can be implemented which address these, it may be possible to achieve considerable energy savings. It is accepted that the number and type of appliances in use today are continually increasing. The ability to manage individual appliances at the building level so they can operate both efficiently and effectively (operative when required) is a research challenge needing to be addressed. If this type of operation can be achieved, there is great potential for savings in energy utilization within the urban environment and ultimately for reducing household expenditure on energy use and potentially mitigating socioeconomic challenges such as fuel poverty. The ability to manage these types of loads can substantively reshape the building load profile to one more favourable to utility or energy-supply companies, to improve the performance of existing power-generating plants. When added to the increasing deployment of green/low-carbon energy technologies, the ability to maximize the utilization of energy produced by these technologies and to synchronize this with the demand control enacted on different appliances makes the challenge of matching demand and supply even greater.

### *5.2.3 Penetration of micro-energy generation systems*

With the growth of small-scale distributed generation at the domestic level, the supply profile becomes more volatile due to the loss of load diversity and the reduction of scale. This is likely to be further exacerbated as a result of recent UK programmes actively supporting enhanced deployment of distributed generation (DG) of various technologies, particularly renewable (RE) and low-carbon (LC) energy systems. RE systems being promoted include photovoltaic (PV), wind turbine (WT) and solar collectors, while LC systems include technologies such as heat pumps (HP) and combined heat and power (CHP). These are all suitably applicable to single-building deployment. Due to the characteristics of RE and LC technologies, the challenge is to satisfy the demand while also maximizing the use of these technologies, increasing their overall efficiency and capacity-utilization factors. Such RE systems are typically dependent on factors such as weather, time and location and are therefore stochastic in their energy supply. However, without proper control, LC systems typically operate less efficiently and as a result emit larger quantities of GHG for the same level of energy supply from a conventional supply network. Without effective control being enacted, the increased emissions within the occupied 'breathable zone' will have a negative impact on local air quality. The research challenge is therefore to develop demand and supply matching and control algorithms, which implement control actions upon each individual load making up the building's demand profile, and to restructure this in order that it is more easily satisfied from RE and/or LC energy supply systems.

### *5.2.4 ICT advancement*

Recent advancements in ICT provide opportunities to facilitate greater roll-out of a range of DSM options. The wider uptake of broadband now provides the greatest coverage of a low-cost, continuous two-way communication system, with government policy aspiring to increase this to more than 90 per cent of the population. Such a widely deployed communication medium provides the ability to acquire information on load status and application and a mechanism to apply control over individual loads.

These advancements make it feasible to use the Internet as the communications portal to build a web-enabled generic energy-monitoring and control platform which merges all aspects, i.e. software, hardware and different communication protocols without time constraints. The wider international deployment of Internet infrastructure is growing rapidly, thereby making it an ideal low-cost platform to reach a global market. This allows Internet-enabled DSM to become an alternative low-cost mass communication and control medium. As such, authorized Internet users located anywhere in the world can acquire requested demand data for specific loads in specific buildings, monitor the whole building system and even activate control over individual devices. Through the use of wired and wireless sensors/actuators, we are able to monitor home conditions and control appliances within a '3A' approach (Any time, Any place within the same building and at Any distributed location). This facilitates the delivery of a low-cost intelligent building with mass international market appeal. This capability provides the opportunity to deliver 'e-services' via the Internet that include indoor climate control, social care for vulnerable people, DSM for saving energy, etc. (Obaidat and Marchese, 2006). In addition, wireless connection of sensors/actuators can widen the application of device monitoring and control because this mitigates the levels of intrusion and disturbance created by a complex wired network and allows flexibility in the deployment and operation within a simple and convenient wireless monitoring and control infrastructure.

## 5.3 DSM

### *5.3.1 Utility level*

Traditionally, most DSM programmes are driven by utilities. Utility-based DSM is defined as 'the planning, implementation, and monitoring of activities designed to influence and encourage customers to modify their level and pattern of electricity usage in such a way that the load profile can be modified by the utility company in order that it can produce power in an optimal way, i.e. changes in the time pattern and magnitude of a utility's load' (Gellings and Chamberlin, 1993; Gellings, 1985). When implementing DSM programmes, aggregated data are normally used to inform the DSM actions to be implemented, with these being implemented on a regional basis as opposed to being building specific. The popular DSM measures employed are peak clipping, valley filling and load shifting, strategic conservation, strategic load growth and flexible load shape. It is widely believed that DSM can reduce electricity consumption and defer the construction of new power plants and transmission lines. DSM can also bring economic benefits in the form of reduced capital expenditure, reduced operating costs, fuel savings, improved system efficiencies and reduced losses. From the customer perspective, DSM can reduce energy bills and improve the service and comfort levels achieved.

However, most of the conventional DSM programmes are carried out through a 'top-down approach' at the macro level. Either the condition of the electrical network, e.g. frequency, or a price signal within the electricity market is the main indicator to trigger such load-management programmes. It is difficult to use this approach to identify the actual DSM resources that would impact less on users. Also, conventional DSM programmes are effective in reshaping the load curve, which limits the energy usage in peak times and encourages its use during off-peak periods. Instead of reducing energy demand, these strategies actually encourage the increased use of energy during the period when the electricity price is low, when sometimes the usage may not be necessary. In such instances, this makes little or no contribution to the reduction of existing high levels of GHG emissions, and potentially exacerbates the problem. It tends to disturb the natural diversity of loads, resulting in the creation of a second peak (i.e. a payback effect). In addition, the 'comfort' and 'functionality' aspects these loads provide to customers are not the first/highest order of priority in deciding when load management is activated. As previous experiences with off-peak heating systems show, many users suffer from uncomfortable environmental conditions, which is one of the main reasons why user participation rates in some DSM programmes remain quite low. Furthermore, the feedback from some demand response programmes is considered, but usually in a qualitative way. There is always a delay period to consider the customers' satisfaction level compared with the time when the actual control actions were enacted. It would be nice if there were some new ways to quantify the control impact on the user/occupant and take control actions on or towards a real-time basis, in order to minimize the inconvenience to users.

### *5.3.2 Household level*

Due to increasing energy use within buildings, several actions, including the adoption of measures to improve building envelope performance and the implementation of energy labelling, have already been implemented to suppress this. Demand-reduction approaches for the building envelope, such as cavity wall insulation, double glazing and loft insulation, can be regarded as 'hard' technical demand measures with the purpose of reducing the magnitude of energy demand during the operational period. Although these 'hard' reduction measures have already played an important role in suppressing the rate of demand increase, as a result of the law of diminishing returns, there are limitations in the ability of continued deployment to maintain meaningful levels of demand reduction, as measures reach saturation point.

Energy labelling has been introduced to force suppliers to provide more information on the electricity consumption of their devices in practice. This in turn is aimed at improving the energy efficiency of appliances and increasing user awareness of appliance-based energy consumption so that consumers can also select appliances based on how efficient they are. However, early assessment of the effectiveness of this approach suggests customers are not always willing to become actively engaged in such behaviour. Two possible reasons, the replacement cost associated with new appliances and the lack of information to understand the energy labels, could be responsible for this.

Another more recent appliance-level DSM measure is network-friendly appliances. By equipping the appliance with an additional controller, a refrigerator for example, is capable of sensing the frequency of the supply network. This simultaneously adjusts its thermostat set-point based on the obtained frequency data in order to switch the appliance either off or on at critical times. The purpose is to ease network pressure by introducing load shedding or load growth control within buildings.

Some 'soft' DSM measures which focus on the management of various end-use devices have been largely neglected. Vast opportunities exist to make better use of, and lower, the energy consumption through better appliance management and control. Demand flexibility exists within the consumption process for every end-use device. Normally end-use devices 'use' electricity to provide a 'service' to the user (Schweppe *et al.*, 1989). Different appliances have different levels of flexibility within their own energy-consumption processes. For example, the flexibility of electrical-based heating and cooling appliances (e.g. refrigerator, air conditioner and electric water heater) is high, as temporary power disconnection does not critically impact on the service/function they are expected to deliver. For some appliances, such as washing machines and dishwashers, energy usage and service may both be rescheduled to another period. This could be acceptable to the customer as long as the quality of service delivered meets with the expectations of the user/occupant. For other appliances, such as those used in lighting and cooking, it may be possible to reduce the quality or level of services delivered, but neither service nor energy usage can be rescheduled without inconvenience to the consumer. For devices such as those used in entertainment (TVs, VCRs, etc.), the flexibility is low since switching off will have an unacceptable impact on users. Empirical evidence suggests that introducing demand flexibility could result in increasing users' tolerance levels when power supplied to a device has to be disconnected for some reason.

However, little research has been carried out on customers' tolerance levels when different types of appliances are controlled. A good DSM system undertakes switching actions upon appliances without notifying the user (Stadler and Bukvic-Schafer, 2003).

## 5.4 Micro-level demand-side management and control (DSM+c)

Micro-level DSM and control means that demand-side management and control can be carried out upon various appliances within single households or individual buildings. Normally, the electricity consumption data typically monitored by utilities are the aggregated consumption of multiple households without knowledge of the activities being enacted within individual households. The fluctuations in electricity consumption concerned with individual households remain largely unrevealed. Users know little about their own energy usage. To redress this requires some form of automated control to be introduced on most/all appliances. This level of control requires the development of new algorithms which, when implemented, apply demand-side measures upon these individual appliances. This will also enable decision makers to analyze various control strategies to identify the extent of contributions demand-side management measures make to ease the load on the supply side, particularly when onsite microgeneration is considered. This is not only suitable for load management at an individual dwelling level but can also be used in large-scale applications. The objectives at a system level can be achieved through a 'bottom-up' approach to DSM.

The system objectives to be achieved through these 'bottom-up' DSM+c algorithms are summarized as follows:

- to maximize the efficiency of energy use, so that energy wastage is reduced;
- to facilitate effective power utilization from building-integrated renewables;
- to create optimal demand profiles for the operation of RE and LC energy systems.

DSM+c algorithms utilize the flexibilities of individual loads to modify their operation processes based on the supply availability at every time step without significantly compromising users' convenience/functionality. Two parameters, 'time constant' and 'control over capacity', are introduced to identify the level of load flexibility that can be achieved. Time constants refer to the corresponding duration of time control that can be is being enacted on a load. This normally depends on the characteristics of the individual load. The longer the time constant associated with a load, the more flexible the load is. The 'control over capacity' parameter defines the potential percentage of load which can be controlled when the device delivers the service to users. Similarly, the higher the value of control over capacity, the more flexible the load is.

These measures could not only lead to carbon dioxide savings and help to facilitate the connection of greater amounts of intermittent renewable energy generation, such as solar photovoltaic, wind power, etc., they could also improve the performance of building-integrated low carbon-emission systems by restructuring the demand profile to one with a more favourable match to the output from the low-carbon energy supply (LCS).

### *5.4.1 Analysis of DSM potential for household appliances*

Based on a 'flexibility' index, the loads of household appliances can be classified into four categories: high flexibility, medium flexibility, low flexibility and no control at all.

The loads with high flexibility are those thermal loads with intrinsic storage capability, such as space cooling/heating systems, water heating and air conditioning, etc., where loads can be controlled without the end-user being aware or without impacting on load functionality. Also included in this category are laptops, mobile phones and other computer devices equipped with an integrated electrical battery. When control on the demand side is required as a result of a mismatch with supply, this type of load is the first choice to be selected for control, and it can be regarded as the load with the least impact upon users' convenience and functionality.

Medium flexibility loads are those such as washing machines, dishwashers and tumble dryers, cooking appliances and lighting. The common features of these types of loads are the shorter time constants but changeable value of control over capacity during the operational process. If we take a washing machine, for example, it can be divided into a heating process, a washing process and a spin-dry process. For the heating process, it can be controlled up to its maximum. However, for the spin-dry process it should not be interrupted.

For cooking appliances, although they work for a limited period, the control availability is low, as interruption to the cooking process will (i) increase the cooking time and (ii) affect the food-cooking process and hence the quality of the food. Loads with low flexibility are those which have a small time constant and little tolerance to control over capacity, such as vacuum cleaners, hairdryers and microwave ovens. If and when control is enacted on such appliances, the results will quickly impact upon user convenience and functionality.

For appliances such as entertainment equipment, there is little or no flexibility of control. The load pattern is rigid and it is hard to impose any changes upon it since the impact of control will quickly compromise

Table 5.1 *Various control priorities, methods and durations for residential appliances*

| | Control method | | | |
|---|---|---|---|---|
| Load | On/Off | Partial | Time | Priority |
| Hot water | √ | √ | Hour/Min | High |
| Washing machine | √ | √ | Hour/Min | High |
| Tumble dryer | √ | √ | Hour/Min | High |
| Dishwasher | √ | √ | Hour/Min | High |
| Fridge/Freezer | √ | | Min | High |
| Towel rails | √ | √ | Min | High |
| Elec. apps (with chargers) | √ | √ | Min | High |
| Lighting | √ | √ | Min/Sec | High |
| Elec. apps (heating) | √ | √ | Sec | High |
| Electric oven/hob | √ | √ | Min | Medium |
| Slow cookers | √ | √ | Min | Medium |
| Elec. heating | √ | √ | Min | Medium |
| Air conditioning | √ | √ | Min | Medium |
| Elec. blanket | √ | √ | Min | Medium |
| Microwaves | √ | | Sec | Medium |
| Extractor fans | | √ | Sec | Low |
| Hairdryers | | √ | Sec | Low |
| Elec. apps (instantaneous) | √ | | | No control |
| Entertainment | √ | | | No control |

the service being delivered and impact greatly on user inconvenience and loss of functionality. This type of load should be a priority one and supplied at the first instance when the service it provides is required. The flexibility of this type of load is regarded as having no control at all. The corresponding detailed data are listed in the Table 5.1.

### *5.4.2 DSM techniques*

Based on the results of a comparison between demand and supply, the appropriate DSM measures are applied to individual loads to flex the total demand and restructure the profile to maximize the DSM potentials for each load to match the available supply. Depending on the level of impact upon user convenience, the DSM methods can be divided into energy efficiency, load shifting and demand-side control (DSC) and from low impact to high impact.

These measures are classified into two fields: (i) energy management and (ii) load management. Energy management refers to managing the demand over a period of time, while load management is a measure to apply switching strategies to individual loads at an instantaneous point in time.

### *Energy efficiency*

Energy efficiency can reduce the magnitude of the demand profile by a certain percentage and results in a reduction in energy consumption over both peak and off-peak periods. This potential is certain to increase in line with the penetration rates of newer, more efficient appliances over the coming years. To assist users in choosing appliances with higher energy efficiency ratings, energy labelling has been introduced which retailers have to display at the point of sale. These measures are suitable for almost all appliances while being informative and having the least impact upon users.

Energy efficiency is a DSM measure which combines specific control approaches with the replacement of existing low-energy efficiency-demand devices within new high-efficiency ones. This could result in levelling down the magnitude of the total demand profile. It maintains the same level of energy service while utilizing less energy and has almost zero impact on users' convenience.

### *Load shifting*

Load-shifting is not a new concept but a novel attempt to apply upon demands to achieve better match with the time-varying, stochastic, supply from RE and LC energy systems. Traditionally, load shifting is a popular classic DSM measure for changing the use patterns of an appliance and shifting the load from an on-peak period to an off-peak period (Gellings and Chamberlin, 1993). In terms of the context of this research (involving RE technologies), the supply from RE energy systems depends on the time and location, and the performance is also vital to the operation of LC energy systems. Shifting the existing loads to the period with sufficient supply is very important because changing the pattern of use might affect users' daily behaviour. This would not affect the whole capacity of the power and would maintain the level of energy consumed. However, this could bring some inconvenience to users, as normal pattern of energy use is changed. Popular applications include water heating, space heating, clothes washing and drying, and customer load shifting. The idea behind load shifting is to identify a time period in which the shared area between the demand and the supply is at its maximum and then to allocate the selected shifting demand to that period:

$$\max Shared = \underbrace{\int^{T} DS_k(t)dt}_{k=1,\dots,N} \tag{5.1}$$

$$DS_k(t) = \begin{cases} Demand_k[t], \text{ if } Demand_k[t] < Supply[t]; \\ Supply[t], \text{ if } Demand_k[t] \geq Supply[t]. \end{cases} \tag{5.2}$$

where: $T$ = simulation period; $N$ = total number of shifting steps; $k$ = the $k$th shifting step; $Demand_k[t]$ = the total demand at the $t^{\text{th}}$ time after the $k$th shifting step; $Supply[t]$ = the total available supply at the $t^{\text{th}}$ time; $DS_k(t)$ = the lower value of total demand and supply at the $t^{\text{th}}$ time after the demand has been shifted by the $k$th step; *Shared* = the shared area between the total demand and total supply profile.

There are several important parameters relevant to load shifting algorithms, as follows.

*Shiftable or non-shiftable*

This depends on the properties of the demand. Some loads with fixed time periods of operational cycles which are not time dependent, such as washing machines, microwaves and dishwashers, can be considered as shiftable (Newborough and Augood, 1999), whereas other loads, for instance lighting, cannot be shifted as this will have a significant impact on the service they provide.

*Load shifting flexibility (whole or partial)*

Another parameter to be defined is the flexibility of the demand, i.e. the ability of the demand to be shifted in time without impacting on the service it provides. The demand profile for a certain load represents the energy use pattern during its operating period. Here the question is whether the total demand or only part of it can be shifted during the control period. The answer significantly affects the load-shifting strategy. There are options to define part of the demand to be shifted within the activation time of the profile.

*Shifting increment*

This parameter defines the period of time the specified load can be shifted, which will affect the results of the match between the total demand and supply curve. The optimal match for a certain combination of demands and supplies can be improved if the loads are

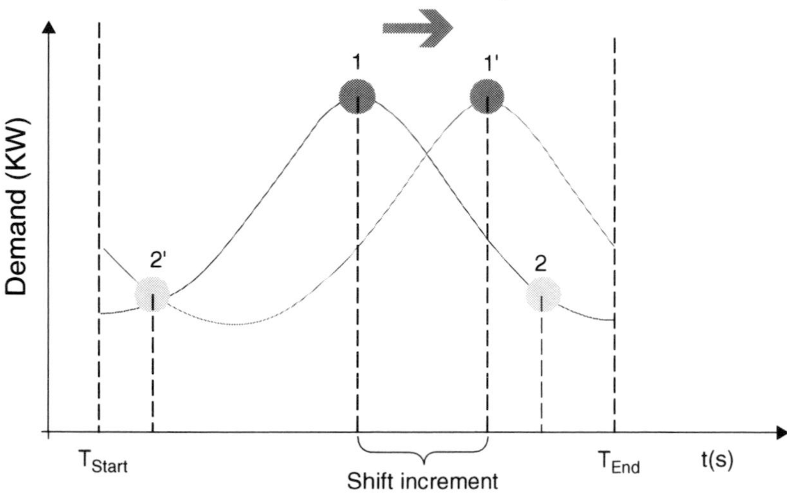


Figure 5.1 Load shift module identifying whole load shift.

shifted with a smaller increment. It is more accurate to shift the loads by less time. However, this means it would take longer to obtain the desired result.

*Shifting boundary and shifting direction*

These two parameters are designed for a situation when the load is not permitted to shift freely within the specified period, and may be shifted only within a certain period of time or shifted in a specific direction (forwards or backwards). In an extreme case, the load may be shifted only in a certain direction and within a certain period. Therefore, the boundary and direction parameters are provided for users to define the load-shifting strategy.

After having defined the above load-shifting parameters, the load-shifting algorithm can run to identify the optimal place for achieving the best match with the given supply profile. Take the whole load-shift module, for example, as demonstrated in Figure 5.1, which shows the mechanism of shifting the whole load. Whole load shifting means that it moves the total profile according to the shift increment, direction and boundary specified. There are two lines in the graph, the leftmost representing the demand profiles before load shifting and the rightmost showing the demand after load shifting. The demand profile is made up of dispersed loads characterized as data points. Therefore the load shifting for the profile requires offsetting the data points. There are usually

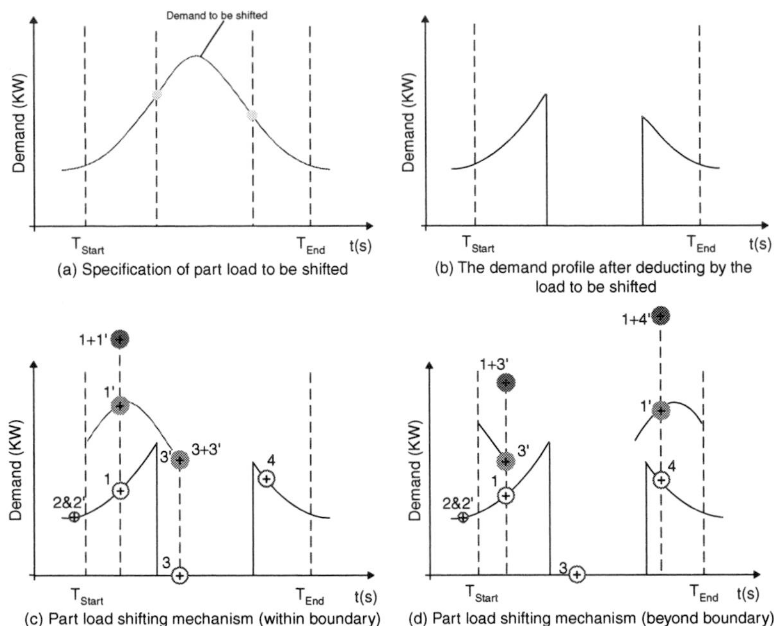


Figure 5.2 Load shift module identifying part load shift.

two situations for the whole load shifting. One is where the data points after being shifted are still within the shifting boundary. This replaces the data point one shift increment ahead each time (such as points 1 and $1'$ in the graph). The other situation is where the data points after being shifted will be outside the shifting boundary (such as point 2). In this case, the data points outside the boundary will subsequently replace the data points on the other side of the boundary (such as point $2'$). At each shifting increment, the shared area of the shifted demand with the given supply is calculated. The data are stored and compared with the results of other shifting increment options. The largest one would be the optimal one for the whole load shifting module. A similar principle can be applied to the part-load shifting algorithm. The difference is that more constraints are applied to the demand. The procedure is shown in Figure 5.2.

*Demand-side control*

DSC is the main DSM method used in a load-management strategy. It manipulates the energy-demand profile of appliances through different combinations of switching strategies, either through on/off or proportional control of individual loads. In general, direct load control (DLC) (Molina *et al.*, 2003) is regarded as the forerunner of DSC. It is used to reduce the demand during the peak period based on the conditions of the electricity grid and the electricity price signal. In terms of the context of this research (involving RE and LC supplies), the capability and flexibility of controlling the loads are vital when there is not enough supply from renewable energy or other low-carbon energy supply sources during a certain period. Popular actions implemented on the demand side to apply DSC methods include water heating, space heating/cooling and refrigeration systems. The idea behind DSC is to find the best switching strategies for the available loads, which will have minimum impact on users' convenience, in order to achieve the minimum difference between demand and supply. This can be described as in Equation 5.3.

$$min\ Diff = \left| \underbrace{\left( Supply[i] - \sum_{j=1}^{n} (Demand[j][i] * \alpha[j][k]) \right)}_{k=1,\ldots,Kctrl} \right| \tag{5.3}$$

subject to:

$$E(n) = f(Demand(n), t)$$

$$E[n][i] \in \left[ E_{low}[n], E_{high}[n] \right], \quad n = 1, \ldots, N$$

where: $i$ = the certain time step; $j$ = the certain demand; $k$ = the control step on a certain demand; $N$ = the total number of environmental variables; $t$ = time; $Diff$ = the difference between demand and supply; $Demand[j][i]$ = the required power for the $j^{th}$ demand at the time step $i$, W; $Supply[i]$ = the available supply at the time step $i$, W; $Kctrl$ = total control steps for demands with similar priority; $\alpha[j][k]$ = control factor applied over the $j^{th}$ demand at the $k^{th}$ control step; $E[n][i]$ = the $n^{th}$ environmental variables ($E(n)$) at time step $i$; $E_{low}[n]$ and $E_{high}[n]$ = the set points for the $n^{th}$ environmental variables.

The approach can improve the match between energy demand and supply from intermittent sources, and reshape the demand profile towards one more favourable for the operation of low carbon energy-supply systems. The summary flow chart is shown in Figure 5.3. In the first instance, all demands are prioritized from high control availability, medium control availability to low control availability and even no control

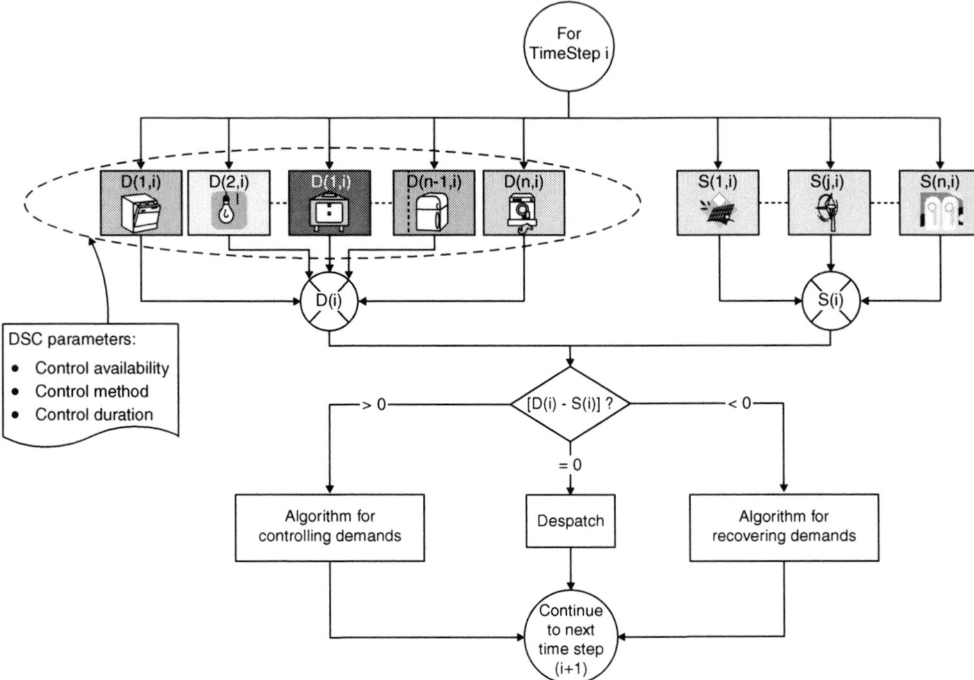


Figure 5.3 Demand–supply appraisal flow chart.

at all. The control methods which can be implemented, either on/off or proportional, will be specified for each individual load. This could result in significant impact upon both the users and the demand environment. Therefore, the maximum control duration for a specific load also needs to be considered, in order to reduce the impact to a minimum.

*DSC parameters*

Three DSC parameters are required, as follows.

- *Load priority* (LP) is one of the most important parameters to be defined in the DSC algorithm. It refers to the control availability for a specific load. It allows the loads to be controlled in the order of the specified load priority, from high control availability through medium to low control availability, and even no control at all. Load priority is set according to the subsequent impact the control will have on users. There are four levels of load priority: high, medium, low and no control. If a specific demand is defined as having a *high load priority*, it means that it has high availability for it to be controlled. Therefore, if at some time supply is less than demand, this demand item is included within the first level of loads to have control enacted upon them. If the demand is defined as *medium load priority*, it has medium control availability. This means that in instances where the total demand is still greater than the supply availability, after having control implemented on each demand listed as a high LP, the demands with medium Load Priority will be considered next. If after the implementation of control over high LP and medium LP demand is still greater than the supply availability, the same rationale applies to the demands with *low LP*. Loads with no control priorities cannot be controlled at any time in the whole control period, even if the supply is less than the demand, as if it is controlled it will have high user impact. Therefore, back-up energy storage/supply needs to be considered at that time.

- *Control method* (CM) is another parameter in the DSC algorithm. This decides how the demands are controlled. There are two main control methods available: on/off control and proportional control. For loads with proportional control, the percentage of maximum available control limit can also be specified. Some loads (such as refrigerators, etc.) can be switched on or off. Some loads (such as lighting) can be adjusted proportionally. Others can be switched both on/off and proportionally. The CM therefore depends upon the properties of the loads themselves.
- *Control duration* (CD) is the maximum period that a certain load can be controlled, which is designed to consider the payback effect (Kurucz *et al.*, 1996) of the demand after being controlled. It indicates the time available for control without adversely affecting the comfort of the users or the functionality of the load. This value can be established from empirical testing, using simulation models or through monitoring the relevant environmental variables on a real-time basis. For demands where relevant internal environmental data are not available, the empirical way is suggested. If the expected control time for a certain demand is beyond the maximum control duration, it cannot be controlled at the next time step (even if control is still required). The definition of CD is based on the maximum tolerance time of users for the particular demand being controlled. It is preferable that the control time for any particular demand is less than the maximum control duration. For demands where the relevant environmental variables are available, the CD will be identified through the use of a simulated model or from real-time monitoring.

*Load control ($Demand_{total} > Supply_{total}$)*

The primary purpose of load control is to control the various loads in order to meet the available supply at all times. This control module automatically sorts the selected demands into three clusters: cluster one – high control availability; cluster two – medium control availability; and cluster three – low control availability. The algorithm will perform the control actions under the decreasing order of control priorities, that is to say, from cluster one, to cluster two and finally cluster three. After having controlled demands within cluster one, the algorithm sums up all the demands (including demands of other clusters both controlled and uncontrolled) to find the new total demand and compares this with total supply. If the total demand is still greater than the total supply, it will move to another cluster and repeat the procedure above. If the total demand is less than supply, it will terminate the control at the current time and move to the next control step.

If there is more than one demand within one cluster, the DSC algorithm treats them equally, applies the possible control factors to each demand within the same cluster and finds the best control combination to achieve the minimum difference between the available supply and new total demand. If the total number of demand clusters with high control availability is two, then a function with the input parameter of the total number within this demand cluster is called to realize the demand-side control capability. After this function is executed, the total demand is recalculated. If the new total demand is less than or equal to the supply, it will terminate the control process and continue to the next time step. If the new total demand at this stage is still greater than the supply, the control of the demand cluster with medium availability will be executed until the total demand is less than or equal to the total supply. If, after the implementation of control over both high and medium demand clusters, demand still exceeds supply, a similar mechanism is subsequently applied to the demand cluster with low control availability.

*Load recover ($Demand_{total} < Supply_{total}$)*

When total energy supply exceeds demand, the aim of the load recover component is to recover the demands as much as possible when surplus energy supplies are available. Within the load recover process, demands are prioritized into three clusters under the ascending order from low to high control availability. Demand clusters with low control availability are recovered first of all, whenever there is surplus supply at the current time step. Depending on the total demand recalculated after recovering the load, the algorithm compares the new total demand with the total supply. If the total supply is still greater than the new total demand, it moves to the next demand cluster with higher control availability to be recovered until the total demand matches the total supply.

*Load despatch ($Demand_{total} = Supply_{total}$)*

When the total demand is equal to the total supply, the load despatch module is invoked to deliver the demand as required.

As shown in Figure 5.3, this procedure is continued until the end of the control period. The whole DSM algorithm is flexible and generic and has the capability to adjust itself to suit the different number of demands.

*Impacts of the DSM+c algorithms*

The impact of the DSM+c algorithm upon the environment the controlled loads are servicing (mainly refers to the users' comfort level) is a vital issue in the roll-out and uptake of demand management. It relates to whether the impact of the control action is acceptable or not to the building occupants. One approach adopted to assess the impact of demand-side management is the survey or questionnaire. People are randomly selected from the population and are questioned on low DSM effects on their lifestyle. This approach can reflect a certain degree of inconvenience that the DSM programmes bring. However, the questionnaire or survey is normally undertaken long after DSM measures are taken. The accuracy of the survey results is doubtful as it depends on people's memories. This approach cannot necessarily reflect the exact time that the DSM measures were taken. Also, this type of approach always takes longer to undertake and report the outcomes than expected. The number of questionnaires completed and returned to the researchers, i.e. the population size, is uncertain. It has some deviation over the feeling of control at the time of occurrence relative to the time when filling out the questionnaire. This method is termed qualitative as opposed to quantitative.

An alternative approach is to design a way to quantify the impact of DSM and control upon the specific environment being impacted through the incorporation of detailed building simulation programmes and the Internet-based monitoring and appliance-control infrastructure. Similar to the nature of the demand profiles, from either statistical data or simulated data, two possible levels of activation can be classified to examine the impact of the DSM+c algorithm: high level and low level.

- *High level*: it is hard to quantify the impact on the high-level demand profile (such as historical or monitoring data, etc.) after the DSM+c algorithm has been implemented. The only possible way to realize this is to build monitoring and control hardware into real buildings. By measuring the parameters relevant to the environment, we know if the control strategy is good or bad. Otherwise we can complement the undesirable impacts only through more intelligent control algorithms.

The high-level DSM+c algorithm described earlier is capable of analyzing the match between supply and demand (including magnitude and phase) after specifying the DSM+c parameters. By specifying different values of the CD parameter, we can compare the match results and see how much the DSM+c algorithm can improve the match. In this way, we can optimize the DSM+c parameters to achieve a better match while minimizing the level of impact on users' comfort or functionality.

- *Low level*: the impact on low-level demand profiles, such as physically based demand models, can be quantified through calculating the relevant environmental parameters within each of the demand models. It can decide the control action by comparing the new values of control variables with the initial settings, and whether the customer's minimum comfort levels are violated. In this way, the CD parameter can be quantified dynamically. Discrepancies between real effects on the load demand curve and preliminary results are mainly due to the incorrect modelling of the loads involved in these control strategies (Molina *et al.*, 2003). Therefore, the more accurate the demand model is, the more realistic is the load-control strategy provided. At the current time, the physically based demand model for a cooling and heating system has been developed for the purpose of informing a low-level load-control algorithm. Physically based load-modelling methods have been widely used because they are able to predict the dynamic response behaviour of individual loads and allow one to obtain the aggregated response of these loads efficiently.

## 5.5 Strategic- and operational-level DSM+c algorithms implementation

At both the strategic and operational levels, DSM+c algorithms have been implemented within simulation-based and ICT-based platforms.

### *5.5.1 Strategic-level DSM+c algorithm*

At the strategic level, the DSM+c algorithm refers to the application of DSM+c measures to historical data on an hourly or half-hourly basis. It is capable of managing both energy supplies and individual loads based on the comparison of demand and available supply resources to generate optimal DSM strategies. The demands at this level are time-series data estimated in advance. Several demand-side measures, such as energy efficiency, load shifting and demand-side control, can be used at this level of DSM+c algorithm application. The resulting impact of DSM measures to be applied is difficult to quantify, as the required internal environmental data relevant to the demand are normally not available. Thus, to

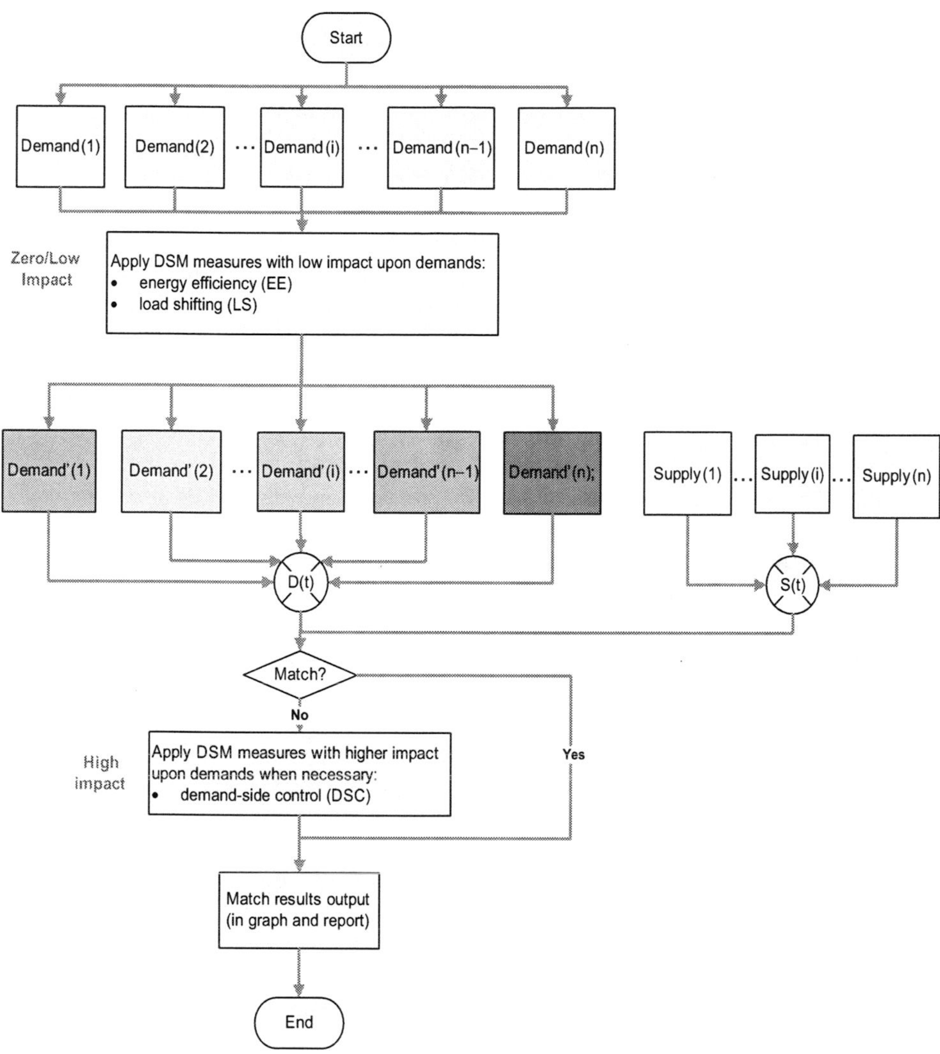


Figure 5.4 DSM+c algorithm when applied at the strategic level.

consider the impact of any DSM+c measures on users' convenience, correlations of empirical experiences against measures can be established. A flow chart representation of the DSM+c algorithm framework to be applied at the strategic level is shown in Figure 5.4.

The general logic behind the strategic-level DSM+c algorithm can be described as follows. The available DSM+c options specified for each demand are checked in the first instance. Depending on its potential impacts on the demand side, the DSM+c options available from zero/low impact level to high impact level have been identified as energy efficiency, load shifting and demand-side control respectively. The demands with the energy efficiency (EE) option (if defined) will be controlled first, followed by the demands with the LS option (if defined), while the demands with the DSC option (if defined) are dealt with last. The match results between the demands and supplies using the DSM+c algorithm are presented in the form of a graph and tabulated data.

For demands with an energy efficiency option, a specific reduction rate throughout the control period is applied, which reduces the magnitude of the demand to a certain level. A good example of this is the replacement of existing incandescent light bulbs with compact fluorescent or LED energy-efficient ones. For demands with a load shift option, similar to the EE option, the strategic-level DSM+c algorithm manages these throughout the specified control period. Based on the same level of energy use, a demand-specific shifting algorithm is employed to find out the maximum shared area with the supply profile. For demands with a DSC option, the strategic-level DSM+c algorithm examines the demands at each time step and compares them with the supply at the same time step. Where a mismatch occurs, control actions are applied based on the comparison results to achieve a demand–supply match.

In order to demonstrate the applicability of demand control, an engineering-focused case study has been undertaken where this approach has been applied to a project looking at the contribution of demand-side measures in the process of designing the low-carbon energy system for multi-family dwellings. Relative to current practice, where it is assumed that supply is demand following and that all loads will be satisfied irrespective of the magnitude and time of occurrence, demand control has been applied to loads which are being partially satisfied from a stochastic supply system containing renewable energy technologies.

The case study demonstrated that up to 20 per cent improvements can be made through different levels of demand-side management activities specified to appliance-specific loads.

### 5.5.2 *Operational-level DSM+c algorithm*

Based on the strategic-level DSC algorithm illustrated in previous sections, a modified DSC algorithm based on the algorithm applied at a strategic level, also called the *operational-level DSC algorithm*, has been developed for the purpose of quantifying the impacts of control on the environmental conditions experienced within the building. This operational-level DSC algorithm is capable of quantifying the post-control impact upon the micro environment, mainly referring to users' comfort levels, after controlling the loads either through simulation or real-time monitoring and control using sensors/actuators applied to each load type. This is an important issue, as the post-control impact dictates the extent to which users will accept the control actions. It also provides a framework for evaluating the expected impacts of the demand-side control strategy. The operational-level DSC algorithm connects supply and demand in much more technical detail and smaller time steps than that at the strategic level. In order to inform the architecture for implementing the DSC algorithm at the operational level, a detailed dynamic building performance simulation program and sensors/actuators in the environment being controlled are required. An integrated building performance computational tool is used to identify relevant environmental variables, while sensors/actuators are employed to measure the environmental conditions or control the devices towards a real-time basis. The operational DSC algorithm takes into account the environmental variables which are established through simulation models or real-time monitoring. Therefore the optimized control actions to be implemented on the loads (e.g. minimizing the users' impact) can be identified. The framework for implementing the operational level DSM+c algorithm is shown in Figure 5.5. It is composed of two outputs: energy impact and the micro-environment impact.

*Energy aspect*

When comparing this with the strategic-level DSM+c algorithm, similar patterns are adopted in terms of energy use at the system level. The difference is that for cases when total demand is less than total supply, a load-recovery module is introduced. The main function of the load-recovery module is to recover some loads when a surplus of energy supply exists. It first recovers the demand cluster with low control availability, when a supply surplus exists at the current time step. Depending on the total demand recalculated after recovering the load, the algorithm then compares the new total demand with the total supply. If the total supply is still greater than the new total demand, it moves to the next demand cluster with higher control availability to be recovered until the total supply is less than or equal to the total demand.

*Micro-environment aspect*

For the micro-environment aspect, internal environmental variables which the demand system has direct impact upon, such as temperature, humidity and illumination level, are used as indicators to determine whether an action can be applied. The value of the internal

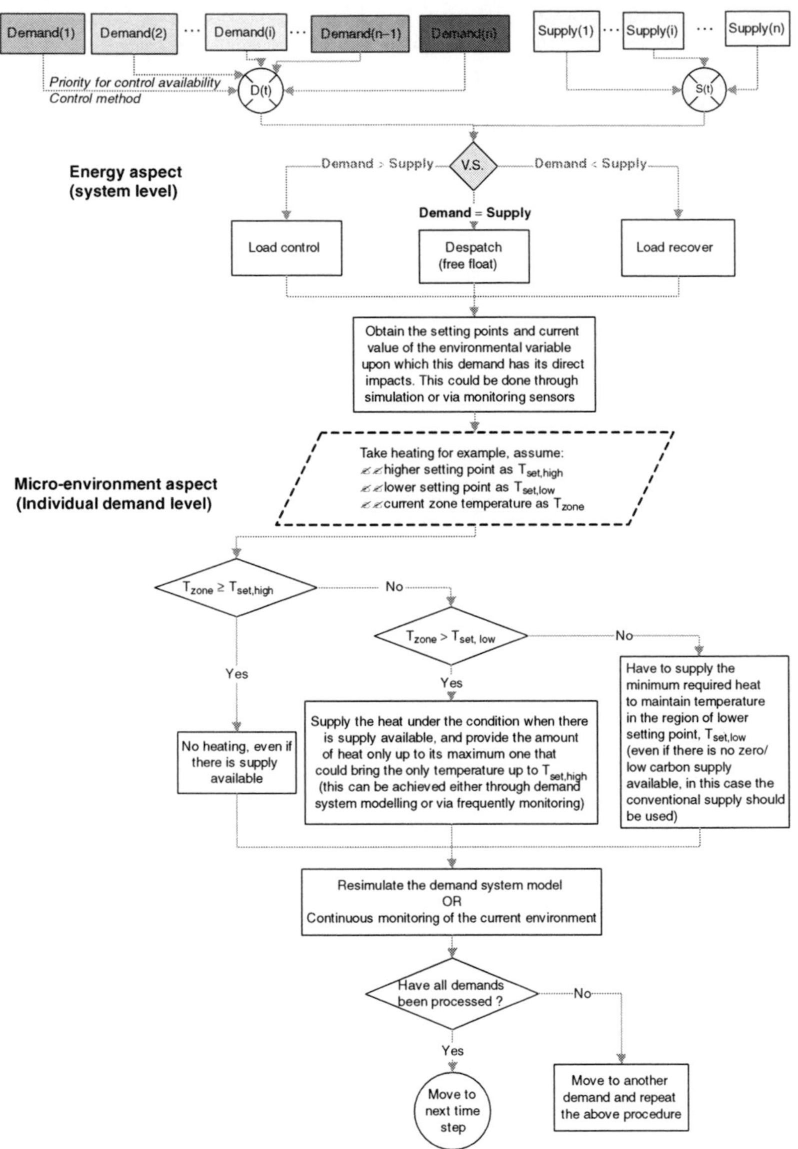


Figure 5.5 Framework for implementing DSM+c at the operational level.

environmental variables at the current time step can be achieved either through simulation of the demand system or via real-time monitoring. Having checked this value against set-point values, appropriate control actions will be taken. This maintains the internal environmental variables within an acceptable range, e.g. users' specified comfort zone, so that loads can be controlled or recovered without sacrificing their convenience.

It is important to select suitable environmental variables as decision criteria. The more influential the variable and the more variables involved, the more sophisticated and realistic demand-side control actions at the operational level will be generated. In order to make it simple and easy to understand, this study mainly considers a single environmental variable for each load within the operational DSC algorithm.

The two aspects illustrated in the above architecture can be best realized through the use of a detailed simulation program and an ICT-enabled energy system. The ESP-r, dynamic building performance simulation software, can be used to implement this operational-level DSM+c algorithm, while an ICT-based wireless Internet-enabled energy system is used as a medium to achieve the operational-level DSM+c algorithm within the real environment.

*Detailed dynamic simulation environment*

To enact more effective demand control without impacting on building occupants/users, discrete DSM+c algorithms have been implemented initially on a number of thermal loads typically found within buildings and the resulting impacts monitored. In order to inform future policy/network planning developments, the DSM+c algorithms have been integrated within a detailed dynamic building simulation platform, ESP-r. The detailed structure of the framework is illustrated in Figure 5.6. This is to facilitate the appraisal of introducing different demand flexing strategies and quantify the user impact when assessed within different building types operating with different tolerance levels and when linked with building integrated renewable/low-carbon microgeneration.

This approach has been applied and tested against a renewable energy-based heat-pump system for different types of dwellings made from a lightweight and a heavyweight construction. The implemented DSC algorithm alters the shape of the demand profile to follow the pattern generated by intermittent renewable sources used to power the heat pump. This demonstrated that a heavyweight building performs better than a lightweight building in terms of the match with the intermittent supply. This is contrary to current building legislation, which focuses on the production of lightweight, fast-responding, climate-adaptive buildings

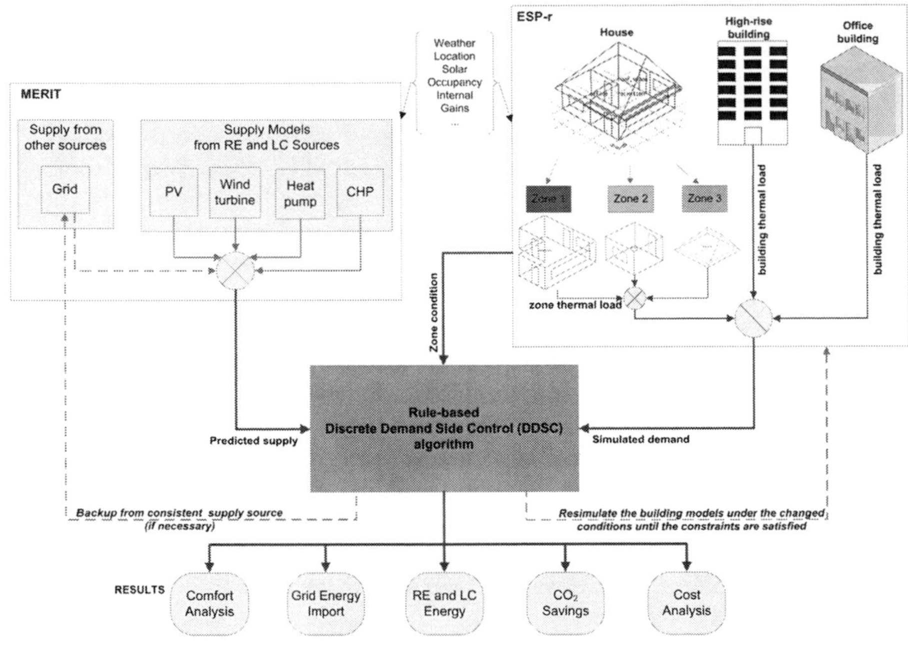


Figure 5.6 Simulation-based DSM+c as applied at the strategic level.

which, if fitted with the necessary HVAC (Heating, Ventilation and Air Conditioning) capacity, can be controlled to respond to differing seasonal conditions. Such buildings may not necessarily result in a reduction in energy demand but, instead, an alteration to the demand type and occurrence, i.e. reducing heating demand in the winter while increasing cooling demands in the summer seasons.

Introducing flexibility to the demand environment can reduce the amount of energy imported from a network without compromising users' comfort. Generally, the greater the flexibility of demand, the more renewable energy can be utilized and less energy imported from the network or from storage. The average comfort index during the occupied period is maintained within acceptable ranges for the user, aided by a certain level of reliable supply. More energy is consumed, compared with supply from an 'available on demand' energy supply.

*Internet-enabled energy system*

The proposed Internet-enabled energy system monitors the power demand and the supply available, together with the environmental variables using wired or wireless sensors connected to an Internet-based communications and control infrastructure. The system architecture, as

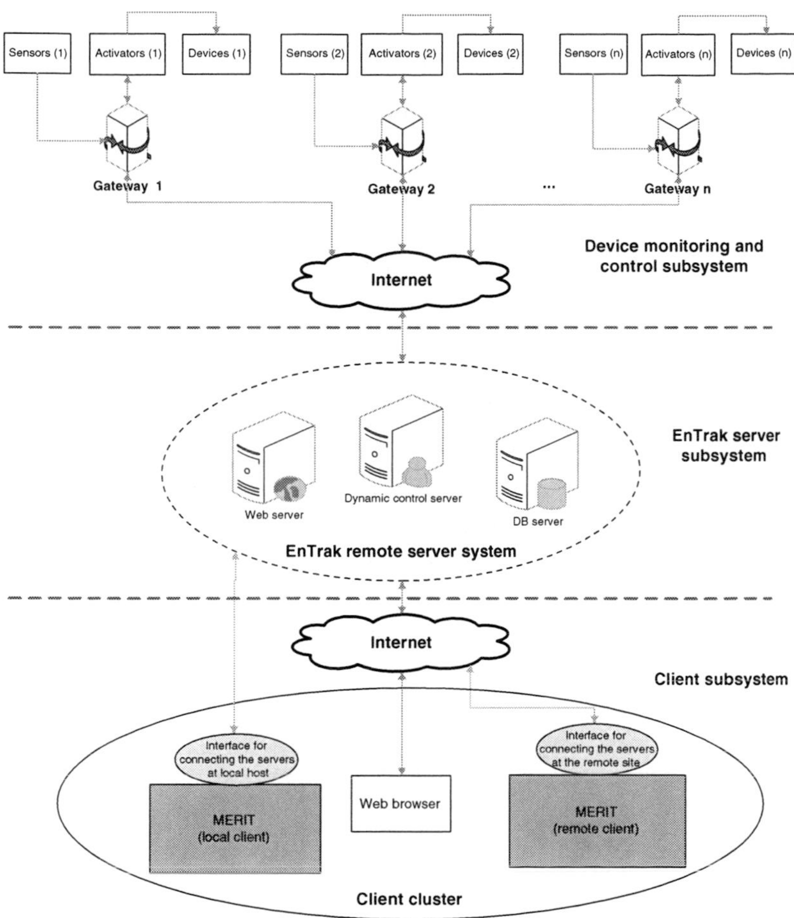


Figure 5.7 Internet-enabled energy system architecture.

shown in Figure 5.7, is divided into three layers: a device monitoring and control network (DMCN) layer, a server cluster layer and a client cluster layer. These layers exchange information via an Internet communications portal. The DMCN layer contains demand and supply devices, distributed sensors/actuators and an Internet gateway device. The server cluster layer, here the EnTrak system, is responsible for data processing and information management. It consists of a database server for storing data from the DMCN layer, a dynamic control server for decoding the control messages from client applications into device-recognizable commands, and a web server for hosting information via a standard

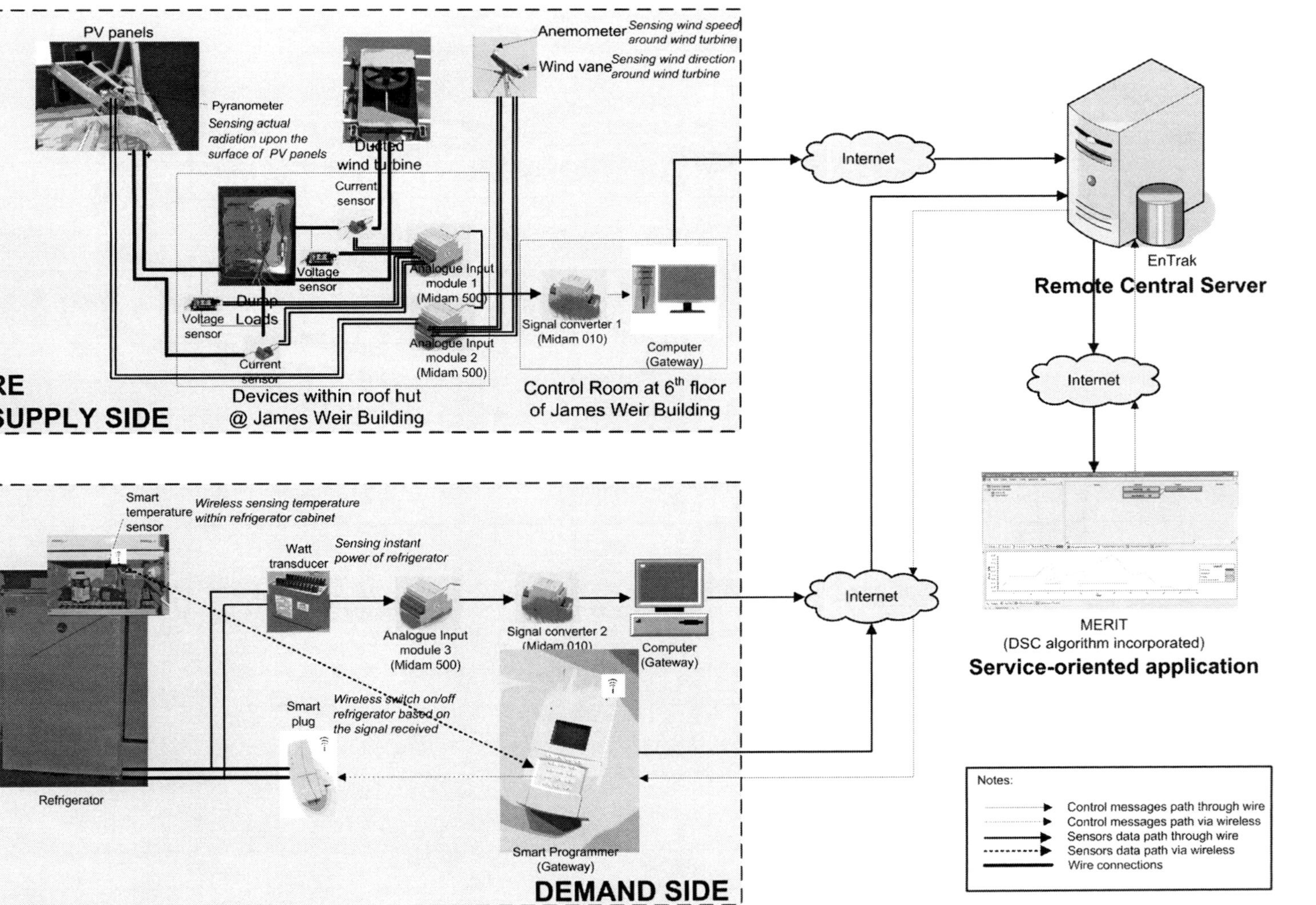


Figure 5.8 Case study architecture for demand control implementation.

web browser. The client cluster layer is composed of service-oriented applications which are responsible for providing different services to end-users, i.e. energy management, health care, security and safety, entertainment, etc.

Each sensor acquires data for electrical and environmental variables, from the demand and supply devices. The sample rate is predefined, which provides flexibility for different data-collection frequencies. Generally speaking, the sample rate for variables with longer time constants can be low, such as temperature, while it is higher for discrete variables in order to achieve a higher accuracy level of monitoring activities, i.e. power and occupancy. These measured data are transmitted to the gateway device through wire/wireless local networks and then stored in a remote database server. The service-oriented client applications can remotely access the database and retrieve the required data for further analysis purposes. The control messages generated by the service-oriented application are sent back to the control server and, after having been decoded, to the device through the Internet. The control actions are applied to the demand or supply devices within the local network to realize a specific service. All these operations can be realized close to a real-time basis. A case study has been carried out to demonstrate the feasibility of applying the proposed architecture in a real system, as illustrated in Figure 5.8. Some initial results after applying the DSM+c algorithm are shown in Figure 5.9.

After having applied the DSM+c algorithm, the demand appliance, here a refrigerator, follows the intermittent supply source, power from the photovoltaic supply. A certain specified level of environmental satisfaction can be maintained. By adjusting the environmental parameter settings and utilizing the conventional energy supply infrastructure as an auxiliary, the specified environmental requirements can be achieved and at the same time the supply can be better matched to the demand.

## 5.6 Future uptake

This chapter has demonstrated that through the use of advanced information communication technology, DSM+c can be applied at different scales in order to work towards a real-time demand–supply match. This can be implemented to maximize the use of renewable energy systems based on a predefined set of environmental parameters. The DSM algorithms are generic so that they can be applied to any heterogeneous mix of devices at various scales. For large-scale DSM applications in respect of heating, cooling and lighting systems, these algorithms can be implemented via an Internet-based communications platform. The use of such

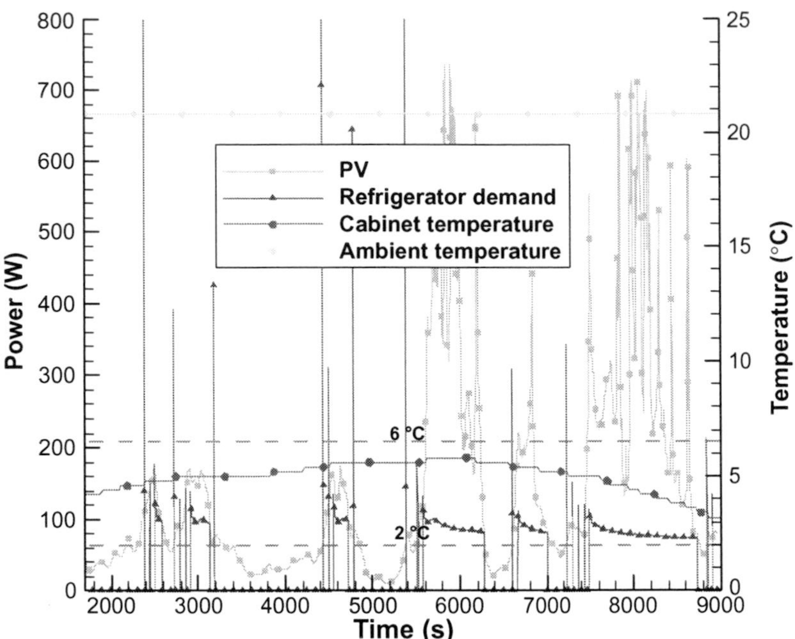


Figure 5.9 Case study results.

a platform enables energy service companies to offer demand-side management as a service. The range of services this facilitates includes managing domestic energy-consuming devices effectively; reducing domestic energy consumption and thus lowering energy bills; the mitigation of fuel poverty; ensuring social responsibility; delivery of the EC Directive on the Energy Performance of Buildings by the production of 'real data' based energy performance certificates (EPCs); and the delivery of wider government policy by reducing carbon emissions from buildings. On the back of the infrastructure installed to deliver the above services, other social services can be provided, including care for the elderly and direct engagement of cold-weather heating intervention and cold-weather payments.

## References

Carbon Trust (2004), Energy Saving Fact Sheet – Retail, Ref. GIL143, The Carbon Trust, London, UK. Available at www.carbontrust.co.uk/Publications, last accessed 23 August 2010.

De Almeida, A.T. and Vine, E.L. (1994). Advanced monitoring technologies for the evaluation of demand-side management programs, *Energy*, **19**(6): 661–78.

DTI (2003). *Energy White Paper: Our Energy Future – Creating a Low Carbon Economy*, London: Department of Trade and Industry.

EU (2002). *On the Energy Performance of Buildings*, Directive 2002/91/EC of the European Parliament and of the Council, *Official Journal of the European Communities*, Brussels: European Communities.

Gellings, C.W. (1985). The concept of demand-side management for electric utilities, *Proceedings of the IEEE*, **73**(10), 1468–70.

Gellings, C.W. and Chamberlin, J.H. (1993). *Demand-Side Management: Concepts and Methods*, 2nd edition, USA: Fairmont Press.

Hawkes, A. and Leach, M. (2005). Impacts of temporal precision in optimisation modelling of micro-combined heat and power, *Energy*, **30**(10): 1759–79.

Hawkes, A.D. and Leach, M.A. (2007). Cost-effective operating strategy for residential micro-combined heat and power, *Energy*, **32**(5): 711–23.

Kim, J. (2004). Integrated information system supporting energy action planning via the internet, PhD Thesis, University of Strathclyde.

Kurucz, C.N., Brandt, D. and Sim, S. (1996). A linear programming model for reducing system peak through customer load control programs, *IEEE Transactions on Power Systems*, **11**( 4), 1817–24.

Liao, Z. and Dexter, A.L. (2004). The potential for energy saving in heating systems through improving boiler controls, *Energy and Buildings*, **36**(3): 261–71.

Molina, A., Gabaldon, A., Fuentes, J.A. and Alvarez, C. (2003). Implementation and assessment of physically based electrical load models: Application to direct load control residential programmes, *IEEE Proceedings: Generation, Transmission and Distribution*, **150**(1): 61–6.

Newborough, M. and Augood, P. (1999). Demand-side management opportunities for the UK domestic sector, *IEEE Proceedings: Generation, Transmission and Distribution*, **146**(3): 283–93.

Obaidat, M.S. and Marchese, M. (2006). Recent advances in wireless networks and systems, *Computers and Electrical Engineering*, **32**(1–3): 1–6.

Rubinstein, F.M., Siminovitch, M. and Verderber, R. (1990). 50 per cent energy savings with automatic lighting controls, Industry Applications Society Annual Meeting, 1990, *Conference Record of the 1990 IEEE*, **2**: 2004–2008.

SBSA (2007), *Technical Handbooks 2007 (Domestic)*, Scottish Building Standards Agency, Denholm House, Almondvale Business Park, Livingston.

Schweppe, F.C., Daryanian, B. and Tabors, R.D. (1989). Algorithms for a spot price responding residential load controller, *IEEE Transactions on Power Systems*, **4**(2): 507–16.

Slater, A.I. (1987). *Lighting Controls: an Essential Element of Energy Efficiency*, Information Paper, Building Research Establishment, London: BRE.

Stadler, I. and Bukvic-Schafer, A.S. (2003). Demand side management as a solution for the balancing problem of distributed generation with high penetration of renewable energy sources, *International Journal of Sustainable Energy*, **23**(4): 157–67.

Williams, E.D. and Matthews, H.S. (2007). Scoping the potential of monitoring and control technologies to reduce energy use in homes, in *IEEE International Symposium on Electronics and the Environment* Orlando, FL, Institute of Electrical and Electronics Engineers Inc., Piscataway, pp. 239–44.

# 6 Smart metering: technology, economics and international experience

*Aoife Brophy Haney, Tooraj Jamasb and Michael G. Pollitt*

## 6.1 Introduction

As we have seen particularly from Part I of this volume, the participation of the demand side is essential in improving the overall efficiency of energy markets. In liberalized electricity markets, active demand-side participation has been limited to date, although there is increasing emphasis on its importance in contributing to a number of energy policy challenges (Bilton *et al.*, 2008; Borenstein *et al.*, 2002; Spees and Lave, 2007). Climate change, security of supply and fuel poverty are the three main areas where a more active demand side has the potential to have both significant and cost-effective impacts (Ofgem, 2006b). The widespread recent interest in smart electricity and gas metering can best be understood in this context. Innovative forms of metering allow for more detailed information to be collected on consumption. Communications technology facilitates greater interaction between the end-user and the rest of the supply chain. Both information and interaction allow for end-users to become more actively involved by, for example, responding to price signals.

Smaller users (domestic, small and medium-sized enterprises (SMEs)) have been the focus of recent smart metering policy debate around the world as they have traditionally not been given the appropriate incentives, means or information to become active participants in energy markets. In the European Union (EU), the 2006 Energy Services Directive (2006/32/EC) has given impetus to the debate by requiring member states to incorporate metering and billing policies into their National Energy Efficiency Action Plans. This has prompted a number of EU countries to explore the costs and benefits of implementing smart metering as well as the appropriate models and regulatory frameworks for deployment. The recent interest in smart grids in both the EU and the US provides a broader framework for looking at some of these issues. Although the definition of a smart grid is a work in progress, the overall aim of developing smart grids is to modernize the electricity system in such a way that it will be able to deal with increased complexity in an efficient and reliable manner. Part of this complexity comes from a more active demand side. Other important factors include the integration of greater amounts of renewable generation, distributed generation and the use of more advanced network control technologies to reduce losses (ERGEG, 2009).

In this chapter, we first discuss the policy context for smart metering in more detail. We then take a closer look at smart metering from a technological perspective. There is often confusion over what actually makes a smart meter smart. Part of this confusion stems from the fact that there is a wide range of available technological options. We will explore some of these options and discuss some of the differences in technology choice in countries where smart meters have already been deployed. In section 6.3, we consider the economic case for smart metering by looking at the main costs and benefits. In section 6.4, we bring together some of the lessons from recent international experience with smart metering policy debates and deployments. We conclude by outlining some of the key challenges that lie ahead, including the question of technology choice and the market model.

## 6.2 Context for smart metering

Smart meters with advanced communications are a gateway to increasing the participation of the demand side in the electricity market through facilitating new pricing structures and overcoming information asymmetry. They can also act as a platform for automated forms of demand response by connecting with smart appliances, such as the smart thermostat, to control loads directly. Improving the flexibility of network operation as a whole will become even more important in the future, particularly due to the integration of intermittent renewable energy resources and distributed generation. More responsive electricity demand is important in contributing to this flexibility (Stadler, 2008). Advanced communications, control methods and information technologies including more sophisticated metering are central to achieving this goal (Strbac *et al.*, 2006).

### *6.2.1 Policy context*

Metering is a central part of the relationship between customers and their electricity and gas suppliers because of the information it provides to both parties. Metering service consists of several activities that do not necessarily have to be carried out by a single party: (i) meter provision (supplying metering equipment), (ii) meter operation (installation, operation and maintenance) and (iii) meter reading and data processing.

Traditionally, meters have been owned and metering activities have been undertaken by network operators. Even since the liberalization of electricity markets this has continued to be the case in many European countries. Several countries, however, have pursued competition in metering. The three main examples are Great Britain, Germany and the Netherlands. Two main models for metering have therefore emerged within the EU: (i) a regulated model where metering activities are treated as a regulated monopoly and (ii) a liberalized model where some or all metering activities are open to competition (ERGEG, 2007). As we will see, these differences in approach have important implications for the smart metering roll-out strategies considered by different countries.

The 2006 EU Energy Services Directive (2006/32/EC) was one of the main policy drivers in Europe for countries to consider more advanced forms of metering and more informative billing. The directive places greater emphasis on the role of the demand side in improving the efficiency of energy markets and in unlocking energy and carbon savings. Smart metering is increasingly seen as a tool in promoting more responsive demand in gas and electricity markets in the context of improving security of supply, reducing $CO_2$ emissions and tackling the growing problem of fuel poverty. The directive requires member states to implement National Energy Efficiency Action Plans. As part of these plans, each country must ensure that metering and billing of energy consumption for all customers reflect actual consumption and provide information on the time of use, as long as it is technically possible and cost-effective to do so (European Union, 2006). This has encouraged much debate and a number of consultations on the costs and benefits of implementing more advanced metering solutions across Europe.

In the US, the drivers for smart metering have been slightly different. Managing peak consumption has been a major driver in states such as California, particularly in the aftermath of the 2001 electricity crisis. There has also been a focus on investment efficiencies within the utilities. In most cases, the individual utilities have been requested to submit detailed business cases to the relevant state's public utilities commission. More recently, action has been taken at a federal level to develop a coherent smart grid policy. The Federal Energy Regulatory Commission (FERC) is responsible for implementing this policy, which was adopted in July 2009. The focus is on providing standards to achieve interoperability in the future electricity system. The goals of FERC's smart grid policy are governed mainly by the 2007 Energy and Security Independence Act, which as its name suggests is primarily concerned with security and reliability of energy supplies (FERC, 2009).

The role of regulation in promoting smart metering has been the subject of considerable debate. This is particularly so in the case of Great Britain, where the regulator has decided that competition in metering is the best way of ensuring that smart metering delivers for customers (Ofgem, 2006b). The UK government set out its initial expectation that all gas and electricity customers would be given smart meters with separate displays in the 2007 Energy White Paper (DTI, 2007). This was followed in October 2008 by a government announcement that smart meters would be rolled out to all homes in Great Britain by the end of 2020. In May 2009, the government launched a consultation to consider some of the important aspects of the roll-out, including the functionality of meters as well as the most appropriate delivery model. The government's response to the consultation and impact assessment were published in December 2009.

One of the most important decisions concerned the delivery model for domestic meters. The government has decided that a central communications model will be used. Under this model suppliers will be responsible for purchasing and installing meters, while communications will be coordinated centrally. Three main alternatives were considered. The first was a fully centralized model where regional franchises would own, deploy and manage meters, with communications coordinated centrally. The second was a fully competitive model where suppliers would be responsible for all metering services. A third model was also investigated where responsibility for metering would return to the distribution companies.

Design of the implementation strategy is due to be completed by 2012 and is a joint initiative of the Department of Energy and Climate Change (DECC) and Ofgem (DECC, 2009b).

### *6.2.2 Technology*

In the UK and most other countries, the traditional electromechanical Ferraris meter is still the predominant means of measuring energy consumption in homes and small businesses. Traditional electricity meters display consumption in kWh only, record consumption cumulatively and are read manually. Because of the need for a meter reader to periodically inspect the meter for an accurate reading or for customers themselves to report a meter reading to the supplier, billing is often based on estimates of consumption rather than on actual consumption and correction of estimates may occur only with a long delay.[1]

Where more advanced electronic meters have been installed, customers with high levels of average annual consumption (typically industrial and large commercial users) and higher levels of peak load are usually the first to be targeted. For example, in Great Britain half-hourly metering (interval metering) is mandatory for users with maximum demand over 100 kW (DTI, 2006). Companies under this threshold can choose to install half-hourly metering once they are prepared to pay the additional charge (Carbon Trust, 2007). Italy is the country with the highest level of installed advanced electricity meters. The roll-out of smart meters to 32 million customers has now been completed by Enel, Italy's largest utility. Enel has also launched a new project to deploy 13 million meters in Spain between 2010 and 2015 (EurActiv, 2010).

Results from ERGEG (2007), a survey of metering across Europe, indicate that although some consideration is being given to promoting smart meters in the gas sector, the current levels of implementation in Europe are very low.[2] In the US, the overall penetration level of advanced metering is relatively low at 6 per cent nationally. However, there are considerable differences across states. Pennsylvania and Wisconsin stand out as front-runners, with 53 per cent and 40 per cent respectively for overall levels of advanced metering in both the electricity and gas sectors (FERC, 2006). There have been further recent developments in other states but mainly in electricity. California's utilities are starting to roll out smart electricity metering, having submitted deployment proposals to the California Public Utilities Commission. In Canada, a province-wide roll-out in Ontario of 4.5 million electricity meters is under way. Comparing countries and regions is difficult, however, because there is no single definition of what it means for a meter or a metering system to be 'advanced' or 'smart'.

The smart gas or electricity meter is a device that forms a small but integral part of a smart metering system. It provides consumption information in more detail than a traditional meter and a range of additional functions once the meter is connected to a communications network. In general, when the term smart meter is used, it is implied that the meter is capable of two-way communications. There are ways of adapting

[1] In the UK, physical inspection of meters is required on a two-yearly basis as part of licence requirements for safety and security reasons. Some changes to this requirement may be necessary to fully exploit the gains of remote reading. The most recent UK impact assessment assumes, however, that this requirement remains in place (DECC, 2009a).

[2] Belgium and Spain were the only countries to report figures for smart meters in the gas sector and both reported percentage shares of 0.05 per cent.

electromechanical meters so that they can give more information to customers. For example, a real-time display unit can be attached that gives information on current and past consumption in monetary or energy units. The metering system remains the same, however, and most customers continue to be billed on an estimated basis. Some suppliers in the UK are offering these kinds of services. British Gas has a new EnergySmart programme where customers are given a real-time electricity display unit as well as an incentive to submit their own meter readings online each month. Online tools are also available for customers to investigate their monthly consumption patterns.

In the rest of this section we will focus on different existing types of smart electricity meters as international experience with the variety of functions and costs is more widespread than in either the gas or water sectors.

An interval electronic meter is most likely to be the metering device in a smart metering system. Interval meters are essentially electronic meters that have the capability to record electricity consumption over a short period of time, usually 15-, 30- or 60-minute intervals. This allows for more complex time-varying pricing structures to be implemented. Beyond this basic requirement, there is a range of functions that can be added to the meter to increase the smartness of the meter and the metering system. The meters can be read manually or they can be equipped with communications technology so that the supplier can read the meter remotely and in some cases also communicate back to the customer/meter. Meters can also be fitted with the functionality to switch between credit and prepayment (FERC, 2006; NERA, 2007).

Electronic prepayment meters are often referred to as 'semi-smart' because although they provide customers with more information on their consumption and a closer connection between the different levels of consumption and their financial implications, their communications capabilities are generally limited. Within the prepayment category, there are, however, an increasing number of technological options and the costs of new prepayment systems relative to previous systems have declined substantially. One of the clearest examples of this is in Northern Ireland. After an initial trial of keypad electricity prepayment meters in 200 homes, Northern Ireland Electricity started to roll out the new meters in the year 2000. There are currently (2010) around 222,000 meters installed, approximately 28 per cent of residential customers (NIE, 2009).

As well as reducing the costs of the metering system, the new prepayment technology offers a range of new functions for customers and suppliers. These include a detailed customized user display with information on credit time in days and information on costs over the previous day, week and month; unit rates and number of units used at these rates; previous purchase information; load limiting rather than disconnection; and the ability to program the meters through vend codes rather than site visits (Ofgem, 2006a). Remotely programming the meters further reduces costs by eliminating the need for site visits to switch the meter between prepayment and credit (Owen and Ward, 2007).

Communications technology is central to the most advanced types of metering systems that are currently available. Initially one-way communication systems were common. This is typically referred to as automated meter reading (AMR) and early versions were widespread in the US. The simplest form of AMR connects the meter temporarily via a radio link to an electronic meter-reading device. Meter readers can then use handheld meter-reading devices to connect remotely to meters as they walk or drive through neighbourhoods.

AMR can also be implemented using a permanent communications link between the meter and the supplier. Various forms of wireless and wired communications technologies can be employed for this purpose. Both the simple and more advanced forms of AMR allow for accelerated meter readings and more accurate billing.

Two-way communications systems, meanwhile, offer a wide variety of extra options for the supplier and services for the customer. These include remote connection and disconnection, outage or loss of supply detection and communication to the supplier, and the ability to interface with load-control technology. Furthermore, some meters have the capability to record electricity that is imported from the grid as well as electricity that is exported to the grid, allowing for the measurement of output from micro-generators. The general term for systems based on two-way communications is automated metering management (AMM). Table 6.1 provides an overview of the wide range of potential functionality that a smart meter can support once there is a two-way communications system in place.

The core set of features creates the foundation for price-responsive tariffs, accurate billing, greater customer awareness and secure two-way communications. The additional features could increase the potential for demand response by providing more frequent information on energy usage and improving how the customer interacts with and responds to this information. One way of doing this is by providing a communications platform in the home through a home area network (HAN). This could allow for more sophisticated forms of load control, for example smart appliances, as well as the potential to integrate other services in the home.

Table 6.1 *Smart meter functionality*

| | Function | Purpose |
|---|---|---|
| *Core features* | | |
| Measurement | Half-hourly measurement and recording | Load-profile measurement; accurate billing; basis for time-differentiated tariffs |
| | Remote reading (weekly) | Accurate billing |
| | Local reading by meter reader or end-user | Back-up in case of communications failure |
| | Remote time synchronization | Clock accuracy |
| Security | Communications and data security | Data are securely transmitted from and to the meter |
| | Tamper detection | Communication of tampering remotely |
| Load management | Support existing load-management arrangements | Continuation of load control via broadcast of turn-on/turn-off commands, e.g. Economy 7 in the UK |
| *Additional features* | | |
| Measurement | Daily remote reading | Potential for greater demand response |
| | Power-factor measurement | Monitoring of power factor and targeted improvements |
| | Import/export metering | Facilitates microgeneration |
| Switching | Remote connection/ disconnection | Facilitates supplier switching |
| | Remote switch between credit and prepayment | Greater customer flexibility |
| Load management | Supply-capacity control | Emergency limits following outages; contractual limits on supply to customers |
| | Interface with load-control technology and smart appliances (white goods), e.g. through a home area network (HAN) | Direct load control through an open standard platform (the HAN) |
| Quality | Detection and notification of supply losses and outages | Faster outage detection; improved quality of service data |
| Customer interaction | Interface to HAN | Potential for integrated additional services, e.g. security, fire safety |
| | In-home display device | Customer awareness; instantaneous information |
| | Interface for other metered data (gas, heat, water) | Integration of other utilities with the existing local communications infrastructure |
| Configurability | Remote reconfiguration | Settings, e.g. times for load control, tariffs, and supply-capacity control, can be changed remotely |

*Source:* Adapted from NERA (2007).

Choosing the appropriate smart metering technology can be difficult. The technology landscape has been changing over time, with new functionality and decreasing hardware costs. Developing an open or interoperable system is important in allowing for future development as well as permitting transparent access and integration among a wide range of equipment and applications. Different countries and regions have adopted different strategies for dealing with technology choice. In Italy, Enel chose to roll out one solution to all its customers. The solution is proprietary in the sense that there are a limited number of meter variations and access to metering data is restricted. Future communication protocols, however, will be non-proprietary (Meeus *et al.*, 2010). In Sweden, Vattenfall took a very different approach. In order to mitigate technology risk, the company entered into contracts with three different technology suppliers for meters with different levels of functionality. Roll-out of the three phases was staggered, allowing for more advanced technology to be implemented in the later stages. By doing this, the company has ensured that other technologies can be introduced in the future without disrupting its business process (Nordgren, 2008). Enel has now recognized the importance of developing an open smart metering communication protocol. In conjunction with Endesa, Enel has created a new initiative called Meters and More that aims to work towards a standardized European smart metering solution (Enel, 2010).

## 6.3 Economic assessment of smart metering

### *6.3.1 The costs of smart metering*

Rolling out a new metering infrastructure is logistically complex. It is also a difficult investment to assess because of the sensitivity of different cost and benefit categories to changes in the roll-out strategy. Table 6.2 provides an overview of the total costs for one completed smart metering roll-out (Italy) and several recent roll-out studies (UK, Australia and France). Though it is not possible to directly compare these numbers due to differing assumptions and technology choices, the overall message is clear: smart metering will require substantial investment over a number of years and will involve millions of electricity and gas customers.

Meter costs tend to be the most significant share of total smart metering project costs. Table 6.3 summarizes recent cost estimates for meters with different levels of functionality in Great Britain. The costs of basic prepayment meters are substantially higher for both electricity and gas than their credit counterparts. In fact, this has been a strong driver for the roll-out of more advanced meters in Northern Ireland where

Table 6.2 *Summary of international costs*

| Country | Total cost* | Meters | Electricity (E); Gas (G) | Roll-out schedule | Status |
|---|---|---|---|---|---|
| Italy | £1.55 billion | 32 million residential | E | 2001 to 2006 | Complete |
| UK | £7.6 billion to £9.1 billion | 47 million residential | E and G | 2010 to 2020 | Impact assessment 2009 preceding roll-out |
| Australia | £2 billion to £2.8 billion | 9.5 million residential and commercial | E | 2009 to 2014 | National roll-out study 2008 |
| France | £3.4 billion to £4.6 billion | 33.4 million residential and small business | E | 5-year and 10-year roll-outs | National roll-out study 2007 |

* Total costs have been converted to GBP using the annual average exchange rate (Bank of England statistics) and then inflated to 2009 using the UK CPI index (Office for National Statistics).
*Source:* Rogai (2006); DECC (2009a); NERA (2008); Capgemini (2007).

prepayment metering is prevalent. There is a wide range of purchase costs for both smart electricity and smart gas meters depending on the additional features that are included. For example, the addition of a separate visual display adds £15 to the base purchase cost of the meter.

Other functions, such as daily remote reading and export/import metering, do not add to the capital cost of the meter itself. They do, however, affect associated IT system and management costs, due to an increase in the volume of data. Smart meters have a shorter technical life than traditional electromechanical meters. A lifetime of fifteen years is typically assumed (NERA, 2007; Carbon Trust, 2007) compared with a twenty-year useful (i.e. certified) lifetime for traditional meters (Frontier Economics, 2007).

The responsibility for and the speed of the meter roll-out may have an impact on meter costs. In theory, due to economies of scale, larger-scale roll-outs where, for example, one party (i.e. a DNO) is responsible for meter purchasing in a geographic area have greater potential to reduce meter unit costs than smaller-scale roll-outs. Consultations with meter vendors in Australia, however, indicated that costs per meter are unlikely to fall considerably for volumes above 250,000 (NERA, 2008).

Table 6.3 *Smart meter costs in the UK*

| Meter/device type | Purchase cost* | Features | Study |
|---|---|---|---|
| *Electromechanical/basic prepayment* | | | |
| Domestic credit electricity | £7–8 | | Owen and Ward (2007) |
| Domestic key prepayment electricity | £45–50 | | |
| Domestic credit gas | £18–20 | | |
| Domestic prepayment gas | £75–100 | | |
| Real-time electricity/ gas display | £15; £14.17 | | Frontier Economics (2007); DECC (2009a) |
| *Smart meter* | | | |
| Domestic electricity | £25–35 | Core plus remote switch credit/prepayment | Owen and Ward (2007) |
| | £72–80 | Core plus separate visual display; remote connect/disconnect; remote switch credit/prepayment; import/export metering | Frontier Economics (2007) |
| | £55.75 | Core plus remote connect/disconnect plus home area network | DECC (2009a) |
| Domestic gas | £40–60 (£70–100) | Core (includes credit/ prepayment switch) | Owen and Ward (2007) |
| | £73–103 | Same as second domestic electricity smart meter | Frontier Economics (2007) |
| | £69.93 | Core plus remote connect/disconnect plus home area network | DECC (2009a) |

* All 2009 costs have been deflated to 2007 using the UK CPI index. For reference, the UK inflation rates for 2007, 2008 and 2009 respectively were 2.3%, 3.6% and 2.2% (Office for National Statistics).
*Source:* Owen and Ward (2007); Frontier Economics (2007).

Meter installation costs are also affected by differences in roll-out strategy. For example, if metering systems are deployed on a new and replacement basis only, lifetime installation costs are relatively low.[3] The coordination of the roll-out can also have an impact on costs. If the roll-out is coordinated by region, travel time between sites can be minimized; and if the roll-out is coordinated so that electricity and gas meters are installed simultaneously, the number of site visits can be reduced (Frontier Economics, 2007). The most recent impact assessment for domestic smart metering in Great Britain assumes a £10 saving for each installation if the roll-out is dual-fuel (DECC, 2009a).[4]

There are a number of potential technology options that could be used to provide a suitable communications platform for a smart metering system. Many countries have chosen to use a combination of different solutions. For example, the Italian communications infrastructure uses both power line carrier (PLC) and public telecommunications. In Sweden, data are transferred from the meters to collection points using PLC or radio communication and then transferred to a central data system using GSM.

Technology trials conducted in Victoria, Australia aimed to investigate some of the factors influencing the cost effectiveness of different communications solutions. The results indicated that customer density is an important factor. In rural and remote areas where customer density is low, PLC tends to be cost effective. Mesh radio communication, where meters are used as repeaters in a mesh configuration, is more suitable and cost effective in areas of high customer density (DPI, 2007).

### 6.3.2 *Benefits of smart metering*

The benefits of smart metering can be divided into two main categories: operational benefits and demand response (DR) benefits. The size of these benefits is influenced by a number of factors, including the level of functionality, deployment speed, coordination and behavioural change.

The main operational benefits for network companies and suppliers come from the improvement in overall efficiency of metering services. The avoided cost of meter reading is one of the most significant operational benefits. In general, slower deployment can have an adverse effect on this and other benefits. With meter reading costs, a slower roll-out

[3] New and replacement basis includes when new and renovated buildings require meter installation and when existing meters need to be replaced. As an example, the replacement rate for electricity and gas meters in Great Britain is approximately 5 per cent per annum (DTI, 2006, p. 21).

[4] The total dual-fuel installation cost is assumed to be £68. Electricity-only installation is £29 and gas-only is £49.

leads to a more costly metering transition period. For example, if roll-out is on a new and replacement basis, the gradually decreasing density of remaining traditional meters will result in a higher cost per meter read over a longer period of time (Frontier Economics, 2007).

Better outage detection, faster response times to outages and accurate billing also improve the efficiency of metering services. The main benefits to the network and supplier come from the reduction in customer service costs due to a lower level of customer complaints. Non-technical loss reduction, losses due to theft for instance, can also be an important benefit. Its magnitude depends on the country context. Where electricity theft has been an important issue, the potential to reduce losses may be a strong driver for smart metering deployment.

The benefits of a more efficient service and a greater level of choice are ultimately passed on to the customer. Operationally, smart meters offer customers more choice in terms of payment options (e.g. easier switching between credit and prepayment to manage debt), improved consumption information and easier supplier switching. They can also facilitate new services such as micro-generation by allowing for exported and imported electricity to be accurately measured.

Smart meters can influence customer demand in a number of ways. Direct load control of appliances and dynamic pricing have the potential to shift consumption from peak to off-peak periods. Dynamic pricing and more detailed consumption information may also lead to changes in average consumption levels. These demand response benefits are subject to a greater amount of uncertainty than the operational benefits of smart metering. Much of this is due to the need for customer acceptance and a certain amount of behavioural change. There have been a number of studies that have tried to quantify the response of customers to increased levels of information on their energy use. Darby (2006), for example, reviews the evidence on the effectiveness of feedback on energy consumption at a household level. Energy savings from direct feedback, i.e. from a meter or display, in the surveyed studies are in the region of 5–15 per cent. There are, however, question marks over applying some of this evidence to the large-scale UK context and over how sustained these changes can be. Studies that assess the benefits of smart metering roll-outs tend to use more conservative estimates of energy savings. The latest impact assessment for Great Britain, for example, assumes 2.8 per cent energy savings from smart electricity meters (DECC, 2009a).

The benefits of dynamic pricing, including real-time pricing and critical-peak pricing, have not received as much attention. Combining smart meters with smarter pricing schemes, however, has the potential to considerably augment the benefits of a smart metering roll-out. Up to now, innovative electricity pricing programmes have typically occurred in regions where summer and winter peaks are central to system management, for example in California. Faruqui, Harris and Hledik (2009) have estimated the benefits of dynamic pricing for the EU as a whole. They suggest that benefits could range from €14 billion to €53 billion depending on how successful policy makers are at overcoming the barriers to adoption. Their estimate of the total cost of an EU smart metering system is €51 billion, with the operational benefits amounting to between €26 billion and €41 billion. These numbers are important. They illustrate that there is in general a gap between the overall costs of a smart metering system and the total operational benefits of the system. Demand-response benefits from smarter pricing are fundamental to the cost effectiveness of smart metering investments.

The value of shifting demand from peak periods is based on a number of benefits. First, shifting demand away from the peak reduces the need to invest in peak generating capacity (see Platchkor and Pollitt, this volume). There would also be a network benefit from the reduction in peak demand. This would reduce the required transmission and distribution capacity (see Jamasb and Marantes, this volume). The estimates calculated by Faruqui *et al.* (2009) include these reduced investment benefits as well as the avoided energy costs that are associated with the reduced peak. More cost-reflective pricing may also help suppliers to minimize their hedging costs, i.e. the premium over wholesale prices that suppliers typically incur to fix the price they pay for energy (KPMG, 2007). Finally, the impact on carbon emissions depends on whether there is an overall reduction in demand. It also depends on the carbon intensities of marginal plants during peak and off-peak periods (Frontier Economics, 2007).

### 6.3.3 *Distribution of costs and benefits*

There are two predominant metering market models in Europe – the regulated model and the liberalized model – although there are many variations between countries. The choice of market model has an impact on the way in which costs and benefits are distributed across the supply chain. This can have a significant influence on the decision of whether and how to implement smart metering. Table 6.4 compares the two extremes of a distributor-led (regulated) and supplier-led (liberalized) roll-out according to the allocation of costs.

Under the distributor-led model, the DNO can recover some of the costs through regulated charges which are then passed on to the customer. When the model is supplier-led, costs are also ultimately passed

Table 6.4 *Allocation of smart metering costs*

| | Distributor | Supplier | Market operator |
|---|---|---|---|
| Distributor-led | Meters<br>Meter data and communications management<br>Communications and IT<br>Distributor systems | Supplier systems | Market meter and data transactions management |
| Supplier-led | Distributor systems | Meters<br>Meter data and communications management<br>Communications and IT | Market meter and data transactions management |

*Source:* Adapted from NERA (2008).

on to the customer but in a competitive setting. Standards for meters, communications and data become even more crucial in a competitive environment. The risks of investing without having standards in place can be prohibitively high. This is because suppliers cannot be sure that their investment will not become stranded, if, for example, a customer switches to another supplier who is not in a position to or does not agree to use the same technology (Wissner and Growitsch, 2007).

Although one party incurs the majority of the costs in both distributor-led and supplier-led scenarios, there is a wide range of benefits for all market actors. Table 6.5 gives an overview of the main benefits for each actor independent of the market model adopted. Reduced meter reading costs are not included in the table. This important operational benefit of smart metering is allocated to the party responsible for meters and meter data and communications management. As a result, it depends on the given market model.

## 6.4 Lessons from international experience

The drivers for rolling out smart meters differ across countries and have in turn shaped international regulatory approaches. Table 6.6 summarizes

Table 6.5 *Allocation of smart metering benefits*

| |
|---|
| *Customer/Society* |
| Bill savings from reducing and/or shifting consumption |
| Accurate billing: better customer service |
| Increased quality of service |
| Easier switching of supplier |
| Reduction in carbon emissions |
| Avoided investment in peak-generation capacity |
| *Supplier* |
| Accurate information for billing purposes; fewer complaints |
| Reduction in unpaid bills |
| *Distribution* |
| Avoided peak investment |
| Reduced technical and non-technical (theft) losses |
| *Transmission* |
| Avoided peak investment |

some of the recent roll-outs in Europe and North America. In most cases, there has been some form of regulatory push. In some cases, this has taken the form of a direct mandate, for example in Ontario where the government set a target date for a full province-wide roll-out. In other cases, intervention has been less direct. In Sweden, for instance, DNOs have been required by law since July 2009 to provide their customers with monthly billing. This type of approach has left technology choice and roll-out strategy open for DNOs to decide individually. In Italy, the initial push came from industry. Enel, the largest Italian DNO, chose to undertake a large roll-out programme in a relatively short period of time.

Deciding between different deployment models has been central to smart metering policy debates in Great Britain and Australia. Both countries have assessed different market models according to their impact on total costs and final net present value. There are tensions between the two extremes of distributor-led and supplier-led roll-outs. On the one hand, distributor-led models offer cost savings, for example in installation and communications costs, thanks to more coordinated regional roll-outs. On the other hand, a model that allows for competition in metering and associated services may be better for innovation and for customers in the long run. There are concerns, however, that a competitive model will slow down the roll-out process unnecessarily. In fact, this is one of the main reasons the Ontario Energy Board cites for choosing a distributor-led model (OEB, 2005).

Table 6.6 *International roll-outs*

| | Meter | Communications | Timeline | Drivers |
|---|---|---|---|---|
| California | Interval and some retrofitting | AMM: PLC and radio frequency (RF) | 2007/2008: three main investor-owned utilities PG&E, SG&E and SCE commencing deployment of approx. 12 million electricity and 5 million gas meters | Management of peak consumption; electricity crisis 2001 |
| Finland | Some retrofitting of existing meters | AMR; wide variations across DNOs; some AMM plans more recently; mobile phone network | 2008: all customers with main fuses >63 A have hourly metering<br>2008: in May Vaasan Sähköverkko Oy announces AMM plans for 60,000 customers<br>2009: Vattenfall expects all of its 900,000 meters to support remote reading | Mandatory hourly metering for customers with fuses >63 A |
| Italy | Interval electronic | AMM: PLC and public telecommunications; proprietary solution | 2001: Enel (largest distribution network operator (DNO) – 85% of low-voltage customers) begins Telegestore project<br>2005: Acea Roma and Asmea Brescia start smart meter installations<br>2007: 32 million digital meters installed | Voluntary initiative by Enel; reduction of non-technical losses (theft) and to control contracted power more effectively |
| Northern Ireland | Keypad pre-payment | Remote management of meters via vend codes | 2000: roll-out by Northern Ireland Electricity (NIE) begins after initial trial in 200 homes<br>2009: approx. 222,000 installed | High costs of prepayment meters compared with credit electricity meters |
| Ontario | Interval | AMM: PLC and public telecommunications; open solution | 2007: target of 800,000 meters (20%)<br>2010: target of 4.5 million meters (100%) | Management of peak consumption to reduce investment in new generating capacity |
| Sweden | Interval; some Zigbee-enabled | AMR to begin with; more recently AMM; PLC and public telecommunications | 2003: legislation requires monthly readings for all electricity users by 1 July 2009 | Requirement to improve the accuracy of customer bills |

*Sources:* Villa (2008); Owen and Ward (2006, 2010); Ofgem (2006a); ERGEG (2007); Metering.com (2008); NIE (2009).

In the UK, the government has decided on a deployment model for households in Great Britain following a number of smart metering consultations. Instead of opting for either extreme, the final decision has been to adopt a centralized communications model. The model is based on suppliers retaining responsibility for the purchase and installation of meters. A separate national communications network will be set up to support the smart metering system. As a result, suppliers will still have strong incentives to provide the best products and services for their customers. The model also provides a standardized communications solution that has the potential to simplify industry processes in the future by centralizing data management (DECC, 2009a).

A centralized communications network is also helpful in providing a standard with which suppliers need to comply. The UK government has, however, also included minimum functionality requirements for meters. These include many of the additional features discussed in section 6.2.2, for example a connection through the home network to an external display, remote connection or disconnection as well as export metering.

Technology choice has differed depending on the specific drivers. Enel's business case was based mainly on improving operational efficiency. As such the demand response functionality of meters did not appear to be a high priority at the time of roll-out. The forthcoming roll-out in Great Britain aims to contribute to energy security and carbon reduction. Helping consumers to reduce their consumption and improve energy efficiency are among the main objectives of the roll-out. Functionality that improves the responsiveness of consumers to information and prices is therefore important. In California, Southern California Edison (SCE) submitted an initial business case for a metering system in 2005 that complied with the minimum requirements set out by the California Public Utilities Commission. The costs, however, outweighed the benefits. SCE decided to wait to develop a fully integrated, open solution with industry collaboration that allowed for two-way communication with devices in the home (SCE, 2005). Peak management and implementing time-varying tariffs were the main drivers behind smart metering in the state. A new business case was submitted by SCE in July 2007. This time, due in part to the improved functionality, the benefits significantly outweighed the costs (SCE, 2007).

The benefits of customer response are the most difficult to assess but have the potential to add a significant amount of value to smart metering roll-outs around the world. In the California utility business cases, the potential of demand response is identified as an opportunity to overcome the gap between total costs and operational benefits. Estimates of how responsive demand would be, as well as participation rates, were based on a state-wide pricing pilot conducted between July 2003 and September 2004. One of the main focuses of the pilot was on the impact of critical-peak pricing. Average prices were about 10 cents/kWh off-peak, 20 cents/kWh at peak times, and 60 cents/kWh during critical-peak hours. The critical peak could be announced on up to fifteen days during the year and customers were notified one day in advance. The average load reduction in response to the critical-peak price was 13 per cent. Response was more than double in hotter compared with cooler climates due to the prevalence of air conditioning (Herter *et al.*, 2007).

A smaller pricing pilot was conducted in Ontario between August 2006 and February 2007. Again, the focus was mainly on assessing the response of customers to different time-varying pricing structures. An average conservation effect of 6 per cent over the pilot period was observed. A critical-peak pricing scheme was also implemented, with critical-peak prices approximately three times off-peak prices. The average load reduction over both summer and winter periods during the critical peaks was 8.1 per cent. Impacts on customer bills were also computed for participants on different pricing schemes. The average savings for customers on a critical-peak pricing scheme were 4.2 per cent in comparison with a 1.8 per cent saving for customers on a simple time-of-use tariff (OEB, 2007).

Another small trial in Oregon, the Olympic Peninsula Project, tested automated demand response for electric water and space heating as well as time-of-use and real-time pricing rates. The trial involved 112 residential customers and ran from early 2006 to March 2007. A small number of commercial and municipal buildings were also involved. The main purpose of the project was to explore how smart grid technologies might allow resources to be despatched more efficiently using load and price signals. The small sample size makes it difficult to compare responses across residential contract types. The results show that overall consumers saved approximately 10 per cent on electricity bills compared with the previous year and that peak demand was reduced by 15 per cent (PNNL, 2007). A larger real-time pricing experiment in Illinois showed similar peak reductions, up to as much as 15 per cent. Findings also suggested that customers respond to blocks of time rather than to hour-by-hour variations (Faruqui, Hledik and Sergici, 2009). The results of these trials are summarized in Table 6.7.

Applying the lessons of international pricing pilots directly to other countries is not advisable due to differences in appliance usage patterns and climate, among other things. It is possible, however, to learn from the questions asked and trial designs implemented internationally. A number of countries, including Great Britain, are starting to undertake

Table 6.7 *Smart pricing trials*

| Trial | Timeframe | Sample size | Tariffs | Demand response |
|---|---|---|---|---|
| California Statewide Pricing Pilot | July 2003 to December 2004 | 2,500 residential and SMEs | TOU and CPP | Average critical peak reduction of 13% |
| Illinois Community Energy Cooperative | Started in 2003, ongoing | 750 initially; 1,500 by 2005 | RTP | Up to 15% peak reduction; 4% energy conservation |
| Olympic Peninsula Project | Early 2006 to March 2007 | 112 residential customers | TOU and RTP | Average peak reduction of 15% |
| Ontario Smart Price Pilot | August 2006 to March 2007 | 373 residential plus control group of 125 | TOU, CPP and RTP | CPP had highest impact on peak reductions (average 8.1%); 6% energy conservation |

TOU = time of use; RTP = real-time prices; CPP = critical peak pricing.

similar trials to assess the value of demand response. The Energy Demand Research Project (EDRP) managed by Ofgem, the British energy regulator, aims to investigate how customers respond to better information on their energy usage. This includes different ways of presenting information, e.g. through in-home displays or more feedback on bills, as well as through pricing interventions. More than 17,000 households had smart meters installed by the end of 2009 as part of the project (Ofgem, 2009). There is a range of other smart metering trials taking place around Europe. Some are centrally coordinated, for example in Ireland where a project with 25,000 homes is being managed by the Commission for Energy Regulation. Others are taking place independently – in Germany, for instance, a number of supplier-led trials are under way (Haney *et al.*, 2009).

## 6.5 Conclusions

There are considerable changes ahead for UK and international metering infrastructures. Deciding on smart metering roll-out strategies has been a complex and lengthy process and will continue to be so for many countries. This is not surprising given the costs and the number of stakeholders involved. So far, regulatory approaches have differed internationally, as have the drivers for smart metering. Going forward, the overarching aim will be to achieve a more responsive demand side that gives future energy systems more flexibility and reliability.

Technology choice is important but difficult. Many regulators have chosen minimum functionality requirements as a means of dealing with this issue. Additional functions, for example those that involve greater levels of interaction with customers and appliances, require more up-front investment but also have the potential to deliver considerable demand-response benefits in the future. An open and interoperable system allows for the integration of a variety of solutions as they develop and become more cost effective. It also helps to avoid lock-in to one specific technology.

Demand response benefits could add significant value to metering systems in Europe and elsewhere if smart meters are combined with dynamic pricing schemes. The operational benefits alone are often not sufficient to cover the costs of investing in smart metering. There is still uncertainty about the size of demand response benefits. We have, however, seen some convincing evidence from North America and we will see more evidence coming from European trials over the next few years.

Finally, there is no one-size-fits-all approach to rolling out smart meters. Deployment across countries has depended on country-specific drivers and also on factors such as existing market structure. Differences in deployment strategies have cost implications. For example, coordinating roll-outs on a regional and dual-fuel basis can reduce installation costs. This also has implications for service innovation and quality. Competition in the metering market has the potential to provide strong incentives to suppliers to offer new and improved services to their customers. The tension between simplifying industry processes on the one hand and providing more choice to customers on the other has been a defining feature of much smart metering policy debate.

Different countries and regions have decided to go in different directions. It will be interesting to follow up and compare how these models perform and how the actual costs and benefits weigh up over time. What we can say for now is that smart metering will facilitate a new and much more active role for energy customers in the coming decades. The extent to which this new role will translate into energy and cost savings remains to be studied.

## References

Bilton, M., Ramsay, C., Leach, M., Devine-Wright, H., Devine-Wright, P. and Kirschen, D. (2008). Domestic electricity consumption and demand-side participation: opportunities and challenges for the UK power system, in

Grubb, M., Jamasb, T. and Pollitt, M. (eds.), *Delivering a Low Carbon Electricity System: Technologies, Economics and Policy*, Cambridge: Cambridge University Press, pp. 207–28.

Borenstein, S., Jaske, M. and Rosenfeld, A. (2002). *Dynamic Pricing, Advanced Metering and Demand Response in Electricity Markets*, Center for the Study of Energy Markets, University of California Energy Institute.

Capgemini (2007). *Comparatif international des systèmes de télé-relève ou de télégestion et étude technico-économique visant à évaluer les conditions d'une migration du parc actuel de compteurs*, Capgemini Consulting.

Carbon Trust (2007). *Advanced Metering for SMEs: Carbon and Cost Savings*, London: Carbon Trust.

Darby, S. (2006). *The Effectiveness of Feedback on Energy Consumption: A Review for Defra of the Literature on Metering, Billing and Direct Displays*, Environmental Change Institute: University of Oxford.

DECC (2009a). *Impact Assessment of a GB-wide Smart Meter Rollout for the Domestic Sector*, London: Department of Energy and Climate Change.

DECC (2009b). *Towards a Smarter Future: Government Response to the Consultation on Electricity and Gas Smart Metering*, London: Department of Energy and Climate Change.

DPI (2007). *Advanced Metering Infrastructure Technology Trials Report*, Victoria, Australia: Department of Primary Industries.

DTI (2006). *Energy Billing and Metering: Changing Customer Behaviour*, London: Department of Trade and Industry.

DTI (2007). *Meeting the Energy Challenge: A White Paper on Energy*, London: Department of Trade and Industry.

Enel (2010). *Smart Meters: Enel and Endesa create 'Meters and More'*, online press release, 18 February, Brussels, Available at www.enel.com/en-GB/media/press_releases/release.aspx?iddoc=1629732, last accessed 9 August 2010.

ERGEG (2007). *Smart Metering with a Focus on Electricity Regulation*. Brussels: European Regulators' Group for Electricity and Gas.

ERGEG (2009). *Position Paper on Smart Grids*, Brussels: European Regulators' Group for Electricity and Gas.

EU (2006). Directive 2006/32/EC of the European Parliament and of the Council of 5 April 2006 on energy end-use efficiency and energy services and repealing Council Directive 93/76/EEC. *Official Journal of the European Union*.

EurActiv (2010). *Enel: Italy reaping first-mover benefits of smart meters*, Euractiv.com, 3 February 2010, Available at www.euractiv.com/en/print/italy-reaping-first-mover-benefits-smart-meters-enel, last accessed 9 August 2010.

Faruqui, A., Harris, D. and Hledik, R. (2009). *Unlocking the €53 billion Savings from Smart Meters in the EU*, The Brattle Group.

Faruqui, A., Hledik, R. and Sergici, S. (2009). Piloting the smart grid, *The Electricity Journal*, **22**(7): 55–69.

FERC (2006). Assessment of Demand Response and Advanced Metering, Federal Energy Regulatory Commission, Staff Report AD-06-2-000, Washington, DC.

FERC (2009). *FERC Approves First Smart Grid Proposal using New Policy*. Federal Energy Regulatory Commission, news release, 17 December, Washington, DC.

Frontier Economics (2007). *Smart Metering: A Report prepared for Centrica*, London: Frontier Economics.

Haney, A.B., Jamasb, T. and Pollitt, M. (2009). Smart Metering and Electricity Demand: Technology, Economics and International Experience, Cambridge: Electricity Policy Research Group Working Paper EPRG 0903/Cambridge Working Paper in Economics 0905.

Herter, K., McAuliffe, P. and Rosenfeld, A. (2007). An exploratory analysis of California residential customer response to critical peak pricing of electricity, *Energy* **32**(1): 25–34.

KPMG (2007). Cost Benefit Analysis of Smart Metering and Direct Load Control – Workstream 3: Retailer Impacts Phase 1 Report. Report for the Ministerial Council on Energy Smart Meter Working Group, KPMG, Australia.

Meeus, L., Saguan, M., Glachant, J. and Belmans, R. (2010). Smart Regulation for Smart Grids, EUI Working Papers 2010/45, Florence: Florence School of Regulation.

Metering.com (2008). *Smart meter deployment for Finnish utility*, 6 May, Available at www.metering.com/node/12385, last accessed 9 August 2010.

NERA (2007). Cost Benefit Analysis of Smart Metering and Direct Load Control: Phase I Overview Report. Report for the Ministerial Council on Energy Smart Meter Working Group, NERA Economic Consulting, Sydney, Australia.

NERA (2008). Cost Benefit Analysis of Smart Metering and Direct Load Control: Overview Report for Consultation. Report for the Ministerial Council on Energy Smart Meter Working Group, NERA Economic Consulting, Sydney, Australia.

NIE (2009). *NIE Energy Limited: Annual Report and Accounts*, Belfast: NIE Energy.

Nordgren, E. (2008). *Sweden: Project AMR – Automatic Meter Reading*, [presentation] Toveiskommunikasjon i Norge 2008, Gardemoen, Oslo, 21 May.

OEB (2005). Smart Meter Implementation Plan, Report of the Board to the Minister, Ontario Energy Board.

OEB (2007). Smart Price Pilot Final Report, Report prepared by IBM and eMeter Strategic Consulting for Ontario Energy Board.

Ofgem (2006a). *Domestic Metering Innovation* [consultation document. Ref 20/06], London: Office of Gas and Electricity Markets.

Ofgem (2006b). *Domestic Metering Innovation – Next Steps* [decision document. Ref 107/06] London: Office of Gas and Electricity Markets.

Ofgem (2009). *Energy Demand Research Project: Review of Progress for period September 2008 to March 2009* [Ref 115/09] London: Office of Gas and Electricity Markets.

Owen, G. and Ward, J. (2010). *Smart Pre-payment in Great Britain*, London: Sustainability First.

Owen, G. and Ward, J. (2006). *Smart Meters: Commercial, Policy and Regulatory Drivers*. London: Sustainability First.

Owen, J. and Ward, J. (2007). *Smart Meters in Great Britain: The Next Steps?* London: Sustainability First.

PNNL (2007). *Pacific Northwest Gridwise Testbed Demonstration Projects: Part 1 – Olympic Peninsula Project*, Pacific Northwest National Laboratory, prepared for the US Department of Energy, Richland, Washington.

Rogai, S. (2006). *ENEL's metering system and telegestore project*, [presentation] NARUC Conference, Washington, 19 February.

SCE (2005). Testimony supporting application for approval of advanced metering infrastructure deployment strategy and cost recovery mechanism: Volume 1 – Business Vision, Management Philosophy, and Summary of Business Case Analysis. Southern California Edison before the Public Utilities Commission of the State of California, Rosemead, California, 30 March.

SCE (2007). Edison Smartconnect deployment funding and cost recovery: Financial assessment and cost benefit analysis. Southern California Edison before the Public Utilities Commission of the State of California, Rosemead, California, 5 December.

Spees, K. and Lave, L.B. (2007). Demand response and electricity market efficiency, *Electricity Journal*, **20**(3): 69–85.

Stadler, I. (2008). Power grid balancing of energy systems with high renewable energy penetration by demand response, *Utilities Policy*, **16**(2008): 90–8.

Strbac, G., Jenkins, N. and Green, T. (2006). *Future Network Technologies: Report to DTI*, London: Department of Trade and Industry.

Villa, F. (2008). The Italian experience in regulating smart metering. Slides from *Energyforum – Smart metering European opportunities and solutions*. Amsterdam, 27–28 February.

Wissner, M. and Growitsch, C. (2007). *Die Liberalisierung des Zähl- und Messwesens*. Wissenschaftliches Institut für Infrastruktur und Kommunikationsdienste, Bad Honnef, Nordrhein-Westfalen.

# 7 Smart domestic appliances as enabling technology for demand-side integration: modelling, value and drivers

*Vera Silva, Vladimir Stanojevic, Marko Aunedi, Danny Pudjianto and Goran Strbac*

## 7.1 Introduction

Decarbonization of future electricity systems requires a significant proportion of electricity consumption to be supplied from nuclear, carbon capture and storage (CCS) plant and renewable sources. Since nuclear and CCS plant are less flexible than, for instance, natural gas-fired combined cycle plants, and renewable sources such as wind, solar and tidal are intermittent, this creates serious challenges to the way the current system is operated. In order to ensure that the system is capable of maintaining a supply and demand balance, the reduction in generation flexibility as a result of incorporating more low-carbon generation technologies has to be balanced with an increase in flexibility from demand. Consequently demand-side flexibility needs to be developed and smart domestic appliances can play an important role (IEA, 2008). In order to gain insight and understanding of the role and value of smart appliances, comprehensive studies of its economic value are required. Such analysis needs to consider relevant parameters such as consumers' behaviour and acceptance, appliance technology and future scenarios of power-system development regarding flexibility of generation and network capacity.

This chapter presents a framework to assess the value of smart appliances, as flexible demand, to increase system flexibility and to provide new sources of ancillary services. The increased flexibility will improve system efficiency, reduce operating costs and carbon emissions, and increase utilization of renewable sources; from these benefits the value of smart appliances will be derived. However, any decrease in the value of energy services received as a result of, for instance, inconvenience caused by curtailment or rescheduling of consumption should, in theory, be deducted from such benefits. At the core of the framework is a model that simulates annual system operation, scheduling simultaneously generation and smart appliances, in order to minimize system operating costs.

This takes into account system security and operational constraints. In addition, the role of smart appliances to support network operation is studied. Realistic appliance data and results from consumer behaviour studies, as well as wind and demand historical data, are used.

In order to investigate the drivers of the value of smart appliances, a set of case studies has been performed, considering a range of scenarios with respect to generation flexibility, wind penetration, smart appliances technology uptake and network constraints. The results obtained suggest that the major drivers for the value of smart appliances are the flexibility of the system's conventional generation mix and wind penetration and network congestion. The value of smart appliances is higher in systems with inflexible generation and high wind penetration. In addition, value increases in highly congested networks. Finally, consumer flexibility and appliance energy consumption were found to influence the value of the technology.

## 7.2 Role of smart appliances

### *7.2.1 Vision of smart appliances implementation*

Household appliances form a significant part of energy consumption, representing around 10 per cent of the total annual energy consumption in the UK (value calculated using data from Stamminger, 2009). The principle of 'smart' operation is to modify appliance operation patterns according to the system's needs. Hence, smart appliances can be used as sources of demand-side flexibility and provide different services to the electricity system, such as generation/demand balancing, frequency control, standing reserve, peak reduction and network-congestion management. A schematic vision of smart appliance implementation is shown in Figure 7.1.

The feasibility of this concept is particularly supported by recent technology developments, such as new information and communication and appliance technologies. The deployment of these technologies also requires strong political and regulatory initiatives, such as the recent decision for the smart metering roll-out in the UK (DECC, 2009).

### *7.2.2 Smart appliance technology*

Many appliances are already equipped with delayed start functions[1] that could be used by consumers to change their starting times, for example,

[1] This is a function that allows the consumer to postpone the start time by a fixed time period.

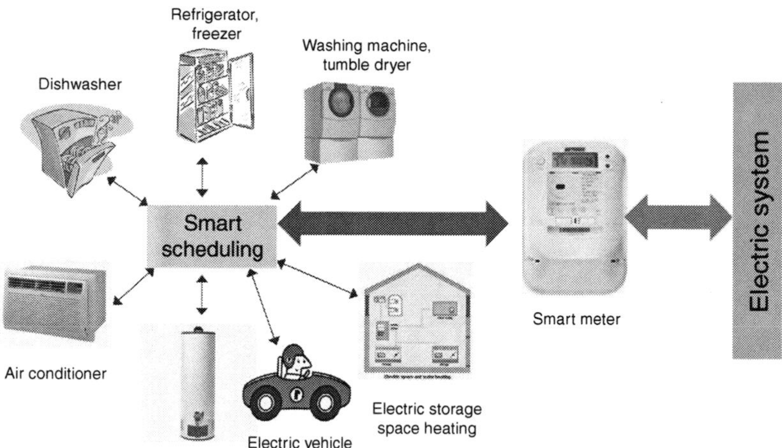


Figure 7.1 Vision of smart appliances implementation structure.

in order to take advantage of time-of-use tariffs.[2] Smart appliances go beyond this by having more decentralized (automatic) intelligent control that may or may not involve the intervention of the consumer.

Smart appliance technology consists mostly of two modifications to the existing technology:

- The more common and less expensive is to enable the appliance to communicate with external sources that will remotely control its operation.
- Recently developed prototype appliances with a larger thermal inertia can be used as a form of electricity storage.

Such appliances are enabled with technologies to allow interaction with the electricity system. Such interaction can involve directions to modify operation cycles, such as shifting them over time or interrupting them for a limited period of time. These appliances will be comparatively more flexible than the existing ones.

The flexibility provided by different appliances depends on operation patterns and uses. Some appliances, such as refrigerators and freezers, have a nearly constant electricity demand. Others, such as water heating and space cooling/heating (air conditioning, space heating and heat pumps), are used during large periods of the day. All these possess thermal inertia. A different type, such as washing machines and dishwashers,

[2] Time-of-use tariffs are different predefined prices of electricity for different blocks of hours. The Economy 7 in the UK is one example.

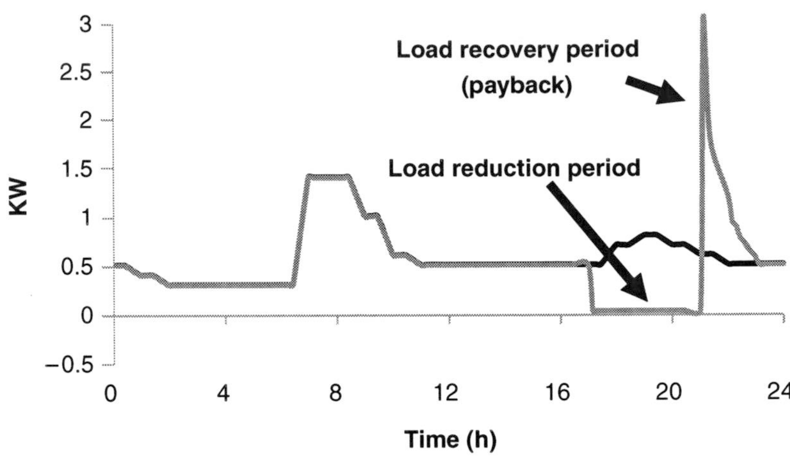


Figure 7.2 Payback effect generated by the process of energy restoration.

consumes electricity during a fixed-duration cycle (for example, two hours) required to perform their task. They are typically operated once per day. The demand of appliances can be modified according to the needs of the system. Based on their characteristics, two main demand-side management actions can be applied:

- Interrupting the demand of appliances with thermal inertia for short periods with minimal impact on consumer comfort.
- Shifting the demand of appliances that operate in limited-duration cycles. Their starting time can be anticipated or postponed within a certain time interval allowed by the consumer.

Every action that modifies the normal operation pattern of a group of appliances needs to be performed with care. Appliances with thermal inertia, if interrupted and simultaneously reconnected, may cause an undesirable impact known as the payback effect, in which loads appreciably increase in subsequent periods.[3] This phenomenon may cause undesirable demand spikes, as shown in Figure 7.2. To avoid this spike the reconnection of load needs to be carefully scheduled.

Appliances that operate per cycle, when shifted, reduce a block of demand that is fully recovered later, once the cycle of the appliance takes

[3] The payback effect is the increase in power demand due to energy restoration of controlled loads that appears in the period immediately after reconnecting to the system the loads that were disconnected. This phenomenon is mainly related with thermal loads and is a function of the duration of disconnection and load characteristics.

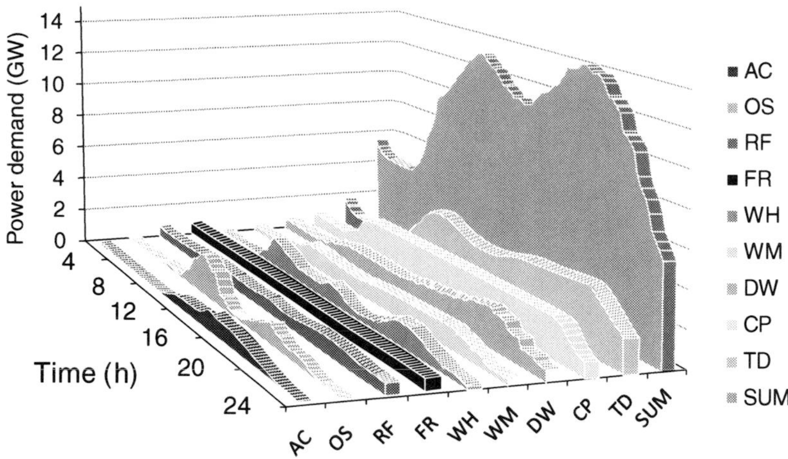


Figure 7.3 Total demand from domestic appliances in the UK. Notes: AC = air conditioner; OS = over and stove; RF = refrigerator; FR = freezer; WH = electric water heater; WM = washing machine; DW = dishwasher; CP = heating circulation pump; TD = tumble dryer; SUM = sum of all appliances.

place. Again the rescheduling of its operation needs to be undertaken with care to avoid the simultaneous operation of all shifted appliances. For instance, the set points for frequency-triggered interruptors for home refrigerators can be randomly set at different values for different homes so as to ensure a smooth decrease and subsequent increase in refrigeration loads in response to a frequency excursion below 50 Hz. Failing to study the impact of all effects of changing appliances' normal operation patterns may give over-optimistic estimates of demand-side management.

The contribution of an appliance to system flexibility depends on its placement within the daily demand profile. The contribution is higher when the operation pattern coincides with more critical operation periods such as peak demand. An estimate of the diversified daily demand of different appliances, in the UK, is based on Stamminger (2009) and is illustrated in Figure 7.3. It is possible to observe that some appliances, e.g. refrigerators (RF) and freezers (FR), have a nearly constant demand, while others, such as dishwashers (DWs), have a higher demand in the evening. The aggregated system demand from domestic appliances is not insignificant, reaching an estimated peak of 14 GW in the UK system.[4] Consequently there is a potential to use this type of load to provide demand flexibility.

[4] Estimate obtained using appliance energy demand and penetration data obtained from Stamminger (2009) and considering a total number of 25 million households in the UK.

Without loss of generality, this work focuses on a batch of shiftable appliances composed of DW, washing machine (WM), washer-dryer[5] (WD) and interruptible appliances composed of refrigerators (RF) and freezers (FR). These are selected based on data availability and flexibility potential. The methodology proposed is sufficiently general to be applied to other appliances.

### *7.2.3 Smart appliances' flexibility potential*

To quantify the value of these appliances, information regarding 'smart' options is required. Taking the example of a WM, the following smart operation options were identified in Stamminger (2009):

1. Delay the start time of the washing cycle.
2. Interrupt the heating phase up to a certain time.
3. Reduce the power demand by automatically choosing a lower temperature for the programme and prolonging the washing time.
4. Prolong the final rinsing phase.
5. Connect the WM to a hot-water supply to avoid the higher demand used during the water-heating phase.

Considering that options 2 to 4 reduce the efficiency of the appliance per cycle and option 5 requires viable alternatives to heat the water, option 1 is chosen for this study. To obtain an approximate estimate of the available capacity from a specific appliance, its diversified demand profile and demand during one cycle are required. An example of these data, for the WM, in the UK, is presented in Figures 7.4 and 7.5, respectively.

The diversified profile represents the aggregated and normalized demand of a WM as seen from the system. Figure 7.4 illustrates that most households use their washing machines early in the morning (around 7 am) and in the evening (around 8 pm), reflecting consumers' habits to wash their clothes before leaving for work or upon returning home in the evening. The distribution of demand per washing cycle (Figure 7.5) shows that demand is larger during the water-heating phase at the beginning of the cycle. A smaller demand rise can be seen in the spinning phase close to cycle completion.

## 7.3 Consumer acceptance

When conducting a study about demand-side flexibility, the role of the consumer cannot be neglected. Even if the smart appliance technology is

[5] The WD is a combination of a WM and a tumble dryer (TD) whose consumption cycle corresponds to the cycle of a WM followed by the cycle of a dryer.

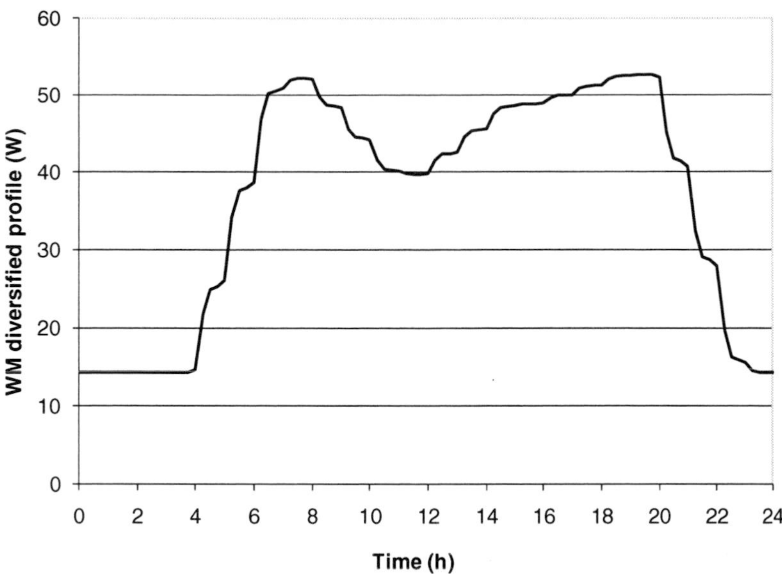


Figure 7.4 Diversified demand of a WM in the UK.

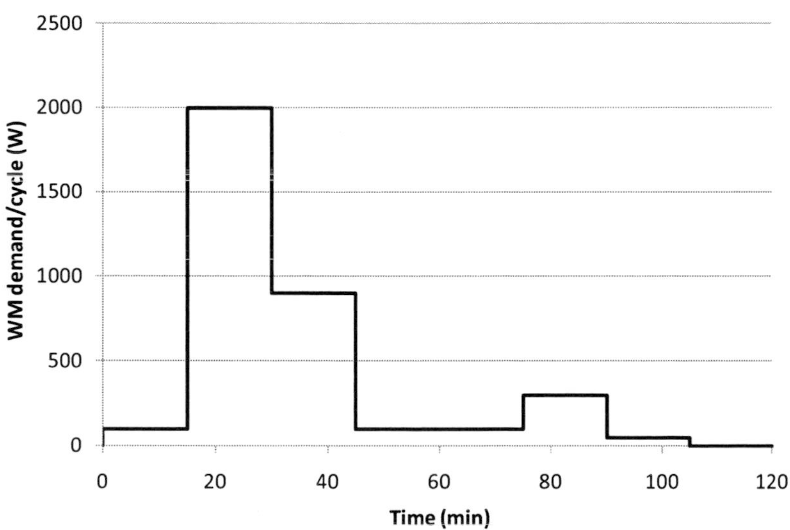


Figure 7.5 Consumption of a WM per washing cycle (reference temperature of 40°).

Table 7.1 *Smart appliances acceptance survey*[6]

| | Shifting operation | |
|---|---|---|
| Device type | Acceptance | Delay |
| Washing machine (WM) | 77% | Up to 3h |
| Washer-dryer (WD) | 77% | Up to 3h |
| Dishwasher (DW) | 77% | More than 3h |

available, economically viable and able to bring environmental benefits, its deployment cannot be achieved without engaging the appliance end-user. A smart appliances consumer acceptance study has been carried out in the SMART-A project (Mert, 2008).

This study is based on quantitative and qualitative consumer research using interviews, questionnaires and focus groups and is conducted in the UK, among other countries. It aims to reveal to what extent consumers will allow load shifting, including, for example, delaying the start of washing cycles or intermediate interruptions of the operation of appliances. The research questions were focused on the readiness and flexibility of consumers to change their behaviour and the benefits they expected. The study concludes that the acceptance level is very high and consumers have a rather positive attitude towards smart appliances. However, there will always be a gap between real actions and attitudes, so these findings have to be interpreted cautiously.

In addition, consumers have many objections and preconditions regarding the use of smart appliances. The acceptance of the smart operation mode is highly appliance-specific and cannot be generalized. These conclusions are reinforced by a set of interviews with appliance industry representatives involved in previous smart appliance consumer research initiatives. Some of the relevant quantitative results are given in Table 7.1.

In all cases the majority (77 per cent) of the consumers would accept postponing operation cycles. The majority would expect an economic compensation for shifting their appliances in the form of reduction in electricity prices or a discount on the electricity bill. A minority would accept shifting their appliances if it was guaranteed that this was contributing to increasing their use of clean energy. The level of flexibility, however, depends on the appliance. Washing clothes is a very sensitive

[6] These results are drawn from a population of 11,000 consumer surveys, ten phone interviews and three focus groups, all in the UK.

area because consumers are reluctant to leave the device operating unattended and the clothes wet inside the machine, so only short delays are allowed. For DW, the flexibility is comparatively higher (more than three hours) because consumers do not attach the same importance to the time when the device operates. Finally, the smart operation of refrigerators and freezers shows very high acceptance as long as the safety in terms of food quality is guaranteed.

The quantitative information about consumer flexibility for different appliances is included in the process of quantification of the value of smart appliances, enabling the understanding of how their attitudes may impact the overall potential of the technology.

## 7.4 Framework to quantify the value of smart appliances as a source of flexibility

The main goal of this section is to outline a framework to provide quantitative estimates of the economic value of smart appliances, as a source of system flexibility, and their contribution to the demand–supply balance and network operation. To this end system operation algorithms have been developed and are briefly described in the following sections.

### *7.4.1 Smart appliances modelling*

Interruption of appliance operation is modelled as frequency-responsive load, referred to as dynamic demand (DD) (Short *et al.*, 2007; Aunedi *et al.*, 2008). In this analysis, domestic refrigerators have been studied as appliances enabling DD, although a much broader range of domestic appliances could participate in the scheme.[7] The mechanism of DD control is to react to frequency deviations from the nominal value by adjusting the operating cycles of refrigerators while at the same time maintaining their inside temperatures within the required range. This has the effect of fast reduction of load in case of sudden frequency drop (e.g. following an unforeseen generation loss), helping the system to contain frequency within the boundaries allowed by the system operation rules.

The contribution of a large number of refrigerators to frequency response is quantified using a dynamic model of the power system, simulating at the same time switching refrigerators on and off under DD control, and the dynamic behaviour of large generators.

[7] Examples of appliances that might be considered for DD include refrigerators, freezers, air conditioners, water heaters, certain types of pumps, ovens and heating systems.

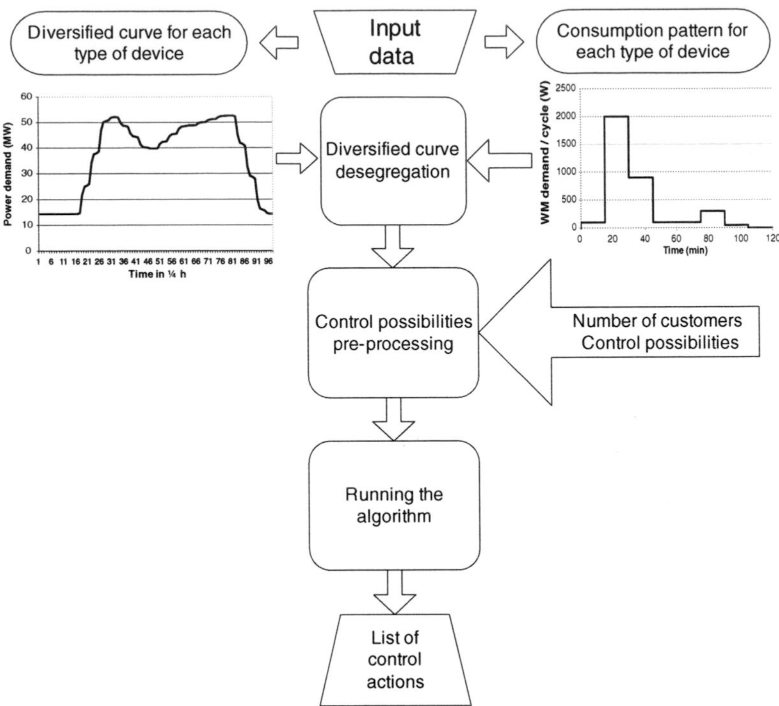


Figure 7.6 Appliance shifting algorithm.

This procedure allowed the response contribution for the entire population of refrigerators in the UK markets to be quantified. A total number of 40 million appliances was assumed to exist in UK households. This value is used in calculations to offset some of the primary and high-frequency response normally provided by part-loaded conventional generators.

Shiftable appliances operation scheduling is modelled taking into account a number of factors. These include the appliance's demand per cycle, an estimate of the number of appliances available for control, at each time period, and the maximum shifting time allowed. Figure 7.6 presents the overall structure of the scheduling algorithm.

This algorithm can be incorporated into larger optimization problems such as the system scheduling and network-congestion models used in this work. The general structure of these tools is described in the following sections and further details can be found in Aunedi *et al.* (2008), Silva *et al.* (2009) and Stanojevic *et al.* (2009).

### 7.4.2 *System scheduling*

The quantification of the value of smart appliances requires a detailed chronologic simulation of power system operation, including all relevant system-operation constraints. Annual studies are carried out to consider all daily and seasonal changes in demand and intermittent generation output.

To this end, the framework developed includes the following features:

- Response and reserve requirements are computed offline taking into account the stochastic behaviour of wind, demand and generation outages.
- Reserve is provided by a combination of spinning and standing reserve. Standing reserve is provided by smart appliances.
- Response is provided by a combination of conventional generators and DD.
- $CO_2$ emissions from fossil fuel-based electricity generation are modelled considering International Panel on Climate Changes (IPCC) emission factors.[8]

The structure of the scheduling algorithm used is presented in Figure 7.7 and is composed of:

- Step 1: commitment and scheduling of generation from generating units to meet the forecasted net demand (demand minus wind forecasted). Response and reserve requirements are incorporated as deterministic constraints.
- Step 2: a synthetic time series of realized net demand is produced by generating random imbalances of wind generation and demand. The system is then redispatched to meet the net demand actually realized. This step represents the deployment of the operating reserves required to cover for wind and demand deviations from the forecasts.

Generation costs include start-up and fuel cost. Generation output is constrained by its technical limits (maximum capacity and minimum stable generation) and dynamic ratings (ramp rates and minimum up and down times). The above steps are repeated for each day in the year.

The value of smart appliances is obtained by comparing the results (operating costs, emissions level, wind curtailment) of the base case with inflexible demand and the case where smart appliances provide demand-side flexibility. The quantification of the value of DD to system response requires the simulation of Step 1, which yields operation costs, emissions and wind curtailed. Assessment of the contribution of smart appliances

[8] Emission factors database: www.ipcc-nggip.iges.or.jp/EFDB/main.php

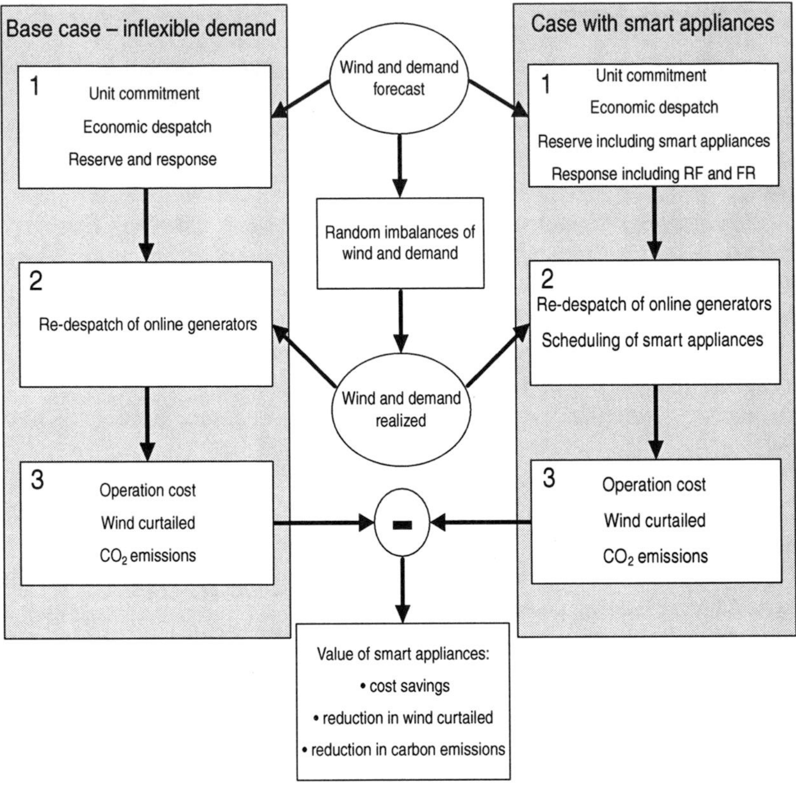


Figure 7.7 Structure of the system scheduling algorithm.

to standing reserve requires the simulation of reserve deployment, i.e. all steps need to be considered.

### *7.4.3 Network congestion model*

To model the impact of the network congestion on generator outputs, an optimal power-flow problem needs to be solved. The methodology is based on a daily scheduling optimization where smart appliances are modelled as a part of the problem constraints, beside generation and network constraints. In this work, a multi-period optimal power-flow model with flexible demand is developed to quantify the value of smart appliances to support network operation. Additional details about the model can be found in Silva *et al.* (2009) and Stanojevic *et al.* (2009).

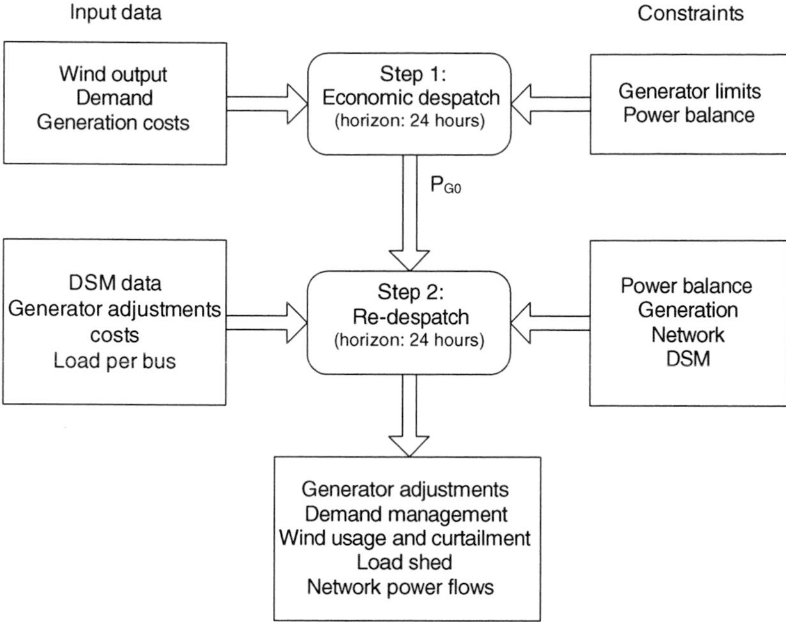


Figure 7.8 Structure of the network congestion algorithm.

The overall structure of the model is presented in Figure 7.8. Broadly the model follows a two-step approach:

- Step 1: generation dispatch considering infinite network capacity. The minimum cost solution is obtained.
- Step 2: adjustment of generation output including network constraints. Whenever network congestion occurs, the generation output (from Step 1) is adjusted and a more expensive solution is obtained, which often leads to wind curtailment. These adjustments are the result of minimization of the total generation costs.

The associated increase in cost is called the congestion cost.

If, to relieve network congestion, the output of wind generators is reduced and replaced by an increase in fossil fuel plants output, wind is wasted and carbon emissions increase.

## 7.5 Quantification of the value of smart appliances

This section presents a set of case studies where the value of smart appliances is estimated for different system applications.

Table 7.2 *Wind-installed capacity and penetration scenarios*

| | | | | |
|---|---|---|---|---|
| Wind installed (GW) | 10 | 20 | 30 | 40 |
| Wind penetration (% of total energy demand) | 8 | 16 | 24 | 32 |

Table 7.3 *Conventional generation plant mix*

| | Must-run (GW) | Low flexible plant (GW) | High flexible plant (GW) |
|---|---|---|---|
| LF – low flexibility | 12 | 26 | 42 |
| HF – high flexibility | 8 | 26 | 46 |

### *7.5.1 Value of smart appliances in system scheduling and balancing*

The set of case studies determines the value of WM, DW and WD for providing standing reserve and contributing to the generation/demand balancing; and the value of RF and FR providing frequency response services. The studies were carried out for different conventional generation mixes and wind penetrations.

The value of smart appliances comes from displacing part of the reserve (Case 1) and response (Case 2), provided by synchronized plant. This reduces the need for part loading plants (having higher efficiency losses) and the total amount of inflexible generation output.[9] This increases systems' ability to accommodate wind generation and thereby reduces operation costs, wind energy curtailed and carbon emissions.

#### *7.5.1.1 Case study 1 – value of shifting appliances operation*

To assess the sensitivity of the value of smart appliances to conventional generation flexibility and wind penetration, four different levels of wind penetration (Table 7.2) are combined with two different conventional generation mixes (Table 7.3), giving a total of eight generation mix scenarios. These generation mixes are used to supply a system with 25 million domestic households, a total annual energy demand of 382 TWh and a peak demand of 66.7 GW.

[9] Inflexible generation output is the total output from conventional generation that cannot be reduced at a specific instant in time. Examples of this are the output of a must-run plant with no ramping capability and the minimum stable generation output of a thermal plant once synchronized to the system.

Table 7.4 *Smart appliances information*

| Type of appliance | Penetration factor | Shifting capabilities | Duration per cycle | No. of cycles per day (million) |
|---|---|---|---|---|
| Washing machine 1h | 20% | 1h | 2h | 5 |
| Washing machine 2h | 20% | 2h | 2h | 5 |
| Washing machine 3h | 20% | 3h | 2h | 5 |
| Aggregated WM | 60% | Up to 3 hours | 2h | 15 |
| Dishwasher | 80% | 6h | 2h | 20 |
| Washer-dryer (WM+TD) | 20% | 3h | 4h | 5.3 |

A batch of controllable appliances composed of WM, DW and WD is considered. A summary of the smart appliances data and allowed shifting times is presented in Table 7.4. These appliances represent an annual demand of 34 TWh, corresponding to approximately 10 per cent of total system annual demand.

To schedule the shifting of appliances, an estimate of the number of appliances connected at different hours of the day is required. This is obtained with an algorithm that uses both the diversified demand profile and demand per cycle for each appliance type, as shown by Figures 7.4 and 7.5, respectively, for the case of a WM. This distribution of the cycles during the day is important to determine when controllable demand is available. Typical appliance usage patterns for the UK are shown in Figure 7.9.

The monetary value of shifting appliance operation, to provide standing reserve[10] and contribute to the demand/balance, is shown in Figure 7.10. This corresponds to the annual fuel cost reduction obtained per appliance for each conventional generation mix and wind penetration.

The trends obtained show:

- the value of appliances increases with wind penetration for each conventional generation mix
- the value is higher for the low flexible conventional generation mix.

The minimum value in all cases is obtained for 8 per cent wind penetration. All systems are able to accommodate this amount of wind without

[10] Deterministic reserve constraints are structurally the same for each run, but they take into account an increased volume of reserve requirements due to wind uncertainty. The unused part of the available smart appliance capacity is assumed to contribute to standing reserve simultaneously with generators, and the model decides on the optimal allocation.

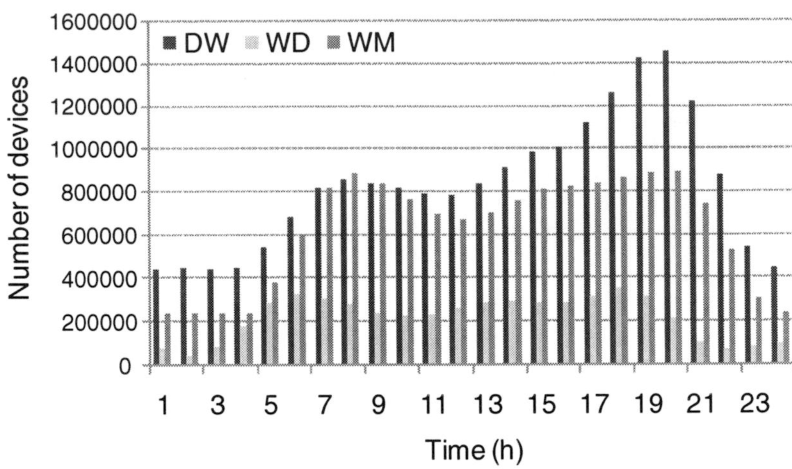


Figure 7.9 Estimated number of appliances starting a cycle during a day.

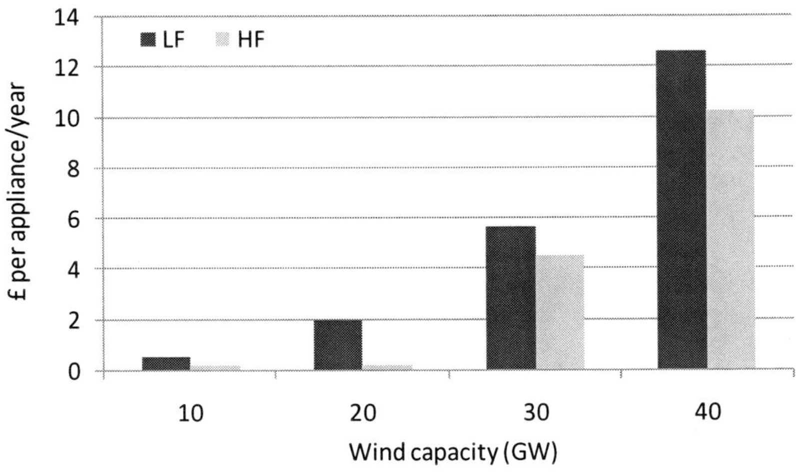


Figure 7.10 Annual value per appliance.

the need for additional flexibility. This reduces the potential of smart appliances.

For high wind penetration (above 25 per cent) the value of appliances increases significantly. For large wind penetrations the system is not able to accommodate all wind generation. The increase in flexibility generated by smart appliances reduces wind curtailed (see Figure 7.11), leading to

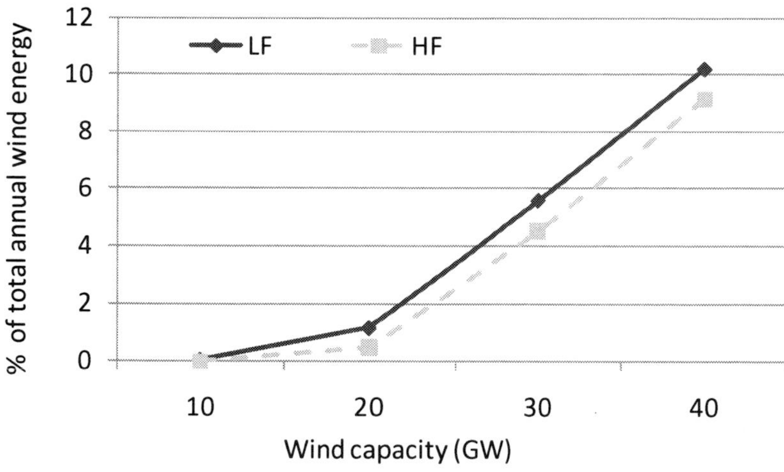


Figure 7.11 Reduction in wind curtailed driven by smart appliances.

a higher value per appliance. Figure 7.11 shows the reduction in wind curtailed. It can be seen that the wind curtailment reduction is higher for the LF system and increases with wind penetration for all cases. There is a clear relation between the increase in system flexibility driven by smart appliances and the system ability for accommodating wind.

Figure 7.12 shows the allocation of the value to different types of appliances. The largest contribution of the smart appliances value is from the DW because this device is the one with higher shifting flexibility. The WD has a comparatively higher value than the WM because it has a higher consumption per operation cycle. Each cycle shifted has a higher impact on demand. The proportion of the total annual energy shifted allocated to each device is as follows: DW 48 per cent, aggregated WM 23 per cent and WD 29 per cent. The shifting flexibility of the appliance plays an important role and for the same WM shifted for 1h is responsible for 6.8 per cent, for 2h 7.8 per cent and for 3h 8.1 per cent of the total shifted energy. These numbers correspond to the LF system with 20 GW wind but the results are consistent for all cases.

Figure 7.13 shows the reduction in carbon emissions. This illustrates that smart appliances bring higher benefits for low flexible conventional generation systems and increasing wind penetrations.

This confirms that in systems with large wind penetration and lower conventional generation flexibility, the value of alternative sources of flexibility, such as smart appliances, is higher.

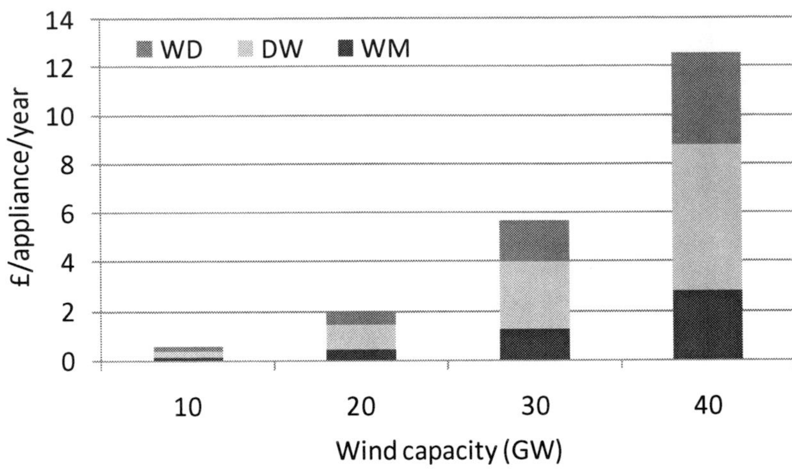


Figure 7.12 Annual value per appliance for different appliances for the LF system.

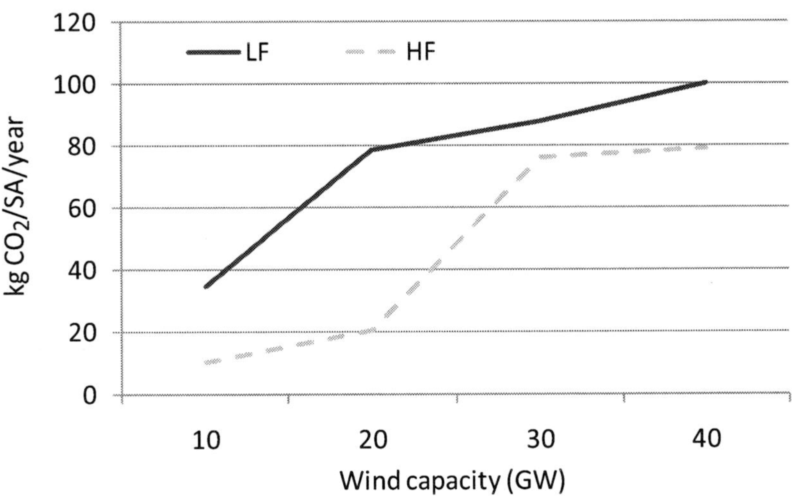


Figure 7.13 Reduction in $CO_2$ emissions driven by smart appliances.

*7.5.1.2 Case study 2 – value of dynamic demand*

The goal of this study is to quantify the value of dynamic demand, represented by FR and RF, used as part of system response. This will alleviate the requirements set upon conventional plants, thus enabling

Table 7.5 *Capacity of different generation technologies in DD studies*

| Type | High ramp rate | Low ramp rate | Must-run | Wind |
|---|---|---|---|---|
| Capacity (GW) | 50 | 20 | 6 / 8 / 10 | 0 / 10 / 20 / 30 |

the units to operate at improved fuel efficiencies and also enhancing the ability to absorb variable wind output.

Two models were used to assess the value of DD. The dynamic response model simulates frequency fluctuations in time (typically second by second) as a result of imbalance between demand and generation. Based on its outputs, the scheduling model quantifies savings in fuel costs, increased wind energy absorbed and the corresponding carbon emissions avoided as a result of using DD. The modelling framework is mostly based on studies performed in DECC (2008).

Table 7.5 summarizes the generation mixes that were tested with respect to the impact of DD (generator types used are the same as in case study 1). A series of simulations for this system was performed for all combinations of wind and must-run capacities. The impact of DD (cost, emissions and wind curtailment) was found by comparing the annual results in cases with and without DD. The value of DD was then quantified per refrigerator. These benefits can in turn be compared with the cost of installing DD control in refrigerators to indicate whether introducing such a scheme would be economically viable.

Figure 7.14 and Table 7.6 show the annual value of DD per appliance. As for the previous study, the value grows with the penetration of must-run and wind generation. This is expected as lower flexibility of the conventional generation yields a higher value of alternative sources of flexibility, and this need increases with high penetrations of wind generation.

Per-appliance savings in a system without wind would be around £2.20 p.a., and for 10 GW this would amount to around £3 p.a., irrespective of must-run capacity (the savings value here refers only to the fuel cost avoided and does not include the economic value of reduced carbon emissions). When increasing wind to 20 GW and 30 GW, the per-appliance benefits increase and start diverging for different must-run capacities. For the highest wind penetration analyzed (30 GW), the benefits increase by an order of magnitude compared with the no-wind case. This

Table 7.6 *Annual savings and emission reduction from dynamic demand*

| Cost savings per fridge (£/app) | | | | Emission reduction per fridge ($kgCO_2$/app) | | | |
|---|---|---|---|---|---|---|---|
| Wind | Must-run | | | Wind | Must-run | | |
| GW | 6 | 8 | 10 | GW | 6 | 8 | 10 |
| 0 | 2.17 | 2.22 | 2.24 | 0 | 12.62 | 9.92 | 8.43 |
| 10 | 2.92 | 2.95 | 2.96 | 10 | 13.02 | 9.88 | 7.98 |
| 20 | 5.31 | 6.53 | 7.98 | 20 | 50.49 | 72.80 | 101.81 |
| 30 | 25.64 | 29.26 | 32.45 | 30 | 386.22 | 448.91 | 513.97 |

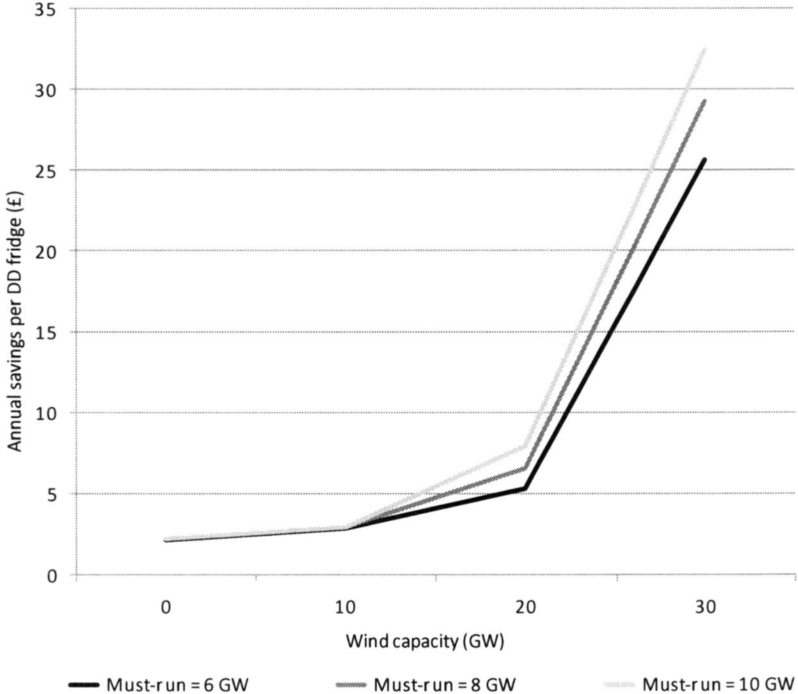


Figure 7.14 Annual savings from DD per appliance.

phenomenon primarily occurs as a result of reduced wind curtailment and is even more evident for the case of carbon emission reductions, which increase almost exponentially when moving from 10 GW to 30 GW of wind.

Table 7.7 *Range of smart appliances' value for different applications*

| Appliance | Service | Value (£/appliance/year) |
|---|---|---|
| WM | Standing reserve | [0.15–2.79] |
| DW | and balancing | [0.32–6.00] |
| WD | | [0.19–3.82] |
| RF and FR | Response | [2.17–32.45] |

The above results allow the identification of key value drivers for DD. One major value driver is the installed capacity of wind: with large wind penetrations, overall response requirements increase. This means that the number of plants needed to operate part loaded will be reduced when DD are applied, bringing benefits to the system. Another key driver is the capacity of must-run units. In a system with large must-run capacity, the room for conventional units to generate electricity and at the same time provide system services would contract, so the value of DD and the flexibility they provide to the system becomes higher.

#### *7.5.1.3 Summary of results from case studies 1 and 2*

The estimated ranges of value of smart appliances for different studies are summarized in Table 7.7. This represents a summary of the results obtained from the studies of the previous sections to give an indication of the broad potential of the technology. More details about these studies can be found in Aunedi *et al.* (2008) and Silva *et al.* (2009).

For the case of response, reserve and system balancing, the lower value of the appliances is obtained for low wind penetrations and more flexible systems. Interruptible appliances present a higher value; however, a direct comparison should not be made as they are used for different applications and the generation mix is not exactly the same. The value of different shiftable appliances depends on the shifting flexibility allowed by the consumer (this explains why the DW has higher value).

The economic benefits need to be compared with the cost of developing and implementing the appliance control technology to determine its economic viability. An estimated range of the cost of smart appliances is obtained from appliance research studies, as presented in Seebach *et al.* (2009). A summary of total investment cost, including appliance and communication infrastructure, is presented in Table 7.8. This cost assumes a mass-market smart appliance deployment and the existence of smart metering in all households. If the cost of smart meters had to be added to the cost of deploying smart appliances, they would not be

Table 7.8 *Investment cost of different smart appliances (taken from Seebach* et al., *2009)*

| | WM | WD | DW | RF and FR |
|---|---|---|---|---|
| Investment cost (£/appliance/year) | [2–4] | [2–4] | [2–4] | [6–8] |

*Source:* Seebach *et al.*, 2009.

economically viable. These values are obtained using an interest rate of 10 per cent and a technology life cycle of twenty years.

Comparing the value obtained with the cost of the technology suggests that the majority of cases are economically viable, however with a low profit margin.

#### *7.5.1.4 Case study 3 – value of smart appliances in network congestion management*

The UK system could be conveniently divided into sixteen areas, representing fourteen major transmission boundaries, as shown in Figure 7.15 (National Grid). Line capacities (in MW) are given in brackets next to each line, and peak demand for each bus is indicated by an arrow. Total installed generation capacity is 95 GW. There are five areas with wind generation (buses 1, 2, 4, 6 and 15). Installed wind capacity is 13 GW and total wind energy forecasted is about 40 TWh. Peak demand for the whole system is 67.7 GW, while yearly energy demand is about 386 TWh. All wind power and demand are given as yearly time series with hourly resolution. In the northern part of the UK (buses 1 to 6) there is less generation and less demand, and high wind penetration, while in the southern part (buses 7 to 16) there is much more conventional generation and also large demand centres. Under such conditions, congestion problems arise. The problem is exacerbated by shipping the intermittent wind energy from the north to the south. Line 6 (L6) is highly congested, being a bottleneck in this system. Assumed installed generation capacity, production costs and bids to alter the scheduled production due to congestion are presented per generation technology in Table 7.9.

Note that instead of using market prices, the model considers the use of a cost-based approach. Depending on the system conditions, some generators may increase their outputs, while the others may decrease relative to their scheduled generation. Volume of congestion is calculated as the sum of annual increased energy on all generators in the system.

The DSM is distributed proportional to the load in the buses. The impact of DSM calculated for various amounts of controllable load, comparing with the base case without DSM, is summarized in

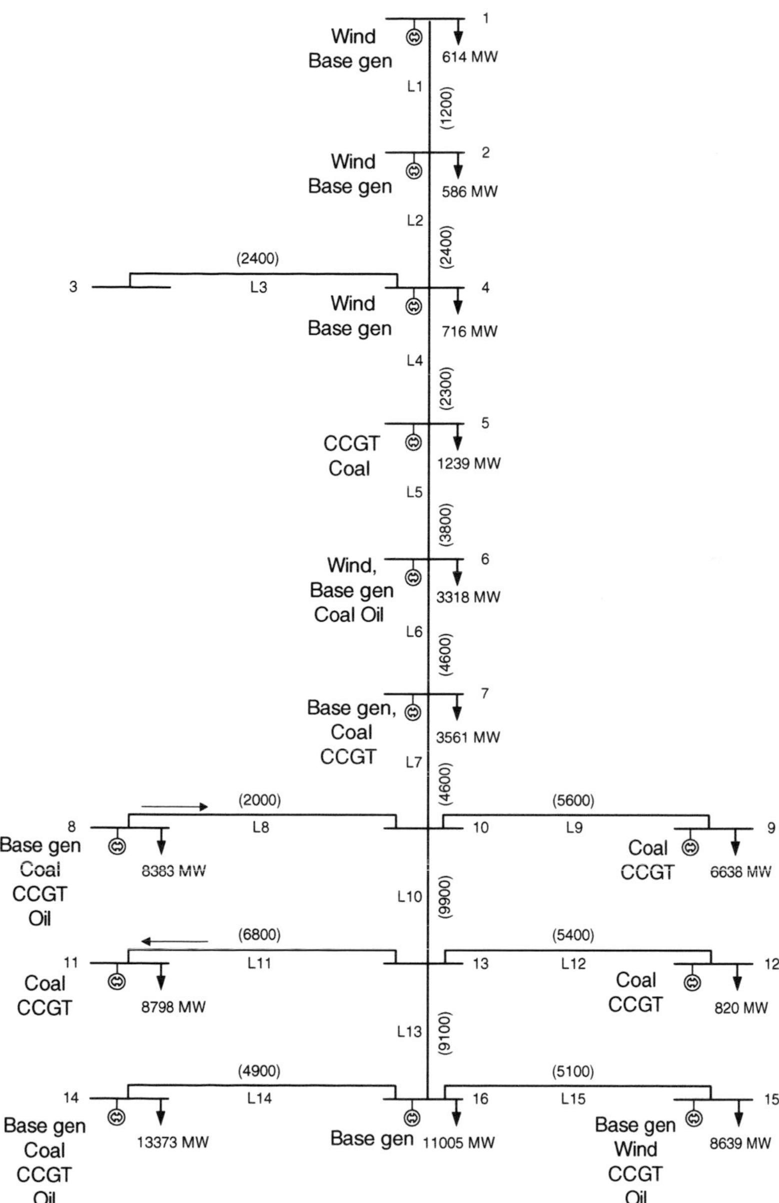


Figure 7.15 Sixteen bus-bar representation of the UK system.

Table 7.9 *Generation data for 16-bus system*

| Type | Inst. cap. [GW] | $c_g$ [£/MWh] | $c_g^+$ [£/MWh] | $c_g^-$ [£/MWh] |
|---|---|---|---|---|
| Base | 15 | 20 | 20 | 15 |
| Wind | 13 | 0 | 0 | 0 |
| Coal | 24.5 | 24 | 24 | 19 |
| CCGT | 30 | 29 | 29 | 24 |
| Oil | 12.6 | 50 | 50 | 45 |
| Total | 95.1 | | | |

Table 7.10 *Impact of DSM on system resources utilization*

| DSM | Value | Reduction in congestion cost | Reduction in wind curtailed | Reduction in volume of congestion |
|---|---|---|---|---|
| [GW] | [£/kW/year] | [$\times 10^6$ £/year] | [GWh/year] | [TWh/year] |
| 1.5 | 34 | 51.49 (7.37%) | 57.45 (0.37%) | 0.606 (1.33%) |
| 3 | 18 | 53.77 (7.69%) | 66.36 (0.43%) | 1.080 (2.37%) |
| 4.5 | 12 | 55.10 (7.88%) | 69.55 (0.45%) | 1.463 (3.22%) |
| 6 | 9 | 55.95 (8.00%) | 71.09 (0.46%) | 1.793 (3.94%) |
| Base values (@ 0 GW DSM) | n.a. | 699 | 15354 | 45.49 |

Table 7.10. The value is defined as a reduction in congestion costs divided by the amount of controllable load. From the results in Table 7.10, it can be observed that the congestion cost reduction tends to saturate for higher penetration of controllable demand. It means that even though there is more controllable load available, it remains unused. This is why the difference between consecutive values in congestion cost reduction becomes smaller and smaller versus higher levels of controllable load.

In general, the operation of DSM leads to less expensive redispatch solutions. DSM changes demand in order to obtain different redispatch solution for all buses in the network, favouring the usage of generators that bid lower redispatch prices.

For this specific system, the amount of controllable load has a large impact on the reduction in congested energy (volume of congestion), while there is a relatively small impact on the reduction in wind spilled. Since wind capacity is mostly installed in the northern part of the network, and there is relatively small demand in that part, DSM is not able to capture all the wind, due to high congestion in Line 6. Yet increasing the amount of controllable load has a larger impact on the reduction in congested energy by mitigating local congestion within the southern part

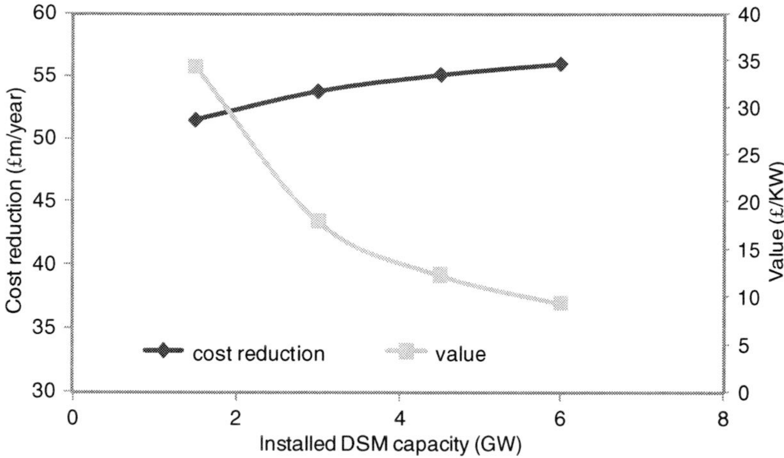


Figure 7.16 Impact of the size of controllable load to the congestion costs and value of DSM.

of the network. For these reasons, a part of the value for DSM comes from more wind generation capture in the north, and another part comes from localized modifications of demand profiles in the south, leading to the more cost-effective redispatch.

Figure 7.16 illustrates the value of DSM as well as the reduction in cost obtained with DSM comparing with the base case. The average value of DSM decreases because cost reductions do not increase in proportion to the installed DSM capacity. The value of DSM for network congestion study is system-specific and in this case varies in range from £9 to £34 per installed kW of controllable load.

### *7.5.2 Summary*

A framework to assess the value of smart appliances, as flexible demand, to increase system flexibility has been described. It has been demonstrated that demand-side flexibility improves system efficiency, reduces operating costs and carbon emissions, and increases utilization of renewable sources. The value of smart appliances is derived from these benefits.

Two types of control actions are studied using different types of appliances applied to different services:

(1) Interrupting operation cycles (DD) is used for modelling the applications of refrigerators (RF) and freezers (FR) to provide frequency response services.
(2) Shifting operation cycle of washing machines, diswashers and washer-dryers (WM, DW and WD): these appliances can be used

to regulate the demand–supply balance and to provide a standing reserve as well as to support network-congestion management. A large number of case studies considering different conventional generation mix flexibility, different wind penetrations and network congestion have been carried out and analyzed to determine the drivers of the value of smart appliances.

## 7.6 Conclusion

In conclusion, the main drivers for the value and economic viability of smart appliance technology are the flexibility of conventional generation and appliances as such, and wind penetration. For the case of network congestion, the value is highly system-specific and there are significant benefits for a stressed system where congestion limits wind integration or when there is a risk of load interruption.

This study shows that there are economical and environmental benefits in using smart appliances to increase system flexibility. Smart appliance technology can support the development of low-carbon electricity systems, composed of a combination of less flexible conventional generation and high wind penetration. Other studies concerning the potential of demand-side flexibility in other countries facing large wind penetrations can be found in Hamidi *et al.* (2008), Lund and Kempton (2008) and Ummels *et al.* (2008).

## References

Aunedi, M., Calderon, J.E.O., *et al.* (2008). *The Potential for Dynamic Demand – Economic and Environmental Impact of Dynamic Demand*, London: Department of Energy and Climate Change.

DECC (2008). *Towards a Smarter Future: Government Response to the Consultation on Electricity and Gas Smart Metering*, London: Department of Energy and Climate Change.

Hamidi, V., Li, F., *et al.* (2008). The effect of responsive demand in domestic sector on power system operation in the networks with high penetration of renewables. IEEE Power and Energy Society General Meeting – Conversion and Delivery of Electrical Energy in the 21st Century, Tampa, USA.

IEA (2008). Empowering variable renewables – options for flexible electricity systems. OECD/IEA. Paris, International Energy Agency.

Lund, H. and Kempton, W. (2008). Integration of renewable energy into the transport and electricity sectors through V2G, *Energy Policy*, **36**(9): 3578–87.

Mert, W., Suschek-Berger, J. and Tritthart, W. (2008). *Consumer Acceptance of Smart Appliances*, Brussels: European Communities.

National Grid, Great Britain Seven Year Statement, Available from: www.nationalgrid.com/uk, last accessed 23 August 2009.

Seebach, D., Timpe, C., *et al.* (2009). *Costs and Benefits of Smart Appliances in Europe*, Brussels: European Communities.

Short, J.A., Infield, D.G., *et al.* (2007). Stabilization of grid frequency through dynamic demand control, *IEEE Transactions on Power Systems*, **22**(3): 1284–93.

Silva, V., Stanojevic, V., *et al.* (2009). *Value of Smart Appliances in System Balancing; Part I of WP 4 from the Smart-A Project*, Brussels: European Communities.

Stamminger, R., ed. (2009). *Synergy Potential of Smart Domestic Appliances in Renewable Energy Systems*, Aachen: Shaker-Verlag.

Stanojevic, V., Silva, V., *et al.* (2009). *Application of Storage and Demand Side Management to Support the Integration of Intermittent Distributed Generation*, Prague: CIRED.

Ummels, B.C., Pelgrum, E., *et al.* (2008). Integration of large-scale wind power and use of energy storage in the Netherlands' electricity supply, *IET Renewable Power Generation*, **2**(1): 34–46.

# 8 The scope for and potential impacts of the adoption of electric vehicles in UK surface transport

*Gregory Marsden and Stephane Hess*

## 8.1 Transport and energy in the UK

In 2008 transport comprised 35.5 per cent of total UK final energy consumption (by user). The breakdown of this demand by energy source is shown in Table 8.1 (BERR, 2009). Electricity provides only 1.2 per cent of the transport sector's energy demands, although it provides almost half of the energy used by the rail sector. The two most important users of energy are road transport (71.7 per cent) and air transport (21.8 per cent). Domestic shipping comprises only 3 per cent of energy consumed. Overall domestic transport was responsible for 131.4 million tonnes of carbon dioxide in 2007, which corresponds to 24.2 per cent of the national total (DfT, 2009a). While the future demand for aviation remains a significant policy issue for climate change, there appears little prospect of switching propulsion technology in aviation or shipping in the medium term and no further consideration is given to them in this chapter.

Traffic has grown by 13.9 per cent over the period from 1997 to 2007 and is forecast to grow by a further 25 per cent by 2025[1] (DfT, 2008a). The key drivers of this growth in demand are income, employment, population and travel costs. Table 8.2 shows how the demand for petroleum products has varied across cars, and light and heavy goods vehicles, over the period 1997–2007 alongside the change in kilometres driven. There have been advances in engine efficiency and a shift to diesel cars, which have kept the rise in energy demand at 2.8 per cent, well below the rise in kilometres. There has been a significant increase in vehicle kilometres in recent years in the light goods vehicle sector. Bus and coach travel accounts for only 4.2 per cent of all petroleum products.

The difficulty in achieving substantial cuts in petroleum consumption from existing technologies, and hence $CO_2$ emissions, is a prime motivation for turning to the potential for electrification of the transport sector.

[1] Relative to 2003 levels.

Table 8.1 *Energy consumption in the transport sector (000s tonnes oil equivalent)*

| Mode | Petroleum | Biomass | Primary electricity | 2008 total | % change 1998–2008 |
|---|---|---|---|---|---|
| Road | 41331 | 821 | | 42152 | +2.8 |
| Rail | 747 | | 725 | 1472 | +9.9 |
| Aviation | 13426 | | | 13426 | +31.1 |
| Domestic shipping | 1764 | | | 1764 | +8.9 |
| Total | 57268 | 821 | 725 | 58814 | +9.4 |

The UK reduced its greenhouse gas emissions by 21 per cent between 1990 and 2007 (DECC, 2009).[2] Despite the overall downwards trajectory for the UK, emissions from transport rose by just over 11 per cent over the same period (EEA, 2009). The UK government has adopted the interim recommendations of the Committee on Climate Change of achieving a 34 per cent reduction in $CO_2$ emissions by 2020 relative to 1990 and, should further international agreements be successfully negotiated, this may be extended to 42 per cent. A longer-term goal of 80 per cent cuts by 2050 also exists. The government's low-carbon transport strategy currently expects to deliver a 10 per cent cut in emissions by 2020 compared with a 5 per cent rise without the policies proposed (DfT, 2009b). The short- to medium-term proposals include adopting more efficient vehicles, increasing the use of biofuels and promoting alternatives to driving. There is also a strong technology push with incentives for ultra-low-carbon cars, vans and buses. This technology push follows from the Treasury-backed King Review of low-carbon cars which concluded that:

*If substantial progress can be made in solving electric or other innovative vehicle and fuel technology challenges and, critically, the power sector can be decarbonised and expanded to supply a large proportion of road transport demand, per kilometre emissions reductions of around 90 per cent could be achievable for cars. If the rate of road transport growth projected by Eddington continues, and road use in the UK approximately doubles by 2050, this would deliver an 80 per cent reduction in total road transport $CO_2$ emissions, relative to 2000 levels.* (King, 2008, p. 4)

Given the importance of technological development in meeting the climate change targets, this chapter reviews the potential for and the potential implications of the widespread electrification of the transport sector.

[2] The reduction in greenhouse gas emissions can, in large part, be attributed to the 'dash for gas' in power generation.

Table 8.2 *Petroleum consumption for road transport 1997–2007 (million tonnes)*

| Mode | 1997 | | 2002 | | 2007 | | % change 1997–2007 | | |
|---|---|---|---|---|---|---|---|---|---|
| | Million tonnes | Billion vehicle km | Million tonnes | Billion vehicle km | Million tonnes | Billion vehicle km | Million tonnes | Billion vehicle km | |
| PTW (petrol) | 0.14 | 4.0 | 0.15 | 5.1 | 0.14 | 5.6 | 0.0 | +40 | |
| Car (petrol) | 20.58 | 365.8 | 19.73 | 392.9 | 16.76 | 404.1 | −18.6 | −6.4 | +10.5 |
| Car (diesel) | 2.42 | | 3.37 | | 4.78 | | +97.6 | | |
| LGV (petrol) | 1.27 | 48.6 | 0.67 | 55.0 | 0.42 | 68.2 | −66.9 | +48.3 | +40.3 |
| LGV (diesel) | 3.13 | | 4.10 | | 6.11 | | +95.3 | | |
| HGV (diesel) | 7.87 | 26.9 | 8.15 | 28.3 | 8.53 | 29.4 | +8.3 | +9.3 | |
| Bus & coach | 1.55 | 5.2 | 1.30 | 5.2 | 1.62 | 5.7 | +4.1 | +9.6 | |
| Total | 36.96 | 450.5 | 37.47 | 486.5 | 38.36 | 513.0 | +4.1 | +13.9 | |

PTW = powered two-wheeler, LGV = light goods vehicle, HGV = heavy goods vehicle, cars include taxis.
*Source:* DfT (2008b).

## 8.2 Technological prospects

Electric vehicles have existed for more than 100 years but the internal combustion engine has dominated vehicle technology since 1910. This dominance presents a major challenge to competing technologies entering the market (Struben and Sterman, 2008). In 2007 in the UK only 2,000 of the registered 28.2 million cars and 4,000 of the 3.2 million light goods vehicles were electric. Interestingly, though, despite some cost disadvantages, 16,000 non-plug-in electric hybrids (such as the Toyota Prius) were registered for the first time in the same year (BERR and DfT, 2008). Demand and supply co-evolve and the market availability of electric vehicles is limited due to the limited range and high battery costs. This section first describes the potential for electric cars before discussing goods vehicles, buses and rail.

Three broad types of electric vehicle are considered in this chapter:

1. Electric vehicles (EV) – driven entirely using a battery and electric motor with recharging undertaken by plugging into the grid.
2. Hybrid electric vehicle (HEV) – in which an electric motor operates in parallel or in series with a traditional combustion engine to power the vehicle.
3. Plug-in hybrid vehicle (PHEV) – a hybrid vehicle which is also able to connect to the grid to recharge its batteries. PHEV can run entirely as electric over shorter ranges, unlike HEVs which require a combination of electric and combustion engine.

A recent study of the potential for EV and PHEV technology suggests that all of the major manufacturers have HEVs either available or in their forward product line (BERR and DfT, 2008). It is anticipated that such products will be competitive up to around 2015–20, when there will be a migration to PHEV (BERR and DfT, 2008). As discussed later, the exact timing and nature of any migration will be strongly determined by the price and performance of the vehicles. The prime focus of this section will therefore be to review the technology issues surrounding EV and PHEV. We acknowledge that a further pathway to electric vehicles is through hydrogen fuel cells and that there is much active research in this area. However, the evidence currently points to nearer-term applications of EV and PHEV, with fuel-cell vehicles and infrastructure unlikely to emerge before 2030 (Kalhammer *et al.*, 2007; Jun *et al.*, 2007). We therefore consider these developments to be beyond the scope of this chapter.

Table 8.3 summarizes the range, charge times and vehicle costs of a sample of early-to-market EVs. Costs and technological capabilities should therefore not be extrapolated.

Table 8.3 *Electric vehicle specifications*

| Model | Range (miles) | Charge time | Total energy | Price |
|---|---|---|---|---|
| Mitsubishi iMiEV* | 100 | 7 hours (200V, 15A) | 16 kWh | £20–25k** |
| Nissan Leaf* | 100 | 8 hours (240V, 13A) | 24 kWh | £20k** + battery lease |
| Telsa Roadster | 244 | 8 hours (240V, 30A) | 55 kWh | £86k |

* Due on the market in 2010/2011.

** Cost estimates from technical press and not yet launch prices.

*Source:* manufacturers' specifications except where indicated.

Both the Mitsubishi and Nissan offers are expected to compete in the small family car market and are therefore expected to be priced at levels similar to those for top-of-the-range petrol or diesel specifications. The range is limited compared with that of a typical petrol or diesel vehicle (around 300 miles), although the Department for Transport suggests that 93 per cent of all two-way journeys are seventy-five miles or less (BERR and DfT, 2008). The extent to which these system attributes are important is explored in the next section.

Crucial to the development and roll-out of EV and PHEV are advances in battery technology. The current HEV market uses nickel metal hydride batteries, which have limited range. Lithium ion batteries have up to twice the energy density (up to 120 Wh/kg) of current batteries and therefore longer range (BERR and DfT, 2008). For PHEV the energy density of the battery determines how long the vehicle can travel in solely electric mode (and therefore the carbon savings) before switching to HEV-style operation. Prices of lithium ion batteries are reportedly at least twice as high as they need to be for widespread adoption. Two studies have estimated that their cost may fall from a level of around $1000/kWh to between $240/kWh and $300/kWh once production levels reach 100,000 per annum (EUROBAT, 2005; Kalhammer *et al.*, 2007) over the next 10–15 years. The degree to which this makes EVs and PHEVs competitive will depend on oil prices, electricity prices, subsidies and consumer preferences as well as battery price. We return to likely forecasts of uptake in section 8.4.

Different options also exist for the charging infrastructure. It is anticipated that most charging would be done at home and that this could be relatively easily facilitated for many homes with an external 240V/13A or 16A connection with a surge protection device (BERR and DfT, 2008). However, only 64 per cent of households park their car in a garage, car port or other off-street parking area (RAC Foundation, 2005). On-street public charging points would therefore be necessary in some residential areas. On-street provision is also necessary to provide confidence in using vehicles away from the home without fear of becoming stranded (for EVs). Current pilot systems are 240V/13A trickle conductive charge systems,[3] although inductive charging is also being investigated. Public charging points also require a payment infrastructure to be established and will require standardization. Trickle charging is likely to be appropriate for locations where vehicles remain for a long period, such as home. Public charging points in particular may need to be able to provide a rapid charge which can take a battery from 20 per cent charge to 80 per cent charge in 10–15 minutes (BERR and DfT, 2008). The substantial roll-out of quick-charge capabilities will have different impacts for the grid (see section 8.5). Other proposals are also actively under development to overcome the problems of limited range for EVs, most notably battery swap stations (e.g. Project Better Place[4]) where, rather than filling up with petrol, an automated battery-swapping station would be used to overcome barriers to longer-distance travel (DfT, 2009c). However, there are concerns over the standardization of batteries for different configurations of vehicles (BERR and DfT, 2008).

After cars, the light goods vehicle market offers some opportunities and electric vehicles are already being sold up to the 7.5–12.5 tonne category (Baker *et al.*, 2009). A technology review of the goods vehicle sector suggested that depot-based operations with daily mileage of less than 100 miles are most suited to the adoption of this type of vehicle (Baker *et al.*, 2009). While the up-front capital costs are substantial, the daily operating costs are around three-quarters lower than a diesel vehicle. Charge times are of the order of 6–8 hours (Smith, 2009). Developments are also possible in the PHEV market for these types of vehicle, but the costs of dual propulsion[5] are higher while the environmental benefits are reduced. There seems little prospect of EVs or PHEVs impacting on the heavy goods vehicle market due to the weight, power and range requirements of these vehicles. There are far more promising technological developments to be made with regards to powering auxiliary units and refrigeration loads in that sector (Baker *et al.*, 2009).

Electric buses have been demonstrated, but hybrid and fuel-cell buses appear to be the major technology development pathways for low-carbon bus technology (London has an aim for all new buses from 2012 to be

[3] Trickle charging means charging a battery at around the same rate that it self-discharges.
[4] www.betterplace.com.
[5] The inclusion of a petrol or diesel engine and an electric motor.

hybrid). Fuel-cell buses have been successfully demonstrated and can work as the fuelling infrastructure can be provided at the depot. The cost of a fuel-cell bus is 3–6 times that of a conventional bus and the near- to medium-term potential for their adoption seems limited, given the need for public transport operators to keep costs down to compete with the car. Low-carbon buses[6] currently make up only 0.2 per cent of the fleet of 179,000 buses and coaches in the UK and while some incentives are in place to encourage uptake, this is anticipated to lead to an increase of 450 low-carbon buses over the next two years, a further 0.2 per cent of the fleet (DfT, 2010).

Table 8.1 shows that rail comprises only 2.5 per cent of all energy use from transport; 40 per cent of the UK's rail network is already electrified and this carries 60 per cent of passenger kilometres (DfT, 2008c). Even if all of the remaining rail network were to be converted to electric, this would have a negligible impact on overall electricity demand. There are plans to electrify the London to Cardiff line and an additional stretch around Manchester (DfT, 2009d). Electric trains are faster, cheaper to run and purchase and are lighter, resulting in lower track repair costs. While there may be strong arguments for a wider electrification programme, however, the scope is limited in the near term. There has already been a significant investment in rolling stock in recent years, such that the average age of the fleet is now thirteen years. As the average operational life of an engine unit is 30–35 years, there will be limited opportunity to replace them. In addition, rail freight operators will continue to choose diesel engines as they require go-anywhere flexibility (DfT, 2009d).

In summary, the main market for the adoption of electric vehicles is likely to be the car market and this is certainly the area which may have the largest potential impact on electricity supply.

## 8.3 Consumer preferences and adoption rates

For a number of years researchers have been seeking to understand the relative preferences of respondents for new vehicle types compared with their conventional internal combustion engine counterparts. Most studies have been framed in a wider alternative-fuel vehicle context rather than just electric. Typically, these applications make use of discrete choice structures belonging to the family of random utility models (RUM), a state-of-the-art technique for analyzing human behaviour

[6] The Department for Transport defines a low-carbon bus as one which has at least a 30 per cent reduction in its greenhouse gas emissions compared with a current Euro 3 diesel bus of the same total passenger capacity.

(cf. Train, 2003). Additionally, given the emphasis on vehicle types with only marginal market shares, the majority of these applications make use of stated preference (SP) data (cf. Louviere *et al.*, 2000), where each respondent is faced with a number of hypothetical scenarios, each time involving the choice between a finite set of mutually exclusive options, in this case different vehicles. The present section provides a brief overview of such studies, focusing on the main factors likely to influence the demand for electric vehicles.

The preferences for electric vehicles are difficult to predict, not least because of the strong relationship between fuel type (i.e. petroleum versus electric) and other attributes such as range, performance, annual costs and incentives (e.g. tax breaks). At the same time, there is a very strong link between fuel type and vehicle type, with certain types of fuels being more appropriate for specific vehicle types. As an example, current-generation hybrid electric cars tend to be small family cars. The aim of studies looking at the potential demand for electric vehicles has thus generally been an analysis of the relative sensitivities to these core factors.

There are numerous examples of studies looking at the choice processes undertaken by potential customers in the context of purchasing a new car. These studies have generally been framed in the wider context of alternative-fuel vehicles, i.e. not limited to just electric vehicles, partly with a view to ensuring a richer choice set.[7] In this chapter, we focus in particular on two studies carried out in California, an area with a long-standing interest in electric vehicles. The first of these two studies is discussed in detail in Train and Hudson (2000), with additional results in Train and Sonnier (2005), with the second study being discussed in Hess *et al.* (2009). The time difference between the two studies conducted in the same general area allows for interesting comparisons, although the two studies were completely independent of one another.

The work by Train and Hudson (2000) is based on a survey in which respondents faced, in each task, a choice between a petrol vehicle, an EV and a HEV. A main aim of this study was to determine the impact of information on customers' choices, where this information related to electric vehicles and hybrid vehicles, and their impact on air quality relative to petrol vehicles. Only half the sample was presented with this detailed additional information, with the respondents being randomly allocated to one of the two groups. The three alternatives were described by body type (ten different types), purchase price, operating cost, performance (in terms of time taken to reach a speed of 60mph) and the range for electric vehicles.

7 (See Mabit (2009) for a recent overview of the literature.)

All else being equal, for respondents without the additional information, hybrid vehicles are about as 'attractive' as petrol vehicles, while electric vehicles are valued significantly below these two other groups. Respondents with the additional information on air quality still value electric vehicles the lowest, although the gap is reduced somewhat, while they now value hybrid vehicles higher than petrol vehicles. A useful comparison in this context is to look at the range required before an electric vehicle is valued as highly as a petrol vehicle. In the base group, electric vehicles would, all else being equal, require on average a range of 460 miles to be valued as highly as petrol vehicles. While this varies considerably across respondents, the required range is clearly unrealistic, compared with those shown in Table 8.3. In the group with additional information, the average required range drops to 338 miles, which is still unrealistic. Additional incentives are thus required to make electric vehicles more desirable. However, the results imply that an average discount of $28,000 would be required to make an electric vehicle with a 100-mile range have the same probability of being chosen as a petrol car in the base group, where this drops to just below $20,000 in the group with additional information. As the authors point out, these results show that possible concerns about recharging and uncertainty about technology or other issues seem to outweigh the air-quality benefits of electric vehicles. Hybrid vehicles, however, receive a far more positive response, especially in the group with additional information.

The study discussed in Hess *et al.* (2009) presents respondents with a choice between a current reference vehicle and three alternative vehicles. This survey makes use of seven different fuel types, namely standard petrol, EV, HEV, PHEV, flex fuel/E85, clean diesel and compressed natural gas. Along with fifteen different body types, the alternatives were described on the basis of vehicle price, maintenance cost, running costs, age, purchase incentives for certain low-emission cars, fuel availability, refuelling time, range and acceleration.

Results show strong vehicle type and fuel type inertia among respondents in the sample.[8] After taking this inertia into account, and using petrol vehicles as the base, EVs are the lowest ranked of seven fuel types, with only compressed natural gas also being ranked lower than petrol. In order of increasing preference, this is then followed by HEV, clean diesel, flex fuel/E85 and PHEV. Across all vehicle types, an EV with a

[8] Inertia in this context explains an underlying preference by the respondent for the vehicle and fuel type of their current automobile. In other words, all else being equal, a respondent is more likely to choose an option that uses the same vehicle type or fuel type as the one they currently possess.

range of more than 100 miles would have to be almost $37,000 cheaper than a petrol car in order to be valued the same way by a respondent in the lowest income group, where this increases with income. HEVs can be $2,600 more expensive than petrol vehicles and PHEVs $6,800 more expensive. All else being equal, a range of more than 1,000 miles would be required for an EV to be valued as highly as a petrol car, though this can be reduced somewhat with the help of incentives, vehicle performance, and the possibility to recharge the vehicles at work or other locations.

The overall findings from these two separate studies by Train and Hudson (2000) and Hess *et al.* (2009) are thus remarkably similar, showing that technically unfeasible ranges or unrealistic subsidies would be required to make EVs as desirable as standard petrol vehicles. While there are of course substantial variations across people in these cut-off points, the overall picture is very negative, and the potential interest in EVs seems to have only decreased further from 2000 to 2009. Yet there is growing interest in HEVs and PHEVs. The importance of range as a constraint on consumer uptake seems very high, explaining the difference between preferences for EV and PHEV.

## 8.4 Impacts on the demand for electricity

A number of studies have attempted to consider the implications of different projections of future EV and PHEV ownership on the demand for electricity under a range of charging assumptions (e.g. Electric Power Research Institute, 2007; BERR and DfT, 2008; Kang and Recker, 2009). In particular, the UK study (BERR and DfT, 2008) considered the impacts of four different vehicle penetration scenarios. The work in section 8.3 suggests that the most extreme positive adoption scenarios for electric vehicles seem unlikely to be realized over the next two decades. While consumer attitudes may change significantly with exposure to the new EV models, this process will take time (Struben and Sterman, 2008). The scale of the demand on the grid is set out in Table 8.4.

In the UK, the average journey length is just under seven miles; 93 per cent of journeys are less than 75 miles round trip (DfT, 2008d; DfT, 2009a). It is therefore anticipated that most vehicles could be used without stopping to charge during the day. Nonetheless, the modelling work in section 8.3 highlights the importance of the availability and option of public charging points (either at work or in parking areas) to provide enhanced range. Such charging facilities are likely to require the delivery of fast charging (i.e. fifteen minutes) as vehicles will be parked for shorter periods of time. The introduction of large numbers of

Table 8.4 *Projections of demand for electricity from EV and PHEV*

| | 2020 | | | | 2030 | | | |
|---|---|---|---|---|---|---|---|---|
| Generating capacity | 100GW | | | | 120GW | | | |
| Projected annual UK demand | 360TWh | | | | 390TWh | | | |
| | EVs | PHEVs | GWh | %NEP | EVs | PHEVs | GWh | %NEP |
| Business as usual | 70k | 200k | 400 | 0.1 | 500k | 2500k | 4200 | 1.1 |
| Mid range | 600k | 200k | 1800 | 0.5 | 1600k | 2500k | 6700 | 1.7 |
| High range | 1200k | 350k | 3500 | 1.0 | 3300k | 7900k | 17000 | 4.4 |

NEP = GB national electric production.
*Source:* Adapted from BERR and DfT (2008).

daytime fast charges may have 'potentially significant impacts on the generation and transmission/distribution networks' (BERR and DfT, 2008, p. 44). Kang and Recker (2009) estimate that with home charging, 40–50 per cent of the distances travelled by internal combustion engine vehicles could be travelled with a PHEV with a twenty-mile range and 70–80 per cent for a PHEV with a sixty-mile range. This rises to between 60 per cent and 70 per cent and 80 per cent to 90 per cent respectively where public charging points are available.

In all of the studies it is anticipated that most people would wish to plug in their vehicles to charge as soon as they return home. Unrestricted charging would place a significant demand on the grid given that this would coincide with the winter peak-hour demands on the grid (BERR and DfT, 2008). It is therefore assumed that smart metering will be introduced before or alongside the widespread adoption of electric vehicles, which will allow charging to occur at night. Smart metering is more than simply a timer switch as it could allow consumers and producers to set parameters which allow the optimization of charging times and tariffs. This will have the potential advantage of spreading the demand for electricity, which will better map to a profile generated by an increasing renewable mix and improve generating efficiency (BERR and DfT, 2008). There is also the potential for vehicles to operate as a storage point for electricity which can be fed back into the grid, although these considerations are beyond the scope of this chapter. The decision to move to a grid which has smart metering technology for managing the consumer–producer interface is far bigger than transport and will not be determined by individual vehicle purchases. In all but the most unlikely high-range scenarios the proportion of the national electricity production required by the vehicle fleet remains below 1.7 per cent by 2030, which suggests that the absence of smart metering in the short to medium term will not be critical.

Overall, it appears that under a mid-range assumption about the adoption of EVs and PHEVs (around 3 million vehicles or 10 per cent of the fleet), the demands for electricity will be less than 2 per cent of total production by 2030. More aggressive assumptions push this to 4.4 per cent by 2030. Given the current reluctance of consumers to adopt EVs in particular, we see this as a probable upper bound. While there remains a degree of uncertainty as to what the standardized charging solutions might be for home and public charge points, it has been suggested that smart metering will be important if this demand is not to place significant extra generation or distribution costs on the grid. While some consumers are currently on dual-rate Economy 7-type tariffs which encourage overnight use of electricity, many are on a flat rate. Further pricing differentiation by the suppliers would assist in making this an attractive option (BERR and DfT, 2008).

## 8.5 Other supporting policies

It is clear from sections 8.3 and 8.4 that the up-front purchase costs of EVs and PHEVs will act as a deterrent to their purchase if left to the market. While PHEVs are currently viewed more favourably than EVs, there is still a price premium to be overcome. This is particularly problematic as the average period of time for which a driver holds a new vehicle is around 3–4 years – which provides a very short payback period. The risks to consumers are also significant as the second-hand market value of these emerging technologies is not yet well understood. This is being countered across Europe with a range of incentives to encourage the purchase of very low-carbon vehicles. In the UK, a long-term programme is scheduled to commence in 2011 with a budget of £250 million set aside to provide subsidies of between £2,000 and £5,000 per vehicle for ultra-low-carbon vehicles. A budget of £30 million is also available for low-carbon buses. Reforms have also been made to the annual circulation tax (vehicle excise duty, VED) to incentivize low-carbon vehicles with a price differential of as much as £435 per year.

The introduction of EVs and PHEVs generates a profound change in the way that users will pay for travel. Fuel excise duty has been levied at the pump since 1909 and currently forms around half of the pump price of fuel (before VAT). In 2007/8 fuel duty from the road sector raised £23.3 billion for the Exchequer. A shift to EVs and PHEVs will mean that travellers are paying VAT only at the rates levied on domestic energy – a substantial reduction on the variable costs of motoring. While this reduction in variable costs helps to offset the additional purchase costs of these vehicles, it also has much broader impacts. A reduction in per-mile driving costs will be economically inefficient as it will further weaken the link between the perceived and full marginal social costs for journeys. Fuel duty currently ensures that drivers pay the average social costs of their journeys, although it is not spatially or temporally targeted and so does little to tackle the externalities of congestion (DfT, 2006). A large shift to EVs and PHEVs will incentivize additional travel, referred to as the rebound effect (Potter, 2009), which will create more delays on the transport network.

Taken together, the reductions in income from VED changes and a loss of fuel duty are forecast to cost the Exchequer £4 billion per annum by 2020, when take-up of PHEV is only just forecast to be beginning (CCC, 2008). While the extent to which this tax loss is offset within transport or elsewhere in the economy is a matter of public policy, leaving variable transport costs to decline will lead to extra traffic and worsen the competitive position of bus and rail. Many studies advocate a shift to a national road user charging scheme (e.g. Glaister and Graham, 2003; DfT, 2006). Such a move would help to ensure that the rebound effect is managed and that prices are brought more in line with congestion costs. However, this is a delicate balancing act as this would likely weaken the running-cost advantage for consumers considering investing in EVs and PHEVS if it is introduced as a part replacement for fuel tax.

## 8.6 Conclusions

The 'dash to electric' will be concentrated largely in the car market with a mix of EVs and PHEVs. There will also be some important opportunities in the light goods vehicle market for urban multi-drop delivery services operating from a depot. Further electrification of the rail network will have very limited impact on overall electricity demand. Even with fairly aggressive assumptions about uptake rates in the car market, recharging is unlikely to require more than 5 per cent of total electric production by 2030. If home charging is managed with smart meters, there will be little impact on the grid and such an approach could even out demand and support more efficient generation. Some local distributional issues may need to be overcome to support a substantial network of publicly available fast-charging points and these seem a necessary part of any full EV future to overcome consumer concerns over operating range.

The research base to date suggests considerable barriers to the uptake of PHEVs and EVs in particular. While governments are proposing a range of incentives to offset the initial higher purchase costs of these technologies to encourage the purchase of ultra-low-carbon vehicles, the technologies are still maturing and consumers have little experience of real marketplace products. The shape and gradient of the adoption curve remain unknown and it is not clear how effective the incentives will be in stimulating widespread uptake. The effectiveness is also dependent on other factors, such as the price of electricity and fuel, the availability of infrastructure and the development of battery technology. The next decade will provide a fertile learning ground in which the real long-term impacts on electricity supply can be more fully understood. For now, the 'dash' to electric looks more like a 'brisk stroll'.

## References

Baker, H., Cornwell, R., Koehler, E. and Patterson, J. (2009). Review of Low Carbon Technologies for Heavy Goods Vehicles. Report prepared for Department for Transport, Ricardo Consulting, RD.09/182601.6.

BERR (2009). *Digest of United Kingdom Energy Statistics*, London: Department for Business, Enterprise and Regulatory Reform.

BERR and DfT (2008). Investigation into the Scope for the Transport Sector to Switch to Electric Vehicles and Plug-in Hybrid Vehicles. Prepared by ARUP and CENEX for the Department for Business, Enterprise and Regulatory Reform and Department for Transport, London.

CCC (2008). *Building a Low-Carbon Economy – the UK's Contribution to Tackling Climate Change*, London: Committee on Climate Change.

DECC (2009). *The UK Low Carbon Transition Plan: National Strategy for Climate and Energy*, London: Department of Energy and Climate Change.

DfT (2006). Transport demand to 2025 and the economic case for road pricing and investment, in Eddington, R. (ed.), *The Eddington Transport Study*, Norwich: HMSO.

DfT (2008a). *Road Transport Forecasts 2008 – Results from the Department for Transport's National Transport Model*, London: Department for Transport.

DfT (2008b). *Transport Statistics Great Britain 2008 Edition*, London: Department for Transport.

DfT (2008c). *Carbon Pathways Analysis: Informing Development of a Carbon Reduction Strategy for the Transport Sector*, London: Department for Transport.

DfT (2008d). *Transport Trends: 2008 Edition*, London: Department for Transport.

DfT (2009a). *Transport Statistics Great Britain: 2009 edition*, London: Department for Transport.

DfT (2009b). *Low Carbon Transport: A Greener Future*. A carbon reduction strategy for transport, London: Department for Transport.

DfT (2009c). *Ultra Low Carbon Cars: Next Steps on delivering the £250 million Consumer Incentive Programme for Electric and Plug-in Hybrid Cars*, London: Department for Transport.

DfT (2009d). *Britain's Transport Infrastructure: Rail Electrification*, London: Department for Transport.

DfT (2010). *Transport Carbon Reduction Delivery Plan*, London: Department for Transport.

EE (2009). Transport at a crossroads – TERM 2008: Indicators tracking transport and environment in the European Union. European Environment Agency Report No. 3/2009, Copenhagen: European Environment Agency.

Electric Power Research Institute (2007). Environmental Assessment of Plug-in Hybrid Electric Vehicles, Vol. 2. United States Air Quality Analysis Based on AEO-2006 Assumptions for 2030. Report #1015326, Palo Alto.

EUROBAT (2005). Battery Systems for Electric Energy Storage Issues. Battery Industry RTD Position Paper, Report Dated July 2005. Brussels: EUROBAT.

Glaister, S. and Graham, D.J. (2003). Transport Pricing and Investment in England. Summary Report, London: Imperial College.

Hess, S., Fowler, M., Adler, T. and Bahreinian, A. (2009). A joint model for vehicle type and fuel type. Paper presented at the European Transport Conference. Noordwijkerhout, The Netherlands.

Jun, E., Jeong, Y.H. and Chang, S.H. (2007). Simulation of the market penetration of hydrogen fuel cell vehicles in Korea, *International Journal of Energy Research*, **32**(4): 318–27.

Kalhammer, F.R., Kopf, B.M., Swan, D.H., Roan, V.P. and Walsh, M.P. (2007). Status and Prospects for Zero Emissions Vehicle Technology. Report of the ARB Independent Expert Panel, State of California Air Resources Board, Sacramento.

Kang, J.E. and Recker, W.W. (2009). An activity-based assessment of the potential impacts of plug-in hybrid electric vehicles on energy and emissions using 1-day travel data, *Transportation Research Part D*, **14**: 541–56.

King, J. (2008). *The King Review of Low-Carbon Cars – Part II: Recommendations for Action*, London: HM Treasury.

Louviere, J., Hensher, D. and Swait, J. (2000). *Stated Choice Methods: Analysis and Applications*, New York: Cambridge University Press.

Mabit, S.L. (2009). Danish preferences concerning alternative-fuel vehicles. Paper presented at the European Transport Conference. Noordwijkerhout, The Netherlands.

Potter, S. (2009). Using environmental taxation for transport demand management, in Milne, J., Deketelaere, K., Kreiser, K. and Ashiabor, H. (eds.) *Critical Issues in Taxation*, Oxford: Oxford University Press.

RAC Foundation (2005). *Parking in Transport Policy*, Pall Mall, London: RAC Foundation.

Smith (2009). Case Study: AG Barr. Smiths Electric Vehicles, Available at www.smithelectricvehicles.com/casestudies_barr.asp, last accessed 04/12/09.

Struben, J. and Sterman, J.D. (2008). Transition challenges for alternative fuelled vehicle and transportation systems, *Environment and Planning B: Planning and Design*, **35**: 1070–97.

Train, K. (2003). *Discrete Choice Methods with Simulation*, Cambridge, MA: Cambridge University Press.

Train, K. and Hudson, K. (2000). The impact of information in vehicle choice and the demand for electric vehicles in California, National Economic Research Associates.

Train, K.E. and Sonnier, G. (2005). Mixed logit with bounded distributions of correlated partworths, in Alberini, A. and Scarpa, R. (eds.), *Applications of Simulation Methods in Environmental Resource Economics*, Dordrecht, The Netherlands: Springer.

*Part III*

# Social dimensions

# 9 From citizen to consumer: energy policy and public attitudes in the UK

*Elcin Akcura, Aoife Brophy Haney, Tooraj Jamasb and David M. Reiner*

## 9.1 Introduction

Interest in the role of the individual and the community in tackling major energy policy challenges has increased significantly over the past decade in the UK and internationally. The main challenges addressed by UK energy policy are climate change and the transition to a low-carbon economy; diversity and security of energy supply; and supporting consumers by overcoming fuel poverty and improving energy efficiency. Long-term continuity of policies concerning the above areas as well as that of liberalization of the energy sector is largely dependent on support from the public. The Department of Energy and Climate Change (DECC) was created in October 2008, mainly in recognition of the fact that these challenges are interlinked and require comprehensive policy making. Each of these challenges also involves an important role for the demand side. For households this includes a role for individuals as consumers of energy as a commodity on the one hand, and as citizens with social and political responsibilities on the other (Devine-Wright, 2007).

The role for consumers in an advanced liberalized energy market such as Great Britain is further augmented due to retail competition: consumers can choose supplier and switch to an alternative supplier if they are dissatisfied with price, quality or customer service. They may also be more exposed to changes in energy prices. As citizens, individuals may participate both privately and collectively in policy-making processes. The degree of participation depends in large part on the willingness of policy makers to engage with the public. Until now, public engagement in UK energy policy making has been based on the information deficit model or the rational choice model. The assumption at the heart of these models is that improving awareness and understanding through providing information is central to encouraging sustainable behaviour and public acceptance for sustainable solutions, e.g. the siting of new wind-turbine developments (Owens, 2000; Owens and Driffill, 2008). This is beginning to change, however, and a number of recent studies have attempted to integrate a more sophisticated approach, acknowledging that the link between attitudes and behaviour is complex and influenced by a range of social, political, institutional and cultural factors (Jackson, 2005; Defra, 2008).

Understanding the attitudes and behaviour of individuals as consumers and citizens and how they change over time is thus becoming increasingly important for UK energy policy. In this chapter, we use the results from the 2006 and 2008 public opinion surveys conducted by the Electricity Policy Research Group (EPRG), University of Cambridge to investigate general attitudes and policy preferences as well as specific opinions on energy prices, service quality and energy conservation.

In section 9.2 we review the existing literature on public attitudes towards energy policy and climate change and the role of behavioural change. Section 9.3 describes the EPRG survey design and the relevant survey questions used here. In section 9.4 we present the survey results and look particularly at the socioeconomic characteristics that determine attitudes and behaviour. In section 9.5 we assess the policy implications of these trends and consider whether there are specific lessons to be learned for the future of energy policy in the UK.

## 9.2 Public attitudes, behaviour and energy policy

Support from the public in any area of policy making is important. In the context of sustainable energy policy and delivering a low-carbon energy future in the UK, the public is expected not only to support but also to actively contribute by changing attitudes and behaviour (Owens and Driffill, 2008). The traditional policy approach has been to rely on voluntary measures to encourage individuals to change their behaviour, with a focus on information provision. Information alone may help to change attitudes and understanding on energy issues but will not necessarily lead to behaviour change (Lorenzoni *et al.*, 2007). Furthermore, the public may not always have the expected response as they receive information from a range of sources.

There are several factors that constrain the ability of individuals to manage, for example, their energy consumption more sustainably or to accept new energy technologies. Some of these can be addressed through regulatory and incentive-based measures targeted at energy consumers, for example appliance standards, building codes and taxes or tax incentives. Policies that have a direct impact on household energy prices, however, tend to be unpopular and as a result politically sensitive. In reality, political dimensions often play a central role in the ultimate choice of policy instruments (Varone and Aebischer, 2001; Pearce, 2006).

As mentioned, energy consumers are also citizens whose actions are shaped by wider social, political and cultural circumstances. The complexity of the link between public attitudes and behaviour, taking these factors into account, has begun to be more widely recognized. The social science literature on attitudes and behaviour in the context of energy continues to grow. There is widespread agreement that engaging with the public needs to move beyond an information deficit model if a sustainable energy policy is to emerge. A more inclusive, participatory model of public engagement; a focus on citizens holding collective responsibility for environmental problems such as climate change; and above all integrative, innovative policy making that recognizes the limitations and context for individual decision making are among the main recommendations (Jackson, 2005; Barr and Gilg, 2007; Faiers *et al.*, 2007). Translating these recommendations into appropriate policy making, however, remains a challenge.

The UK Climate Change Committee (CCC) has analyzed the potential for carbon-emissions reductions in all areas of the economy as part of its independent, advisory role to the UK government on reaching the 2050 targets. The potential for low-cost carbon savings in the residential sector comes first from energy-efficiency improvements (e.g. insulation, lighting and appliances) and second from lifestyle change (e.g. turning down the thermostat). Although the technical potential identified by the CCC in these two areas is 43 $MtCO_2$, the realistic potential given barriers to action is in the range of 9–18 $MtCO_2$ or between 6 per cent and 12 per cent of residential emissions. There is greater potential still from microgeneration and renewable heat. However, realizing even a small fraction of the total technical potential (105 $MtCO_2$) will require addressing the current limited willingness and ability of consumers to install such technologies (CCC, 2008). In short, there is a significant role for energy policy making in improving the potential gains from the residential sector.

Achieving these changes will depend on how successful policy makers are at influencing existing public attitudes and behaviour. Promoting any type of behaviour change is and always has been a challenge across various areas of public policy. There are several examples, for instance, in the area of public health where behaviour change is crucial to policy success, e.g. tackling obesity and smoking. Economists have traditionally approached these problems from a rational choice perspective, i.e. that individuals make rational decisions on the basis of maximizing their welfare. This type of approach has led to public policies that aim to inform as a way of encouraging behaviour change.

Increasingly, however, social psychologists, behavioural economists and policy makers are drawing attention to the many dimensions involved in individual decision making beyond the availability of adequate information. Social norms, routines and habits, institutional and infrastructural constraints, and the capacity for individuals to make bad choices even when provided with the correct information are all factors that make policy interventions to change behaviour extremely complex (Jackson, 2005; Thaler and Sunstein, 2008).

Instead of focusing on information provision alone, experts from a number of disciplines encourage policy makers to create an enabling environment in recognition of these complexities. Ultimately it is not so much about changing behaviour as it is a question of acknowledging the challenges at hand and finding a sustainable way forward. Many believe that sustainable progress in the area of energy can be achieved only if members of the public become active rather than passive stakeholders (Devine-Wright, 2007; Owens and Driffill, 2008).

Understanding the audience is an essential part of communicating any message and indeed this has become a central tenet of UK domestic policy making in recent years (Bird, 2008). As a result, public attitude surveys in the areas of energy and climate change have become more prevalent in the UK and internationally. The European Commission has undertaken public opinion surveys on aspects of energy policy since the 1980s. In recent years, the focus has been firmly on climate change. In 2008 and 2009, Eurobarometer surveys have investigated public attitudes to climate change in significant detail across the twenty-seven member states. In the most recent survey, all countries except Sweden show a decrease in the share of respondents mentioning climate change as a serious problem facing the world. The economic downturn dominates, but climate change still ranks as the third most serious problem across the EU. The UK has the second highest percentage of people who believe that climate change is not a serious issue (17 per cent); and yet the UK also has one of the highest shares of people who say they have taken action against climate change (77 per cent) (Eurobarometer, 2009).

In the US, attitude surveys with questions related to climate change also started becoming prevalent in the 1980s, with more interest from the late 1980s onwards (Bord *et al.*, 1999). More recently, the focus of survey-based studies has been to investigate the barriers to lifestyle or behaviour change and to explore the socioeconomic characteristics that determine a willingness or unwillingness to act. For example, a 2007 study of individuals in two very different US cities, Portland and

Houston, finds that although awareness of climate change is high in both cities, younger people and those from Portland are more likely to change their behaviour. The study concludes that messages to encourage change and initiatives that support sustainable energy use need to target individuals at different stages of awareness and action in different ways.

The question of the actual impact that behavioural responses can have on energy consumption is also crucial. Switching off appliances and lights when not in use is an easy first step to conserving energy but will not have a large impact overall on a country's energy demand (especially as technological changes reduce the significance of lighting demand – see Platchkov and Pollitt, this volume). Changes to heating, i.e. turning down the thermostat, and travel behaviour have larger potential savings, as does improving building insulation (McKay, 2008).[1] By improving energy efficiency of appliances, cars, heating or homes, we also make energy services cheaper. This may encourage an increase in energy consumption, often referred to as the direct rebound effect, and may offset some of the potential energy savings. Estimating the size of this effect is complex and depends on the energy service in question. Sorrell *et al.* (2009) provide a comprehensive review of studies that attempt to estimate the rebound effect and conclude that the average value of the long-run direct effect is likely to be less than 30 per cent (i.e. actual demand for energy falls by 0.7 per cent for every 1 per cent reduction in per-unit energy use) and may be closer to 10 per cent for transport (see also Steinbuks, this volume).

There is increasing evidence that individuals' intentions and their subsequent actions in response to climate change do not always align. The most popular activity undertaken out of concern for climate change in a 2003 survey of residents in southern England was recycling. Direct energy conservation, for example reducing travel-related or domestic energy use, was also widespread but is generally undertaken for reasons other than concern for the environment, such as health or to save money (Whitmarsh, 2009). These findings reinforce other work on understanding attitudes in the context of energy and the environment, which emphasizes how energy consumption is embedded into everyday lifestyle practices. Effective and sustainable policy making should recognize this rather than trying to compartmentalize consumption behaviours into multiple categories (Barr and Gilg, 2007).

[1] In David McKay's analysis of individual action, turning down the thermostat to 15° or 17° C and turning off the heating when no one is at home has a possible saving of 20 kWh per day compared with a saving of 4 kWh per day from switching off appliances, lights, etc. when not in use. Changing lights to fluorescent or LED has an additional saving of 4 kWh per day (McKay, 2008, pp. 229–30).

Timing can also have a critical influence on the results of public-attitude surveys and on related public support for energy policies. In the UK, research by Ipsos MORI shows that economic pessimism during 2008 has had a negative impact on concerns about the environment overall (Ipsos MORI, 2008). We would expect a similar impact on the results of the 2008 EPRG survey and will explore this further in the following sections. By doing so, we contribute to understanding how sensitive public opinion is to short-run changes. We also discuss the impacts of this on energy policy making in the UK and draw lessons for other countries with advanced liberalized energy markets.

## 9.3 EPRG survey design and implementation

In May 2006 the Electricity Policy Research Group commissioned a survey that covered a number of areas relating to energy policy in the UK. In October 2008, EPRG conducted a follow-up survey that addressed many of the same areas as the 2006 survey. The results from these two surveys form the basis for this chapter.

The execution of the 2008 survey coincided with a highly volatile and uncertain period in the UK economy. During the months prior to the survey, there was a period of sharp falls in asset prices, as well as increasing fears of job losses. The financial crisis which in the UK was highlighted by the collapse of Northern Rock in February 2008 escalated further in September 2008 (a month before the survey was conducted) with Lehman Brothers filing for bankruptcy. Coincidentally, energy prices, which had begun an upward course with the onset of the Iraq War in 2003, reached record levels by mid-2008, with oil prices approaching $150 per barrel. Although prices had begun to fall markedly by autumn 2008, many consumers would have vivid memories of the winter of 2007. It is highly likely that the responses to the survey were affected by the rise and fall of the economy and fuel prices, which will be discussed further in the results section.

Both surveys were administered in England, Wales and Scotland. The 2006 survey was conducted by YouGov, which specializes in the application of Internet-based opinion surveys. For the survey, YouGov contacted 2,254 UK residents over the age of eighteen, of whom 1,019 responded, representing a 45 per cent response rate. The respondents were randomly selected from YouGov's panel of more than 200,000 individuals who are on the electoral list in the UK. The YouGov panel is recruited through non-political websites and recruitment agencies and seeks to make the pool as representative of the UK populace as possible. The respondents were given a small monetary incentive to participate in the survey, ranging from 50 pence to £1 per survey completion. The 2008

EPRG survey was administered by Accent, which specializes in stated preference surveys for public utility sectors. The sample size for the 2008 survey was increased to 2,000 individuals to improve the statistics for the split samples.

Both surveys were conducted over the Internet, in contrast to more traditional methods such as by mail, over the phone, or face-to-face interviews. There are a number of advantages to Internet surveys (or e-surveys), which led to the selection of this method. Internet-based surveys in general are less expensive as they involve fewer and less time-consuming administration and processing procedures. Internet-based surveys also have faster response times as well as higher response rates (Lazar and Preece, 1999; Oppermann, 1995) compared with the traditional approaches. Furthermore, respondents in Internet surveys are under no time pressure when completing surveys online, which can improve the validity of responses to complex questions. They also avoid the 'interviewer effect' as people responding to the survey are filling in their questionnaires on a computer screen rather than talking to a person.

While Internet-based surveys are now widely used, there are some concerns over their representativeness as the whole population does not have access to the Internet. However, this is not such a significant issue in the UK, where 63.9 per cent of households have access to the Internet at home (ITUI, 2007). According to the communication regulator, Ofcom, approximately 69 per cent of the population has some form of access to the Internet either at home, work, in a library or some other such setting. Moreover, the traditional formats of survey execution can lead to higher biases than those observed in e-surveys. For instance, telephone and interview surveys tend to be biased towards those who spend most of their time at home, such as the retired or the unemployed. In contrast, Internet surveys can be accessed in any location with an Internet connection.

However, there is a certain degree of regional and age bias associated with Internet surveys. In the UK, as in many other countries, a higher percentage of people under the age of thirty use the Internet compared with other age groups, especially compared with people over sixty-five. The National Statistical Office conducts the National Statistics Omnibus Survey annually, which is a survey of Internet usage of the population. The results of the survey in 2006 and 2007 are presented in Table 9.1. The table displays the skewed distribution of Internet usage by age. In the 2006 survey only 15 per cent of those over sixty-five had used the Internet in the past three months compared with 83 per cent of those aged between sixteen and twenty-four.

Although the UK is ranked among the countries with the highest Internet penetration rate, there are some regional disparities. According to National Statistics' 2007 report on Internet access, Scotland, Northern

Table 9.1 *National Statistical Office survey results on percentage of sample that used the Internet in the past three months prior to the survey*

| | Used Internet in the past three months | |
|---|---|---|
| Age groups | 2006 | 2007 |
| 16–24 | 83 | 90 |
| 25–44 | 79 | 80 |
| 45–54 | 68 | 75 |
| 55–64 | 52 | 59 |
| 65+ | 15 | 24 |

Table 9.2 *Households with Internet access by region (%), UK, 2006, 2007*

| Regions | 2006 | 2007 |
|---|---|---|
| South East | 66 | 65 |
| East of England | 64 | 67 |
| London | 63 | 69 |
| South West | 59 | 69 |
| East Midlands | 55 | 59 |
| North West | 54 | 56 |
| North East | 54 | 52 |
| West Midlands | 53 | 56 |
| Wales | 52 | 57 |
| Yorks & Humber | 52 | 52 |
| Northern Ireland | 50 | 52 |
| Scotland | 48 | 60 |

Ireland, Northern England, Wales and the West Midlands have lower rates of Internet usage at home compared with the rest of the country (Table 9.2).

The problem with the skewed nature of Internet penetration by age and region is not in its impact on representativeness per se. In the 2006 YouGov survey, each respondent is weighted so that the sample as a whole is representative (and the weighting is restricted to account not only for age or region but also for other key variables such as newspaper readership). In the 2008 Accent survey, quotas were imposed for key sociodemographic variables (age, gender, region, social class) to ensure that the sample was representative of the British population. Thus, the

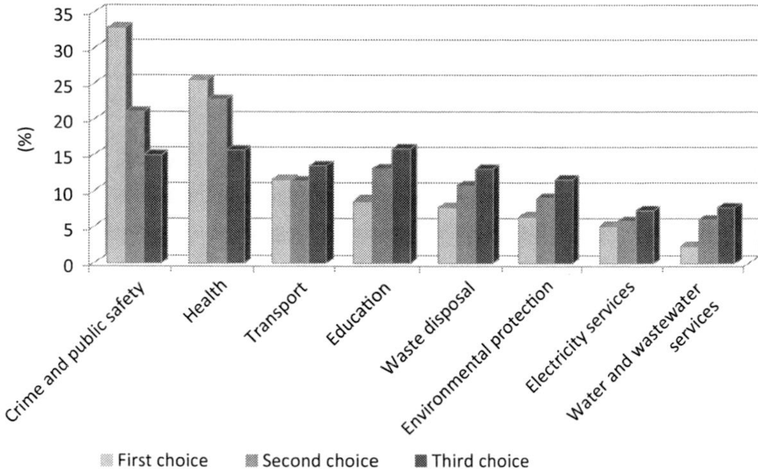


Figure 9.1 Top three choices of respondents on areas in need of urgent attention and improvement.

real concern is not so much representativeness of the national sample but whether the relatively small fraction of the older population (or any other demographic of interest) which uses the Internet is biased in some way even after ensuring that the sample itself is representative. One might surmise that Internet users might be biased on certain questions, for example on the use of technology. Any such bias would be most pronounced on questions to do with the use of the medium itself, such as media or shopping preferences. Respondents to Internet surveys also might display a wider pro-technology bias, even if the sample might be perfectly representative on questions regarding national politics, brand awareness or morality.

## 9.4 Survey results

### *9.4.1 General attitudes*

One of the questions in the EPRG 2008 survey asked the respondents to prioritize three areas from among a set of public services that in their opinion needed urgent attention and improvement in the UK. Figure 9.1 summarizes the priorities of the respondents. 'Crime and public safety' and 'health' were respondents' predominant choices. Around 33 per cent of our sample selected 'crime and public safety' as the area most in need of urgent attention, while 26 per cent thought it should be 'health services'. Only 5 per cent of respondents chose electricity services as the area most

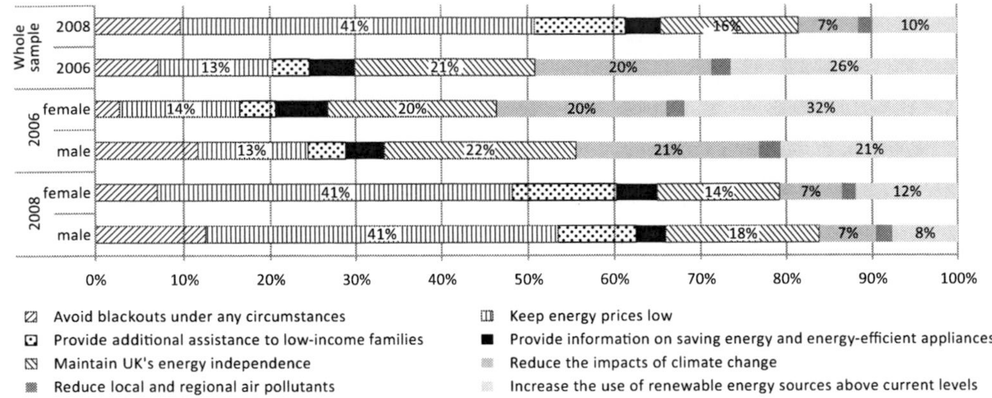


Figure 9.2 National energy policy priorities.

in need of attention, while around 2 per cent of the respondents chose water and wastewater services as their first choice. Electricity and water services were the least popular first choices and although they received higher second- and third-choice ratings, they remained the two least frequently cited concerns overall.

Respondents in the 35–44 age group chose health, electricity and water services as having a higher priority compared with other groups. Respondents who were between fifty-five and sixty-four years old were more likely to choose transport and waste disposal as a priority. Compared with males, a higher proportion of female respondents chose environmental protection, waste and health as top priorities. Compared with other regions, a higher proportion of respondents from Wales selected ‘health’ as their first choice.

### 9.4.2 *Energy policy preferences*

The respondents were asked to identify what in their opinion should be the top priority for a national energy policy. This question was asked in the 2006 survey as well and as Figure 9.2 displays, there was a dramatic shift in the priorities. In 2006 the top priorities for households were ‘increasing the use of renewable energy’ (26 per cent) and ‘reducing the impacts of climate change’ (20 per cent), both falling by almost a factor of three to 9 per cent and 6 per cent respectively. By 2008, we see a significant drop in the number of people choosing these two options. Instead we observe that people are far more concerned about ‘keeping energy prices low’ – around 41 per cent of our sample indicated this should be the

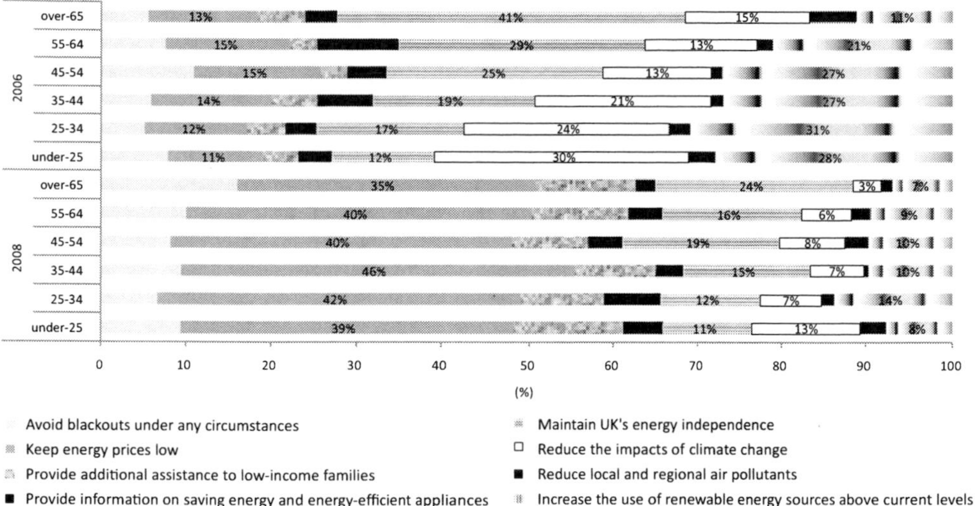


Figure 9.3 National energy policy priorities split by age.

main priority. The number of respondents choosing 'maintaining energy independence' and 'providing assistance to low-income families' also rose significantly – almost twofold since 2006. These changes in sentiment are not surprising considering the economic climate and volatile energy prices in 2008 when the survey was administered, as discussed earlier.

Overall there are no significant differences between male and female respondents, although there was a shift in sentiment between the years (Figure 9.3). Around one-fifth of both male and female respondents chose either 'reduce the impact of climate change' or 'maintaining UK's energy independence' as the top priority in 2006. In 2008, this share had shrunk to 7 per cent for 'maintaining UK's energy independence' and to around 14 per cent for 'reduce the impact of climate change'. The main difference between the genders was that a higher proportion of females chose increasing the use of renewables as their top priority compared with males in both 2006 and 2008.

Overall, the number of respondents with a preference for reducing the impacts of climate change as their top priority decreased with age, while the number of people indicating maintaining UK's energy independence as the top priority increased with age. The same pattern is observed on the issues of increasing the use of renewable energy sources.

We also observe some slight changes in the level of concern over the UK's energy dependence, with a higher proportion of people expressing that they were 'fairly concerned' about this issue than in 2006

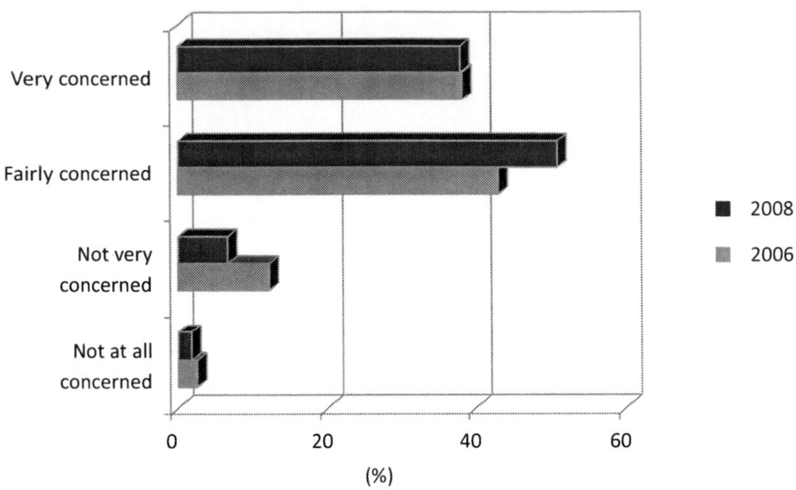


Figure 9.4 How concerned are you that UK is becoming dependent on foreign sources of energy?

(Figure 9.4). The share of those reporting that they were 'not very concerned' about the UK's energy dependence had shrunk by nearly half, from 12 per cent in 2006 to 7 per cent in 2008.

### 9.4.3 *Energy price effects on households*

The respondents were also asked how energy prices were affecting their household finances. In 2008, a higher share reported that energy prices were having a serious or moderate impact on their finances compared with 2006. Close to 18 per cent of our sample in 2008 indicated that energy prices were imposing a serious financial impact, while 33 per cent said they were imposing a moderate financial impact (Figure 9.5). A higher number of female respondents reported having serious hardship due to energy prices compared with male respondents. The difference between the two groups increased significantly in 2008.

### 9.4.4 *Household satisfaction with services*

In the 2008 survey we included a few questions on respondents' overall satisfaction with their electricity and water service providers and on the measures they were implementing to reduce their energy demand. One of these areas of focus was price.

We asked respondents to rate their electricity providers on maintaining reasonable prices. Atlantic and Scottish Hydro achieved the highest proportion of favourable ratings by their customers and npower had the

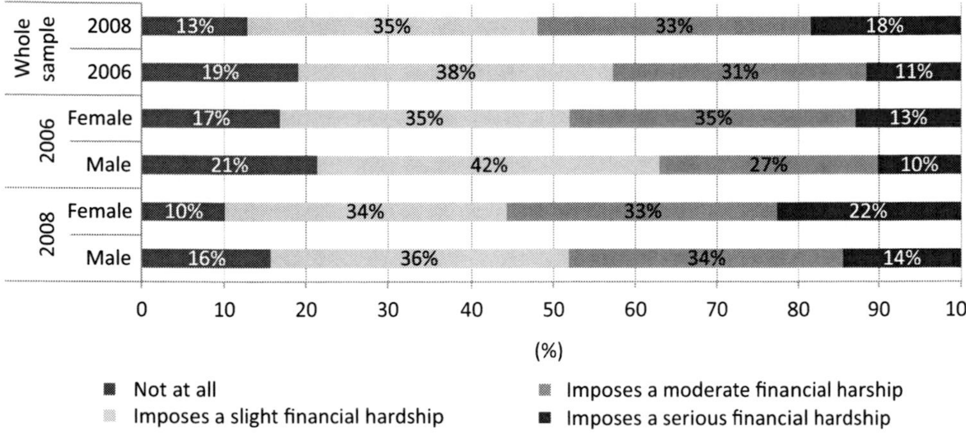


Figure 9.5 To what extent are energy prices affecting your overall financial situation?

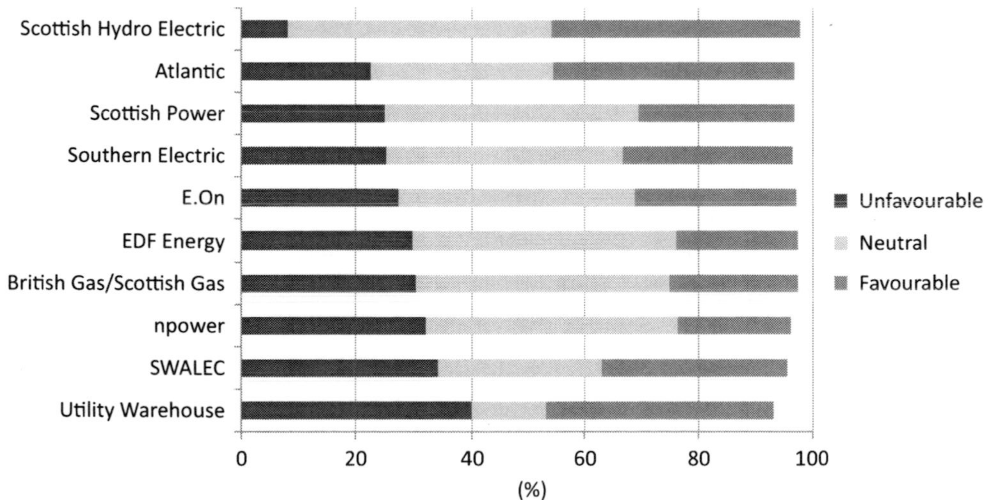


Figure 9.6 Household rating of electricity suppliers on maintaining reasonable prices.

lowest favourable ratings. Utility Warehouse customers had the most divergent opinions, with 40 per cent giving the provider a favourable rating and another 40 per cent giving an unfavourable rating (Figure 9.6). Scottish Hydro and Atlantic had the highest number of respondents reporting a favourable rating in terms of price. Overall, electricity companies received less favourable ratings than water companies.

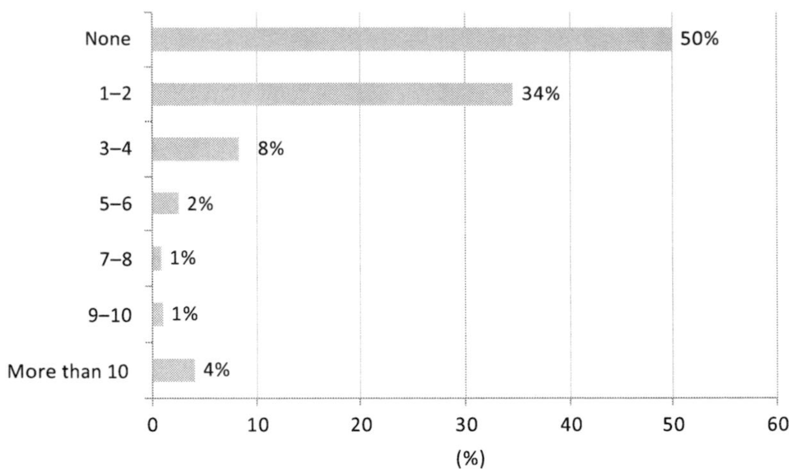


Figure 9.7 Number of blackouts experienced in the past year.

We also asked respondents whether they had experienced any power outages in the past twelve months (see Figure 9.7). Of our sample, 50 per cent did not experience any blackouts. Of those who had power cuts, the majority had only one or two during the year. Around 8 per cent experienced 3–4 blackouts during the year, while 4 per cent reported experiencing more than ten.

Close to 10 per cent of the respondents from London reported having more than ten outages in the past year. The second highest share was in South Eastern England, with 4 per cent of the respondents reporting more than ten outages. Respondents whose electricity supplier was EDF energy (23 per cent), npower (16 per cent) or Scottish Power (16 per cent) stated that they had a higher number of outages.

We also asked specific questions in the survey related to supplier switching (Figure 9.8). In terms of switching behaviour, 52 per cent of respondents said they had changed their gas or electricity provider in the past five years without moving home (45 per cent did not change and 4 per cent did not know whether they had switched). The number of people who reported switching suppliers was slightly higher in 2008 than in 2006, when 48 per cent of the sample reported that they had switched suppliers.

Respondents were allowed to choose multiple reasons for switching supplier. Price was the primary reason in both the 2006 and 2008 surveys. More than 80 per cent of those who switched said they did it for a lower price – about the same as in 2006. However, we see a higher number of people switching for price guarantees in 2008. The number of people

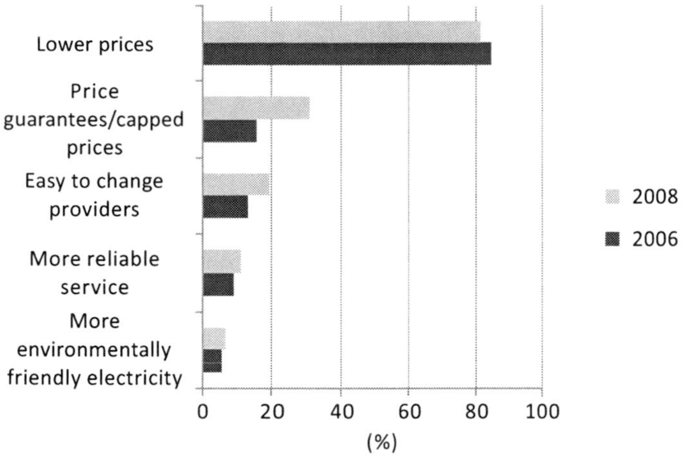


Figure 9.8 Reasons for switching suppliers.

who said they switched for price guarantees/caps had nearly doubled since 2006 (30 per cent in 2008 versus 15 per cent in 2006). This is again a likely effect of energy price increases experienced in 2008.

We also asked those respondents who had not switched suppliers about their reasons for not doing so. Most respondents stated that they were satisfied with the reliability (36 per cent) and price (21 per cent) of their existing supplier. Around 25 per cent of the non-switchers said that it was too much trouble to change suppliers. Only 1 per cent of this group stated that they were not aware of the possibility that they could switch.

### 9.4.5 *Household adoption of energy-efficiency measures*

The survey also asked questions about respondents' adoption of energy-efficiency measures. In 2008 we find a much higher proportion of the sample reporting that they were taking action to reduce energy use. More than 90 per cent of our sample said they were deliberately taking action to reduce their use of energy compared with 75 per cent of the sample in 2006.

The most popular measures adopted by the respondents included:

- turn off lights when leaving the room/house (92 per cent)
- fit energy-efficient light bulbs (85 per cent)
- turn down the thermostat (70 per cent)
- drive less than usual (50 per cent)
- insulate home (46 per cent)
- purchase energy-efficient appliances (41 per cent).

The only significant change occurring between 2006 and 2008 was that a higher number of respondents stated they were driving less than usual. This group comprised 50 per cent of those who said they were trying to reduce their energy demand compared with 39 per cent in 2006.

## 9.5 Conclusions

The two public opinion surveys conducted in mid-2006 and late 2008 bracket a volatile period in the history of UK energy markets. By the time of the 2006 survey, energy prices had been increasing for several years. It was over the subsequent two-year period up to the middle of 2008 that prices (and speculation over ever-higher prices) reached record levels. The cost of energy over the winter of 2007/8 in particular helped to transform the UK public from one which prioritized climate change and renewable energy in 2006 to one where 'keeping prices low' and 'assistance to low-income families' rose dramatically. Those expressing concern over the hardship imposed by energy prices also increased over this period. Still, energy prices were in the process of declining at the time the 2008 survey was held and fell throughout the second half of 2008, although prices did rise again, though less dramatically, in 2009. At the same time, 2006 was a time of bullish markets and healthy economic growth in the UK and globally, whereas 2008 was a time of exceptionally high insecurity.

The results show how susceptible attitudes to energy and the environment are to exogeneous factors. They also point to the limits of such shifts since it would be hard to find a more dramatic shift in conditions over the past three decades. The other clear difference that emerges is the dichotomy between consumer and citizen. Some of the questions were clearly intended to ask about priorities as citizens, such as national policy priorities or service provision. Others focused instead on respondents' role as consumers, such as changing utility providers or claimed individual behaviour. Clearly, the priorities expressed as citizens did not always translate into consumer behaviour – the strong concerns expressed about climate change in the 2006 survey did not translate completely into action. Nor did the record energy prices provoke significant changes in consumer behaviour, such as switching suppliers, although some of the reasons for switching suppliers (such as price guarantees) did change.

There is clearly a need for more research in the future to better understand the relationship between citizen opinion and consumer behaviour and the implications of this relationship for energy policy making. We observe that the opinions of citizens do not necessarily translate into significant changes in behaviour as consumers. This does not mean that the importance of the former can be discarded altogether. On the contrary, public opinion still plays an important political-economy role in the formation of energy policies. However, our indicative results suggest that shifts in public opinion alone have apparent limits in delivering desirable energy-policy objectives.

This in turn leads us to conclude that economic instruments aimed at altering consumer behaviour should have a central role in achieving these objectives. Just as the public can separate their roles as citizens versus consumers, energy policy making should also recognize this distinction and relate to these two spheres accordingly.

## References

Barr, S. and Gilg, A.W. (2007). A conceptual framework for understanding and analyzing attitudes towards environmental behaviour, *Geografiska Annaler, Series B: Human Geography*, **89 B**(4): 361–79.

Bird, C. (2008). Strategic communication and behaviour change: Lessons from domestic policy, *Engagement: Public Diplomacy in a Globalised World*, London: Foreign and Commonwealth Office.

Bord, R.J., Fisher, A. and O'Connor, R.E. (1999). Public perceptions of global warming: United States and international perspectives, *Climate Research* **11**(1): 75–84.

CCC (2008). *Building a Low-carbon Economy: The UK's Contribution to Tackling Climate Change*. London: Climate Change Committee.

Defra (2008). *A Framework for Pro-environmental Behaviours*, London: Department for Environment, Food and Rural Affairs.

Devine-Wright, P. (2007). Energy citizenship: Psychological aspects of evolution in sustainable energy technologies, in Murphy, J. (ed.), *Governing Technology for Sustainability*, London: Earthscan, pp. 63–86.

Eurobarometer (2009). Europeans' attitudes towards climate change. Special Eurobarometer 313. Brussels: European Commission; European Parliament.

Faiers, A., Cook, M. and Neame, C. (2007). Towards a contemporary approach for understanding consumer behaviour in the context of domestic energy use, *Energy Policy*, **35**(8): 4381–90.

Internet Communications Union (ITU) (2007). World Telecommunications Indicators 2007. Available at www.itu.int/ITU-D/ict/statistics/.

Ipsos MORI (2008). *Public Attitudes to Climate Change, 2008: Concerned but still Unconvinced*, London: Ipsos MORI Social Research Institute.

Jackson, T. (2005). Motivating Sustainable Consumption: A review of evidence on consumer behaviour and behavioural change. A report to the Sustainable Development Research Network.

Lazar, J. and Preece, J. (1999). Designing and implementing web-based surveys, *Journal of Computer Information Systems*, **39**(4): 63–7.

Lorenzoni, I., Nicholson-Cole, S. and Whitmarsh, L. (2007). Barriers perceived to engaging with climate change among the UK public and their policy implications, *Global Environmental Change* **17**(3–4): 445–9.

McKay, D.J. (2008). *Sustainable Energy – Without the Hot Air*, Cambridge: UIT.

Oppermann, M. (1995). E-mail surveys: potentials and pitfalls, *Marketing Research*, 7(3): 28.

Owens, S. (2000). 'Engaging the public': information and deliberation in environmental policy, *Environment and Planning A*, **32**(7): 1141–8.

Owens, S. and Driffill, L. (2008). How to change attitudes and behaviours in the context of energy, *Energy Policy*, **36**(12): 4412–18.

Pearce, D. (2006). The political economy of an energy tax: the United Kingdom's climate change levy, *Energy Economics* **28**(2): 149–58.

Sorrell, S., Dimitropoulos, J. and Sommerville, M. (2009). Empirical estimates of the direct rebound effect: A review, *Energy Policy*, **37**(4): 1356–71.

Thaler, R. and Sunstein, C. (2008). *Nudge: Improving Decisions about Health, Wealth and Happiness*, London and New Haven, CT: Yale University Press.

Varone, F. and Aebischer, B. (2001). Energy efficiency: the challenges of policy design, *Energy Policy*, **29**(8): 615–29.

Whitmarsh, L. (2009). Behavioural responses to climate change: asymmetry of intentions and impacts, *Journal of Environmental Psychology*, **29**(1): 13–23.

# 10 The local dimension of energy

*Scott Kelly and Michael G. Pollitt*

## 10.1 Introduction

More than half of the world's population lives in urban centres and this is projected to reach two-thirds by the middle of this century (OECD 2009, p. 21). Cities alone consume about two-thirds of the world's total energy production and account for more than 70 per cent of global $CO_2$ emissions through heating, transport and electricity use (IEA, 2008c, p. 179). Many urban centres are now making strides to mitigate greenhouse gas emissions (GHGs) and take control over energy consumption and generation. In this chapter, we postulate that some of the best opportunities for reducing energy demand and carbon emissions are through stronger involvement and leadership from local government. We show that local government can and does have a significant impact on both energy production and energy consumption and is an important participant for the implementation of distributed energy.

While the theory of free-riding goes some way to explain the difficulties in getting local governments to unilaterally cut carbon emissions, it neglects to account for many of the co-benefits of implementing such policies. For instance, the costs and the benefits of carbon mitigation are difficult to measure and thus introduce large uncertainty about the aggregate economic and welfare impacts different policies may have. Such uncertainty leads to inefficient decision making and to councils adopting a 'wait and see' policy rather than deriving direct benefit from more immediate implementation. While such a strategy may seem rational from a unilateral perspective, in aggregate it leads to inefficient outcomes where the majority of players choose to 'wait and see' rather than 'acting now'. Councils which choose not to adopt carbon-mitigation strategies are therefore 'free-riding' and benefiting from the knowledge and implementation strategies created by other first movers. While free-riders adopting status quo policies derive some secondary benefits from first movers, we show that first movers who have self-imposed and targeted local energy strategies do indeed derive direct benefit from self-imposed implementation strategies. In addition, local governments which work with and include local business and residents in carbon-mitigation strategies have a larger impact and a greater probability of success. Not only are synergies created and direct benefits derived for the climate but these partnerships are often financially rewarding to local government, business and the residents who participate in them.

In many parts of Europe, local government involvement in energy generation is well developed (e.g. Denmark, Sweden and Finland) and already accounts for a significant proportion of energy supply. In contrast, there are only a few leading examples of local authority-led energy schemes in the UK (e.g. Kirklees, Peterborough, Woking, Leicester, Aberdeen, Nottingham, Southampton). Interestingly, however, the localization of energy services in the UK is evolving more systematically than in many other parts of Europe. For example, in addition to the development of more local and distributed energy, local governments in the UK are considering demand reduction as a key component of their long-term energy strategies.

Local governments are shown to take responsibility over local energy matters for a number of reasons. First, local governments have a genuine and direct concern for residents exposed to fuel poverty. Second, they have an increasing awareness about the effects of pollution and GHG emissions, both locally and globally. And finally, they recognize that ambitious early action pre-empts future central government regulation. Equally important are the many ancillary benefits created when local sustainable energy strategies are adopted. These include regional economic regeneration, increased employment, improved energy security, lower energy costs, improved local environments and stronger connections between people and energy, thereby encouraging further energy-demand reduction. However, such strategies manifest only when there is clear political leadership from within an elected council and a genuine willingness from employees within the institutional hierarchy.

In this chapter, we will first discuss the development of local energy governance in a global political context and, importantly, how locally driven energy solutions are making an important contribution to meeting energy and emissions targets. We follow this with a discussion on how to reconcile the conflicting benefits of an asymmetric centralized energy system with a more balanced and distributed energy system within the UK. We then look at the implementation of distributed energy solutions in Europe and discuss how localised energy systems have evolved in several European states. Learning from both local and international experience, several bespoke energy strategies are identified that have significant potential to contribute to local energy-demand reduction and lower $CO_2$ emissions in the UK. The strategies identified include combined heat and power with district heating (CHP-DH), energy from waste facilities (EfW) and demand-side solutions using targeted financial instruments. For each of these technological strategies we show how energy services companies (ESCOs) can be employed as an appropriate vehicle for delivering each of the above strategies. Even with the heterogeneity of governance structures within the UK the opportunities and barriers for wider adoption of such energy strategies still apply.

## 10.2 Defining local energy

Climate change is widely regarded as a global problem requiring a global solution (Bulkeley and Kern, 2006; Defra, 2007; EU Insight, 2009; HM Government, 2006). It is on these foundations that multilateral agreements such as Agenda 21 and the Kyoto Protocol have been ratified. It is also the reason that such emphasis and political attention were directed at reaching an agreement during the Copenhagen Climate Change negotiations in 2009. With such immense political, economical and environmental inertia behind the present carbon-intensive socioeconomic system, concerted action at every level of society is necessary. This is particularly true for the local level for it is at the local level where policies are ultimately implemented, unique local solutions are found, the benefits of distributed generation are realized and the associated gains from social cohesion and cooperation manifest in both society and the economy.

Given the significant discrepancies in both scale and function of centralized versus distributed power system infrastructure, it is necessary to discuss the differences between such systems (Bouffard and Kirschen, 2008). Distributed generation (DG) is already well defined (see Bouffard and Kirschen, 2008; Woodman and Baker, 2008; Mitchell *et al.*, 2009; Pollitt, 2009; BERR, 2008) and typically refers to energy that is generated close to the point where it is finally used. DG systems can usually be defined as systems with capacities under 50MW that connect directly into a distribution network or the part of the network with an operating voltage between 240V and 400V (sometimes even up to 110kV). Distributed generation can thus be further categorized into three distinct groups (Figure 10.1):

1. Microgeneration is generation that occurs at the household level and includes technologies such as solar photovoltaics, micro-CHP and micro-wind.
2. Community energy initiatives usually evolve through grass-roots community-led organizations and typically build power facilities

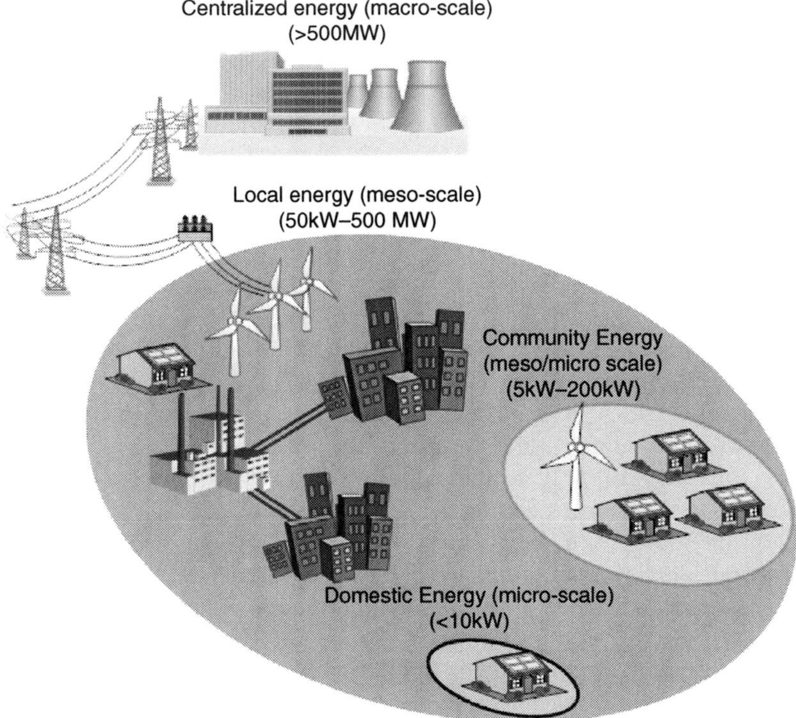


Figure 10.1 Graphical representation between centralized energy, local energy, community energy and micro-energy.

under 200 KW but may include heat schemes (e.g. biomass boilers and ground-source heat pumps (Hoffman and High-Pippert, 2005; Walker, 2008a, 2008b).

3. Local energy systems tend to be led by local or regional government, district network operators, existing energy companies or ESCOs and operate at the meso-scale. Because of this, local energy systems tend to be much larger in capacity than both microgeneration and community energy, usually with sufficient capacity to supply a town, city or region. Because locally led solutions are often created with support from local government, they usually have strong organizational structures and develop strong networks with other locally based organizations and businesses. Due to their size they are also able to leverage economies of scale usually afforded only to large centralized power plant.

Figure 10.1 is a graphical representation showing how the scale between different energy projects can vary. As shown by Walker and

Devine-Wright (2008), the process for defining what community energy represents is complicated and involves an understanding for how the project was implemented (who the project is developed and run by) as well as the intentions and purpose for the project once it is completed (who are the beneficiaries of the project). Thus using similar principles to those outlined above, it is possible to compare and contrast the distinction between local energy and community energy. Although there are clear overlaps between these two energy categories, there are also several distinctions; one clear distinction is the scale of the project. Community energy projects are typically below 200 KW in capacity while local energy projects can be defined as any energy source not connected to the national transmission grid and therefore can range in size from a few KW to 500 MW. The second distinction comes from the process of implementation and management. Community energy projects are typically developed via grassroots community organizations in consultation and sometimes in partnership with existing organizations through an organic bottom-up system. Local energy projects are developed by well-established large institutions such as local government or existing energy companies in partnership with local businesses, residents and sometimes government departments. One similarity between community energy and local energy is that they share the same outcome objectives; the beneficiaries of the energy project are the businesses and residents in the locality where the energy project is deployed.

Local energy solutions are typically guided by local government but can also be established by cooperative organizations, non-profit organizations or an ESCO where the ESCO represents the interests of multiple parties, via either a profit or a non-profit motive. A further distinction of local energy from other forms of energy generation is that local energy generation must first typically meet local demand. Depending on the system charges imposed on an embedded generator – which may be significant – it may even prove competitive for an energy project to sell excess electricity production on the open market. A further distinction and advantage of local energy solutions is that local energy incorporates both demand-side and supply-side solutions to maximize energy service delivery and therefore local benefit (Torriti *et al.*, 2010). For example, Aberdeen County Council implemented home-energy efficiency upgrades to its social housing stock before connecting these same homes to a district heating (DH) scheme. The key element of any local energy project is that it provides a bespoke solution for the locality and reflects the specific needs and characteristics where it is deployed.

Electricity generation and distribution in Great Britain, similar to other industrialized countries, relies on a centralized energy system to meet

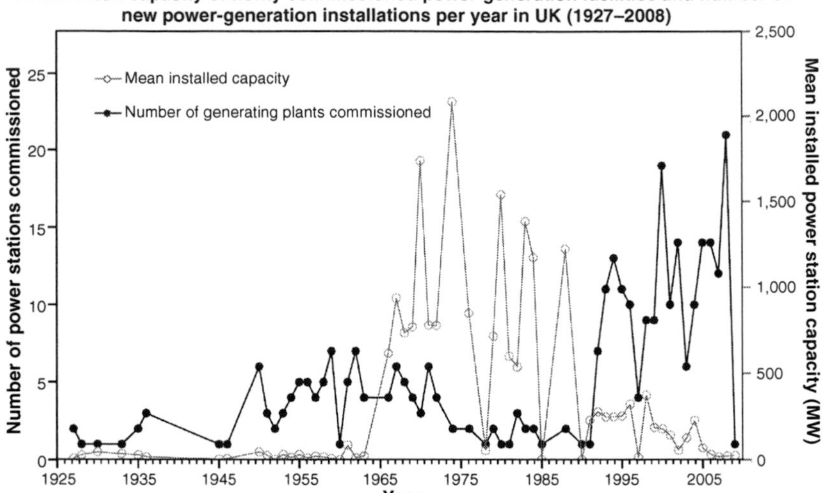


Figure 10.2 Trends in the annual mean installed power generation capacity of new power-generation facilities compared with the annual total number of new installations.
*Source:* DUKES Table 5.7.

the nation's growing demand for electrical power. Even today, the UK relies largely on power produced by aging centralized power infrastructure. However, analysis of data from recent history reveals things have already begun to change. It appears the trend for installing large, centralized power infrastructure has been diminishing since 1975, at which point the annual mean installed power station capacity in Great Britain reached its all-time peak (Figure 10.2). In addition, the number of new power stations commissioned each year, albeit at much smaller per-unit capacities, has been steadily increasing since the 1990s. Such trends can be explained by the increasing attractiveness of smaller and more localized power systems such as combined cycle gas turbines (CCGT), wind, biomass and CHP installations.

## 10.3 The context for local energy solutions

It is a well-established notion that global problems require global solutions. In general, this has been the mantra adopted by the EU and other international conventions on climate change (Collier and Löfstedt, 1997). However, an opposing view that has been advocated by several leading authors (i.e. Schumacher (1973), *Small is Beautiful* and Lovins

(1979), *Soft Energy Paths*) is only now beginning to gain wider support. Global problems, such as climate change, not only require global agreement and leadership but also rely heavily on local action. This intuitively simple idea was notably recognized by the Brundtland Commission and later ratified by the United Nations in 1987 with the publication of 'Our common future' (Brundtland and WCED, 1987). This recognition of the importance of localization and participatory processes for improving the world's environmental problems received renewed recognition when the majority of countries at the Rio Earth Summit signed Agenda 21 in which it was recognized that effective participation of local government is a determining factor in fulfilling the objectives of Agenda 21 (United Nations, 1992).

Recognizing that local government represents the closest form of governance to people, it therefore plays a vital role in educating, mobilizing and responding to the challenges of sustainable development. A key component to fulfilling this objective was 'Local Agenda 21' (LA21), where local governments in each country were asked to undertake a consultative process with their respective communities. The initiative was designed not only to create stronger rapport and participation in communities but also to promote cooperation and coordination between local governments, both locally and internationally. The UK is just one of a small number of countries with a coordinated national LA21 strategy, with more than 93 per cent of municipalities having developed LA21 strategies. This is encouraging when compared with France, where less than 1 per cent of local governments have a strategy (ICLEI, 2002). Despite the widespread acceptance of Agenda 21 in the UK, as a process it remains under-resourced and at the margin of many local government structures. Furthermore, it receives little support among senior officers and is frequently undermined by the top-level strategic plans of councils (Chatterton, 2001).

The growing emphasis of local decision making is in direct conflict with the increasingly prominent role of supranational organizations, such as the European Union, and multi-national energy companies that are assuming increasingly prominent roles in national and international energy policy (Burton and Hubacek, 2007). In contrast, it remains the case that local governments in the UK and elsewhere have limited influence over national and international energy policy (Collier, 1996). Bulkeley and Betsill (2003) argue that in spite of this, global environmental governance is a multi-level process and subnational governments play a crucial role, especially in the formation of transnational networks (see the Cities for Climate Protection (CCP) programme). They claim that such transnational networks of subnational governments represent a new form of environmental governance that simultaneously takes place at both global and local scales, seeming to bypass the nation-state. Such processes are frequently overlooked when defining strategies for delivering environmental governance (Bulkeley and Betsill, 2003). If programmes like the CCP do indeed present a new form of environmental governance, do they then provide a means for overcoming the barriers and reducing local GHG emissions? If so, there will be an increasing role for political and institutional leadership for the management and delivery of energy resources directed at the local level.

## 10.4 Reconciling local government strategy with local energy solutions

In both academic literature and public policy arenas, many well-supported arguments have been put forward that explain why local governments are important for the supply and delivery of and demand for energy services. Given that public administration accounts for approximately 5 per cent of total energy demand in the UK[1] (DECC, 2009a), significant savings can be made in the energy that is consumed in public buildings, hospitals, recreational facilities, council offices and other associated services. The Office of Government Commerce claims that local government consumes at least 26 TWh of energy per year, resulting in more than 6.9 Mt of $CO_2$ emissions and subsequent energy expenditure in the order of £750 million. More importantly, additional energy savings can be made from the more than 3.6 million council-owned homes in the UK classified as 'social rented' where it is estimated a further 5 per cent of total UK energy demand is consumed. Energy is one of the most controllable overheads in many local government buildings, thus providing many opportunities for savings. Space heating, for example, is responsible for more than two-thirds of local government energy consumption, making it an ideal target for further reductions (Figure 10.3). Some facilities managers have even shaved up to one-third off their building energy costs through the implementation of energy-saving measures. Street lighting is the next largest contributor of $CO_2$ emissions, responsible for approximately 41 per cent of local government $CO_2$ emissions (Figure 10.4). Thus, simply replacing the street lighting can have a significant impact on $CO_2$ emissions.

[1] In 2008 total energy consumption in the UK was 225 Mtoe, public administration and services alone accounted for 11.5 Mtoe where 0.9 Mtoe came from electricity, 0.3 Mtoe came from renewables, 7.3 Mtoe came from gas, 0.7 Mtoe came from petroleum and 2.3 Mtoe came from other solid fuels.

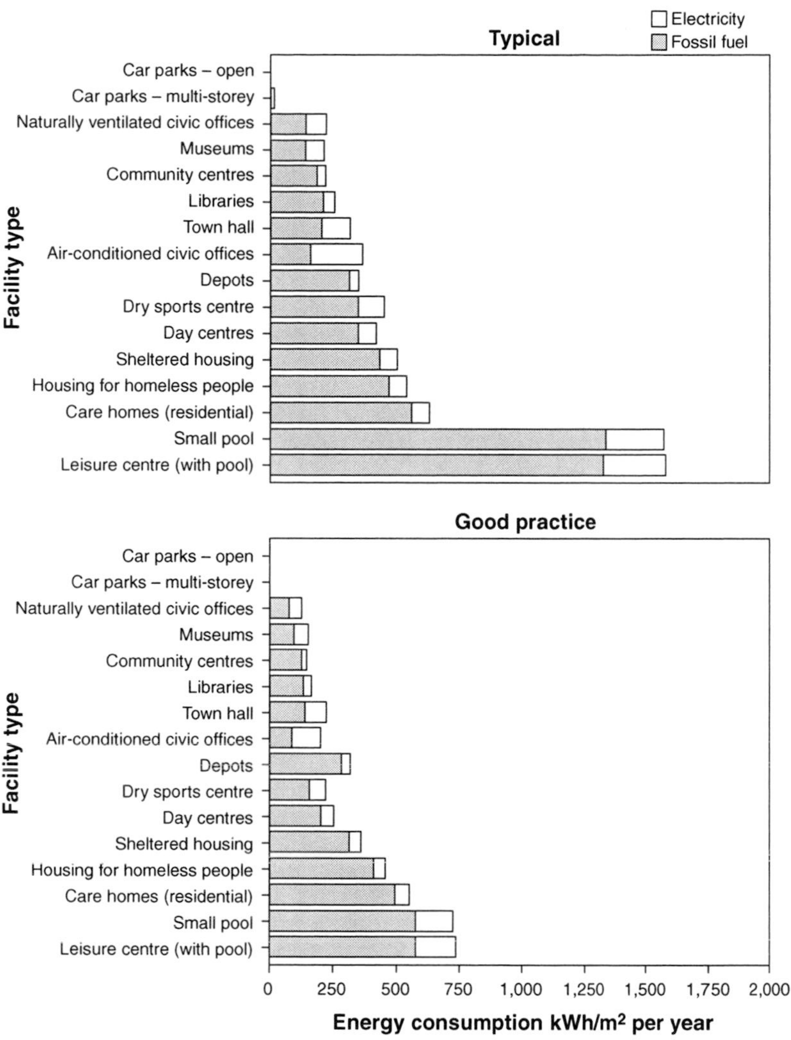


Figure 10.3 Energy consumption from local authority buildings and facilities.
*Source:* Carbon Trust (2004, p. 13).

It is not just through direct means that local governments have the power to reduce energy. As the layer of government closest to the citizen, local governments have an important role in leading by example, communicating and creating opportunities for demand reduction and increased efficiency. Furthermore, local governments are responsible for large areas

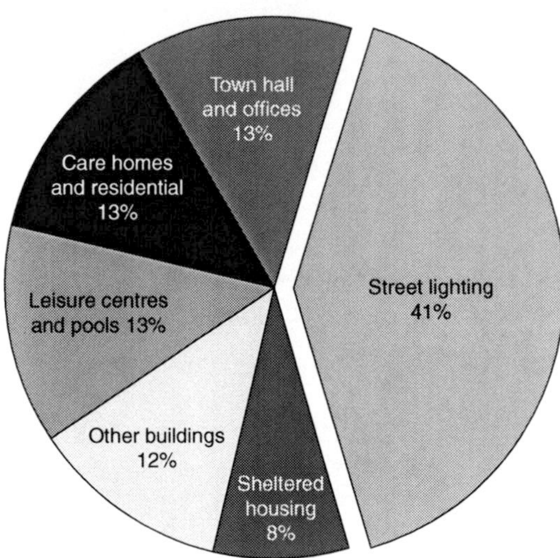


Figure 10.4 Breakdown of $CO_2$ emissions from local authority-owned infrastructure (excluding social housing energy consumption).
*Source:* Carbon Trust (2004, p. 21).

of policy that could be reformed to encourage significant behavioural change in business and residential sectors alike. They are also responsible for granting planning permission for local renewable-energy sites as well as the renovation of old and the construction of new buildings. Consequently, local governments can reduce energy consumption within their region by creating opportunities for and influencing the behaviour of residents to change their energy-consumption patterns (Coenen and Menkveld, 2002).

Increasingly it is recognized that energy and climate policy go hand in hand. In the UK this is shown by the recent formation of the Department of Energy and Climate Change (DECC), established to combine the policy objectives of both climate change and energy into a single government department. Although this department is at the national level, such synergies and organizational efficiencies can also be achieved at the local level. Local governments are increasingly given responsibility for meeting $CO_2$ mitigation targets. Given the significant contribution of GHGs coming from energy production it makes sense that local governments have influence over energy production and consumption from within their localities. Commentators also show that although climate change issues are a multi-level intra-national process, the implementation and practice of meeting targets is best achieved at the local level (Collier and Löfstedt, 1997; Allman *et al.*, 2004; Bulkeley and Kern, 2006; Bulkeley and Betsill, 2005; Burton and Hubacek, 2007; Hopkins 2008). As energy use is an important contributor to climate change, it follows that local governments need greater jurisdiction over the supply, distribution and consumption of local energy. Indeed, it has been clearly identified by three consecutive government white papers on energy that a more devolved approach is required to meet future energy and climate change targets (DTI, 2003, 2007b; DECC, 2009b).

The ability of local governments to respond to energy objectives within their district depends on many factors. Elements such as the demography, geography, culture, urbanization, the economy and resilience to climate change are all important, but perhaps the most critical factor is an authority's legal jurisdiction and political capacity to initiate change in its own locality. Coenen and Menkveld (2002) describe the framework in which a local government operates as its *playing field*. They identify two possible paths to enlarge the role of municipal involvement and therefore its capacity to initiate change for reducing emissions. The first is to increase the size of the playing field in which the local government operates and the second is to use the existing playing field as advantageously as possible. The former relies on a greater devolution of power and responsibility from central government or alternatively an increased willingness on the part of the local government to accept more responsibility in areas traditionally outside the council's remit – such as energy. The latter implies better management of existing governing responsibilities and processes. With this in mind, there is considerable scope to enhance the playing field of local government in the UK in both dimensions: local governments can do what they are already doing better but they can also take control over new areas traditionally thought to be outside their remit. Energy is a particularly important example because historically this has been outside the remit of local government, thus leaving considerable scope and opportunity for local governments to start having a significant influence over energy consumption within their district. For this to happen, the 'lock-in' from the present centralized system will need to be overcome.

Bulkeley and Kern (2006) contribute further to this discussion by identifying four modes of governance used by local government to implement change:

> *Self-governing* – the capacity of local government to govern themselves and is accomplished through better self-management.

*Governing by provision* – the shaping of local government practice through the delivery of particular forms of service or resources implemented by practical, material and infrastructural means.

*Governing by authority* – the use of traditional forms of regulation and direction through sanction and law.

*Governing through enabling* – when local governments facilitate, coordinate and encourage action through partnerships, private voluntary-sector agencies and various forms of community engagement.

Using such a framework allows us to categorize local government influence over energy and emissions (Table 10.1).

## 10.5 Lessons learned from the localization of energy generation in Europe

Denmark, Finland, Sweden, Norway and the Netherlands were among the first countries to take action on greenhouse gas emissions, agreeing to stabilize emissions at 1988 levels by the year 2000, two years before the Kyoto Protocol was conceived (van den Bergh, 2002; Alfsen, 2000). Today, Denmark is one of the most energy-efficient countries in the world[2] and Sweden has one of the lowest $CO_2$ emissions per capita among all OECD countries. Part of what made these countries unique and set them apart from other industrialized countries was their internal governance structure. For instance, the level of political jurisdiction of a local government can be placed on a spectrum ranging from those countries where local governments have considerable power to those where power is concentrated centrally. Sweden, Denmark, the Netherlands, Germany and Austria are countries with significantly devolved power and where local urban planning and municipal energy-management policy is commonplace. In the United Kingdom, Ireland, France, Belgium, Spain, Portugal and Greece, local governments have much less influence over energy policy and a more centralized energy system dominates (Coenen and Menkveld, 2002, p. 110). Norway is one exception as traditionally it has a centralized system, but approximately 50 per cent of energy capacity in Norway is owned by local government, a further 30 per cent by the national government and the remainder by private enterprise. This is predominantly explained by Norway's significant hydro-electricity resource managed primarily at the local level (Ministry of Petroleum and Energy, 2007).

[2] As measured by energy intensity in 2006 (gross inland consumption (GDP)/kg of oil equivalent). *Source:* IEA statistics, http://esds80.mcc.ac.uk/wds_iea/TableViewer/tableView.aspx

Table 10.1 *A framework to identify modes of governance for implementing local energy solutions*

| Governance | Strategy | Efficacy/Acceptability (Fair, Good, Excellent) |
|---|---|---|
| Self-governing | Self-imposed carbon budgets. | Excellent/Excellent |
| | Monitoring and managing own energy and carbon emissions. | Excellent/Excellent |
| | Energy efficiency schemes for local government buildings (schools, halls etc.). | Excellent/Excellent |
| | Using CHP (combined heat and power) to supply energy to municipal buildings. | Good/Excellent |
| | Purchasing green energy from the market. | Fair/Excellent |
| | Procurement of energy efficient appliances and technology. | Good/Excellent |
| | Installation of eco-house demonstration projects. | Fair/Excellent |
| | Increasing the minimum efficiency standards for council owned social housing. | Excellent/Good |
| | Installation of renewable energy projects for meeting own energy demand. | Excellent/Excellent |
| Governing by provision | Installation of energy efficiency measures in council owned housing. | Excellent/Excellent |
| | Implementation of new organizational structures such as energy service companies (ESCOs) | Good/Excellent |
| | Support for community level projects. | Fair/Excellent |
| | Interest free loans for installing energy-efficiency measures. | Excellent/Good |
| | Provision of CHP with district heating | Good/Good |
| Governing by authority | Minimum efficiency standards for new buildings. | Excellent/Fair |
| | Minimum levels for energy conservation in the renovation of old buildings. | Excellent/Good |
| | Strategic planning to enhance energy conservation. | Excellent/Excellent |
| | Regulated connection to CHP or renewable energy. | Good/Fair |

(*cont.*)

Table 10.1 (*cont.*)

| Governance | Strategy | Efficacy/Acceptability (Fair, Good, Excellent) |
|---|---|---|
| Governing through enabling | Campaigns for energy efficiency to the general public. | Fair/Good |
| | Advice on energy efficiency and demand reduction to business and citizens. | Good/Excellent |
| | Provision of grants or other financial incentives for energy efficiency projects. | Good/Good |
| | Promotion of renewable and decentralized projects. | Fair/Excellent |
| | Supplementary planning advice for energy efficient design. | Good/Excellent |
| | Supplementary planning and guidance for CHP and renewable installation. | Good/Excellent |

Reproduced from Bulkeley and Kern (2006).

In order to understand the economic effects of decentralization it is necessary to compare the energy intensities of these two groups of countries (Table 10.2). Therefore a two-sample t-test was created to test the null hypothesis that there is no difference between the level of centralization and the energy intensity of countries. The null hypothesis was rejected with 98 per cent confidence that the results were not down to chance alone. We can therefore state the degree of centralization of an economy is positively correlated with a country's energy intensity (i.e. countries considered to be highly decentralized have correspondingly low energy-intensity levels). This result is clearly shown in Table 10.2 where countries with more decentralized energy and political structures generally have much lower energy intensities and thus produce less $CO_2$ for each unit of GDP created.

Comparing two international examples – the USA and Japan – this distinction becomes even more striking. Within literature, it is generally agreed that during the latter part of the twentieth century Japan went through a process of democratization and decentralization, which led to local governments achieving a level of autonomy over policy and regional development agendas (Shun'ichi, 2003; Yagi, 2004). In contrast, the USA has a somewhat centralized political administration where power for the most part of the twentieth century was directed at state level and

Table 10.2 *Energy intensity of the economy: gross inland consumption of energy divided by GDP at constant prices in 2006 (kilogram of oil equivalent per 1000 euros)*

| | |
|---|---|
| Countries in Europe with greater devolution of power to local government bodies | |
| Denmark | 118 |
| Austria | 145 |
| Germany | 155 |
| Sweden | 188 |
| Netherlands | 188 |
| Countries in Europe with greater central government control | |
| Norway | 160 |
| France | 179 |
| United Kingdom | 193 |
| Greece | 205 |
| Spain | 211 |
| Belgium | 219 |
| Portugal | 225 |
| Other international examples | |
| Japan | 115 |
| United States | 291 |

*Source*: Eurostat (2009).

towards central government. In federalism, the federal government shares power with semi-autonomous states, which in turn devolve power to municipalities. Thus comparing these two diametrically different political structures, the USA being an example of centralization and Japan being an example of decentralization, it is informative to compare their energy intensities. Interestingly, Japan has one of the lowest energy intensities in the world and the USA has one of the highest, the USA producing only half as much economic output for each unit of energy input when compared with Japan.

During the 1970s, Denmark's energy system was highly centralized, consisting of a small number of large plants. Today the country receives heat and power from 16 centralized and 415 decentralized CHP plants (Odgaard, 2009). Such rapid deployment of CHP-DH during the 1990s can largely be attributed to proactive energy policy that targeted energy saving, technological development and the involvement of energy-distribution companies (MURE Network, 2002). The root of government policy to focus more on decentralization and CHP-DH was triggered by the 1970s' oil crisis when more than 90 per cent of energy demand was met by oil imports. District heating now forms the backbone of the Danish energy system, with almost all heating networks served by CHP plant and the vast majority of those owned by local government and cooperatives. With so many people reliant on the Danish heat networks, heat prices are heavily regulated to ensure consumer protection against natural monopolies. For example, the heat-supply law stipulates that DH networks must operate on a non-profit basis and heat and electricity prices must be cost reflective (IEA, 2009).

Unlike Denmark's heavily regulated approach, Sweden adopted a more market-based and local government-led approach not underpinned by a strong central government incentive regime. In Sweden, for example, local government brought together the owners of high energy-consuming buildings such as apartment blocks and company-owned office buildings so they could collaborate in the investment of DH where it may have been too expensive for one entity to consider it alone. In Sweden during the early 1970s, DH networks were heavily dependent on fossil fuels, but now more than 70 per cent of fuel for DH comes from renewable feedstocks such as biomass and municipal waste. In Finland, aside from a small initial tax rebate to kick-start the sector, minimal regulation was required to support the introduction of CHP-DH networks. Nevertheless, more than 65 per cent of Finland's thermal electricity production now comes from CHP plant (IEA, 2008a). The Finnish government has also maintained low barriers to entry for producers wishing to enter the electricity market. Any competitor that conforms to the necessary safety legislation can connect to the grid, paving the way for large CHP schemes that under normal conditions would have taken years to receive planning approval. Figure 10.5 represents the proportion of CHP generation capacity throughout Europe averaged between 2001, 2005 and 2006.

## 10.6 Local dimensions of energy demand in the UK

### *10.6.1 Political realities*

In the UK, in contrast to many other parts of Europe, the relationship between central government and local government is governed by the principle of *ultra vires*. Accordingly, local governments have permission to do only what they are statutorily permitted to do. This is in contrast to many parts of Europe where local governments can undertake any activities that they consider to be in the interests of their communities, unless they are statutorily *not* permitted to do so. This has considerable implications for local energy projects in the UK. However, as will be shown, the political structure is shifting and the implications of this shift could lead to significant changes to the energy sector in the UK.

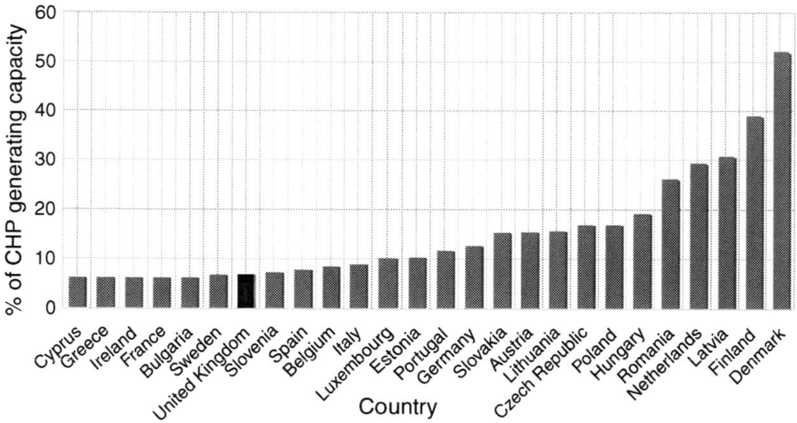


Figure 10.5 The EU share of generating capacity coming from CHP. *Source:* IEA data and analysis; data merged from years 2001, 2005, 2006.

Local governments in the UK are democratically constituted bodies that assume multi-functional roles covering such areas as education, health, social housing, planning, waste management, regeneration and in some limited cases the provision of energy. Prior to 1970, local government in the UK enjoyed a high degree of discretionary power with considerable say in the delivery of public services (Bulkeley and Betsill, 2003). With the introduction of the Local Government Act (2000) and more recently the Sustainable Communities Act (2007), local governments have faced significant reform to their organization, function and finance. With this new modernization agenda, municipalities have gained a new level of financial independence and responsibility, leading some commentators to suggest that local governments in the UK now have 'partial autonomy' (Bulkeley and Kern, 2006). Worthy of particular mention is the conferment to local government of the *power of wellbeing* with the Local Government Act (2000). With this new devolved power, local governments have the powers to act on any area 'likely to have a positive impact on the lived experience of the people in the area' (Communities and Local Government, 2009b, p. 32). This relatively new piece of legislation gives local governments wide-ranging powers in a number of new areas, but unfortunately, local governments are moving far too slowly to make any real or lasting impact. For example, NI188 is a national indicator that measures a locality's progress in planning to adapt to climate change and is measured on a scale from 0 to 4. In 2009, more than 50 per cent of authorities had a rating of 0 and just 15 out of

334 had a rating greater than 1. It is predicted the trend for increased devolution of power from central government to local government for the economic and social wellbeing of localities will continue and ultimately lead to increasing roles for local government in the management and governance of local energy resources (Communities and Local Government, 2009a). Local governments' willingness to accept and implement such powers is another matter altogether and may require deeper consideration.

### *10.6.2 Opportunities for introducing local energy solutions for the UK*

#### *10.6.2.1 Local government experience*

Local governments have the potential to exploit many distributed generation and local energy solutions. The first step for an authority implementing energy strategies is to learn from the experience of other local governments (see Kelly and Pollitt, 2009). For example, Kirklees council and Woking borough provide advice and consulting services to other local governments wishing to learn from their own experience. The second step is to gain thorough understanding for how energy is produced and consumed within the locality. The following questions are generally answered during this stage:

Where is the demand located – spatial?
When is it required – temporal?
How can demand match supply – spatially and temporally?
How much is required – physical capacity?
What type of energy is required – resource availability?

After this information has been collected, bespoke strategies for the locality can be planned. Several of the most common solutions implemented by local governments include CHP-DH, EfW, the establishment of ESCOs and the introduction of financial incentives for installing energy-efficiency measures. The opportunities and potential barriers of each of these core strategies shall now be discussed.

The district of Kirklees has long been recognized as a pioneer for implementing sustainable development and has featured as a case study in several peer-reviewed journal articles (Bulkeley and Kern, 2006; Burton and Hubacek, 2007). Located on the western border of Yorkshire and Humberside, Kirklees was the only local government to enrol in the UK emissions trading scheme (UK ETS) (Kirklees Council, 2010). This commitment required the council to reduce in-house emissions by 12 per cent between 2002 and 2006. During the first stages of implementation, the council learned about the importance of accurate and frequent monitoring of fuel consumption across all of its sites. It achieved this by installing an electronic data interchange (EDI) and billing system, thus enabling the council to get monthly energy-consumption statistics for all of its sites. By receiving this information electronically, the council was able to monitor energy-consumption patterns and identify high-consumption areas and peaks in demand. Properties that were identified as high-energy consumers were then targeted for energy-efficiency technologies and upgrades.

Similarly, Peterborough Council, located on the border of the East Midlands, in 2009 identified the need to develop a county-wide local energy strategy and set about collecting accurate data on energy consumption and emissions for lower super output areas (LSOAs) for the entire council (Peterborough Council, 2010). It is thought this data-collection exercise is the first occasion an energy audit of this scale has been conducted by any local government in the UK (Harker and Chatterton, 2009). Armed with new, highly disaggregated information about energy consumption, the authority could develop baseline energy projections and construct future energy options for the council. A main finding from this analysis was that a single county-wide energy strategy would not work across all LSOAs within the city. Instead, more targeted energy strategies for each zone would produce optimal results.

Local governments which have made the decision to reduce emissions and take leadership on local energy matters have succeeded by implementing targeted programmes. For example, in Kirklees a new corporate change programme was established to meet the targets established in the local area agreements (LAA). The programme aimed to raise local awareness, reduce greenhouse gas emissions, improve energy management of buildings and support the business community in working together through a 'green network' (Kirklees Council, 2007). Within the strategy both mitigation and adaptation issues were addressed in parallel and included long-term strategies such as developing biomass wood stocks for district heating and the completion of a climate impacts profile to quantify extreme weather events for climate-change adaptation. In order to implement these targets a new reporting and organizational structure was established within the council, incorporating a low-carbon board of senior managers reporting directly to the executive management and the council cabinet. In this new reporting structure, six climate-change sub-boards are responsible for meeting targets in key strategic areas.

The following sections will discuss key benefits and barriers to complementary and competing strategies for implementing sociotechnical energy solutions. At this point it is worth noting the inseparable connection between social networks and technology deployment (Guy, 2006). For instance, CHP-DH can be made viable only if a critical mass of actors (organizations) agree to participate in the network. Crucially, the viability of a scheme depends as much on the relationships between the actors (issues of trust) as on the technology itself.

*10.6.2.2 Strategy: CHP with district heating (CHP-DH)*

Although CHP and DH networks do not necessarily go hand in hand, the majority of local governments which have pioneered DH systems have also installed CHP plant to meet local base-load heat demand (Aberdeen, Nottingham, Southampton, Leicester, Woking, Barkantine). The decision by a local government to install a CHP-DH network is made for several reasons. First, CHP-DH networks provide affordable and manageable onsite energy generation and distribution for council-owned infrastructure such as halls, schools and swimming pools. They also provide affordable heating and electricity for council-owned housing as a way to reduce energy costs and alleviate fuel poverty (BERR, 2007). Finally, CHP-DH is a proven technology that has real potential to reduce $CO_2$ emissions, both through energy-efficiency gains and through the combustion of low-carbon fuels such as biomass and waste (Torchio *et al.*, 2007; DTI, 2007a; IEA, 2008b). In addition, CHP-DH provides increased energy security because it can be operated in island mode (independent from the grid) but also because when local low-carbon fuels are used, susceptibility to the volatility of international energy markets is mitigated. Ancillary benefits include a more robust and better-managed heat infrastructure, increased employment opportunities and therefore local economic regeneration and development of local capacity. Unfortunately, the number of CHP-DH networks in the UK has stagnated despite a significantly decreasing heat-to-power ratio and increased government intervention to encourage CHP development (Figure 10.6).

*10.6.2.3 Strategy: energy from waste (EfW)*

Fuelling CHP-DH networks using municipal waste is increasingly becoming a method of choice for local governments. This is driven by (1) central government's ambitious target to reduce waste sent to landfill by 50 per cent by 2020, (2) an increasing landfill tax, (3) environmental problems arising from poorly managed landfill sites, and (4) a government target to have 12 per cent of all heat coming from renewable resources by 2020 (DECC, 2009c). Although the mix of waste-disposal options is primarily driven by the government's Waste Strategy (Defra, 2008), local governments have increasing responsibility for meeting targets through significant increases in both recycling and EfW facilities (Biffaward and C-Tech, 2003). In 2006, waste processed in EfW accounted for 8 per cent of total waste or 2.8 Mt, sufficient to heat and

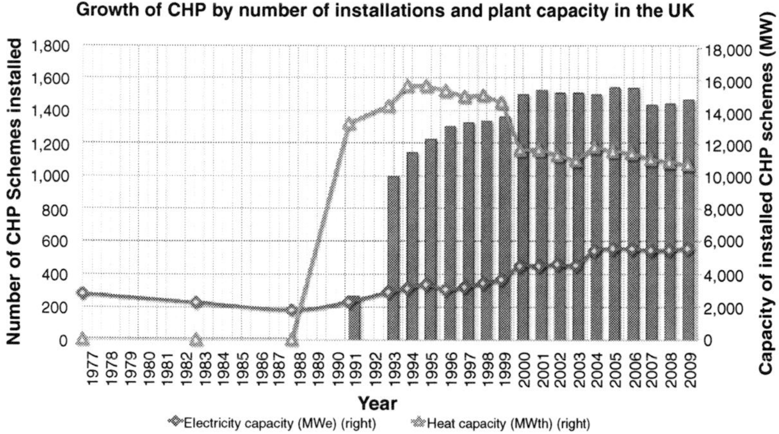


Figure 10.6 Growth of CHP capacity in the UK (1977–2006).
*Source:* Graph created from data on the DUKES database (2008).

power 250,000 homes; in 2020, EfW facilities are expected to process at least 25 per cent of total waste generated, providing heat and power for more than 1 million homes (Environmental Services Association, 2009).

It is clear why municipalities increasingly choose EfW facilities. First, waste is regarded as a semi-renewable energy resource, since approximately 70 per cent of municipal solid waste (MSW) is defined as being carbon neutral (Energy Future Solutions, 2005). Second, there is strong evidence from Europe that countries that rely heavily on EfW have high recycling rates (Defra, 2008, p. 78). Third, EfW is seen as a win–win solution where waste and energy problems are solved simultaneously. Finally, waste not being sent to landfill sites eliminates the creation of methane – a GHG twenty times more potent than $CO_2$. Evidence for the competitiveness of EfW is shown by the success of the existing twenty operational facilities in the UK and the growing number of predicted or planned new installations. In 2007, 29 Mt of MSW was produced, where 31 per cent was recycled, 11 per cent was used in EfW facilities and the remainder, 58 per cent, went to landfills (Defra, 2009). Using conservative estimates, at least 25 TWh of heat and power[3] can be produced from MSW in the UK annually. This equates to about 5 per cent of present UK domestic energy demand (heat and electricity), estimated

[3] Approximately 30Mt of MSW is produced each year where we assume 10Mt are recycled and 20Mt can be used for the generation of heat and power. Using a net calorific value (NCV) for MSW of 2.5 MWh/t and a 50 per cent conversion efficiency, we estimate that approximately 25 TWh of heat and power can be produced annually.

at 500 TWh per year (DECC, 2009a). Supplementing municipal waste with industrial and agricultural waste could significantly increase this unexploited energy resource.

There are, however, many barriers for implementing EfW. For example, all EU states must meet stringent regulatory requirements concerning pollutant emissions to air, land and water (EU Directive 2000/7/76/EC). Such demands require costly abatement, monitoring and control equipment, thus making large plants more cost effective through economies of scale. Despite strict anti-pollution regulations, local opposition has hampered many EfW facilities and remains a significant hurdle for local governments to gain public acceptance (Franchini *et al.*, 2004; Greenpeace, 2004). There are also serious shortcomings in plant efficiencies with some EfW plant rated with efficiencies below 25 per cent. However, coupling EfW with CHP and district heating could help with this dramatically. Large plant size together with unpopular public opinion has driven EfW facilities outside population centres and away from heat consumers, making heat delivery through district heating not cost effective, or impossible. In order to combat this trend Scotland has now introduced minimum efficiency standards for all new EfW facilities (Scottish Environment Protection Agency, 2009).

When the benefits of CHP and EfW are combined with DH, synergy in the delivery of more sustainable energy can be demonstrated. Local governments are shown to assist these schemes first by connecting their own buildings but also by acting as a financial guarantor for the scheme by offering long-term energy-demand contracts for the supply of heat and power to council-owned infrastructure. Local governments can influence local planning laws to facilitate the installation of pipework and the connection of new buildings to a heating network. Furthermore, as coordinators and representatives, local governments can offer encouragement and other incentives for residents and local businesses to connect to heating networks. Finally, local governments have access to both national and international funds that can be used to offset some of the high up-front capital expenses required for installing CHP-DH networks, thus making them more attractive.

#### *10.6.2.4 Strategy: establishing an energy service company (ESCO)*

Among local governments in the UK there is an increasing trend to use ESCOs for managing local energy services. This trend is also supported by the government with one of the major recommendations coming out of the government's heat and energy saving strategy for a new focus on delivering local low-carbon heat and electricity. There is also growing acceptance that ESCOs are a viable and appropriate special purpose vehicle (SPV) capable of delivering 'energy services' such as heat and light rather than merely units of gas and electricity. This is shown by the increasing interest and recent establishment of ESCOs throughout the UK (e.g. Woking (1999), Birmingham (2007), Leicester (2003), Kirklees (2005), Peterborough (2010)). Usually ESCOs are collaborative ventures owned by both public and private organizations, and can be either profit or non-profit motivated. ESCOs provide many benefits, but most importantly they allow for the organization and ownership of the supply, delivery and consumption of energy locally. The benefits of creating an ESCO include bulk purchases of energy efficiency measures, implementation of creative financial mechanisms, energy performance contracting and the direct specialist management of energy resources. Because an ESCO is an independent company at arm's length from the owners, they lower risk on large projects and provide a legal mechanism for the apportionment of shares and profits. For example, in Peterborough an ESCO is proposed to bring together the interests of several parties, including EDF, Peterborough City Council, British Gas and Opportunity Peterborough (Harker and Chatterton, 2009). Indeed, in the government's 'renewable heat and energy saving strategy' it is clear ESCOs will play an increasingly important role for delivering future energy services in the UK.

Two categories of legal contracts are used in the creation of ESCOs that represent the varied interests of parties involved. One of the most common contracts in the UK is 'energy supply contracting' (ESC), where consumers are sold energy at pre-agreed rates. The ESCO guarantees a level of energy service and is then free to act and make decisions for energy efficiency purposes to reduce its own costs. The ESCO or contractor is responsible for maintenance and offers support for the life of the project. These schemes are frequently financed using the Build Own Operate Transfer (BOOT) financing model. The second category of contracts usually implemented by ESCOs is energy performance contracting (EPC). Using EPC methods, it is possible to drawdown on future savings gained from installed energy efficiency measures in order to provide sufficient finances to invest in the energy efficiency measures up-front. ESCOs are thus able to provide energy performance guarantees for the provision of energy, the cost of energy and energy savings. The energy savings can then be distributed in a pre-arranged agreement between the ESCO and the client, where the client can choose to reinvest in more improvements if desired. This approach differs from pure ESC methods because savings in both energy production and delivery are targeted (Energy Saving Trust, 2008; Smith, 2007; TNEI, 2008; Werner and Dhcan, 2008).

Increasingly, ESCOs also offer services to improve household efficiency or provide finance for the development of district heating networks. In sum, ESCOs are seen as an appropriate way to minimize risk, increase revenues, appropriately apportion ownership rights and provide specialist energy services typically outside of public experience.

*10.6.2.5 Strategy: creative financial instruments*

Local governments also have significant potential to encourage and implement energy-saving strategies in residential homes within their district. Usually schemes administered by central government are available only for the elderly or those people on qualifying benefits (e.g. Warm Front). In Kirklees, however, Warm Zone Plus was established to provide free cavity wall insulation to all residents, not just those in fuel poverty. In the first two years of Warm Zone Plus (until July 2009), more than 143,000 homes engaged with the scheme and 43,000 homes received free insulation, with the average householder saving £209 per year, equating to total annual savings in the order of £8.9 million (Kirklees Council, 2009).

Similar schemes often provide the up-front capital, sometimes as a grant (Warm Zone Plus) but more commonly as a loan with little or no interest being demanded from the resident. Any balance remaining on the loan is then paid back when the property is sold – when there are sufficient funds to cover the expense. Examples of such schemes include the Kirklees Re-Charge scheme or Suncities project (Environment Unit and Browne, 2008). Alternatively, the energy savings achieved during the life of the investment can be used to pay back the initial capital (as in the UK government's proposed 'Green Deal'). There are, however, several barriers preventing these schemes from being more widely adopted. Large sums of up-front capital are usually required to finance the scheme and although this sum is usually paid back over time, the interest is generally written off. Overcoming these barriers requires securing finance from multiple sources and innovative accounting methods. Kirklees Council managed to do this with grants from Scottish Power, the National Grid, the Regional Housing Board and the British Gas Energy Trust. Implementing and managing these financial arrangements can be complicated and administratively burdensome and generally leads to local government outsourcing the management of financial schemes to external management companies, including ESCOs.

### *10.6.3 Discussion*

The UK government has recognized that distributed generation can make a significant contribution to reducing the UK's carbon emissions

(Woodman and Baker, 2008). Moreover, when municipalities make the decision to implement energy strategies they have many tools and opportunities at their disposal, such as planning and regulation, waste-disposal systems, grants and subsidies, district-wide energy strategies and energy consumption in council-owned buildings. In addition, municipalities which have implemented energy strategies have seen cost savings, increased employment and improved quality of life for their citizens. For example, since 2001 the Cornwall Sustainable Energy Partnership – comprising local government, universities and private companies – has been working to reduce $CO_2$ emissions. In 2009, funding was agreed for a £42 million wave-energy facility. An economic impact assessment estimated that the project would create almost 1,000 jobs and boost the local economy by a further £332 million over twenty-five years (and a further 800 jobs and £228 million elsewhere in the UK) (Audit Commission, 2009).

There are many co-benefits for local authorities adopting these types of solution. For example, local governments receive increased energy resilience through a more diverse energy supply; they mitigate uncertain and volatile international energy prices; and they secure the regeneration of local economies through the sourcing of local energy supplies such as biomass and waste. When local governments have responsibility over local energy systems, they create economies of scale through supplying energy to their own infrastructure but also through economies of scope by providing demand-side efficiency solutions and developing creative opportunities for reduced energy consumption.

Since 2008 two-thirds of all local area agreements (LAAs) have specific targets for reducing $CO_2$ emissions from a 2005 baseline; however, only one in five has a stretching target and fifty have no target at all, including fifteen of the highest emitting localities. Targets range from 1 per cent reduction in Bristol to 15 per cent in Kirklees with the median reduction target being 10.6 per cent. If all areas where targets are set achieve the anticipated level of reductions this will achieve just 6 per cent of the $CO_2$ savings required to deliver the UK 2050 target. A small number of local governments have made GHG inventories, developed strategies and implemented energy solutions despite such measures not being a legal requirement (Audit Commission 2009, p. 18).

The lack of implementation of local energy solutions may be explained partly by the significant barriers that need to be overcome. These include:

*Significant upfront capital costs* inhibit investment from public and private sectors in supply and distribution infrastructure such as district heating pipe work or high-volume efficiency programmes.

*Long payback periods* are typical of high-cost and large-scale renewable energy projects, making investment in such projects unattractive compared with other high-return and low-risk investments.

*Increased risk* due to high up-front capital costs and long payback periods of energy-saving projects commands higher financial returns for a project, increasing the initial hurdles a project must reach before it is even deemed viable.

*Hidden costs and high transaction costs* that are a result of brokering and maintaining public–private partnerships or establishing organizations such as ESCOs discouraging investment.

*A convoluted and difficult national subsidy and rebate system* acts as a deterrent for new entrants, thus preventing competition and lower energy prices.

*Political and economic 'lock-in'* from existing centralized infrastructure disadvantages small, variable or unpredictable power.

*Insufficient information or 'know-how'* among public bodies for creating and implementing local energy systems is low and requires national programmes to build capacity.

*Policy restrictions* on private wire networks (PWNs) and an insufficient market for heat provide little incentive for large industry to supply waste heat into DH networks.

*Principal–agent problems* inhibit investment in energy efficiency because the owner of the home does not pay the energy bills and is therefore not interested in making the investments in energy efficiency.

*Consumer preference problems* occur when a consumer resists change to more efficient alternatives such as energy-saving light bulbs.

*Negative externalities* such as locating renewable energy projects close to city centres may encourage local opposition and prevent projects moving forward.

*Many local governments lack good quality data* about the housing stock in their region, making it difficult to target effectively and assess opportunities to get the best value for money.

As shown, a number of barriers act to prevent local energy deployment (Kousky and Schneider, 2003), but as presented by Allman *et al.* (2004), these barriers change depending on the stage or level of progress a local government has made towards implementing local energy strategies. While local governments provide many of the answers for increasing the uptake of distributed generation, they also sometimes become part of the problem. Planning rules and regulations need to appropriately reflect the benefit that distributed renewable energy and local demand reduction measures provide to society. Without such support the roll-out of distributed renewable energy infrastructure may not take hold.

## 10.7 Conclusion

The progress being made by successful local governments can be narrowed to three key factors. First, they have all recognized the co-benefits of a local energy strategy: a reduction in fuel poverty, increased employment, improved quality of life and mitigation of uncertain fuel supplies and prices. Second, successful councils have strong political leadership and employee support to implement the structural change to bring about change. Third, leading councils have gained momentum by working in partnership with utilities, private companies, NGOs, DNOs and government departments to raise finance and garner support. With increasing uncertainty over international global climate change negotiations and similar challenges facing national energy targets, locally led solutions are set to be an increasingly important dimension for both the supply and demand of energy. It is therefore imperative that regulation reflects the benefits that local energy systems can deliver.

## References


Alfsen, K.H. (2000). A trip down memory lane: Looking back on climate targets, Available at: www.cicero.uio.no/media/558.pdf, last accessed 3 August 2010.

Allman, L., Fleming, P. and Wallace, A. (2004). The progress of English and Welsh local authorities in addressing climate change, *Local Environment*, **9**: 271–83.

Audit Commission (2009). Lofty ambitions. Available at www.audit-commission.gov.uk, last accessed 3 August 2010.

BERR (2007). *Meeting the Energy Challenge: A White Paper on Energy*. London: Stationery Office, Available at: www.berr.gov.uk/files/file39387.pdf, last accessed 3 August 2010.

BERR (2008). Renewable energy strategy, Available at: www.berr.gov.uk/energy/sources/renewables/strategy/page43356.html, last accessed 3 August 2010.

Biffaward and C-Tech (2003). Thermal methods of municipal waste treatment, Available at www.massbalance.org/downloads/projectfiles/1826–00237.pdf, last accessed 3 August 2010.

Bouffard, F. and Kirschen, D.S. (2008). Centralised and distributed electricity systems, *Energy Policy*, **36**(12): 4504–8.

Brundtland, G. and WCED (1987). *Report of the World Commission on Environment and Development: 'Our Common Future'*, New York: United Nations.

Bulkeley, H. and Betsill, M. (2003). *Cities and Climate Change: Urban Sustainability and Global Environmental Governance*, London: Routledge.

Bulkeley, H. and Betsill, M. (2005). Rethinking sustainable cities: multilevel governance and the 'urban' politics of climate change, *Environmental Politics*, **14**(1): 42.

Bulkeley, H. and Kern, K. (2006). Local government and the governing of climate change in Germany and the UK, *Urban Studies*, **43**(12): 2237–59.

Burton, J. and Hubacek, K. (2007). Is small beautiful? A multicriteria assessment of small-scale energy technology applications in local governments, *Energy Policy*, **35**(12): 6402–12.

Carbon Trust (2004). Local authorities: saving energy in local authority buildings, Available at www.carbontrust.co.uk/energy.

Chatterton, P. (2001). Putting sustainable development into practice? The role of local policy partnership networks, *Local Environment*, **6**(4): 439–52.

Coenen, F. and Menkveld, M. (2002). The role of local authorities in a transition towards a climate-neutral society, in Kok, M., Vermeulen, W., Faaij, A. and de Jager, D. (eds.), *Global Warming and Social Innovation: The Challenge of a Climate Neutral Society*, London, Sterling, VA: Earthscan.

Collier, U. (1996). The European Union's climate change policy: limiting emissions or limiting powers? *Journal of European Public Policy*, **3**(1): 122.

Collier, U. and Löfstedt, R.E. (1997). Think globally, act locally?: Local climate change and energy policies in Sweden and the UK, *Global Environmental Change*, **7**(1): 25–40.

Communities and Local Government (2009a). *National Indicators for Local Authorities and Local Authority Partnerships: Handbook of Definitions*, London: Communities and Local Government.

Communities and Local Government (2009b). Well being power – local government – communities and local government, Available at www.communities.gov.uk/localgovernment/localregional/localcommunity/wellbeingpower/, last accessed 18 November 2009.

DECC (2009a). Energy statistics: total energy – Department of Energy and Climate change, Available at www.decc.gov.uk/en/content/cms/statistics/source/total/total.aspx, last accessed 25 November 2009.

DECC (2009b). Heat and energy saving strategy consultation, Available at http://hes.decc.gov.uk/, last accessed 26 March 2009.

DECC (2009c). *Renewable Energy Strategy*, Available at http://tinyurl.com/2v4e5ee, last accessed 3 August 2009.

Defra (2007). UK energy efficiency action plan, Available at www.defra.gov.uk/environment/climatechange/uk/energy/pdf/action-plan-2007.pdf, last accessed 23 April 2009.

Defra (2008). *Waste Strategy for England*, Available at www.defra.gov.uk/environment/waste/strategy/strategy07/documents/waste07-strategy.pdf, last accessed 3 August 2010.

Defra (2009). Defra, UK – environmental protection – recycling and waste, Available at www.defra.gov.uk/environment/waste/index.htm, last accessed 24 November 2009.

DTI (2003). Our energy future: creating a low carbon economy, London: Stationery Office, Available at www.dti.gov.uk/files/file10719.pdf, last accessed 3 August 2010.

DTI (2007a). *Energy Trends March 2007*, Department of Trade and Industry, Available at www.berr.gov.uk/files/file38674.pdf, last accessed 3 August 2010.

DTI (2007b). *Meeting the Energy Challenge: a White Paper on Energy*, London: Stationery Office, Available at www.berr.gov.uk/files/file39387.pdf, last accessed 3 August 2010.

Energy Future Solutions (2005). Renewable heat and heat from combined heat and power plants – study and analysis, Available at www.berr.gov.uk/files/file21141.pdf, last accessed 3 August 2010.

Energy Saving Trust (2008). Energy services and renewable energy, Available at www.est.org.uk/housingbuildings/servicepackages, last accessed 3 August 2010.

Environment Unit and Browne, M. (2008). Recharge scheme, Available at: www.kirklees.gov.uk/community/environment/green/greenliving/home/re-charge.shtml, last accessed 10 November 2009.

Environmental Services Association (2009). Energy from waste – Environmental Services Association, Available at www.esauk.org/publications/briefings/energy_from_waste.asp, last accessed 6 April 2009.

EU Insight (2009). Climate change: a global problem requiring a global solution, Available at http://tinyurl.com/2vr2s7j, last accessed 3 August 2010.

Franchini, M., Rial, M., Buiatti, E. and Bianchi, F. (2004). Health effects of exposure to waste incinerator emissions: a review of epidemiological studies, *Annali dell' Istituto superiore di sanità*, **40**(1): 101–15.

Greenpeace (2004). Pollution and health impacts of waste incinerators, Available at www.greenpeace.org.uk/MultimediaFiles/Live/FullReport/3809.pdf, last accessed 3 August 2010.

Guy, S. (2006). Designing urban knowledge: competing perspectives on energy and buildings, *Environment and Planning C: Government and Policy*, **24**(5): 645–59, Available at http://dx.doi.org/10.1068/c0607j, last accessed 15 June 2010.

Harker, P. and Chatterton, J. (2009). Interview by author. Opportunity Peterborough, November.

HM Government (2000). *Local Government Act 2000: Chapter 22*. London: The Stationery Office.

HM Government (2006). Climate change – the UK programme, Available at www.defra.gov.uk/environment/climatechange/uk/ukccp/pdf/ukccp06-all.pdf, last accessed 24 April 2009.

HM Government (2007). *Sustainable Communities Act 2007: Chapter 23*. London: The Stationery Office.

Hoffman, S.M. and High-Pippert, A. (2005). Community energy: a social architecture for an alternative energy future, *Bulletin of Science Technology Society*, **25**(5): 387–401. Available at http://dx.doi.org/10.1177/0270467605278880, last accessed 12 September 2009.

Hopkins, R. (2008). *The Transition Handbook: From Oil Dependency to Local Resilience*, Totnes: Green Books.

ICLEI (2002). *Local government's response to Agenda 21: summary report of Local Agenda 21 Survey with regional focus*, Available at www.iclei.org/documents/Global/la21summary.pdf, last accessed 3 August 2010.

IEA (2008a). CHP/DHC score card – Finland, Available at www.iea.org/G8/CHP/profiles/Finland.pdf, last accessed 1 March 2010.

IEA (2008b). *Energy Technology Perspectives: Scenarios & Strategies to 2050: in support of the G8 Plan of Action*. Paris: OECD/IEA.

IEA (2008c). *World Energy Outlook 2008*. Paris: OCDE/IEA.

IEA (2009). The international CHP/DHC collaborative: scorecard Denmark, Available at www.iea.org/G8/CHP/profiles.asp, last accessed 5 October 2009.

Kelly, S. and Pollitt, M. (2009). The economic competitiveness of combined heat and power (CHP-DH) networks in the UK: a comparative approach, University of Cambridge, Available at www.eprg.group.cam.ac.uk/wp-content/uploads/2009/11/eprg09251.pdf, last accessed 3 August 2010.

Kirklees Council (2007). 2025 Kirklees environment vision, Available at www.kirklees.gov.uk/you-kmc/kmc-policies/environmentvision.pdf.

Kirklees Council (2009). Visions and strategies related to energy and climate issues, Available at www.kirklees.gov.uk/you-kmc/kmc-policies/environmentvision.shtml

Kirklees Council (2010). Kirklees Council, serving Batley, Dewsbury, Huddersfield, Holmfirth, Available at www.kirklees.gov.uk, last accessed 27 April 2010.

Kousky, C. and Schneider, S.H. (2003). Global climate policy: will cities lead the way? *Climate Policy*, **3**(4): 359–72.

Lovins, A.B. (1979). *Soft Energy Paths: Toward a Durable Peace*, Cambridge, MA: Ballinger Publishing.

Ministry of Petroleum and Energy (2007). Owners and organisation in the power sector – regjeringen.*no*, Available at www.regjeringen.no/en/dep/oed/Subject/Energy-in-Norway/Owners-and-organisation-in-the-power-sec.html?id=444386, last accessed 18 February 2010.

Mitchell, K., Nagrial, M. and Rizk, J. (2009). Network benefits of embedded solar systems: a case study from western Sydney, *Renewable Energy*, **34**(12): 2592–6.

MURE Network (2002). MURE Part II backcasting, Available at: www.mure2.com/doc/MURE_Backcasting.pdf, last accessed 24 April 2009.

Odgaard, O. (2009). Large and small scale district heating plants, Available at www.ens.dk/en-us/supply/heat/district_heating_plants/Sider/Forside.aspx, last accessed 7 December 2009.

OECD (2009). Competitive cities and climate change. Available at http://dx.doi.org/10.1787/218830433146, last accessed 3 August 2010.

Peterborough Council (2010). Peterborough City Council home page, Available at www.peterborough.gov.uk, last accessed 27 April 2010.

Pollitt, M. (2009). Does electricity and heat network regulation have anything to learn from fixed line telecoms regulations? Available at www.ofgem.gov.uk/Networks/rpix20/forum/Documents1/Telecoms%20Pollitt.pdf, last accessed 28 June 2009.

Schumacher, E. (1973). *Small Is Beautiful: Economics as if People Mattered*, New York: Harper & Row.

Scottish Environment Protection Agency (2009). SEP as thermal treatment of waste guidelines 2009, Available at www.sepa.org.uk/waste/waste_regulation/energy_from_waste.aspx, last accessed 3 August 2010.

Shun'ichi, F. (2003). *Decentralisation in Japan: Japan's Road to Pluralism*, Tokyo: Japan Center for International Exchange. pp. 21–45.

Smith, C. (2007). *Making ESCOS Work*, London: London, Energy Partnership.

TNEI (2008). ESCO feasibility study, Available at www.micropower.co.uk/publications/esco.pdf, last accessed 3 August 2010.

Torchio, M.F., Genon, G., Poggio, A. and Poggio, M. (2007). Merging of energy and environmental analyses for district heating systems, *Energy* **34**(3): 220–7, Available at DOI: 16/j.energy.2008.01.012, last accessed 14 June 2011.

Torriti, J., Hassan, M.G. and Leach, M. (2010). Demand response experience in Europe: policies, programmes and implementation, *Energy*, **35**(4): 1575–83.

United Nations (1992). Agenda 21, in *AGENDA 21*, United Nations Conference on Environment & Development Rio de Janeiro, Brazil, 3–14 June.

Jeroen C.J.M. van den Bergh (2002). *Handbook of Environmental and Resource Economics*, Cheltenham: Edward Elgar Publishing.

Walker, G. (2008a). Community renewable energy: What should it mean? *Energy Policy*, **36**(2): 497–500.

Walker, G. (2008b). What are the barriers and incentives for community-owned means of energy production and use? *Energy Policy*, **36**(12): 4401–5.

Werner, S. and Dhcan (2008). *District heating system institutional guide*, Available at www.euroheat.org.

Woodman, B. and Baker, P. (2008). Regulatory frameworks for decentralised energy, *Energy Policy*, **36**(12): 4527–31.

Yagi, K. (2004). Decentralization in Japan, *Policy and Governance Working Paper Series*, **30**.

# 11 Centralization, decentralization and the scales in between: what role might they play in the UK energy system?

*Jim Watson and Patrick Devine-Wright*

## 11.1 Introduction

The scale of future energy systems in the UK will have a significant impact on the evolution of the built environment. Yet, the scale at which energy systems emerge is closely connected with social and economic values and behaviours and the nature of governance at local and national levels. Today's centralized energy system has a particular relationship with the built environment through the way people understand and use energy services. Electricity is centrally generated in remote power plants; the majority of heating systems are fuelled by gas which is centrally distributed; and petrol for vehicles is refined and distributed through a few large depots. Electricity generation within the built environment is rare, while district heating networks are virtually absent.

A key issue for decision makers is whether the strongly centralized approach to energy provision that developed in the post-war period can continue to meet the needs of the economy and society over the coming decades. The current pattern of mainly large-scale power plants and centralized delivery infrastructures for electricity, gas and oil may be sufficiently flexible to meet the dual challenges of energy security and climate change, but this is by no means certain. Meeting these challenges could require a significant shift so that energy systems are located at a range of scales. Indeed, some government strategies such as those to increase the role of renewables imply that such a shift needs to start soon.

This chapter explores the scope for deploying energy systems that are both centralized and decentralized. Since there is considerable confusion over the meaning of the term 'decentralized', the chapter first

This chapter is based on Chapter 5 of the final report from the UK government Foresight programme's *Sustainable Energy Management and the Built Environment* project (Foresight, 2008). The authors were lead experts with this project, and were the main authors of this particular chapter.

sets out some definitions and explores the range of scales that this term encompasses. The chapter then considers some of the critical drivers for future energy systems and what they might mean for system scale. The chapter also focuses in some detail on the relationship between citizen engagement and the provision of energy services at different scales.

## 11.2 What is 'decentralized energy'?

The defining characteristic of decentralized energy is that energy is generated close to the place where it is used, so that transmission of electricity, heat and other energy carriers is minimized. A broad technical definition, offered by the former DTI and the energy regulator Ofgem, includes distributed electricity, usually defined as power generation that is connected to the low voltage distribution network at 132 kV and below (Department of Trade and Industry, 2006b). It also includes combined heat and power (CHP) technologies that are similarly connected, and decentralized applications of technologies that provide heat, such as biomass, solar thermal and heat pumps. In addition to this technical definition, decentralization has organizational, regulatory, governance and social components. It might mean that the ownership of energy infrastructure is in the hands of businesses, individuals, community groups and local authorities as well as energy companies. This would contrast with the centralized ownership that exists today where multi-nationals dominate in most parts of the energy system (e.g. oil extraction and supply, electricity generation, household appliances and power plant equipment). In addition, markets and regulations could be decentralized so that different regional or local priorities are reflected in devolved policy for energy systems. Rather than the current dominance of national and international policy, a decentralized future might be one in which the policies of local authorities and local or regional trading systems are more important.

As these definitions suggest, decentralized energy is a wide-ranging category that encompasses energy systems at different scales. Each can involve different technologies, institutions, policy and behavioural issues. Decentralized energy can mean a solar hot water panel on a house, a CHP system for a block of flats, or a larger power plant in a city centre or a rural area. It can also mean new roles for building occupants, not only as consumers of power, but as 'co-providers' (van Vliet and Chappells, 1999) blurring the distinction between producer and consumer. Co-provision suggests new behavioural practices, for example householders checking the levels of heat or power produced by their own systems using 'smart' metering technology (Keirstead, 2008) and scrutinizing

Table 11.1 *The spectrum of energy system scales*

| | Geography | Technologies | Institutions | Regulations and incentives |
|---|---|---|---|---|
| Centralized | International | Electricity inter-connectors | International Energy Agency | EU emissions trading scheme |
| | National | National gas grid | | 'BETTA' electricity trading rules |
| Decentralized | Region/City | | London climate change agency | |
| | Town/ Neighbourhood | Woking district heating system | | Merton rule |
| | Building | Microgeneration | Household | |

*Source:* the authors, adapted from original in (Foresight, 2008).

tariff levels to decide whether to directly use their energy or to sell it to utilities by exporting it back into the grid. Decentralized energy also suggests new organizational structures involving community ownership to different degrees and in different ways, including cooperatives, development trusts and community charities. These implicate different forms of community – both of locality and of interest (Walker, 2008b).

These different dimensions are explored in Table 11.1. Each row of the table represents a different scale at which energy systems can be deployed – from international to household. The columns distinguish between the technical, governance and regulatory characteristics of energy systems at these different scales. The cells of the Table provide some brief illustrative examples of the technologies, institutions and regulations that might apply at each scale. An energy system in the future might combine centralized and decentralized elements. For example, a hybrid energy system could include centralized power plants, a mixed transport system fuelled by oil and locally produced electricity, and significant heat and power generation in towns and cities.

Institutionally, hybrid organizations could become more prevalent, with large-scale wind farms being co-owned by multi-national companies and communities, when one or more turbines are 'gifted' to the community as a way of ensuring local benefit (Centre for Sustainable Energy *et al.*, 2007). Here the ability to influence investment choices and behaviour by citizens and firms would be shared between international, national and local institutions.

## 11.3 Scale and the current energy system

Decentralized energy has been important in the past in the UK, but the nation's current energy supply is highly centralized. Two thirds of UK heating demand is met by natural gas from a centralized network (Department of Trade and Industry, 2007). Less than 10 per cent of heat demand is met by off-grid heat generation – i.e. by sources other than gas or electricity. Furthermore, less than 10 per cent of the UK's electricity is supplied from renewable energy or CHP plants connected to the electricity distribution network (Department of Trade and Industry, 2006b).

The potential advantages of decentralized energy for meeting current and future challenges have led to extensive discussion and research in the policy, business and academic communities. The focus of much of this activity has been on electricity. Heat has only been analyzed in detail by government relatively recently. An important sign that these advantages were being taken seriously was the government–industry Embedded Generation Working Group, which reported in 2001 on a range of issues on network access (Embedded Generation Working Group, 2001). This was followed by a series of other committees and reviews such as a call for evidence on barriers and incentives for decentralized energy in 2006 (Department of Trade and Industry, 2006a).

Despite this significant activity, there have been only marginal changes in the contribution of decentralized energy in the UK. The deployment of CHP plants grew relatively quickly in the 1990s, but their total capacity has levelled off at about 5.5GW in recent years (Department of Energy and Climate Change, 2010). Most of the heat that they generate is for industrial processes rather than to heat buildings. Investment in microgeneration is growing slowly, despite the availability of government grants. The number of installations remains at about 100,000. The contribution of renewable electricity is limited, having increased from 2 per cent of UK electricity in 1990 to 6.7 per cent in 2009 (Department of Energy and Climate Change, 2010). However, not all of this is decentralized since it includes output from relatively large hydro stations.

There are many reasons for this limited progress (Wolfe, 2008; Woodman and Baker, 2008). CHP investment has slowed due to a rise in the relative costs of gas and the absence of the local utilities that normally install district heating networks in other northern European countries. For microgeneration, the need for planning permission (which has now been removed), the hassle factor, high up-front costs and a stop-start grant programme have all mitigated against investment. Larger-scale

Table 11.2 *Scale in the Foresight 'SEMBE' scenarios*

| | Geography | Resourceful regions | Sunshine state | Green growth | Carbon creativity |
|---|---|---|---|---|---|
| Centralized | International | [modest] | | [major] | [significant] |
| | National | [significant] | [modest] | [major] | [major] |
| Decentralized | Region/City | [major] | [significant] | [modest] | [modest] |
| | Town/ Neighbourhood | [modest] | [major] | [modest] | |
| | Building | [modest] | [major] | [modest] | [modest] |

*Key:* [black shading] denotes a major contribution from technologies, institutions and/or regulations; [dark grey shading] denotes a significant contribution; [light grey shading] denotes a modest contribution; no shading denotes little or no contribution.

renewables have faced significant planning barriers and still have to contend with long waits for grid connection.

## 11.4 Drivers for changes in scale

Future changes in energy systems and the built environment could have a variety of impacts on the scale of energy systems. This can be illustrated by looking at some of the different future scenarios for the UK which have dealt with this issue. For example, the Long Term Electricity Network Scenarios commissioned by Ofgem included both a centralized 'big transmission and distribution' scenario and a highly decentralized 'microgrids' scenario (Ault *et al.*, 2008). The Foresight Sustainable Energy Management and the Built Environment project explored four scenarios with significantly different patterns of energy system scales (Foresight, 2008). In some of these Foresight scenarios, the current centralized energy system prevails, meaning that there is little energy generation embedded within the built environment. In others, the built environment changes to absorb significant energy generation. Table 11.2 summarizes the scale of energy systems in 2050 within each of the four scenarios. Within the table, darker shading is used to denote scales which are particularly prominent in a given scenario.

How might these changes in scale come about? There are a number of critical drivers of energy systems and the built environment, many of which will have implications for the scale of energy systems in the future. In this section, five drivers are analyzed to understand better their impact on energy system scale: climate change, energy security, technology trends, the governance of energy markets and social change.

### *11.4.1 Climate change*

Climate change has been emphasized as the major priority for UK energy policy since the 2003 Energy White Paper (Department of Trade and Industry, 2003). There are a number of reasons why decentralization might help to meet the UK's ambitious targets for reductions in greenhouse gas emissions. Increasing the efficiency of energy use through CHP implies locating more electricity generation capacity near to the end-user, something in which the UK lags behind many other northern European countries (Hinnells, 2008; Roberts, 2008).

Many renewable energy options such as solar (photovoltaic and thermal), biomass (for heat and power) and wind can be deployed on a small scale, either close to or within urban areas. Such options can help to reduce carbon emissions from buildings alongside behavioural changes and efficient end-use technologies. Substantial investment programmes would be needed to upgrade the performance of existing buildings in this way (Power, 2008).

However, a low-carbon energy system can continue to be centralized too. Future scenarios to explore how the UK can cut its emissions to meet climate change targets have shown that there are different ways this can be achieved. For example, the Royal Commission on Environmental Pollution's influential scenarios which led to the original 60 per cent emissions reduction target for 2050 elaborated both centralized and decentralized scenarios (Royal Commission on Environmental Pollution, 2000).[1] Similarly, a scenario exercise by the Tyndall Centre (e.g. Tyndall Centre for Climate Change Research, 2005) and scenarios commissioned by Ofgem (Ault *et al.*, 2008) also explored the implications of different scales of low-carbon technology deployment.

It is possible that the current centralized energy system can be adapted to help meet stringent climate change targets. Low-carbon supply options such as nuclear, CCS and centralized renewable energy such as offshore wind could be deployed in large volume to do so. It is an open question whether such centralized scenarios would leave room for more decentralized governance structures and service-based business models that could foster significant demand-side cuts in energy use.

The costs of meeting climate change targets will be significant, but are expected to be much lower than the costs of inaction (Stern, 2006). When considering alternative pathways for the 'decarbonization' of the UK, it is inherently difficult to predict which pathway might be more or less costly than the others. Some voices within the debate on scales of

[1] This target was subsequently revised upwards to an 80 per cent reduction in all greenhouse gas emissions by 2050 compared to 1990 levels.

energy systems have claimed that decentralized systems could be cheaper than centralized ones (Greenpeace, 2006). Whilst there are economic benefits to be gained from siting energy generation closer to centres of demand, the costs of transition from our current centralized system are sometimes underplayed. A significant change of direction in energy system development will often look more expensive to governments and investors whose financial models are designed to optimize the current system. For example, a new wind farm in the North Sea looks expensive at present partly because it requires new infrastructure. However, if it were considered as part of broader change in the UK electricity system to include many offshore wind farms, the costs of system change would be shared among many projects – and would be much smaller for individual investors.

### *11.4.2 Energy security*

While energy security has always been an important goal of energy policies, it has become more salient in the UK in the past few years. This is due to a combination of factors including the UK's shift from a net exporter to a net importer of energy in 2004, high fossil fuel prices, geopolitical events (especially the Iraq war) and the blackouts in electricity systems in summer 2003 (Ofgem, 2004).

One dimension of energy security that has been prominent in recent government statements on energy policy is the need for timely investment in new power plant infrastructure. The 2007 Energy White Paper stated that 30–35 GW of new power plant capacity will be required over the next two decades due to the expected retirement of existing plant (Department of Trade and Industry, 2007). This implies that almost half the current power plant stock will be replaced – and has been further reinforced by the more recent Low Carbon Transition Plan which stated that 40 per cent of electricity should come from low-carbon sources by 2020 (HM Government, 2009). There will also be a need to replace and extend other energy infrastructure such as electricity transmission lines. The development of offshore transmission networks is particularly important to connect up to 35 GW of offshore wind capacity to help meet both climate change and renewable energy targets.

While meeting this need for new capacity will be a major challenge for decision makers in government, industry, wider civil society and energy companies, it also offers new opportunities. Infrastructure could be replaced on a 'like for like' basis, with a preference for low- or zero-carbon technology. This would mean little change for today's towns and cities. Alternatively, investment could be made at a variety of different scales, including much more decentralization. This could include measures to manage and reduce demand more actively than in the past, and a different geographical coverage, for example allowing connection of substantial offshore wind farms. One possible advantage of this more diverse approach to scale is that it might introduce more flexibility into investment patterns, and counter the inherent irreversibility of many energy system investments (Fielder, 1996).

There is no clear answer to the question of whether centralized or decentralized energy systems are more secure. For some analysts, more decentralized systems could be less prone to security risks because they can contain more redundancy. In other words, they are likely to contain many more power and heat-producing plants, more grid interconnections and more technological variety (Coaffee, 2008). However, managing such systems will be more challenging, and is likely to require new models for control and coordination. While centralized systems may not need more sophisticated incentive and control technologies or changes in governance, these could be vulnerable if they do not include multiple energy sources, supply routes and adequate energy storage.

In all cases, costs will be an important consideration. There is often a trade-off between the inclusion of more redundancy within energy systems and society's willingness to pay for this (NERA, 2002). For example, centralized gas supplies can be made more secure if governments mandate the construction of strategic (but non-commercial) storage facilities. By contrast, decentralized power grids might still need to rely on centralized power infrastructure to help balance supply and demand patterns within (and between) local areas.

### *11.4.3 Trends in technology*

The architecture of future energy systems will depend on the availability of technologies and the political, market and regulatory frameworks that are adopted. This includes technologies for energy supply and generation (e.g. solar thermal for hot water, wave power or CCS); for end-use (e.g. LED lighting); for network management with new information, communication and control systems; and for storage, for example using hydrogen. One of the reasons that decentralized energy is on the agenda again in the UK is that there are more decentralized technologies available and their costs have reduced. As noted earlier, their deployment has been very slow to date (Roberts, 2008).

Most investment in energy supply is still centralized. But the technologies to operate complex networks and markets with large amounts of decentralization have improved significantly as a result of developments in information technology (Bouffard and Kirschen, 2008). A key issue is the integration of decentralized technologies with the built environment. Buildings in the UK will need widespread retrofitting to improve their energy and emissions performance, especially to help them adapt as the climate changes (Smith and Levermore, 2008).

Retrofitting this building stock with microgeneration or perhaps with larger 'community-scale' energy supply technologies will be an important target alongside measures to reduce energy demand through energy efficiency and other means. Different technologies will be appropriate for different locations. A relatively large but still decentralized power plant to generate heat and power for a large number of houses and other buildings would make the most sense in densely populated areas. This form of decentralization is more efficient than deployment at the household scale. However, such projects would have implications for urban design. Space would be needed for new generation and heat network infrastructure. Retrofitting has an important social dimension, particularly at the larger 'community scale'. Changes to familiar built environments may be opposed by local residents if public engagement is poorly managed. Public acceptance of disruption to homes and gardens, and the switch from building to neighbourhood-scale heat and power systems will be contingent upon levels of trust in the institutions implementing change.

At the household level, geography and local circumstances also matter. A micro wind turbine is much more likely to generate significant amounts of electricity if it is deployed in rural areas with good wind resources (Watson *et al.*, 2006). Some microcombined heat and power technologies produce too much heat for apartments and are better suited to poorly insulated detached houses. As energy performance is improved in both existing and new buildings, some energy generation technologies will become less attractive because the demand for heat might be too low (Pitts, 2008).

Enabling technologies such as information, communication and control are vital to the security of decentralized systems. Another related set of supporting technologies for energy storage could influence the direction of the energy system in the future (Baker, 2008). Storage of electricity or heat is possible using a variety of technologies at a range of scales. In some cases, such as domestic hot water tanks, it is already widespread although combination boilers may reduce their prevalence. Other forms of storage such as electric batteries in plug-in hybrid vehicles could be important in the future. There is also the option of 'virtual storage', which uses control systems to manage loads as well as energy sources in electricity systems (Hemmi, 2003).

Storage could open up possibilities for future energy systems. For example, the electricity system could integrate more intermittent renewable energy, which could be centralized or decentralized. Solar heat collected in summer could perhaps be stored for months at a time until it is needed in winter. However, many storage technologies are limited by a combination of factors such as cost, storage capacity and durability (Baker, 2008). While incremental developments are envisaged for the future which will help to improve the attractiveness of storage technologies, it is difficult to foresee radical breakthroughs in the short to medium term.

### *11.4.4 The governance of energy markets*

Part of the reason why investment has continued to focus on centralized technologies, particularly in electricity, is the structure of electricity and gas markets and the way in which they are regulated. While the liberalization of electricity and gas markets since the late 1980s has opened them up to competition, there is a widespread recognition, not least in government, that the current system includes many barriers to decentralized options. Some of these are due to market rules, which are designed to suit large-scale power plants. Some are due to the regulatory approach to monopoly networks which has been concerned with cost reductions rather than innovation.

Many government policy statements talk in terms of levelling the playing field for decentralized investments such as CHP and small-scale renewables (Department of Trade and Industry, 2006c; Department of Trade and Industry, 2006a). Some changes to assist decentralized electricity generation have been included in regulations for electricity distribution networks by the regulator, Ofgem. These provide some economic incentives for network operators to connect distributed electricity generators. However, the accompanying incentives to encourage research and demonstration of new network technologies have only produced modest results so far (Woodman and Baker, 2008). More recent regulatory reforms, implemented in 2010, include much greater incentives for innovation – particularly through a new £500 million Low Carbon Network Fund (Ofgem, 2009).

Other bodies have called for more fundamental reform of regulatory systems, for example, a change to the energy regulator's duties so that they place more emphasis on government environmental and social targets (Helm, 2007; Sustainable Development Commission, 2007). This is partly informed by the observation that the UK is locked in to centralized systems and their associated institutions, rules and regulations (Wolfe, 2008; Woodman and Baker, 2008). For example, domestic microgenerators cannot sell their power to the main electricity wholesale market and take advantage of time-of-day pricing. Demand-side investors enjoy less favourable tax treatment than those on the supply side (Watson *et al.*, 2006). The implication is that action beyond the removal of barriers or the 'levelling of playing fields' might be required to open up the possibility of widespread decentralized investments.

Other regulatory developments also have implications for decentralized energy. Some of the most interesting and potentially radical regulations cut across traditional divisions within energy systems. New obligations on energy suppliers could lead to a more integrated approach to investments in energy supply and demand. Meanwhile, building regulations have been strengthened to mandate zero-carbon homes by 2016. This is likely to focus developers' minds on the energy performance of buildings, including the integration of low-carbon supply options, much more than in the past (Boardman, 2007). While many of these regulations are national, they have been pushed and reinforced by a series of EU Directives on buildings and energy services (Ekins and Lees, 2008).

The increasing obligations on energy suppliers in the UK to encourage carbon-saving measures within households are in line with the EU's 2006 Directive on energy services (see Chapter 16, this volume). These obligations could be met through a combination of traditional efficiency measures and microgeneration. The current phase of these regulations (known as the Carbon Emissions Reduction Target or CERT) is not expected to lead to large numbers of new microgenerators. However, the decision to introduce feed-in tariffs for small-scale renewables (below 5 MW) in April 2010 is starting to have an impact – and has now made renewable energy much more attractive for householders and other small investors. The proposed Renewable Heat Incentive may have a similar effect on renewable heat if it is implemented as originally planned in April 2011.

Looking beyond current policy proposals, changes in governance could have a critical impact on the scale of energy systems in the future. There is significant scope for subnational institutions (e.g. local authorities and regional bodies) to play a greater role. While there are some notable examples of energy system development led by local authorities (e.g. in Woking and London), these stand out as the exception rather than the rule (see Chapter 10, this volume). New powers and greater guidance to local authorities from central government in areas such as planning, finance and regulation may be required for other areas to follow suit (Local Government Association, 2007). The new government has already started to recognize this, with the lifting of a ban on the sale of electricity by local authorities.

Table 11.3 *Routes for public engagement and scales of energy systems*

| | |
|---|---|
| 1. **Centralized engagement** Deployment of smart metering technologies enables building occupants to track their levels of consumption and shape behavioural patterns in response to different time-of-use tariffs offered by utilities. Appliances are designed to enable efficient use and bills provide details of where heat and power is generated, what fuels are used and what carbon gases are emitted as a result. | 2. **Centralized disengagement** Building occupants are disengaged with energy beyond bill payment. Bills provide minimal levels of information about the energy system and its environmental impacts. Meters are inaccessibly located and not user-friendly. Heat and power plant are 'out of sight and out of mind'; individuals have little idea where their energy comes from or how the system functions. |
| 3. **Decentralized engagement** Energy is more 'visible' in everyday lifestyles as people prefer to have energy technologies 'in their back yard'. Deployment of both smart meters and small-scale heat and power systems enables individuals and communities to play a stronger role in managing energy and the built environment. | 4. **Decentralized disengagement** Small-scale heat and power systems become common through a 'company control' business model, maximizing convenience for building users who benefit from, but have little everyday involvement with, energy systems. Billing and metering systems provide minimal levels of information to users. |

### *11.4.5 Broader social change*

Decentralized energy has been consistently advocated by environmentalists since the 1970s on the grounds of increasing public participation, empowerment and self-sufficiency (Lovins, 1977; Willis, 2006). However, opinions on the social advantages or disadvantages of decentralized energy are often polarized. For example, industry and policy makers tend to emphasize the convenience of centralized energy systems, arising from an 'information-deficit' perspective of the public (Owens, 2000) which presumes a lack of awareness, knowledge, interest and time to be the norm among energy users (Devine-Wright and Devine-Wright, 2006). In contrast, advocates of decentralization tend to demonize centralized systems as inevitably 'bad', imagining a decentralized energy future where energy is 'democratized' (Greenpeace, 2005) and increased engagement is the norm.

It is useful to disentangle the interrelations between the scale of energy systems and the level of public engagement. Table 11.3 illustrates four divergent routes with a particular focus on electricity and heat. For analytic purposes, it simplifies system scale into a single dimension from centralization to decentralization, and characterizes levels of engagement along a continuum varying from high to low. This produces four stylized possibilities for public engagement with energy systems: centralized engagement, centralized disengagement, decentralized engagement and decentralized disengagement. Of these, perhaps the most notable are the ones typically overlooked: engaged centralization and disengaged decentralization. These are discussed further below.

In route 1, large-scale power plants remain the conventional way to generate heat and power, with supply enabled by continued use of a national grid of gas and power infrastructure. But within buildings, the installation of technologies such as smart meters transforms the potential for engagement, enabling individuals and households to shape behavioural patterns of energy consumption across the day and week, for example to benefit from different time-of-use tariffs offered by energy utilities, and to track their levels of consumption over time. In this case, the meters are characterized as 'smart' not because they provide utilities with increased data about energy use but because they are designed and located in such a way as to promote and maximize user engagement.

In route 4, disengaged decentralization highlights a scenario where building occupants benefit from small-scale energy technologies but have little or no input into their installation or operation, perhaps for reasons of convenience. The details of technology operation and management are handled by a service company that takes charge of all aspects of decentralization, in a similar fashion to the 'company driven' model of decentralized energy identified by previous research (Watson *et al.*, 2006). Technical systems are decentralized but this does not occur in parallel with a shift in norms of engagement and behavioural patterns.

These routes suggest two things: that increased levels of public engagement are not an inevitable outcome of decentralized energy technologies, and that centralized systems are not inevitably 'disengaged' with by energy users.

While it has been claimed that our current system is one of centralized disengagement (Greenpeace, 2005), there is evidence that this is beginning to change. First, the government has committed to rolling out 'smart meters' in all UK homes by 2020 (HM Government, 2009). Second, as stated earlier, new financial mechanisms, such as feed-in tariffs, aim to boost the numbers of household and community-level schemes for low-carbon energy generation (DECC, 2009). Third, policy support for the community level of deployment is manifest by various support schemes and funding programmes (Walker *et al.*, 2007), in order to realize a range of potential benefits, including the economic regeneration of urban and rural areas, social cohesion, enhanced public understanding and support for renewable energy, and the triggering of behavioural change (Wüstenhagen *et al.*, 2007; Keirstead, 2008).

Notably, the Low Carbon Communities Challenge[2] has provided £10 million of funding to twenty selected communities in England and Wales with the aim of testing different methods of achieving significant cuts in emissions through an area-based approach. In Scotland, the emergence of Community Energy Companies has signalled policy support for the view that a shift towards decentralized energy can bring socioeconomic benefits in marginalized communities.

These policy-led initiatives operate in parallel with grassroots initiatives such as The Transition Towns network, which includes groups in many towns across the UK, and provide a clear example of decentralization in the political and social sense, signalling a trend that could develop alongside more technical decentralization over the next decades. However, despite the diversity of potential benefits, significant community activity and the development of publicly funded support schemes, many barriers towards increased decentralization remain to be solved (Walker, 2008a).

## 11.5 Conclusions

This chapter has explored the possible evolution of scale within the UK energy system. This energy system has been developed in an increasingly centralized way in recent decades – with technical infrastructures, institutions, policies and regulations being designed to support large-scale technologies. While this system has generally worked well – for example, by delivering reliable, affordable energy services to the majority of consumers – the need for deep cuts in emissions offers an opportunity to re-evaluate this inheritance.

In order to analyze the potential and desirability of decentralization within the UK's low-carbon transition, it is important to be clear about definitions. As this chapter has argued, a dichotomous debate about 'centralization vs decentralization' is simplistic and unhelpful. There are a range of possible scales for energy system development and deployment – from large scale (international and national) through regional scale (e.g. in cities) to small scale (e.g. neighbourhood and household). These scales do not only apply to technologies and infrastructures, but can also apply

[2] See www.decc.gov.uk/en/content/cms/what_we_do/consumers/lc_communities/lc_communities.aspx

to institutions and policies. Furthermore, different scales of energy systems have a range of possible implications for public engagement.

It is also important to bear in mind that more decentralized energy options and systems are not necessarily more sustainable than centralized options. Decentralized energy technologies can be high carbon (e.g. diesel engines) or low carbon (e.g. wind turbines). Decentralized energy systems can be more resilient, with greater levels of energy security (Coaffee, 2008). But they could also introduce new risks to energy security – for example, by making local electricity systems more complex and difficult to manage. As this chapter has demonstrated, the common assumption that decentralized energy provision is automatically correlated with high levels of public engagement can also be questioned. Therefore, the extent to which decentralization leads to a lower-carbon, more secure energy system with high levels of public engagement depends on the kind of decentralization that is pursued.

In principle, energy systems can be deployed in the UK across this range of scales. Recent policy strategies such as the Low Carbon Transition Plan (HM Government, 2009) and the Renewable Energy Strategy (DECC, 2009) envisage this. To meet the 15 per cent renewable energy target, the Renewable Energy Strategy envisages a strong emphasis on large-scale wind power complemented by a range of other technologies which vary widely in their scale of deployment. However, public policies to implement this and other strategies need to take into account the phenomenon of lock-in. As other authors have observed, lock-in to high-carbon energy systems is a particular challenge for countries wishing to transition to much lower carbon systems (Unruh, 2000). For the UK, historic centralization leads to a further dimension of lock-in. This means that it is not necessarily straightforward for energy systems to be deployed at other scales. This is because policies, regulations, institutions and infrastructures have been understandably oriented to support the incumbent centralized system. For example, local authorities in the UK have very little influence over the shape of energy systems – and local energy generation is rare.

Despite their apparent diversity, there is continued lack of appreciation of the importance of lock-in in official UK energy strategies. There are statements about the value of actions by households and local communities, and there are also some greater incentives for these actors to invest in energy systems (for example, through new feed-in tariffs). However, the policy process has not fully understood the way in which lock-in may frustrate ambitions for a more plural energy system. There is no suggestion that policy making and governance itself should be more plural for example, with a greater role for regional and local actors. This suggests that a predominantly centralized system may well continue into the future, perhaps with increasing 'pockets' of decentralization emerging ad hoc as a result of particular local circumstances.

## References


Ault, G., Frame, D., Hughes, N. and Strachan, N. (2008). *Electricity Network Scenarios for Great Britain in 2050*, London: Ofgem.

Baker, J. (2008). New technology and possible advances in energy storage, *Energy Policy*, **36**(12): 4368–73.

Boardman, B. (2007). *Home Truths: A Low Carbon Strategy to Reduce UK Housing Emissions by 80% by 2050*, Oxford: Environmental Change Institute.

Bouffard, F. and Kirschen, D.S. (2008). Centralised and distributed electricity systems, *Energy Policy*, **36**(12): 4504–8.

Centre for Sustainable Energy, Garrad Hassan, P. Capener and Bond Pearce LLP (2007). *Delivering Community Benefits from Wind Energy Development: A Toolkit*, London: Department of Trade and Industry.

Coaffee, J. (2008). Risk, resilience and environmentally sustainable cities, *Energy Policy*, **36**(12): 4633–8.

DECC (2009). *The UK Renewable Energy Strategy*, London: DECC.

Department of Energy and Climate Change (2010), *Digest of UK Energy Statistics 2010*, London: The Stationery Office.

Department of Trade and Industry (2003). Energy White Paper: Our Energy Future – Creating a Low Carbon Economy. CM 5761. London: HMSO.

Department of Trade and Industry (2006a). *Distributed Energy: A Call for Evidence for the Review of Barriers and Incentives to Distributed Electricity Generation, including Combined Heat and Power*, London: DTI.

Department of Trade and Industry (2006b). *The Energy Challenge: Energy Review Report*, London: The Stationery Office.

Department of Trade and Industry (2006c). *Our Energy Challenge, Power from the People: A Microgeneration Strategy*, London: Department of Trade and Industry.

Department of Trade and Industry (2007). *Meeting the Energy Challenge*, London: The Stationery Office.

Devine-Wright, H. and Devine-Wright, P. (2006). Social representations of intermittency and the shaping of public support for wind energy in the UK, *International Journal of Global Energy Issues*, **25**(3–4): 243–56.

Ekins, P. and Lees, E. (2008). The impact of EU policies on energy use in and the evolution of the UK built environment, *Energy Policy*, **36**(12): 4580–3.

Embedded Generation Working Group (2001). *Report into Network Access Issues, Volume I*, London: Department of Trade and Industry.

Fielder, F. (1996). Integrating financial thinking with strategic planning to achieve competitive success, *The Electricity Journal*, **9**(4): 62–7.

Foresight (2008). *Powering Our Lives: Sustainable Energy Management and the Built Environment*, London: Government Office for Science.

Greenpeace (2005). *Decentralising Power: An Energy Revolution for the 21st Century*, London: Greenpeace.

Greenpeace (2006). *Decentralising UK Energy: Cleaner, Cheaper, More Secure Energy for the 21st Century. Application of the WADE Economic Model to the UK*, London: Greenpeace UK.

Helm, D. (2007). *The New Energy Paradigm*, Oxford: Oxford University Press.

Hemmi, K. (2003). *Energy Storage and its Role in the Further Integration of Renewable Energy Sources into the UK Electricity Grid*, Brighton: University of Sussex.

Hinnells, M. (2008). Combined heat and power in industry and buildings, *Energy Policy*, **36**(12): 4522–6.

HM Government (2009). *The UK Low Carbon Transition Plan*, London: The Stationery Office.

Keirstead, J. (2008). What changes, if any, would increased levels of low-carbon decentralised energy have on the built environment? *Energy Policy*, **36**(12): 4518–21.

Local Government Association (2007). *A Climate of Change*, London: Local Government Association.

Lovins, A. (1977). *Soft Energy Paths: Towards a Durable Peace*, Harmondsworth: Penguin Books.

NERA (2002). *Security in Gas and Electricity Markets*, London: NERA.

Ofgem (2004). *London and Birmingham Blackouts Decision*, London: Ofgem.

Ofgem (2009). *Electricity Distribution Price Control Review: Initial Proposals*, London: Ofgem.

Owens, S. (2000). 'Engaging the public': information and deliberation in environmental policy, *Environment and Planning A*, **32**(7): 1141–8.

Pitts, A. (2008). Future proof construction – Future building and systems design for energy and fuel flexibility, *Energy Policy*, **36**(12): 4539–43.

Power, A. (2008). Does demolition or refurbishment of old and inefficient homes help to increase our environmental, social and economic viability? *Energy Policy*, **36**(12): 4487–501.

Roberts, S. (2008). Energy, equity and the future of the fuel poor, *Energy Policy*, **36**(12): 4471–4.

Royal Commission on Environmental Pollution (2000). *Energy: The Changing Climate*. London: Royal Commission on Environmental Pollution.

Smith, C. and Levermore, G. (2008). Designing urban spaces and buildings to improve sustainability and quality of life in a warmer world, *Energy Policy*, **36**(12): 4558–62.

Stern, N. (2006). *Stern Review: The Economics of Climate Change*, London: HM Treasury.

Sustainable Development Commission (2007). *Lost in Transmission? The Role of Ofgem in a Changing Climate*, London: SDC.

Tyndall Centre for Climate Change Research (2005). *Decarbonising the UK: Energy for a Climate Conscious Future*, Norwich: Tyndall Centre.

Unruh, G.C. (2000). Understanding carbon lock-in, *Energy Policy*, **28**: 817–30.

van Vliet, B. and Chappells, H. (1999). The Co-provision of Utility Services: Resources, New Technologies & Consumers, Reader distributed for the

Consumption, Everyday Life and Sustainability Summer School 1999, Lancaster University.

Walker, G. (2008a). Decentralised systems and fuel poverty: Are there any links or risks? *Energy Policy*, **36**(12): 4514–17.

Walker, G. (2008b). What are the barriers and incentives for community-owned means of energy production and use? *Energy Policy*, **36**(12): 4401–5.

Walker, G., Hunter, S., Devine-Wright, P., Evans, B. and Fay, H. (2007). Harnessing community energies: explaining and evaluating community-based localism in renewable energy policy in the UK, *Global Environmental Politics*, 7(2): 64–82.

Watson, J., Sauter, R., James, P., Myers, L., Bahaj, B. and Wing, R. (2006). *Unlocking the Power House: Policy and System Change for Domestic Microgeneration in the UK*, Brighton: University of Sussex.

Willis, R. (2006). *Grid 2.0: The Next Generation*, London: Green Alliance.

Wolfe, P. (2008). The implications of an increasingly decentralised energy system, *Energy Policy*, **36**(12): 4509–13.

Woodman, B. and Baker, P. (2008). Regulatory frameworks for decentralised energy, *Energy Policy*, **36**(12): 4527–31.

Wüstenhagen, R., Wolsink, M. and Bürer, M.J. (2007). Social acceptance of renewable energy innovation: An introduction to the concept, *Energy Policy*, **35**(5): 2683–91.

# 12 Equity, fuel poverty and demand (maintaining affordability with sustainability and security of supply)

*Catherine Waddams Price*

## 12.1 Introduction

Fuel poverty has been the subject of campaigns and government policy for more than twenty years. The target for its eradication among vulnerable households in 2010 was missed because of rising fuel prices and the environmental agenda. This chapter examines how the concept of fuel poverty fits with other aspects of the energy policy agenda and the extent to which the government's official targets and policy correspond to more subjective measures of 'affording fuel'. In the UK this discussion is placed in the context of developing competition in retail energy markets, and raises questions about whether choice of supplier at the household level, long a prized achievement of the UK regulator and government, remains the most appropriate way to deliver the current social and environmental objectives.

The next section of the chapter explains the background to the current debate. Section 12.3 considers different concepts of fuel poverty, including one derived from interview data with households. Section 12.4 describes the official policy and its development in the UK. Section 12.5 draws on the experience of other countries; first among developing countries, then narrowing the scope to those who seek entry to the EU, and then those who are already EU members. Section 12.6 concludes.

## 12.2 The citizen and consumer in energy markets

The current challenges for energy policy in the domestic market, acknowledged in the government's July 2010 Annual Energy Statement (DECC, 2010c), are sustainability in the face of climate change, security

The support of the Economic and Social Research Council and able research assistance by Hieu Tran are gratefully acknowledged. This chapter is dedicated to the memory of Karl Brazier who died on 27 November 2009, and whose research on reconciling measures of fuel poverty is reported in this chapter.

of supply as investment in new sources of energy and its transportation is required, and affordability.

The first two have received considerable attention, and both imply increasing energy prices, posing a direct challenge to the third objective. This chapter considers the issue of energy affordability at a time of rising cost pressures, both in the UK and elsewhere, and the ways in which the UK government and regulator have addressed this issue. Energy markets represent an intriguing meeting place of consumer and citizen issues. This largely arises from the history of the sector, whose legacy is a significant and powerful lobby group, and strong pressure on and among policy makers to pay special attention to this sector (Helm, 2003).

The characteristics which give the energy sector this particular focus exist in other sectors, but their combination in energy is particularly powerful. Energy is seen as essential to health (and perhaps life), a characteristic shared with food and housing. Like many essentials, demand increases with income, but less than proportionately, so poorer households spend a higher proportion of their income on energy than richer ones.

The average expenditure on fuel and power in the home did not change substantially between 1992 and 2008 (the latest year for which figures are available from the Expenditure and Fuel Survey), but is likely to have increased in 2009 when energy prices rose considerably. In 1992, the average spend was 5 per cent of total expenditure (a reasonably reliable indicator of income), falling to 4 per cent in 1995–98, 3 per cent in 1998–2006, and rising again to 4 per cent for 2006–8. This compares with a figure in 2008 of 16 per cent for food and non-alcoholic drinks, and 20 per cent for net housing costs. Clothing and footwear accounted for 5 per cent of total expenditure in 2008, and motoring for 14 per cent.

Recent interest in the effect of energy prices on household expenditure on other products, particularly food, is captured in work by Cullen *et al.* (2005) on US data and Beatty *et al.* (2009) on UK data. Both find evidence that unexpected increases in energy expenditure caused by unseasonably cold weather result in lower food expenditure by lower-income groups. However, neither is able to identify the effect of unanticipated increases in energy prices. Such a study would be complicated by two factors: the need to know the particular tariff which applied to any household, since some may be on fixed-price deals and so face any price increase with a lag; and where households do face increased prices, the extent to which these were indeed anticipated by the consumers concerned. Cullen *et al.* (2005) present convincing evidence that where higher expenditure is anticipated, for example, because of expected seasonal cold weather, even households with limited financial resources do not reduce expenditure on food.

On the supply side, there is a tradition of provision by publicly owned companies, in the UK at least since the nationalization of the electricity and gas companies in the middle of the twentieth century. Municipal provision was common before that date, and in many European countries public provision has been a longer tradition; the US has a history of mixed ownership. Energy provision has also traditionally been provided by monopolies (whether public or private), raising the need for more consumer protection than in markets where there is a choice of suppliers.

Energy is often seen as strategic, particularly in terms of security of supply, since so much domestic and commercial life depends on a continuous and good quality supply, which may be jeopardized if there are insufficient sources. In the UK, coal was seen as the engine of the industrial revolution and continuing industrial production, and troubled labour relationships over decades made this industry particularly politically sensitive. The discovery of a substantial amount of gas and oil in the North Sea enabled the UK to be self-sufficient in energy for almost forty years, but as these fields become exhausted, concerns about reliance on overseas supplies are again surfacing.

And in recent years the climate change agenda has raised additional questions and challenges, in particular how society can reduce its greenhouse emissions without placing an unacceptable burden on users. In particular, how can low-income households be protected while ensuring that UK firms can remain competitive? This new combination of environmental and social pressures makes for difficult choices in the industries, and new attitudes by governments and the energy regulator, Ofgem.

The main fuels used by households in Britain for light, power and heating are gas and electricity. Oil and bottled gas are much more commonly used in Northern Ireland, where there is no tradition of piped gas supply, and in some parts of rural mainland Britain. Explicit economic regulation was instituted in both the gas and electricity industries when they were privatized in 1986 and 1990–91 (Gas Act, 1986; Electricity Act, 1989) respectively, including a cap on prices charged to households. The cap was a response to the duty of the regulator 'to protect the interests of customers of gas' (Gas Act 1986 4(2)(a)).

The model of regulation followed that devised for telecoms (Littlechild, 1983) and was based on a traditional economic model which focused on the product concerned, the protection of consumers from high prices charged by suppliers with market power in that market, and the efficiency of the industry. Regulation was seen as a substitute for competition, and where the latter could be introduced, the former was withdrawn. There is a tension between regulation and competition, since if an efficient monopolist is regulated so that there are no excess profits, there is also little incentive for others to enter the market. However, the model of regulation did not envisage that it should provide for wider social needs. The energy regulator's duties to protect consumers were themselves secondary to those securing that all reasonable demands for gas would be met and that gas suppliers should be able to finance the provision of gas (Gas Act 1986, 4(1)). In particular, these secondary duties encompassed taking account of the needs of certain consumers, including those who were disabled or of pensionable age (Gas Act 1986, 4 (3)), a group to which was added the chronically sick in 1995 (Gas Act, 1995, 4(3)), and individuals residing in rural areas and those with low incomes under the 2000 Utilities Act (9 AA (3) (d) and (c)).[1] The 2000 Utilities Act also instituted a new primary duty for the regulator 'to protect the interests of consumers . . . , wherever appropriate by promoting effective competition . . . ' (Utilities Act 2000 9 – 4AA (1)); securing demand and financing activities were relegated to a secondary duty (Utilities Act 2000 9 – 4AA (2)).[2] But until 2008 obligations to particular groups of consumers were very much secondary to concern for efficiency and competition, especially in the retail markets.

Competition was introduced into retail gas and electricity markets from 1996 and 1998 respectively, and by 2002 there had been sufficient entry for the regulator to remove the last price caps (though prices of transmission and distribution continue to be regulated). While there was considerable entry into both the national gas market and the fourteen regional electricity markets in England, Scotland and Wales, there was also considerable exit, merger and takeover, so that from 2003 the market was dominated by six large suppliers which were the consolidated descendants of the pre-competition monopolists in each of these markets. There was more switching than in any other national domestic energy market, and a decade after the last markets were opened to competition, more than three quarters of consumers had switched at least one of their energy suppliers at least once, with incumbents retaining on average just under half of their markets. But this competitive landscape also included a number of consumers who had never switched at all, and a majority of switchers had changed supplier only once; there were concerns that the benefits of the competitive market were not being shared fairly across households.

[1] Note that these statutory duties encompass a different group of households from those described as vulnerable under the fuel poverty policy definition (see footnote 3).

[2] The Utilities Act 2000 also included duties on the regulator to take account of environmental and social guidance provided by the government (Utilities Act 2000, 10).

Worries were also expressed about the competitiveness of the market, with six large firms, each dominant in its own home market, and interacting across the gas and electricity markets; these issues were explained and examined by Ofgem in their 2004 market report (Ofgem, 2004, Chapter 6). While Ofgem found no cause for concern in 2004, and there was little suspicion of any explicit or illegal agreements, worries were raised by the almost textbook conditions for firms to avoid head-on competition by tacitly agreeing not to indulge in aggressively rivalrous behaviour. Ofgem explained these theoretical conditions in appendix 18 of its 2004 market report, and in his evidence to the Business and Enterprise Committee in 2008, the chief executive of Energywatch (the consumer body responsible for the sector) elucidated concerns about how this was operating in practice (House of Commons Business and Enterprise Committee, 2008a, especially pp. 24–7). These suspicions were exacerbated by a link between wholesale and retail prices which was obscured by both vertical integration and extensive forward contracts and hedging.

As the environmental agenda was addressed more seriously by policy makers around the turn of the millennium, it became clear that if the ambitious targets for carbon reduction and renewable energy were to be realized, it could only be at the cost of considerably higher energy prices. Indeed higher energy prices themselves were likely to be a crucial instrument in achieving many of the goals for reducing domestic demand. Here a dilemma arises from the nature of energy demand. The households whose demand is most responsive to increases in energy prices are low-income households (Baker *et al.*, 1989), but there was concern that some households used too *little* energy, particularly the elderly. If this group was to be encouraged to use more, and low-income households were to be protected from the adverse effects on income of higher energy prices, a major instrument to achieve lower consumption would be sacrificed.

At the same time, just before the financial collapse of 2008, oil prices soared, pushing up not only the price of oil used for domestic heating, but also gas and electricity prices. Households that were already struggling with rising food prices faced gas price increases of over 50 per cent in the year to January 2008, and electricity price increases of 30 per cent over the same period (BIS, 2009). The regulator, who had previously maintained that the retail market was working well, was persuaded by the government to announce a 'supply probe' into the market in March 2008 which reported in October the same year. During this period the regulator's attitude changed from one of reiterating that the competitive market was working well ('Market is Sound, Ofgem Assures Chancellor'

(Ofgem, 2008a)) to a focus of concern about the areas that were working less well ('Ofgem puts industry on notice to make markets work better for all' (Ofgem, 2008b)). While these approaches are not mutually exclusive, the regulator's emphasis has been increasingly interventionist since the report of the probe in October 2008. Beyond the regulator's office, by the end of 2008 the market model of energy regulation was seen to have 'failed' by many commentators (see, for example, Allan Asher's evidence, House of Commons Business and Enterprise Committee, 2008a) in the same sense that financial regulation based on minimal intervention was seen to have been deficient following the financial collapse in the same period. Both were seen as needing 'fixing'.

The regulator's role was perceived, by both itself and others, to be no longer focused on a narrow purpose of protecting the energy consumer and ensuring the efficiency of the industry, but to have a broader remit to ensure equity in some wider sense. For example, the regulator followed other commentators, mainly from charities working with low-income groups, in judging that it was unfair that some consumers benefited from competition by switching suppliers, while those who did not do so had been paying around 10 per cent more for their electricity (Ofgem, 2008c). Ofgem's objective was to ensure that everyone had equal opportunity to switch, and many of its remedies were addressed precisely to ensuring that such opportunities were equally available to all. But it was impatient to see the results of these changes, and also enacted licence changes which will hamper the development of competition (Hviid and Waddams Price, 2010), showing clearly that it is now paying much more attention to its role of protecting certain citizens, than focusing broadly on consumers in general.

Fuel poverty had also traditionally been linked to payment method, with particular concern for prepayment consumers, who were charged more than those who paid either by standard credit or direct debit. Following the energy probe, the regulator made changes in line with a European directive that charges to households should reflect the costs of the payment methods used. In the UK, the 'original' standard credit scheme provided for meters to be read every three months to generate a bill which was then paid (quarterly) in arrears of the consumption. This sometimes led to large bills and difficulties in payment, particularly for low-income households after the winter quarter. To enable consumers to repay their debt while still supplying energy (and to avoid difficulties in payment for households without a good credit record) companies introduced prepayment meters (or pay as you go) where a card is charged in advance and inserted in a meter to release the flow of energy. Any debt can also be recovered by deducting a set amount per week from the credit registered

Table 12.1 *Characteristics of gas and electricity prepayment households, £s, 2004–5*

| Characteristics | Gas | Electricity | All |
|---|---|---|---|
| Weekly income | | | |
| *Average* | 303.41 | 311.11 | 479.57 |
| *Standard deviation* | 219.10 | 223.63 | 509.70 |
| Income support (%) | 27.94 | 25.89 | 6.22 |
| *Household type* (%) | | | |
| *Head retired* | 47.66 | 46.95 | 38.58 |
| *Head unemployed* | 7.38 | 6.20 | 1.81 |
| Total cases | 705 | 1097 | 6798 |

*Source:* Family Expenditure Survey 2004–5, authors' calculations.

on the card. Such payment is more expensive for the companies than standard credit both because of the slightly more complex meters and because of the cost of handling frequent small cash payments. By 2010, 14 per cent of electricity and 12 per cent of gas consumers had prepayment meters (derived from Ofgem, 2010 and DECC, 2010a). A third cheaper way for the company is to receive payment from monthly direct debit arrangements, based on anticipated consumption, with differences reconciled annually.

Prepayment meters are more likely to be installed in low-income households. A report for Consumer Focus (Mummery and Reilly, 2010) found that more than half PPM households received some kind of means-tested benefit or benefit for disability, and were over-represented among properties rented from local authorities and housing associations. Table 12.1 shows that in 2004–5 the average income of gas and electricity prepayment households was lower than average (£303 and £311 per week, compared with an average for all households of £480); PPM households are more likely to be in receipt of income support and to have a head of household who is retired or unemployed. Ofgem's own figures (Table 12.2) confirm a similar pattern.

Because potentially vulnerable customers were more likely to use prepayment (and less likely to use direct debit because of fear of becoming overdrawn, which attracts high penalties from banks), concerns have been raised that they were being overcharged. The implementation of the directive was therefore welcomed by many consumer lobbyists, who believed that the predominantly lower-income prepayment consumers had been paying more than the costs they were incurring.

Table 12.2 *Characteristics of prepayment and other domestic consumers*

| | Prepayment % | All % |
|---|---|---|
| *Income* | | |
| <£10K | 38 | 32 |
| >£10K, <£25K | 46 | 37 |
| >£25K, <£50K | 13 | 22 |
| >50K | 2 | 8 |
| Total | 100 | 100 |
| *Social class* | | |
| AB | 7 | 16 |
| C1 | 23 | 26 |
| C2 | 25 | 21 |
| D | 20 | 17 |
| E | 25 | 19 |
| Total | 100 | 100 |
| *Characteristics* | | |
| Long-term illness/disability | 21 | 10 |
| Single parent | 15 | 6 |
| Unemployed | 12 | 6 |
| Receiving other benefits | 16 | 9 |
| Retired, occupational pension | 5 | 16 |
| Retired, state pension only | 9 | 26 |
| Owner occupier | 32 | 72 |
| Tenant | 59 | 31 |

*Source:* Domestic Retail Market Report June 2005 (published by Ofgem, 2006).

## 12.3 Fuel poverty in the UK

The concept of fuel poverty developed in the UK following the rapid rises in energy prices in the 1970s, largely related to oil price increases, and initially referred to a general concern about affordability of energy (including inadequate expenditure to support good health by some low-income households). As research into the nature of fuel expenditure developed, the concept of fuel poverty became defined in terms of the proportion of household expenditure which was spent (or should be spent) on warmth (Bradshaw and Hutton, 1983). A number of political, campaigning and action groups grew up around the concept and kept the issue close to the political consciousness. Over the following decades the notion of fuel poverty came to be defined as needing to spend more than 10 per cent of income on household energy, and the official government

Table 12.3 *Overlap between fuel poverty and other measures of deprivation, average 2003–5, millions of households*

| Measure of deprivation | Households in fuel poverty but without this deprivation measure | Households who are both in fuel poverty and suffer this deprivation measure | Households who are not in fuel poverty but suffer this deprivation measure |
|---|---|---|---|
| Income poverty* | 1.1 | 1.9 | 1.6 |
| Working-age households without work | 0.2 | 0.4 | 1.7 |
| Vulnerable households by fuel poverty definition | 0.3 | 1.0 | 14 |
| Vulnerable households by usual government definition | 0.6 | 0.8 | 5.1 |
| Living in deprived areas | 1.0 | 0.3 | 3.7 |

* updated to 2007.
*Source:* Palmer *et al.* (2008), from various diagrams pp. 14–20.

definition is that fuel poverty occurs when a household 'needs to spend more than 10 per cent of its income on all fuel use to heat its home to an adequate standard of warmth' (InterMinisterial Group on Fuel Poverty, 2001, p. 6). A household is more likely to be in fuel poverty the lower is its income, the higher are fuel prices, and the worse the insulation conditions of the home. Thus the concept of fuel poverty is closely related, but not identical, to other measures of deprivation. Palmer *et al.* (2008) estimated that in 2007, 1.9 million English households were in both fuel poverty and income poverty, 1.1 million households were in fuel poverty but not in income poverty, and 1.6 million households were in income poverty but not in fuel poverty. They argue that the link becomes weaker as the number in fuel poverty rises, which we know has occurred since 2007. Table 12.3 shows the overlap between fuel poverty and other measures of deprivation, which emphasizes both how different measures will identify different households in need of assistance, and the difficulty of targeting effectively one measure through other categories.

### *12.3.1 Expenditure fuel poverty*

Since energy shares the characteristic of many necessities that expenditure increases with income, but at a less than proportionate rate, the rich spend more on energy than the poor, but the expenditure forms a much

Table 12.4 *Households in fuel poverty 1996–2010, UK, millions of households*

| | 96 | 98 | 01 | 02 | 03 | 04 | 05 | 06 | 07 | 08# | 09# | 10# |
|---|---|---|---|---|---|---|---|---|---|---|---|---|
| Households in fuel poverty | 6.5 | 4.8 | 2.5 | 2.2 | 2.0 | 2.0 | 2.5 | 3.5 | 4.0 | 4.5 | 5 | 4.6 |
| Vulnerable* households in fuel poverty | 5.0 | 3.5 | 2.0 | 1.8 | 1.5 | 1.4 | 2.0 | 2.75 | 3.25 | | | |

# estimates from Neighbourhood Energy Action (House of Commons Business and Enterprise Committee, 2008b; NEA, 2009; Fuel Poverty Advisory Group, 2010).
* This measure of vulnerability is the one defined in the fuel poverty policy, see footnote 3.
*Source:* Fuel Poverty Advisory Group (2010).

lower proportion of their income. In 2007, the most recent year for which figures are available (at the time of writing), the poorest 30 per cent of households spent an average of 7 per cent of their income on household energy, while this absorbed less than 2 per cent of the income of the richest 30 per cent (Fuel Poverty Advisory Group, 2009). The concept of fuel poverty includes both the expenditure of more than 10 per cent of income on energy, and the need to do so, a need which may not be met because of expenditure constraints. Assuming that all those who spend more than 10 per cent of their income do, indeed, need to do so, expenditure data can reveal those households where spending is higher than this limit, which, following Bennett *et al.* (2002), we can name 'expenditure fuel poor'. Analysis of expenditure for 1997–8 showed that a 1 per cent increase in income was associated with a 9 per cent reduction in the probability of being expenditure fuel poor, and that household size raised the probability of fuel poverty (unsurprisingly if income is not itself 'equivalized' to allow for different household structures). If the household is retired, this also increases the probability of fuel poverty by just under 1 per cent (Bennett *et al.*, 2002). While the magnitude of these relationships may have changed with the increase in energy prices, their nature is likely to remain the same.

Official figures for fuel poverty are produced with two years' lag, and the most recent trends in measuring fuel poverty show that fuel poverty in England doubled between 2003 (where it was at its lowest measured levels) and 2007. By 2010 the Fuel Poverty Advisory Group estimated that fuel poverty had risen to 4.6 million households (FPAG, 2010), compared to 2.0 million in 2004. In Northern Ireland the rate is even higher, placing more than a third of households in fuel poverty (Public Health Agency, 2009). The government's own advisory group suggests the increase is 'largely due to gas and electricity bills increasing by 125 per cent' (FPAG, 2010, p. 4). It is estimated that every 1 per cent increase in energy prices pulls another 40,000 households into fuel poverty (House of Commons Environment, Food and Rural Affairs Committee, 2009).

Changes in income and housing conditions will clearly help to alleviate fuel poverty in the long term, and the energy regulator has instituted obligations on the suppliers to deliver energy savings investment, including a proportion to low-income households, to help with both the environmental and social agendas. But it is difficult to measure the direct effect of such programmes on fuel poverty, partly because some of the benefit is taken in greater comfort rather than lower expenditure. In the shorter term, fuel poverty is driven strongly by changes in energy prices. Where assistance is provided this is calculated as additions to income rather than reductions in expenditure (Palmer *et al.*, 2008), and so this has a relatively small influence on whether a household is counted as fuel poor or not. There are two main direct benefits currently associated with assisting with energy costs, both directed at pensioners. All who are over 60 receive a winter fuel payment (£250 in 2010, and £400 for those who are over 80), and its universal nature renders it a poorly targeted benefit. The House of Commons Environment, Food and Rural Affairs Committee recommended that it be taxed, and that those who paid higher-rate tax should not receive the payment at all, estimating that this would save £250 million. The total cost of the scheme was £2.7 billion in 2007–8 (House of Commons Environment, Food and Rural Affairs Committee, 2009). The second benefit, cold weather payment, is paid at the rate of £25 a week when there is exceptionally cold weather, and is available only to low-income pensioners (based on their eligibility for other benefits). In 2009–10 at least £261 million was committed to the scheme, considerably more than in previous years.

However, the Mandatory Social Price Support Scheme announced by the Labour government in 2009 aims to provide direct reductions in fuel expenditure, and so is likely to have a more substantial effect on the level of fuel poverty. As part of this scheme, for example, certain low-income pensioners over the age of 70 will receive an £80 rebate on their bills (Department of Energy and Climate Change, 2010b), which will have a direct effect on the numbers in fuel poverty. However, without substantial social tariffs for low-income households, the expected long-term rise in energy prices is likely to pull more households into fuel poverty.

### *12.3.2 A subjective concept of 'fuel poverty'*

One alternative concept of fuel poverty is to assess whether the household itself feels able to afford sufficient heat; the relationship between this measure and the more traditional 'expenditure fuel poverty' was explored through a household survey of 2,578 low-income households in 2000 (Waddams Price *et al.*, 2007). While there is a positive relation between those classified as fuel poor by the two definitions, some surprising differences emerge which may have important implications for both government policy in this area and the behavioural response of households. A household was said to be subjectively fuel poor if the respondent felt unable to heat their home adequately because they found it difficult to afford the fuel. At the time of the survey, fewer households felt unable to afford heating than spent more than 10 per cent of their income on energy (16 per cent compared to 28 per cent). Of this 16 per cent, just under half spent less than 10 per cent of their income on household energy (compared with 24 per cent of the group who did not feel fuel poor); the remaining half of those who felt unable to afford sufficient heating may have been fuel poor in the sense of needing to spend more than a tenth of their household income in this way, but budget constraints prevented them from doing so. In contrast, nearly three quarters of those who spent more than 10 per cent of their income on energy did feel able to afford sufficient heating; those who felt fuel poor spent no more on their energy than those who did not, though they were likely to have lower income. These insights into how households feel about energy affordability are likely to be important in meeting the government's targets both on carbon reduction through lower household demand, and in increasing affordability, and reflect similar findings from the Fuel Poverty Advisory Group (2009).

## 12.4 Public response and policies for reducing fuel poverty

'The End Fuel Poverty Campaign **wants energy efficient homes, decent incomes and low cost fuel for low income households**' (Consumer Focus, 2009, their emphasis), and while the first two of these are aligned with many social aspirations, we have seen that the last is not consistent with a market which includes all households and reflects true carbon costs. For many years there has been no official acknowledgement of these contradictions, but recent developments do seem to address these concerns more realistically.

The focus of the UK government's energy affordability debate has, until recently, been on eliminating fuel poverty. While the Conservative governments of 1979–97 had taken some initiatives to assist with fuel poverty, in 2001 the Labour government committed to eradicating fuel poverty, as far as was practicable, among vulnerable[3] households by 2010 and all households in England by 2016 (similar pledges exist for Wales, Scotland and Northern Ireland). A combination of rising incomes, falling energy prices and schemes to improve the housing stock saw good progress being made towards the government's targets until 2004, but rising energy prices since then, exacerbated by some fall in incomes towards the end of the decade, have seen fuel poverty levels increasing dramatically as reported above.

In 2008 two voluntary organisations (Help the Aged and Friends of the Earth) challenged the government over its anticipated failure to meet its self-imposed targets. The UK High Court ruled that as long as the government was making reasonable efforts to eliminate fuel poverty, it could not be considered in breach of its duties, and the case was dismissed. The concerns raised by the case reflect a growing belief that low-income households have gained little from the opening of the UK's retail markets to competition. Such concerns contributed to measures which marked new interventions by the regulator, including the introduction of non-discrimination clauses in 2009.

Addressing fuel poverty and domestic sector emissions more directly, the regulator and successive governments have introduced several initiatives to help low-income households through energy savings investment. Suppliers were obliged to offer energy savings measures through the Energy Efficiency Standards of Performance from 1994 to 2002, and later the Energy Efficiency Commitment. This was succeeded in 2008 by the Carbon Emissions Reduction Target (CERT), which adds about 3 per cent to a typical household bill (Ofgem, 2009), thus providing a cross subsidy from most consumers to those who qualify for subsidized assistance.

In addition the government and the regulator negotiated voluntary agreements with companies to offer assistance to vulnerable customers through social programmes. The cost of this exercise was at a smaller scale – just over a tenth of the CERT commitment – and was made statutory by the 2010 Energy Act. These measures acknowledge and address the difficulty for low-income households in a period in which energy prices will continue to rise, and the coalition government elected in May 2010 is committed to continuing and extending these measures (DECC, 2010c). Perhaps just as importantly, they locate the responsibility for the redistributive policies which are envisaged with the elected government rather than with the unelected regulator or the private retail suppliers,

[3] The definition of a vulnerable household for fuel poverty policy is any household with a child, an older person or someone receiving state benefits, which constitutes around 75 per cent of households.

though the latter remain responsible for their delivery. Thus they do not sit comfortably with the development of a competitive market, whose importance seems to be taking an increasingly subsidiary role. The interaction between social programmes which are adequate to deliver relief in a period of rising energy prices and competitive market depends partly on the attitudes of the companies. Sharratt *et al.* (2007) show that companies have taken a variety of attitudes to such programmes, from 'embracing social obligations' to finding that they 'conflict with commerce'. The possible need to (re)introduce direct regulation in the retail market will depend on the outcome of the government's review of the market and the regulator, announced in July 2010 (DECC, 2010c).

The wider issue for low-income policies which arise from the fuel poverty debate is whether focus on an industry (energy)-based measure and particular types of household (with children, the elderly, receiving state benefits) is the most effective way to reduce either poverty or fuel poverty. Palmer *et al.* (2008) show that other households, particularly single households and the rural poor, are liable to suffer from fuel poverty. Moreover, their analysis shows that even if fuel poverty had been eradicated in 2005 through a combination of higher incomes and better insulated houses, the combined effect of these measures would have been reversed by the rise in energy prices between 2005 and 2007. Higher energy prices are crucial if the environmental agenda is to be realized, and focus on fuel poverty rather than more general issues affecting low-income households may lead to distortions both within the market and between households.

Other regulators are being drawn into 'product poverty' measures; for example, the Walker Review concluded that 'Ofwat should track the affordability problems facing the water industry and should then take appropriate action and/or provide advice to the UK Government and Welsh Assembly Government, to ensure that water and sewerage services remain affordable over both the medium and longer term. Ofwat should report on the position on affordability in an Annual Report on affordability and debt' (Walker, 2009, p. 130). There is a real danger that if individual regulators and industries each address deprivation problems individually, those most in need will be faced with a complex, confusing, inadequate and inequitable patchwork of assistance.

## 12.5 Fuel poverty and policies in other countries

Because the level of energy prices in the UK has broadly recovered the costs of supply to the companies (a necessary condition if supply is to be provided by unsubsidized private companies) the emphasis in fuel poverty discussions has up to now been on reducing the bills paid by particular households, rather than on subsidizing the industry as a whole (see, for example, Defra, 2004). More serious problems are looming through the much higher 'real' price of energy if it is to reflect the environmental cost of its carbon content, which will require increases in energy prices across the board, with serious implications for affordability. This problem is exacerbated in countries where even the much lower private costs of energy have not been fully reflected in charges to households. The issue surfaced particularly in countries which planned to reform their energy supply industry, often because of pressure from international organizations such as the World Bank or, for aspiring members, the European Union.

As well as the sensitivities outlined above for the UK, in many developing countries the need for substantial investment to deliver power supplies to scattered communities has raised additional problems. The industry itself, usually state owned, has often been subsidized, and the wish to please urban voters has frequently resulted in particularly low prices in cities, subsidized from the industrial sector. Non-technical losses in the form of theft of electricity have also been common in some countries. To introduce private capital and ensure that the companies do not benefit from 'state aid', substantial increases in tariff levels would be necessary to make the sector self-sufficient in the sense of covering the 'private' costs of supply, including often needed investment, repair or strengthening of fragile generation and distribution systems. If competition were to be effective, it would threaten any persistent cross-subsidies between different consumers (for example, lifeline tariffs to support low-income consumers) as entrants avoided such consumers in favour of more profitable alternatives.

Household expenditure surveys have been used to identify the challenges of fuel poverty for a selection of Latin American and South Eastern European countries. Such surveys are not without difficulties but they do identify some of the issues.

In Latin America, where the issue is often that of investing for new supplies, reforms have generally raised prices for customers, but provided additional benefit for those newly connected to the system. In Bolivia and Peru, reforms left existing consumers worse off, but new consumers gained; in Argentina both existing and new consumers were better off, though the rich gained most of the benefits (Ugaz and Waddams Price, 2003).

The challenge for countries which seek entry to the European Union is less likely to be to connect new consumers, but rather to be strengthening existing networks; and if they are to offer all householders a choice of energy supplier as required following the European Commission's directive, reform will be needed to avoid subsidies both to the energy sector as a whole and between consumers within it. Three countries in South East Europe (one member state, one potential candidate country and one candidate country) provide a contrast in the challenge for fuel poverty. In Bulgaria, which entered the European Union in 2007, electricity tariffs increased considerably between 2001 and the year of accession; these increases represented over 7 per cent of the income of the average household. In contrast, Albania was, at the same date, charging average prices which were only half of the World Bank's estimated long-run marginal cost, indicating that substantial additional price rises would be necessary if accession were to become a reality (Waddams Price and Pham, 2009). The proportional changes would be particularly high for low-income consumers, representing almost an eighth of total household expenditure for the poorest tenth of consumers, compared with a much more modest one twenty-fifth for the richest tenth.

Turkey is a candidate country for accession to the European Union and faces different issues in its energy markets. The main challenge on residential tariffs is their structure rather than their level (though levels have also been somewhat below costs). Adjusting prices to reflect regional losses would impact more severely on the low-income households in each region (Bağdadioğlu *et al.*, 2009); and adjusting the tariffs to reflect cost structures, which would be an inevitable result of competition, would inevitably result in the current flat tariff being replaced by one which reflected the fixed costs of supplying consumers, i.e. with a standing charge or a higher rate for low-consumption households. This is exactly the reverse of a lifeline tariff or rising block tariff, which offers all households (or those with particular characteristics) initial energy consumption at a lower price. Here low-income consumers lose out because their absolute level of consumption is lower than for richer households. A revenue neutral introduction of a standing charge which collected 10 per cent of revenue (a conservative estimate – the average in the UK is around 15 per cent) would increase the energy bills of the poorest tenth of consumers by 2 per cent of their disposable income, while the richest tenth would benefit (from the lower per unit energy charges) to the tune of 0.15 per cent of their income.

Within Europe it will also be important to avoid overall subsidies to a sector and any potential accusations of 'state aid'. Scott *et al.* (2008) estimate higher rates of fuel poverty in the Republic of Ireland than in the UK, and attribute this to poor housing stock. They find little consistent quantified description of fuel poverty on a consistent basis in other European countries, and a wide range of policies to address the problems associated with fuel poverty.

All these examples show the challenge for affordability of bringing the charges made to households close to the 'private' costs of supply as these costs rise. If prices are to reflect fully the environmental damage from burning carbon fuels, household energy prices would need to rise still further in all these countries, a serious challenge at a time of increasing austerity following the financial crisis of 2008–9. One solution is a 'virtuous tax', whose revenues would be returned as an 'environmental dividend' (Hansen, 2009). If this were distributed on a per capita basis, the higher prices for energy would prove generally progressive rather than regressive, since a greater proportion of the tax would be generated by the rich who tend to use more energy, though low-income households in large and/or badly insulated homes and which therefore use more energy would make a disproportionate contribution.

## 12.6 Concluding remarks

The UK government's targets to remove households from fuel poverty, while they seemed appropriate in the early years of the twenty-first century, are being overtaken by more general issues of affordability which are becoming increasingly pressing with the environmental agenda. We have shown both how feelings of affordability may differ from those which are recorded as 'formal' fuel poverty, and the challenges across the world for reforming energy markets. The overlap between fuel poverty and other measures is partial and likely to be weakening as fuel poverty increases with rising prices.

The changed emphasis is reflected in the Energy Act 2010, where the regulator's duties to protect consumers, wherever appropriate by competition, are enhanced by new obligations to take account of security of supply and sustainability, and where considering alternatives to competition is more explicitly signalled. The coalition government in the UK produced a 32-point 'Energy Statement' which includes a review of energy markets and the role of the regulator in the context of both social and environmental concerns (DECC, 2010c). Finding an appropriate balance should indeed be the responsibility of government rather than the regulator or individual supply companies, and in this context it is somewhat surprising that the suppliers remain mandated to deliver social programmes, albeit now by government, rather than the regulator. Whether competitive markets remain the best vehicle to deliver such social programmes to increase affordability and reduce fuel poverty (and address other affordability issues in utilities) remains to be seen; but the recognition of the tension by all parties in the Energy Act 2010 passed by the Labour government, and in the review announced later by the

Conservative and Liberal coalition, and by the regulator in its judgements on non-discrimination, should at least provide for a more honest debate on this crucial aspect of energy and social policy.

## References


Baker, P., Blundell, R. and Micklewright, J. (1989). Modelling household energy expenditures using micro-data, *Economic Journal*, **99**: 720–38.

Bağdadioğlu, N., Başaran, A. and Waddams Price, C. (2007). Potential impact of electricity reforms on Turkish households. Centre for Competition Policy Research Paper 07–8. University of East Anglia.

Bağdaldioğlu, N., Başaran, A., Kalaycioğlu, S. and Pinar, A. (2009). Integrating poverty in utilities governance. UNDP Turkey and Haceteppe University Center for Market Economics and Entrepreneurship, Ankara.

Beatty, T., Blow, L. and Crossley, T. (2009). Heat or eat? An empirical analysis of UK cold weather income support, presented at the Agricultural & Applied Economics Associations 2009 AAEA and ACCI Joint Annual Meeting, Milwaukee, 26–28 July.

Bennett, M., Cooke, D. and Waddams-Price, C. (2002). Left out in the cold? New energy tariffs, low-income households and the fuel poor, *Fiscal Studies*, **23**(2): 167–94.

BIS (2009). Retail prices index: fuels components monthly figures, Available at www.berr.gov.uk/whatwedo/energy/statistics/source/prices/page47818.html, last accessed 29 August 2009.

Boardman, B. (1991). *Fuel Poverty: From Cold Homes to Affordable Warmth*, London: Belhaven Press.

Bradshaw, J. and Hutton, S. (1983). Social policy options and fuel poverty, *Journal of Economic Psychology*, **3**: 249–66.

Consumer Focus (2009). End Fuel Poverty Campaign, Available at www.consumerfocus.org.uk/campaigns/end-fuel-poverty, last accessed 28 December 2009.

Cullen, J.B., Friedberg, L. and Wolfram, C. (2005). Do households smooth small consumption shocks? Evidence from anticipated and unanticipated variation in home energy costs, Working Paper No. 141, Center for the Study of Energy Markets, Berkeley, CA.

DECC (2010a). *Digest of United Kingdom Energy Statistics 2009 (DUKES)*, London: Department of Energy and Climate Change.

DECC (2010b), Up to £20 million off fuel bills for poor pensioners as energy rebate scheme gets underway (press release), Available at www.decc.gov.uk/en/content/cms/news/dwp10_084/dwp10_084.aspx, last accessed 3 August 2010.

DECC (2010c). *Annual Energy Statement, DECC Departmental Memorandum, 27 July 2010*, London: DECC.

Defra (2004). *Fuel Poverty in England: The Government's Plan for Action London*, London: Department for Environment, Food and Rural Affairs.

DTI Energy Group (2001). InterMinisterial Group on Fuel Poverty, the UK Fuel Poverty Strategy, London: Her Majesty's Stationery Office,

Available at http://webarchive.nationalarchives.gov.uk/+/http://www.berr.gov.uk/files/file16495.pdf, last accessed 21 February 2011.

Electricity Act (1989). Chapter 29, Her Majesty's Stationery Office.

Energy Act (2010). Available at www.opsi.gov.uk/acts/acts2010/pdf/ukpga_20100027_en.pdf, last accessed 9 August 2010, London: The Stationery Office.

Fuel Poverty Advisory Group (2010). *Annual Report on Fuel Poverty Statistics, London*, London: Department of Energy and Climate Change.

Gas Act (1986). London: The Stationery Office.

Gas Act (1995). London: The Stationery Office.

Hansen, J. (2009). *Storms of my Grandchildren*, USA: Bloomsbury.

Helm, D. (2003). *Energy, the State, and the Market: British Energy Policy since 1979*, Oxford: Oxford University Press.

House of Commons (2010). Cold Weather Payments, Briefing Paper Standard Note SN/SP/696: The Stationery Office.

House of Commons Business and Enterprise Committee (2008a). Energy prices, fuel poverty and Ofgem, *Eleventh Report of Session 2007–08*, 2, London: The Stationery Office.

House of Commons Business and Enterprise Committee (2008b). Energy prices, fuel poverty and Ofgem, *Eleventh Report of Session 2007–08*, 1, London: The Stationery Office.

House of Commons Environment, Food and Rural Affairs Committee (2009). Energy efficiency and fuel poverty, HC 37: The Stationery Office.

Hviid, M. and Waddams Price, C. (2010). Non-discrimination clauses in the retail energy sector, University of East Anglia, Centre for Competition Policy Working Paper, 10–18.

Littlechild, S.C. (1983). *Regulation of British Telecommunication's Profitability.* Department of Trade and Industry, London: The Stationery Office.

Lloyd, C.R. (2006). Fuel poverty in New Zealand, *Social Policy Journal of New Zealand*, **27**, 142–55.

Mummery, H. and Reilly, H. (2010). Cutting back, cutting down, cutting off: self-disconnection among prepayment meter users, London: Consumer Focus, Available at www.consumerfocus.org.uk/files/2010/10/Cutting-back-cutting-down-cutting-off.pdf, last accessed 21 February 2011.

NEA (2009). Radical action needed to help millions who cannot afford their energy bills (press release), Available at www.nea.org.uk/radical-action-needed-to-help-millions-who-cannot-afford-their-energy-bills, last accessed 22 December 2009.

Next Generation Utility Forum (2010). Working Group Manifesto, Available at www.communityni.org/sites/files/communityni/NGUF%20Manifesto%20final%20v3%20and%20final.doc, last accessed 13 May 2010.

Ofgem (2004). *Domestic Competitive Market Review 2004, A review document April 2004*, Chapter 6 and appendix 18, London: Ofgem.

Ofgem (2006). *Domestic Retail Market Report June 2005*, London: Ofgem.

Ofgem (2008a). Market is sound, Ofgem assures chancellor, London: Ofgem, Available at www.ofgem.gov.uk/Pages/MoreInformation.aspx?file=Ofgem%202.pdf&refer=Media/PressRel, last accessed 28 December 2009.

Ofgem (2008b). Ofgem puts industry on notice to make markets work better for all, London: Ofgem, Available at www.ofgem.gov.uk/Pages/MoreInformation.aspx?docid=209&refer=Media/PressRel, last accessed 28 December 2009.

Ofgem (2008c). *The Energy Supply Probe, Ref: 140/08*, London: Ofgem.

Ofgem (2009). *A Review of the First Year of the Carbon Emissions Reduction Target, Ref: 88/09*, London: Ofgem.

Ofgem (2010). *Domestic Suppliers' Social Obligations 2009 Report*, July 2009, London: Ofgem.

Palmer, G., McInnes, T. and Kenway, P. (2008). *Cold and Poor: An Analysis of the Link between Fuel Poverty and Low Income*, London: New Policy Institute.

Public Health Agency (2009). Press release: Seminar focuses on tackling fuel poverty in Northern Ireland, Monday 23 November 2009, Available at www.publichealth.hscni.net/lnews/47%20Press%20release%20-%20Seminar%20focuses%20on%20tackling%20fuel%20poverty%20in%20Northern%20Ireland%20-%2023%20November.html, last accessed 22 December 2009.

Scott, S., Lyons, S., Keane, C., McCarthy, D. and Tol, R. (2008). Fuel poverty in Ireland: extent, affected groups and policy issues, Economic and Social Research Institute Working Paper No. 262, November, Dublin.

Sharratt, D., Brigham, B.H. and Brigham, M. (2007). The utility of social obligations in the UK energy industry, *Journal of Management Studies*, **44**:8.

Ugaz, C. and Waddams Price, C. (eds.) (2003). *Utility Privatisation and Regulation: Fair Deal for Consumers?* Cheltenham: Edward Elgar.

Utilities Act (2000). The Stationery Office, Norwich, UK.

Waddams Price, C. and Pham, K. (2009). The impact of electricity market reform on consumers, *Utilities Policy*, **17**(1): 43–8.

Waddams Price, C., Brazier, K., Pham, K., Mathieu, L. and Wang, W. (2007). Identifying fuel poverty using objective and subjective measures. Centre for Competition Policy Research Paper 07–11, University of East Anglia.

Walker, A. (2009). *The Independent Review of Charging for Household Water and Sewerage Services Final Report*, London: Department of Food, Environment and Rural Affairs.

# 13 Energy spending and vulnerable households

*Tooraj Jamasb and Helena Meier*

## 13.1 Introduction

As with most goods and services there are significant variations in the energy use and spending levels among different households. Most of these differences can be explained by specific household characteristics such as income, the number of family members, the type and size of a family's home, or geography. As a consequence, the effect of changes in energy prices, incomes, or energy policy measures on household energy spending can vary across different types of families. In recent years, fuel poverty among vulnerable households and energy equity has occupied an important place in the energy policy debate.

In this chapter we focus on the UK. A discussion of the significance of the issue in other countries can be found in the previous chapter, by Waddams Price, in this book. In Britain, according to the official definition, households that spend more than 10 per cent of their incomes on energy are described as 'fuel poor' and having difficulties in warming their homes adequately. The fuel poverty ratio is calculated as fuel costs (usage multiplied with price) divided by income. If this ratio is larger than 0.1, a household is considered as being fuel poor (DECC, 2009c).

Vulnerable households are at especially high risk in terms of being affected by fuel poverty (Defra and BERR, 2008). A household is considered as vulnerable if some of its members are children, elderly, sick or disabled. The number of families that spend a large share of their income on energy has increased again since 2004 (DECC, 2009b). Three factors play a major role in fuel poverty: income, energy prices and energy efficiency. Currently about 4 million households in the UK are considered fuel poor and more than 80 per cent of these are vulnerable households (DECC, 2009c).

The authors would like to acknowledge the generous support from Electricity Policy Research Group (EPRG), University of Cambridge, for this work.

At the same time, there is concern that efforts towards achieving renewable energy and climate change policies can result in higher energy prices and higher fuel poverty. It is therefore important to design policies to help the most affected groups. However, the wrong types of policies can also lead to inefficient use of energy. In this chapter we explore energy spending among households on very low incomes, including pensioners, female single parent households and benefit recipients. We describe how energy spending of these households has changed over time in order to shed light on energy spending more broadly.

## 13.2 Background and past studies

Household energy spending and consumption has been in the focus of research since the 1970s. As the energy efficiency in the industrial sector has gradually improved, the potential for reducing energy usage in the domestic sector has become more important. The availability of micro data has enabled researchers to analyze and compare the energy usage and behaviour of households. The literature can be divided into two main groups according to the modelling approach. First, discrete-continuous models describe a two-step decision by households. Households first choose the energy consuming appliances they need and then decide the extent to which they actually use their appliances. Studies in this area are available for the UK (Baker and Blundell, 1991) and several other countries (Dubin and McFadden, 1984; Nesbakken, 1999 and 2001; Vaage, 2000; Liao and Chang, 2002).

Second, conditional demand models focus on the usage of energy consuming appliances. Energy demand is modelled as being conditional on the existing appliance stock. The conditional energy demand or spending approach has been explored for Great Britain (Baker *et al.*, 1989; Meier and Rehdanz, 2009), Denmark (Leth-Petersen and Togeby, 2001), Germany (Rehdanz, 2007) and for developing countries (Wu *et al.*, 2004). Baker *et al.* (1989) present an extension of this approach. The study uses a two-stage budgeting model where, independent from their stock of appliances, households first allocate their income between energy and all other goods and then distribute the share of their income on energy spending among the different fuels.

Independent from the modelling approach, most of these studies analyze the income and price responses of households. Income elasticities of energy demand show how energy demand changes with income and could indicate the possible effects of income-supporting policy measures on energy spending. The estimated income elasticities are mainly positive but are not larger than 1 suggesting that energy demand increases with income but this increase is less than proportionate. Some studies estimate price responses for different fuels. Their main findings indicate that own price elasticities are negative but are well below 1 (in absolute value). Price increases thus do not lead to strong demand reductions. Moreover, the demand for one type of fuel is found to be affected by the price of other fuels. The strength of the response is given by cross price elasticities which are mainly positive – i.e. the demand for one type of fuel increases when the price of another fuel increases (Dubin and McFadden, 1984; Baker *et al.*, 1989; Baker and Blundell, 1991; Nesbakken, 1999; Vaage, 2000; Rehdanz, 2007; Meier and Rehdanz, 2009).

More differentiated results can be found in studies that analyze specific groups of households separately. Different household income groups react differently to changes in income and energy prices. Using British panel data, Jamasb and Meier (2010) find that households on low incomes have lower income elasticity of energy spending than those with higher incomes. Baker *et al.* (1989) estimate income elasticities for heads of households older than sixty-five and show that these households react weakly to income changes. Households with at least one child younger than the age of five in comparison have very high income elasticities (Baker *et al.*, 1989). Price responses also differ across household groups. Nesbakken (1999) finds that high-income households in Norway react more sensitively to energy price changes. Jamasb and Meier (2010) estimate a similar link for gas prices and gas spending and find low-income households to be more responsive to electricity price changes than those with high incomes.

Belonging to a specific socioeconomic group can also lead to a higher probability of being affected by fuel poverty (Bennett *et al.*, 2002). In particular, low incomes lead to fuel poverty even though not all low-income households are fuel poor (Palmer *et al.*, 2008) or consider themselves as being fuel poor (see Waddams Price, this volume). Next to income, other socioeconomic characteristics such as household size, age, number of children, employment status or tenancy are drivers of the energy spending level of households (see, for example, Meier and Rehdanz, 2010).

In addition to income levels, some studies have shown that age has a significant influence on energy spending. Elderly households tend to be more energy intensive than other groups of households. They generally consist of a smaller number of occupants but live in more spacious dwellings. Hence they tend to demand more space heating than other households (Liao and Chang, 2002). Elderly people as vulnerable households face two problems: they often live on very low incomes and their larger than average dwellings are often poorly insulated. Thus, they have high energy consumption and bills in order to sustain a certain level of warmth and as a result cause higher than average carbon emissions (Roberts, 2008).

Policy measures to reduce carbon emissions might thus affect fuel poor households relatively more. Dresner and Ekins (2006), for example, analyze the effect of carbon taxation on fuel-poor households. These households may have to pay relatively higher taxes if they live in poorly insulated homes and already face high energy bills. Compensating these households with a simple benefit system is rather difficult. In addition there is a difference between the objective measure of fuel poverty and the perception of households facing difficulties in warming their homes adequately. Waddams Price *et al.* (2007) show that while some households feel fuel poor they are not a policy target group, thus the current policy measures will not improve their condition.

The space heating expenditures of welfare recipients in Germany is analyzed in Rehdanz and Stöwhase (2008). The study shows that welfare recipients have significantly higher heating expenditures than other households as their spending is fully covered by benefit payments. Hence the incentives to reduce heating consumption among this group of households are low, leaving some scope for devising suitable policy measures to reduce overall domestic energy consumption.

Altogether, we can conclude from the evidence provided by the existing literature that households are likely to differ in their energy usage according to some specific socioeconomic characteristics. In the rest of this chapter we further explore the energy spending of vulnerable groups of households and give some insights into how these households differ from the average population and analyze some household characteristics that seem to lead to the observed differences in energy spending.

## 13.3 Types of vulnerable households

Officially, low-income households are defined as households with an income below 60 per cent of median disposable income (ONS, 2009). These households are regarded as at high risk of spending a great share of their incomes on fuel. It is noteworthy that low-income households often fall into more than one category of vulnerable households. For example, single persons aged sixty years and older also belong to a large extent to the low-income group (DECC, 2009b). The UK government has implemented a range of measures to improve the income situation and to tackle poverty. These include income support and energy efficiency measures aimed at tackling pensioner poverty and child poverty (DECC, 2009b).

Elderly people run a particular risk of being affected by fuel poverty. Tackling fuel poverty of the elderly is expected to become a growing concern as the group of elderly people becomes larger in the UK. For example, between 1983 and 2008 the population aged sixty-five and older increased by 1.5 million. In the same period, the number of people aged eighty-five and over increased at an even faster rate (ONS, 2009). This demographic change has several implications. In 2007 almost 25 per cent of fuel-poor households had at least one occupant aged seventy-five years or older (DECC, 2009a). In response, policy makers have developed measures that especially address the elderly groups. In England, for example, householders qualify for the Warm Front Scheme if they are aged sixty or over and receive one or several of specified benefits, for example Pension Credit which tops up the weekly income to a guaranteed minimum level. Warm Front Grants cover insulation and heating measures with a maximum value of £3,500 (or up to £6,000 if fuels other than gas are used, DECC, 2009c). Pensioners should automatically receive Winter Fuel Payments if they are sixty and over. These payments are even higher if a householder is at least eighty years old (DECC, 2009c).

Another group of households that we are interested in are the benefit recipients. In the context of this chapter benefit recipients are defined as households that receive Jobseeker's Allowance or Income Support. In Britain, income support is an extra payment to people who satisfy all of the following criteria: being on low incomes if they are between sixteen and fifty-nine years old while not full-time employed or full-time students; not receiving Jobseeker's Allowance; and not having savings above £16,000. Recipients of income support are, for example, sick or disabled or lone parents responsible for a child up to twelve years old. A part of income support also covers certain housing payments. Jobseeker's Allowance is another working age benefit and is paid to those available for work and actively seeking it. Individuals working less than sixteen hours per week are also eligible for this benefit (Jobcentre Plus, 2010). Benefit recipients tend to live on low incomes and in addition they are likely to spend more time at home than full-time employees. Both of these factors could contribute to a higher than average energy spending over income share.

We also examine the case of female single-parent households in our analysis as these have a high probability of being affected by fuel poverty as some members of these households are children. Most of the lone parents do not work full time and thus these households live to a large extent on lower incomes. Moreover, lone parents tend to be mainly single mothers. Consequently in our analysis we specifically concentrate on this group of single parent households.

## 13.4 Data

We base our study of household energy expenditures and analysis of their characteristics on the British Household Panel Survey (BHPS). The BHPS data consist of an unbalanced[1] panel of about 5,500 households that have been re-interviewed over a period of seventeen years, running from 1991 to 2008. The main purpose of the survey is to understand the dynamics of change in the British population. In order to collect a representative sample for Great Britain, household addresses have been clustered and stratified. The main selection criteria for the sample are age, employment and retirement.

While the dataset covers several social and economic domains it is not certain that it is statistically fully representative of the British population concerning, for example, the distribution of income levels. We use the Consumer Price Index (CPI) of the UK Office for National Statistics (ONS) with 2005=100 (ONS, 2009) in order to adjust all monetary values relative to price developments in the wider economy.

The developments of household energy spending over time are influenced by movements of gas and electricity prices. Figure 13.1 shows the average yearly gas and electricity price developments for the UK during the period of our study. The data are drawn from the IEA (1997) and IEA (2008).[2] Both prices have developed rather similarly, and were below their 1991 levels until 2005 and reached their lowest levels in 2003.

The restructuring of the electricity market started in 1989 with the British Electricity Act that went into force in March 1990. Consumers seem to have profited from efficiency gains after 1995 as reflected in the rather strong reduction in electricity price from 1995 (Newbery and Pollitt, 1997). Also, in 1993 the Value Added Tax (VAT) on domestic fuels was introduced at a rate of 8 per cent (Fouquet, 1995) but this was then reduced again to 5 per cent in 1997 (Boardman, 2010). Since 2005 electricity and gas prices have both significantly increased in real terms impacting the link between energy spending and income. Figure 13.1 also shows that electricity prices largely follow the price of gas reflecting

[1] An unbalanced panel is a panel that does not have the same number of observations in every period (balanced panel), i.e. the number of interviewed households varies over time.

[2] The IEA data are also published by the Department of Energy and Climate Change (DECC).

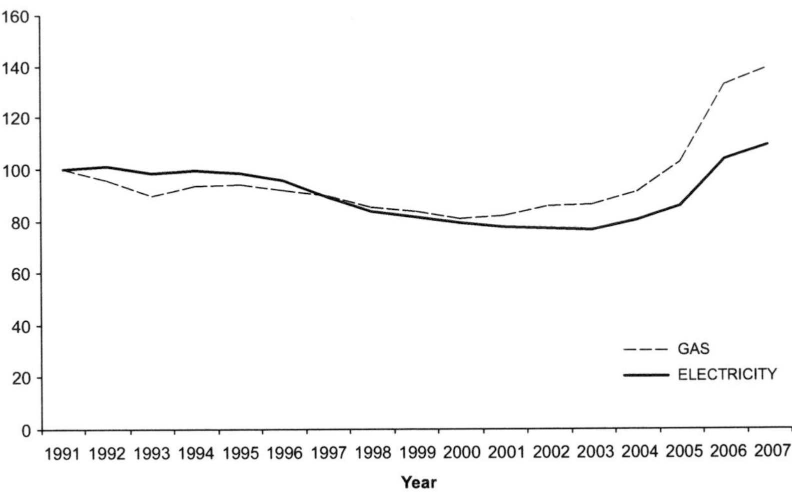


Figure 13.1 Real gas and electricity price index, 1991=100.
*Source:* IEA 1997 and 2008; ONS, 2005.

the rapid increase in the share of combined cycle gas turbines (CCGT) as the preferred generation technology by new entrants in the post liberalization period in the UK (Green and Newbery, 1992; Green and Newbery, 1993).

Although privatization and competition initially led to an overall decrease in energy prices, an analysis of distributional impacts on consumers has shown that some consumers did not gain from these. Thus privatization and competition have not been a better solution for all consumers. Paying more attention to distributional and social impacts would have led to better policy design and should be taken into account in the future. An analysis of the different tariffs that came into effect after the liberalization of the energy markets indicates that a mix of fuel poverty and specific household characteristics might lead to some households being worse off than before. In particular, large households with low incomes seem to have been adversely affected by the new tariff structures since they have comparably large energy expenditure (Bennet *et al.*, 2002).

## 13.5 Vulnerable households and energy spending

The number of (vulnerable) fuel-poor households decreased up until 2003–4 and then increased again in recent years. Figure 13.2 presents the development of fuel-poor households subdivided into different vulnerable groups based on the BHPS data. It can be seen that the named household groups altogether make up almost all of the fuel-poor households.

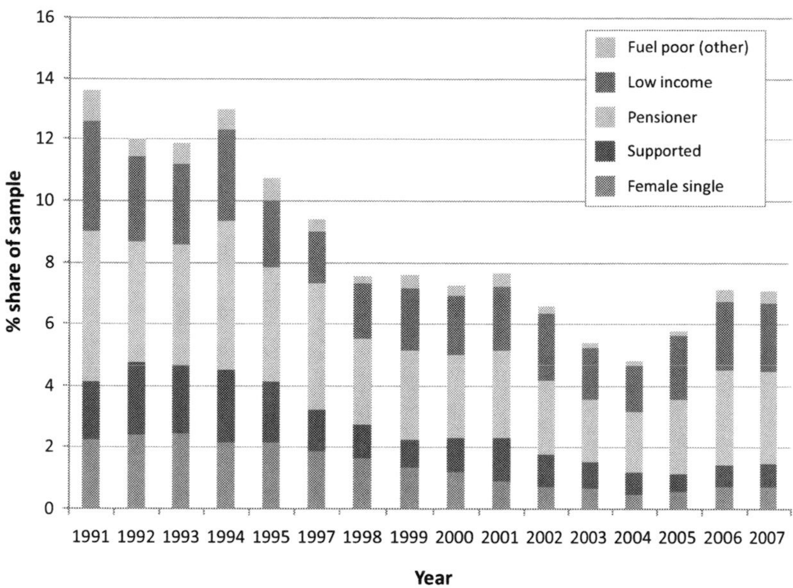


Figure 13.2 Share of fuel-poor households subdivided into vulnerable groups.
*Note:* Data on household energy spending is not readily available for 1996.
*Source:* Own presentation, based on BHPS data.

Also, the development over time represents the trend as described by the Fuel Poverty Advisory Group, 2009 which is based on the English House Condition Survey (EHCS), and similar datasets for Scotland, Wales and Northern Ireland.

While in 1996 almost 6.5 million households in the whole UK were fuel poor (five million fuel-poor vulnerable households), numbers decreased to two million in 2003 (1.5 million vulnerable households) and increased again to four million (3.25 million vulnerable households) in 2007 (see Waddams Price, this volume, and Fuel Poverty Advisory Group, 2009). A similar development can be observed for energy spending over income shares for different household types. Using the BHPS data we compare income, and energy spending as a share of income for the whole sample as well as for different subsets of households:

- Low-income households are defined as having an income below 60 per cent of median income in the sample. Since the survey does not provide information on disposable income (used in the official definition of low-income households) we use annual household income instead. At the same time, we ensure that observations from this group do not overlap with any other social groups in focus.

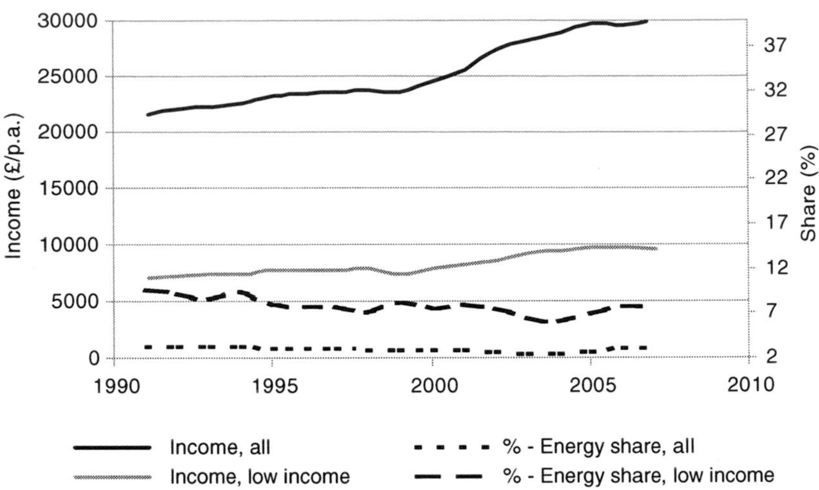


Figure 13.3 All and low-income households.
*Source:* Based on BHPS data.

- Pensioner households are defined as those with a retired head of household. These households might also be low-income households.
- Supported households are those who receive income support or jobseeker's allowances. These households might be on low incomes but do not include female single parents or pensioners.
- Female single parent households have a female single parent and at least one child. These households might be on low incomes as well but are not retired or recipients of income support or jobseeker's allowances.

Figures 13.3 to 6 show how income levels and energy spending shares have developed over time. The average annual household income for the whole sample has increased from £21,370 in 1991 to £29,000 in 2007 (in 2005 prices) though it stagnated in 2005–6. The share of energy spending over income was highest for all households in 1991 (3.4 per cent), lowest in 2003 (2.4 per cent) and reached 2.9 per cent in 2007. Figure 13.3 shows similar developments for low-income households though income levels are at much lower levels and percentage of energy spending shares much higher.

For pensioners (Figure 13.4) and Income Support (IS) and Jobseeker's Allowance (JSA) recipients (Figure 13.5), similar movements are observable, although the difference in income levels and spending shares is not as high for low-income households. Female single parent households show a rather marked development (Figure 13.6), and their income

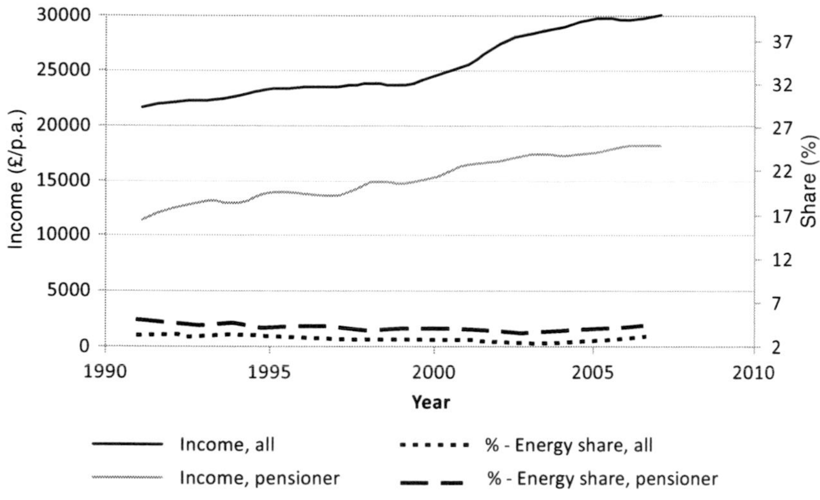


Figure 13.4 All and pensioner households.
*Source*: Based on BHPS data.

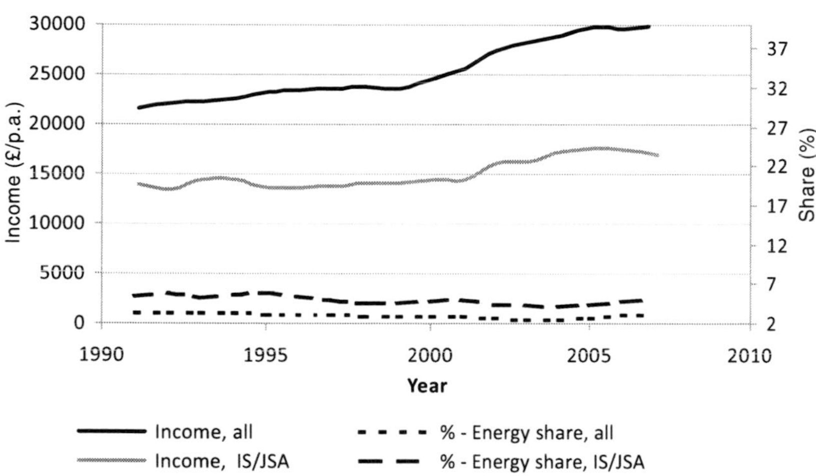


Figure 13.5 All and IS/JSA recipient households.
*Source:* Based on BHPS data.

decline after 2005 is comparatively high. Pensioner households and female single headed households with children form a high proportion of low-income households. However, the average disposable income for these households decreased by 1 per cent in 2005–6 and in 2006–7. Real income from benefits did not increase and this might explain the strong

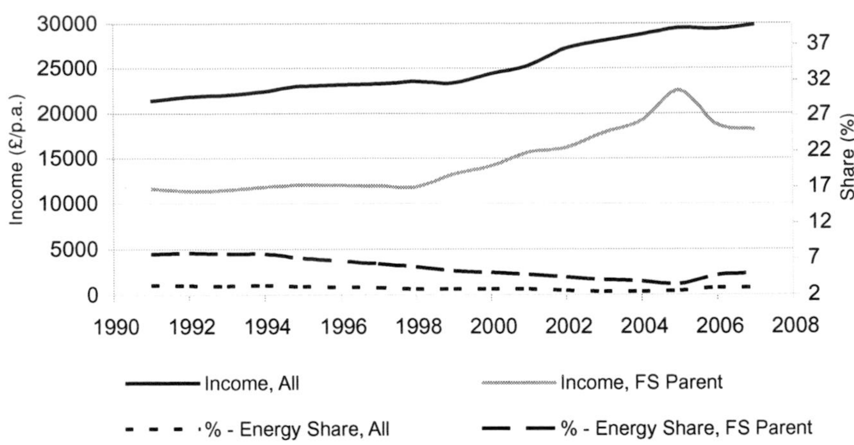


Figure 13.6 All and female single-parent households.
*Source*: Based on BHPS data.

reduction in income for female single parent households as they were not compensated by a real increase in the child benefit or education benefit they receive (Jones *et al.*, 2008).

## 13.6 Drivers of fuel poverty

Following the above descriptive results we present an empirical analysis using the BHPS data and explore the drivers of the fuel-poverty ratio, i.e. of the energy spending over income share. In our model we control for price impacts, socioeconomic characteristics such as household size and ownership of a property, the development over time, different building types and for the different vulnerable household groups discussed above. Our findings show that the specific characteristics of these household groups have a positive significant effect on their energy spending over income share. In other words, these household groups have higher energy spending over income shares independent of the other variables that we control for within our model. Among these household groups, low-income households in particular tend to have the highest energy spending over income share.

Table 13.1 summarizes some household characteristics of the specific groups of households. It shows that different vulnerable households are rather heterogeneous. As depicted in the table, fuel-poor households belonging to any of the vulnerable household groups on average have

Table 13.1 *Mean values for different household types*

| Mean values | INCOME (£ p.a.) | | ENERGY (£ p.a.) | | AVERAGE AGE | HHSIZE | CHILDREN | ROOMS | SHARE (in whole sample) % |
|---|---|---|---|---|---|---|---|---|---|
| Whole sample | 25,671 | | 728 | | 44 | 2.5 | 0.6 | 4.4 | 100 |
| Whole sample, fuel poor | 6,797 | (26.5)* | 1,021 | (140.3) | 49 | 2.0 | 0.5 | 1.8 | 8.06 |
| Low Income | 8,178 | | 624 | | 44 | 1.8 | 0.3 | 1.6 | 7.27 |
| Low Income, fuel poor | 5,830 | (71.3) | 960 | (153.8) | 43 | 2.1 | 0.5 | 1.8 | 2.16 |
| Retired | 14,839 | | 620 | | 70 | 1.6 | 0.0 | 4.1 | 27.12 |
| Retired, fuel poor | 6,207 | (41.8) | 876 | (141.2) | 72 | 1.3 | 0.0 | 4.1 | 3.05 |
| Supported | 14,879 | | 713 | | 37 | 2.6 | 0.7 | 3.8 | 6.25 |
| Supported, fuel poor | 6,211 | (41.7) | 954 | (133.7) | 40 | 1.9 | 0.5 | 3.6 | 1.22 |
| Female single | 15,459 | | 783 | | 19 | 3.0 | 1.7 | 1.3 | 5.92 |
| Female single, fuel poor | 6,996 | (45.3) | 1,073 | (137) | 17 | 2.9 | 1.8 | 4.1 | 1.25 |

* Numbers in brackets: percentages of income (energy spending) of different groups of fuel-poor households in relation to overall income (energy spending) in different groups of households, e.g. 26.5 = (6,797/25,671) * 100.

*Source:* BHPS survey data.

lower incomes and at the same time higher levels of energy spending than the average (not fuel-poor) households in the sample.

There are some possible explanations for the higher energy spending levels among these households. For example, households living in poorly insulated accommodations are at a higher risk of fuel poverty. It has been shown that households on low incomes live to a large extent in homes with poor energy efficiency (Palmer *et al.*, 2008). In order to maintain an adequate level of warmth at home those households have to pay larger than average energy bills (Roberts, 2008). Moreover, low income levels contribute to a lack of capital which would be necessary to pay for insulation measures to improve the energy efficiency of heating systems.

Another reason for higher energy spending among these groups of households is their actual use of energy. Besides the energy used for heating which makes up the largest share of a household's energy consumption, electricity is needed for lighting and appliances. The amount of electricity used per unit of energy service tends to be higher for fuel-poor households as they tend to have older and less energy efficient appliances than higher-income households. A major reason for this is that some fuel-poor households often buy second-hand appliances rather than new appliances that comply with the highest energy efficiency standards (Boardman, 2010).

Moreover, not all households have access to all different fuels. In particular some households living in rural areas do not have access to piped gas and only use electricity, even for heating purposes. These households are likely to pay higher electricity prices than households that have access to both fuel types (Jamasb and Meier, 2010). Fuel poverty rates in rural areas are in general higher than in urban areas as houses in these areas tend to be larger but at the same time less energy efficient (Boardman, 2010).

In addition, different payment methods can also be a reason for a higher probability of some household types being affected by fuel poverty. For example, households using prepayment metres tend to pay more for each energy unit than households which pay by direct debit (Bennett *et al.*, 2002). Finally, low-income households might also have high energy bills because of a large number of family members who use many appliances. In contrast, single person households have a higher risk of being affected by fuel poverty (Palmer *et al.*, 2008). In these households relative energy costs per capita are much higher because single persons live on their own (Boardman, 2010). Overall, our findings indicate that energy spending over income share decreases with household size.

## 13.7 Discussion and conclusions

As discussed above, low-income households, pensioners, benefit recipients and female single households spend significantly more of their incomes on energy in comparison to other households. In particular, low-income households differ most from all other households. This can be explained by three arguments. First, vulnerable households live on lower than average incomes and in order to reach a certain level of comfort or to heat their homes adequately they need to spend a larger share of their income on energy. A second reason could be that these households spend more time at home than households that consist mainly of full-time workers and thus use more energy than others. The third reason may be that these households are not able to improve the energy efficiency of their homes. Thus the energy efficiency of their homes is lower and their energy-using appliances may be less efficient.

Independent from reasons that cause higher energy spending to income shares, these higher spending shares are directly linked to these households being more severely affected by energy price increases. However, it is not the actual percentage of energy spending over income share that matters in this context. Rather, it is the household type that often appears to predetermine a worse than average outcome in energy spending and in particular the degree of affliction by energy price increases.

Different approaches are now undertaken to reduce the energy bills of these consumers and to reduce fuel poverty and help vulnerable households. One such recent development affecting all customers is the UK government's plan to introduce smart meters for all electricity customers in the coming ten years. Next to financial support paid to vulnerable households and in particular elderly people, smart metering and social tariffs can play an important part in eradicating fuel poverty and helping the vulnerable households. Smart metering can provide consumers with information on the actual energy consumption and might lead to behavioural changes. At the same time, energy suppliers no longer have to estimate bills, servicing costs can be reduced and thus there are potential consumer benefits.

Since many low-income households only have access to electricity (and not piped gas), the introduction of smart meters can help these households as they can provide information on usage patterns while benefits from time-of-use tariffs can be realized. Low-income households and single parent households use prepayment meters to a larger extent which are more costly. Introducing smart technologies can contribute to the reduction of energy bills. In addition, smart meter technologies can facilitate switching of suppliers and lead to lower energy bills for vulnerable households (Owen and Ward, 2007).

Some combined efforts are undertaken by the government, energy suppliers and Ofgem. The 'Smart Metering Implementation Programme' is a joint approach by DECC and the energy regulator. They focus on standardization and coordination to promote competition and enable consumers to switch suppliers easily. At the same time the creation of innovation incentives for energy suppliers is aimed at offering products and services that meet the needs of consumers (DECC and Ofgem, 2010). Also, the extension of the gas networks is part of measures undertaken by the regulator to help fuel-poor households without access to gas. In addition, some grants are available for installation of efficient gas central heating and gas appliances (Ofgem, 2010).

The impact of the further changes and new technologies such as smart meters on vulnerable households needs to be carefully examined, and in particular behavioural changes need to be accompanied by measures to improve the energy efficiency of homes. Decision makers should pay ample attention to the equity aspect of the expected future price increase that will affect certain households more severely and could widen the existing 'energy gap' and inequality among households.

## References

Baker, P. and Blundell, R. (1991). The microeconometric approach to modelling energy demand: some results for UK households, *Oxford Review of Economic Policy*, **7**(2): 54–76.

Baker, P., Blundell, R. and Micklewright, J. (1989). Modelling household energy expenditures using micro-data, *Economic Journal*, **99**(397): 720–38.

Bennett, M., Cooke, D. and Waddams Price, C. (2002). Left out in the cold? New energy tariffs, low income households and the fuel poor, *Fiscal Studies*, **32**(2): 167–94.

Boardman, B. (2010). *Fixing Fuel Poverty – Challenges and Solutions*, London: Earthscan.

DECC (2009a). Annual Report on Fuel Poverty Statistics. Department of Energy and Climate Change, Available at www.decc.gov.uk, last accessed 13 August 2010.

DECC (2009b). UK Energy Sector Indicators 2009. Department of Energy and Climate Change, Available at www.decc.gov.uk, last accessed 13 August 2010.

DECC (2009c). Addressing Fuel Poverty. Department of Energy and Climate Change, Available at www.decc.gov.uk/en/content/cms/what_we_do/consumers/fuel_poverty/fuel_poverty.aspx.

DECC and Ofgem (2010). Smart Metering Implementation Programme, Prospectus. Department of Energy and Climate Change. Office for Gas and Electricity Markets, July, Available at www.decc.gov.uk, last accessed 13 August 2010.

Defra and BERR (2008). The UK Fuel Poverty Strategy 6th Annual Progress Report 2008. Department for Environment, Food and Rural Affairs, Department for Business, Enterprise and Regulatory Reform, Available at www.berr.gov.uk/energy/fuel-poverty/strategy/index.html, last accessed 13 August 2010.

Dresner, S. and Ekins, P. (2006). Economic instruments to improve UK home energy efficiency without negative social impacts, *Fiscal Studies* **27**(1): 47–74.

Dubin, J.A. and McFadden, D.L. (1984). An econometric analysis of residential electric appliance holdings and consumption, *Econometrica*, **52**(2): 345–62.

Fouquet, R. (1995). The impact of VAT introduction on UK residential energy demand, *Energy Economics*, **17**(3): 237–47.

Fuel Poverty Advisory Group (2009). Annual Report on Fuel Poverty Statistics, London: Department of Energy and Climate Change.

Green, R.J. and Newbery, D.M. (1992). Competition in the British electricity spot market, *The Journal of Political Economy*, **100**(5): 929–53.

Green, R.J. and Newbery, D.M. (1993). The regulation of the gas industry: lessons from electricity, *Fiscal Studies*, **14**(2): 37–52.

IEA (1997). Energy Prices and Taxes, Quarterly Statistics, Fourth Quarter 1997. International Energy Agency.

IEA (2008). Energy Prices and Taxes, Quarterly Statistics, Third Quarter 2008, International Energy Agency.

Jamasb, T. and Meier, H. (2010). Household Energy Spending and Income Groups: Evidence from Great Britain. Cambridge Working Papers in Economics 1011, Faculty of Economics, University of Cambridge.

Jobcentre Plus (2010). Working Age Benefits, Available at www.jobcentreplus.gov.uk/JCP/Customers/WorkingAgeBenefits/index.html, last accessed 6 February 2010.

Jones, F., Annan, D. and Shah, S. (2008). The distribution of household income 1977 to 2006/07, *Economic and Labour Market Review*, **2**(12): December, Office of National Statistics (ONS).

Leth-Petersen, S. and Togeby, M. (2001). Demand for space heating in apartment blocks: measuring effects of policy measures aiming at reducing energy consumption, *Energy Economics*, **23**(4): 387–403.

Liao, H.C. and Chang, T.F. (2002). Space-heating and water-heating energy demands of the aged in the US, *Energy Economics*, **24**(3): 267–84.

Meier, H. and Rehdanz, K. (2010). Determinants of residential space heating expenditures in Great Britain, *Energy Economics*, **32**: 949–59.

Nesbakken, R. (1999). Price sensitivity of residential energy consumption in Norway, *Energy Economics*, **21**, 493–515.

Nesbakken, R. (2001). Energy consumption for space heating: a discrete-continuous approach, *Scandinavian Journal of Economics*, **103**(1): 165–84.

Newbery, D. and Pollitt, M. (1997). Restructuring and privatisation of the CEGB – was it worth it? *Journal of Industrial Economics*, **45**(3): 269–304.

Ofgem (2010). Social Action Strategy: 2009–2010 Update. Office for Gas and Electricity Markets. July 2010, Available at www.ofgem.gov.uk, last accessed 13 August 2010.

ONS (2009). Office for National Statistics, Available at www.statistics.gov.uk.

Owen, G. and Ward, J. (2007). Smart meters in Great Britain: the next steps? *Sustainability First*, July.

Palmer, G., MacInnes, T. and Kenway, P. (2008). Cold and poor: an analysis of the link between fuel poverty and low income, *New Policy Institute*, July.

Rehdanz, K. (2007). Determinants of residential space heating expenditures in Germany, *Energy Economics*, **29**(2): 167–82.

Rehdanz, K. and Stöwhase, S. (2008). Cost liability and residential space heating expenditures of welfare recipients in Germany, *Fiscal Studies*, **29**(3): 329–45.

Roberts, S. (2008). Energy, equity and the future of the fuel poor, *Energy Policy*, **36**(12): 4471–4.

Vaage, K. (2000). Heating technology and energy use: a discrete continuous choice approach to Norwegian household energy demand, *Energy Economics*, **22**(6): 649–66.

Waddams Price, C., Brazier, K., Pham, K., Mathieu, L. and Wang, W. (2007). Identifying Fuel Poverty Using Objective and Subjective Measures. Centre for Competition Policy Research Paper 07–11, University of East Anglia.

Wu, X., Lampietti, J. and Meyer, A.S. (2004). Coping with the cold: space heating and the urban poor in developing countries, *Energy Economics*, **26**(3): 345–57.

*Part IV*

# Policy and regulation

# 14 Demand-side management strategies and the residential sector: lessons from the international experience

*Aoife Brophy Haney, Tooraj Jamasb, Laura M. Platchkov and Michael G. Pollitt*

## 14.1 Introduction

Policies and measures targeting energy demand took off over the last three decades in response to the oil shocks of the 1970s. Since then, concerns about the sensitivity of economies to energy prices, oil dependency and more recently climate change, contributed to the development of energy efficiency (EE) policies.[1] Demand-related policies that aim to influence quantities or patterns of energy use have traditionally been referred to as demand-side management (DSM) programmes. They include both energy efficiency policies and demand response (DR).[2] Energy efficiency improvements can bring many benefits in terms of reduced energy infrastructure investments, decrease in electricity prices, increased energy security, improved environmental quality and other ancillary benefits.[3] Scientists estimate that by 2050, we will need to have reduced our greenhouse gas emissions (GHG) by 50 per cent to avoid the worst-case scenarios of climate change. In such a context, the building sector appears as the 'cornerstone of every national climate change strategy', as it is responsible for up to 30 per cent of global annual GHG emissions, and 40 per cent of all energy consumption (UNEP, 2009). Furthermore, there is widespread evidence of the cost-effectiveness of energy efficiency measures as compared to renewable programmes (IEA, 2006). In parallel, load growth; increased intermittency due to renewable generation; and, in the UK in particular, the renewal and reconfiguration of the electricity network pose challenges to the electricity sector never seen before. These

[1] By EE we refer to the amount of energy needed for a given service (heating, lighting etc.) or level of activity. See section 14.2 for a discussion of EE indicators.

[2] Pricing is at the heart of DR, which aims at increasing the elasticity of demand, including the cost-reflectivity of prices.

[3] For instance, reduced air pollution, increased health quality and energy security are among important co-benefits.

challenges increasingly lead to the recognition of the importance of active consumer participation in load shifting, and hence interest in influencing quantities or patterns of energy demand.

There is now substantial experience particularly among OECD countries in using policy instruments to improve the overall efficiency with which energy is used. Several recent studies have assessed these experiences. For example, Geller *et al.* (2006) review energy intensity trends in the OECD from 1973 to 2003. They focus on the specific policies adopted by Japan, the US and a selection of European countries to improve energy use per unit of GDP across sectors. The World Energy Council (WEC) has conducted a review of energy efficiency policies using a survey of seventy countries, including examples of the most effective types of policy measures (WEC, 2008). Similarly, the United National Environment Programme Sustainable Buildings & Climate Initiative (UNEP-SBCI) published several reports assessing the implemented policies in various countries. A number of International Energy Agency (IEA) publications have also looked at energy use trends (IEA, 2007; IEA, 2008); reviewed the implementation of energy efficiencies policies in general (IEA, 2009b); and in the residential sector in particular (IEA, 2008).

Some areas of general consensus emerge from these cross-country studies. First, the so-called 'energy efficiency gap'[4] of the building sector is particularly highlighted, together with the huge potential for cost-effective or 'negative cost' measures. Second, as we will discuss in this chapter, some features of the residential sector hinder optimal energy choices. These studies also show that there is still little understanding of the impacts of a specific measure and, more crucially, of the reasons behind those impacts (UNEP, 2009), as shown by the differences in experiences from one country to another. Last but not least, packages of integrated, complementary policies are much more effective in addressing barriers to energy efficiency than single measures. Several countries are mentioned as having successfully achieved integrated policy making: Germany; Denmark; Japan; the US, particularly states such as California; and Australia (de T'Serclaes, 2007; Uihlein and Eder, 2009). Even if the relative 'success' of certain countries needs to be matched to the specific original level of discretionary load, a closer examination of their strategies can offer useful lessons. In addition to policy packages, engaging the private sector is acknowledged as being central to ensuring long-lasting

[4] A simple definition of the energy efficiency gap reads as the difference between current or expected future energy use and the optimal current or future energy use (Jaffe and Stavins, 1994).

impact. The importance of institutional framework and national context are also emphasized in relation to policy stability and sustainability.

In this chapter we focus on DSM policies – i.e. including both energy efficiency policies and demand response – targeting residential demand for electricity and heat, i.e. household energy demand from buildings and appliances (see also Silva *et al.*, this volume and Torriti *et al.*, this volume). The objective is to understand why an integrated policy package is more likely to be successful than single policies. In section 14.2 we discuss some limits to aggregated energy indicators and to cross-country comparisons. This reveals the importance of the residential sector in energy demand. We then review past and recent energy demand trends in this sector, and uncover large untapped potential. This is due to specific barriers to energy demand reduction, discussed in section 14.3. In section 14.4, we present examples of policy responses to overcome those barriers. This leads us to discuss, in section 14.5, policy packages and the importance of comprehensiveness in DSM demonstrated by several case studies. We then draw some lessons for the UK from international experience.

## 14.2 The residential energy demand: key features

### *14.2.1 Energy-efficiency measures and the residential sector*

Greater energy efficiency is an essential part of overcoming the challenges facing the energy sector and considerable improvements are needed compared to recent trends (IEA, 2008). Here, energy efficiency improvement is defined as a reduction in the energy used for a given service (heating, lighting, etc.) or level of activity (WEC, 2008), typically without affecting the level of end-use service. Comparing energy efficiency performance across countries is difficult.

First and foremost, energy indicators at the scale of the whole economy, such as the ratio of total final consumption to GDP, are often used as proxies for energy efficiency and to assess how successful countries have been at reducing demand. Such a high level of aggregation conceals specific trends and makes the measure very rough. Nowadays, a bottom-up approach is becoming increasingly popular. Such an approach distinguishes between the structural components of energy demand and the intensity with which energy is used (Unander *et al.*, 2004; Ang, 2006; Taylor *et al.*, 2010).

As an example, the structural components of residential energy demand include floor area per capita; persons per household; and appliance ownership per capita. Each of these drives the demand for energy services which in turn drives absolute, as well as per capita, energy use.

Those components are dependent on demographics, income distribution, prices and climate and cannot all necessarily be influenced by energy efficiency measures. Energy intensity, on the other hand, refers to the energy used in producing a given level of output or activity. It is measured by the quantity of energy required to perform a particular activity (service) expressed as energy per unit of output or activity measure of service (EERE, 2010). In the residential sector, energy intensity can be measured per household or capita. Increases in energy efficiency help to reduce energy intensity; and changes in other factors can sustain or counteract improved efficiencies, e.g. changes in usage patterns (Unander *et al.*, 2004). In UK households, for instance, there has been a reduction of 9 per cent in energy consumption per household between 1990 and 2009, but only 1 per cent if measured per capita (DECC, 2010). This is explained by structural changes – an increase in the number of households – as well as an increase in the number of appliances, both of which have gradually offset the improvement in energy efficiency in insulation and heating.

Second, turning to the performance in terms of policies, ex post evaluation studies are difficult to find, often not publicly available or not translated, if not non-existent (Koeppel and Urge-Vorsatz, 2007). When available, challenges arise due to the lack of data and differing evaluation methods[5] or measurement and verification (M&V) protocols (Ramesohl and Dudda, 2001; Gillingham *et al.*, 2006; IEA, 2008). It is also difficult to agree on the quantification of ancillary benefits (IEA, 2008). Gillingham *et al.* (2006) review ex ante and ex post studies assessing the cost-effectiveness of different policies implemented in the US. Regarding appliances standards, for instance, the studies display a wide range of assessments.

A third important caveat to bear in mind is due to country-specific factors when analyzing demand-side strategies. Policies are implemented within complex political, economic and cultural environments. They interact with other policies from which synergies can trigger or weaken their effect (Koeppel and Urge-Vorsatz, 2007).

Looking at disaggregated energy indicators reveals the importance of the residential sector. Energy demand from residential buildings represented 40 per cent of the world's total primary consumption (IEA, 2008). Projections suggest that following the global economic downturn, demand for electricity from buildings is expected to grow at 3.1 per cent between 2007 and 2020 (McKinsey, 2009). In the UK, households

[5] For instance, differences occur in the inclusion or not of transaction and administrative costs or – when known – differing baselines.

account for around 30 per cent of final energy consumption (petajoules) with an increase of 5.8 per cent between 1990 and 2006; and only a recent decline of 6.5 per cent from 2000 to 2007 (BRE, 2008; Utley and Shorrock, 2008; MURE, 2009). Hence, the residential sector should be a major component of a demand-side energy strategy. Furthermore, it offers cost-effective opportunities with the lowest investment needs. Its potential has, however, traditionally been largely intractable due to a range of barriers discussed below (McKinsey, 2008; IEA, 2009c).

### *14.2.2 Historical residential energy trends and the potential for demand reduction*

Energy efficiency improvements for households in IEA countries have been significantly lower since 1990 (Taylor *et al.*, 2010) than during the period starting in 1973, when responding to the oil shocks was a driving force behind energy policy. Besides, total final consumption in 15 countries of the IEA increased between 1990 and 2004 due mainly to a rapid rise in electricity demand from appliances. As a result, there has been a 15 per cent increase in residential $CO_2$ emissions over the same period (IEA, 2007). In the UK, factors pushing energy demand upwards include the increase in the demand for space heating (6°C since 1970), which today accounts for 60 per cent of total residential energy demand; an increase in the number of households (30 per cent), and the poor quality of buildings (Boardman, 2005; Clarke *et al.*, 2008; MURE, 2008; Utley and Shorrock, 2008).

Taylor *et al.* (2010) provide an overview of household energy use per capita for 19 IEA countries for 1990 and 2005, space heating being by far the largest end-use category, accounting for 53 per cent of final household energy use in 2005. The shares by different end-use categories vary a little among countries, but the variation is the greatest as regards water heating. What is also interesting is to examine the decomposition over time. Figure 14.1 shows that decomposition for the UK from 1970 to 2008. As we can see, household energy use from lighting and appliances is the category which has increased most.

Taylor *et al.* (2010) further show that the differences among countries in per capita household energy use are much less pronounced when climate is controlled for, i.e. when values are normalized based on heating degree-days. Hence, further decomposing the effects of structure and end-use intensities gives a much more accurate picture of how countries compare to each other. Taking space heating as an example, Figure 14.2 decomposes the changes in heating per capita in the IEA 15. For most countries, the intensity effect, i.e. a reduction in energy

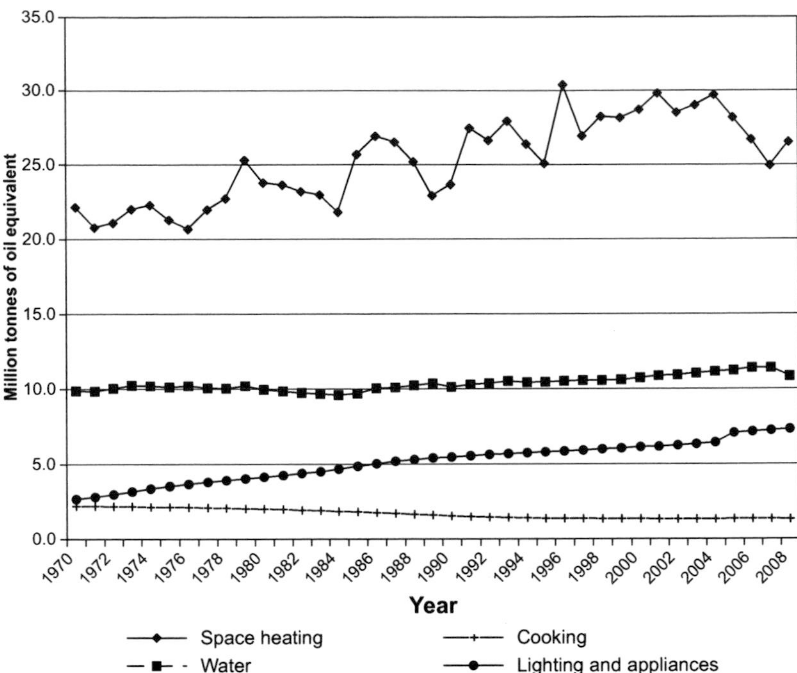


Figure 14.1 UK energy consumption by end use, 1970–2008.
*Source*: DECC (2010).

intensity mainly from improved insulation, has dominated and has in general led to reductions in space heating per capita. Structural effects have been dominant, however, in the UK larger dwellings and fewer occupants have led to an increase in per capita space heating.

Figure 14.3 shows the changes in space heating intensity[6] for the same period for nineteen countries in the IEA. The most significant reductions in intensity have been in the Netherlands and South Korea. Countries with milder winter climates dominate the left-hand side of the graph, i.e. those with higher space heating intensities. This is probably due to lower levels of insulation in older buildings (Taylor *et al.*, 2010). Building codes and minimum energy performance standards (MEPS) have a central role to play (and indeed have already been central) in further increasing space heating efficiency. Even with this type of

[6] Space heating intensity is defined as the 'useful energy' – i.e. final energy minus loss estimated for boilers – for space heating per square metre. To allow for comparisons across countries with different climates, the space heating intensity is divided by each country's yearly number of heating degree-days (Taylor *et al.*, 2010).

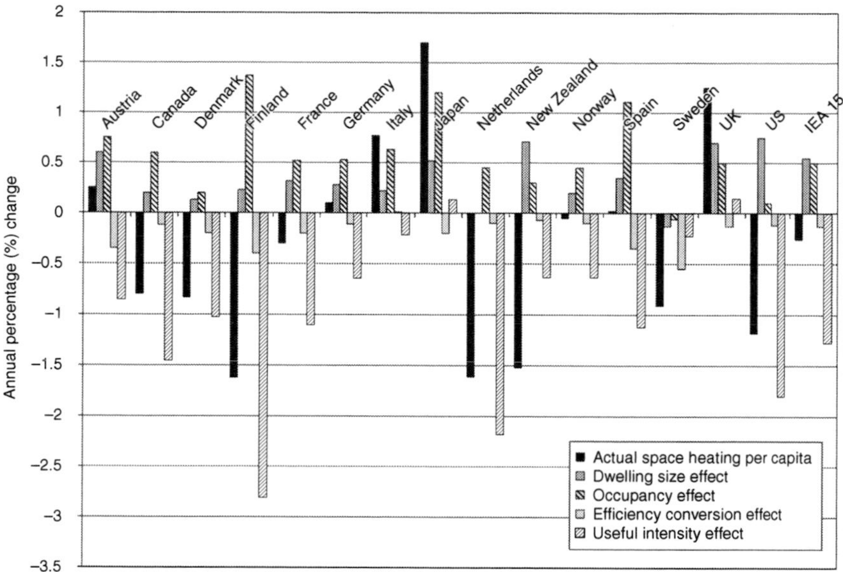


Figure 14.2 Decomposition of changes in heating per capita, 1990–2005.
*Source:* IEA (2007).

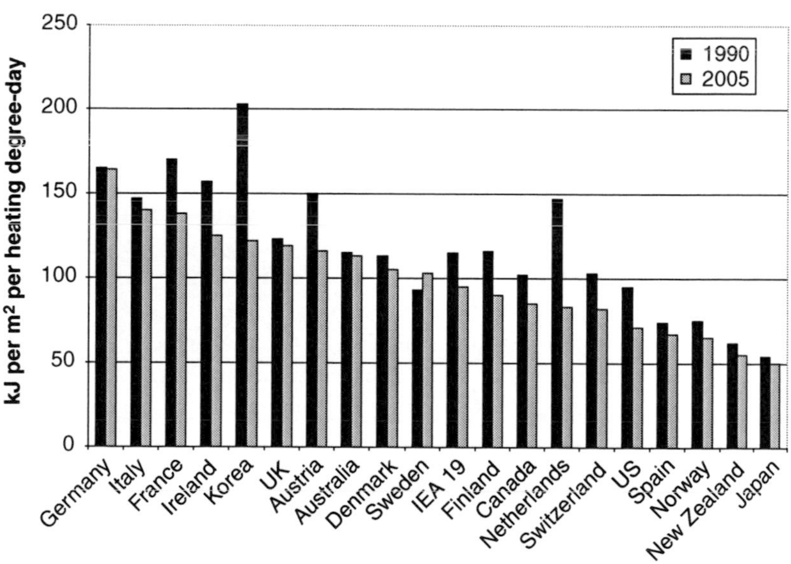


Figure 14.3 Useful space heating intensity.
*Source:* Taylor *et al.* (2010).

end-use specific indicator, however, it is not possible to identify the exact impact of such policies (IEA, 2008).

## 14.3 Barriers to energy efficiency in the residential sector

The trends in energy use discussed above reflect a number of barriers to energy efficiency and demand response[7] in the residential sector. There is a substantial literature on the barriers to EE and on the importance of appropriate policy responses in overcoming these. Several authors have emphasized the distinction between market failures, e.g. stemming from a flaw in the operation of the market, and market barriers, e.g. stemming from obstacles other than market driven (Brown, 2001). Intervening to correct market failures improves both energy efficiency and economic efficiency, whereas overcoming a market barrier improves energy efficiency but at a cost to consumers (Jaffe *et al.*, 1999; Brown, 2001). Others have sought to supplement the market failure approach with insights from areas such as transaction costs and behavioural economics. Sorrell (2004) offers a comprehensive overview and advocates a broader understanding of barriers to energy efficiency which includes organizational and behavioural barriers as well as a more realistic view of the consumer decision-making process. He suggests that the importance of overcoming these additional barriers is often underestimated.

Table 14.1 collates the main barriers to energy efficiency affecting the residential sector which result in suboptimal investments, and possible generic remedies based on this literature.[8] Even a cursory glance shows how complex and interrelated many of the barriers and responses are. Market barriers, in particular access to capital due to high up-front costs, are among the most important barriers to energy efficiency in the residential sector. By contrast, behavioural barriers are perhaps among the most difficult to address as changing behaviour and lifestyle is very difficult.

Many policies have been implemented to varying degrees internationally. At the same time, considerable potential remains for both energy efficiency and demand response in the residential sector. This suggests that overcoming many of the barriers in an effective way has yet to be achieved. Barriers to demand response are closely linked to the market failure barriers, particularly imperfect information and split

[7] With barriers to EE and to DR, we are referring to characteristics or circumstances that prevent consumer behaviour from being economically as well as energy efficient (Sorrell, 2004).

[8] Due to space constraints, we only briefly mention those barriers and rather focus on policy responses.

Table 14.1 *Barriers to energy efficiency in the building sector*

| Category | Barriers | Description | Examples/Possible causes | Generic remedy |
|---|---|---|---|---|
| *Market failure* | Imperfect information | When information is expensive, unreliable and/or difficult to obtain | Lack of or incomplete real pricing and/or consumption information | Increase and/or improve quantity & quality of information |
| | Negative externalities/ absence of markets for EE | When there is a lack of effective pricing (e.g. negative impacts, social costs or benefits are unpriced) or when EE is a by-product/ attribute for which the consumer has no choice | Costs of $CO_2$ emissions not included in fuel prices; retail price of electricity does not reflect real-time costs of production; failure to capture the benefits of R&D investments by private entities; absence of choice in EE levels | 'Internalization' of unaccounted costs |
| | Split incentives | When an agent has the authority to act on behalf of a consumer, but does not reflect consumers' best interests | Principal-agent problem (e.g. landlord–tenant split or utilities versus clients, fees structures for engineers and architects); involvement of intermediaries in the purchase of energy technologies | Re-align incentives |
| *Market barrier* | Access to capital | When the ratio of investment cost to value of energy savings is large | High up-front costs for more efficient equipment; lack of access to financing; insufficient access to low-interest loans[9]/ energy subsidies; information gap; unfamiliarity of financiers with EE investments; institutional barriers, etc. | Reduce interest rates and opportunity costs |

(*cont.*)

[9] Energy producers and consumers may also have varying access to financial capital and at different interest rates, with low-income households usually having virtually no ability to borrow funds.

Table 14.1 (*cont.*)

| Category | Barriers | Description | Examples/Possible causes | Generic remedy |
|---|---|---|---|---|
| | Risk | When risks (real or perceived) are not captured directly in financial flows | Length of the payback period;[10] uncertainty about future energy prices/regulations | Reduce real/perceived uncertainty and risk |
| | Transaction costs – hidden costs | When costs (real or perceived) are not captured directly in financial flows | Costs involved in finding appropriate information/ equipment, costs due to potential incompatibilities/ mistrust on appliance or building energy performance | Reduce real/perceived uncertainty and risk |
| *Behavioural economics* | Bounded rationality | When individuals do not make decisions in optimal way, and hence neglect EE opportunities | Constraints on time, resources and ability to process information, even when good information is available | Raise awareness and available information |
| | Low priority/ interest of energy issues | When EE opportunities are missed as a consequence of lack of awareness and interest | Energy costs are a small percentage of total household costs; energy subsidies in developing countries[11] | Raise awareness and available information |
| *Others* | Political and structural barriers | When structural characteristics of the political, economic, energy system make EE investments difficult | Differences in degree of liberalization of the electricity market (Blumstein *et al.*, 2005); differences in economic level across regions; lack of technical skills, detailed guidelines, tools and experts; inadequate energy service levels | Enhance the institutions, capacity-building cooperation |

*Source:* Brown (2001); Deringer *et al.* (2004); Sorrell (2004); McKinsey (2007); IEA (2008); Grubb and Wilde (2008); UNEP (2009).

[10] The short payback period means that consumers expect very high rates of return on energy efficiency investments.

[11] Such subsidies can provide disincentives for rational use of energy (Alam *et al.*, 1998).

incentives. Indeed, asymmetries of information and inelasticity of demand, mainly due to a lack of cost-reflective pricing, are the two main obstacles to a more responsive demand-side. Demand response has been largely neglected in policy making until very recently. Policy support is now growing, however, in the European Union (EU) and within individual member states as well as in the US (Torriti *et al.*, 2010).

## 14.4 Demand-side management policies

### *14.4.1 Overview of demand-side policies*

The barriers outlined in Table 14.1 above justify some form of action. Policies should aim to encourage both energy and economic efficiency (Sorrell, 2004). Timing is particularly important for electricity, where generation prices fluctuate significantly according to the time of day. At times of peak demand, for instance, electricity production costs are significantly higher because peak-load generators must be despatched to satisfy demand. Most residential customers are not exposed to these changes so that there is little incentive to shift consumption away from times when it is most expensive to produce. Future peak-load plant investment decisions are affected by this lack of demand response, as is the ability to match demand and supply reliably. DSM includes demand response and energy efficiency measures, such as load management, energy efficiency and electrification activities and has evolved in response to changes in industry structure and policy priorities since the oil shocks in the 1970s (CRA, 2005). DSM can be administered by utilities, state agencies or non-profit organizations. More recently, dynamic demand-side activities such as time-of-use (TOU) or critical-peak pricing (CPP) and other forms of demand response, e.g. interruptible loads, have become central to improving market efficiency and system control (Bilton *et al.*, 2008).

We are interested in analyzing the wide range of demand-side policies implemented internationally. This includes policies that seek to reduce demand and improve overall energy efficiency as well as those that aim to improve the economic efficiency with which energy is used. Our focus is on demand-side strategies, i.e. packages[12] of measures that aim to overcome barriers in a coherent and coordinated way. This type of approach lends itself well to demand-side policy making where there is a range of barriers, several policy goals and a vast array of potential policy instruments that need to work simultaneously and in support of each other.

[12] Here, a package refers to programmes combining different policies.

The literature on cross-country and cross-state analyses of policy packages identifies 18 major policies targeting the residential sector, which we classify into six general policy categories that we would expect to see in a comprehensive strategy (see Table 14.2). Some policies are strongly linked together and/or might overlap; however, all categories are important. In our discussion, we follow the evaluation criteria proposed by the UNEP-SBCI initiative, where policies are evaluated according to their strengths, weaknesses and effectiveness: the achievement of their goal, i.e. increase in energy efficiency and/or reduction of GHG emissions, their cost-effectiveness where data are available[13] and the factors triggering or hindering their success. Market transformation[14] offers guarantees of success and should be one of the ultimate objectives. Table 14.3 offers an overview of the latter, and Table 14.4 gives some examples of cost estimates. Care should be taken when evaluating and selecting policies, given the difficulty of quantifying costs and benefits, and data availability (Lee and Yik, 2004; Uihlein and Eder, 2009). Technological changes and energy prices might also alter the attractiveness of programmes (IEA, 2006). Significant double counting exists in energy savings, and disentangling the effect of single programmes is a major, if not irreducible, challenge. Modelling assumptions including baseline scenarios differ across programme and country evaluation studies, rendering comparisons very difficult and baseline scenarios can be debatable. The assessment hence entails important uncertainties.

### *14.4.2 Regulatory and control measures*

Regulatory and control measures are the most common measures in the residential sector. *Normative* measures include appliance standards,[15] buildings codes and EE obligations and quotas. Building codes can target the whole building, the envelope and/or major equipment, and are more difficult to apply to old buildings. Energy efficiency obligations and quotas oblige gas and electricity suppliers to achieve certain energy savings or demand peak reduction. Suppliers meet those targets by taking actions such as insulation, or improved heat pumps to save energy on the customer's premises. In the US, twenty-two states have energy saving targets

[13] Depending on the perspective taken, cost effectiveness estimates can include the costs for the programme administrator, the individual or the society, the latter being the preferred measure.

[14] Market transformation is defined as 'the reduction in market barriers due to a market intervention, as evidenced by a set of market effects that lasts after the intervention has been withdrawn, reduced or changed' (Eto *et al.*, 1996, p. xii).

[15] Products targeted by standards in the residential sector include appliances, ICT, lighting, heating and cooling equipment.

Table 14.2 *Major demand-side policies in the residential sector and their definition*

| Category | | Example of policies | Definition – policies |
|---|---|---|---|
| *Framework policy* | | | |
| A general and more abstract set of principles and long-term objectives that guide the development of and form the basis of specific policies, and that may demonstrate a holistic and/or broader strategic approach | | National EE strategies and action plans (NEESAP) | Sets a national strategy and creates institutions establishing relevant laws and programmes, including M&V[16] guidelines and methods |
| *Regulatory/control measures* | | | |
| Laws and implementation regulations (e.g. qualitative/quantitative requirements) that require certain devices, practices or system design to improve energy efficiency (IEA, 2005) | Normative | Appliance standards | Define a minimum EE level for a particular product class such as refrigerators, to be fulfilled by the producer (Birner *et al.*, 2002, cited by Koeppel and Urge-Vorsatz, 2007) |
| | | Building codes for both new & existing buildings | Address energy use of an entire building or building systems such as heating or air conditioning (Birner and Martinot, 2002) |
| | | EE obligations & quotas | Legal obligations for electricity and gas suppliers to achieve EE targets in households (Lees, 2006) |
| | Informative | Mandatory labels & certification programmes | Mandatory provision of information to end-users about the energy-using performance of products such as electrical appliances and equipment, and even buildings (Crossley *et al.*, 2000) |
| | | Mandatory audits, M&V of energy performance | Mandatory audits, monitoring and energy management in commercial, industrial, or private building, sometimes subsidized by government |

*(cont.)*

16 M&V (measurement and verification) is discussed below.

Table 14.2 (*cont.*)

| Category | Example of policies | Definition – policies |
|---|---|---|
| *Economic/Market based instruments* | | |
| | Energy performance contracting (EPC) | A contractor, typically an Energy Service Company (ESCO), guarantees certain energy savings for a location over a specified period: implements the appropriate EE improvements, and is paid from the actual energy costs reductions achieved (EFA, 2002) |
| *Financial and incentive-based measures* | | |
| Correct energy prices either by a Pigouvian tax or by financial support to address cost-related barriers | Direct provision of financing (e.g. preferential loans/ subsidies and grants) | Financial support for the purchase of EE appliance or buildings refurbishments |
| | Fiscal measures (taxations/tax exemptions/tax reductions) | A specific tax exemption/ reduction/increase at any point in the supply/demand chain used to provide signals promoting investment in EE/EE behaviours to end-use costumers |
| | Public benefit charges (PBC) | Funds raised from the operation of the electricity or energy market, which can be directed into DSM/EE activities (Crossley *et al.*, 2000) |
| | Utility based programmes (e.g. load control programmes; time-varying pricing tariffs) | Planning, implementing, and monitoring activities of EE programmes among/by utilities targeting the price of electricity and/or usage pattern of end consumers |
| *Voluntary agreements and partnerships* | | |
| Aim at persuading consumer to change their behaviour | Public–private partnerships (PPP) | Formal partnerships between public and private actors involving specific actions targeting households' energy services demand |
| | Voluntary labelling & certification | Voluntary provision of information by producers to end-users about the energy-using performance of products such as electrical appliance and equipment, and even buildings (Crossley *et al.*, 2000) |

Table 14.2 (*cont.*)

| Category | Example of policies | Definition – policies |
|---|---|---|
| | Voluntary & negotiated agreements | Formal quantified agreement between a government body and a business or organization which states that the business or organization will carry out specified actions to increase the efficiency of its energy use (Crossley *et al.*, 2000) |
| *Information and capacity-building* | | |
| Aim at persuading consumer to change their behaviour by providing information and examples of successful implementation and building capacity | Education and public outreach campaigns/ awareness raising campaigns | Policy instruments designed by government agencies with the intention to change individual behaviour, attitudes, values, or knowledge (Weiss and Tschirhart, 1994) |
| | Training programmes | Policy instruments designed by government agencies to build/strengthen capacity through training of energy managers, energy auditors and other energy professionals to effectively manage energy with minimum external assistance |
| | Utility DSM/DR programmes (counselling and general information[17]) | Planning, advisory, informational and monitoring activities of EE programmes among/by utilities |
| | Detailed billing and disclosure programmes (e.g. smart metering, smart energy boxes,[18] dynamic pricing) | Display detailed information related to energy consumption to the user either on bill and/or directly on appliance or meter |

*Source:* adapted from Koeppel and Urge-Vorsatz (2007); Eldridge *et al.* (2008); IEA (2008); WEC (2008); UNEP (2009).

[17] Counselling includes: individual advice and counselling, conversion of electrical heating, appraisal of electrical heating, advice on heat pump installation; and general information includes activities changing energy behaviour, education of schoolchildren, lending out of meters and low-energy bulbs, show- and display rooms, articles, advertisement, magazines, PC-programmes about energy use and saving (Hein Nybroe, 2001; cited by Koeppel and Urge-Vorsatz, 2007).

[18] Utilities and telecommunications companies have started developing 'smart energy boxes' to allow customers to plan and manage directly the use of electric appliances, and manage decentralized generation facilities (Torriti *et al.*, 2010).

Table 14.3 *Assessment of individual policies*

| Policy | I | C | Strengths | Weaknesses | Identified success factors |
|---|---|---|---|---|---|
| National EE strategies and action plans (NEESAP) | | | – facilitates integrative approach towards EE and DSM | | |
| Regulatory/control measures | | | | | |
| *Normative* | | | | | |
| Appliance standards | H | L | – reduces transaction costs<br>– easy administration<br>– can trigger market transformation<br>– eliminates worst practice by imposing a minimum | – no incentives for innovation<br>– rebound effect<br>– problem of enforcement | – regular updates<br>– independent control<br>– clear communication<br>– quality testing<br>– 'Top Runner Approach'<br>– enhanced effect when combined with information & capacity-building instruments<br>– should be maintained over time to phase out inefficient technologies |
| Building codes | M-H | M | – reduces transaction costs<br>– imposes min. threshold<br>– can be very clear and effective | – lack of compliance, partly due to lack of standardization/ market fragmentation<br>– rebound effect<br>– difficult to target existing building<br>– difficulty to respond rapidly to market changes<br>– no incentive for over performance | – flexibility, e.g. through regular updates (e.g. UK EEC)<br>– need to be adapted to local context<br>– should reward over performance (e.g. Japan GHLC)<br>– should be maintained over time for genuine market change/phase out inefficient technologies<br>– need to be combined with capacity-building measures/ demonstration programmes<br>– enhanced effect when combined with mandatory (common) M&V (e.g. California audits) |
| EE obligations | H | L | – relatively simple and flexible, as suppliers choose the measure<br>– cheap administration<br>– no public expenditures<br>– can trigger market transformation<br>– can avoid regressive social impacts | – can bring some increase in energy prices (1–2%)<br>– can bring rebound effect | – effects are maximized if government decides target and discount<br>– regular updates<br>– need to be combined with mandatory M&V and capacity-building<br>– should be combined with financial incentives and information measures |

I: Impact, C: costs.
H: high, M: medium, L: low.

Table 14.3 (*cont.*)

| Policy | I | C | Strengths | Weaknesses | Identified success factors |
|---|---|---|---|---|---|
| *Informative* | | | | | |
| Mandatory labels & certificates | H | L | – can achieve market transformation<br>– can be more effective than voluntary labelling<br>– can be used for appliances and increasingly whole buildings as well<br>– can be used as a marketing tool and basis for reporting performance | – evidence of case of lack of compliance<br>– rebound effect | – stakeholder involvement in supervisory systems<br>– should be open-ended labelling, but with regular updates<br>– enhanced effect when combined with financial incentives and M&V (e.g. Japan) |
| Mandatory audits, M&V | L-H | L-M | | – difficult application to residential sector | – stakeholder involvement in supervisory systems<br>– regular updates<br>– enhanced effect when combined with financial incentives |
| *Economic/market based instruments* | | | | | |
| EPC (by ESCOs) | H | L | – cost-effective (repaid through savings, no public spending)<br>– co-benefits: improved competitiveness<br>– no need of market intervention<br>– long term effects<br>– reduce risks, bounded rationality and financial barriers<br>– reduce transaction costs by bundling small size projects and filling the gap between energy specialist and financier<br>– can be relevant, impactful and clear | – often lack of equity capacity to endure risk and uncertainty<br>– difficult to standardize small projects | – need financial partners (e.g. private investors/ public fund)/mature financial sector willing to lend for EE projects<br>– need unsubsidized and regionally uniform energy prices<br>– enhanced when combined with PPP with large institutional investors/government support |
| *Financial/incentive-based measures* | | | | | |
| Direct provision of financing | M-H | L-H | – flexibility in the tools, but not in the targets<br>– rapid effect while can push market transformation<br>– can effectively target access to initial cost barriers | – no flexibility for the targets<br>– sometimes unclear<br>– difficult implementation on a wide scale<br>– may create only short term | – need to be combined with information campaigns<br>– adapted to changing need of the markets<br>– should be limited in time and to specific segments |

(*cont.*)

Table 14.3 (*cont.*)

| Policy | I | C | Strengths | Weaknesses | Identified success factors |
|---|---|---|---|---|---|
| | | | – can specifically address social issues e.g. fuel poverty by targeting vulnerable households<br>– can have strong impacts (e.g. DK) | 'artificial' demand, impact may last only until programme ends<br>– lack of flexibility due to narrow targets in some cases<br>– risk of free-riders<br>– lack of awareness<br>– rebound effect<br>– administrative burden | – should not be introduced once penetration rate of the products is high<br>– need to be clear<br>– training and awareness campaign for sustainable impact (e.g. Denmark)<br>– better when involves PPP, which combines resources |
| Fiscal measures | L-H[19] | L-M | – effective indirect financial tool<br>– can create demand<br>– flexible as market left to respond to the demand<br>– can reinforce other instruments such as regulations and standards<br>– affect the whole building life<br>– raise revenue<br>– tax exemption can stimulate introduction of highly efficient equipment/appliances and building materials | – can encourage rebound effect if scope too broad (e.g. France)<br>– often lack clarity<br>– free-rider problem<br>– difficult to address the vulnerable household which still lacks the extra cash provision<br>– depends on price elasticity of demand | – need to last to induce market transformation<br>– level and design – including the use of the revenues – of the tax are crucial<br>– taxation is more effective when combined with other measures |
| Public benefit charges | M | L | – raise funds for EE measures/investments (through taxation) | | – involvement of stakeholders, but independent administration of the funds<br>– regular evaluation and adjustments<br>– clear and simple programme design<br>– well designed use of the funds<br>– need training programmes (e.g. of the programme administrators) and M&V measures |

[19] Higher impact with tax exemptions.

Table 14.3 (*cont.*)

| Policy | I | C | Strengths | Weaknesses | Identified success factors |
|---|---|---|---|---|---|
| Utility-based programmes (load control programmes; RTP, tariffs) | | | – can effectively shave peak demand and shift load | – can encourage rebound effect | – need awareness campaigns |
| *Voluntary agreements and public–private partnerships* | | | | | |
| PPP | L-M | M | – faster decisions and implementation<br>– more flexible and cost-effective for the companies | – often lower outcomes than with mandatory actions | – can be effective when regulation is difficult to enforce/combined with threat of regulation<br>– effective when industry-wide/all stakeholders are involved<br>– effective when clear quantitative targets and effective monitoring |
| Voluntary labelling & certificates | M-H | L-M | – relevant contribution to other instruments<br>– can have a great impact and enhance sustainability<br>– can affect upstream and downstream actors<br>– can have impact on consumers' behaviour<br>– sends clear messages/ information<br>– desirable when mandatory labels are not possible/difficult to implement<br>– can be adapted to local conditions | – not very flexible (no internal mechanism to adapt to the evolution of the market and response)<br>– weakened by lack of international standards and may lack credibility<br>– only efficient products are labelled<br>– testing mechanisms may be of variable quality | – international labelling/testing standards can improve their effectiveness<br>– label can be more efficient when combined with awareness raising campaigns, fiscal incentives and/or regulations<br>– label should involve stakeholders and be backed by government to be credible |
| Voluntary and negotiated | L-M | L | – more flexible and potential to be more up to date than order forms of agreement | – can be used to strategically | – incentivize private companies |
| *Information and capacity-building* | | | | | |
| Education and public outreach campaigns/ awareness raising campaigns | L-M | M-H | – strengthens long-term impact of most other policy measures<br>– particularly needed as regards residential sector<br>– sends clear messages | – can fail if not targeted to the needs | – message must be clear, credible, and relevant to the target audience<br>– must complement other measures |

(*cont.*)

Table 14.3 (*cont.*)

| Policy | I | C | Strengths | Weaknesses | Identified success factors |
|---|---|---|---|---|---|
| Training programmes | H | | – fill an important gap in terms of competence, both upstream/downstream<br>– relevant contribution to other instruments<br>– can enhance sustainability<br>– can have impact on consumers' behaviour<br>– sends clear messages | | – should be adapted to local conditions and target audience<br>– in complement to a wide range of other measures |
| Utility DSM/DR programmes (counselling and general information) | H | L | – can be effective (usually lower in the residential sector) and cost-effective | – may be hampered by electricity market restructuring | – project must be carefully designed – adapted to local context and market<br>– stakeholders must be involved<br>– objectives must be clear and some pilot programmes first<br>– enhanced when triggered by regulatory incentives, and combined with mandatory charges on electricity prices<br>– need complementary capacity-building/ awareness raising measures |
| Detailed billing and disclosure programmes | M | M | – can induce long-term behavioural change | – may be hampered by imperfect information<br>– first cost<br>– uncertainty about rate of return on investment | – combination with other measures<br>– regular assessments |

*Source:* adapted from de T'Serclaes (2007); MURE (2010); UNEP (2009).

Table 14.4 *Estimated impacts of some implemented policies*

| Policy | Estimated Impact | Costs |
|---|---|---|
| Regulatory/control measures | | |
| *Normative* | | |
| Appliance standards | JP: 31 M $tCO_2$ in 2010<br>US: 1990–97: 108$MtCO_2$, 65$MtCO_2$ in 2000 (2.5% of electricity use) | JP: Top Runner Programme: actual and projected EE improvements: TV sets (25.7% actual, 16.4% projected); Videotape recorders (73.6% actual, 58.7% projected); Air conditioners (67.8% actual, 66.1% projected); Electric refrigerators (55.2% actual, 30.5% projected); Electric freezers (29.6% actual, 22.9% projected)<br>US: −65$/$tCO_2$ in 2020 |
| Building codes for both new & existing buildings | UK: 7% less energy use housing, 14% with grants and labelling,<br>UK: 70% increase in EE since 1990<br>US: 15–16% of BAU (79.6$MtCO_2$ in 2000)<br>EU: up to 60% for new buildings | US: buildings and appliances standards: saved more than $56 billion in energy bills since 1978, estimated $23 billion savings by 2013. |
| EE obligations | UK: 1.63% of total domestic $CO_2$ (2.16 $MtCO_2$/yr) | UK: £17/$tCO_2$ (DECC estimates) |
| *Informative* | | |
| Mandatory labels & certification programmes | DK: insignificant (Kjaerbye, 2009) | |
| Mandatory audits, M&V | US weatherization programme: 22% savings after audits, 30% according to IEA | US: 2.4 (benefit/cost ratio) |
| *Economic/Market-based instruments* | | |
| EPC | US: 20–40% of building energy saved, 3.2 $MtCO_2$/yr | EU: Negative costs or less than 22$/$tCO_2$<br>US: cost benefits ratio in private sector: 2.1 |
| *Financial and incentive-based measures* | | |
| Taxations/tax exemptions/ tax reductions | *Taxation:* GE: household consumption reduced by 0.9%, 1.5 $MtCO_2$ in 2003 | US: benefit-cost ratio of tax exemptions for new homes: 1.6 |
| Subsidies and grants | UK: 6.48 $MtCO_2$ per year, 100.8 $MtCO_2$ in total, 0.4% in average | DK: −20$/$tCO_2$<br>UK: 29$/$tCO_2$ |

(*cont.*)

Table 14.4 (*cont.*)

| Policy | Estimated Impact | Costs |
|---|---|---|
| PBC | US: 0.1–0.8% of total electricity sales saved per year, 1.3 kt$CO_2$ in 12 states | US: form −53\$/t$CO_2$ to −17\$/t$CO_2$ |
| Utility-based programmes | US: 3.1% in 2000 (36.7 Mt$CO_2$)<br>DK: 42% of energy saving from 2006 to 2008 (0.8 Mt$CO_2$) | US: (average costs) −35 \$/t$CO_2$<br>EU: −255\$/t$CO_2$<br>DK: −209.3 \$/t$CO_2$ |
| *Voluntary agreements and partnerships* | | |
| voluntary labelling & certification | US: Energy Star: 43 millions metric tons GHG since 2000, 13.2 Mt$CO_2$ in 2004, 4% reductions by 2010, 884 Mt$CO_{2equ.}$ in total by 2012 | US: −53 \$/t$CO_2$ |
| Voluntary & negotiated agreements | US: 5.6% of total emissions (66.45 Mt$CO_{2equ}$ in 2000)<br>EU: 50kt$CO_2$, 100 GWh/yr (300 buildings) | |
| *Information and capacity-building* | | |
| Education, public outreach/ awareness raising campaign | UK: around 0.8% of total residential emissions in 2009 (10.4 kt$CO_2$ per year)<br>California: 6.7% energy use reduction | UK: 8\$/t$CO_2$ for all Energy Trust programmes |
| Detailed billing & disclosure programmes | Direct feedback: 5–15%, up to 20% (Darby, 2006)<br>UK: 3% | |

UK: United Kingdom, JP: Japan, GE: Germany, US: United States, DK: Denmark.
Data may include savings from buildings in other sectors.
*Source:* Lee and Yik (2004); Geller *et al.* (2006); Koeppel and Urge-Vorsatz (2007); Energy Star programme website; Defra website.

imposed on electricity utilities. Most of them are legally binding, and some of them are reinforced by large penalties if targets are not met (ACEEE, 2010).[20]

[20] Hence, in the state of Pennsylvania for instance, the Electricity Act 129 of 2008 requires distribution companies to meet specific levels of energy savings and demand reduction (1 per cent by 2011, and 3 per cent by 2013, compared with 2009–10 sales). In the event of failing to reach those targets, distribution companies can face a fine of at least \$1 million, and up to \$20 million (Act 129, 2008).

*Informative measures* include mandatory labels and certifications, originally used for appliances, but increasingly for whole buildings, as shown with the EPBD, for instance (see Clarke *et al.*, this volume, for a discussion of the EPBD). The updating and tightening – as technology improves – and coverage expansion, in particular with respect to household electronics, are crucial (Fonseca *et al.*, 2009). Standby consumption, for instance, should also be included, as it is estimated to account for 6 to 10 per cent of residential electricity demand (EST, 2006).

Numerous studies report evidence of the strong impact from regulatory and control measures. Today, building codes vary widely across countries. Regulatory and control measures can reduce transaction costs to end-users, and provide high energy savings at low costs, sometimes at negative cost to society.[21] They can address many of the barriers outlined above, such as imperfect information, hidden/transaction costs, access to capital, and behavioural barriers such as lack of interest in energy issues. However, their success depends on several factors. The quality of enforcement is crucial. Appliance standards are easier to enforce than building codes, which in turn are easier to enforce in new buildings.[22] The potential for rebound effect[23] should be addressed. Constant monitoring and regular updates to reflect technological progress are also needed (see also Steinbuks, this volume, for more analysis).

In the US, some estimates suggest that current federal building standards should further account for $23 billion savings by 2013 (CPUC, 2008). However, federal appliance standards are rarely updated and are not very tight. By contrast, 30 per cent of energy saved is attributed to product standards in California (IEA, 2007), and regular updates of buildings codes (every three years) might in part account for the great impact that building codes have had.[24] In the UK, despite the claim that

[21] Some costs estimates range from −65\$/t$CO_2$ (US) to −190\$/t$C0_2$ (EU) for appliances standards – hence a net benefit.

[22] This can be a major weakness as regards building codes, as the largest part of the building stock is composed of existing buildings in the UK.

[23] The rebound effect refers to the actual difference between improvements in the energy efficiency and reduction in energy consumption. The idea is that the rebound (or 'take-back') effect will lead to increases in consumption, due to the decrease in the per unit price of energy services. As a result, consumption of energy services should increase, partially offsetting the impact of the efficiency improvement. This basic mechanism is widely accepted, and numerous empirical studies suggest that these rebound effects are real and can be significant (Greening *et al.*, 2000). However, the magnitude of this effect is disputed.

[24] The last update of the Title 24, Part 6, of the Building Energy Efficiency Standards, effective since 1 January 2010, includes a 15 per cent increase in energy efficiency savings compared with the 2005 standards; and incorporates regulations targeting lighting and heating, ventilation and air-conditioning (HVAC), as well as a load control programme, the Programmable Communicating Thermostats, which enables the operators to reduce electricity load at peak times.

building regulations have led to an increase of around 70 per cent in the energy efficiency of buildings since 1990 (IEA, 2008), a more aggressive approach towards standards is needed (Hartley, 2006). From September 2007, performance certificates are required for both new and existing buildings put into the market, as part of a Home Information Pack (CLG, 2010), and the government announced its intention to extend their use (DECC, 2009), although the new coalition government decided to scrap them. Key challenges remain in the UK: the low level of compliance – estimated to amount to only one third; the lack of clarity due to frequent and sporadic updates of regulations (in 2002, 2005, 2006, 2007); and finally, a lack of capacity to implement the regulations (IEA 2008b; Clarke, 2008). Data availability has also been a challenge, partly due to the division of responsibilities between Defra and BERR, which lasted until 2008. Also, the financial crisis has increased the ratio of energy efficiency investments to house values, reducing incentives for refurbishments (IEA, 2009a).

There is evidence that the impact of regulatory and control measures is enhanced when combined with specific measures addressing their weakness or side-effects. For instance, mandatory labelling can increase the benefit of appliance standards, which otherwise fail to incentivize innovation. For instance, standards have the benefit of imposing a minimum, but in principle do not provide any incentive to go beyond. Combinations with labelling can overcome this. In Japan, an innovative feature of the latest update of the Energy Conservation Law, in 2009, is the implementation of sectoral benchmarking to target the efficiency performance of companies. Targets are set at the level of the top 10–20 per cent best performing companies, and the names of these companies are published (IEA, 2010). This 'top-runner approach' was originally set in the 1990s to promote continuous energy-efficiency improvements in end-use appliances. Its coverage has been expanded several times, and has included appliances since 2005. This is an obligation on manufacturers of domestic appliances to produce products as efficient as the most efficient product in the product class by a specified date and a corresponding restriction on imported products. The regulator has a key role as it decides the categories of products and specific targets – after consultation with stakeholders (Nordqvist, 2007). In 2007, twenty-one home appliances were covered. In 2009, further products were considered for addition or revisions (routers, lighting, TV sets, computers and magnetic disk units). The targets have been reached, with sometimes higher than expected improvements (IEA, 2010). The measure has several strengths. First, it targets manufacturers. Second, this is complemented by mandatory labelling which increases consumer awareness.

Third, the instrument is flexible and targets can be tightened if achieved ahead of time. Finally, the programme is clear and the standards are set with the active involvement of the manufacturers. Claims of the risk of gaming seem unfounded, as Japan's continued fame for innovative technologies demonstrates. Implementation of a top-runner approach in the EU, at the national level, could be much easier than at the European level, given the difference in purchasing capacity across countries.[25] However, a strategy based on reputation might be more successful in a Japanese context, where social pressure is very strong.

Insulation requirements can also be enhanced by specific measures targeting low-income households, such as preferential loans or measures to incentivize their implementation. In Germany for instance, tenants are eligible for rebates on their rent if the landlord does not comply with some building codes. Some building labelling systems are combined with the issuance of mortgages or upgrades of homes, hence addressing financial barriers, while increasing awareness. For instance, in the US, the Home Energy Rating System (HERS) is used to guide energy efficient investments, to obtain energy efficiency mortgages, and to check for compliance with building standards. Despite being almost completely financed by federal funds, HERS is flexible because it is administered at the state level with standards developed by the states.[26]

### *14.4.3 Economic and market-based instruments*

Economic and market-based instruments essentially amount to energy performance contracting (EPC) and support from energy services companies (ESCOs). ESCOs usually guarantee certain energy savings for a location over a specified period (see Kelly and Pollitt, this volume). The revenues are earned from the reduced energy costs achieved. Various barriers hamper ESCOs' expansion in the residential sector, in particular, the existence of split incentives, suspicion among customers, the difficulty for contractors to find financing sources or high transaction costs due to the small size of the projects[27] – which, however, can be reduced with the bundling of similar projects.

Interest in EPC and the promotion of ESCOs is increasing, partly due to the fact that it avoids public spending or market intervention. In

[25] Germany is the proponent of a similar approach at the European level.

[26] Amendment expanded the HERS to include energy efficiency ratings of smaller size homes and establish a systematic process for the rating for houses put on the market, including the evaluation of the options to increase EE (CEC website). Such measures have been found to be effective (IEA, 2008).

[27] For a complete list of barriers to EPC including other sectors, see Koeppel and Urge-Vorsatz (2007).

general, the development of ESCOs in the residential sector is promoted by any measure which triggers a market for energy efficiency, e.g. the UK government's proposed 'Green Deal' which seeks to provide a new financial instrument to finance energy efficiency investments. The presence of investors willing to lend to ESCOs as well as facilitating financial and market conditions is crucial. The success of EPC varies from country to country, but the case of the US demonstrates its potential, with an estimated 3.2 $MtCO_2$ saved through EPC (Koeppel and Urge-Vorsatz, 2007).

### *14.4.4 Financial/incentive-based measures*

Financial/incentive-based measures aim to correct, energy prices so that they are more cost-reflective. They also address access to capital barriers, in particular the high up-front costs of energy efficiency investments. They can facilitate the introduction and commercialization of energy efficiency products. *Energy taxes* equalize compliance costs, and bring revenues for the government which can be invested in energy efficiency under the form of public benefits charges (PBC) (Koeppel and Urge-Vorsatz, 2007). *Direct provision of financing* includes preferential loans, grants and subsidies. *Time-varying pricing* refers to tariffs that vary according to the time electricity is used to reflect more accurately the costs of generation. This includes time of use (TOU), or real-time pricing (RTP), for instance.[28] Other types of tariff worth mentioning are block tariffs. These tariffs vary with the amount of energy consumed. A common example of these is inclining block rates where a higher rate is charged per unit of consumption beyond a certain amount. These have been applied for a long time in California to encourage conservation.

In the US, the four-year benefits charge, a small tax on electricity sales, is used to fund DSM programmes operated by utilities that include grants, loans and rebates (IEA, 2008). Taxes have several advantages. They can reinforce the impacts of other tools such as regulation and standards or be reinforced themselves when combined with other measures. In Denmark, taxes complemented with subsidies have resulted in a 15 per cent $CO_2$ reduction between 1977 and 1991 (Koeppel and Urge-Vorsatz, 2007). In the UK, the impact of the Landlord's Energy Saving Allowance, introduced in 2004, as a VAT reduction of 5 per cent

[28] TOU refers to tariffs that are based on the time of the day when electricity is being consumed. TOU are fixed and set in advance, in contrast to RTP, a dynamic tariff which can vary up to every half hour, being directly linked to the wholesale power markets.

for grant-funded installation of energy-saving materials in priority homes and microgeneration technologies is not clear yet. Some concerns remain as regards its clarity and lack of sustainability (IEA, 2008). Taxes address market barriers such as risk, or uncertainty related to energy efficiency investments, and importantly, they affect the whole building life, by contrast to other instruments. However, they can be difficult to implement politically and can also be socially undesirable due to adverse effects on vulnerable households.[29]

Evaluation of the impact of taxes or time-varying pricing in the household sector is difficult, due to a lack of quantitative data. Factors such as the price elasticity of demand are important determinants of the impact whose estimated median values are low.[30] For instance, the US federal tax has been found to be too small and short term to induce changes in behaviour (IEA, 2008). The US Energy Tax Act of 1978, including a 15 per cent tax credit for residential conservation and renewable energy measures, was not effective as the total amount was capped to $300 and was not applicable to the newest technologies (Koeppel and Urge-Vorsatz, 2007). Hence, taxes must be high enough and flexible enough to cover the best available technologies.

More than half of the measures targeting the residential sector identified in the MURE database[31] (MURE, 2010) are grants, preferential loans and rebates. Evidence suggests that they have a strong impact – with the majority of measures rated as having a high or medium impact. They are particularly useful for the introduction of new energy efficiency appliances/equipment and/or for targeting access to capital in vulnerable households. However, such measures require financial resources, and are threatened by free-riding; hence they need to be carefully designed. Their effectiveness increases with information/awareness raising campaigns.

### *14.4.5 Voluntary action and public–private partnerships (PPP)*

There is some evidence of the impact of voluntary action and public–private partnerships (PPP). Voluntary labels and certification are

[29] This concern is particularly important in the UK nowadays. See Waddams Price, this volume, and Jamasb and Meier, this volume, for a discussion of fuel poverty.

[30] Estimates of elasticities in the literature range from −0.15 to −0.39 in the short run and −0.09 to −0.579 in the long run.

[31] MURE II Database (MURE, 2010) provides information on EE policies implemented (including some impact assessments) in EU countries. It hence enables comparisons across countries. The MURE II Database is constructed in five sections, including the household sector and general cross-cutting measures.

commonly used for appliances. The US Energy Star labelling programme is often cited as a particularly successful example, with an estimated saving of around 833 $MtCO_2$ by 2010 (Gillingham *et al.*, 2006). There has also been a continuous increase in the number of sales of Energy Star products since 2000, a saving estimated at 43 million metric tons of GHG in 2008 and more than $19 billion on utility bills US wide (Energy Star, 2008). This success was among others attributed to the combination of the measure with the obligation for public bodies to buy Energy Star appliances, and the governmental back-up needed to enhance trust among consumers (Banerjee and Solomon, 2003). It involves the interaction of the federal and state levels, as it can incorporate state-developed initiatives. The programme is found to be more effective when ratings are used as benchmarks for other financial measures such as loans, grants and rebates (IEA, 2008).

The impact of voluntary agreements between companies and governmental bodies is more contested, as they can be used as a strategy by businesses to prevent stringent regulatory actions. On the positive side, as the company itself commits to a certain action, voluntary actions can be effective, more flexible and more cost-effective than regulatory measures. Moreover, when such actions are taken at the industry-wide level, they can drive competition for EE. However, the level of commitment can be lower than what would be socially desirable, although the threat of regulation can ensure some level of commitment.

PPP offer the best opportunities in terms of relevance, flexibility, impact, clarity and sustainability (de T'Serclaes, 2007; UNEP, 2009). They enable the combination of the strength of private and public actors. In many cases, PPP have enhanced the impact of financial and incentive-based measures, such as in the case of Germany with the KfW schemes. In other cases, PPP can take place in the very elaboration of framework policies, as the case of the US 2008 National Action Plan for Energy Efficiency (NAPEE) illustrates, which included the collaboration of states, gas and electric utilities, utility regulators, and other partner organizations.

### 14.4.6 *Information and capacity-building measures*

Information and capacity-building measures include utilities DSM/demand response programmes and education, public outreach and awareness campaigns. They are administered by a range of actors, including governmental agencies, regulators, local agencies, housing associations or utilities. They are soft measures, rarely impactful alone, and often complement other tools, in particular as they help to minimize possible rebound effects and induce long-term behavioural change. They can nevertheless have significant impacts and address a range of informational and behavioural barriers particularly acute in the residential sector. In the US, non-governmental organisations[32] play an important role in conveying information at state levels. In the UK, capacity-building measures need to be enhanced, as seen with the low implementation of current building regulations (Clarke *et al.*, 2008); and quality of feedback (Pyrko and Darby, 2009).

Utilities' DSM measures are flexible and foster market creation. In California, they were considered to be the most effective measures (Eto *et al.*, 1996). Such impact was made possible through a strategy that decouples the amount of electricity sold from revenues and hence realigns incentives between utilities and consumers in efficient resource allocation decisions. In particular, they can overcome market barriers such as the initial cost barriers (IEA 2008). Still today, the California Public Utilities Commission (CPUC) allocates 83 per cent of its funds to utilities' programmes (IEA, 2008). However, competition brought by the restructuring of electricity markets can significantly reduce utilities' incentives to spend money on such programmes, despite the new opportunities opened up in new market structures.

The impact of awareness raising campaigns is difficult to disentangle from joint measures, and possible short and long term effects. Campaigns are particularly successful when the message is clear, carefully adapted to the targeted population, relevant to its needs, and creates a social context which strengthens the impact (Weiss and Tschirhart, 1994). The Californian 'Flex your power' campaign clearly stands out as a huge success: it induced an 8.9 per cent reduction of peak demand and 6.7 per cent reduction in energy consumption. The initiative involved partnerships with businesses, manufacturers, retailers, media organizations, and schools, targeting a large share of the population through specific means. However, such programmes can have adverse effects, for example in the UK, where the free distribution of compact fluorescent lamps has discouraged the purchase of energy efficiency products and undermined market transformation. In the UK, the Energy Saving Trust centralizes all the information on available grants at all levels, and promotes partnerships for the supply of energy efficiency products, complementing other policies.

Detailed billing and smart meters provide consumers with detailed information about their consumption, either real time (smart-meters/

[32] They include the American Council for an Energy Efficient Economy (ACEEE), the Alliance to Save Energy (ASE) and the National Commission on Energy Policy.

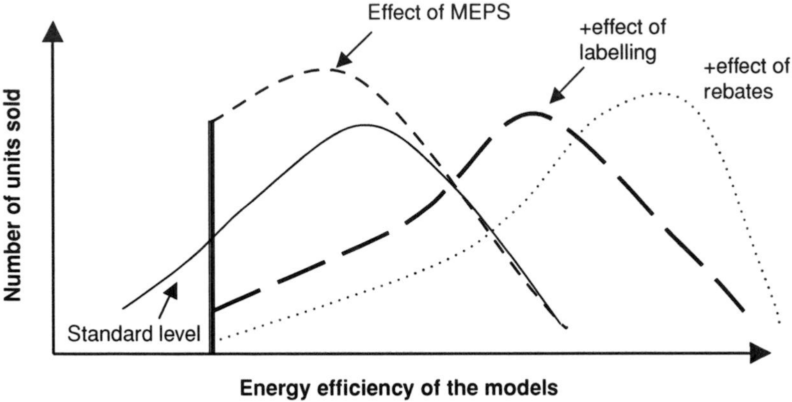


Figure 14.4 Combined effects of MEPS, rebates and labels.
*Source:* UNEP (2007); CLASP (2005).

real-time displays) or deferred (detailed/more frequent billing).[33] The electricity savings induced with direct feedback range from 5–15 per cent[34] (Darby, 2006). Factors that hamper the take-off of direct feedback tools can include the up-front costs of the device, imperfect information, specific regulatory barriers and uncertainty. The ownership structure of the networks also complicates the roll-out. In the UK, the rolling-out of smart-meters in every home by 2020 has recently been decided (DECC, 2009). However, some crucial issues remain unresolved, especially regarding the treatment of consumption data, including the possibility for utilities to discriminate between consumers. Full results of Ofgem's Energy Demand Research Project (EDRP), a series of large-scale trials across Great Britain, will be available in 2011 and might shed some light on these issues.

In brief, regulatory and economic instruments have a high potential, but their outcomes are ambiguous. Fiscal instruments can bring some savings if well designed, but the distributional impacts should be well understood. Subsidies are less cost-effective; and voluntary instruments' impact depends on the context and the accompanying measures. In general, they need to be accompanied by capacity-building and educational measures. Timing is also important, as illustrated by Figure 14.4, which shows the combined effect of minimum energy performance standards (MEPS), rebates and labels.

[33] For a discussion of smart meters technologies and economics, see Haney *et al.*, this volume.

[34] The highest impacts were achieved with interactive displays units, with smart-meters being more effective than innovative billings.

Finally, concerns over distribution of the costs and benefits further highlight the importance of policy design. Underlying the policy mix, the institutional framework must be designed to address specific barriers. In the US, transaction costs are reduced, as the Environment Protection Agency (EPA) centralizes all the information and guidelines related to the National Action Plan. By contrast, up until the creation of the Department of Energy and Climate Change (DECC) in 2008 which brought together energy and climate policies, the UK institutional organization might have implied additional costs, complexity, risk of duplication, and opacity in terms of the overlapping roles and responsibilities of the Department for Business, Enterprise and Regulatory Reform (BERR) and the Department for Environment, Food and Rural Affairs (Defra), both involved in energy policy.

## 14.5 Policy packages and the importance of comprehensiveness

### *14.5.1 Integrated policy strategies*

There is now increasing awareness about the interactions between single policies and the recognition that energy efficiency targets require the coordination of a myriad small actions across society. In terms of designing an optimal integrated strategy, two of the main aims are: to pursue multiple policy goals coherently; and to adopt mixes of policy instruments that are consistent and mutually supportive (Rayner and Howlett, 2009). An optimal integrated demand-side strategy should seek to impact different parts of the market, and enhance the strengths of individual mechanisms while compensating for their weaknesses through the use of complementary measures (Gunningham and Sinclair, 1999; Jollands and Pasquier, 2008).

Hence, so-called ‘integrated policy strategies’ have received much attention in various fields of late, materialized through the now numerous national energy efficiency strategies and action plans (NEESAP). Barriers to energy efficiency and demand response are diffuse and, as a result, policy mechanisms will rarely operate effectively in isolation (Sovacool, 2009). Many cross-country studies of demand-side policies come to the conclusion that comprehensive policy packages are a necessity if barriers are to be successfully overcome (Brown, 2001; Geller *et al.*, 2006; IEA, 2007; Koeppel and Urge-Vorsatz, 2007).

The US EESP is an insightful example of such a package, based on a synergistic underlying approach that targets all sectors, including the residential sector. The report is elaborated on four overarching strategies[35] and calls for integration across all sectors along three levels: (1) comprehensive and unified information campaigns to reduce transaction costs and increase public awareness; (2) ex post evaluations documentation and advice for consumers; and (3) the integration of technology and information systems to achieve multiple DSM options and create synergies (CPUC, 2008). Such an integrative approach manifests itself on the institutional side, with a division of energy responsibilities among the federal – with the Department of Energy (DOE) and the Environmental Protection Agency (EPA)[36] – and state level, including the collaboration of non-governmental institutions, including utilities. Regional initiatives, such as the Western Governors' Association (WGA), make it possible to address barriers such as transaction costs through the elaboration of common targets at the regional level, through sharing similar challenges and needs and the sharing of information across states (www.westgov.org; IEA, 2008).

Of course, a number of country-specific factors have an influence on or may constrain optimal outcomes. There are important political dimensions involved in the choice of policy instruments, and so it is rarely just a case of matching appropriate policies against barriers. Institutional context can also be a determinant of policy success and may vary widely across countries. The transferability of policy experience from one country to another is, as a result, far from straightforward (Varone and Aebischer, 2001). Different stages of electricity and gas reform can influence the incentives for different actors to engage in energy efficiency and demand response. The introduction of competition is the most complex stage and is likely to have a net negative effect on end-user incentives to adopt energy efficiency measures. This is because wholesale competition creates price signals based on short-term costs which tend to be more variable, thus making energy savings more uncertain. Competition also increases a supplier's incentive to maximize sales and provide the lowest rates to retain and attract customers. At the same time, policy mechanisms to overcome these barriers may be more effective under competition and may allow for more innovative solutions given a supportive policy framework (Vine *et al.*, 2003). Denmark illustrates well

[35] (1) pilot programmes such as the utilities' demand response portfolios; (2) collaboration with stakeholders to develop and implement a long-term approach; (3) the development of new technologies for DSM options and to provide synergies; (4) coordinated DSM marketing for the development of smart meter systems and dynamic pricing tariffs that are being deployed state-wide during 2009–11.

[36] The DOE is concerned with the United States' policies regarding energy and safety in handling nuclear material. The EPA's main roles are to develop and enforce regulations, manage and allocate grants, and raise awareness about environmental issues.

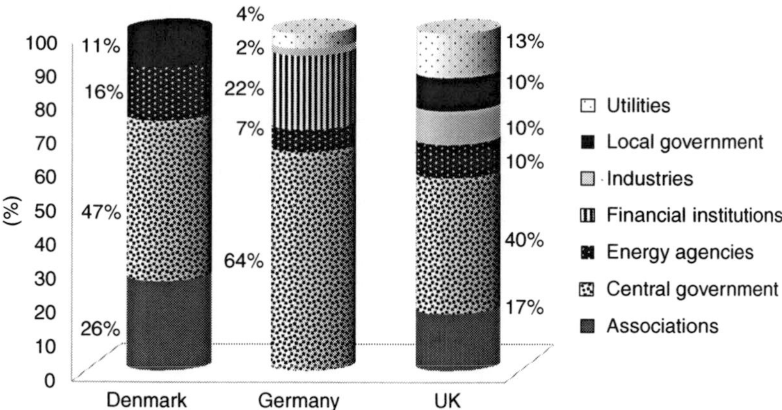


Figure 14.5 Actors involved in DSM policies in the UK, Denmark and Germany.
*Source:* MURE (2010).

the case that electricity liberalization can go hand in hand with energy efficiency.

The existing barriers, the resource limits, the need for accountability and the recognition of the need to integrate energy efficiency policies within broader economic, social and environmental policies all provide a strong case for the development of a strategy that: (1) exhibits 'a system perspective', i.e. linking energy efficiency to the broader policy context; (2) addresses important strategic questions; (3) prioritizes measures; (4) includes specific actions and targets; (5) takes a 'learning approach',[37] i.e. monitoring and evaluating to expand or discontinue policies; (6) ensures accountability;[38] and (7) encourages consultation and stakeholder engagement (Jollands and Pasquier, 2008). In addition, (8) a long-term view to ensure sustainability/market transformation is often advocated in the literature.

### 14.5.2 *The UK versus international experience*

When compared to the policies of Germany and Denmark, as listed in the MURE II database, the UK seems to have a balanced set of policies, with the participation of diverse actors. This contrasts with, for instance,

[37] Defined as the process of deliberately monitoring and evaluating the effectiveness of EE measures and the NEESAP in order to expand successful measures and redevelop or discontinue poor performing measures (Jollands and Pasquier, 2008).

[38] While accountability is a cornerstone, its optimal allocation – centralized or distributed across agencies – may depend on the context (Jollands and Pasquier, 2008).

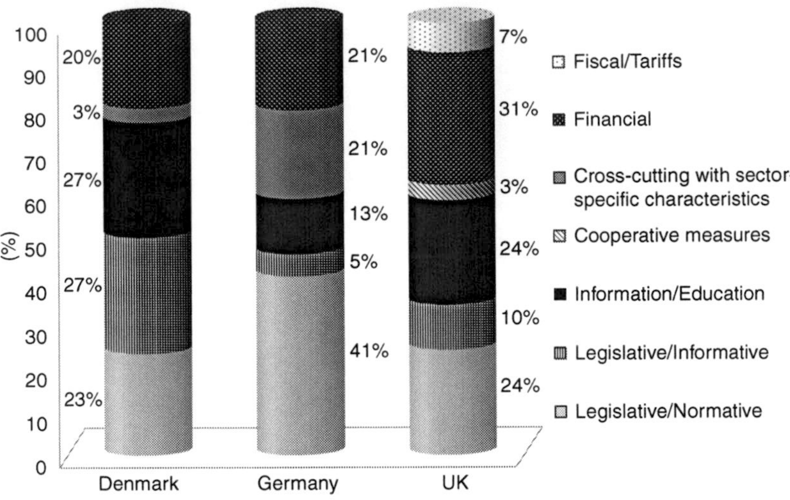


Figure 14.6 Type of measures implemented in the UK, Denmark and Germany.
*Source:* MURE (2010).

Germany's more centralized implementation (Figure 14.5). Similarly, the range of policies is wide. However, there is still large potential and scope for improvement. So what explains the still poor performance of energy use in households in the UK compared with, for instance, Denmark or Germany? We suggest that untapped potential in the UK remains particularly large because of a lack of an underlying holistic approach to energy policy, which, by extension, permeates all dimensions of DSM.

A strategic view should manifest itself in an integrative policy package that is coherent, coordinated and has a long-term perspective. In Denmark, for instance, energy savings in buildings has been a major focus of energy policy since 1975. Environmental preservation, awareness and concern is embedded in Danish culture (Figure 14.6). Primary supply of energy for heating has decreased by more than 20 per cent despite a 34 per cent increase in heating space (IEA, 2006). Building regulations to curb heating needs have been tightened since 1977, offering predictability to construction companies. Enforcement of these codes as well as strict labelling demonstrate an underlying coherent view, complemented by a strong policy with respect to CHP and district heating.

In the US, the 2008 National Action Plan for Energy Efficiency (NAPEE) calls for a sustainable national commitment in all sectors. Such goals are also adopted in state-level reports: the 2009 Integrated Energy Policy Report (IEPR) and the 2008 California Long-term Energy

Efficiency Strategic Plan (EESP). Both announce the ambitious target of making all new residential constructions 'Zero Net Energy'[39] by 2020 (CPUC, 2008; CEC, 2009). The case of California illustrates the necessity of involving all three levels: federal, regional and local. The federal level builds capacity by providing funding, guiding strategies and toolkits for state and local authorities, thereby reducing state-level costs to enact policies. Building and appliance standards, necessary at the federal level, benefit from some flexibility at the state level, as states have better information and can target the standards to state characteristics. Regional associations, such as WGA, can add clarity and harmonize targets. All this requires simultaneous initiatives at all three levels.

The Californian policies demonstrate several strengths in terms of relevance, flexibility, clarity and sustainability. Also, coherence is visible, as some policies are coupled together, and hence, their impact strengthened. The Energy Star labels are used as criteria for loans and grants. Building regulation updates go hand in hand with increased usage of energy efficient appliances (IEA, 2008). Finally, it also shows the necessity of public awareness, an essential element in the strategy. Future challenges include developing data gathering in order to improve future energy demand forecasts as well as assessing the quantitative impacts in post-evaluation studies, and distinguishing between the different factors influencing outcomes (Vine *et al.*, 2006).

Although the Japanese policies show some weaknesses, such as the need to target more rural households – responsible for 52.5 per cent of the total residential building sector – and to extend the scope of some measures (Ashina and Nakata, 2008), they reveal an underlying integrative conceptual approach, where policies are combined and target multiple barriers. Innovative features include, for instance, the use of regulations as benchmarks for voluntary labels and the provision of subsidies. The Top Runner standard, for instance, has been used as a reference point for voluntary labels. Specific measures such as labels or grants simultaneously address several barriers at the same time – access to capital or behavioural barriers – while targeting a wide range of actors at different levels – from consumers to manufacturers and local governments – through effective partnerships.

On the contrary, UK policies seem heavily shaped by short-term politics and a particular conceptual rationale. The UK government recognizes the need for a combination of policies and enhanced coordination (DTI, 2007; IEA, 2008; NAO, 2008). However, the wide range of

[39] Zero Net Energy buildings would contain generation technologies and be connected to the grid so as to export energy when there is a surplus and import when not enough is produced (CPUC, 2008).

measures adopted in general, and elaborated in the EEAP 2007 for instance, bears the risk of resource dispersion as well as difficulty in evaluation. Small, incremental steps still take priority over a more comprehensive and integrative approach which would have the advantage of enhancing market transformation. Also, clearer and longer-term targets would strengthen the latter.

For instance, a confusing number of different measures specifically target fuel poverty – the Warm Front, Reduced VAT for energy-saving materials, Decent Homes, Warm Zones, the Low Carbon Buildings Programmes. Differences between them seem rather small. They could achieve more with increased flexibility and continuous funding (Pyrko and Darby, 2009). Besides, and perhaps more importantly, constant incremental updates and changes in framework policies, evidenced through serial publications of 'long-term' energy white papers and plans – 1998, 2003, 2006, 2007, 2008, 2009 – affect credibility and unhinge a sector traditionally known for its long-term investments, and need for certainty and predictability. Frequent changes of Secretaries of State responsible for energy who remained for on average fifteen months are also detrimental to a long-term perspective.

Furthermore, our discussion has demonstrated the need for data gathering and ex post evaluations. The Danish Energy Saving Trust, an independent body itself, is subject to frequent reviews by an independent body. UK measures unveil a lack of focus and understanding of the actual impact of policies, with very few evaluations and ex post studies. Modelling of building performance, compliance to building regulations and ex post evaluation studies would facilitate the monitoring of the impacts and progress of measures. Dedicated reviews need to be put in place.

However, no one size fits all in terms of the approach to DSM. Japan provides a very good illustration of a 'horizontally driven' policy package, targeting a wide range of actors. The measures are multi-dimensional and address multiple barriers. Californian policies, by contrast, are vertically articulated, with a multi-stage implementation: federal, regional and state, including utilities' participation.

## 14.6 Conclusion

In its review of programmes targeting financial barriers, de T'Serclaes (2007) finds that the challenges to energy efficiency rather lie in more carefully designing policy packages than in increasing financial resources. A successful strategy is the combination of 'sticks' (regulations) with 'carrots' (incentives) and 'tambourines' (awareness raising campaign) (Warren, 2007, cited by Koeppel and Urge-Vorsatz, 2007). Our review of policies has provided some evidence on this. We have shown that an integrated demand-side strategy is based on the recognition that no single policy alone can overcome the barriers to energy efficiency, which are diverse and spread out over a wide range of actors and sectors. Policies may address several barriers at the same time and treating them as complementary strengthens their impact (Lee and Yik, 2004; Sovacool, 2009).

This requires an 'integrated policy strategy', i.e. a holistic underlying approach. We suggested that packages of policies reveal different cultural and conceptual approaches, as well as methodologies and that policy making might benefit from departing from a focus on the strengths and weaknesses of isolated instruments towards a more comprehensive analysis accounting for their interactions. This also opens new avenues for research, as in dynamic modelling, for instance; and the need to create a market for energy efficiency. In the UK, for instance, the reliance on marginal abatement cost curves (MACC) as an aid to policy making might explain the existing lack of coherence. On the contrary, Denmark's culture for environmental preservation which goes far beyond the energy sector could well facilitate an integrative approach. The Japanese example reveals an explicit focus on and exploitation of policy interactions.

'Success' factors of a well-designed energy efficiency strategy have been provided, such as the existence of clear objectives and mandates; the participation of stakeholders; the ability to combine flexibility and sustainability; and the ability to adapt and integrate adjacent policies (Harmelink *et al.*, 2008). Flexibility is required as policies interact with each other, and their impact evolves over time. Sustainability creates certainty and can be fostered through the integration into market transformation strategies (Sovacool, 2009). The most successful packages are clear, effective and sustainable while remaining flexible. The importance of post-evaluation studies and benchmarking has also been highlighted repeatedly (Lee and Yik, 2004; IEA, 2009a). As regards the specific mix of policies, particularly effective combinations involve both private and public actors, e.g. through PPP. Effective DSM measures rarely emerge from private actors alone, and government action is often needed to encourage action and investments by private actors. Hence, political will is required, in order to reduce uncertainty. In general, policy makers show a move towards a holistic approach (Lee and Yik, 2004). In the US, Denmark and Japan, integrated packages of DSM do not duplicate energy efficiency measures in the residential sector, but rather augment and strengthen them, as illustrated in the case of California (CPUC, 2008).

These countries can provide useful lessons for the UK. UK policies show a move towards packages of integrated policies, yet there is still scope for improvement, especially in terms of M&V, clarification and coordination. However, as we have seen, given the poor quality of buildings, capacity-building measures should be strengthened, refurbishments promoted, and building regulations better enforced. The plethora of existing tariffs and grant programmes offers a rather confusing impression and may miss its targets. In general, weaknesses must be identified and targeted. Some policies need to be complemented through awareness measures, as shown by the SAP ratings, for instance. Product policy should precede higher prices; tax reductions should be a means to enable low-income families to buy more energy efficient products. As regards behaviour, the ideal condition would be a mix of consumer 'pull' and manufacturer 'push' measures (Boardman, 2007). This focus on single policies alone might have been the result of a reliance on a 'Marginal Abatement Cost Curves' approach, which indicates which measures are most cost effective individually. However, such disaggregation conceals the interactions between measures, which can imply the need for a very different strategy.

On the institutional side, the recent creation of the Department for Energy and Climate Change (DECC) might reduce hidden costs and facilitate coordination. Its role and functions could make DECC the leading department in the development of a holistic strategy taking explicitly into account dynamic interdependencies and based on empirical evidence and the regulator's independent advice. However, the particular administration and implementation of specific policies should be carried out by the most appropriate governmental and non-governmental bodies exploiting their capacities strategically. For example, the Energy Saving Trust local energy saving centres have experience and knowledge on local conditions as well as a privileged relationship with citizens; the Department for Communities and Local Government has established collaboration with local authorities; and Ofgem has advisory capacities and extended knowledge of the energy supply market. The latter could promote further PPP opportunities and ensure the independent measurement and evaluation of future and existing policies.

## References

ACEEE (2010). State Energy Efficiency Resource Standards, (EERS) Activity, Available at www.aceee.org/energy/state/State%20EERS%20Summary%20Jan%202010.pdf, last accessed 2 August 2010.

Act 129 (2008). Available at www.puc.state.pa.us/electric/pdf/Act129/HB2200-Act129_Bill.pdf, last accessed 2 August 2010.

Alam, M., Sathaye, J. and Barnes, D. (1998). Urban household energy use in India: efficiency and policy implications, *Energy Policy*, **26**(11): 885–91.

Ang, B.W. (2006). Monitoring changes in economy-wide energy efficiency: from energy-GDP ratio to composite efficiency index, *Energy Policy*, **34**(5): 574–82.

Ashina, S. and Nakata, T. (2008). Energy-efficiency strategy for $CO_2$ emissions in a residential sector in Japan, *Applied Energy*, **85**(2–3): 101–14.

Banerjee, A. and Solomon, B.D. (2003). Eco-labeling for energy efficiency and sustainability: a meta-evaluation of US programs, *Energy Policy*, **31**(2): 109–23.

Bilton, M., Ramsay, C., Leach, M., Devine-Wright, H., Devine-Wright, P. and Kirschen, D. (2008). Domestic electricity consumption and demand-side participation: opportunities and challenges for the UK power system, in Grubb, M., Jamasb, T. and Pollitt, M. (eds.), *Delivering a Low-Carbon Electricity System: Technologies, Economics and Policy*, Cambridge: Cambridge University Press, pp. 207–28.

Birner, S. and Martinot, E. (2002). The GEF Energy-Efficient Product Portfolio: Emerging Experience and Lessons. Washington DC.

Blumstein, C., Goldman, C. and Barbose, G. (2005). Who should administer energy-efficiency programs? *Energy Policy*, **33**(8): 1053–67.

Boardman, B. (2005). *Domestic Energy Fact File*. ECEEE Summer Study – What works and who delivers? France: Côte d'azur.

Boardman, B. (2007). *Home Truths: A Low-Carbon Strategy to reduce UK Housing Emissions by 80% by 2050*, Oxford: ECI.

BRE (2008). *Domestic Energy Fact File 2008*, UK: BRE Housing.

Brown, M.A. (2001). Market failures and barriers as a basis for clean energy policies, *Energy Policy*, **29**(14): 1197–207.

CEC (2009). *2009 Integrated Energy Policy Report, Final Commission Report, December 2009*, California: California Energy Commission.

Clarke, J.A., Johnstone, C.M., Kelly, N.J., Strachan, P.A. and Tuohy, P. (2008). The role of built environment energy efficiency in a sustainable UK energy economy, *Energy Policy*, **36**(12): 4605–9.

CLASP (2005). *A Standards & Labeling Guidebook for Appliances, Equipment, and Lighting (2nd Edition) – English Version*, Washington, DC: The Collaborative Labeling and Appliance Standards Program (CLASP), Available at www.clasponline.org/clasp.online.resource.php?sbo=289, last accessed 28 August 2010.

CLG (2010). Communities and Local Government website, retrieved 2 August 2010 from www.communities.gov.uk/corporate.

CPUC (2008). *California Long Term Energy Efficiency Strategic Plan*, California: California Public Utilities Commission.

CRA (2005). *Primer on Demand-side Management*, Oakland, CA: Prepared for the World Bank by Charles River Associates.

Crossley, D., Maloney, M. and Watt, G. (2000). Developing mechanisms for promoting demand-side management and energy efficiency in changing electricity businesses, Hornsby Heights, Task VI of the IEA Demand-Side Management Program.

Darby, S. (2006). *The Effectiveness of Feedback on Energy Consumption*, Oxford: Environmental Change Institute, University of Oxford.

de T'Serclaes, P. (2007). *Financing Energy Efficient Homes: Existing Policy Responses to Financial Barriers*, Paris: International Energy Agency.

DECC (2009). *The UK Low Carbon Transition Plan: National Strategy for Climate and Energy*, London: Department of Energy and Climate Change.

DECC (2010). Energy consumption in the United Kingdom, retrieved 16 August 2010, from www.decc.gov.uk/en/content/cms/statistics/publications/ecuk/ecuk.aspx.

Deringer, J., Iyer, M. and Huang, Y.J. (2004). Transferred just on paper? Why doesn't the reality of Transferring/Adapting Energy Efficiency Codes and Standards come close to the potential? ACEEE Summer Study on Energy Efficiency in Buildings, Pacific Grove, California, US, ACEEE.

DTI (2007). *Meeting the Energy Challenge: A White Paper on Energy*, London: Department for Trade and Industry.

EERE (2010). US Department of Energy, Energy Efficiency and Renewable Energy, retrieved 27 July 2010 from www1.eere.energy.gov/ba/pba/intensityindicators/trend_definitions.html.

Eldridge, M., Neubauer, M., York, D., Vaidyanathan, S., Chittum, A. and Nadel, S. (2008). *The 2008 State Energy Efficiency Scorecard*, Washington, DC: American Council for an Energy-Efficient Economy (ACEEE).

Energy Star (2008). *2008 Annual Report*, Energy Star.

EST (2006). *The Rise of the Machine: A Review of Energy Using Products in the Home from the 1970s to Today*, London: Energy Saving Trust.

Eto, J., Prahl, R. and Schlegel, J. (1996). *A Scoping Study on Energy-Efficiency Market Transformation by California Utility DSM Programs*. LBNL 39058.

Fonseca, P., de Almeida, A., Feilberg, N., Markogiannakis, G. and Kofod, C. (2009). Characterization of the household electricity consumption in the EU, potential energy savings and specific policy recommendations. ECEEE 2009 Summer Study, France.

Geller, H., Harrington, P., Rosenfeld, A.H., Tanishima, S. and Unander, F. (2006). Policies for increasing energy efficiency: thirty years of experience in OECD countries, *Energy Policy*, **34**(5): 556–73.

Gillingham, K., Newell, R. and Palmer, K. (2006). Energy efficiency policies: a retrospective examination, *Annual Review of Environment and Resources*, **31**(1): 161–92.

Greening, L.A., Greene, D.L. and Difiglio, C. (2000). Energy efficiency and consumption – the rebound effect – a survey, *Energy Policy*, **28**(6–7): 389–401.

Grubb, M. and Wilde, J. (2008). Enhancing the efficient use of electricity in the business and public sectors, in Grubb, M., Jamasb, T. and Pollitt, M.G. (eds.), *Delivering a Low-Carbon Electricity System: Technologies, Economics and Policy*, Cambridge: Cambridge University Press, pp. 207–28.

Gunningham, N. and Sinclair, D. (1999). Regulatory pluralism: designing policy mixes for environmental protection, *Law and Policy*, **41**(1): 49–74.

Harmelink, M., Nilsson, L. and Harmsen, R. (2008). Theory-based policy evaluation of 20 energy efficiency instruments, *Energy Efficiency*, **1**(2): 131–48.

Hartley, N. (2006). The 2006 review of energy policy: the main issues, *Political Quarterly*, 77(1): 117–23.

IEA (2005). Evaluating energy efficiency policy measures and DSM programmes: Volume II: Country reports and case examples used for the evaluation guide book. Sittard, the Netherlands: IEA.

IEA (2006). *Denmark 2006 Review*, Paris: International Energy Agency.

IEA (2007). *Energy Use in the New Millenium: Trends in IEA Countries*, Paris: International Energy Agency.

IEA (2008). *Promoting Energy Efficiency: Case Studies in the Residential Sector*, Paris: International Energy Agency.

IEA (2009a). *Financial Crisis and Energy Efficiency*, Paris: OECD/IEA.

IEA (2009b). *Implementing Energy Efficiency Policies: Are IEA Member Countries on track?* Paris: International Energy Agency.

IEA (2009c). *Progress with Implementing Energy Efficiency Policies in the G8*, Paris: International Energy Agency.

IEA (2010). Energy Efficiency Policies and Measures Database, retrieved 3 February 2010 from http://www.iea.org/textbase/pm/?mode=pm.

Jaffe, A.B., Newell, R. and S.R.N. (1999). *Energy-efficient Technologies and Climate Change Policies: Issues and Evidence*, Washington, DC: Resources for the Future.

Jaffe, A.B. and Stavins, R.N. (1994). The energy-efficiency gap: what does it mean? *Energy Policy*, **22**(10): 804–10.

Jollands, N. and Pasquier, S. (2008). Innovations in National Energy Efficiency Strategies and Action Plans. Workshop on Innovations in National Energy Efficiency Strategies and Action Plans. International Energy Agency, Paris, France.

Koeppel, S. and Urge-Vorsatz, D. (2007). Assessment of Policy Instruments for Reducing Greenhouse Gas Emissions from Buildings. Budapest, Hungary: Central European University.

Lee, W.L. and Yik, F.W.H. (2004). Regulatory and voluntary approaches for enhancing building energy efficiency, *Progress in Energy and Combustion Science*, **30**(5): 477–99.

Lees, E. (2006). Evaluation of the Energy Efficiency Commitment 2002–05, ADEME-WEC Workshop on Energy Efficiency Policies, Oxon/London.

McKinsey (2007). *Curbing Global Energy Demand Growth: The Energy Productivity Opportunity*, San Francisco, CA: McKinsey Global Institute.

McKinsey (2008). *The Case for Investing in Energy Productivity*, San Francisco, CA: McKinsey Global Institute.

McKinsey (2009). *Averting the Next Energy Crisis: The Demand Challenge*, San Francisco, CA, Houston, TX: McKinsey & Company and McKinsey Global Institute.

MURE (2008). *Energy Efficiency Profile: UK*, MURE.

MURE (2009). *Energy Efficiency Policies and Measures in the UK 2009*, MURE.

MURE (2010). Mesures d'Utilisation Rationnelle de l'Energie, retrieved 3 February 2010 from www.isisrome.com/mure.

NAO (2008). *Programmes to Reduce Household Energy Consumption*, London: National Audit Office.

Nordqvist, J. (2007). The Top Runner policy concept: Pass it down? ECEEE 2007 Summer Study: Saving energy – just do it!, La Colle sur Loup, France.

Pyrko, J. and Darby, S. (2009). Conditions of behavioural changes towards efficient energy use – a comparative study between Sweden and the United Kingdom. ECEEE 2009 Summer Study: Act! Innovate! Deliver! Reducing Energy Demand Sustainably, Côte d'Azur, France, ECEEE.

Ramesohl, S. and Dudda, C. (2001). Barriers to energy service contracting and the role of standardised measurement and verification schemes as a tool to remove them. European Council for an Energy Efficient Economy 2001 Summer Study proceedings.

Rayner, J. and Howlett, M. (2009). Introduction: understanding integrated policy strategies and their evolution, *Policy and Society*, **28**(2): 99–109.

Sorrell, S. (2004). Understanding barriers to energy efficiency, in Sorrell, S., O'Malley, E., Schleich, J. and Scott, S. (eds.), *The Economics of Energy Efficiency*, Cheltenham: Edward Elgar, pp. 25–95.

Sovacool, B.K. (2009). The importance of comprehensiveness in renewable electricity and energy-efficiency policy, *Energy Policy*, **37**(4): 1529–41.

Taylor, P., d'Ortigue, O.L., Francoeur, M. and Trudeau, N. (2010). Final energy use in IEA countries: the role of energy efficiency, *Energy Policy*, **38**(11): 6463–74.

Torriti, J., Hassan, M.G. and Leach, M. (2010). Demand response experience in Europe: policies, programmes and implementation, *Energy*, **35**(4): 1575–83.

Uihlein, A. and Eder, P. (2009). Towards additional policies to improve the environmental performance of buildings. Luxembourg: European Communities and Institute for Prospective Technological Studies.

Unander, F., Ettestøl, I., Ting, M. and Schipper, L. (2004). Residential energy use: an international perspective on long-term trends in Denmark, Norway and Sweden, *Energy Policy*, **32**(12): 1395–404.

UNEP (2009). *Buildings and Climate Change*, Paris: United National Environment Programme Sustainable Buildings & Climate Initiative (UNEP-SBCI).

Utley, J.I. and Shorrock, L.D. (2008). *Domestic Energy Fact File 2008*, UK: BRE Housing.

Varone, F. and Aebischer, B. (2001). Energy efficiency: the challenges of policy design, *Energy Policy*, **29**(8): 615–29.

Vine, E., Hamrin, J., Eyre, N., Crossley, D., Maloney, M. and Watt, G. (2003). Public policy analysis of energy efficiency and load management in changing electricity businesses, *Energy Policy*, **31**(5): 405–30.

Vine, E., Rhee, C.H. and Lee, K.D. (2006). Measurement and Evaluation of energy efficiency programs: California and South Korea, *Energy*, **31**(6–7): 1100–13.

WEC (2008). *Energy Efficiency Policies around the World: Review and Evaluation*, London: World Energy Council.

Weiss, J.A. and Tschirhart, M. (1994). Public information campaigns as policy instruments, *Journal of Policy Analysis and Management*, **13**(1): 82–119.

# 15 Electricity distribution networks: investment and regulation, and uncertain demand

*Tooraj Jamasb and Cristiano Marantes*

## 15.1 Introduction

Electricity distribution networks are highly capital-intensive systems and timely investments to maintain and upgrade the assets are crucial for long-term reliability and expansion of their service. In the coming years, in the UK, and elsewhere in Europe, many distribution networks will be in need of extensive investments in their aging assets. At the same time, aspects of energy policy concerning climate change, renewable energy sources, energy efficiency, demand-side management (DSM), network energy loss reduction, quality of service standards and even security of supply (Jamasb and Pollitt, 2008) require active, flexible and smart networks that can be achieved only through significant investments.

At the same time, the utilities' investment decisions are dependent on the regulatory framework within which they operate. Following the liberalization of the electricity sectors around the world, the introduction of incentive regulation regimes based on RPI-X models and benchmarking has in most cases improved the efficiency of network utilities. Cost savings can be achieved in operation and maintenance (Opex) and in capital expenditures (Capex). Evaluation of the efficiency potential in Capex is a challenging task. The main difficulty in incentivizing investments is in the discrepancy between the long economic life and the cyclical nature of network assets on the one hand and the considerably shorter (five years in the UK) distribution price control periods on the other. Here both better planning and implementation of investments, or a mere reduction in investments, can appear as achieving efficiency improvement in the short and medium term while the implications of under-investment become apparent in the long run.

Most of the efficiency improvements in the UK Distribution Network Operators (DNOs) have been in the form of savings in Opex which have been subject to stricter regulatory benchmarking and incentives. However, capital investments are not an integrated part of the cost benchmarking exercise and individual utility investment plans need to be approved by the regulator. The regulator has developed incentive schemes resembling a menu of options to encourage efficiency in capital investments based on engineering consultants' assessments. Nevertheless, assessing the effectiveness of investment efficiency incentives remains a difficult task due to the long time horizons involved in network investments, information asymmetry between the regulator and the utility, and the five-year focus of distribution price control reviews.

The investment needs of the different regions of a network can vary greatly mainly due to differences in asset age and load growth. At the same time, the investment needs of meeting some of the above mentioned requirements from active and flexible networks can have mainly localized effects on the networks. For example, an increase in distributed or microgeneration in parts of the network or an interest in power generation activities by councils and communities can lead to such local network effects. Therefore, there is a need for models that can be used to assess and regulate investments at the subnetwork level.

This chapter describes and utilizes the use of a network investment assessment model developed as a practical tool to identify and assess the investment requirements of a particular group of distribution networks in the UK. A broadening of the scope of network investments to include demand-related measures such as microgeneration, distributed generation and energy efficiency is likely to achieve overall investment reductions. However, the regulatory framework also needs to adapt to the changing role of the future networks and in order to harness the benefit of a wider range of investment possibilities.

The next two sections provide the main features of the current UK distribution network regulation. Section 15.4 then discusses demand for distribution network services and drivers for capital investments. Section 15.5 describes a network model developed by EDF Energy for assessing local investment needs of networks which is used for the analysis in this chapter. Section 15.6 offers some discussion of future distribution regulation frameworks and conclusions.

## 15.2 Distribution networks and their operating environment

### *15.2.1 Background*

This section describes the role of electricity distribution networks and their operating environment emphasizing the importance of capital investments in the networks and the role of regulation for achieving the appropriate type and level of investments in the networks. The features of the UK incentive regulation and benchmarking regime are described in detail elsewhere in the literature (see, e.g., Pollitt, 2005; Jamasb and Pollitt, 2007).

The electricity system consists of generation, transmission, distribution and supply activities. Generation comprises production and conversion of electric power. Transmission involves long-distance transportation of electricity at high voltage. Distribution is transportation of low-voltage electricity through local networks from the transmission network to customers' premises. The supply function consists of metering, billing and sale of electricity to end-users. The generation and supply activities are generally regarded as potentially competitive. The transmission and distribution networks are characterized as natural monopolies and are hence subject to economic regulation.

Distribution networks consist of overhead lines, cables, switchgear, transformers, control systems and meters to transfer electricity, making them capital-intensive activities. Much of these assets have long economic lives and become sunk costs upon investment. Also, distribution networks have a diverse set of residential, commercial and industrial customers in terms of usage level as well as consumption patterns. As demand for electricity service continues to increase the existing networks need to gradually be replaced and expanded and the utilities can experience investment cycles.

Due to their strategic position in the electricity system – as the main physical interface to end-users as well as to distributed generation (DG) sources, microgeneration units, smart meters and the transmission network – distribution networks will have a central role to play in enabling an active demand side and a future low-carbon electricity system. Living up to this expectation requires that these utilities undertake substantial investments in new technologies and solutions that transform them into active, flexible and smart networks.

As electricity distribution is a capital-intensive activity the efficiency with which the required investments are undertaken is a concern for the regulator. The main aim of electricity reform in general and incentive regulation of networks in particular is to provide utilities with incentives to improve their operating and investment efficiency and at the same time to ensure that consumers benefit from the gains. However, despite progress in economic regulation of networks in recent years, devising suitable incentives for network investments still remains a work in progress and a challenge for the regulators (see Joskow, 2008; Ofgem, 2010).

### *15.2.2 The regulatory framework*

As a result of regulatory reform, there have been significant changes in the way that DNOs structure their business and the range of activities in which they are involved. For example, in the UK, several DNOs have active second-tier supply businesses and most are active in the supply of gas as well as electricity. This provides opportunities for joint marketing of the two fuels. Meanwhile, some DNOs are now in different ownership from their former supply businesses. Following a series of mergers, the distribution businesses of the fourteen original regional electricity companies (RECs) are currently (late 2010) owned by seven independent companies.

The regulation model of distribution networks in Britain consists of a hybrid of incentive schemes. Under the current arrangements, the operating expenditures, capital expenditures, quality of service and network energy losses are incentivized separately and under different types of schemes within a building block framework. The utilities' controllable operating expenditures (Opex) are incentivized by benchmarking these against an efficient frontier that is made up of the best-practice DNOs in the sector. The allowed Opex of individual DNOs is set such that it requires them to close a specific proportion of their performance gap relative to the frontier during the price control period. In addition, the DNOs are given a general technical efficiency improvement target that is common to all DNOs (Pollitt, 2005; Jamasb and Pollitt, 2007).

In response to regulators' incentives and benchmarking, operating expenditures of DNOs have fallen significantly while new investments are added to a growing regulatory asset base. As a result, capital investments are increasingly driving the regulated revenue of the DNOs.

### *15.2.3 The price control process*

The process for assessing the required level of capital expenditure over a price control review period is as follows. Utilities must draft business plans which include projected capital expenditure. These are then audited by a firm of engineering consultants, working for Ofgem. Usually these consultants recommend lower levels of capital expenditure than that proposed by each utility. This gives a base level of required capital expenditure to which an incentive scheme is applied. The incentive scheme resembles a menu of contracts regulation model. The menu of contracts approach is appealing to the presence of strong information asymmetry. However, this approach is not widely used in practice with the main difficulty being the development of a suitable menu of options (Pollitt, 2005).

In addition, quality of service and network energy losses are incentivized separately through performance standards and targets. The targets for each DNO are individual and deviation from these results in company-specific penalties and rewards calculated based on an elaborate system. The rewards and penalties directly affect the total allowed revenue. In order to avoid jeopardizing financial viability of the companies, the maximum amount subject to quality of service reward and penalty scheme is capped as a percentage of allowed revenue. The 2004 distribution price control (for the period 2005–10) review introduced a sliding scale system to incentives capital investments by which the DNOs are rewarded by higher rate of returns if their actual investments are lower than the predicted levels (Ofgem, 2004). Collectively, these separate incentive schemes for Opex, Capex, quality of service and network energy losses amount to a revenue cap incentive regulation.

Due to the presence of potential trade-offs between Opex, Capex, quality of service and network losses, from an economic efficiency point of view, it is preferable to use an integrated benchmarking model. Such a model would be based on a single total expenditure measure where all cost measures as well as some measure of the monetary values of service quality and network losses are added together. The hybrid system in Britain is contrary to the notion of integrated overall incentive regulation. However, the adopted approach – segmented regulation – gives more control to the regulator to address specific and urgent areas of focus. It also involves less complicated modelling than a fully integrated benchmarking model would require and is more transparent and easier to implement. At the same time, the current incentive system cannot account for the potential trade-off between the specific regulated aspects of the utilities.

The investment efficiency incentive scheme adopted by Ofgem as part of distribution price control reviews offers some flexibility for the utilities to perform better than their allowed and expected investment needs. This approach also, to some extent, enables the utilities, when possible, to take the trade-offs with operating expenditures into consideration. For the most recent distribution price control period (2010–15) there has been an equalization of the incentive rate for Opex and Capex reductions, which should reduce the incentives to inefficiently substitute capital expenditure for operating expenditure (see Ofgem, 2009).

## 15.3 Regulation of active network and demand

Ofgem's benchmarking model of DNOs can be described as a short-term efficiency model as it only addresses the companies' operating expenditures. This is in contrast to the long lead times necessary for the firms to change their asset structure. Capital expenditures are controlled and incentivized under a separate scheme.

Achieving long-term efficiency improvements can require short-term increases in Capex and/or Opex expenditures that may not generate immediate efficiency improvements. Indeed, such expenditure increases by a given firm can weaken its short-term performance relative to other firms. This can prevent firms from embarking on types of investments that have long-term efficiency gains. Such efficiency improvements can be facilitated with incentives allowing the firms to keep a larger share of the benefits of the efficiency gains. This is particularly the case with investment programmes in active networks and DSM which are capital intensive and investment projects can have long lead times that can exceed the current five-year price control reviews.

The mismatch between the long-term horizon of investments and short price control periods can also have a negative effect on the cost of financing investments (see Ofwat/Ofgem, 2006). Longer regulatory periods (e.g. seven or ten years) can reduce uncertainty with regards to long-term investments and retaining their benefits. However, even substantially longer regulatory price control periods will likely not fully incentivize investments if the innovations appear to have even longer payback periods.

The current regulatory framework will need to evolve in order to enable the transition of the networks from passive system components to active and flexible actors. For example, Niesten (2010) discusses some aspects of regulation that can help encourage the required investments in distribution networks to connect distributed generation (DG). Among others, for example, the study argues that DG can pay capacity-based network connection charges and be paid for the amount of energy that they supply to distribution networks.

Saplacan (2008) describes how the perception of the activities of the DNOs has evolved and distinguishes between network ownership and network operation, the former being a natural monopoly while the latter can potentially be open to 'competition for markets'. The study outlines a detailed breakdown of the different types of activities of distribution networks some of which can potentially be subject to competition. In the coming years, due to technological progress, the dividing lines between regulation and the market can be redrawn so that more functions can be subjected to competition. Such a trend may result in a larger role for the use of market-based solutions for some aspects of active networks and demand.

Ofgem has been conducting a review of its price control processes. This has already led to proposals for a move towards 'Sustainable Network Regulation', which will seek to strengthen incentives for network companies to facilitate low-carbon investments in their networks (e.g. of local distributed generation from renewable resources). This will be based on a wider definition of network outputs than in the past where regulated revenue will be based on incentives, innovation and outputs (so called RIIO regulation) (see Ofgem, 2010).

## 15.4 Demand for distribution services and drivers of investment

### *15.4.1 Background*

There is an extensive body of literature on electricity demand modelling and forecasts. Steinbuks (this volume) presents a review of the recent literature and references on this topic. However, the literature on electricity demand is predominantly focused on generation, capacity and, occasionally, related investments. The investment requirements of distribution networks are generally assumed to be a rough function of demand growth and typically at the macro level, and only a small subset of studies are concerned with demand for distribution network services and related investments. Also, in the past utilities have mainly used simple demand forecast methods and technical analysis to predict and plan their investment requirements.

In this paper we assess the drivers of demand for distribution network services and investments. Demand for electric energy and related services is initiated by end-users. Generators provide the required electricity in real time which is then delivered through the high voltage transmission and medium-low voltage distribution networks. The need for services of distribution networks can therefore be characterized as a 'derived demand' where network investment requirements are driven by end-users' demand for electricity.

The distribution networks provide the final physical link to the electricity system allowing grid-connected electricity generation to be delivered to end-users at the required location, quantity and time. The need for load-related investments of distribution utilities is linked to demand for electricity. It is useful to distinguish between the two main types of investments in distribution networks.

i. Asset replacement and upgrading – these investments are aimed at maintaining the services of the network to existing customers. Asset renewal needs arise from aging assets that need to be renewed. In addition, demand growth from existing customers can lead to replacement and upgrading of certain asset types such as transformers. Asset registers and probability-based methods can be used to determine their optimum renewal time. The technical useful life of typical main network assets is long and their economic life may sometimes extend beyond their technical life.

ii. Network expansion – the size and shape of distribution networks evolve gradually in response to changes in demand and the customer base. Over time, some customers or sites may be disconnected and/or leave the network while new customers and sites are constantly connected to the network. Demand for new connections in existing parts of the service area lead to investment in expansion of the system.

The relative share of investments in asset replacement and new investments can vary among utilities, for example, depending on the age profile of assets and network reinforcement and expansion requirements in their service areas.

A question that arises is the extent to which macroeconomic type of variables can be used to forecast uncertain demand for network investment at the level of utilities' service areas. Indeed this is a difficult task. In particular, the degree of difficulty increases for smaller service areas as the high-level or macroeconomic-type relations between the main factors become less reliable. An appealing approach is to use correlation analysis to identify accurate drivers for demand. However, the available data and previous studies are not sufficient for detailed service area analysis where indivisibilities of network capacity and demand at individual nodes in the distribution network may be large. For example, the length of the time-series used in correlations is too short to draw firm conclusions. Moreover, some correlations of potential driving factors of demand and investment among the service areas as, for example, used in CEPA (2009) and Frontier Economics (2007) reveal considerable regional differences which cannot be readily explained without further detailed studies.

In particular, investment planning under economic uncertainty is difficult. Much of the historical data that can be used in forecasts are from periods of relatively stable economic and demand growth. The energy demand and the economy relationship under the recent economic downturn (at least in the short/medium term) may be very different from those of past trends. However, the nature of this relationship at times of economic downturn is not well understood. For example, the effect of economic activity on demand for electricity can be asymmetric – i.e. the negative effect of GDP reduction on demand for energy is not simply the inverse of a positive effect of GDP growth as shown in Mork (1989) in the case of oil prices.

In short, past trends are unlikely to provide good indicators for planning future network investment in particular for short-term applications to the economic environment such as that of the late 2000s with negative economic growth. For example, in recent years, the adoption of flexible work arrangements in some sectors of the economy marks a new trend in labour–energy–economy relationships.

### *15.4.2 Drivers of load-related investments*

In this study we assess the load growth and associated investment requirements for two main customer groups – i.e. 'residential' and 'non-residential sectors'.[1] A number of indicators can be considered as drivers of residential and non-residential demand and investment. The investment drivers differ in terms of the directness of their effect on demand and the tangibility of their relationship to actual investments in network assets. In addition, a recurring issue with many of the commonly used variables in energy forecasting models is that there is often a strong degree of correlation among them making the identification of accurate demand and investment drivers more difficult.

The choice between the above mentioned demand and investment drivers can depend on the level of analysis. In the absence of extensive data and inconclusive evidence on specific drivers for utility-level investments we need to turn to economic reasoning and engineering experience in order to select key indicators of demand and investment.

## 15.5 Model description

This section describes a comprehensive long-term maximum electricity demand forecast methodology developed by EDF Energy Networks, UK. It produces highly disaggregated outputs as it attributes unique demand growth values to every single primary substation depending on their geographical location. Electricity demand is assumed to have a domestic and non-domestic component. This methodology is based on publicly available information and is therefore applicable to all DNOs in the UK.

In the UK, all DNOs have an obligation under their distribution licence to plan and develop the distribution networks in accordance with a standard not below that set out in the Engineering Recommendation P2/6 of the Energy Networks Association. This prescribes the level of redundancy in the distribution network needed for various magnitudes of demand and specifies the speed with which service to customers should be restored when these fail. Moreover, maintaining future P2/6 compliance influences the longer-term investment in distribution networks by indicating when reinforcement is necessary.

[1] By non-residential demand we mean commercial and industrial demand.

A key factor when carrying out a reinforcement assessment is the prediction of future network demand. Knowing the existing demand on a substation, the underlying growth rate and any future demand increases due to specific known developments allows an estimate to be made as to when a substation capacity will be insufficient to support demand in the future. With this knowledge, strategies can be developed to achieve optimal timing of network reinforcement.

Although network reinforcement is driven mainly by demand growth, other factors such as energy efficiency and integration of distributed generation have the potential to defer some demand-related network reinforcement. However, the networks should be provided with appropriate incentives to consider active network and demand type investments alongside conventional network development investments. Developing a robust investment assessment tool based on demand forecast methodology is of paramount importance for DNOs to meet their long-term licence conditions as economically and efficiently as possible.

### *15.5.1 Forecasting domestic electricity demand*

It is common practice within the electricity industry to calculate domestic electricity demand based on the combination of the annual average electricity unit consumption (kWh/year) and the maximum demand profile of a set of consumers. Studies of detailed demand data have indicated that daily demand profiles of consumers of the same type have a similar shape and also that the demand of a group of consumers is closely related to the annual electricity consumption of those consumers. This is the basis of a statistical analysis approach termed Demand Estimation Based on Units and Time (DEBUT),[2] which uses the above information to calculate the average maximum demand of a group of consumers while recognizing that the maximum demand of individual consumers may not occur at the same time. This measure of maximum average individual demand is called After Diversity Maximum Demand (ADMD), specified in kW, which is commonly used by distribution network planners to design new distribution networks.

One of the benefits of basing ADMD calculation on annual average electricity unit consumption is that it takes into account demand-influencing factors such as the size of dwellings and the availability of gas supply. This is depicted in Figure 15.1, which shows the annual average electricity unit consumption (kWh/year) for all Local Authority Districts (Boroughs in London) within EDF Energy Networks licensed

[2] Engineering Technical Report 115 (1988).

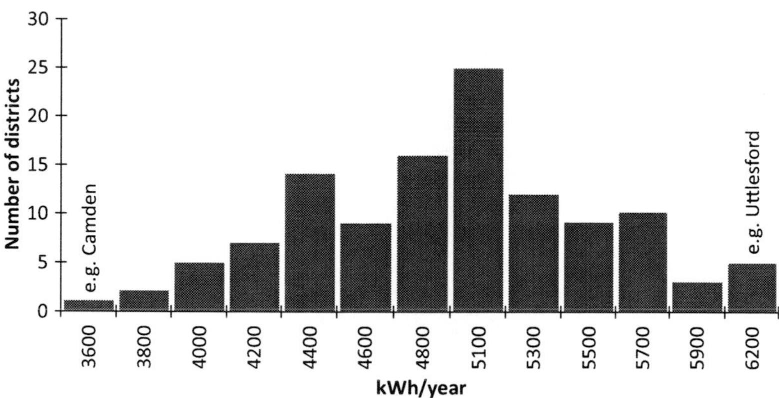


Figure 15.1 Average annual domestic electricity consumption per meter point (kWh).

areas. This information is published by the Department of Energy and Climate Change (DEEC) on an annual basis.[3]

As can be seen, average electricity consumption can range from 3,600 to 6,200 kWh/year and therefore using a single notional average would misrepresent regional consumption variations. For example, the average electricity consumption per dwelling in Islington is substantially less than in mid-Suffolk, as average properties in Islington would be smaller and proprieties in mid-Suffolk would have limited access to gas networks.

A crucial step in estimating the average domestic electricity demand going forward involves forecasting the growth in the number of electricity customers or the number of electricity meters since each electricity consumer has a meter, referred to as MPAN (Metering Point Administration Number). However, forecasting the number of MPANs directly is not always practicable and therefore alternative variables are required as a proxy to MPANs growth. On a theoretical level, dwellings, household numbers and MPANs are strongly related variables (see Table 15.1).

However, a study commissioned for EDF Energy Networks shows that the growth of households appears to overestimate the growth in MPANs, most notably in London. On the other hand growth in the number of MPANs appears to follow growth in the number of dwellings (Figure 15.2).

[3] DECC subnational energy consumption statistics (www.decc.gov.uk/en/content/cms/statistics/).

Table 15.1 *Measures of residential electricity demand*

| | |
|---|---|
| Household | One person or group of people living at the same address who share a living area or at least one meal per day. |
| Dwelling | A self-contained accommodation unit that contains all of its rooms and essential facilities – e.g. a shared dwelling could be made up of households that share a kitchen (but not a living area, otherwise they would be only one household). |
| MPAN | Metering point administration number – a unique number given to every electricity customer. |

Although the above analysis is based on the relatively short period of time for which EDF Energy Networks MPAN data are available, the one-to-one relationship between dwellings and MPANs seems reasonable as, in broad terms, new dwellings are expected to have their own electricity meter (MPAN) and hence represent a single new connection.

In the UK, long-term dwelling provision targets are set by the government and this information is publicly available at Local Authority District level (Boroughs in London).[4] Therefore using this information, together with the ADMD figures described previously, allows the expected long-term domestic demand to be derived at a Local Authority District level (Boroughs in London) as described in Equation 15.1:

$$\text{Domestic demand (kW)} = [\text{Number of dwellings}] \times [\text{ADMD/dwelling}] \qquad \text{Equation 15.1}$$

### *15.5.2 Forecasting non-domestic electricity demand*

Production theory in economics generally regards energy, labour and capital as the main input factors in the production processes. Within this framework, energy and labour can be viewed as complementary inputs. However, a change in the relative prices of labour and energy can, in the long run, lead to substitution of the relatively more expensive factor with the cheaper one (see Platchkov and Pollitt, this volume, for a longer-run perspective on this). Theory also suggests that in the short run the stock of capital is fixed while the use of labour can be more flexible. Hence an upward energy price shock in the short term can result in some reduced use of labour. In the long run the stock of capital becomes more flexible

[4] Regional Spatial Strategy Plans such as 'East of England Plan' (www.eera.gov.uk), 'South East of England Plan' (www.southeast-ra.gov.uk) and 'The London Plan' (www.london.gov.uk/thelondonplan).

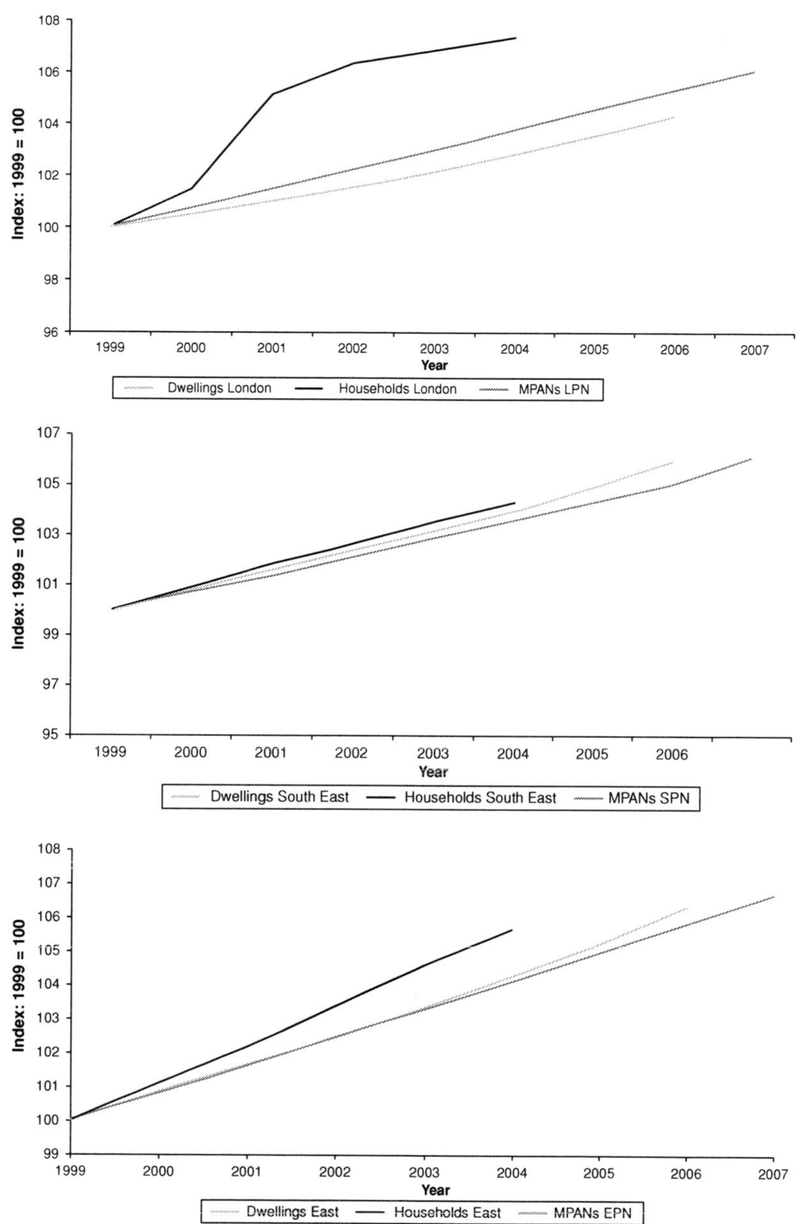


Figure 15.2 Comparison of measures of residential demand in three EDF energy networks service areas: LPN, SPN and EPN.

and some factor substitution in response to changes in relative prices can take place.

Gross Value Added (GVA) is a measure of economic activity that in principle encompasses all energy use in production processes whether these are substitutes for or complementary with the amount of labour input. A workplace-based measure of GVA (that allocates the income of commuters to the region in which they work) can be a good indicator of the industrial and commercial activity within the service area of a given DNO. However, local GVA is currently not available. Moreover, although GVA has interesting theoretical properties, the suitability of it for the purpose of the present model is uncertain and needs to be examined carefully in future versions of the model. The main concern is the extent to which the theoretical relationships between labour, energy and GVA or production still hold at disaggregated and fairly small geographic areas as required by the model.

Hence in this chapter the described methodology uses the number of jobs as a proxy for non-domestic demand growth as detailed projections at the appropriate level are publicly available. A practical advantage of using labour as a driver of non-residential demand is that it is more easily observable and measurable in physical terms and hence is more easily translatable to specific investments in load-related network assets where past engineering knowledge and experience can also aid the investment decisions.

The electricity consumption statistics in the form of kWh/employee for all Local Authority Districts in the UK are published by the Department of Energy and Climate Change (DECC) on an annual basis.[5] As can be seen in Figure 15.3, the average annual electricity consumption per employee varies significantly among the Local Authority Districts within EDF Energy Networks' area of operation. The figure illustrates the diversity of non-domestic activity, which must be taken into account while forecasting non-domestic demand.

In order to translate the above information into demand (kW/employee), as opposed to energy (kWh/employee), the current methodology assumes a notional load factor, which takes a view of the average usage profiles of employees. The baseline figure assumes a usage profile of eight hours/day, six days/week, fifty weeks/year, which is equivalent to 2,400h a year.[6] The latter together with regional electricity consumption

[5] DECC Subnational energy consumption statistics (www.decc.gov.uk/en/content/cms/statistics/).

[6] The assumptions reflect the fact that some industrial and commercial users work for six or seven days/week – i.e. more than the average five days/week.

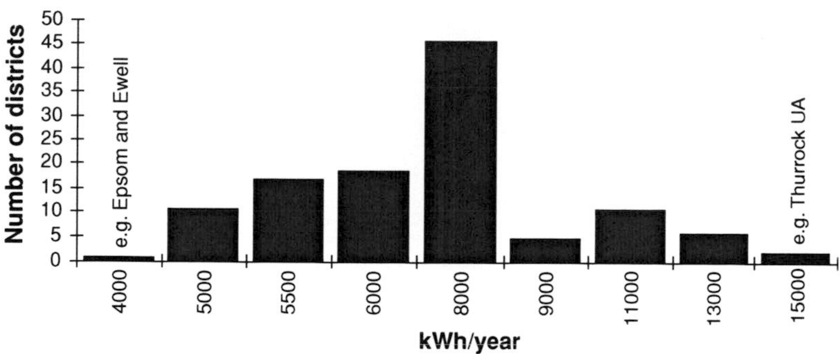


Figure 15.3 Average annual industrial and commercial electricity consumption per employee (kWh).
*Source*: Oxera analysis.

per employee (Figure 15.3) produces a regional demand per employee (kW/employee) as in equation 15.2.

$$\text{kW/employee} = \text{kWh/employee} \div \text{usage profile} \qquad \text{Equation 15.2}$$

The regional annual employment targets for all Local Authority Districts are currently published by the UK government. This information provides a strong indication of the level of non-domestic activity, which can then be converted into electricity demand. This is achieved by multiplying regional employment targets by the regional demand per employee as in equation 15.3:

$$\begin{aligned}&\text{Regional non-domestic demand (kW)}\\&\quad = [\text{regional annual employment targets}]\\&\qquad \times [\text{regional demand per employee (kW/employee)}]\end{aligned} \qquad \text{Equation 15.3}$$

### *15.5.3 Regional electricity demand growth*

The above sections describe the main factors that have an impact on domestic and non-domestic demand growth. A strength of the methodology described here is that it is based on publicly available information published by the Department of Energy and Climate Change, Regional Development Agencies and other UK government institutions. Moreover, it allows all UK DNOs to take into account UK government housing and employment targets and convert this information into electricity demand growth.

(a) 2010

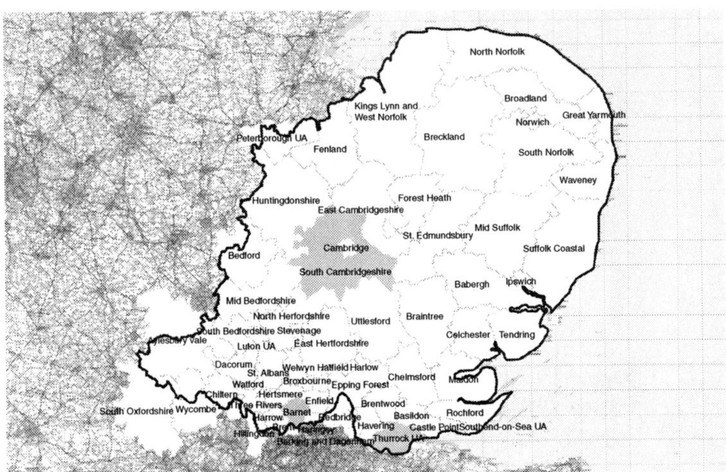


(b) 2015

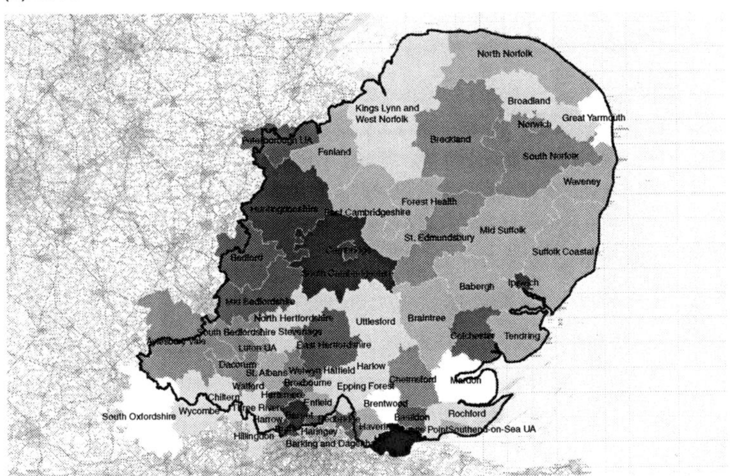


Figure 15.4 Regional demand growth in 2010, 2015 and 2020.
*Scale:* 1:1,500,000.

Figure 15.4 illustrates the outcome of this regional electricity demand growth methodology. It depicts the regional demand growth for one of EDF Energy Networks' licensed areas, EPN,[7] up to 2020. Housing and

[7] Available at www.edfenergy.com/products-services/networks, last accessed 31 August 2010.

(c) 2020

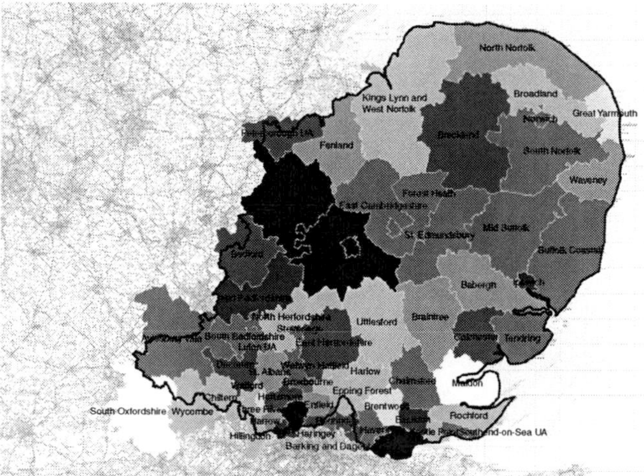


Figure 15.4 (*cont.*)

employment long-term targets were obtained directly from the East of England Plan.[8]

Figure 15.4 depicts the growth in maximum demand (MW) for all local authority districts within EDF Energy Networks' EPN distribution network. Darker shades reflect higher demand growth. This provides a clear view of sections of the network where demand growth will be more significant in coming years, which in turn provides a high-level indication of where demand-related network investment might be required.

### *15.5.4 Disaggregated electricity demand growth*

Regional demand growth forecasts are important as they provide a high-level indication of the main electricity demand growth areas. However, as part of any network reinforcement assessment, knowing the existing demand on an electrical substation, and consequently being able to estimate when its capacity will be insufficient to support predicted demand, is of paramount importance.

The next stage of the demand growth methodology here described is to calculate demand growth at a primary substation level (typically 33/11 kV), directly from the local authority district (regional) demand

[8] East of England Plan (available at www.eera.gov.uk, last accessed 31 August 2010).

(a) 2010

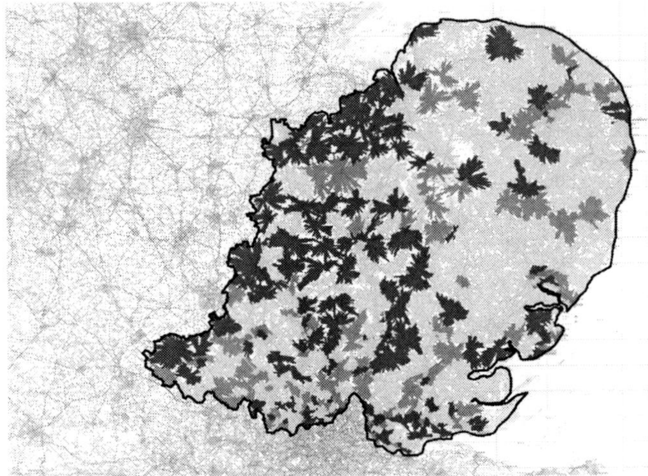

Figure 15.5 Primary substations risk level in 2010, 2015 and 2020. *Scale:* 1:1,500,000.

growth described above. This is achieved using the transformer rating and geographical location of the secondary substations (typically 11/0.4 kV), fed from each primary substation. Initially, the regional demand growth is spread across all secondary substations in a pro rata way. For example, this means that a 100 kVA secondary substation will be allocated twice as much load as a 50 kVA. This demand is then aggregated back to a primary substation level, producing highly disaggregated demand growth forecasts. This is an important step in the overall methodology as it allows for primary substations that supply neighbouring local authority districts which have different housing and employment targets. This has been possible through the use of GIS (geographic information system) tools, as they take into account the geographical location of district boundaries and primary and secondary substations.

Once demand growth forecast at a primary substation level is obtained, it is possible to identify those substations whose capacity would be insufficient to support predicted demand. Figure 15.5 depicts the level of risk that each primary substation within EDF Energy EPN distribution network would be subject to due to the regional demand growth portrayed in Figure 15.4 above.

Each primary substation is shown as an irregularly shaped cluster which represents the area it supplies. Here risk is defined as demand as a

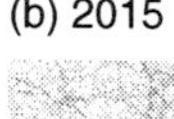

(b) 2015

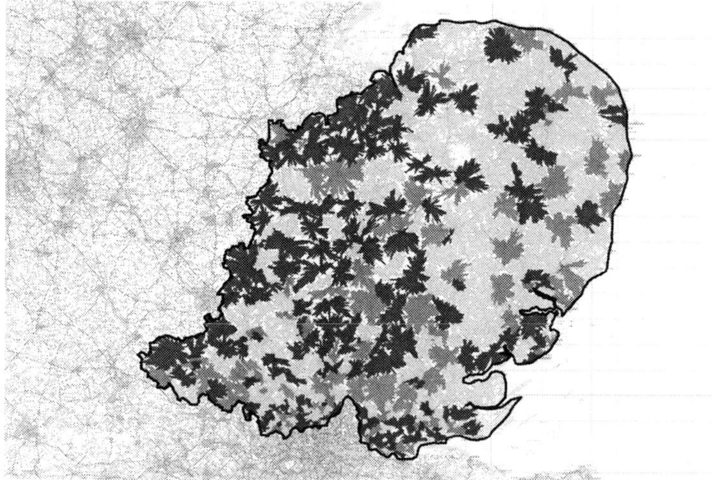

(c) 2020

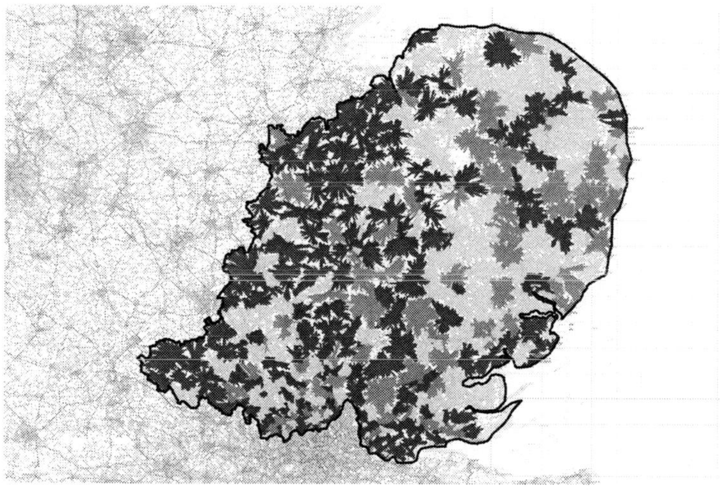

Figure 15.5 (*cont.*)

percentage of the primary substation capacity under N-1 conditions[9] (firm capacity). Because of confidentiality reasons the firm capacity of the primary substations shown in Figure 15.4 has been randomly generated and does not therefore represent their real firm capacity. Risk higher than

[9] Note that this is a simplification of N-1 conditions set in ER P2/6.

100 per cent is shown in the darkest shade, greater than 85 per cent in the middle shade and risk levels lower than 85 per cent are shown in the lightest shade.

As shown in the above illustration, the model produces a clear picture of the primary substations that might need reinforcement, due to demand growth, in order to maintain an acceptable level of risk. This risk level is set by the Engineering Recommendation P2/6. Moreover, the model outputs provide planning engineers with an analytical and visual aid to identify low-risk primary substations adjacent to high-risk ones. With this information, the possibility to transfer load from high-risk primary substations to neighbouring low-risk ones could be assessed. This could be a cost-efficient way to support demand growth, defer reinforcements and reduce the level of risk of capacity-constrained substations.

## 15.6 Relevance of the model for active network and demand and concluding remarks

As demonstrated in the previous section, companies can use models (such as that of EDF described above) as subsystem network investment planning tools. The EDF model (for example) can use historical load development data and demand-growth prognoses to determine emerging load-related investments in specific parts of the network at a detailed level. We also noted that network investment needs are capital intensive, most of the assets have long economic lives, and are often sunk costs upon investment.

The EDF model has practical applications for the evaluation of active network and demand options by coordination of these with the need of the network for upgrade and expansion in response to load growth. It can do so by feeding into other models and assessments of the need for conventional investments at network and subnetwork levels. In particular, the model can be used to assess the potential for the use of competing generic network and demand activating options in relation to the characteristics and expected future needs of specific parts of the network.

Given the right regulatory incentives, such a holistic approach to investments can increase the long-term economic and operational efficiency of the network. Such a view of investment assessments will be fairly similar to the concept of integrated resource planning (IRP) used by some public utility commissions in the US. Under IRP, regulated utilities are required to evaluate their generation capacity expansion plans not only in isolation but also in relation to alternative supply sources such as other suppliers or demand-side options.

Similarly, the corresponding factors in the context of load capacity expansion in distribution networks in response to demand growth are DG sources, combined heat and power (CHP) microgeneration technologies, active demand and smart meters, and various energy-saving and efficiency alternatives.

At the same time, the level and nature of demand for electricity services is likely to change. For example, the expected emergence of the large-scale adoption of electric vehicles (EVs) will add a fairly unknown but important type of demand to the system. As discussed in Marsden and Hess (this volume), the effect of large-scale electric vehicles on total energy demand may not be very significant. However, their effect on system load could be considerable. A large-scale adoption of EVs will require domestic as well as public charging facilities. In particular, provision of public charging facilities is likely to require fast-charging and load-intensive facilities in order to encourage their use. The development of the infrastructure required for this will be costly and will need careful assessment with regards to network planning. Similarly there may be significant effects as a result of the electrification of space heating via heat pumps (as discussed in Clarke *et al.*, this volume).

A site-specific but integrated approach to network investment that includes the range of new supply and demand options will be clearly beneficial and can be aided by the type of modelling discussed here. Achieving the full potential of the above options requires development of new suitable regulatory incentives. However, a discussion of such appropriate regulation and incentive models is outside the scope of the present chapter.

## References

CEPA (2009). Ofgem: Research into Volume and Input Price Uncertainty for Electricity Distribution Price Control Review 5, Submitted to Ofgem by Cambridge Economic Policy Associates Ltd.

Frontier Economics (2007). The Association between Unexpected Changes in Electricity Volume and GDP Growth for Residential Customers, Report prepared for IPART, May.

Hyndman, R.J. (2007). Extended Models for Long-Term Peak Half-Hourly Electricity Demand for South Australia, Business and Economic Forecasting Unit, Monash University.

Jamasb, T. and Pollitt, M. (2007). Incentive regulation of electricity distribution networks: lessons of experience from Britain, *Energy Policy*, **35**(12): 6163–87.

Jamasb, T. and Pollitt, M. (2008). Security of supply and regulation of energy networks, *Energy Policy*, **36**: 4584–9.

Joskow, P. (2008). Incentive regulation and its application to electricity networks, *Review of Network Economics*, 7(4): 547–60.

Mork, K.A. (1989). Oil and the macroeconomy when prices go up and down: an extension of Hamilton's results, *Journal of Political Economy*, **97**(3): 740–4.

Niesten, E. (2010). Identifying Options for Regulating the Coordination of Network Investments with Investments in Distributed Electricity Generation, CPB Discussion Paper, No. 141.

Ofgem (2004). *Electricity Distribution Price Control Review Final Proposals, Ref. 265/04*, London: Ofgem.

Ofgem (2009). *Electricity Distribution Price Control Review Final Proposals, Ref. 144/09*, London: Ofgem.

Ofgem (2010). *Regulating Energy Networks for the Future: RPI-X@20 Recommendations Consultation*, Ref. 91/10, London: Ofgem.

Ofwat/Ofgem (2006). *Financing Networks: A Discussion Paper, Office of Water Regulation/Office of Gas and Electricity Markets*, London: Ofgem.

Pollitt, M. (2005). The role of efficiency estimates in regulatory price reviews: Ofgem's approach to benchmarking electricity networks, *Utilities Policy*, **13**(4): 279–88.

Pollitt, M. and Bialek, J. (2008). Electricity network investment and regulation for a low carbon future, in Grubb, M., Jamasb, T. and Pollitt, M. (eds.), *Delivering a Low- Carbon Electricity System: Technologies, Economics, and Policy*, Cambridge: Cambridge University Press, pp. 183–206.

Saplacan, R. (2008). Competition in electricity distribution, *Utilities Policy*, **16**(4): 231–7.

# 16 The potential impact of policy and legislation on the energy demands of UK buildings and implications for the electrical network

*Joe A. Clarke, Jun Hong, Cameron M. Johnstone, Jae Min Kim and Paul G. Tuohy*

## 16.1 Introduction

The EU has promoted energy efficiency in the built environment through policy and legislation such as the Energy Performance of Buildings Directive (EPBD) (EU, 2002) and also through funded research projects including several focused on the definition, validation and dissemination of the EU Passive House standard for new and renovated buildings. The UK and its devolved parliaments have developed their own policy and legislation aimed at reducing energy use and carbon emissions associated with the built environment largely in synergy with the EU. In this chapter we review a selection of the EU and UK legislative approaches.

Building on this review, the types of new and renovated buildings that these policy initiatives will tend to promote are illustrated; and an analysis of some of these probable future buildings is undertaken to illustrate the likely changes in energy demands that will result. Some key factors which have large future uncertainties are identified and potential consequences of these uncertainties projected. Finally we discuss the potential increased use of heat pumps for heating and cooling and the increased deployment of photovoltaic and CHP (combined heat and power) generation systems and discuss some of the potential challenges for the generation, grid and distribution network.

## 16.2 EU policy, legislation and standards relating to energy performance of buildings

A major milestone in the ongoing promotion of energy efficiency by the EU was the adoption into legislation of the 2002 Energy Performance of Buildings Directive (EPBD) (EU, 2002). One of the key elements of this legislation made it mandatory for all member states to implement the rating of energy performance and for these energy performance ratings to be available at the point of sale or rental of a building. The member states were given a number of years to implement the legislation with almost all having completed this implementation by January 2009.

In support of the EPBD implementation the European Committee for Standardization (CEN) reviewed and revised the relevant standards. A total of thirty European (EN) and twenty-four international (EN ISO) standards were drafted or updated including those relating to calculation methods, minimum performance levels, energy performance certificates and inspections of heating and cooling equipment (Roulet and Anderson 2006). These standards are in general not prescriptive but allow a range of options giving member states freedom to tailor implementation to local circumstances. Some of the key elements that are open for member states to decide on are: the use of calculated (known as 'asset') ratings or actual monitored energy use (known as 'operational') ratings, the use of primary energy or carbon-related factors for aggregation of performance for the different energy uses and fuel types, the selection of the calculation method (simplified or more complex methods) and the selection of input parameters for the performance calculations representing local climates and patterns of building use for each building type. The choices made by member states can have a large influence on ratings and the types of buildings that are ultimately realized as explained later in this chapter.

To promote competitiveness and innovation in the area of energy efficiency the EU funds a wide range of research and dissemination projects through the Intelligent Energy Europe (IEE) programme largely aimed at the development of new solutions and the establishment and dissemination of best practice. Within the IEE programme, projects relevant to energy demand and supply in the built environment are grouped under both energy efficiency (EU 'SAVE' projects) and alternative energy supply areas (EU 'ALTENAR' projects) with hundreds of separate projects having been funded.

Since 1998 the EU has funded projects aimed initially at validating and then disseminating the Passive House standard for adoption across the EU. While in English the name 'Passive House' would suggest a standard only for dwellings, in fact the Passive House standard is applicable to all building types including offices, supermarkets, schools, sports facilities, etc. The first EU project related to Passive House was the Cost Effective Passive Houses as EU Standard (CEPHEUS) project from 1998 to 2001 (CEPHEUS, 2010). Under the CEPHEUS project around 250 dwellings were built and monitored across five central and northern EU countries with very positive results showing a 90 per cent reduction in space heating energy demands. The Passive Houses were compared to standard buildings and some dwellings built to an alternative low-energy standard. Based on these positive results the EU funded a further raft of projects aimed at extending and disseminating the Passive House standard across the whole of the EU. These projects include: the extension of the Passive House standard to southern EU countries (PASSIVE-ON project) and northern EU countries (NORTHPASS); the development of a Passive House retrofit kit (E-RETROFIT-KIT); the promotion of EU Passive Houses (PEP) and creation of a Passive House network of promoters (PASS-NET); and the development of training and accreditation as Passive House Designer (CEPH).

The Passive House standard involves demand minimization through high-quality construction methods and equipment that maximize the use of passive energy gains and minimize but do not eliminate the need for energy inputs. The approach is aimed at delivering a building with excellent comfort and high cost effectiveness. Principles are: excellent insulation, e.g. wall, roof and floor thermal transmittance (U-value) less than 0.15 $W/m^2.K$;[1] excellent construction details (thermal bridge free, air-tightness of construction better than 0.6 air changes per hour at 50 Pa);[2] excellent glazing (U-value less than 0.85 $W/m^2.K$ including installation, solar radiation transmittance greater than 50 per cent); high-efficiency ventilation system with heat recovery; comfortable summer temperatures; and high-efficiency appliances and lighting. Compliance with Passive House criteria is demonstrated through the use of the Passive House Planning Package (PHPP) calculation method and submission of construction details and construction air-tightness test results. The PHPP calculates the space heating energy demand and the total operational primary energy demand for all energy uses. To achieve the Passive House standard the calculated heating and cooling energy demand must be less than 15 $kWh/m^2$ per year and the primary energy demand less than 120 $kWh/m^2$ per year. The PHPP uses the CEN standard monthly calculation method and was found to give good agreement with actual monitored energy use in the CEPHEUS project. The Passive House standard aims to minimize the requirement for delivered and primary energy, but while it allows the contribution of building integrated or local renewable energy generation to be quantified, it does not allow the renewable electricity generation to be used as an offset for primary energy use – rather, the Passive House standard focuses only on demand reduction.

[1] $W/m^2.K$ is a measure of thermal conductivity, giving the number of watts lost per metre squared for a given temperature differential (K, in degrees kelvin).

[2] Pa is a measure of pressure (in Pascals).

The EU is currently formulating an update to the EPBD (EPBD2) with a target date of 2011 for legislation. The details are in consultation phase and not yet finalized; however, there are strong indications that there will be a strengthening of the criteria for application of energy performance standards to renovations and an increase in the building types that will be required to display energy rating certificates to include shops and other buildings with public access. Additionally it is probable that minimum standards will be defined for 'nearly zero energy buildings' that will have to be met by new or renovated public buildings by 2018 and all new or renovated buildings by 2020. This 'nearly zero energy building' category is described in consultations as a very high-performance building with significant energy supply from renewable sources. Member states will define this category themselves for their local context and take account of cost effectiveness, but it is proposed that it be mandatory that they include a numeric indicator of primary energy use in kWh/m$^2$ per year.

## 16.3 UK policy, legislation and standards relating to energy performance of buildings

Since the 1970s the UK building regulations have included energy performance, initially through prescriptive standards for insulation of building elements such as walls, roof, etc., but since the 1990s the regulations for dwellings have been based on a performance calculation taking account of building dimensions and the properties of building constructions and systems for heating and hot water, etc. The calculation method established in the 1990s was the government's Standard Assessment Procedure for dwellings (SAP) (BRE, 2010). Initially the calculated performance was output as a SAP score based on the predicted running cost per m$^2$ assuming a standard occupancy pattern and climate; since 2002 SAP has been extended to output additional parameters representing the calculated $CO_2$ emissions. The 2005 version of SAP also included calculations to be used for the implementation of the EPBD requirements for energy performance certificates (EPCs). The format of EPCs for dwellings in the UK includes the rating of performance against an A to G scale for both the SAP score (based on running cost) and a $CO_2$-based Environmental Index (EI) score (1 to 100 based on $CO_2$ emissions). The $CO_2$-based EI score satisfies the EPBD requirement for an aggregation including downstream energy conversion. Building regulations for dwellings have been revised at roughly five-year intervals and since 2002 have been based on the calculated carbon performance output from SAP (Dwelling Emissions Rate, DER) compared to a target emissions rate (TER). The target emissions rate to be achieved is incrementally improved with each generation of the regulations with the 2006–7 regulations achieving around a 28 per cent improvement over 2002 regulation minimum performance. The scope of the UK SAP calculations includes space and hot water heating, auxiliary energy for pumps and fans, ventilation systems and lights but does not include energy used for appliances or cooking.

There are some important differences between the EU Passive House PHPP calculations and the UK SAP calculations – although both use the simplified underlying calculations given in the CEN Standard 13790 the input assumptions are significantly different. The result is that the SAP method predicts significantly less space heating energy demand than PHPP primarily due to lower gains assumed than in SAP (Scottish Government, 2010). The PHPP calculation method was found to predict around 80 per cent more heating than that predicted by SAP. The PHPP calculations have been validated for Passive Houses through the monitoring of actual energy use in Passive Houses in the EU CEPHEUS project.

Non-domestic buildings in the UK are beyond the scope of the SAP calculation method and for non-domestic buildings the regulations relied on elemental performance standards until the EPBD implementation drove the development of the UK National Calculation Method (NCM) for non-dwellings (BRE 2010a). The NCM is aligned with the CEN standard 13790, which allows performance of non-domestic buildings to be calculated either using a simplified monthly energy balance calculation or with a more complex dynamic simulation method where a building is beyond the scope of the simplified method. Dynamic simulation takes more detailed account of physical processes and shorter timescale effects. NCM-based calculations are the basis of regulation compliance and EPCs for non-dwellings; EPCs and compliance are based only on the NCM-calculated $CO_2$ emissions and include space and hot water heating, auxiliary energy for pumps and fans, ventilation systems and lights but do not include energy used for equipment (IT, etc.) appliances or cooking. Some limited comparison between the UK NCM calculations and the EU PHPP calculations for an office building has been carried out with both methods giving similar space heating demand results (Scottish Government, 2010).

For public buildings in England and Wales a different strategy has been adopted from that in the other UK regions. While in the other regions all EPCs are from asset ratings based on calculated emissions for regulated energy uses, in England and Wales the EPCs for public buildings over 1,000m$^2$ are generated from operational ratings based on all actual energy used. This is providing a useful data source as the energy use data for the

18,000 public buildings are available in the public domain and are providing interesting comparisons between predicted energy use by architects and what is actually achieved in practice (Booth, 2008), with some buildings advertised as virtually non-polluting achieving only an 'E' rating.

In Scotland and in England and Wales the governments have proposed future building regulations for consultation which demand improvements in $CO_2$ emissions beyond the current minimum performance levels. In Scotland a 30 per cent reduction in regulated energy uses (which excludes energy used for appliances as stated above) has been proposed for 2010; a 60 per cent reduction for 2013; and a 100 per cent reduction by 2017 (Sullivan, 2007). In England and Wales there is a proposal of net zero carbon for all energy uses including appliances by 2016 which equates to a calculated 140 per cent reduction in regulated energy uses (i.e. 100 per cent reduction in regulated energy use plus 40 per cent from local electrical generation technologies such as PV to offset the currently unregulated energy use by appliances) (Communities-Gov, 2010). The UK government has announced a tax incentive for achieving this net zero carbon standard in new buildings (to become effective in 2016) and is also proposing a raft of payments and feed-in tariffs as incentives for those who install renewable generation equipment.

The net zero carbon 2016 standard is mirrored in level 6 of the UK government's Code for Sustainable Homes (CSH) which defines voluntary levels of performance (code levels 1 to 6) that go beyond the building regulations (Communities-Gov, 2010a). The CSH has only been adopted so far in England and Wales. The Passive House standard which is based on demand minimization achieves around code level 4; significant local generation from renewable technologies is required to achieve levels 5 and 6 (one code level 6 demonstration house deployed 46m$^2$ of PV on a large curved roof structure to achieve the standard). Although the code level 6 building has a calculated net carbon performance of zero, this building requires a robust grid connection as the generation and consumption are not synchronized.

The Scottish government has not adopted the CSH. One concern is that it may not be appropriate or cost effective in the Scottish context to aim to install building-integrated generation technologies to achieve the higher code levels (Scotland has many flats without large roof areas per dwelling; it has many larger-scale renewable generation opportunities such as wind, hydro, tidal and wave – these larger-scale generation opportunities would appear to have some potential cost advantage). The difference in approach between Scotland and England can be viewed as two distinct policy options: 1. Minimize demand plus decarbonize the grid through large-scale renewable generation, or 2. Minimize demand plus generate locally on buildings. Currently in the UK both approaches are being promoted in parallel.

## 16.4 The probable buildings of the future?

In order to support their policy on future building regulations and quantify the impact of improved carbon emission limits on the construction industry and consumers, the Scottish government commissioned a number of research projects, some of which we explore here as examples of the types of buildings that may result from proposed future regulation.

A joint study was carried out comprising cost analysis by Turner & Townsend, architectural analysis by the Holmes Architects and energy and carbon performance analysis by the University of Strathclyde (Turner & Townsend Ltd, 2008). The study investigated a range of options for achieving carbon reductions beyond the 2007 minimum regulatory performance for a typical detached house, a typical mid-floor flat and a typical two-storey naturally ventilated science park-type office building. The baseline buildings were all naturally ventilated and space and water heating was with a gas condensing boiler. The research brief specified that the current regulatory calculation methods were to be used to quantify the carbon emissions (BRE, 2010a, 2010b).

Initially the impacts of individually applied improvement measures on building performance were analyzed and then some combinations of improvement measures applied together. Some of the analysis is summarized below in sections 16.4.1 and 16.4.2. Two levels of improvement to the building insulation and glazing standards were evaluated 1. Passive House, and 2. An intermediate insulation and glazing level – approximately half way to Passive House. The system improvement measures considered included the application of heat pumps; in this study two heat pump types were evaluated: ground source (GSHP) and air source (ASHP), and in this evaluation the seasonal co-efficients of performance (COP) for the systems were set at 3.2 and 2.5 for space heating respectively, and the COPs for water heating were de-rated appropriately (×0.7) to account for the reduced efficiency of typical heat pumps at higher output temperatures. The study also looked at the deployment of combined heat and power (CHP) systems (fuelled by either gas or biomass), biomass boiler systems, photovoltaic (PV) electricity generation systems and solar thermal systems for hot water. It should be noted that the COPs of the heat pumps used in the Scottish government study are current typical values and that heat pumps with significantly higher performance are possible.

### *16.4.1 Improvement measures applied to a dwelling to achieve future standards*

For the typical 90m$^2$ detached house built to meet the 2007 regulations in the Scottish government study to achieve the 30 per cent improvement in $CO_2$ emissions proposed for 2010 regulations, the following options appeared feasible:

Individual measures that achieved the 2010 30 per cent improvement target:

- Biomass boiler.
- Gas or biomass CHP.
- Passive House standard building envelope.

Combined measures that achieved the 2010 30 per cent improvement target:

- Heat pump (high COP) plus solar thermal system.
- Intermediate building envelope plus heat pump.
- Intermediate building envelope plus solar thermal system.
- Intermediate building envelope plus PV.
- Any other combination which includes the above individual or combined measures.

For the detached house to achieve the 60 per cent improvement in $CO_2$ emissions required by the proposed 2013 regulations, the following options appeared feasible:

Individual measures that achieved the 2013 60 per cent improvement target:

- Biomass boiler or biomass CHP.

Combined measures that achieved the 2013 60 per cent improvement target:

- Passive House building envelope plus heat pump (high COP) plus solar thermal plus heat recovery ventilation (high efficiency).
- Passive House building envelope plus heat pump (high COP) plus solar thermal plus PV.
- Passive House building envelope and gas CHP.
- Any other combination which includes the above individual or combined measures.

For the 2007 detached house to achieve the 100 per cent reduction in regulated emissions proposed in Scotland or 140 per cent reduction targets suggested for the 2016 net zero carbon house proposed in England

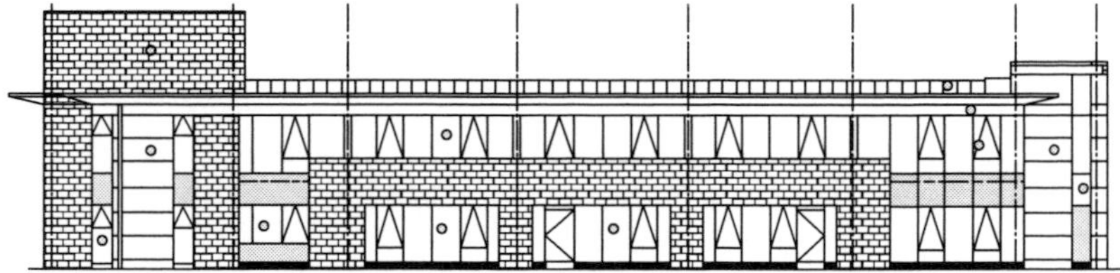

Figure 16.1 The example office.
*Source:* Tuohy (2009).

would require either biomass CHP or combinations of the above measures combined with much larger local generation systems such as PV, CHP or wind turbines. An example of a zero net carbon house is the CSH level 6 'Lighthouse' built at the Building Research Establishment (BRE) innovations park. The Lighthouse is similar to a Passive House with added electrical generation (Kingspan, 2010).

Measures that achieved the 2016 target (code level 6) in the 'Lighthouse':

- Passive House building envelope.
- High-efficiency heat recovery ventilation system.
- Solar thermal hot water system.
- Biomass heating for winter use.
- High-efficiency appliances.
- High-efficiency lighting.
- 46m$^2$ PV electrical generation (approx 5 kW peak of PV (kWp)).

### *16.4.2 Improvement measures applied to a naturally ventilated office to achieve future standards*

The same study for the Scottish government investigated options to achieve the targeted 30 per cent and 60 per cent $CO_2$ emissions reductions for a two-storey naturally ventilated office (Figure 16.1); a brief summary is given here.

Individual measures that achieved the 2010 30 per cent improvement target:

- No individual measures achieved 30 per cent; however, Passive House standard building envelope on its own achieved 26 per cent improvement and mechanical ventilation with heat recovery (MVHR) on its own achieved 21 per cent.

Possible combined measures that achieved the 2010 30 per cent improvement target:

- ANY combination that included both a fabric improvement plus MVHR achieved a 30 per cent improvement over 2007 standards.

Individual measures that achieved the 2013 60 per cent improvement target:

- No individual measures achieved 60 per cent target.

Possible combined measures that achieved the 2013 60 per cent improvement target:

- Passive House envelope plus MVHR plus Heat Pump (high COP).
- Intermediate envelope plus MVHR plus gas CHP or biomass heating.
- Intermediate envelope plus MVHR plus Heat Pump plus PV.

### *16.4.3 Improvement measures applied to a naturally ventilated office to achieve future standards – possible adoption of mechanical cooling systems?*

The same science park office was used in another study which looked at the possible adoption of cooling in future office buildings (Tuohy, 2009). This looked at the calculated performance of the office for three service strategies: naturally ventilated (NV), mechanically ventilated (MV) and mechanically ventilated and cooled (HVAC). Three levels of building fabric and building systems performance were analyzed based on current typical, 2008 best available and an advanced level of performance representing the probable future best practice. The advanced level of fabric was again set as the Passive House standard. The 2007 typical systems all have heating through an 87 per cent efficiency gas boiler while the 2008 best available and advanced system performance scenarios assume reversible variable refrigerant flow (vrf) heat pump systems. The high-level results are summarized in Figure 16.2, Figure 16.3 and Figure 16.4, and the key to these figures is explained in Table 16.1.

It can be argued from this analysis that it is easier to achieve building regulation compliance for new buildings where a services approach with mechanical cooling is chosen than a naturally ventilated approach due to the higher allowed emissions in the regulations. The adoption of cooling also avoids the need to demonstrate comfortable summer temperature performance and avoids the perceived risks associated with the performance of natural ventilation. Overall it appears likely that there will be increased adoption of mechanical cooling.

The study shows, similar to the earlier analysis, that to achieve future emission reduction targets mechanical ventilation with heat recovery and heat pump technologies will be possible solutions. The study also suggests that with 2008 best practice systems the performance of all service strategies is approximately equivalent at 17 $kgCO_2/m^2$ p.a. (this

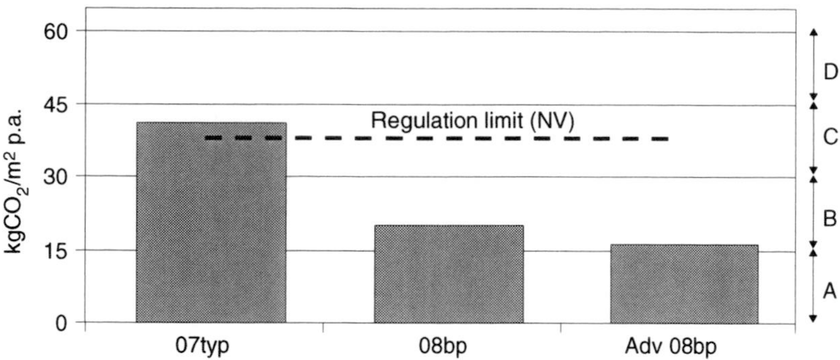


Figure 16.2 Carbon performance and energy ratings for the naturally ventilated (NV) design options calculated using SBEM.
*Source:* Tuohy (2009).

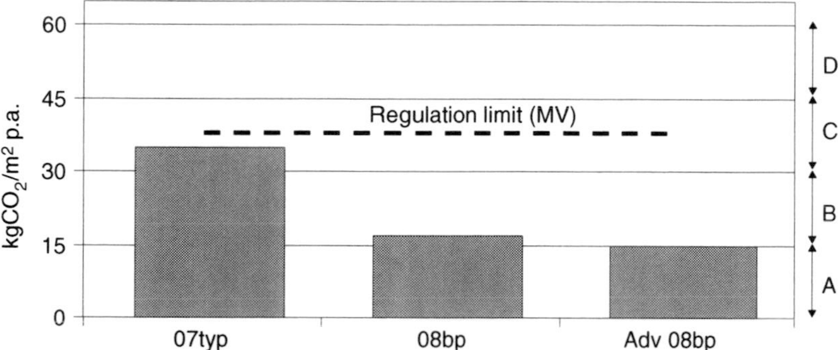


Figure 16.3 Carbon performance and energy ratings for the mechanically ventilated (MV) design options with heat recovery and no cooling.
*Source:* Tuohy (2009).

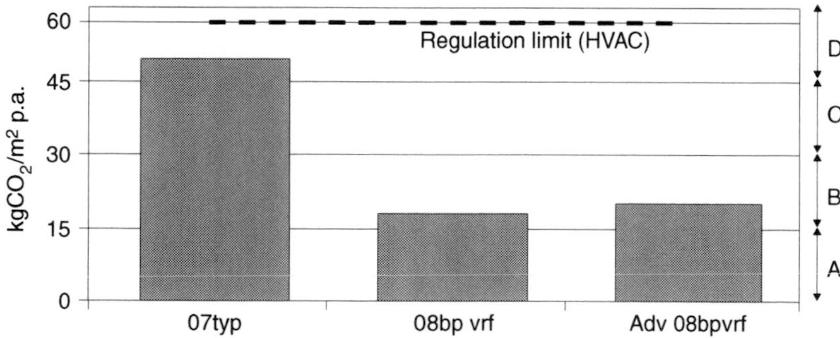


Figure 16.4 Carbon performance and energy ratings for the mechanically ventilated and cooled (HVAC) design options.
*Source:* Tuohy (2009).

Table 16.1 *Key to graph labels for combinations of construction and system performance levels*

| | | Construction performance level | |
|---|---|---|---|
| Key to graph labels: | | 2007 typical | Advanced |
| System performance level | 2007 typical | 07typ | Adv 07typ |
| 2008 best practice | 08bp | Adv 08bp | |
| Advanced | Adv | Adv Adv | |

equivalent calculated result may be optimistic given that historically more highly serviced buildings when monitored have been found to use higher levels of energy).

### *16.4.4 Summary of probable characteristics of future building types*

The current building regulation compliance calculations do not include emissions from appliance and equipment energy use despite their increasing importance. In the future it is likely that these energy uses will be included in regulations, as the EU Passive House, the voluntary Code for Sustainable Homes and the Operational Ratings for public buildings all do include these emissions and are likely to inform future regulations. Separate EU and global initiatives on energy performance and labelling of energy-using appliances and IT equipment (such as Energy Star, etc.) are already well established.

In summary the improvements in the requirements for compliance with building regulations and other standards suggest that future new and renovated dwellings will increasingly have the following characteristics:

- Passive House standard of thermal envelope
- Mechanical ventilation with heat recovery
- Solar thermal hot water
- Heat pump systems for heating and hot water
- CHP systems for heating and hot water
- Biomass systems for heating and hot water
- Energy efficient appliances, IT equipment and lights
- Photovoltaic electricity generation.

And future non-domestic new build and renovated buildings will increasingly have the following characteristics:

- Mechanical ventilation with heat recovery
- Heat pump systems for both heating and cooling
- Energy efficient IT equipment, appliances and lights

- CHP or biomass systems for heating and hot water
- Photovoltaic electricity generation.

## 16.5 Other factors influencing the probable buildings of the future

Grid carbon emission factors (or primary energy factors) and also cost-effectiveness (impacted by fuel costs and feed-in tariffs) will have significant impact on the measures chosen for future new build and renovation.

In the UK government's legislation the $CO_2$ emissions calculation on which the building standards are based is dependent on the emissions factors allocated to each of the different fuels ($kgCO_2$ per kWh of fuel used). The emissions factor associated with the electricity supplied from the grid is extremely important and has been the subject of much recent debate. In the UK calculation method grid electricity consumed in the building is associated with one emissions factor related to the overall grid generation mix while there is a second higher emissions factor which is derived only from the fossil fuel generated portion of the grid; this higher emissions factor is applied to electricity generated in the building (e.g. PV, wind turbine or CHP) as it is expected that this will reduce grid generation through fossil fuels as these would be adjusted down first.

The UK grid as a whole has been gradually reducing its carbon intensity from around 1.1 $kgCO_2$/kWh in 1970 to around 0.55 $kgCO_2$/kWh today largely through the switch to gas from more carbon-intensive fuels such as coal and oil. There are several differing projections for how the grid will perform in the future and a wide range of possible scenarios; actual outcome will depend on UK and global political and economic factors. UK government projections range from 0.29 to 0.43 $kgCO_2$/kWh for the 2020 UK grid.

The value of the emission factors has a large impact on the calculated performance of different technologies which use or generate electricity and will have a large impact on which technologies will be selected. To illustrate this effect two grid scenarios representing a high-carbon future grid (0.54 and 0.73 $kgCO_2$/kWh for whole grid and fossil fuel portion of the grid respectively) and a low-carbon future grid (0.3 and 0.4) are investigated. The building heating systems considered for the two grid scenarios include a range of CHP systems (gas-fuelled micro-CHP (uCHP), community CHP (comCHP) and fuel cell CHP (FCCHP) with different overall and electrical efficiencies, (i.e. 87 per cent (12e) implies 87 per cent overall fuel efficiency with 12 per cent electrical generation efficiency and 75 per cent heat generation efficiency, etc.) and heat pumps of different co-efficient of performance (COP) levels (air source heat pumps

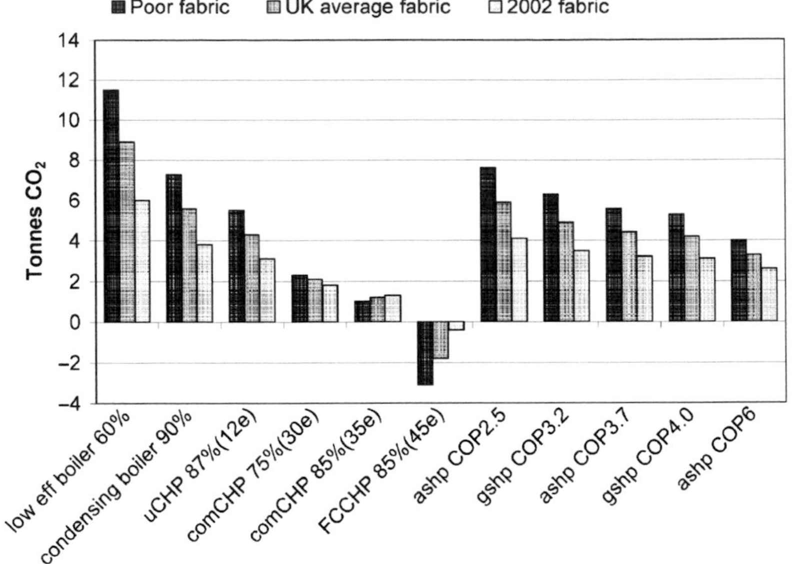


Figure 16.5 High-carbon-intensity grid similar to current situation with overall grid and carbon-fuelled generation intensities of 0.54 and 0.73 $kgCO_2/kWh$ respectively.
*Source:* Clarke *et al.* (2008).

(ashp) and ground source heat pumps (gshp) with COPs between 2.5 and 6 are considered); two gas boilers with efficiencies of 60 per cent and 90 per cent are included as a comparison. The technologies are deployed in the analysis for a UK average dwelling (labelled 'UK average fabric'), an unimproved pre-1981 dwelling (labelled 'Poor fabric') and a dwelling built or already renovated to the 2002 building standards ('2002 fabric'). Figures 16.5 and 16.6 capture the results in tonnes $CO_2$ from all energy uses calculated using the ESRU Domestic Energy Model (Clarke *et al.*, 2008). In the high-carbon intensity grid scenario the CHP technologies which export electricity to the grid are relatively more attractive than the heat pump technologies which use grid electricity, while the converse is true in the low-carbon intensity case.

The cost of fuels and also the revenue received from selling electricity fed into the grid have a potentially very large influence on which approaches will be adopted in practice to meet the future standards for new buildings and renovations as well as the capital costs of the measures themselves. In general the cost savings from improvements are greater for buildings with poorer initial performance; this could potentially mitigate against a strategy of incremental improvements as investments

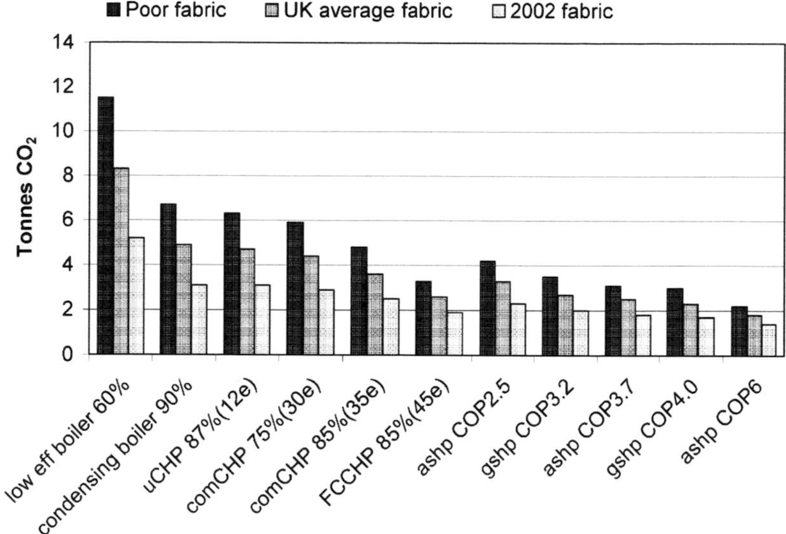


Figure 16.6 Carbon intensity of grid with significant decarbonization, overall grid and carbon-fuelled generation intensities of 0.30 and 0.40 $kgCO_2/kWh$ respectively.
*Source:* Clarke *et al.* (2008).

become incrementally less attractive, while in contrast a combined single improvement to a higher standard could still meet financial investment criteria while delivering a better overall result. The cost-effectiveness of electricity generating technology is obviously highly dependent on the feed-in tariffs received for this electricity. Figure 16.7 shows the simple paybacks in years calculated for a range of technology improvements; the improvements have been applied to the Poor fabric dwelling with a 60 per cent efficient gas boiler, the UK average fabric dwelling with a 76 per cent efficient gas boiler and the 2002 regulations dwelling with a 90 per cent efficient gas condensing boiler. The improvement of the Poor fabric and UK average dwellings with a fabric upgrade to 2002 standard of fabric with no change in systems is also shown. While the costs used in this analysis are subject to variation over time, the general conclusion is that the heat pump and CHP technologies are generally cost-effective especially when applied to older buildings with a poorer initial performance. The capital cost of heat pump technologies for dwellings, particularly air source heat pumps, is likely to be relatively low compared to ground source heat pumps or CHP given the already mature supply chain for domestic heat pumps for cooling already established over large areas of the world which deploys largely similar technology.

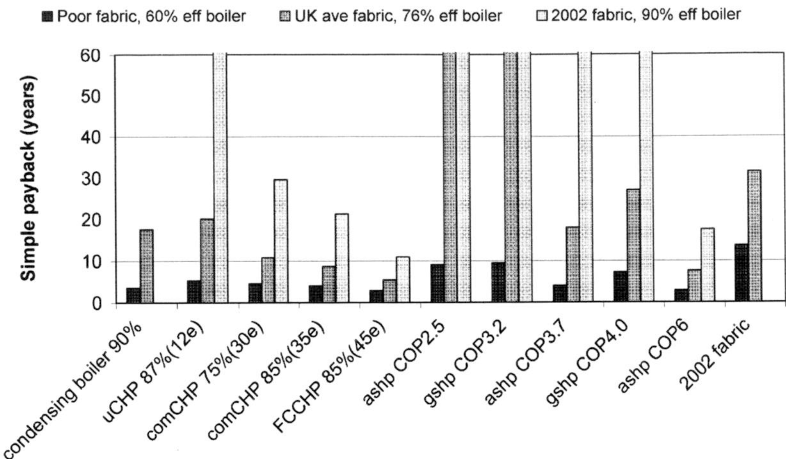


Figure 16.7 Payback (years) analysis for individual measures applied to three different dwelling types for the higher feed-in tariff case.
*Source:* Clarke *et al.* (2008).

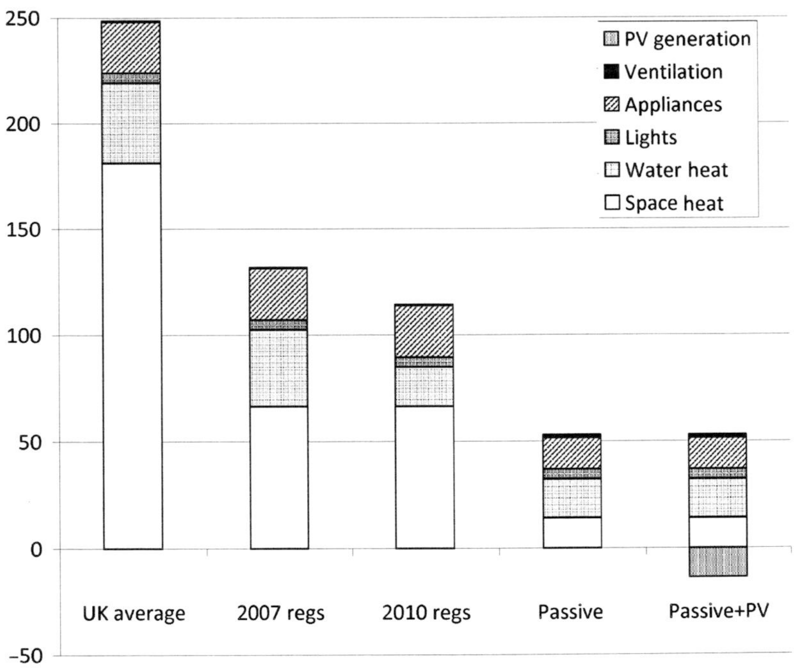


Figure 16.8 Energy demand (kWh/m$^2$ p.a.) for semi-detached dwelling to different standards.
*Source:* Clarke *et al.* (2008).

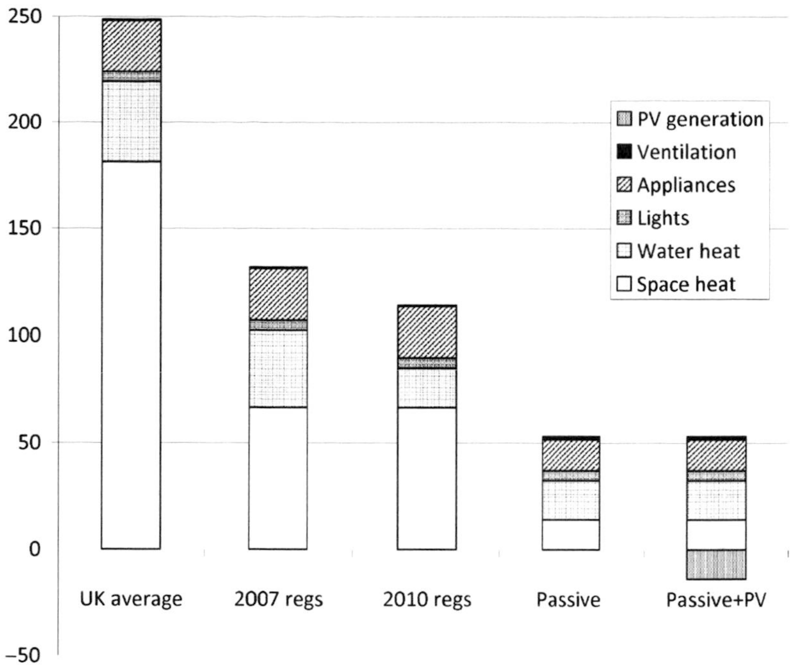


Figure 16.9 Delivered energy (kWh/m$^2$ p.a.) for semi-detached dwelling to different standards.

## 16.6 Impact of probable future buildings on energy demand and supply choices

Figures 16.8, 16.9 and 16.10 show (1) the energy demands for different uses, (2) the delivered energy as input to the systems which meet those demands, and (3) the delivered energy by fuel type, for a UK average dwelling, the same dwelling built to the current (2007) building regulations, a further version built to meet the probable 2010 regulations (solar thermal hot water system and a heat pump system COP = 3.2 for space heating 0.7 × 3.2 for water heating), a further version built to meet the EU Passive House standard (including an air source heat pump compact unit (COP = 2.5) for space and water heating) and finally a version of the Passive House with a 2 kWp PV panel. Calculations in this analysis were again outputs from the University of Strathclyde's ESRU Domestic Energy Model (EDEM) as used in section 16.4.

The reduction in energy demand between the UK average and the 2007 regulations is around 50 per cent primarily driven by the improved

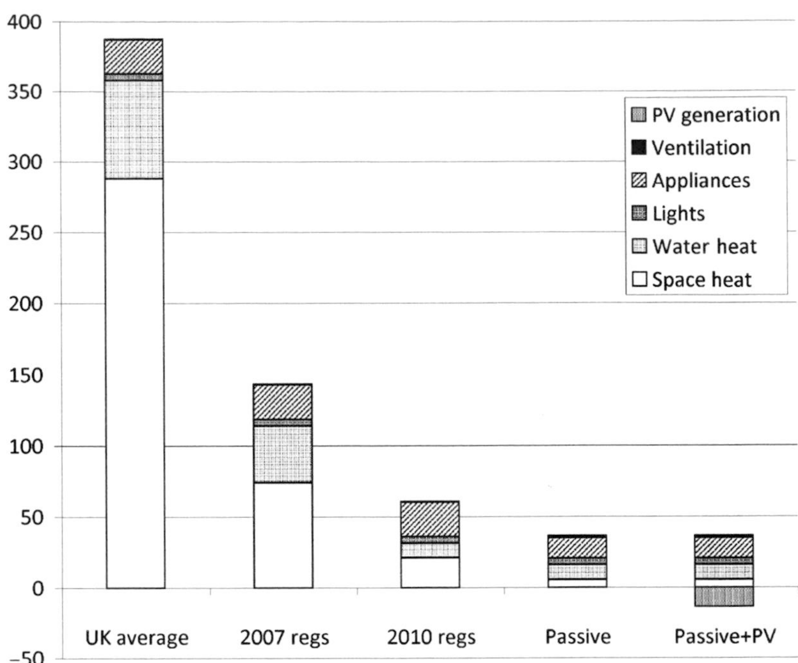


Figure 16.10 Delivered energy (kWh/m$^2$ p.a.) by fuel type for semi-detached dwelling to different standards.

thermal envelope reducing the need for space heating; no further reduction in space heating demand is required by the chosen method of meeting the 2010 regulations, the required reduction in emissions being achieved by a change in the service strategy rather than through improving building envelope. The Passive House shows a 90 per cent and 75 per cent reduction in space heating demand respectively when compared to the UK average and the 2007 regulations. We have shown the PV contribution as a negative value; some calculation methods and standards (e.g. CSH, UK building regulations) allow this generated electricity to be offset directly from the energy demands; however, as the generation is not coincident with the demands then this subtraction is not done here.

While the energy demand of the 2010 regulations version is only reduced by the solar thermal contribution to the hot water supply, the delivered energy is significantly reduced through the use of the heat pump technology for space heating and hot water (Figure 16.9). This reduction in total delivered energy is combined with a fuel switch from gas to electricity (Figure 16.10 and Table 16.2). Table 16.2 shows the delivered

Table 16.2 *Delivered energy by fuel type (kWh/m² p.a.) for semi-detached dwelling to different standards*

| | UK average | UK average with HP | 2007 Regs. | 2010 Regs. | Passive House | Passive + PV |
|---|---|---|---|---|---|---|
| Electricity | 29.5 | 109.5 | 29.5 | 60.9 | 36.7 | 36.7 |
| Mains gas | 358 | 0 | 114 | 0 | 0 | 0 |
| Electricity generation | 0 | 0 | 0 | 0 | 0 | −14 |

energy by fuel type. It is apparent that electricity demand increases with the fuel switching from gas to electricity; that may be one response to the 30 per cent reduction in carbon emissions required by the 2010 regulations. The increased deployment of heat pump technology on otherwise unimproved UK average dwellings would have a much greater impact due to the higher demand for space heating.

The Passive House building fabric, solar thermal water heating and efficient appliances approach acts to mitigate the increased demand for electricity.

While the focus in this analysis is a UK domestic building, the same arguments could be put forward for non-domestic buildings where fuel switching (gas boiler to heat pump as discussed in section 16.3) to meet future standards in addition to increased adoption of air conditioning could lead to a large increase in electricity demand and also potential network quality issues caused by heat pumps and generation devices on the distribution networks. Again the adoption of passive demand reduction measures could act to mitigate this in the non-domestic sector.

## 16.7 Discussion

To meet future building standards there is a high probability of a widespread adoption of electric heat pump technology as a replacement for gas-fuelled heating in both the domestic and non-domestic sectors. In the non-domestic sector there is also a potential for increased adoption of heat pump technology for cooling. There is also a high probability of increased adoption of MVHR and PV. This potential change in the servicing of buildings could substantially increase the demand and peak loads on the electricity grid and distribution network.

Although local generation has the potential to offset some of the electricity demand and this offset is counted in the government's regulatory calculations, the reality is that the PV panels will not necessarily act to reduce the peak demands on the grid as the PV-generated electricity will not necessarily provide a good match with the peak loads in the UK. While small-scale heat pumps are common in refrigeration in current buildings, the increasing deployment of larger-scale systems for heating, hot water and cooling may require action on the electrical distribution networks. The larger-scale deployment of PV panels will also pose challenges to the UK grid.

The rate at which buildings will be replaced or retrofitted to the future standards described in this chapter is uncertain; however, we are increasingly seeing these advanced low-carbon emission specifications being applied to new developments including eco-towns and also to large-scale renovation projects. The scale of the increase in the demand for electricity will depend on the approach taken to renovation; the worst case scenario would be the widespread deployment of heat pump technology in buildings with high heating demands. For example, the implementation of heat pumps to a dwelling of UK average fabric could lead to a more than three-fold increase in electricity demand; applying heat pumps to buildings after they were renovated to 2010 regulation standards could lead to a two-fold increase in electricity demand, etc. Renovation to Passive House standard or similar would appear to have two positive effects: reducing space heating demands and reducing the size of the heat pump required to meet that demand with less potential impact on grid quality. While the rate of new build and major renovation of the UK building stock is quite slow, the replacement rate for heating and hot water systems is much shorter (of the order of 15 years), so there is the potential for widespread adoption of heat pump technology in a relatively short timeframe.

The analysis presented here is one possible scenario. Grid carbon factors, fuel costs and capital costs as well as government incentive programmes among others will have a large effect on which route is followed to achieve the desired carbon reductions from the built environment and comply with future building standards. Also, we focus here on the whole building performance and include the energy used in appliances and equipment while the UK regulations do not. The EU Passive House standard and the England and Wales operational EPC does include these emissions in its criteria, and it would seem reasonable for all energy uses to be included in UK regulations in future.

The analysis here looks at the regulatory calculations of energy use but the use of the existing regulatory calculation methods such as SAP and SBEM to predict the performance of future building types has to be viewed with some caution. The Passive House calculation method predicts significantly higher space heating demands in dwellings (80 per cent higher) and has been validated by a significant monitoring study on exemplar buildings built to the Passive House standard in several

European countries. UK methods need a similar validation for future building types in UK contexts.

The feedback from monitoring of actual highly insulated Passive Houses – as in the CEPHEUS project – will allow the calculation methods (PHPP in the case of Passive House) to include the 'take-back' effects which are often cited as a limitation of current UK calculation methods; the take-back effects may not be represented in the UK methods and be part of the explanation of the much higher space heating energy demands calculated by PHPP.

The operational rating for public buildings in England and Wales is based on actual billed energy and would appear to be a very useful 'truth model' against which the non-domestic calculation methods could be compared. For the operational ratings to be adopted across more building types would be of potentially great benefit.

There is a requirement to predict in advance building performance and the alignment of operational and calculation performance is the ultimate goal. The UK regulations, EU standards and Passive House methods recognize the limitations of the simple calculation methods; it is expected that there will be a shift towards more detailed dynamic simulation methods in future.

## 16.8 Conclusions

EU and UK policy and regulations on the built environment are aimed at delivering reductions in $CO_2$ emissions, and reductions in the primary energy associated with the UK building stock and aggressive reduction targets have been set. The translation of these policies into standards will potentially lead to increasing adoption of heat pump technologies for space and hot water heating and also cooling with a resultant increase in demand for electricity.

These policies and standards will also act to increase the adoption of distributed PV and CHP electrical generation technology which will also provide a challenge to the future grid. The likely adoption rates of these technologies will be dependent on grid carbon intensity and other economic and political factors. Finally, current regulatory calculation methods to predict actual energy performance of future building types need to be improved.

## References

Booth, R. (2008). Halls of shame: biggest $CO_2$ offenders unveiled, *The Guardian*, 2 October.

BRE (2010a). The UK Government's Standard Assessment Procedure, Building Research Establishment Publication, Available at http://projects.bre.co.uk/sap2005/, last accessed 23 August 2010, London: BRE.

BRE (2010b). National Calculation Methodology, Available at www.ncm.bre.co.uk/, last accessed 23 August 2010.

CEPHEUS (2010). Cost Efficient Passive Houses as European Standards, Available at www.cepheus.de/eng/, last accessed 23 August 2010.

Clarke, J.A., Johnstone, C.M., Kim, J.M. and Tuohy, P.G. (2008). Energy, carbon and cost performance of building stocks: upgrade analysis, energy labelling and national policy development, in *Advances in Building Energy Research*, Santamouris, M. (editor in chief), London: Earthscan.

Communities-Gov (2010). Building Regulations: Energy efficiency requirements for new dwellings – a forward look at what standards may be in 2010 and 2013, Available at www.communities.gov.uk/publications/planningandbuilding/energyefficiencynewdwellings, last accessed 23 August 2010.

Communities-Gov (2010a). Code for Sustainable Homes, Available at www.communities.gov.uk/planningandbuilding/buildingregulations/legislation/codesustainable/, last accessed 23 August 2010.

EU (2002). Directive 2002/91/EC of the European Parliament and of the Council on the Energy Performance of Buildings, European Parliament, *Official Journal of the European Communities*, **4**(1): L1/65–71.

Kingspan Ltd (2010). Kinspan Lighthouse: Climate for Change, zero carbon future, Available at www.kingspanlighthouse.com/Achieving_Code_Level_6.htm, last accessed 23 August 2010.

Roulet and Anderson (2006). CEN standards for implementing the Energy Performance of Buildings Directive, Proceedings of the 23rd Conference on Passive and Low Energy Architecture, Geneva, Switzerland, 6–8 September. Geneva: PLEA.

Scottish Government (2010). Benchmarking Scottish energy standards: Passive House and CarbonLite Standards: A comparison of space heating energy demand using SAP, SBEM, and PHPP methodologies, Available at www.scotland.gov.uk/Resource/Doc/217736/0091333.pdf, last accessed 23 August 2010.

Sullivan, L. (2007). A Low Carbon Building Standards Strategy for Scotland, Available at www.scotland.gov.uk/Topics/Built-Environment/Building/Building-standards3/publications/sullivan, last accessed 23 August 2010.

Tuohy, P.G. (2009). Regulations and robust low-carbon buildings. Building research and information, *Special Issue: Cooling in a Low-Carbon World*, **37**(4): 433–45.

Turner & Townsend Ltd (2008). The Impact on Costs and Construction Practice in Scotland of Any Further Limitation of Carbon Dioxide Emissions from New Buildings. Livingston, Scotland – Report for the Scottish Building Standards Agency.

# 17 The ADDRESS European Project: a large-scale R&D initiative for the development of active demand

*François Bouffard, Régine Belhomme, Alioune Diop, Maria Sebastian-Viana, Cherry Yuen, Hannah Devine-Wright, Pedro Linares, Ramón Cerero Real De Asua and Giovanni Valtorta*

## 17.1 Introduction

In less than twenty years, we have seen tremendous changes in the demand mix worldwide spurred primarily by the dawn of the digital age with its ever more energy-hungry computers, server farms, telecommunication equipment, etc. The expected evolution in the electricity demand for the next 10–20 years is even more radical. While efficiencies in current electricity-using devices are expected to improve (e.g. lighting being the most prominent example), electricity demand has the potential to increase significantly because of the electrification of road transportation, combined with the demise of fossil fuels for space heating and the ever growing need for space cooling. Electricity is the energy carrier par excellence in a low-carbon world; therefore, demand for it will increase, if not significantly in the UK (see Ault *et al.*, this volume), then certainly globally.

Electric power systems have been designed and built to allow for the supply side to follow demand quite well (aside from the rare blackout in most advanced countries). Currently, most low-carbon generation technologies (like wind power and even nuclear power stations) are not well suited to follow the constant fluctuations of demand. Hence, in a power system dominated by generally uncontrollable low-carbon generation, keeping the same operating paradigm may be increasingly unreliable and overly costly.

Hence, the expected demand growth and the decreasing supply-side controllability provide an opportunity to explore how demand for electricity can be made more flexible and participate fully in the operation of the electricity system (as discussed in Torriti *et al.*, this volume). In fact, this is not only an opportunity, this is indeed needed if ambitious climate change targets are to be met. The ongoing developments in information and communication technologies, advanced metering systems, energy management at the local level (in houses, commercial buildings, etc.) as well as intelligent household technologies open new opportunities for demand-side initiatives in the electricity business. At the same time, there is a growing need for a more active participation of demand in the electricity supply chain, and consumers are increasingly aware of environmental and energy efficiency issues.

In light of these new opportunities and challenges, the European project ADDRESS ('Active Distribution networks with full integration of Demand and distributed energy RESourceS') was launched in June 2008 and will last until the end of May 2012. The project consortium consists of twenty-five partners from eleven European countries spanning the entire electricity supply chain, qualified R&D bodies, and Small and Medium Enterprises and manufacturers, and its coordinator is ENEL Distribuzione SpA (Belhomme *et al.*, 2008).

The goal of the ADDRESS project is the development of an integrated platform for the emergence and deployment of Active Demand (AD). AD here entails active participation of domestic and small commercial consumers in electricity markets and in providing services to the other participants of the industry like generation companies, transmission and distribution system operators, retailers, etc.[1] Within ADDRESS, Active Demand involves all types of equipment that may be installed at the consumers' premises: electrical appliances (pure loads), distributed generation (such as photovoltaic arrays or microturbines) and thermal or electrical energy storage systems.

The salient feature of the ADDRESS project is its combined size in terms of resources and breadth in terms of R&D coverage. The project funding is of the order of €16 million with a €9 million contribution from the European Commission. ADDRESS was the first flagship industrial collaborative research project in the electricity networks area to be funded under the EU Seventh Framework Programme. The underlying objectives of the European Commission with ADDRESS are the development of some near-to-market enabling technologies and the establishment of regulatory and commercial templates for making active demand possible in Europe in the 2020–30 horizon.

It is clear that only an industry-led initiative like this one can deliver that kind of impact in such a short amount of time. Moreover, it is most certain that a collaborative R&D effort like this one is best to leverage niche and

[1] In this chapter, we use the generic terms 'participant'/'participants' to designate an organization/organizations involved in the electricity supply chain.

national knowledge and expertise leading to higher-value technologies and practices. ADDRESS' modus operandi is really its integrated and multi-disciplinary approach. It covers the entire spectrum of issues: from the details of the operation of distribution and transmission networks with active demand, down to the sociological and cultural aspects relating to the introduction of active demand principles in people's lives; and this is without neglecting its business, regulatory and policy implications.

Another important feature of the project is its planned package of demonstration activities which will be carried out in three test sites in Europe (namely France, Spain and Italy). The demonstration activities will not just provide exceptional opportunities to validate some of the technologies and principles developed in the project, but they will serve also to showcase to its stakeholders and the public the potential of active demand in enabling tomorrow's low-carbon electricity networks.

This chapter outlines some of the key developments and achievements of the first eighteen months of the project as we focus on the design of a commercial architecture enabling the materialization of AD. What has emerged from the work so far is that the potential success of this architecture relies on the following three pillars:

1. The need for aggregation of demand-side flexibilities.
2. The need for market outlets for demand-side products and services.
3. The need for significant benefits and acceptance of active demand across the electricity supply chain, especially with consumers.

In the remainder of the chapter, we scrutinize in detail the commercial side of the ADDRESS architecture. In addition, we present the case for the development of solutions and businesses for aggregation and viable market outlets for active demand. Finally, we outline the results of a stakeholder enquiry about the potential for benefits and acceptance of active demand.

## 17.2 The ADDRESS architecture

Figure 17.1 shows the ADDRESS scope along with a simplified representation of the proposed architecture. It shows the participants and the main components, and in a very simplified way how they interact, i.e. via technical and commercial channels. In this architecture, the aggregators are a central concept. The aggregators are the key mediators between consumers on one side and markets and other power system participants on the other:

- The aggregators collect the requests and signals for AD-based flexibilities to be used as services coming from the markets and power system participants.

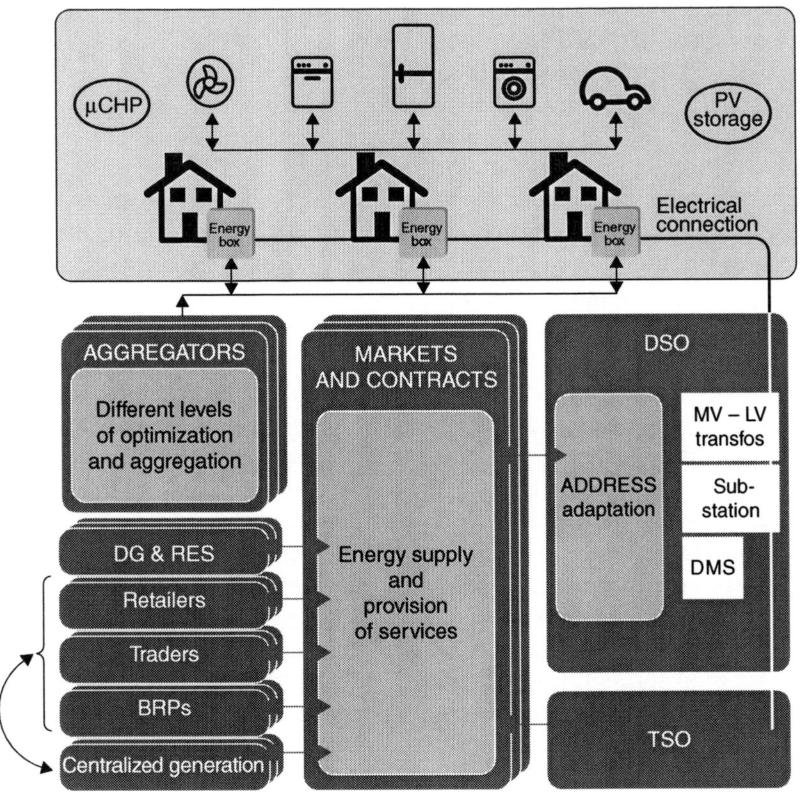


Figure 17.1 Scope and simplified representation of the ADDRESS architecture.

- They gather and package the flexibilities provided by consumers to form AD-based products, and they offer them to the different power system participants through various markets.

It should be emphasized that the flexibilities of consumers are provided in the form of modifications of their consumption profile. Therefore, aggregators form specific instances of AD products using price-driven consumer demand modifications and not consumer energy profiles as such. In other words, an aggregator's commercial mission is to sell demand deviations from forecasted levels.

At the consumer level, the Energy Box is the interface between a consumer and an aggregator. It carries out the optimization and the control of the loads and local distributed energy resources at the consumer's premises. It represents the consumer from the aggregator's perspective.

The Distribution System Operators (DSOs) also play an important role because AD stems out of consumers connected to distribution networks. DSOs still have to ensure secure and efficient network operation in the ADDRESS paradigm as they do today. Hence, they keep on doing so mainly through interactions with other power system participants and, in particular, with aggregators via market-based channels. Likewise, DSOs maintain and extend their direct interactions with Transmission System Operators (TSOs) for this purpose.

## 17.3 Needs and expectations of power system participants with respect to active demand

All the power system participants seen in Figure 17.1 (other than the aggregators and consumers) should see AD as a potential resource to address some of their fundamental needs in running their business.

For system operators, whose profits are regulated, AD represents an opportunity to improve the economics of operations and planning as well as enhance the reliability and the resilience of their networks. Within the set timeframes for aggregator actions (up to 15–20 minutes ahead, which essentially excludes emergency situations), active demand can provide for the regulated participants three basic services (Belhomme *et al.*, 2009):

- *Voltage regulation and power flow control*: DSOs and TSOs can resort to AD services to carry out voltage regulation and power flow control. They can accomplish these functions by foreseeing production/consumption plans for a target period and rearranging them if they do not comply with network constraints.
- *Tertiary active power control*: tertiary reserves are used as non-automatic actions to restore adequate control margins. Frequency control is under the responsibility of TSOs. However, with the development of distributed generation on distribution networks and the evolution towards active distribution networks, DSOs may be involved, directly or indirectly, in the provision of the services for this control.
- *'Smart' load reduction*: both TSOs and DSOs might need some form of load reduction in a certain area of their networks when, due to maintenance issues or following network failure, a load reduction is needed. Nowadays, if such a problem occurs, entire feeders or substations are disconnected.

These services then map to the particular needs of the system operators, as shown in Table 17.1. In the case of the commercially driven participants the analysis always boils down to using AD to increase commercial returns and/or decrease risk. For instance, in the case of an electricity retailer, AD can serve to help minimize consumption when the retail price

Table 17.1 *Needs of system operators and their fulfilment by means of AD*

| | Type of AD service | | |
|---|---|---|---|
| Needs | Voltage Regulation and Power Flow Control | Tertiary Active Power Control | 'Smart' Load Reduction |
| Power flow control/network congestion solution | X | | X |
| Frequency control/power reserve | | X | |
| Network restoration/black start | | | X |
| Voltage control and Reactive power compensation | X | | |
| Reduction of system losses | X | | X |
| Optimized development and usage of the network | X | | X |

is lower than the wholesale price of electricity while doing the opposite when this margin is positive. Likewise, a retailer can use AD to minimize the risk of being out of balance with respect to its previously announced consumption schedules. The interested reader is invited to consult the work by Belhomme *et al.* (2009) for the complete details.

## 17.4 Active demand services and products

The bottom line here is that AD has the potential to be of use across the industry. The exercise on the needs and expectations of system participants with respect to AD led to the identification of a large number of different possible AD services (twenty-four different services for the nine deregulated participants and seven services for the above three categories of services provided to DSOs and TSOs). It turns out, however, that all those *services* can be provided through three standard aggregator-based *products*.

An *AD product* (or *product* for short) is what an aggregator provides (sells) to the participants and which the participants use to create their own services. It is a specific 'power against time' demand response shape to be provided by an aggregator during a specific time period. In the case of AD and ADDRESS, we are talking about changing the consumption pattern of groups of consumers, in other words 're-profiling' the demand, via appropriate price and volume signals broadcast by aggregators.

AD products become *AD services* (or *services* for short) when they are acquired and used by participants. It is a specific instance of the use of basic AD products. The terminology here is such that the services actually refer to the fulfilment of specific needs of the participants.

This differentiation stems from the fact that an identical AD product can have different applications (i.e. provide different services) when used by different participants. This could even be argued further by seeing that a given product may have a different application when used by one participant depending on the prevailing circumstances.

The primary characteristics of AD products are:

- The conditionality of the delivery of a specified product power shape:
  - Conditional delivery: the power delivery associated with the product has to be 'triggered' by the buyer. The buyer has the *option* to call for a pre-agreed power volume to be delivered by the aggregator.
  - Unconditional delivery: the buyer does not need to do anything. The aggregator has an *obligation* to deliver the specified power shape during the specified delivery period; this means that the product delivery is effectively 'scheduled'.
- The allowance for delivery within a range of power or the delivery of a specific amount is another differentiator.
- Bidirectional (i.e. allowing for both demand reduction and increase) or a unidirectional (i.e. allowing for demand reduction or increase only) delivery volume range for the specified power shape in the case of conditional delivery products. One could argue that a bidirectional flexibility product is simply the combination of two unidirectional ones with their appropriate calling conditions.[2]

Keeping these characteristics in mind, the three basic AD-based products defined in ADDRESS are *Scheduled Re-Profiling* (*SRP*), *Conditional Re-Profiling* (*CRP*) and *Bi-directional Conditional Re-Profiling* (*CRP-2*) and are summarized in Table 17.2. These define the most basic characteristics of the AD products. However, the products need to be further specified with respect to parameters which specify the demand response process associated with the product. This is done in the product description template below.

Before proceeding to the complete description of active demand products, it is necessary to be reminded of a key characteristic of electricity demand as a source of flexibility. When demand is reduced (increased) at some point in time, for instance, there is a high likelihood that demand

[2] However, in order to reduce transaction costs, it may be more reasonable and practical to allow for bidirectional conditional products. In the end, the markets should decide the fate of such products.

Table 17.2 *AD products and their main characteristics*

| AD product | Conditionality | Typical example |
|---|---|---|
| Scheduled re-profiling (SRP) | Unconditional (obligation) | The aggregator has the obligation to provide *a specified* demand modification (reduction or increase) at a given time to the product buyer. |
| Conditional re-profiling (CRP) | Conditional (real option) | The aggregator must have the capacity to provide *a specified* demand modification during a given period. The delivery is called upon by the buyer (similar to a reserve service). |
| Bi-directional conditional re-profiling (CRP-2) | Conditional (real option) | The aggregator must have the capacity to provide *a specified* demand modification during a given period in a bidirectional range [$-y$, $x$] MW, including both demand increase and decrease. The delivery is called upon by the buyer of the AD product (similar to a reserve service). |

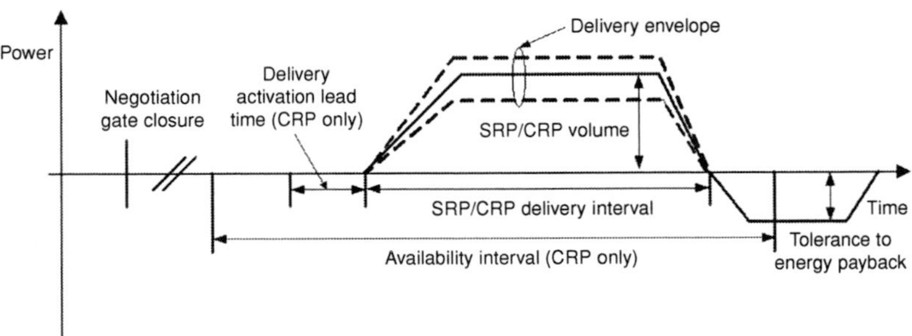


Figure 17.2 AD product standardized delivery process.

will increase (decrease) at a later time or even beforehand; this is called the *payback effect* (Lee and Wilkins, 1983; Kurucz *et al.*, 1996; Ruiz *et al.*, 2009). This payback may have adverse consequences on the electricity system and the participants from both the technical and economic points of view if it is not managed in the AD product itself.

We designed a product template as the basic format of a product description. It lists the basic set of parameters necessary to specify any product as shown in Figure 17.2. This three-product approach to the provision of AD-based services is very powerful. It has the advantage of greatly simplifying the inner workings of aggregators by not requesting them to be able to cater for twenty-one different services. In addition, it has the potential to better fit the current workings of actual energy markets which already deal only with a few simple products (e.g. on-peak

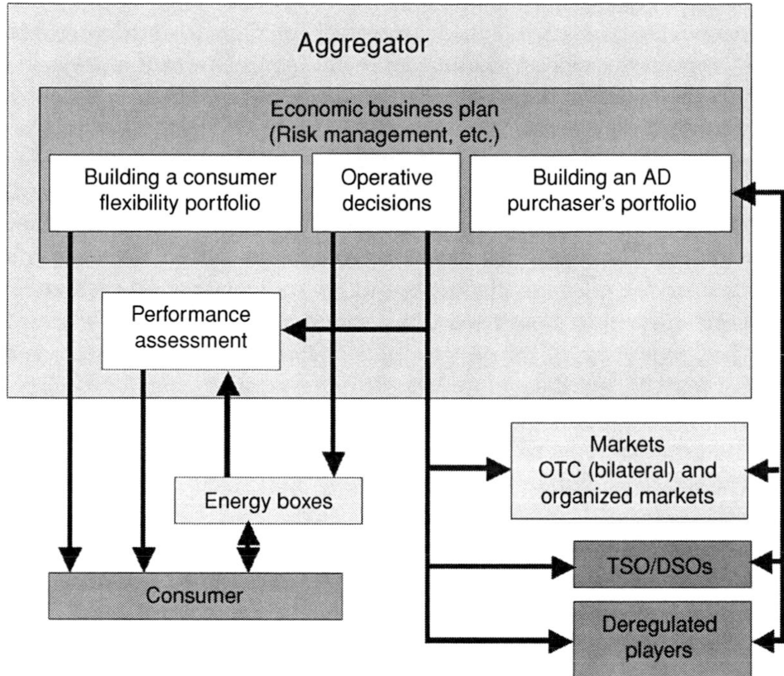


Figure 17.3 Overview of an aggregator's internal functionalities.

and off-peak electricity in 1 MWh blocks) while ultimately increasing the liquidity of markets for AD and other competing sources of flexibility.

## 17.5 The need for aggregation

In the ADDRESS architecture, the aggregator purchases small consumers' flexibility, packages it into tradable products and sells them. To achieve those seemingly simple tasks, the aggregator needs to have the following set of functionalities which map onto the set of relationships illustrated in Figure 17.3.

- *To gather the flexibilities of domestic and small commercial consumers.* For this purpose the aggregator is expected to have a high expertise in consumer demand flexibilities. It must also develop an active role on advising and proposing technical and commercial solutions to consumers, so that the maximum flexibility capabilities are made available when most needed. Most fundamentally, however, the ADDRESS approach assumes that the aggregator generates tailored price and volume signals for stimulating specific consumer response. This, unlike other approaches based on direct load control (Ruiz, Cobelo and Oyarzabal, 2009), represents a major challenge for the aggregator as it must assess not only the available flexibility of consumers, but also their willingness to surrender it at a price.

- *To be aware of the AD requests and opportunities.* The aggregator should have an active role looking for opportunities to sell AD in the appropriate markets and proposing its products to regulated and deregulated participants. Therefore, the aggregators have to collect requests and signals from the different electricity system participants via markets to build offers meeting those needs. In particular, the aggregator's knowledge and awareness of the geographical location of its consumers and of the regulated and deregulated participants requiring flexibility could be important to match the right request with the right source of flexibility. The aggregator should also be able to properly manage its portfolio of requests, identifying synergies, overlaps and maybe even inconsistencies between different requests.
- *To maximize the value of its consumers' flexibility.* The aggregator's main objective should always be to maximize the value from gathering and packaging consumers' flexibility to its final sale to a third party. This should lead aggregators to search for the AD requests with the highest potential added value.
- *To manage risks associated with uncertainties.* The aggregator should face price risks in upstream flexibility markets, and it faces volume risks because of the uncertain responsiveness of its consumer base (risk of non-delivery or poor-quality delivery of forward purchased demand-side flexibility). Different schemes for allocation of such risks may be adopted, but the aggregator should in any case deal with a large part of them. In some cases, the aggregator might negotiate transferring these risks to other participants which might have a better control of them with standard financial and insurance products.

These functions are to be performed while the aggregator is competing against other aggregators for the 'highest-value' consumers providing flexibility (for instance, consumers with certain desirable flexibility characteristics or consumers located in strategic areas known for their tight network margins) for the 'highest-value' end-market deals.

## 17.6 The value of active demand and its markets

Each participant in the electricity system has his own fundamental needs. It gives relative importance to each one; in other words it gives them value. To meet those needs, participants are willing to spend effort and money.

But the participant generally has different alternatives: it may invest in new assets, change its operating procedures, buy services from a third party or do nothing and pay the associated fines for non-fulfilment of an obligation.

The hypothesis is that AD can meet some of the participants' needs and that if at least one participant has given to its need a value that is superior to the cost of an AD solution, it may be willing to implement it by buying the corresponding product to implement the needed service. But it is not certain that AD will be the best solution to answer a given need. In fact, the AD solution is in competition with all other possible solutions, and the choice will result from a comparison of both efficiency to meet the need and the cost of the different solutions. For each of the needs, evaluating:

1. the cost of the other solutions that the participant has at its hand;
2. the expected economic gains or savings that the use of AD can bring;

will help determine the price the participant is willing to pay for an AD service and therefore the price signals that will be exchanged to and from the aggregators via markets.

Of course, the AD solution valuation process also has to take into account the technical characteristics (power, energy, time) as well as non-technical characteristics (communication, predictability, contracts, tariffs) of the needs because these cannot generally be dissociated from the economic aspects, since they have a direct or at least an indirect impact on the cost of the various solutions.

### *17.6.1 Market valuation of AD*

We consider here the case of a market participant that is contemplating purchasing an amount $u$ of SRP to satisfy a need at a given future time (i.e. to solve a technical or a commercial problem).[3]

This problem can be modelled as solving the system of inequalities $F(u, x) \leq b$ for $u$, where $x$ represents a vector of the participant's state variables. That is, the participant should find $u$ to ensure that the equation is satisfied. The inequalities $F(u, x) \leq b$ can represent any number of conditions and requirements, which the participant has to satisfy in solving its problem.

Finding some $u$ does not necessarily require any optimization as the participant may already know how much it needs to meet its need from experience and field information. However, more realistically, the

[3] This argument is for SRP, without loss of generality. A similar reasoning is applicable for CRP; see Belhomme *et al.*, 2009 for the corresponding development for CRP.

participant should attempt to acquire the optimal amount of SRP, which would maximize its overall profits (and possibly also minimize its own risks). To do so, however, would require an exogenous price for the SRP product. In the absence of an exogenous price for the SRP, this becomes complicated. What the participant has to do then is determine up to how much it would be willing to pay for a given amount of SRP, *that is formulate its price and volume signals*. The signals are indicators of the participant's willingness to pay and willingness to buy. In the actual markets, depending on the settlement rules, the participant will earn a surplus in the event the clearing prices for the products are less than its bid prices.

The classic unconstrained result that applies here is that a participant will acquire SRP up until the marginal benefit from purchasing one more unit of SRP becomes equal to the marginal cost of that extra unit. In the case where constraints become active restricting the quantity of AD that it can buy, the participant would have to resort to other resources on top of AD to fulfil completely its need. In that case, the value of an extra unit of AD goes to zero and so does its corresponding incremental demand for AD.

### *17.6.2 Market clearing of AD*

As mentioned earlier, the choice made to standardize AD into three products makes AD essentially identical to energy as a tradable commodity. However, AD has technical peculiarities which make it radically different from energy. It remains, though, that AD can be traded like a standard commodity as it is standardized. Therefore, the hypothesis is that the markets structures and the associated market clearing mechanisms for AD should be no different than those for energy. We illustrate this later.[4]

## 17.7 Active demand process architecture

In this section, we explain the whole process of active demand generation in Figure 17.4 illustrating the ADDRESS Active Demand process in a chronological order, with the process progressing from the left to the right. The top half of the diagram shows the individual internal processes of system participants while the bottom half shows the interaction between the participants themselves. The procedure horizon shows only the sequence of events or subprocesses and does not reflect the actual duration or the time differences between these events.

[4] We point out, nonetheless, that further research is needed in demonstrating this hypothesis.

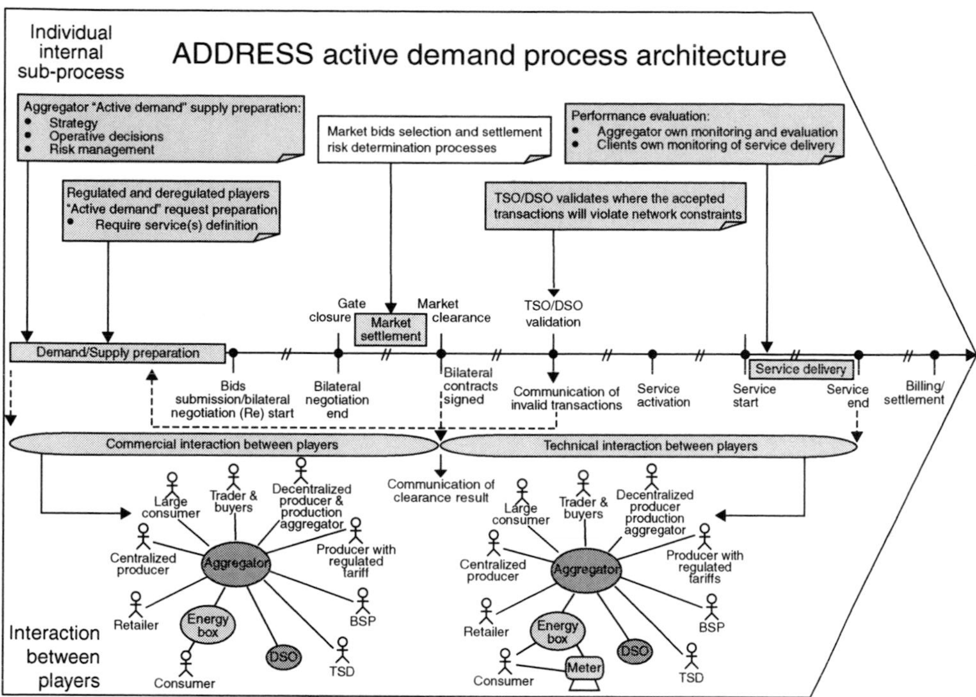


Figure 17.4 Process architecture diagram.

### *17.7.1 Internal subprocesses (top half of Figure 17.4)*

During demand/supply preparation:

- The aggregator prepares offers according to its portfolio of consumers who exhibit different levels of flexibility. The aggregator follows a certain number of internal subprocesses. They are:
  - Strategies' definition
  - Operative decision making
  - Risk management.
- Other participants who might be in need of AD prepare their requests according to defined service templates.

During market settlement and bilateral contract negotiations:

- The context of 'Markets' in ADDRESS covers all kinds of commercial activities, which can result potentially in a transaction and involves a central entity which monitors and registers such activities, while

'Bilateral Contracts' refer to the deals struck without a central entity. It has been identified that the subprocesses of the market operation mechanism are part of the whole AD process.

After the market is cleared or the bilateral contracts are agreed, the TSO/DSO need to validate the transactions to find out if the AD delivery will violate any network constraints:

- If the DSO/TSO detect a network constraint violation, the transactions causing the violations will be refused. In this case, the participants requesting the service as well as the aggregator might rework their offers/requests and attempt to bid or negotiate a bilateral contract again.
- If the DSO/TSO does not detect any network constraint violations, the participants can proceed to the next process or event on the procedural horizon.

During service delivery:

- Once the accepted and validated service is activated, the AD product is ready to be delivered. Note that in the diagram the subprocess 'service delivery' includes any possible energy payback associated with the service. During this subprocess, both the aggregator and the AD buyer monitor the delivery for performance evaluation.

### *17.7.2 Interaction between participants (bottom half of Figure 17.4)*

This is roughly divided into two phases: commercial and technical. Commercial interactions cover the preparation phase up to market clearance. Technical interactions cover the phase immediately after market clearance all the way up to the end of service delivery. The enlarged interaction diagrams are shown in Figure 17.5 and Figure 17.6.

Figure 17.5 shows the commercial interactions between the participants. In this figure, the market has the most general meaning, i.e. it covers open markets/exchanges, call for tenders, bilateral contracts, etc. It is at the centre of the figure since the interactions represent:

- The interactions of the aggregators:
  - Sending offers for AD products to the markets and other power system participants.
  - Negotiating contracts with other power system participants.
  - Possibly buying AD products from other aggregators (or even other types of products from other power system participants).
- The interactions of the other regulated and deregulated power system participants:
  - Sending requests for AD products to the markets and to aggregators.
  - Negotiating contracts with aggregators.

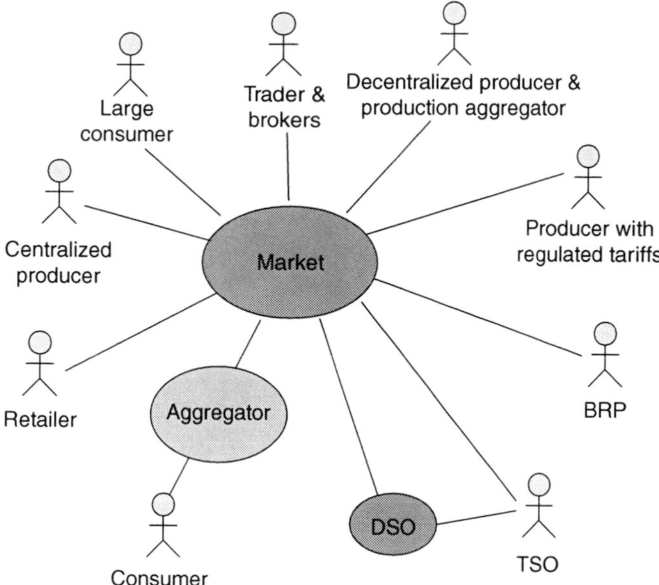


Figure 17.5 UML diagram showing the commercial interaction between players.

- Possibly buying products competing with AD from other power system participants or possibly making offers for competing products.
- The interactions between DSO and TSO, exchanging information for coordination needs.

Another type of interaction also represented in the interaction diagram concerns the commercial interactions between the aggregator and its consumers which include:

- The preparation and sending of offers (i.e. price and volume signals) by the aggregator to the consumers.
- The negotiation of contracts for AD flexibility.

Figure 17.6 shows the technical interactions between the participants. The aggregator is at the centre of the figure since the interactions represent:

- The possible sending of activation signals (call option triggers) by the AD product buyer in the case of CRP.
- The delivery of the AD products by the aggregator to the buyers.
- The monitoring and performance assessment of the service delivery.

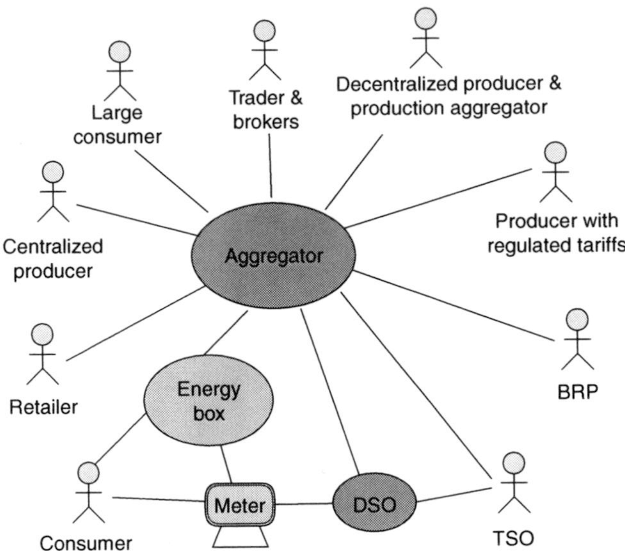


Figure 17.6 UML diagram showing the technical interaction between players.

- The exchange of information between the aggregator and the DSO for the technical validation of the AD transactions.
- The further exchange of information between DSO and TSO for the purpose of technical validation.
- Depending on the regulation and market rules, the possible exchanges of information with the TSO and the Balancing Responsible Parties about possible imbalances.
- The exchanges of signals between the aggregator and the Energy Boxes of consumers: activation signals, sending of other types of information, collection of information on the consumers and their consumption, etc.
- The interaction between the Energy Box and the equipment in the house and with the electricity meter.
- Provision of the consumer AD flexibility and monitoring of consumers' response.

## 17.8 A simple example of market clearing process

The market clearing process shown in the process diagram is elaborated as follows. It should be noted that it is a simple example of how AD products can be traded, and not necessarily the only means of achieving this. Market mechanisms will be studied in much more depth in later stages

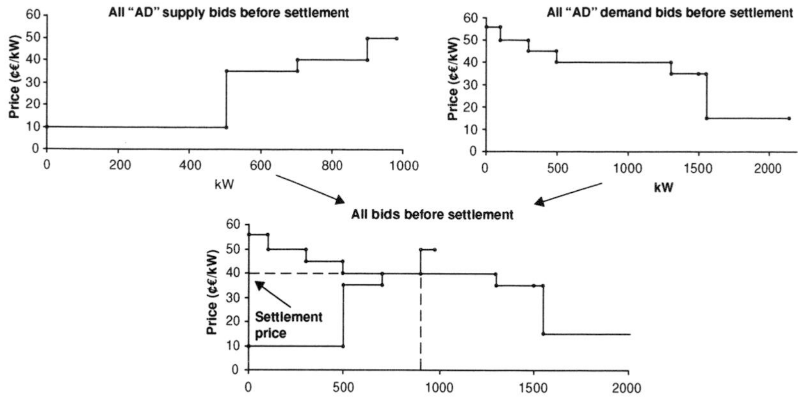


Figure 17.7 Uniform price market clearing.

of the project. The purpose of the example is to illustrate the concepts of ADDRESS by showing the information flow between participants for AD and cash flow between participants acquiring and supplying AD. It is a market simulation programmed in Excel which focuses on cash flow illustration to study the business case and potential profits as well as to help calculate the revenue and net income of the participants.

We adopted a uniform pricing auction which means that all accepted bids settle at one market clearing price (see Figure 17.7). The reason that it is chosen is because it is an auction mechanism which is simple and widely adopted in existing European energy markets.

Special technical constraints are integrated into the market clearing process which comprises the introduction of 'All-or-Nothing' bids[5] to reflect the technical needs of those participants requiring AD. For example, if a DSO wants to have at least 100 KW of AD from the market, anything less is of no practical use. These technical constraints are checked during the bid selection process and a similar procedure could be applied for other technical validation such as congestion management, etc. With these special constraints all accepted bids will still clear at one price.[6]

To illustrate this concept, we now present an example of bid selection based on pre-defined technical constraints as shown in Figure 17.8. The highlighted AD request bid is rejected since the remaining supply

[5] These are similar to the block orders in the Amsterdam Power Exchange (APX), for instance.

[6] However, the market clearing price may not be an equilibrium price because of the non-convexities introduced by the all-or-nothing bids. See Bouffard and Galiana (2005), which develops a similar example in the context of an electricity market with unit commitment decisions.

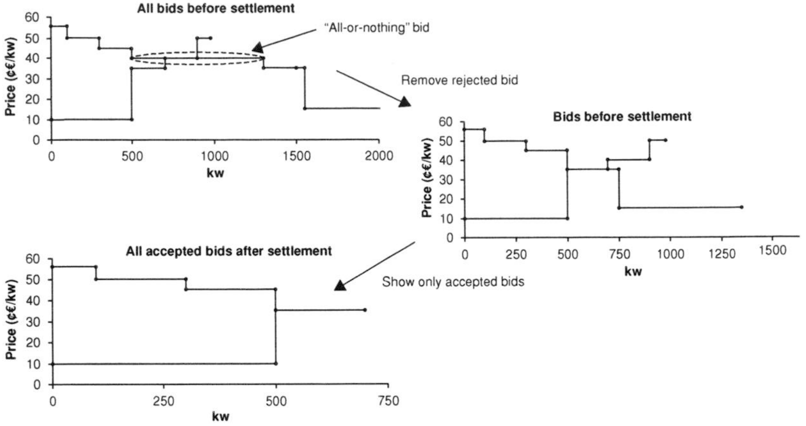


Figure 17.8 Principle of 'all-or-nothing' bids.

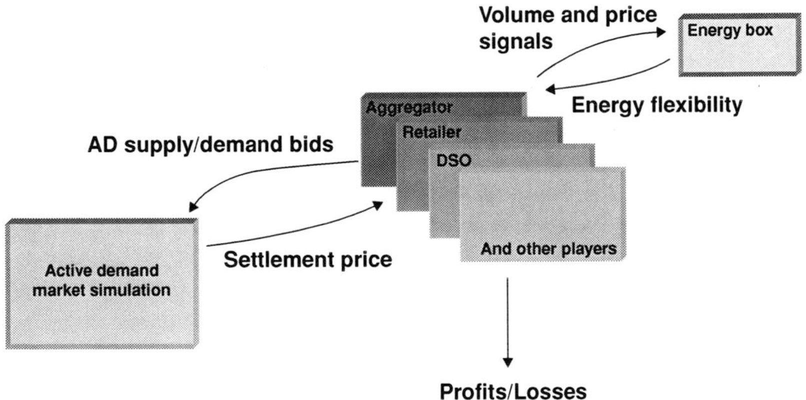


Figure 17.9 Relationships between the market and its participants.

bids cannot fulfil the minimum quantity requirement, and the next AD demand bid gets considered instead.

Once the market clearing results have been obtained, they are used to accept the bids from different participants who work out their own optimal bids based on their own internal processes. For example, the aggregator coordinates with the Energy Box(es) using close-to-real-time volume price signals in order to acquire the energy flexibility of the active demand consumers. The market simulation returns the accepted bids and the clearing price to the participants which can then calculate their financial gains or losses as illustrated in Figure 17.9.

## 17.9 The potential benefits and acceptance of active demand

As already mentioned in sections 17.3 and 17.5, AD may provide useful services to the power system participants, who may be willing to pay for them according to the value they bring. These many benefits have already been highlighted by many studies (e.g. DOE, 2006; Linares and Conchado, 2010; see also Silva *et al.*, this volume). They include, in the short term, a more efficient operation of the generation system, a lower environmental impact – depending on the configuration of the system – and an easier real-time balance of supply and demand – something which will become more relevant as more intermittent generation is added to the system. Regarding networks, AD may help alleviate network constraints and avoid outages. Moreover, AD can reduce line losses and even provide ancillary services for system operators (as already mentioned in section 17.3).

In the long term, AD can reduce the need for network reinforcements or new investments. It can also decrease installed capacity in peaking units, and in capacity reserves. It may also enable a higher penetration of intermittent sources.

Active demand also allows for a more active participation of the demand side in power markets, thereby achieving significant improvements in market efficiency: a better allocation of resources, a lower capacity to exercise market power, and a reduction in price volatility.

The existence of these potential benefits is agreed upon by most stakeholders in the power sector, as shown by the survey carried out within the ADDRESS project (Devine-Wright and Bouffard, 2010). The survey was carried out by interviewing twenty-eight stakeholders familiar with AD concepts, and involved in the ADDRESS project. Results show that consumers believe that AD will increase their opportunities to receive new services, and to increase their awareness of energy use. They also agree that AD will help manage grid overload and congestion, will reduce investments in generation and grids, and also bring about environmental benefits and better quality and security of supply.

However, in spite of all these possible benefits, AD will only be broadly adopted if the power system participants – and particularly final consumers – are willing to participate in such a scheme. This will depend on the one hand on the possibility of materializing the benefits already mentioned (more about this below); and on the other hand, it will need to address some of the other qualitative issues, such as acceptance. Of course, stakeholders also recognize that AD will entail costs for the deployment of the infrastructure required, which have to be balanced with the potential benefits.

The qualitative aspects have been identified by the already mentioned ADDRESS survey, which focused particularly on the acceptability and type of participants likely to engage in active demand. The survey identified several elements which need to be addressed carefully. One of the major issues regarding acceptance is that the outcome on consumer comfort is not clear. AD basically requires consumers to shift loads, something which will always entail a reduction in comfort or convenience unless it is fully automated and integrates all consumers' constraints and preferences. In addition, having to calculate and decide between complex and multiple AD options may also create discomfort to the consumer – in fact, most consumers prefer fixed rather than TOU tariffs because of their simplicity. Again, this can be solved through better ICT technologies and interfaces.

A second aspect which greatly influences acceptance is trust: there is a need to increase consumer trust in power system participants: this may be achieved by informing and co-opting consumers as participants in the system. Related to this, consumers feel that they need to be able to control and validate the accuracy of their own consumption data, not only for the data themselves, but also for privacy issues. Another important issue is the current low cost of energy for many consumers: if costs are low, so will be the savings provided by AD, and hence the incentives for its adoption.

Therefore, in order to increase acceptance of AD, the following factors have been highlighted: a smart, flexible and cost-effective AD; an increased trust in aggregators by regulating them to act in a fair and transparent manner; to deliver energy services rather than units of electricity; to emphasize the environmental benefits of participation; to provide information that is affordable and easy to use; flexible contracts; ICT and control technologies which enable consumer control; no negative impact on comfort or convenience; reasonably priced technologies; and appropriately designed and implemented user interfaces.

Finally, as mentioned before, these benefits have to be balanced against the costs of the deployment of AD infrastructure (for a discussion see Silva *et al.*, this volume). And a critical issue here is that, since benefits are unequally distributed among the agents, costs have to be carefully assigned so that agents have the right incentives to participate. There is an important need therefore for good regulation of the system, which does not create perverse incentives – such as those existing in some countries, where the current regulation of distribution discourages the use of AD in spite of it being a more economic option – and that allows the benefits of AD to materialize. This regulation should also address the greater need for coordination between participants.

## 17.10 Conclusion

This paper has outlined some of the key developments and achievements of the first eighteen months of the ADDRESS European project. We focused on describing the design of the commercial architecture enabling the materialization of active demand. The potential success of this architecture relies on the following three pillars, about which we provided the main results regarding their developments:

1. The need for aggregation of demand-side flexibilities.
2. The need for market outlets for demand-side products and services.
3. The need for significant benefits and acceptance of active demand across the electricity supply chain, especially with consumers.

Ongoing phases of the work in the project are developing the enabling technologies and methodologies for deploying the ADDRESS architecture. Specific work is dedicated also to the study of market mechanisms and regulatory changes required by active demand, while we are conducting extensive activities investigating the social, cultural and behavioural challenges related to the deployment of active demand principles with small domestic and commercial consumers. Illustrative scenarios of evolution of active demand in Europe have been developed and these are driving the elaboration of business models for active demand (Bouffard *et al.*, 2010).

### Acknowledgement

The research leading to the results has received funding from the European Community's Seventh Framework Programme (FP7/2007–2013) under grant agreement no. 207643.

### References

Belhomme, R., Cerero Real de Asua, R., Valtorta, G., Paice, A., Bouffard, F., Rooth, R. and Losi, A. (2008). ADDRESS – Active demand for the smart grids of the future, in *Proc. CIRED Seminar 2008: Smart Grids for Distribution*, Prague, Czech Republic.

Belhomme, R., Sebastian, M., Diop, A., Entem, M., Bouffard, F., Valtorta, G., *et al.* (2009). *ADDRESS technical and commercial architecture – core document* (ADDRESS Deliverable D1.1), Brussels, Belgium: European Commission, Available at www.addressfp7.org/config/files/ADD-WP1_Technical_and-Commercial_Architectures.pdf.

Bouffard, F. and Galiana, F.D. (2005). Generalized uplifts in pool-based electricity markets: coordinating time-dynamic markets, in Boukas, E.K. and Malhamé, R.P. (eds), *Analysis, Control and Optimization of Complex Dynamic Systems*, pp. 193–214, New York: Springer.

Bouffard, F., Gonzalez-Longatt, F., Su, C.-L., Jimeno, J., Laresgoiti, I., Noce, C. and Russo, M. (2010). *Application of the ADDRESS conceptual architecture in four specific scenarios* (ADDRESS Deliverable D1.2), Brussels, Belgium: European Commission, Available at www.addressfp7.org/config/files/ADD-WP1_ADDRESS_scenarios-v1.0.pdf.

Devine-Wright, H. and Bouffard, F. (2010). *Interview study of stakeholder beliefs about consumer benefits of active demand* (ADDRESS Internal Report I5.1), Brussels, Belgium: European Commission.

Kurucz, C.N., Brandt, D. and Sim, S. (1996). A linear programming model for reducing system peak through customer load control programs, *IEEE Trans. Power Syst.*, **11**(4): 1817–24.

Lee, S.H. and Wilkins, C.L. (1983). A practical approach to appliance load control analysis: a water heater case study, *IEEE Trans. Power App. System*, **102**(4): 1007–13.

Linares, P. and Conchado, A. (2010). The economic impact of demand response programs on power systems. A survey of the state of the art, in Pardalos, P.M., Pereira, M.V.F., Iliadis, N.A., Rebennack, S. and Sorokin, A. (eds.), *Handbook of Networks in Power Systems: Optimization, Modeling, Simulation and Economic Aspects*, New York: Springer.

Ruiz, N., Cobelo, I. and Oyarzabal, J. (2009). A direct load control model for virtual power plant management, *IEEE Trans. Power Syst.*, **24**(2): 959–66.

United States Department of Energy (2006). *Benefits of Demand Response in Electricity Markets and Recommendations for Achieving Them*, Washington, DC: Department of Energy.

# 18 Daylight saving, electricity demand and emissions: the British case

*Yu-Foong Chong, Elizabeth Garnsey, Simon Hill and Frédéric Desobry*

## 18.1 Introduction

In the years following the introduction of official standard time in the nineteenth century, efforts to promote daylight saving time were resisted in Britain and elsewhere in the world. Daylight saving time (DST) was finally introduced under wartime conditions in the twentieth century to save fuel. But only recently has the urgency of energy issues redirected attention to the issue of DST and electricity demand. A review of the literature on the impact of daylight saving on electricity demand shows that those advocating a change in DST are charged with providing detailed proof of expected energy benefits, while the assumed benefits of historic standard time are taken as given. Britain provides a case study of institutional inertia in this domain (Cronin and Garnsey, 2007).

We take up the British case in this chapter. After a brief review of the literature on the impact of DST on electricity demand, we report here on a modelling exercise undertaken using National Grid data to estimate the electricity savings that would result from a change in the clock time regime in Britain. The study demonstrates the change in electricity demand that would result from extending daylight saving over the months when clock time is currently on Greenwich Mean Time (GMT). Effects of advancing the current clock-regime by an additional hour are also estimated, using an experimental method.

## 18.2 Background

DST was first introduced in order to save fuel during the First World War. During the Second World War, DST was advanced by a further hour,

Acknowledgements to Professor Mark Franklin of the European Institute University, Florence, for sharing his expertise in regression analysis and piloting an exploratory methodology.

with clock time on GMT+1 during the winter months and GMT+2 during the summer, known as British Double Summer Time (BDST) or Double Daylight Savings Time (DDST), with a reversion to DST in 1947. Between 1968 and 1971, year-round DST (YRDST) was adopted in Britain for a trial period. However, following vocal opposition and a free vote in the House of Commons the experiment was abandoned. This change occurred even though, as explored in section 18.4, the weight of evidence was in support of the continuation of year-round DST. The UK put back the date of onset of DST by two weeks in 1981 to align with clock-change dates in EU countries on Central European Time (CET), remaining one hour behind CET year-round. This was formalized by an EU Directive on summer-time arrangements in January 2001.

Successive UK governments maintained this clock time regime despite a series of attempts to introduce private bills reforming clock time policy. The rationale for the government position was expressed during the House of Lords debate on the 2006 'Lighter Evenings Bill', when the UK government's position was that the current clock time regime is: '*a satisfactory compromise between those who prefer lighter mornings and those who prefer lighter evenings*.' Evidence is summarized here to inform preferences and policy making, making it clear that the preference for morning light has been protected at considerable cost.

## 18.3 Evidence and policy

The reason for introducing Daylight Saving Time (DST) was highlighted by Benjamin Franklin in 1784, as the mismatch between daylight hours and activity patterns. In a letter to the editors of the *Journal of Paris*, he asked why Parisians lived by the '*smoky, unwholesome, and enormously expensive light of candles [when] they might have had as much pure light of the sun for nothing?*' (Prereau, 2005). Today it is easier for policy makers to alter official clock time than to change the habits of the population. But in the literature on clock time, few authors analyze clock time in relation to the daily activity patterns of today's urban population, for whom noon is much earlier than the mid-point of their waking day.

The most cited studies on DST are summarized in Table 18.1. However, their findings do not provide direct guidance to policy makers on clock time policy for Britain in the twenty-first century because of differences in methodology, region, season, timeframe and demand measures:

- *Methodology* – studies can be categorized into following one of two main approaches: bottom-up or top-down.

Table 18.1 *Studies on the impact of extending DST on electricity usage*

| Region | Time Regime | Method/ Evidence | Impact on Electricity Demand due to DST (S = Savings, C = Costs, N = Neutral results) | Author |
|---|---|---|---|---|
| UK | YRDST | Electricity System | **S** – Reduction in electricity consumption of 0.5% in evening peak demand of 3% | HMSO (1970) |
| UK | YRDST | Electricity system | **S** – 2.5% increase in mornings, but 3% reduction in the higher evening peak | Hillman and Parker (1988) |
| UK | YRDST | Electricity system | **S** – 0.8% decrease in domestic lighting. Afternoon peak reduced by 3% | Hillman (1993) |
| UK | DDST | Light switch simulation | **N** – 5% increase in *commercial* lighting energy use, and 5% decrease in *domestic* lighting use during GMT+2 summer months | Littlefair (1990) |
| UK | YRDST & DDST | Building simulation | **C** – Energy consumption increase by 1% under YRDST and 2% under DDST | Pout (2006) |
| Germany | DST | Building simulation | **S** – Savings of 3.9% in residential buildings. 1.8% overall reduction | Bouillon (1983) |
| Germany | DST | Daylight analysis | **N** – Overall neutral effect on lighting energy | Fischer (2000) |
| EU | DST | Simulation | **S** – Electricity savings ranging from 0% to 0.5% depending on country | Reincke and Van den Broek (1999) |
| Japan | DST & DDST | Building simulation | **S** – Reduction in lighting electricity consumption varies from area to area. DDST offered greater savings than DST | Fong *et al.* (2007) |
| Osaka | DST | Building simulation | **C** – 0.02% decrease in lighting, but 0.15% increase in heating. Overall, 0.13% increase in residential electricity consumption | Shimoda *et al.* (2007) |

*(cont.)*

Table 18.1 (*cont.*)

| Region | Time Regime | Method/ Evidence | Impact on Electricity Demand due to DST (S = Savings, C = Costs, N = Neutral results) | Author |
|---|---|---|---|---|
| Mexico | DST | Theoretical study | **S** – Annual savings from 0.65% to 1.10% from reduction in artificial lighting | Ramos *et al.* (1998) |
| Mexico | DST | Empirical analysis | **S** – Overall electricity savings of 0.83% (exclusively from residential buildings). Annual maximum demand reduced by 2.6%. Monitor of 560 residential, 28 commercial and 14 industrial customers from 12 cities | Ramos and Diaz (1999) |
| US | YRDST | Electricity system | **S** – Savings in order of 1% (in March and April) | Ebersole *et al.* (1974) |
| US | YRDST | Electricity system | **N** – Did not support Ebersole (1974), with inconclusive results | Filliben (1976) |
| US | YRDST | Electricity system | **S** – Savings in order of 1% (in March and April) | Binder (1976) |
| US | DST & YRDST | Building simulation | **C/S** – DST increases electricity usage by 0.24%. YRDST decreases usage by 0.02%. | Rock (1997) |
| US | DST | Empirical analysis | **S** – 0.5% reduction in daily electricity consumption | Belzer *et al.* (2008) |
| California | DDST | Demand simulation | **S** – YRDST reduces winter peak by an average of 3.4%, and consumption by 0.5%. DDST reduces summer peak by 0.6% and consumption by 0.2% | Kandel and Metz (2001) |
| California | DST | Empirical analysis | **S** – 0.18% savings, with a 95% confidence interval ranging from 1.5% savings to 1.4% increase | Kandel and Sheridan (2007) |
| Indiana | DST | Empirical analysis | **N** – No definitive or conclusive changes in electricity consumption | Indiana FPI (2001) |
| Indiana | DST | Empirical analysis | **C** – Overall increase in residential electricity demand of 1% to 4% | Kotchen and Grant (2008) |

Table 18.1 (*cont.*)

| Region | Time Regime | Method/ Evidence | Impact on Electricity Demand due to DST (S = Savings, C = Costs, N = Neutral results) | Author |
|---|---|---|---|---|
| New Zealand | DST | Electricity system | **S** – Decrease of 3.5% (cf. average 2% decrease in weeks before). Peak decrease of 7.5%, and on average 5.5% over the previous three years | Small (2001) |
| Australia | DST | Empirical analysis | **N** – Reduction in evening peak demand, but with a higher morning peak. No overall reduction | Kellogg and Wolff (2007) |
| Estimated effect of extended period of DST on electricity use | | | Fourteen of twenty-three studies find extension of DST would save electricity<br>Three of twenty-three studies find extension of DST would incur additional costs<br>Six of twenty-three studies find extension of DST would be energy neutral | |

*Note:* YRDST = year-round daylight savings time; DDST = double daylight savings time.

- Building simulation methods represent the lighting behaviour of users in buildings (Bouillon, 1983; Rock, 1997; Pout, 2006; Fong *et al.*, 2007; Shimoda *et al.*, 2007). Estimates that have been aggregated from individual buildings to system level are subject to error from the use of an unrepresentative base for estimates and from stylized assumptions about behaviour in the absence of evidence. Building types and behavioural patterns vary from region to region, making these studies regionally specific (see below).
- Top-down approaches based on system-wide data draw on recorded electricity usage at the regional or national level (HMSO, 1970; Hillman and Parker, 1988; Hillman, 1993; Ebersole *et al.*, 1974; Filliben, 1976; Binder, 1976; Ramos and Diaz, 1999; Small, 2001; Kellogg and Wolff, 2007; Kandel and Sheridan, 2007; Indiana FPI, 2001; Kotchen and Grant, 2008; Belzer *et al.*, 2008). Isolating the impact of DST on electricity demand presents problems, given the number of other variables affecting demand. However, a variety of regression methods have been used to eliminate 'noise' and identify the impact of clock time on energy demand.

- *Region* – daily and seasonal electricity demand profiles vary by region (Reincke and Van den Broek, 1999). Differences in demand profiles for electricity are revealed by studies of Californian electricity demand (Kandel and Metz, 2001), which show that annual demand peaks at midday in summer when use of air-conditioning is heaviest. In contrast, in the UK, annual peak demands occur in the late afternoon during the winter. Changes to DST depend on demand for lighting, which also varies from one region to another.
- *Season* – DST has different effects at different times of year, and it is essential to specify time-of-year effects to guide policy on optimum length of DST versus standard time.
- *Timeframe* – economies have changed significantly in the past forty years, and studies from the 1970s cannot accurately reflect the impact of DST on current electricity demand. Deindustrialization, new appliances and changes in lifestyle have affected the magnitude and shape of the UK's electricity demand profile. The timings of off-peak lower electricity tariffs have been altered, affecting the timings of peak electricity demand.
- *Demand measures* – some studies have not clearly distinguished or measured the difference between the impact of DST on peak demand versus its effect on overall electricity consumption. Reductions in peak demand result in significantly higher marginal savings on system costs and carbon emissions than reductions in overall electricity consumption for reasons explored in section 18.6.

Nevertheless, the literature is useful in providing parameters in terms of which to assess expected orders of magnitude of response to clock time change. A number of studies featured in Table 18.1 report savings in overall electricity consumption of between 0.5 per cent and 1 per cent from a better alignment of clock time with the activity patterns of consumers. Setting these in context, lighting accounts for around 9 per cent of residential electricity consumption in the US and studies suggest similar orders of magnitude in other advanced economies (Seiferlein and Boyer, 2005). For commercial buildings in the US, more electricity is consumed by lighting than any other individual end-use, amounting to 36 per cent of energy used in the buildings surveyed by the Energy Information Administration (EIA, 2003).

## 18.4 US and UK clock time policy

Clock time regimes have shown great continuity in the US and UK, as elsewhere. In the US, a two-year period of year-round DST (introduced to save energy) was discontinued in 1975 and it was not until 2007 that the US changed its clock policy, extending the period of DST by adding an extra three weeks of DST in the spring and one week in the autumn. A study by the US Department of Energy in 2008 found that from this four-week period, a total of 1.3 TWh were saved, corresponding to 0.5 per cent of daily consumption during this period (Belzer *et al.*, 2008). This extensive inquiry concluded that electricity savings in the evenings as a result of DST more than offset small increases in usage during morning hours. The effects varied by region, with savings higher in northern and eastern states, but overall there were benefits for US national electricity consumption, and hence a reduction in carbon emissions, from extending the period of DST.

The effects of the UK trial year-round DST period from 1968 to 1971, when the clock was advanced by one hour in winter, were investigated in 1970. This study concluded that there was a 0.5 per cent reduction in overall electricity consumption and a 3 per cent decrease in the afternoon peak over the trial period to date (HMSO, 1970). Later studies also found savings in energy use over the trial period (Hillman and Parker, 1988; Hillman, 1993). The 1970 study did not have policy impact at the time because the media focused on the increase in morning accidents during the trial period, without taking into account the greater fall in evening accidents and hence the beneficial net impact on accidents of GMT+1 all year (Hillman, 1993). At the time there was little interest in energy savings.

A UK-based study, from the Building Research Establishment in 2005 (Pout, 2006), has been cited by Department of Trade and Industry officials as justifying clock time policy. This study used a building simulation approach, based on modelling software devised for other purposes. Behavioural variables were based on assumptions which did not accommodate evidence that there is higher demand for electric lighting around sunset than around sunrise. The BRE study concluded that energy consumption would increase by 1 per cent under year-round DST and 2 per cent under Double DST (GMT+2). However, this report exemplifies the use of assumptions and aggregation methods not grounded in empirical evidence, which call into question the inferences drawn.

There were no recent studies using system-wide lighting demand data to assess the impact of DST on demand in Britain, justifying the study reported here.

## 18.5 Activity patterns of the UK population

A key issue is the alignment of clock time with the activity patterns of the population. Although not carried out to inform clock time policy,

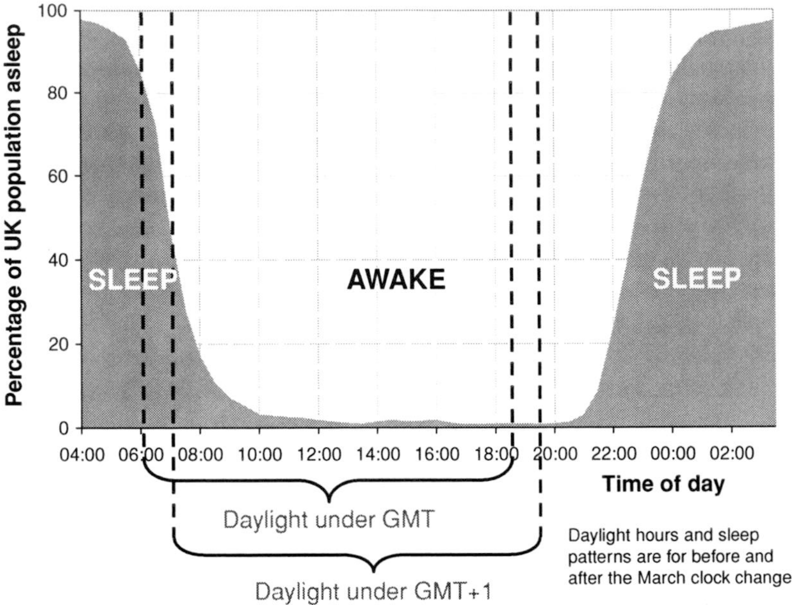


Figure 18.1 Sleeping and waking patterns for selected sunrise and sunset times.

the UK Time Use Survey in 2000 (Office for National Statistics, 2000) provides relevant evidence. Analysis of diurnal activity patterns shows that throughout most of the year, the large proportion of the UK population are asleep during the hours of early morning light after sunrise while most people are still active during the early evening period after sunset. For example, during the month of March, illustrated in Figure 18.1, under GMT the sun rises just after 6am when a large proportion of people are asleep, whereas one would find that most people are still awake after sunset at 6.30pm. Research on demand for lighting by other researchers shows a peak in demand in the evening that is higher than morning demand for lighting (Stokes *et al.*, 2004).

Seasonal activity patterns of the UK population are illustrated in Figure 18.2. This shows that morning activity patterns vary little across the year, revealing the way morning schedules are dictated by clock time rather than timing of sunrise. Leisure activities in the UK make relatively little use of early morning light. Late afternoon and evening activity patterns alter from winter to summer. During the warmer and lighter evenings of summer months, a decrease in electricity consumption coincides with increased time spent out of doors. With recreation occurring

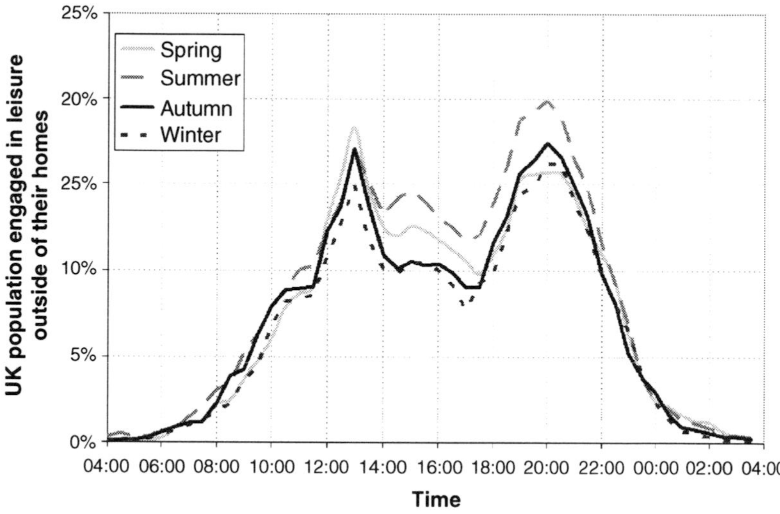


Figure 18.2 UK leisure patterns – percentage of respondents engaged in leisure pursuits outside the home.

mainly after work, it can be inferred that later sunset makes possible a longer period of outdoor activity, with consequent health, tourism and leisure benefits.

## 18.6 Analyzing the potential for winter daylight saving

Daily profiles of British demand[1] for electricity are illustrated in Figure 18.3 and Figure 18.4 for the weeks preceding and following the spring and autumn clock changes. The demand profiles shift from week to week with seasonal changes in light and temperature, but there is a strong discontinuity in the rate of change in seasonal demand immediately after the clock changes of spring and autumn. This discontinuous shift in the rate of change of demand at the time of the clock change is associated with higher energy consumption under GMT than GMT+1 in both spring and autumn.

The demand profiles are based on pooled data on half-hourly demand for electricity over the course of the day for all working days from January 2001 to April 2008. The discontinuous shift in the rate of change of

[1] The data analyzed are British half-hourly electricity demand data for weekdays excluding bank holidays, supplied by National Grid, beginning on 1 January 2001 and analyzed until 30 April 2008.

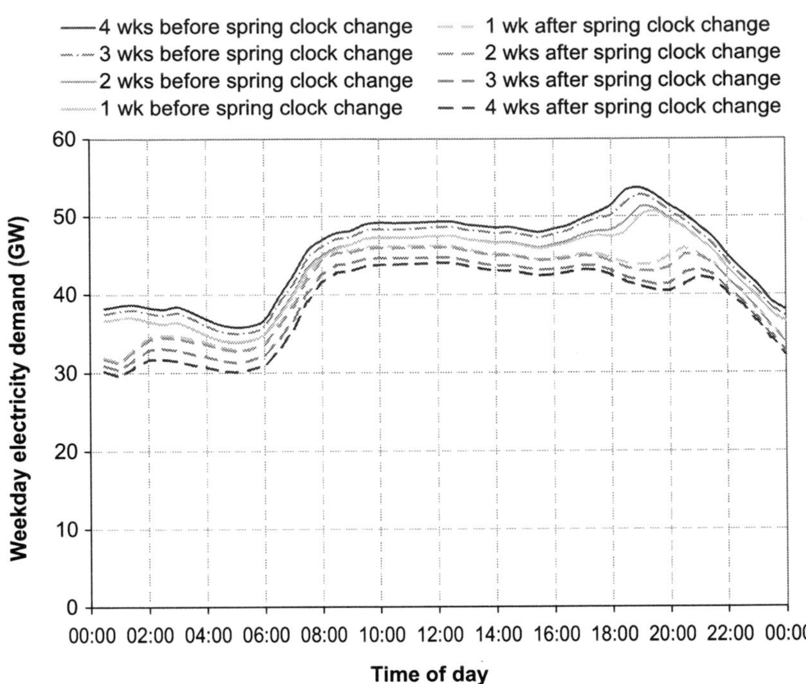


Figure 18.3 Changes in average demand during weeks on spring clock changes.

demand at the time of the clock change is associated with higher energy consumption under GMT than GMT+1 in both spring and autumn (Hill *et al.*, 2010).

To examine effects beyond the clock change weeks during winter months, a regression model called Support Vector Regression (SVR) was used, built on forecasting techniques (Chen *et al.*, 2004). The model estimated the potential saving of electricity in Britain that would have occurred if clock time had been on daylight saving (GMT+1 hour) during the years 2001–8, holding the main determinants of demand constant.[2]

The model found that daily peak demand could have been reduced by up to 4.3 per cent and that a net reduction in electricity consumption would have occurred, had the clock regime stayed on GMT+1 instead

[2] Analysis was based on data supplied by National Grid, consisting of British demand data and average temperature and illumination data for half-hourly time intervals for weekdays (excluding bank holidays) from January 2001 to April 2008.

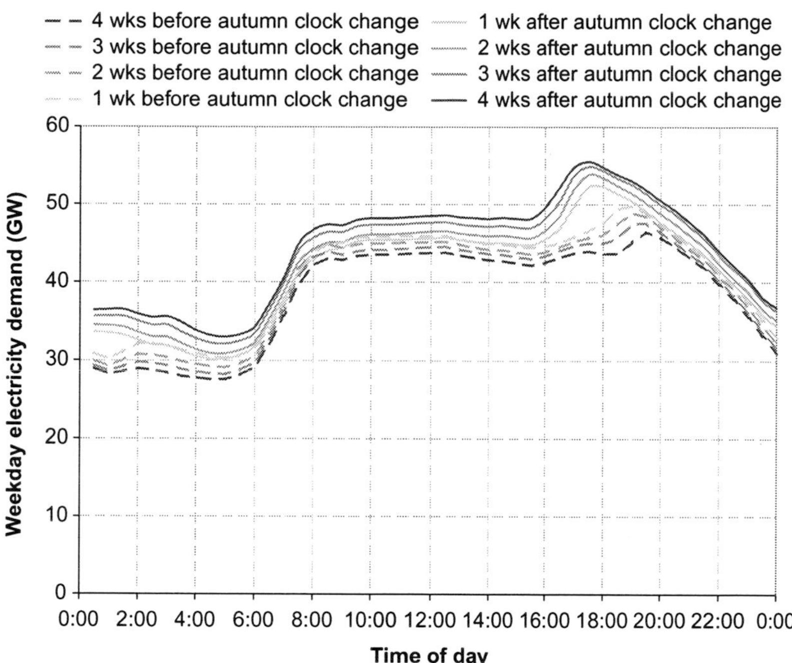


Figure 18.4 Changes in average demand during weeks on autumn clock changes.

of GMT during the winter months. As a percentage of British daily electricity consumption, these savings averaged 0.32 per cent in November, 0.22 per cent in December, 0.32 per cent in February and 0.32 per cent in March.[3] Based on these average savings, the adoption of GMT+1 during the winter could result in a reduction of electricity consumption by 450 GWh per annum. This is equivalent to continuous baseload generation from a 120 MW power plant or a wind farm of approximately 300 turbines.[4] The associated reduction in carbon emissions is 375,000 tonnes $CO_2$ per annum, based on peaking generation when changes in demand mainly occur.[5]

[3] January effects could not be modelled as they were too far removed from existing GMT+1 data.

[4] Based on wind turbines of 1.5 MW capacity and 28 per cent capacity factor.

[5] Based on average emissions of 833 tonnes of $CO_2$ per GWh of generation from open cycle gas turbines (OCGT) generation.

## 18.7 Peak demand and cost effects

The impact on peak time demand of advancing the clock by an hour would be greater than the effect on national daily consumption. The SVR methodology estimated that the reduction in peak demand (for electricity for artificial lighting) resulting from the extension of the period of DST could be as high as 4.3 per cent of daily peak demand over the winter period.

Peak demand differences are of great operational significance for forecasters and savings reported above are a higher proportion of peak demand than of daily national demand. Peak demand generally occurs at 5.30pm when there is an overlap of office and domestic electricity demand, and also at the onset of dark after sunset. When the timing of sunset results in these two sources of demand coinciding, the resulting peak is significantly higher. To deal with transitory peaks in demand, methods of power generation with short powering-up times are employed, including pumped storage, open cycle gas turbines (OCGT) and oil generators. These provide rapid ramp-up in power supply but have much higher marginal system costs and higher marginal carbon emissions as a result of their lower efficiencies and higher fuel prices. Reductions in demand for electricity during hours of peak demand are thus of particular benefit, reducing carbon emissions, generation costs and electricity price.

The price implications are considerable, but it is difficult to estimate precisely the effect on the privatized UK electricity market of changes in clock time because a diversity of forward contracts is agreed between utility companies and suppliers. As a rough estimate, we used half-hourly electricity market price data over the course of the day and the change in electricity demand predicted by the SVR algorithm to estimate the corresponding electricity price change on the electricity trading market.[6] We then expressed the overall change in price as a percentage of the daily price of electricity and averaged this over a whole month, taking November as the exemplar, for the years 2002–7, the period for which data were available. This analysis showed that an electricity price reduction of between 0.6 per cent and 0.8 per cent over a day was associated with clock time on GMT+1 instead of GMT in November over these years. The market price of electricity was found to be higher by 0.8 per cent as a result of higher peaks in demand over the period in question.

[6] SBP and SSP data from Elexon Best View Prices 2009. This analysis does not take into account forward contracts between utility companies and energy suppliers, which have a major influence on electricity pricing.

This has an indirect effect on the price paid by consumers (because of forward contracts between utility companies and suppliers), but consumers all over the UK, including consumers and businesses in Scotland, face higher electricity prices from higher generation costs associated with higher peaks in demand. Conditions of recession would reduce overall demand and hence peak demand.

## 18.8 The impact of advancing the clock by an hour all year

The method reported above focused on a change in winter clock time because the forecasting method could use data on GMT+1 effects from adjoining months. The method requires that the prediction equation be trained on appropriate data, but no such data are available in summer since GMT+2 has not been used since the Second World War when it was introduced in an attempt to save fuel. An experimental regression model, which lacked the proven record of the SVR method, was developed to estimate effects year round, by modelling the effect of setting the clocks forward by one hour throughout the year.[7] This model simulated the effect of GMT+1 in the winter and GMT+2 in the summer (as on Central European Time). The method aimed to estimate effects for all days, not just working days. The percentage reduction in peak demand could not be estimated by this method, but would be higher than savings estimated for daily demand. This experimental methodology estimated average annual savings from advancing the clock by one hour ahead of current clock regime all year to be 934 GWh (equating to 0.27 per cent reduction in electricity consumption). This average daily demand reduction is somewhat above the estimate for changing the clocks to GMT+1 all year reported above, using the SVR method which looked at working days only.

## 18.9 Scottish and European Union issues

Clock time policy must take into account how Scotland and the European Union would be affected by any changes. Scottish MPs have consistently opposed all private members bills in Parliament calling for extension of daylight saving time (Cronin and Garnsey, 2007). In Scotland the trial period of 1968–71 on DST in winter is strongly associated with memories of child road casualties resulting from later timing of sunrise. However, the net figures show there was a decrease in Scottish road

[7] Professor Mark Franklin of the European University Institute, Florence, helped to devise this method and to pilot the exploratory regression analysis.

casualties during trial years on DST in winter, taking into account the fall in casualties in the evenings in Scotland.[8] This data were questioned by Scottish MPs in 1970, but studies since then have repeatedly confirmed that traffic patterns in Scotland result in road users, including children, being at greater risk from heavier road use later in the day than in the early morning, as shown by casualty data together with road traffic flow data for Scotland.[9] It follows that later timing of sunset can do more to reduce accidents in Scotland than keeping clock time in winter on GMT. Alternatively, there could be further seasonal adjustment of local school and working hours in the north of Britain and Scotland, as is practised in Scandinavian countries on Central European Time.

In 2001, the European Parliament formally synchronized the dates of clock change throughout Europe. It was required that the Commission of the European Communities report back the implications of standardized DST (EurLex, 2000). This report stated that the savings (from DST) actually achieved are difficult to gauge and relatively small. The report may reflect the bias in favour of the status quo found in the literature: the report found compelling the fact that no member state was calling for changes to the current arrangements. But benefits described as 'relatively small' from extending the period of clock time on DST are in relation to very large national demand figures and overlook the extent to which the high marginal savings in electricity costs and carbon emissions have cumulative impact. Moreover, if harmonization is the only certain benefit of the current system, studies should be undertaken to assess the effects of extending the period of DST throughout the EU, especially in view of US findings that a longer period of DST resulted in a net 0.5 per cent saving in electricity nationally over the weeks concerned (Belzer *et al.*, 2008).

Since 2002, the UK and the rest of the European Union countries have applied daylight saving time at 1am GMT on the last Sunday in March, ending at 1am GMT on the last Sunday of October. The

[8] 'We have the statistics of the casualties. In England and Wales there was a betterment of 3 per cent. In Scotland ... there was a betterment of 8.6 per cent.' House of Commons Hansard, 02nd Dec 1970 c.1340. In the 1960s street lighting was not computer controlled or relit for morning darkness, whereas today computerized lighting can ensure that streets are not darker before sunrise than after sunset.

[9] If a GMT+1/GMT+2 regime had been adopted during the 1990s in Scotland, there would have been an annual reduction on Scottish roads of all casualties of 57 persons per year and a reduction of killed and seriously injured persons of 41 persons per year, according to the Transport Research Laboratory's study (Broughton, 1998). Scottish Government publication *Road Casualties in Scotland 2009*, Table 27 provides data for 2003–7 showing casualties by time of day (www.scotland.gov.uk/publications/2009/03/20124132/40). Traffic flow data are available from www.transportscotland.gov.uk/.

Directive sets out these arrangements for an unspecified period.[10] Keeping clock-change dates the same as the rest of the European Union, the UK could institute GMT+1 during the winter and GMT+2 in the summer (as on CET). In addition to savings in electricity consumption and carbon emissions, there would be obvious trade benefits from being on the same clock time as the UK's main trading partners in Europe.

## 18.10 Implications and conclusions

Our research and studies show that advancing the clock to align better with activity patterns could unquestionably result in savings in electricity consumption with associated carbon emissions. We found no evidence that increased costs are to be expected from advancing the clock. On the contrary, extension of DST should result in lower peak demand, which in turn would lower generation costs by reducing recourse to reserve generating capacity to cover peaks in demand, which is both expensive and highly polluting.

A consistent finding of the methods reported here is that timing sunrise and sunset an hour later would accord better with the activity patterns of the population and would have a net favourable effect on electricity usage over the course of the day. The principle of aligning clock time with activity patterns applies to other countries where the sun rises before electricity usage reaches a high point in the daily demand profile but peak demand occurs near sunset.

Our findings should be viewed in relation to wider benefits of shifting light to the evening period in line with activity patterns. These include evidence found consistently since 1971 on the reduction in road accidents from advancing the clock, which leads the Royal Society for the Prevention of Accidents, on the basis of analysis by The Transport Research Lab and other analysis of the timing of road accidents, to favour extension of Daylight Saving Time (ROSPA, 2006). Economists often have to weigh up differences in death rates associated with alternative policies. But in this case there is no trade-off to show that current accident figures are justified by any other benefits from clock time on GMT. Taken together since 1971, avoidable road fatalities in Britain associated with early sunset on GMT at the time of peak road use amount to around 5,000 (Cronin and Garnsey, 2007). Quite independently of energy costs (to which they contribute), these tragedies justify the later timing of sunset.

[10] Directive 2000/84/EC of the European Parliament and of the Council of 19 January 2001 on summer-time arrangements.

Local opening hours and school hours could be adjusted to seasonal changes in local daylight. An education campaign could be undertaken to encourage the population to make better use of early morning light by changing their daily routines. Given the marked disparity between activity patterns and daylight hours, especially in summer, such an initiative could be justified whether or not policy on official clock time is changed, but has never been attempted outside wartime.

Clock time on GMT+1 all year would remove the forecasting difficulties associated with the twice-yearly clock changes, and would be popular in removing the disruption of clock change. On the other hand, it would fail to capitalize on anticipated energy savings and leisure benefits from advancing the clock by a further hour in summer and the benefits of shared clock time with the UK's primary trading partners in the European Union. However, EU Directives enforce the harmonization of the clock-change dates by member states. This has been interpreted by the UK government as prohibiting the UK from adopting year-round GMT+1, although the UK is at liberty to adopt CET.

The issue of extending DST in the EU with the aim of reducing both energy consumption and carbon emissions could be raised in Brussels. Extension of the period of DST can result in savings in electricity consumption, as demonstrated in the US where the period of DST has been extended by three weeks in the spring and one week in the autumn since 2007. This has been shown by the US Department of Energy to amount to savings of 1.3 TWh (0.5 per cent of daily consumption) during this four-week period.

Climate change concern has created a strong political drive for the reduction of energy consumption and the reduction of carbon emissions worldwide. Billions of pounds are being spent on low-carbon technologies and energy efficient solutions aimed at abating climate change. Contributions of all kinds are needed, but not least from measures which constitute 'low-hanging fruit' – requiring minimal time, investment and effort to yield tangible results. Clock time that achieves daylight saving is the epitome of a 'low-hanging fruit' in combating global pollution. What is required is the political will to overcome inertia that holds back institutional innovation.

## References

Aries, M.B.C. and Newsham, G.R. (2008). Effect of daylight saving time on lighting energy use: a literature review, *Energy Policy*, **36**(6): 1858–66.

Belzer, D.B., Hadley, S.W. and Chin, S.-M., (2008). *Impact of Extended Daylight Saving Time on National Energy Consumption: Report to Congress*, USDOE: Office of Energy Efficiency and Renewable Energy.

Binder, R. (1976). Testimony of Robert H. Binder, Assistant Secretary for Policy, Plans, and International Affairs, U.S. Department of Transportation, before the House Subcommittee on Transportation and Commerce, on Legislation concerning Daylight Saving Time, Available at http://testimony.ost.dot.gov/test/pasttest/76test/Binder1.PDF, last accessed November 2008.

Boardman, B. (1991). *Fuel Poverty: From Cold Homes to Affordable Warmth*, London: Belhaven Press.

Bouillon, H. (1983). Mikro- und Makroanalyse der Auswirkungen der Sommerzeit auf den Energie-Leistungsbedarf in den verschiedenen Energieverbrauchssektoren der Bundesrepublik Deutschland. IFR Schriftenreihe 13, Dissertation, Technical University, Munich (in German).

Broughton, J. and Stone, M. (1998). A New Assessment of the Likely Effects on Road Accidents of Adopting SDST. TRL Report 368, Transport Research Laboratory, Crowthorne.

Chen, B.-J., Chang, M.-W. and Lin, C.-J. (2004). Load forecasting using support vector machines: a study on EUNITE competition 2001, *IEEE Transactions on Power Systems*, **19**(4): 1821–30.

Cronin, B. and Garnsey, E. (2007). Daylight Saving in GB, The Case for Institutional Innovation, Available at www.ifm.eng.cam.ac.uk/people/ewg, last accessed November 2008.

DECC (2008). *Energy Trends*, London: Department of Energy and Climate Change.

Ebersole, N., Rubin, D., Hannan, W., Darling, E., Frenkel, L., Prerau, D. and Schaeffer, K. (1974). *The Year-Round Daylight Saving Time Study, vol. I. Interim Report on the Operation and Effects of Year-Round Daylight Saving Time*, Cambridge, MA: US Department of Transportation, Transportation Systems Center.

Energy Information Administration (US), (2003). *Lighting in Commercial Buildings*, Available at www.eia.doe.gov/emeu/cbecs/cbecs2003/lighting/lighting1.html, last accessed November 2008.

EurLex (2000). EU Directive 2000/84/EC of the European Parliament and of the Council of 19 January 2001 on summer-time arrangements, Proposal for a Directive of the European Parliament and of the Council on summer-time arrangements, Official Journal C 337 E, 0136–0137.

Filliben, J.J. (1976). Review and technical evaluation of the DOT daylight saving time study, US National Bureau of Standards, NBS Internal Report Prepared for the Chairman Subcommittee on Transportation and Commerce, Committee on Interstate and Foreign Commerce, US House of Representatives, Washington.

Fischer, U. (2000). Hilft die Sommerzeit beim Sparen von Energie?, *Licht*, **52**(5): 574–7 (in German).

Fong, W., Matsumoto, H., Lun, Y. and Kimura, R. (2007). Energy savings potential of the summer time concept in different regions of Japan from the perspective of household lighting, *Journal of Asian Architecture and Building Engineering*, **6**(2): 371–8.

Hansard Report (2005), *Hansard Report, House of Lords for 24 April 2005, Publications and Records*, London: Parliament.

Her Majesty's Stationery Office (1970). *Review of British Standard Time*, Command Paper Cmnd 4512, London: The Stationery Office.

Hill, S., Desobry, F. and Chong, Y.F. (2009). *Quantifying the Impact of Daylight Saving Clock Changes on Energy Consumption*, University of Cambridge Engineering Department CUED/F-INFENG/TR.620.

Hill, S.I., Desobry, F., Garnsey, E. and Chong, Y.F. (2010). The impact on energy consumption of daylight saving clock changes, *Energy Policy*, **38**(9): 4955–65.

Hillman, M. (1993). *Time for Change: Setting Clocks Forward by One Hour Throughout the Year; a New Review of the Evidence*, London: Policy Studies Institute.

Hillman, M. and Parker, J. (1988). More daylight, less electricity, *Energy Policy*, **16**(5): 514–15.

Indiana Fiscal Policy Institute (2001). *Interim Report: The Energy Impact of Daylight Saving Time Implementation in Indiana*, Indiana Fiscal Policy Institute.

Kandel, A. and Metz, M. (2001). *Effects of Daylight Saving Time on California Electricity Use*, California Energy Commission, Staff Report, P400–01–013.

Kandel, A. and Sheridan, M. (2007). *The Effect of Early Daylight Saving Time on California Electricity Consumption: A Statistical Analysis*, California Energy Commission, Staff Report CEC-200–2007–004.

Kellogg, R. and Wolff, H. (2007). *Does Extending Daylight Saving Time Save Energy? Evidence from an Australian Experiment*, Center for the Study of Energy Markets Paper CSEMWP-163.

Kotchen, M.J. and Grant, L.E. (2008). Does daylight saving time save energy? Evidence from a Natural Experiment in Indiana (draft), NBER Working Paper No. W14429.

Littlefair, P.F. (1990). Effects of clock change on lighting energy use, *Energy World*, **175**: 15–17.

ONS (2000). *United Kingdom Time Use Survey 2000*, UK Data Archive, SN 4504, Office for National Statistics, London: UK.

Pout, C. (2006). *The Effect of Clock Changes on Energy Consumption in UK Buildings, Building Research Establishment*, London: Building Research Establishment.

Prereau, D. (2005). *Seize the Daylight*, New York: Thunder's Mouth Press.

Ramos, G.N. and Diaz, R.A. (1999). A methodology to classify residential customers by their pattern of use, in *Proceedings of the Power Engineering Society Summer Meeting*, **1**: 226–31.

Ramos, G.N., Covarrubias, R.R., Sada, J.G., Buitron, H.S., Vargas, E.N. and Rodriguez, R.C. (1998). Energy saving due to the implementation of the daylight saving time in Mexico in 1996, in *Proceedings of the International Conference on Large High Voltage Electric Systems*, CIGRE '98, Paris, 13, 6 pp.

Reincke, K.-J. and Van den Broek, F. (1999). Summer time, thorough examination of the implications of summer-time arrangements in the Member States of the European Union. Executive summary, Research voor Beleid International (RvB) EC DG VII.

Rock, B.A. (1997). Impact of daylight saving time on residential energy use and cost, *Energy and Buildings*, **25**: 63–8.

Royal Society for Prevention of Accidents (2006). Single/Double Summer Time. Policy Paper.

Seiferlein, K.E. and Boyer, R. (2005). *Annual Energy Review 2005*, Energy Information Administration, US Department of Energy.

Shimoda, Y., Asahi, T., Taniguchi, A. and Mizuno, M. (2007). Evaluation of city-scale impact of residential energy conservation measures using the detailed end-use simulation model, *Energy*, **32**: 1617–33.

Small, V. (2001). Daylight saving idea to beat cuts, The New Zealand Herald, Available at www.nzherald.co.nz/topic/story.cfm?c_id=187&objectid=207726, last accessed May 2007.

Stokes, M. and Rylatt M., Lomas, K. (2004). A simple model of domestic lighting demand, *Energy and Buildings*, **36**: 103–16.

The Scottish Government (2009). *Road Casualties in Scotland*, Available at www.scotland.gov.uk/publications/2009/03/20124132/40, last accessed November 2009.

# 19 Concluding reflections on future active networks and the demand-side for electricity

*Tooraj Jamasb and Michael G. Pollitt*

## 19.1 Introduction

As this book has made clear, the landscape for active networks and an active demand-side in future electricity systems appears promising and suggests scope for various benefits and untapped potentials. There are a wide range of solutions and measures through which flexible electricity networks and active customers can contribute to energy saving and efficiency. As technology continues to progress and practical experience accumulates, even more types of solution can become possible. Two key questions arise. What can be done to facilitate the emergence of smarter networks and more active demand? What pitfalls are there that can hinder this more active world from emerging? These are important but difficult questions and this chapter aims to highlight some of the main issues related to them.

At the conceptual level a rather significant issue is the lack of a coherent vision of smart networks and active demand. At present there are different, and at times conflicting, conceptions of active networks and demand and a well-defined and unified understanding of them is yet to emerge. A common understanding of these concepts is clearly important for policy making, sector regulation, corporate planning, consumer participation and public opinion support.

However, substantive progress may in practice take longer to materialize than first anticipated. It is helpful to recall that since its inception, the electricity system has evolved over a period of well over 100 years. During this time the level of demand has increased rapidly while the nature of demand for electricity services has changed significantly, but *in general* the pace of change in the industry itself has not been as rapid as that experienced in other consumer services sectors, such as telecommunications. However, there have also been short periods during which the sector experienced rapid transformations. For example, privatization, liberalization and the subsequent dash-for-gas changed the landscape and dynamics of the industry within a few years in the UK in the 1990s; while the energy security-inspired French nuclear power programme radically changed their power sector in the 1980s. The unidirectional and passive flow of power from network to end-users has, however, seen little change. Hence, while the sector is susceptible to change, it is difficult to predict the speed of this change and rapid change is the exception rather than the norm. Past experience suggests that clear (and focused) objectives and economic incentives can greatly facilitate and speed up the pace of changes in the sector that otherwise would not have happened.

The need for change will not be limited to the electricity system and its customers. Future regulation and policies towards the sector also need to adapt to the changing technological possibilities and environmental challenges. In order to increase the effectiveness of new technologies and policies it is important to provide a greater role for economic, social and behavioural factors. Information, incentive and behavioural failures are still widespread in energy efficiency and end-use. Also, the development of suitable economic instruments can still at best be regarded as work in progress. The behavioural dimension of energy consumers is complex and our understanding of these and how to promote sustainable behaviour is still limited. Furthermore, only in recent years have we begun to explore the potential of social capital and community-based approaches to energy supply and demand. In short, when it comes to the demand-side for energy, while technological progress can enable change, it will in no way guarantee it.

## 19.2 Technology and R&D

An important issue is what type of research and development (R&D) is needed and for what purpose. Important innovations will include integration of existing power and design of communications technologies. In addition, there is a need for validation and demonstration of emerging technologies through large and commercial-scale experimentations. Such experimentation needs to pay due attention to the way people in particular places interact with technology as much as the technology itself.

The British electricity sector reform has been in most respects at the forefront of liberalization efforts in the world. While there are clear benefits to having a home-grown reform and oversight model, this also means that lessons of experience from other parts of the world may to a lesser degree be applicable to Britain. The obvious response to this is to promote the type of in-house R&D efforts that are specifically suited for the needs and circumstances of the British sector.

This also means that sufficient physical and human research capacity in relevant technical and non-technical fields needs to be built up and maintained over time. The R&D capacity building in Britain declined sharply following the liberalization of the sector. In recent years there has been an increase in R&D activities mainly as a result of government and regulatory decisions, albeit building up from a low base. An important question is whether this positive upward trend will be maintained in the long run as a matter of strategy or may fall back again due to the recent economic downturn.

While the central role of technical progress in achieving future energy objectives should not be underestimated, we need to place emphasis on developing technologies that have commercial prospects, are economical and consumers need and want. Building up and maintaining an effective research capacity requires a significant and long-term commitment to a programme of research in the relevant disciplinary and interdisciplinary areas. In particular, in the emerging climate of economic austerity there are good reasons to be mindful of signs of possible investment imbalances that may emerge between research in 'harder' (e.g. electrical engineering) and 'softer' sciences (e.g. sociology and psychology) relating to the future of energy supply and demand.

## 19.3 Utilities, consumers and communities

A common thread among most of the proposed ideas for active and smart demand is that they are to differing degrees rooted in 'market-based' or incentive regulation solutions and private sector involvement. This means that private actors – including both suppliers and customers – are subject to the costs and risks of their decisions through market prices as the main organizing principle. The role of the demand-side in a market-oriented sector is a rather important one. However, this role has so far mainly been limited to switching electricity suppliers. Greater flexibility for demand to adjust to constantly changing supply and market conditions will enhance the role of customers in balancing the future market and increasing the economic efficiency of the sector.

In order to achieve the active future electricity demand we need to develop and deploy a wide range of different technologies and non-technical solutions. In order to be effective, these diverse technologies will in turn need to be integrated in different parts of the system and then be coordinated across different actors with differing interests and incentives.

It follows that the development of an active demand-side will require innovative business models, such as those followed by energy service companies (ESCOs), virtual utilities, aggregators, etc., and to be extended to new areas that have not been envisaged yet. New business models can also include market participation of new actors at the individual level, for example, enabled by microgeneration, electric car batteries or community-based generation (such as combined heat and power CHP), microgrids or demand management (for example, through ESCOs). However, ultimately, the consumers will decide which products and services offer value to them and as a result which business models are successful and pass the test of time.

## 19.4 Economics and policy

The real potential and benefits of technical solutions will only be achieved by applying appropriate technologies across the whole of the value chain, coherent economic instruments, and a predictable regulatory and policy framework. In order for the active demand to be effective the measures taken will need to be coherent and internally consistent across the whole supply chain from generation to end-user.

However, at a fundamental level, the ability to use price-based mechanisms in order to activate the networks and users is to a large degree dependent on having the main elements of a liberalized electricity sector in place. This in turn requires managing and resolving the, so far implicit, tensions between the liberalization paradigm and climate change policies in such a way that they are not in constant conflict or even mutually exclusive (see Noel and Pollitt, 2010).

A glance at the technologies being proposed reveals that the technical solutions are generally capital intensive and the costs associated with development and deployment of them will be non-trivial. Therefore, economic efficiency and cost-effectiveness in how the investment funds are raised, spent and recovered will also play a prominent role in enabling the efforts.

Some of the actors in the active energy demand economy will be active in competitive markets and will bear the risk of their investment and pricing decisions. Other actors such as the distribution network operators (DNOs) are natural monopolies operating under incentive regulation schemes and periodic price control reviews. Some of the costs and risks associated with the substantial investment requirements in the networks are therefore passed on directly and indirectly to customers. However, while there is ample need to develop better investment regulation and incentive schemes and there have been new developments in recent years, this can be regarded as work in progress (Joskow, 2008).

## 19.5 Society and political economy

We also need to be mindful of some of the pitfalls that can delay or prevent effective demand-side measures. The technological progress and economic innovations in future energy demand can offer cost-effective benefits to many consumers. However, these developments also carry with them the potential for an increase in 'energy-divide' in society. It is important to avoid the possibility that the suite of implemented energy demand technologies and policies only benefits some groups of consumers and in the process increases the existing energy divide between the fuel poor and low-income consumers, and other users.

This is because higher income and resourceful consumers are often better placed to invest in new technologies and pay for the beneficial products and services offered to them. Active demand can potentially reduce or increase the energy divide in society. The deciding factor is in the details of implementation of active demand. It is also important to note that the existing 'digital divide' in the use of and access to information technology in society can contribute to an increased energy divide as some technical solutions for active demand build on digital platforms such as the internet.

The distributional effects of the changes in energy demand are not only important from an equity point of view in the economic sense. Given the current level of fuel poverty in Britain and the expected future price increases associated with efforts aimed at achieving climate change targets, the importance of energy equity and its political economy for the direction of active energy demand policies cannot be underestimated. Against this background far-sighted strategies towards the demand-side need to be accompanied by public support for their component policies.

## References

Joskow, P. (2008). Incentive regulation and its application to electricity networks, *Review of Network Economics*, 7(4): 547–60.

Noel, P. and Pollitt, M. (2010). Don't lose power, *Parliamentary Brief*, **12**(11): 6–8.

# Index

Lightning Source UK Ltd.
Milton Keynes UK
UKOW041349010313

207022UK00001B/66/P